The GRAIL RIDER

RETURN TO THE HEART OF THE WILD DIVINE SOPHIA

An Unbridled Memoir

INAIYA RAY

The Grail Rider: Return to the Heart of the Wild Divine Sophia
Copyright © 2022 by Inaiya Ray
First published January 10, 2017
Second edition published by Inaiya Ray, 2022

www.inaiyaray.love
www.thelivingchalice.com

This is a work of creative nonfiction. The events are portrayed to the best of Inaiya Ray's memory. While all the stories in this book are true, some names and identifying details have been changed to protect the privacy of the people involved.

Printed in the United States of America.

ISBN   (Paperback):   978-0-578-91673-6
         (Hardback):   978-0-578-91696-5
         (Ebook):   978-0-578-91674-3

XX-V22

Dedicated to Gaia Sophia and her band of wild divine beloveds.
To Rael and Quoia, my eternal blue star companions,
and to my beloved Mother, bestower of endless heart smiles.

"In The Grail Rider, Inaiya weaves the ineffable, intangible and eternal with edge-of-your-seat, real life fairy tale sagas in a language that invites the reader into sumptuous, riveting divinity. Truly, a must read for all those on the path of spiritual awakening, and the Wayshowers of the New Earth."

– Caitlin Naramore, *The Modern Queen*

"To read this book is to pick up the lucid thread of one's own death and rebirth. It can be a frightening thing to stand at the gates of transformation, but within the primal womb of darkness, there is always a bright lantern guiding us home. Journey with Inaiya Ray and enter the heart of the Grail. Jump into the Alchemical Kiln and become like ember! The family of the vine is spinning the threads of special destiny, reweaving the alchemy of sacred union between the divine Christos Sophia. Join with them on the grand loom. Drink the Mead of Memory from the Golden Chalice and reclaim the codes of remembrance for each of us is a special thread within the Tapestry of Life. Inaiya's story reminds us we are all destined to return to the heart of eternal love within the centre of the nation, to feel the bliss of homecoming rise and interlock amid the shimmering, vibrating pattern of the entire web of the One."

– O'ran Ruadh, *author of The Last Ember*

"Once the Mysteries were reserved for initiates. As we are called now to step into a new paradigm, stories must emerge that remind us of how we realign with the realms of the soul and find wholeness again. Inaiya Ray has written such a tale, a Grail quest to help us find the way back home to our awakened Heart."

– Ayn Cates Sullivan Ph.D. *author of Legends of the Grail Series*

"The Grail Rider is a memoir inspired by Inaiya's real-life experience and teachings. Over the last few years I have had the great fortune to work with her. During that time, she has repeatedly opened the doors of the Akashic Records to reveal the wonder of my inner universe and I am forever grateful for the transformational work we have done.

Inaiya has written something whose value is grounded in the universal and whose wisdom and clarity changes the fabric of reality as the page turns. Her words convey a powerful vibration that carry depth and passion while embodying a pristine essence whose value promises lasting impact for the hero's and heroine's of our time. Her memoir traverses other places and events that may have passed temporally but whose essence continues to breathe life from the Masters and Mystics of long ago. These individuals lived, taught and passed on their legacy into the archives of human consciousness. As if preserved in a time capsule buried in the ocean, awaiting rediscovery for this poignant moment in humanity's collective awakening. Inaiya stands here amongst us as a Wayshower of these ancient future mysteries and brings to our time the length, depth and breath of her message steeped in universal truth, love and timeless wisdom."

– Stefan J. Malecek Ph.D. *Mankind Project,*

CONTENTS

FOREWORD

The Grail Rider is an epic travel adventure and intoxicating romance that can help guide souls through the twisting labyrinth of the trials and tribulations of the heart...toward ultimate liberation into the Heart of Hearts and greater understanding into the nature of true love.

I was drawn into the story by a compelling sense of common origin...like a family tree whose budding spring branches emerge from wild roots, offering succulent fruits from seeds planted long ago. Likened to reading a legendary mythic tale, the memoir enlivens fresh sap into my own spring branches, awakening memories and weaving its magic into my own myth and legend.

The story is rich with magic and meaning. The narrative carries one along from one adventurous chapter to the next. Like a river flowing and turning across a continually changing landscape, one is toured across space, time, and synchronicity on an archetypal magic carpet journey that nourishes both the mind and heart, offering an abundant shower of insightful gems, pearls of wisdom, and golden reflections along the way.

Opening the book, you climb aboard a global transcendental roller coaster ride! The story travels both 'horizontally' across new vistas of historic and enchanting locations in Europe, while simultaneously moves 'vertically' across psychological and spiritual landscapes—continuously climbing to lofty peaks of idealistic spiritual love, then descending again into the dirt-hard realities and seemingly impossible dualistic dynamics of male and female relationship. Overall, this undulating pattern entrains toward a more encompassing awakening to the ultimate relationship with one Self and the Divine.

The Grail Rider is an alchemical dance through the theme of personal empowerment while alchemisxsing the evolutionary balance between the Divine Feminine with the Divine Masculine. The story is relevant for any reader, female or male and delivers a universal message that speaks to each of us individually according to our unique Mythos. Inaiya weaves a common language for our tender hearts to come home to true love and in so doing join the collective Heart as a whole. Enjoy the ride!

– Michael Gaio, michaelgaio.com

ACKNOWLEDGMENTS

I am beyond grateful for my chosen parents Sheila and Shayle, whose big love and belief in my soul's calling continues to bless my life. To my cherished soul family who light up my life wherever I may be wandering in the world. Deepest bows to my beloved teachers who inspire me daily to create a legacy of love that uplifts and enlivens all beings. To the musicians and poets who have shared their creative brilliance to illuminate this story. To The Living Chalice global community whose hearts beat with mine throughout this birth and beyond. Thank you, Jenna Palden, Norie Libradilla and Jomar Ouano, my editors, who dotted my i's with ongoing patience and compassion. And to my temple cats, Rael and Quoia, companions of my eternal heart smile. I will always cherish the precious love, life and joy that we shared throughout our journey together.

To my beloved Family of Light, who show me the way to grow my wings and live my life as an offering of Big Love that blesses the whole. I am forever grateful for your unwavering presence and unending inspiration in my life. It is my greatest joy and honour to join you in ushering in a new way of living and loving the beauty way.

MITAKUYE OYASIN

Aho Mitakuye Oyasin...
All my relations. I honor you in this circle of life with me today.
I am grateful for this opportunity to acknowledge you in this prayer...
To the Creator, for the ultimate gift of life, I thank you.
To the mineral nation that has built and maintained my bones
and all foundations of life experience, I thank you.
To the plant nation that sustains my organs and body
and gives me healing herbs, I thank you.
To the animal nation that feeds me from your own flesh and
offers your loyal companionship in this walk of life, I thank you.
To the human nation that shares my path as a soul
upon the sacred wheel of Earthly life, I thank you.
To the Spirit nation that guides me invisibly through the ups and downs of life
and for carrying the torch of light through the Ages, I thank you.
To the Four Winds of Change and Growth, I thank you.
You are all my relations, my relatives, without whom I would not live.
We are in the circle of life together, co-existing, inter-dependent,
co-creating our destiny.
One, not more important than the other.
One nation evolving from the other, each dependent upon the one above
and the one below.
All of us a part of the Great Mystery.
Thank you for this Life.

– Lakota Sioux Prayer

INTRODUCTION

RESURRECTION *of the* MAGDALENES

When Magdalene comes into your life, you know you are being asked to not only be the 'rainbow bridge' of the feminine between Earth and Spirit world, you are also being asked to become the cup or chalice – the Holy Grail – of a Queen of heaven on Earth. This means healing at a relational, embodied, physical and sensual level – this restores your primordial birthing template, which Yeshua and Magdalene referred to as being "clothed in light." Jesus refers to a "root" or "primordial template" of form, which he calls an image – disconnection from this root or blueprint of original Womb Consciousness causes physical, emotional and spiritual disease. On this "royal road," you are being invited to take the journey of descent into the Underworld, to reclaim your wisdom throne so that, if you choose, you can also unite with your soul half and experience the journey of merging here on Earth.

– Azra Bertrand, MD and Seren Bertrand, *Womb Awakening*

The tidal wave of love that is pouring forth to the Earth is coming from the heart of our Divine Mother and is the supernal light of the Goddess. This light is the sacred core of purification and life that will release the binding and heavy lower nature from the souls who have chosen to live in heart consciousness. There will be a sense of renewed connection to the Source energy of creation and an understanding of our relationship to the cosmos. The light that is coming to Earth can only be fully received as we have prepared our physical, mental and emotional bodies to hold it.

Every human being has a body of pain that holds the trauma and lower emotions of the many incarnations in physical life. Until we have become conscious of our self and our limiting patterns, they own us and keep us from knowing the fullness of our Divine Self. Our emotions have the power to take us deeper into the dark and debilitate our spiritual body — or they can elevate us to the perception of the full spectrum of Creation. As we wake up, we begin to consciously use the power of our emotions to join Heaven and Earth in Sacred Union within our heart. This is truly a time of receiving higher communication and wisdom from the womb of Creation; the heart of our Divine Mother.

– Shannon Port, *Art of the Feminine*

In the year of 2015, I was called to Aotearoa to honour the Waitaha nation and visit the sacred site of Castle Hill. This is a very sacred place that reflected back to me some of the first soul memories of living in harmony with Gaia, my star ancestors and the awakened heart of creation. This pilgrimage was my way of paying homage to the pantheon of spiritual lifetimes and lineages that have initiated me into divine sovereign embodiment and brought me to be here now. While visiting a sacred retreat centre in the North of Auckland, I was met by Grandmother Eyla, who upon greeting me for the first time, placed a picture of the Divine Mother Sophia into my hands and told me that she had been awaiting my arrival while keeping this picture on her altar for me. It was during this death and rebirth pilgrimage journey that I made an offering of my prior name, this story, and received a new spiritual name, *Inaiya*, which means, 'she who comes from beyond the beyond to midwife a New Earth humanity'. Prior to embracing Inaiya as my new name, I was called *Ambé* and this is *her* memoir dedicated to the heart of the Wild Divine Sophia and the love that shines forth from the hearts of all beings.

The Grail Rider was born from a life-altering encounter with the Divine Mother Sophia, whom I encountered during a shamanic journey in June of 2003. It is *Her* illuminated consciousness that guides me on an epic travel adventure to reclaim the unified heart through revisiting multiple timelines and places where my soul had splintered off from it's Divine source and monadic core.

It was on that ceremonial twilight evening that I asked Creator the one question that I had asked throughout the course of my life: *How may I best serve this planet and this precious human life?* The answer came flooding in as a single epiphany while laying face down in the dirt, utterly motionless for over nine hours while the Divine Mother Sophia infused my being with an all-embracing love-light and multi-dimensional transmission that has forever changed the nature of my life.

As this high voltage frequency blazed through my body, my Family of Light appeared to me and revealed that they were one consciousness that have incarnated over lifetimes to pollinate the Earth with the seeds of Universal Christ Consciousness. These are the very light seeds now blossoming within me and the hearts of all those who feel called as I have to join in ushering in the Golden Age of Gaia.

The Grail Rider follows a series of initiatory and serendipitous events that were put into motion after this ceremonial encounter with the Sophianic Christ consciousness. She transmitted to me that life on Earth would evolve into its next phase of awakened heart-centred unity through each being undergoing the inner alchemy of sacred union known as *Heiros Gamos* or the Divine Inner Marriage. *Heiros Gamos* is a rite of spiritual passage, a gnostic term that describes the complete balance, restoration and unification of polarity throughout all layers of our consciousness, architecture and light body.

Divine Sophia went on to transmit; *Your soul purpose is to remember the truth of who you are. This re-membrance invites you to heal the unconscious split between the Masculine and Feminine. It is through the alchemy of integrating the light and the dark, that peace on Earth is made possible. The harmonic union of the Masculine and the Feminine within will propel you along with countless others to give birth to your Christ child and become the change you so long to see in the world.* Little did I know at the time, that this burning desire to offer my life in service to the whole would in turn cost me all that I once knew myself to be.

The over-lighting vibrational presence of the Divine Sophia, known by her many names, continues to weave her wisdom in a myriad of wondrous ways throughout this story. I invite you to relate to her by the name that is in highest resonance and affinity for you. As my constant travel companion, I refer to her as the Goddess, Feminine Christ, Soul of Nature and Gaia Sophia in her Earthly form. Legend has it that she once walked upon this Earth as the embodiment of Isis, the re-assembler of lost knowledge. The Egyptian goddess Isis was known for her healing and resurrection powers. She is often associated with the life force, fertility and creational energy of the sacred womb chalice within us all. She was entrusted with the sacred task of reassembling the scattered wisdom of the Goddess into a body of knowledge that would bring life back to the wasteland of a dying Earth. It is told that She took off her crown, wrapped her hair in a scarf and went in search of the remnants of lost wisdom throughout many foreign lands. Dressed in the mode of a woman traveler, the pilgrim Goddess wore a cloak to prevent drawing attention to herself. Over the course of thousands of years and countless lifetimes, Sophia has now emerged from each culture and country, having retrieved a part of her soul's memory of Sacred Union to remind us all of our true nature as love, lover and beloved.

We are all Divine Sophia's children and when the time is ripe, she may call upon you according to your unique mythos and divine destiny. The labyrinth of the initiates journey is well traversed by all those called to journey through the unknown internal and external landscapes of the soul. It is ultimately this burning desire to return home to the origin of Love – driven by the relentless calling to serve this precious life on Earth – that motivates the initiate to give oneself in entirety to this quest and in turn be delivered to the wellspring of one's own awakened heart.

Likened to Sophia and the countless pilgrims who have travelled before me, I had a profound spiritual experience that propelled me to journey into strange and unfamiliar lands, to the legendary places where the sacred initiates of the past planted seeds of divine consciousness for me to magically stumble upon. As I retraced the footsteps of the Magdalene, daughter of Isis and bride of Yeshua, I was empowered to excavate and reclaim the lost facets of my soul, which were buried deep within the unconscious and wounded parts of my cellular memory. Eventually, the unpredictable labyrinth of the Great Mystery led me to wed the Divine and forge an abiding relationship that continues to evolve and grow in intimacy to this very day!

The mystic's journey of wedding the Divine is often referred to as *alchemy*, by which we transform the lead of our lives into gold. By each embarking upon our unique alchemical journey, we come to embody the remedy to the atrocities of our individual and collective past. The reward is one of becoming one with our essential nature while dancing in symbiotic union with all of creation. This is the legacy of our time, where each unique facet of the whole awakens within the soul of nature and join in the co-creation of a planet that flourishes together as one unified Family of Light.

I am grateful you are here with me to share in the story of how I followed a stream of synchronistic events into the mythic lands of England, France, Italy and Greece to discover the origin of the Divine Beloved, who is called by many names throughout this book. This memoir was written in partnership with the over-lighting wisdom of the Christos Sophia as an offering of Love to assist individuals on their return journey home.

I invite you to travel along with me through inner and outer alchemical landscapes to discover the source of the living Grail. This tale serves as a richly encoded treasure map that will lead you on a journey through the legendary ley-lines to retrace the footsteps of the spiritual Wayshowers of the past who have left timeless clues and universal light codes for those who are called, as I was to remember my eternal roots.

I feel moved to share a little of how this whale of a tale into the heart of the living Grail all began, at least in this lifetime. I was born in the sprawl of Los Angeles in the late 1960s. At that time, I was unaware that I was one of the first wave of Indigo Blue Starseed children, who incarnate to pioneer and anchor the New Earth energies. These races were sent to the Earth as guardians and protectors of the living light library and to prevent this planet from descending into the fallen or false Phantom Matrix. Indigos are often the system busters and harbingers of the huge paradigm shift of consciousness that is upon us now. They come to anchor a vibrational frequency of unified love and harmonic balance for their families, community and the collective. The Starseeds are here to fulfill this planetary Ascension cycle by anchoring the frequencies and light codes required to activate the planetary grid and support individuals to embody their sovereign Divinity. Over time, I have come to know that this particular blueprint requires a lifetime of learning how to balance polarity and embody the light so that I may become an integral part in raising the vibration of the whole.

From the onset of my birth, I was a highly empathic and aware child and extremely sensitive to discordant and inorganic energies. I can remember how rattled I felt living amongst the weight of unconscious denial that governed my family and their fast-paced Los Angeles lifestyle. All to often, I would become emotionally upset when I felt people to be disconnected from their heart, each other, Mother Nature and Great Spirit. At times, it was excruciating, as I was psychically open and acutely aware of the unspoken impact of the overly materialistic lifestyle that people would often refer to as living the "California dream".

Even though my mother and father did their very best to provide me the luxuries of a middle-class lifestyle, I often felt like an estranged child in my own reality television show – one that closely resembled the television series *Madmen*. As far as I could tell, humans were all 'mad'. And no matter how much we consumed, shopped, prayed or popped happy pills, this hunger to fill the insatiable void seemed to only get more pervasive. I can still recall feeling the unconscious energies of the people around me living in a state of perpetual dissatisfaction and chronic disappointment. To cope, people were often taught and encouraged to look 'good' and 'keep up appearances' at an extreme cost that often ruptured their connection with their authentic Self. All the while they lived inside a bubble of well-disguised pain and chronic shame. I rarely felt safe enough to simply relax and be myself around most people. Never mind breathe, as I recall being surrounded by clouds of cigarette smoke considered to make adults look ultra-cool and attractive. *Glad those days are over!* Meanwhile, the number one hit Rolling Stone song, 'Satisfaction', played on the radio: *'I can't get no* satisfaction. *I can't get no satisfaction. Cuz I try and I try and I try. I can't get no, no, no, no!'*

For the most part, this extreme sensitivity was profoundly misunderstood and served as a driving force for my longing for deep, meaningful and authentic connection. It was around 1975, when the barrage of nightmares began for me. They lasted well over a year. Night after night, after an intense struggle to soothe my racing heart, I would eventually fall asleep to the sound of fire trucks, only to have lucid dreams of Earth's inevitable destruction – horrifying scenes of earthquakes, tidal waves, atom bombs, massive floods, pandemics and uncontrollable wild fires flooded my inner landscape. I watched skyscrapers crumble like pastry and atom bombs explode like giant fiery mushrooms. This onslaught of Earth Armageddon imagery convinced me that we were nearing the end of the world and that life on Earth was in grave and imminent danger. At this young age, I felt an unceasing pressure to wake up and change the course of the world that could potentially destroy me along with all of life's precious creatures – that is, if *I* didn't do something about it.

At the age of ten, I had a vivid revelation that humanity's disconnection from their authentic core and creative passion corresponded to the visions of Earth Armageddon that had haunted me night after night. I sensed that people's split from their Divine Self and the living consciousness of Mother Nature had created the enormous death urge that was now turning the human race into the greatest weapon of mass destruction ever known.

At times the discomfort was unbearable as I observed humanity's unconscious shit being buried, exploded, blown up, and dumped upon our precious Earth. Meanwhile, humans continued to harvest her most precious resources in order to covet and consume more and more, never quite getting that elusive 'satisfaction'. In those early days, sheer terror motivated me to live in that incessant burning question: *How can my life be in service to the whole?* This question consumed my every waking and sleeping hours. So much so that I spent hours in meditation, attempting to glimpse an answer in those rare gaps of silence that existed between a barrage of erratic thoughts. I would dive into the void with some hope of retrieving a magical key that would in some miraculous way, show me the way before it was all too late.

In those formative days, I tossed and turned in an ocean of helpless desperation that created an ongoing low-grade anxiety within me. *How was anyone going to understand the urgency I felt for myself and humanity to wake up before it was all too late?* I can still remember the night, terrified of being caught up in yet another catastrophic barrage while sleeping, I decided to never go to sleep again until I could find a way to help shift the course of Earth's potential fatal destiny. As everyone around me seemed preoccupied with the latest celebrity fashion, my quest to do my part *consciously* began at the ripe age of ten and most likely over countless lifetimes.

Eventually, my brilliant mom enrolled me in a transformational seminar. At ten years old, I attended my first personal growth seminar called, The Children's Training, in which the fierce and feisty female seminar leader told me loud and clear, 'You have the power to change what you find unbearable in this world by taking full responsibility and changing your thoughts!'

Even though I was quite skeptical at first, I was intrigued by the idea, because the seminar leader felt like one of the first human beings that really saw me and acknowledged that there was a highly sensitive and aware person living inside my tomboy body. At last, there was someone I could entrust with my visions and along with her guidance, begin my journey of self- empowerment and steering the course of my life beyond the doom and gloom scenarios that haunted my dreamtime.

During those three weekends (which felt nothing like my lazy days at summer camp), the trainer would remind the children, 'You will never be able to transform your life circumstances by feeling like a victim, nor from worrying, fretting and complaining about life. You must realise that on some level, you chose this life, your parents, your challenges and all of the unique circumstances. Behind every nightmare is an opportunity to create a happy dream. The key is to find your magic powers instead of waiting for someone or something to rescue or save you. If you want to be happy and have a fulfilling life, you best get on with creating that life from inside of you! As soon as you do, you will discover the power and resources to change your reality has been inside you all along. Abracadabra! Just like that. Magic!' She added, as she handed us each our own magic wand and 'get of jail free' card.

Admittedly, this was more than a tall order for a child to come to terms with. The Children's Training was the beginning of a lifelong quest to becoming the change I so passionately sought to see in the world. From then on, I taught myself how to ground into the Earth, calm my nervous system and create a peaceful night's sleep by placing my attention on something more pleasant and desirable that I wished to experience. I sought out ways to embody solutions as my way of making a difference in a world that was seemingly destroying its own home at an accelerated pace. I vowed that I would devote my life to the art of waking up to the truth of who and what I am rather than blindly follow the collective trance of mass distraction.

As wondrous *and* tumultuous my upbringing was, I know deep down that my parents did their very best. They provided me with an abundance of love, support, core values and cultural experiences that continue to enrich and bless my life. I now stand in a place of immense gratitude and bless the mess that has made me into the person I am today.

Throughout the course of my life, I have been led by this intrinsic love and reverence for life and an unceasing passion to heal the roots of my own and humanity's disconnection from Source, the Earth and from one another. I have travelled the globe to sacred sites as a pilgrim of the Divine and have woven my love of art, nature and spirit into becoming an Evolutionary Priestess of the Beauty Way.

My global journeys have led me to immerse myself in a plethora of Eastern and Western spiritual traditions, wisdom cultures and multi-dimensional healing modalities. I have delved deeply into Tibetan Buddhism, Taoism, Yoga, meditation, Holistic Health, Rebirthing, Chi Nei Tsang, Shamanism, Energetic healing, Conscious Evolution, Akashic Clairvoyant studies and immersed myself in a vast array of Evolutionary Temple Arts. Feeling highly motivated to heal and empower myself and others to embody the majesty of our Divine nature, I have dedicated my life to being a clear and conscious conduit for the awakening of a Divine New Earth humanity.

With deep humility and boundless love, I offer this timeless tale to all of the courageous pioneering souls who have gone before me, for those who are with me now and for those who are yet to come. Each one of us has said 'yes' to embarking upon our uniquely encoded Hero or Heroine's journey. May we always return to the central fire to share our magnificent stories of discovery as the very gifts that bless each other and this ever-evolving world that we are gifted to share. Finally, on behalf of all those who are called, as I have to live in the open-ended inquiry of *'How may I best serve this planet and precious human life'*, may this journey inspire and serve as an alchemical treasure map that leads you to the greatest treasure of all.

SUGGESTIONS *for your* GRAIL RIDE

Woven throughout this story are universal healing codes and vibrational words that carry the potential to alchemise you along the way. As you travel along, you may experience an aspect of your own story come up for reflection and review. I invite you to stay open, curious and grounded throughout. With bold and tender curiosity, please receive only that which feels in highest affinity and resonance for you. And just in case your feathers get a wee ruffled along the way, I invite you to use these triggers as opportunities for deep inquiry that serve to expand the love that you are and always have been.

As you embark upon this Grail ride, you may find that your own story begins to unravel and transform as a new one is being born – one where self-responsibility, dignity and abiding respect replace the heartbreak of victim, betrayal and separation from Source. As hidden shadows may surface, be compassionate, kind and gentle with yourself, as you may go through a metamorphosis of birthing the monarch butterfly that you are.

The Grail Rider highlights a plethora of spiritual lineages that have blessed and contributed to my journey of awakening. I wish to clarify that within this quest, I relate to a variety of spiritual masters and deities as benevolent guides and friends that graciously guide and support me along the way. I wish to honour your special relationship to each one of them and invite you to receive their presence as a vibrational gift that inspires to awaken these Divine qualities within you. It is my highest intention to share with you universal codes of awakening that enrich and compliment your journey, no matter what your religious or spiritual orientation may be. In essence, I have the greatest respect for your sovereign journey and vital contribution to the whole.

It feels vital to highlight that just because the story of the Grail Rider was in part catalysed by a shamanic journey, I am in no way endorsing their usage as the pathway to spiritual awakening and Christ Consciousness. With the greatest honour and respect for our plant medicine allies, I recognize that there are countless ways to access awakened states of consciousness and multi-dimensional realms without engaging in mind-altering substances. For some, they are supportive and for others, they may lead to adverse side-effects.

We are going to take a journey that conspires to bring out the greatest potential in all of us as we cultivate intimacy with ourselves in the seen and unseen realms. You may find, as I have, that this narrative evolves along with you, ever revealing its deeper mysteries along the way with refreshing epiphanies and insights. And just as one reaches the end of a spiral of soul growth, we come to arrive as beginners in the next. This story continues to alchemise and prepare me to embody the sacred covenant of the Inner Marriage while discovering the ever-evolving nuances of Sacred Union and Evolutionary Relationship.

May you love yourself relentlessly, embrace the power of your innermost heart in the knowing that everything that happens to you is designed and destined to bring you into absolute Sacred Union with the eternal Beloved. Blessings on your journey beloved one. I am ever so grateful that you are here.

The names of characters in this book and some of the locations have been modified to respect the privacy of those who participated in the creation of this story. I am forever grateful and honour the invaluable soul lessons and gifts that each being has contributed to my life and this spiritual memoir in service to the whole.

PART
I

CHAPTER ONE

HER WILD MAJESTY

BLESSING

We call upon the celestial realms, the Angelic beings, the planetary
guides and protectors, and the ascended ones to bless all beings
and to be present here with us. We call upon the Divine light of
Love, Truth and Harmony to shine in places that need healing and
guide our way. We ask for these blessings with great reverence,
from our Mother – the Earth, the Sky, the Moon, the Stars, the Sun
– our Father. May we always remember we're pure consciousness,
the essence of Life, the source of all things. May we find the
courage to let go fear and the pain of past conditioning. Let us walk
upon the Earth gently, as true spiritual warriors, inter-dimensional
midwifes giving birth to our true Self. Letting go of separation,
evolving beyond limitation into divine self-expression thereby
assisting into a co-creation of a dawning light filled world.
Om Shanti, Shanti, Shanti...

– Darpan, *LoveLight*

Mount the stallion of Love
And do not fear the path
Love's stallion knows the way exactly
However black with obstacles the path may be
With one leap Love's horse will carry you home

– Jelaluddin Rumi

Once upon a time on a beautiful twilight evening, my eleven housemates and I gathered together around a campfire as the last rays of the setting sun streamed forth through the luscious forest amphitheater. Gaia's Grove was nestled in a little town just north of the Golden Gate Bridge of San Francisco and one of the many places throughout the world that I had come to lovingly call home. Even at that twilight hour, I can still recollect the feeling of imminent change looming in the air as my heart quickened with anticipation for all that was yet to be unraveled and undone.

Like loving and protective guardians, the majestic trees towered over my eclectic soul family casting beams of shimmering golden light upon their faces. The trees swayed in unison to a celestial rhythm reminding me to stay rooted in my core, fluid in my limbs and true to my essential nature.

In preparation for our ceremony, each person in our circle created a personal altar by placing inspirational pictures, crystals, and sacred objects upon the leaf-covered ground before them. As I attuned to our unified field, I sensed that each one of us quietly anticipated a death of sorts, an ending to who and what we once knew ourselves to be. After all, one is never quite the same after communing with such a wise and sacred plant medicine.

As the ceremony commenced, a gentle wind rustled through the fern leaves and two hawks screeched and encircled overhead. Otherwise, all was silent and still, that is, apart from my thunderous heart. Out of my commitment to heal and come into greater wholeness, I humbly surrendered to the Divine, and sent out a prayer that I may come to know a deeper truth of who I am and how I might serve this precious human life.

As the sun descended behind the mountain, we wrapped ourselves up in a colourful array of blankets to ensure we stayed warm throughout the night. I took a moment to look around the circle and admire the radiant soul light emanating from this eclectic group of friends. Over the last seven years of living in community together, each magnificent being had profoundly touched my life and I had grown to cherish their unique essence and beauty. This precious tribe of kindred hearts had become the brothers and sisters I never had as a child. Full-body goddess bumps raised the tiny hairs on my arms as my eyes went around the circle as if for the very last time to offer a final farewell to each one of them – *at least for now, that is.* My instincts told me we would each be very different people in the morning. I could feel a quivering in the marrow of my bones as I offered up a silent prayer before surrendering into the company of my own sovereign being: *Journey well, beloved star family. May the long time sun, shine upon you, all love surround you and the pure light within guide our way home.*

Santiago and Aisha were our Shamanic guides for the evening. They prepared for our ceremony with precision like intent and other worldly reverence. Tobacco, rose water and bundled leaves used for purification were placed on his left side while a variety of indigenous instruments sat in front of him. To the right of him stood an unusual glass bottle filled with a dark amber, molasses-like liquid accompanied by two empty coconuts hulls. Santiago lit the sage, cedar and copal to purify the space. It felt like hours of silence had passed before Santiago visited each one of us with the chakapa. He used the bundled leaves to tenderly brush over the front and back of our bodies serving to cleanse our auras while bringing comfort with their rustling sound. He then resumed his seat next to Aisha and commenced the ceremony by invoking the spirit guides and celestial beings with his lullaby-like kalimba and gentle Icuru chant. He then called upon the seven directions and offered a prayer to honour the guardian spirits of the land and plant medicine. We joined in by offering our heart-felt gratitude for the gift of this ancient Amazonian vine that would guide us with Her all consuming love, omniscient wisdom and ruthless grace that dissolves the cobwebs of illusion.

Even though her body was petite and delicate, like the hummingbird feather she held between her thumb and forefinger, Santiago's partner, Aisha, was fiercely present and acutely aware of the slightest movements within our circle. She held the ground with precision-like focus and kept the steady rhythm of her rattle while whistling a welcome prayer to the Divine Mother and Father of Creation. She summoned their presence to bless our ceremonial circle such that each may receive precisely what was needed for our highest soul growth and evolution. Her humble innocence and crystalline voice soothed and comforted the butterflies flittering within the pit of my belly.

We were told that this was no ordinary medicine. 'This particular plant is the descendant of a five-hundred-year-old vine,' Santiago shared with the circle as if he was forewarning us for what was to come. We were being blessed by this benevolent plant intelligence more ancient than the old-growth trees that surrounded us. Santiago passed a macaw feather around the circle; that represented the opening of our psychic and spiritual abilities. We were each invited to hold the blue and green iridescent feather, and share our deepest prayers and intentions for the ceremony. He then walked around the circle and purified our auras with splashes of rose and tobacco water and then poured a portion of it into our cupped palms. We sipped the cleansing water in preparation for our communion with the uncompromising love of *Madre Tierra*.

With the nimbleness of a lion, Santiago rejoined Aisha in the circle. He gently shook the glass bottle filled with amber nectar and poured a small portion into the coconut chalice. As I prepared myself to leave behind all that I knew myself to be, I summoned the courage to offer my life in service to this precious Earth and my highest purpose within it. One by one, we approached our shamanic guides with a humble reverence to receive our dose of medicinal tea in a sacred way. When my turn came, I composed my beating heart and approached Santiago with all the bravery I could muster up at the time. As I drank from the coconut-shell cup, I did my best to swallow the thick syrupy elixir that was all together bitter, pungent and sweet. The sludge-like liquid went down my throat with an intensity that made me squirm and shiver all at once, while leaving an unforgettable aftertaste in my mouth. There was no denying it, I was consciously choosing to die so that I may truly know what it was to be fully alive.

The central fire sparked and sputtered as our circle of twelve sat transfixed in the tenuous wonderment of what was to become of each one of us. The gentle rhythms of Santiago's kalimba and Aisha's angelic voice continued to soothe and carry me, helping to guide the poignant medicine into the river of my blood, where it would slowly, layer by layer, unwrap my DNA and unravel the ancient codes of remembrance encrusted between my etheric feathers.

Whoa, Mamacita! Suddenly, the first wave of *Madre Ayahuasca* came rushing in – quick, strong and fierce like a tidal wave, insisting

I let go of any resistance to her all-consuming presence. Even though I preferred to sit upright with the others, my body swiftly folded into child's pose, with my forehead facedown toward the fire. As I lay motionless in prostration upon the forest floor, I became lucidly aware that I had arrived at a point of no return. With an unapologetic announcement, the plant spirit oozed into every sub-atomic particle of my being. She demanded nothing less than my complete presence and simultaneous surrender. Deep full breaths was all I could draw upon to keep me centred as I whirled down a bottomless wormhole. I landed in *Her* multi-dimensional world of rainbow fractal light complete with undulating plant spirits who communicated through the language light and pure feeling frequency.

Her purpose was inexorable: to turn my DNA inside out and upside down, revealing the divine codex encapsulated within it. This five-hundred-year-old vine ruthlessly wrapped itself around every fiber of my being. She unstrapped me from all human assemblage points and then took me into her intergalactic bosom on the most highly transpersonal, cosmic unraveling of my entire existence. Breath by breath, I descended into more expanded states of lucid awareness as I communed with Pachamama, the soul of the natural world. As *Her* presence intensified, I found myself riding a majestic white lion that whisked me away on one of the wildest, inter-dimensional, cosmic rides of my entire life. At some unidentifiable point, I had reached the point of no return. I had gone, gone, gone beyond all that I once knew myself to be.

What followed was a continuous download of vivid imagery accompanied by an all-consuming, love-beauty intelligence that flooded my awareness with rainbow, pearlescent, aqua-marine and golden-white diamond light that can be best described as 'home'. A multi-dimensional pantheon of extremely lucid, movie-like clips played out in full-spectrum colour upon the inner screen of my mind's eye. Within this influx of vivid impressions, each representative from this Christ Council of Light paid me a warm and congenial visit. One by one, they greeted me with their interchanging expressions, making it crystal clear that they were unique expressions of one over-lighting soul. Each embodied a vital thread of the tapestry of the Divine Christos Sophia. They telepathically conveyed to me through vibration, vivid images, symbols, sacred geometries, and deep-feeling frequencies that penetrated my heart and reminded me all the while that I too, was a part of their beloved family.

They proceeded to download my consciousness with a pictorial journey of the Divine Feminine and Divine Masculine as they've incarnated throughout lifetimes to self-initiate and seed the planet with the eternal codes of Sacred Union and the Law of One. Isis, Mother Mary, Mary Magdalene, Sarah, Grandmother Anna, and Yeshua were the main beings that appeared to me predominantly because I was the most familiar with them. They showed me images of a treasure chest that held a golden chalice along with majestic caves, wooden boats, turquoise seas, star tetrahedrons, wild white horses, dolphins, whales and so much more. I was infused with a feeling of crystalline presence, the energetic signature of my family of Divine origin. This was a reunion and homecoming unlike anything I had ever experienced before. Each star being felt to be an intimate friend, undeniably familiar as they flooded me in a waterfall of sublime love and homecoming. And yet, this undeniable feeling of majestic belonging was simultaneously accompanied by a longing in the centre of my heart as vast as the night universe. *Would I ever come to truly belong?*

Over the next nine hours, the interchanging faces of my Family of Light occupied my lucid awareness, transmitting to me the authentic story of who they really are, where they came from, and the higher purpose for their various incarnations on Earth. They revealed that they too had to face countless challenges of navigating the terrain of their human emotions while staying anchored to the Divine plan. They strived as I did to stay awake, aware and connected to Source through tumultuous waves of darkness and uncertainty.

I was in awe of how in the midst of unfathomable devastation they had remained resilient and loyal to their larger purpose as Divine Wayshowers in service to a greater unfolding plan. They reminded me that humanity was at a vital crossroads and that the key to bringing the beloved Earth back into harmony and balance was through each undergoing the Inner Marriage; the process of wedding one's authentic Self to the Divine Beloved within. In turn, this alchemical wedding would end the war within and usher in a New Earth anchored in abiding love and respect for *all* of life.

Just like when I was a child and stayed awake for countless nights, I saw how once again Mother Earth was on the verge of total destruction and Gaia was calling to me and each one of us to awaken to a deeper truth and reality. They revealed that my larger purpose was to assist humanity to cross the river of separation and join with the ocean of Oneness.

After countless hours of lying face down in the Earth, I slowly emerged at dawn to gently touch my face and find it covered in moist dirt, leaves and twigs. While the others remained motionless under their blankets, I reoriented myself to my surroundings and realised I had barely moved from lying face down in child's pose. Feeling massively altered, I slowly sat upright amongst the towering redwoods and noticed a singular image blazing within my third eye. It was of a white marble statue tucked away within a silvery cave that was dripping with water. As I focused my awareness the image became clearer of a woman wearing a long cascading robe. She held a singular ruby red rose between her delicate fingers.

As the dawn was breaking, I managed to drag my limp body to the outdoor shower next to our hot tub. I peeled off my soiled clothes and rinsed off in the refreshing cool water. Still meandering between worlds, I snuggled into my cozy nest that I had carefully prepared the day before as my post-ceremony lily pad. As I lye there under my feathered duvet, my consciousness continued to dance between the dimensions, gently gathering epiphanies like wild flowers from which I made a vibrant spiritual bouquet. Before long, I was consumed by a tidal wave of high frequency Love that enveloped my being in a coccoon of diamond light. This was a LOVE as bright as the radiant sun, so familiar and yet unlike anything I had ever experienced before. Wave upon wave of nectarous bliss-light coursed through my being like dazzling sunlight making love to the crystalline sea. As I continued to drift between worlds, my Family of Light flooded my awareness with the full-bodied knowingness that I was made of the same eternal stardust...and it was time to come home once *and* for all.

CHAPTER TWO

DOWN THE RABBIT HOLE

*The future of the world depends on the full restoration
of the Sacred Feminine in all its tenderness, passion,
Divine ferocity and surrendered persistence.*

– Andrew Harvey

Everyone had their own vision and experience of the Holy Shekinah's many gifts, not the least of which was the unmistakable presence of the Mother of all Life. Regardless of her many names, the Holy Spirit came, according to each one's belief. She was felt within every heart and body, according to each one's capacity to hold Her mighty presence, which was like being consumed in flames of light. Then, when the capacity was reached, each was stretched and stretched until all in equal measure received the gifts of Spirit their Soul had long awaited since the beginning to incarnate in flesh.

The feminine creative aspect of the Godhead came down and alighted upon each of us with the softness of a white dove. Her embrace was both incredibly sweet and terrible. Sweet, because her Divine Love is the milk of eternal life. Her countenance was only 'dark and terrible' to those who chose to resist her embrace. For it is that when her intoxicating nectars are drunk, everything dissolves into formless being. In the moment of her coming, we became one with the Birther of All Life. We became one with God, the Mother-Father! In those precious hours, we knew only One.

It was that fiery, consuming anointing of Holy Spirit that sustained us throughout our remaining days! Regardless of our outer circumstances on the Earthplane, whether we witnessed joy or suffering, the Holy Spirit, like a dove of eternal peace, carried us into our destiny, each in our own way.

– Claire Heartsong, *Anna, Grandmother of Jesus*

Nearly three weeks had passed since I lay face down in the redwood grove, drooling unabashedly in the dirt. I spent some days integrating my experience and doing my best to adjust to 'normal life'. I tended to gravitate toward the practical and mundane tasks as if to dilute the magnitude of what I had experienced in the grove. Yet, deep down, I knew my life would never be the same. The images, feelings and frequencies that downloaded into me from the Divine Mother and my Family of Light continued to circulate within my body and mind like shimmering encoded clues to a mysterious puzzle. I felt like I was being summoned by a future memory, along with a deep sense of imminence that pulsated from my heart-womb.

In truth, my home at Gaia's Grove was far from ordinary, nor was my life. I was living amongst an eclectic community of Evolutionary Change Agents, Cultural Creatives and New Earth Engineers, each of whom surfed the leading edge of consciousness in his or her own unique and creative way. Gaia's Grove was a community epicentre for all kinds of visionary artists, sacred musicians and guardians of the New Earth. I was mostly known as the yogini/priestess/healer of the bunch and at the time taught Dolphin Flow yoga, practiced integrative healing arts and guided transformational Temple Art trainings at a variety wellness centres and sacred sites throughout the world.

Several weeks after my shamanic journey, I was surprised and elated to see my old friend Jahrusha turn up unexpectedly at the Grove. He was passing through our little town on his way to pay a visit to the renowned Divine Mother, Ammachi, popular throughout the world for her immense global charity and giving life-changing hugging Darshan. Jahrusha and I shared a warm fondness for each other that spanned over lifetimes. In all honesty, I admired his free spirit and mystical whimsy and had a kind of soul-mate crush on him. People would often comment on how we looked like an old indigenous married couple or twin-star siblings. I was anxious to consult with him and hear what he had to say about my recent experience in the redwood grove.

A tingly warmth washed through me as we embraced. As always, the timeless familiarity between us made me grin from head to toe. Jahrusha would typically turn up out of the blue weeks and sometimes days before one of my sacred site journeys. His appearance typically heralded a massive change in my life. Although our visits were infrequent and unpredictable, they were always life changing and highly pivotal. His gift of vision was beyond impressive as he allowed a streaming of clear impressions that served to illuminate significant signposts along the way. I prayed that we would get some solo time together so that I may receive his wise and intuitive counsel. He was the one who could make sense of it all while highlighting my part and planetary assignment to bring healing to the grid and consciousness of a particular place.

Over the last eighteen years, I had made several excursions to sacred sites around the world. Each of them began with a relentless beckoning that eventually grew into a loud siren. The calling would inevitably become so strong that it was impossible to ignore until it eventually rendered me choiceless to do anything but go and let myself be guided by the invisible hand of Gaia. More often than not, I was called to travel to a sacred site where the ancient and the future would converge to be recalibrated and rebalanced to serve in the restoration of harmony and peace throughout the world. Thus far, each excursion was inexplicably interconnected and shared a common thread of creating greater coherence, connection and communication between each sacred site that I visited. Each place that I was called to go held specific key codes to assist humanity to awaken and activate their Divine Human blueprint. Pieces of a greater puzzle would reveal themselves where the ancient and new worlds intersected. Before each of these journeys, Jahrusha would offer me his gift of intuitive vision and precision-like guidance. He would share about some of the potential challenges I might encounter along the way, as well as what transformation might be called forth in relationship to these challenges. All that I knew was that I was being called out once again to venture into the vast unknown.

I gently closed my bedroom door behind us and prayed we would not be disturbed by my eleven roommates or summoned by any other surprise visitors. I might add, this kind of privacy was nearly impossible in my fun-loving tribal community.

Jahrusha sat cross-legged in front of me, adjusted his long embroidered tunic and cleared his throat, followed by a long pause. This radiant Texan-born mystic was a true shaman, a medicine man who beamed a huge gregarious grin and deep brown eyes that glistened with the light of his smiling heart. My wizard-like, elven friend walked in several worlds at one time. I watched his big brown eyes roll back behind his eyelids to rest in a place of extraordinary vision. After a long silence, he let out a deep chuckle of amusement that could only come from tapping into a vision of cosmic proportions. I paid close attention as his gaze refocused upon my restless eyes and then spoke the following words:

'There is a place somewhere in the South of France surrounded by bright turquoise waters. Spain sits close to one side, Italy on the other side, the Italian Alps tower behind. Here, in a small town, your true homecoming and awakening awaits you. It is a place where the dark and light flow into one and returns you to the Source, the Source where the waters converge. This place is a home for you, where you will kiss the feet of the Beloved and remember something that has long been forgotten.

'A pod of etheric dolphins will escort you, and you will be accompanied by many high masters and celestial beings. This is a culmination journey for you. You have taken many prior journeys to this point of self-realization. A silver mirror will go out from your third eye and call forth your significant other and soul mate. There will be times you will be romantic, but mostly, he will be more like a friend. Be careful not to have strong expectations.

'Upon this journey, you will be called to be strong and yield your sword of truth as you walk as an emissary of peace, planting seeds for a more harmonious and unified future. There will be times you will be placed in cities and you will not like them at all. These cities will test your capacity to maintain your balance and centre in the face of chaos and uncertainty. Be in integrity and this will ease your experience greatly.

'Wanderer of truth, you will go as an Wayshower of light to bridge the worlds and meet the Goddess in her most cherished form. There is a golden child stirring within your heart-womb who represents a being of immense purity and light. You will meet her there and guide her to open and trust so that she can help many to awaken to their own divine innocence and childlike nature.

'You are tracing the footsteps of the Divine Christos Sophia to the source of the true Beloved. When you have finally surrendered all last traces of resistance, a beautiful whale in the form of your grandfather will leap from the sea and assist you to remember your true place of origin, which is always within your own innermost heart.

'In truth, this journey began several lifetimes ago. It is the story of the Feminine Christ and her initiatory journey into divine sovereignty and Sacred Union. There is a beautiful price for this communion, which is the willingness to offer oneself up to the complete unknown. This is your enlightenment journey, in which you will conceive and give birth to a beautiful golden child. Prepare yourself to be gone for three months to a year. Pack lightly, have faith and remember – the white horses and dolphins that you encounter along the way are a sign of the Goddess who is with and within you.'

I felt the enormity of Jahrusha's reading, which stirred both excitement and apprehension in me all at once. *Best not to over think this too much,* I advised myself, feeling the need to let it seep in slowly rather than taking the shot all at once. Instead, I chose to refocus my attention on the practical reality of what it was going to take to fly out of my cozy yet crowded nest. Jahrusha and I embraced, my heart swollen with gratitude for the gift of his gift to see the unseen realms. I then excused myself to get ready for our evening together.

I could not imagine a better time to receive the blessing of the Divine Mother, Ammachi, I thought to myself, as I changed into my long, white cotton dress. Receiving one of her warm, sparkling hugs and chocolate kisses was exactly what I needed to settle the newly hatched butterflies swarming inside my belly. Within the hour, my van was filled with giddy housemates. Jahrusha sat in the passenger seat next to me, maintaining his mischievous, all-knowing grin. I was grateful to have some time to integrate the reading over the long drive to Ammachi's ashram. After all, this was the beginning of the end of my life as I knew it and there was no other place to be than in the arms of the Divine Mother.

CHAPTER THREE

GONE, GONE, GONE BEYOND

After a large shift, there is an attempt to return to life as we once knew it
– to go back to where it is safe and secure and predictable.

– Joseph Campbell, *The Hero's Journey*

The Grail is a way of being and will always remain true
to its essential nature: a marriage of paradox, a mysterious
and sacred courtship that reveals itself as an improvisational dance
between the awakened heart and luminous mind.

– Inaiya Ray

We returned home from Amma's ashram around 2am. Weary to the bones, I dove into bed and pulled the covers over my head as if to hide from the intensity of my encroaching destiny. Before the first light of the morning sun, I was startled awake by a lucid dream. It had been a stormy night. I had tossed and turned in my sleep, just like the boat in my dream, which was lost at sea in a tumultuous storm. Tormented and alone in my capsized boat, I awoke, startled and strained to remember the details of my dream, sensing its prophetic nature.

My beautiful white boat was sinking in a giant whirlpool of turbulent ocean water. Everything physically and materially that I had created in my life thus far was sinking along with the boat, bubbles and all – *bloop, bloop, bloop*. Struggling to save whatever I could, I observed in shock and awe as all of my material possessions representing different parts of my life, were swallowed up by the mouth of the foamy sea. While still deep in the dream, I desperately strategised how I could replace the missing pieces of myself. The struggle felt like it went on and on, until in the end, it proved to be completely futile. My boat was sinking, and along with it, my entire identity and all of my precious belongings. I could do nothing but succumb and come to accept my apparent loss.

The following morning, I sat straight up in bed with my heart pounding wildly, feeling completely overwhelmed by my prophetic dream. Yet, another part of me recognised that this catastrophic end- to-life feeling was also a clear sign that I was being led to the most mysterious new beginning. Still, I was in a kind of existential shock. On that Saturday morning, I decided to use my creative energy to shift this feeling of fear and overwhelm to a place of excited anticipation about the adventure that was yet to come. With the determined will of a fierce lioness, I jumped out of bed, threw on some yoga clothes and headed off to Sausalito to dance out my prophetic nightmare at a Sweat Your Prayers ecstatic dance class.

On that particular day, the parking lot was overflowing with vehicles. It was 9.11am and there were yellow ribbons strung across the entrance doors with a sign that read, 'Do not enter. Capacity full.' The large gymnasium was throbbing with hundreds of bodies grooving to the rhythms of electronica world beats. It felt like the whole structure of the building was shaking from its very foundation and core. My heartbeat was erratic from the trauma of my dream, combined with the strong urge to lose myself inside the gyrating pool of wildly abandoned dancers. Quickly scanning through my possible options, I was overcome by a kind of supernatural survival instinct and decided to walk around to the back of the building to try to sneak into the throbbing gymnasium via the emergency door exit.

A tall lanky woman wearing a blue spandex unitard, covered by a large canary yellow tank top spotted me immediately. I froze as she approached and reprimanded me in a Rhonda Righteous meets New Age Nelly kind of tone and said, 'Sorry, sister, we are already over our legal capacity and there is absolutely no room left for you. Please come back next week.' Noticing the look on my face, she added, 'You should have come earlier.'

Feeling outcast, I was washed in rejection and sheepishly retreated from the scene of my ecstatic-dance tribe. I proceeded to seek comfort in the local health food store down the road. A cacao ball and green juice would do the trick. As I was sucking down my Super Green smoothie, the used bookstore across the street caught my eye. Replete with a spirulina moustache, I darted across the street and went straight to the travel section where two guidebooks glistened like precious jewels amongst the rubble. One book was a travel book on France and the other on Spain. I pulled them off the shelf and then impulsively purchased them, ignoring their pricey price tag.

The energy of my dream lingered on, festering in the background of my restless mind. A part of me wanted to deny the fact that my world was beginning to crumble around me. I much preferred to feel normal and in control again. Then I heard a loving and reassuring voice bubble up from the depths of my being. It whispered to me, *You, my dear, are on the brink of leaving behind all that you have known yourself to be. The tide is rising. This is your destiny. You might as well surrender and ride current into the mystery.*

A moment of brave acceptance washed through me. My life had taken a new course and there was no going back. Suzanne Sterling's song, 'The River', wailed in the background on the CD player in my car. 'Somebody's holding your hand... Somebody's holding your heart. Somebody's holding your hand... Somebody's holding your heart. Take a chance on love... Take a chance on love.'

I decided to window shop for good travel shoes for the mysterious journey twinkling on the not-too-distant horizon. I had just enough time to find the perfect pair before going to Shiva Rea's vinyasa flow workshop at the Yoga Studio. With the remains of my smoothie in hand, I pulled into the parking lot, sprinted to the studio with mat in hand at exactly 2pm and said enthusiastically, 'Hi, I'm here for Shiva Rea's yoga workshop!'

'Oh, I'm so sorry, that workshop happened last Saturday,' the receptionist replied in a sympathetic voice.

The 'Twilight Zone' theme song began playing out in my head as my heart sank a little deeper into my chest. I thought to myself, *This is one trippy day. I seem to keep missing the boat wherever I go. What on Earth is going on?*

I stepped outside the posh Yoga Studio, took a deep breath and inhaled the familiar scent of Tibetan incense drifting in from the building across the courtyard. I followed the musky perfume trail to a gallery-like shop with large glass bay windows. Peering inside, I could see several large Tibetan tankas hanging from the high ceiling. A handful of people congregated inside the large open room, whispering reverently amongst themselves. Tibetan monks in maroon and yellow robes bustled about like elves in Santa's toyshop, busily preparing for something that carried an air of paramount importance. I was magnetically pulled into the gallery where I discovered an exquisite rainbow-coloured sand mandala radiating from a square wooden platform in the centre of the room. Instantly, one of the monks caught my eye. His deep brown eyes pierced my heart. He greeted me, as if he had been expecting me all along. It became immediately apparent that this was exactly where I was meant to be. I sat down upon a burgundy zafu pillow in the front row to meditate on the intricate design that depicted the five stages of enlightenment. Its complex beauty was comprised of natural sand, dyed in an array of rainbow colours.

The monks were chanting prayers and mantras in preparation for the Green Tara, Sand Mandala Dissolution Ceremony. 'Tara', in Sanskrit means, 'to cross over'. She is known as the Mother of Liberation. She will do anything to help us cross over from suffering to awareness. She vows right then and there to always reincarnate as a female Buddha until all beings are freed from the suffering that this illusion perpetuates. The intricate mandala represented the realms of enlightened consciousness that symbolises the emptiness of all phenomena and true nature of existence. I overheard the whisper of the middle-aged woman sitting behind me, 'Can you believe in only moments the monks are going to destroy this magnificent masterpiece after ten whole days of continuous round the clock prayers and intricate construction?'

The entire multi-dimensional sand mandala, which represented the stages of enlightenment and the cosmos, would soon be swept into a jar, turning all of its colours into a murky shade of brown. A light went on inside me as I remembered my dream and recognised that I was witnessing the ultimate Buddhist ritual of impermanence!

I recollected the Heart Sutra prayer that I had been initiated into and recited daily while residing in Dharamsala, India, and immersing myself in Tibetan Buddhism.

When Bodhisattva Avalokitesvara practiced the deep Prajnaparamita, he saw that the five skandhas were empty; thus, he overcame all ills and suffering.

O Sariputra! Form does not differ from the void, and the void does not differ from the form. Form is the void, and the void is form. The same is true for feelings, conceptions, impulses and consciousness.

O Sariputra, the characteristics of the void are not created, not annihilated, not impure, not pure, not increasing, not decreasing.

Therefore, in the void, there are no forms and no feelings, conceptions, impulses and no consciousness: there is no eye, ear, nose, tongue, body or mind; there is no form, sound, smell, taste, touch or idea; no eye elements, until we come to no elements of consciousness; no ignorance and also no ending of ignorance, until we come to no old age and death; and no ending of old age and death.

Also, there is no truth of suffering, of the cause of suffering, of the cessation of suffering or of the path. There is no wisdom, and there is no attainment whatsoever. Because there is nothing to be attained, a Bodhisattva relying on Prajnaparamita has no obstruction in his heart. Because there is no obstruction, he has no fear, and he passes far beyond all confused imagination and reaches Ultimate Nirvana.

All Buddhas in the past, present and future have attained Supreme Enlightenment by relying on the Prajnaparamita. Therefore, we know that the Prajnaparamita is the great magic Mantra, the great Mantra of illumination. It is the supreme Mantra, the unequalled Mantra, which can truly wipe out all suffering without fail.

Therefore, he uttered the Prajnaparamita mantra, by saying:

'Gate, Gate, Paragate, Parasamgate Bodhi-svaha! Form is emptiness, emptiness is form. Form is no other than emptiness.'

Aha, I recognize you, dear bittersweet sonnet of impermanence, radical detachment and full-bodied surrender, I reminded myself as I flashed upon my dream of my boat sinking along with all of what made me, 'me' inside of it. Like the boat capsized at sea, I was now being swallowed up, enveloped by the ocean of my destiny and carried into the vast unknown. *Bloop, bloop, bloop – all is gone, gone, gone beyond.*

With this sinking feeling, my eyes gently closed and I dropped into a quiet meditation. I recollected my special connection to the Mother of all Buddhas, Green Tara, to whom this Sand Mandala was being offered and dedicated. I felt so much love and adoration for this deity who returned to Earth through her compassion to assist humanity in clearing away all ignorance, the greatest obstacle to our enlightenment. She is here to liberate all beings from misguided perception that form illusion, which is the cause of all physical, emotional and spiritual suffering.

I then invoked my beloved teacher, Lama Yeshe, who once appeared to me in a lucid vision to offer me these words of wisdom and compassion:

'My dear, even the sun has to die and all things must eventually come to an end through changing forms. Impermanence is the true nature of all living phenomena. Seek that which exists beyond the comings and goings of the temporal world and offer your life to that which can never die.'

I remained as still as I possibly could and held back the tears as wave upon wave of raw vulnerability washed over me. It made the marrow of my bones feel hollow and vibrate with a kind of spiritual heebie-jeebies. And then I heard the distinct all-loving voice of the Great Mother, the same voice that had visited me during my recent medicine journey.

'*Dear child, it is time to let go and trust all that is being orchestrated by the hands of the Divine. Like nature, your life has a way of fulfilling what is destined to be. In just moments, this beautiful sand mandala will be completely washed away, returned to the ocean of Oneness. All things must change, dear one. Change is nature's way of regenerating itself over and over again.*'

I nearly burst, but I continued to hold back my tears, not wanting to create a scene. I reached for my journal and pen to find refuge from the waves of emotion threatening to swallow me whole. I asked myself, *If I am to totally release my life to the unknown, then what purpose does my life serve here and now?* I fervently scribbled down my thoughts and excerpts from the dream. A little girl of around eight years old strutting new designer jeans interrupted me. I noticed her shiny hot-pink lip-gloss and her thick ponytail that hung from the back of her head. She stood in front of me with her hand on her waist and then asked me in a very direct and authoritative voice, 'What are you doing?'

'I am writing about the dream I had last night and how, just like this beautiful mandala in front of us, everything in life must one day return to dust.'

'Nah-uh,' she said confidently. 'Not in this movie I just saw where these people drank this special water and they could live on forever and ever.'

'Wow. I'd like to find some of that magical water that creates everlasting life.'

Then she said, 'Well, it's not that great because then you have to watch your kids and everyone you love die and you will just be left there all alone.'

'Point well taken,' I answered, and smiled warmly at the sassy little princess who came to set me straight. I stewed in the perplexity of the paradox of life. Again, the mysterious voice gently whispered to me, '*You must relinquish the old life for the new one to be born.*'

I looked up at the bustling monks in complete awe and admiration. Their precise and graceful movements expressed an aura of unwavering confidence as they swept up the intricately coloured sand into one small jar, without a flinch of remorse or regret.

The Tibetan monks concluded the Dissolution Ceremony with a procession down the street to the edge of the breezy ocean bay. I joined the procession along with a handful of Western bystanders. We stood at the edge of the bay and observed the Lama pour the jar of brown sand that once held the cosmos and all of creation into the swift ocean current. As I witnessed the sand disappearing into the deep blue sea, I could have sworn that two dolphins swam by, bobbing their heads to pay homage to the blessed sand as it returned to the source from which it once came.

This was the day my life would surely change. Like the spinning of a Tibetan prayer wheel, my life began to accelerate a thousand fold. Everything that proceeded to happen served the singular purpose of submitting to what mysteriously called me forth. A cascade of unseen forces and synchronistic events continued to unfold, postmarked and labelled, *'Special delivery for Ambe' Ray, c/o her destiny calling.'*

CHAPTER FOUR

DREAM OF A DREAM

The Weaver Dreamer is She who dreams and weaves reality with the Great Mystery. She acknowledges and empowers through reweaving patterns of reality in the Dream Time. The way of the Weaver is the way of relationship and connectedness. Thus, the loom is Her sacred tool. Her transcendent function is the nurturance of the soul, ensoulment. She weaves the pattern that connects everything to the ONE. The function She holds in the cycle of creativity is the entry into timelessness that allows for direct connection to the Mythic realms of being from which all creation springs. She offers non-causal, non-linear associations through dreams and other means that are the basis of creative insight. She reweaves the patterns in our lives to present possibilities that unfold our highest evolutionary potential. Her loom encompasses all possibilities. She supports particular probable realities through synchronicity and connecting individual destinies with the pattern of the whole.

In understanding these unifying principles, one learns to become the empty loom on which the Divine plays with the elements of time and space. In this position of receptive awareness, one becomes a conscious dreamer, dreaming the dream of the Divine into reality. The Dreamer's dream of the Great Miracle that is now manifesting in 'time' is being realised and facilitated through the conscious Dreamer's awakening and dancing the new dream for an awakened New Earth. The Weaver offers us the sacred thread that guides us through the apparent maze and multifarious appearances of existence to unity consciousness. She shows us the pattern that connects even between seemingly irreconcilable pairs like love and death.

– Ariel Spilsbury, *The Alchemy of Ecstasy*

After a week of teaching and playing in the life-giving waters of Harbin Hot Springs, I returned to the Bay Area via a brief stop at the Health and Harmony Festival in Santa Rosa, California. I pulled into the parking lot in my silver Toyota van, grabbed my straw hat and dove into the eclectic crowds perusing the bustling vendors. This was the first of a long slew of summer festivals that began in late spring and ended in the fall with Earth Dance. My departure to Europe was set for less than a month away. I felt called to say a brief hello to my friends, knowing I would probably not see them again for a whole year. The infamous Casbah Tea House was a large Bedouin tent brimming with people. These finely feathered Fungineers resembled a large flock of exotic birds, each uniquely adorned in an array of tribal regalia and glittery face paint. Jah Levi, an Essene priest, musician, and beloved friend of mine, strummed his guitar to the rhythm of his well-known song, 'Pacha Mama.'

I warmly recollected how we first met and clearly recognised him as someone I've shared countless lifetimes with, spanning the mystery schools throughout the world. When visiting him in the privacy of his home, he allowed his dreadlocks to hang to the ground. I marveled as I watched them gently sweep the floor behind him as if to sweep away all of life's illusions. Tonight, they were neatly piled up onto the top of his head so he wouldn't trip on them while playing music on stage. He once told me that it was the life force from his Essene practice that rejuvenated his cells and gave him the appearance of looking half his linear age. His prophetic music had a way of seeping under one's skin and vibrating one's soul codes into remembrance.

The last of the twilight sun illuminated the faces of my tribe as we swayed to the hypnotic rhythms, which wove an etheric web of our collective prayers. I reveled in the feeling of being amongst my star family, unified in our shared purpose to awaken and be conscientious guardians of Mama Gaia. Many of us had been gathering for over thirteen summers to share our creativity, unique offerings, and heart songs by the sacred fire. I silently sent out my gratitude and love, knowing that this year, I would not be joining them around the fire. I was being called to venture overseas and

Goddess willing, return home with stories and newfound gifts of embodied wisdom to share.

The evening chill was rapidly setting in. I took this as a sign to head home to Gaia's Grove. Before I made my getaway, I was guided to go by the performer's parking lot and say goodbye to my friends from the Mystic Family Circus who were camped out there. Clusters of mythically costumed people were engaged in juggling, whimsical play and fire dancing. Several of these magical beings, which I often referred to as my Bay Area 'tribe', went all the way back to my college days of living in San Francisco. We had been celebrating life together over many years, sharing mutual passion for the sacred arts, music, and the global dance culture. I spotted my old roommate and DJ friend, Moon Doggy, standing next to a noticeably striking man wrapped up in an oversized South American blanket. I noticed something different about him as he stood out amongst the other circus folks frolicking about the campground. His aura glowed in golden light. My heart immediately sped up as I sensed a mysterious magnetic connection.

'Hey, Sista Ambe´, ahwoooh!' Moon Doggy howled as we gave each other a giant bear hug. 'Have you met my friend Tomas? [pronounced 'to'-moss'] He recently returned from living in Costa Rica and now he's on his way to Spain to take a course in visionary painting.'

My heart skipped a beat as a future memory of Tomas flashed before me. Had we met before?

'Hello,' I uttered, trying hard to hide my excitement. 'Wow! I'm also headed over to that part of the world. I'm leaving in less than a month,' I said in a nonchalant way, attempting to restrain my excitement at the first sign that this was actually happening and I was quite literally on my way.

'I'm going to Cadeques. Have you heard of it? It's a beautiful town tucked away on the Spanish Mediterranean Coast. Where are you going?' he asked curiously.

Time stood still. As soon as he said the word *Cadeques*, I flashed back on a dream I had several months ago where a beautiful man wrapped in a red and white Shipibo medicine blanket was telling me of a course in Spain that he was on his way to take. I always pay close attention when I realize I am reliving a part of a dream that I have already dreamt. The word *Cadeques* sounded so familiar to me, as if I had waited my whole life to hear this one simple word – *Cadeques.* I whispered to myself. Here was a mysterious clue, rolling in like thunder to point me in the direction of my destiny. Tomas's green eyes pierced mine and for an instant, we met in a place that transcended space and time, a place where stars collide, and miracles are made manifest.

Then with a twinkle in his eye, he said, 'I am a visionary painter. What is it that you're up to in this life?'

Hmmm, I thought. This question was always a tricky one to answer, as nothing ever seemed to capture what I really felt I was up to. Cheekily, I ran through a list in my head, *Oh, I'm presently in the business of releasing all that I know myself to be, shedding all identities and transmuting as many holy shits into hallelujahs along the way!*

I then politely replied, 'I'm an Akashic intuitive, teach yoga and facilitate transformational workshops around the world. From time to time, I'm called to go to sacred sites to assist in clearing and rebalancing the energies. In essence, I tend to offer that which I feel most inspired and passionate about learning and embodying myself. I'm presently being called to return to France where I'm told, I'll meet my beloved.' *Whoa, that was a lot I just spewed out on the table!* 'Lovely to meet you, Tomas. I hope to run into you in Spain!' I added.

I decided to mingle a little with the rest of my circus friends so as not to seem as blown away as I really was. All the while, I felt my heart beating a mile a minute. I was having an extreme déjà vu feeling. I wandered toward the fire and stood gazing at it, appreciating its warmth and immediate comfort. Tomas casually walked to the fire and stood across from me. We continued to energetically feel each other through the dancing flames. I sensed that we shared a mysterious future memory that beckoned us both to venture out into the great unknown and so the familiarity was palatable for both of us. I felt an alluring golden thread gently pulling my heartstrings and whispering to me a familiar Rumi poem, 'Come, come, whoever you are. Wanderer, worshiper, lover of leaving. It doesn't matter. Ours is not a caravan of despair. Come, even if you have broken your vows a thousand times. Come, yet again, come, come.'

I surrendered to the divine flow, relying on trust and patience to balance my anxious anticipation. Just as I was feeling the call to go back to my car, Tomas sauntered over to me nice and slow, and relaxed. He asked, 'Hey, would you like to see some of my paintings?'

'Absolutely,' I responded in a heartbeat.

We squatted down on the dark pavement while he pulled out his black leather book portfolio. He opened it up and illuminated the pages with his headlamp along with the misty light of the full moon. I nearly fell over when he revealed his first painting. Through colours, interconnected shapes, symbols and sacred geometry, a universal mythic story unfolded before my astounded eyes. Each multi-dimensional image depicted a symbolic transmission of Divine consciousness and Sacred Union alchemy that I recognised was encoded to blossom within me. Over the last several years, I had been given several spiritual visions that illuminated an aspect of this collective cosmic birthing of Universal Christ Consciousness. And yet until that evening, I had never seen such an accurate multi-dimensional depiction of what I had envisioned in my mind's eye. My molecules seemed to light up as I absorbed these paintings as living illustrations of what the Divine Mother had just transmitted to me during the ceremony at Gaia's Grove. The moment I saw them, I knew that they were a visual map that held the key codes to some mysterious alchemy that would eventually lead my soul home.

'What are the chances of getting a copy of this one?' I asked, excitedly pointing to the royal blue and gold star tetrahedron.

'Here you go,' he said while handing me a shiny colour copy of the painting.

'Wow! Thank you, Tomas. This means more to me than you can ever imagine!'

I walked back to my car while looking up to the stars in complete awe, astonished by the synchronicities unfolding. I had said 'yes' to going on this mysterious quest, and the universe was meeting me every step of the way. And now, thanks to my serendipitous encounter with Tomas, I was just a little closer to the Mediterranean Sea and meeting my future destiny.

CHAPTER FIVE

CROSSING OVER

Our lives are the story of how we remember. It is the dance that was woven into the fabric of our being from the beginning. The presence of the Great Mystery is always with us. I have only to turn my face toward it, and it is there— as a voice beneath the sound of the pale grey waves crashing on the shore, as a touch of the unseen on the back of my neck that makes me pause and turn as I cut carrots on my kitchen counter, as a kiss that lingers as I come up out of dreams in the midst of dark mornings.

– Oriah Mountain Dreamer, *The Dance*

Without any real logical explanation, I proceeded to close my life down piece-by-piece and person-by-person. In only three weeks, I managed to move out of my room at Gaia's Grove, give up my healing office in San Raphael, sub out my yoga classes and create a going-away party with over forty friends and loved ones. 'Where are you going?' they would ask.

All I could say was, 'I'm off on an adventure for an indiscernible amount of time to a place I know nothing about to meet my beloved. All that I know is that I have been clearly guided not to leave any loose ends behind.'

I cleverly enticed my closest friend and fellow housemate Eva to accompany me on the first leg of the journey. She was excited to check out the festival scene in Europe and I thought this would be a good way to ease into my mysterious calling to go abroad. Eva was a budding, beautiful, tall, strawberry blond maiden with large, hypnotic blue-green eyes that shot out sparkles when you caught her glance. Best described as a blossoming Fairy and Queen of the Muses, she had too many divine gifts to name. As a self-proclaimed Enchantress of twenty-three, she applied herself to poetry, fire dancing, singing, song writing, and performance art. Eva played many roles in my life. I admired her passion and her pursuit of all things creative, and I was inspired by her guile to hypnotically enchant the most reluctant of beings into the magic of life lived free of inhibition.

Eva was my best friend with whom I shared the sacred and mundane nuances of life while conspiring all matters if magical adventures. I found it impossible to fathom anything ever coming between our mutual adoration for one another. But strangely enough, Jahrusha had warned me in his vision of some unavoidable strain to come in our relationship at some point during our travels together. He said this turbulence would cause us to separate for a time, but eventually we would come back together stronger than ever. I was reluctant to see how anything could ever come between us. We were inseparable. The truth is that I made a conscious choice to override and ignore that part of his reading. Little did I know that his premonition would catch up with me and I would be faced with a heart-wrenching challenge to overcome.

Meanwhile, in high spirits, Eva and I frugally purchased our 'dirt cheap' Airtech plane tickets on the Internet. Before the big flight overseas, I scheduled a three-day layover in Los Angeles to pay a quick visit to my mother and father. We were set to depart from LAX on 23 July 2003, and to land at Heathrow Airport in London on the morning of the 24th.

Two things stand out vividly from those brief few days we spent in Los Angeles before flying out to London. The first was a lucid dream I had in which I was an Egyptian priestess. I recollected being sexually ravished by a man who felt to be a combination of my father, my husband and my brother. He left me with the devastating sense that I had been taken apart, betrayed and deceived by the man I once loved and cherished the most. Consequently, out of my outrage in reaction to being raped, I murdered and buried this man alive. And then, I felt horribly ashamed about this dark secret. All of my priestess power was demolished from the shame of the murder and the raw powerlessness of being raped. So in the dream, I set out on a grand search to find the man I had once loved, who now carried a vital missing part of my soul. I pursued him feverishly, knowing that if I found him, I could then set myself free and reclaim my sovereignty, wholeness and innocence once again. I recognized that the dream echoed the mythos of the Goddess Isis whose partner Osiris was murdered and his body went missing. Isis set out to gather the pieces of him scattered throughout the lands. Once all of his pieces were retrieved and re-assembled, she resurrects him.

That morning, I awoke in a cold sweat as if I had actually gone through the whole massive ordeal. The dream created a terror and trepidation in me as to what might lay ahead on my journey. I had a strong intuitive feeling that my pilgrimage abroad was leading me to my very own demise. Waking up on that particular day, I had to muster an inner courage that stretched far beyond my ordinary life. I had glimpsed my greatest nightmare along with my salvation – all in one long vivid dream. In a mere twenty-four hours, I would be flying across the ocean in search of the Masculine part of me that I had once buried – these missing pieces were clearly of the dark *and* the light.

On the evening prior to our departure, my mother and I went out to see the film *Whale Rider*, while Eva visited her uncle who resided in the area. The film told the story of a young Maori girl's journey of reclaiming her cultural identity and power within her ancestral bloodline and family clan. My soul stirred in familiar resonance with her challenge and her quest.

Even though the little girl felt a strong affinity with her Maori lineage, she was treated as an outcast, by her family and relatives. Determined to find her place of belonging amongst her people, she underwent a series of initiatory experiences that challenged every aspect of who she knew herself to be. Because she was born a girl, she was rejected and banished from participating in the traditional Maori warrior training, to which she felt deeply called to engage in. And as most heroine's journeys go, her calling persisted until she found the courage, strength and conviction to face her demons and stand in her truth through countless trials and tribulations.

She chose to trust the undeniable resonance that came from her connection to the spirit of the whales. To claim her birthright, she had to disconnect from her own blood family in order to access her innate power to transcend generations of ancestral karma.

In the end, she found the courage and faith to trust herself above and beyond the familial pressure to conform to the status quo pressures of their ways. In the end, she became the very thing that infused her family and tribe with a deeper connection to the heart and spirit of their treasured traditions. Her courageous choice to go on a vision quest to discover her true Self eventually became the very catalyst that allowed all of her clan to evolve and grow into greater alignment with their spiritual values. In the end, it was through individuating from her people and trusting her heart's calling that she was able to restore the ancient familial bond that had been painfully ruptured along the way and fulfill her highest destiny.

Mom and I clutched hands until the very end of the movie when the credits rolled by. Teary eyed and speechless, we left the theatre and drove home in a timeless silence that could only be shared between mother and daughter. We both felt into the significance of the core message portrayed in this prophetic movie along with the magnitude of tomorrow's flight to London. We shared in the unspoken knowing that I too was born to be a Whale Rider on her way to becoming a Grail Rider.

24 July 2003, LAX Airport, Mayan Day Out of Time

Eva and I sat poised on the airplane, fiddling with the content of our carry-on bags as a way to distract ourselves from our shared trepidation of the long journey ahead. I pulled everything out of my travel pack and placed it back, one item at a time, as if that would put my life back in some semblance of order. I pulled out my journal, Mayan oracle deck, CD Walkman, *Tantra of the Beloved* book, amber rose oil, citrus lip balm, a pen and two of my favourite crystals. Somehow, I felt much calmer after doing that. Once the big jet roared into the sky, we relaxed and even slept until we landed in London. Once there, we connected with a small flight to the West Country. The plan was to catch a bus from the airport and then take a taxi into the town of Glastonbury. I was feeling so much gratitude for having Eva as my travel companion, and I secretly wondered what could ever possibly tear us apart.

Giddy from travel and excitement, we headed straight into the heart of Glastonbury, also known as the gateway into the mythic realms of Avalon. Many believe that the etheric isle of Avalon is accessed through the town of Glastonbury and that it still exists in a parallel reality. Once in Glastonbury, our destination was a haven called Saint Michael's Cottage, situated just above the famous Chalice Well. I had arranged this serendipitous lodging one rainy day when I met Simon back in Marin County.

I recalled this short wiry man, whose face told the story of a thousand hero's journeys. One rainy day, he randomly showed at my yoga class. Simon and I immediately recognized one another and hit it off as ancient new friends. Among his many life accomplishments was his esteemed title, Druid Priest of Avalon. When he heard of my travel plans, he graciously invited Eva and I to stay at his historic home, St. Michael's Cottage, as his honourary guests. He then proceeded to warn me that his humble abode had recently undergone a small accidental fire and that it was currently undergoing renovation. 'You ought to come anyway,' he said enthusiastically, assuring us we would be comfortable enough amongst the renovation. Being the overly optimistic traveling fools that we were, Eva and I gladly accepted his generous offer.

The journey from Los Angeles to Glastonbury was brutally long, to say the least. Eventually, we arrived and found ourselves dropped off on Park Street where our lodgings were located, via a Czech cabbie who knew very little of the area. He managed to get us painfully lost before finally locating our street. At this stage, we were exhausted and more than ready for the comforts of home and a hot shower. Eva and I grabbed our ridiculously excessive baggage from our confused cab driver and stood bewildered on the steep hill under the moonlight. We looked around for the address but in the misty fog couldn't make out any of the numbers. I made a silent prayer to my guardian angel to guide us to our lodgings.

Within seconds, we heard a chipper voice sneak up behind us and announce himself, 'Ello, you must be friends of Simon's from America!' he said with a strong English accent that reminded me of a Dickens' story.

We let out a simultaneous sigh of relief and relaxed instantly. Our escort's quirky appearance had us feel right at home. He sported an oversized faux-fur leopard-print women's coat, colourful quilted Balinese overalls and a ripped-up white cotton tank top revealing his nicely toned biceps. Stylish, silly and sexy – I liked him at first glance.

His big green eyes sparkled like emeralds in the light of the rising full moon. 'Allow me to introduce myself,' he said in his funny accent and then bowed politely like any good Englishman would. 'My name is Ra. Your 'ost Simon regrets that 'e could not be 'ere to greet you tonight, but I am ever so 'appy to stand in for 'im. Now, ladies, allow me to 'elp you across the road. We are just over there,' he said as he pointed across the street through the misty night air.

We followed him to the front door of the cobblestone house that looked just like something Snow White and the Seven Dwarfs may have once inhabited. A young woman with blond hair came to greet us at the front door wearing a one-piece grey painter's jumpsuit and large combat boots. She introduced herself as Nicola. We soon came to know that she was also a yoga teacher and an old friend of Simon's who was staying at the cottage to assist in its renovation from the fire that left little of the interior structure intact.

As we entered and looked around, Eva and I were taken aback by what we found. The charred house had been completely burnt out and gutted from the core. Only a few distinguishable features made the house livable at all. The only sign of comfort in sight was in the tiny little kitchen where a dimly lit fire cast strange shadows on the charcoaled walls. A lonely white painter's bucket served as the toilet. So much for a hot shower and a cozy bed! I sighed. One look at Eva's crestfallen face confirmed that she was thinking wistfully about the lack of shower too. In the former living room, an old, scrappy mattress lay on the floor, which was Nicola's makeshift bedroom.

Upstairs was a tiny loft space, where only a few of the floorboards had escaped charring from the recent flames.

As we continued our tour, I envisioned the gutted house like a great phoenix that would soon rise from the ashes, freshly birthed into its brand-new resurrected form. My deeper knowing told me that Archangel Michael had done a little spring cleaning with the purifying element of fire to ensure that the cottage continued to live up to 'his' name of St. Michael and wield the sword of truth for all those who would inhabit it. Despite the initial surprise, I was simply relieved to find shelter for our road-weary bodies in this sooty sanctuary amongst kindred souls.

Our gracious hostess, Nicola, stoked the kitchen fire while Ra began to talk in a never-ending run-on sentence, at which he would occasionally come up to take a breath and swallow a gulp of English tea from his bulky mug. Ra gave us a running download on his unique and truly rarefied insights into the Egyptian mysteries. He reminded us that the symbols embedded within the Egyptian glyphs are a holographic language of light that lead us into an experience of the quantum light field that exists beyond time and space – like having access to all places, times, spaces and dimensions from a singular point in consciousness. Realms of ancient wisdom poured from his bright eyes and zealous tongue. Like some kind of cosmic evangelist, Ra had the gift of talking for hours, with or without a listening audience. It didn't take long for my politely nodding head to grow weary from the exhaustion of our long travels. I was glad that Eva was willing to hold strong and keep up her polite presence as an enthusiastic audience for Ra's meta-download of the Egyptian mysteries. I felt the significance of his generous transmission and yet I was simply too exhausted to take it all in at the time.

With a gigantic yawn, I quietly excused myself and climbed the small wooden ladder to the upper loft. I had just enough energy left to spread out my yoga mat and sleeping bag onto the dusty, scorched floorboards. As my body gave way into the hard wooden floor, I became acutely aware that all of my bones ached all at once. I overheard Ra referring to the Goddess Isis downstairs as I recollected my dream from the night before. I noticed my heart rate was still somewhat erratic from the spooky Egyptian nightmare that I had experienced prior to leaving Los Angeles. My head felt swollen with pain. It pounded with a steady, rhythmic throbbing, as if keeping up with the beat of my disoriented heart. Quite frankly, I felt as cooked as the scorched house I laid my weary bones upon.

Much to my relief, I dreamt of a beautiful pod of dolphins. Hundreds of them came to welcome me in a crystalline, blue-green bay. They swam around me and lovingly nuzzled me as if to show me the way to a hidden treasure. I flashed back to my earlier vision counsel with Jahrusha and remembered him prophesising, 'You will be going to Europe accompanied by a great pod of etheric dolphin friends. They will lead the way for you on your journey.' At the time, I thought to myself, *Dolphins in Europe? Hmmm, I wonder where I might encounter wild dolphins in Europe.* Yet, I felt them with me now. It was as real as anything else I could feel. Somehow, they had made their way to Glastonbury to guide and be with me. *Imagine that! I could not have asked for any better travel companions.*

CHAPTER SIX

CHALICE WELL

If you want to awaken all of humanity, then awaken all of yourself.
If you want to eliminate the suffering in the world,
then eliminate all that is dark and negative within yourself.
Truly the greatest gift you have to give is that of your own self-transformation.

– Lao Tzu

*The Grail is Sophia's cup, the feminine vessel
of the all-containing manifest world.
It is her loving wisdom that sustains it.
We must yoke the opposites of duality
rather than choose one side over the other,
to hold on to both of them consciously
and heal the splits apparent in the world within
our own individual psyches.
Only in this way can we hope to love and heal our world.*

– Alice O. Howell, *The Dove and the Stone*

After a very long and restless night, the morning finally came to greet us. As I lay on the singed floorboards, I pondered the personal symbolism of beginning my pilgrimage in a burnt-down house. Nevertheless, I was grateful that Eva and I had managed to get through our first night in Glastonbury, even amongst soot and ashes. Now the sun was shining and our bright, blue-eyed hostess Nicola greeted us. 'Would you ladies like to join me for a session of yoga and lunch at the Shekinah Ashram just beyond the Chalice Well?'

'Yes!' we both accepted her cheery invitation in stereo. What a perfect way to begin our first day in Avalon. Before doing anything else, we enthusiastically chose to love up our body temples and replenish ourselves. Eva and I proceeded to wash the black smudges off our faces, have a cup of strong English tea and then walked down the road in high spirits to meet Nicola at the neighbouring Ashram.

The inside of Shekinah's Ashram was comprised of a quaint bright purple room with a small stack of yoga blankets, meditation pillows, and a modest rectangular altar covered in a royal purple cloth. Centred on the altar table was a golden chalice, a small vase with a single red rose and a picture of a vesica piscis, symbolizing the Inner Marriage and the Grail Mysteries echoed in this land. As we stretched open our stiff bodies, the sounds of chopping and blending serenaded us from the adjacent kitchen. Limb by limb, we blissfully unfurled our tightly wound muscles until a vibrant young lady peaked her head out through the wooden door and announced, 'Time for our midday meal, ladies, if ya care ta join us.'

Eva, Nicola and I completed by chanting three long-drawn-out 'om's', before transitioning to partake in some love-infused nourishment. Upon entering the dining hall, we simultaneously gasped as we noticed the large drawing that hung from the ceiling. My cells quickened as I recognised that the image was a symbolic depiction of what had called me to these mythic lands in the first place. I stood transfixed, while gazing up at this sacred bird drawn with a precise configuration of geometrical shapes. The Shekinah Dove radiated vital keys and master codes that stirred awake a cellular memory of my Feminine Christ blueprint. With excited anticipation, my heart quickened in the knowing I was being summoned to enter into her mystery.

Eva and I sat down at the wooden picnic table in the garden with a gentleman from the north of England, who introduced himself as Louie. As we sipped herbal tea and ate the beautifully prepared organic meal, the conversation sparkled with our shared recognition of meeting yet another kindred soul. Louie looked like a bald version of Lawrence of Arabia. He proudly touted his passion and undying loyalty to three things: Time as Art, Zero Point Energy, and blooming young goddesses. As we began to reveal more of ourselves to one another, we came to discover that we shared some common friends in the fields of cosmology and consciousness. Once again, we were awed and amazed to discover yet another connective link into our greater unfolding destiny. I began to pay extra attention to the dovetailing of seemingly random events and chance encounters that were threads of a larger tapestry. We soon recognised that each of us had been called to be initiated by the living Mythos of these lands. To be truly in service to the whole, it was essential to undergo our own inner alchemy of transforming the lead in our lives into gold. In other words, evolution was having her way with each of us and it was our soul's purpose to show up for our sacred marching orders each and every day.

After the meal, Eva and I focused on our immediate plans. We were going to ease into our travels by attending some of the epic summertime festivals in the Glastonbury area. We were excited to build rainbow bridges between our home tribe and the new friends we made from this part of the world. At lunch, Louie informed us that a huge storm was on its way and was due to hit the first day of the Healing Fields festival. Eva and I were in no way prepared to camp out in the English rain, so Nicola kindly volunteered to take us to the nearest town to peruse the charity shops, otherwise known as thrift shops.

While Eva and Nicola scoured the shops for camping gear, I went to use the loo at the bakery next door. I had to wait outside as it was occupied. To my great amazement, my dear friend Stella sauntered out of the loo and our jaws dropped. We nearly collided into each other. Once again, I was astounded by yet another exquisitely timed convergence.

Stella is an amazing sound healer, singer, and star sister from the UK who had frequented Gaia's Grove to partake in our festive ceremonies and celebrations. She and I had recently been communicating about co-creating a sound healing and ecstatic dance journey in Brighton. It was lovely to see her and her new beloved sporting their brightly coloured rainbow regalia. Stella's long crimped hair cascaded over her bum, and her long-lashed eyes sparkled with glitter and love. She wore furry white boots, a colourful short skirt and a leather waist belt that had several attached pouches to house her festival trinkets. She and Ananda had come all the way from London to attend the Healing Fields festival and were picking up some last-minute gear at the charity shops. In our short excited visit, Stella graciously offered to lend Eva and I her extra tent and said that she would be more than happy to bring it along to the festival for us. I returned to the charity shop elated by my discovery and with a big grin on my face for finding us a tent – all in the time it took to go for a pee! I gathered up a few pairs of warm woolly socks and a heavy wool jumper. As we headed back to Glastonbury, the afternoon chill began to set in all too quickly. Nicola recommended we stop at the bakery to pick up some freshly baked pastry to enjoy back at home over the fire along with a nice hot cuppa. We heartily agreed. Soot and all, my mouth watered at the very thought of it.

CHAPTER SEVEN

THE HEALING FIELDS

This is our starting place: right in that raw fissure of our lostness, down in the ache to find our place in the family of things. Before we even ask ourselves how to heal our estrangement, we must first sink down into the wound itself and apprentice ourselves to it. We must enter into the question of what has been missing from us. Of what are we being deprived? Only when we lower ourselves down into that holy longing can we get a glimpse of the majesty we are meant to become.

– Toko-pa Turner,
Belonging: Remembering Ourselves Home

Live life as if everything is rigged in your favor.

– Jelaluddin Rumi

Luckily, the festival was not far from Glastonbury and Nicola was able to drop us off the next day, just in the nick of time. We met up with Stella to retrieve our tent and proceeded to set it up on a patch of grass in the large meadow amongst a sea of other tents. Moments after we set up camp, the rain came pouring down. Luckily, we had the smarts to tuck our excessive belongings inside the tent to keep them dry. A damp English chill seeped into my bones that no Californian girl could have ever properly prepared for. I had to surrender to the reality that most of my clothes and bedding would be damp and cold for the duration of the festival. The only place I found to stay remotely warm was across the field at the Lost Horizons Café.

Appropriately named after my present state of mind, the Lost Horizons Café and its adjacent sauna became my toasty haven for the duration of the miserably rainy festival. The nomadic café was run by an eclectic group of global expats, variously from Australia, Israel, Italy, Ireland and Pakistan. The café had a reputation for late-night fireside music in the adjacent tipi. Delicious homemade chai, organic soups, and vegan treats were available throughout the day and into the late evenings. They ran a wood-burning sauna, which easily fit eight and sometimes eleven if standing up. I especially liked the multi-tiered altar dedicated to the goddess that served as a home for a variety of maha crystals collected from around the world. Based on their moods, the staff would throw a spontaneous party and keep the fire and music going till dawn. Over the course of three days, this place became my refuge. I became quite friendly with everyone as they graciously provided me with warmth and comfort throughout those long, bone-chilling days. I was beyond grateful to have a place of refuge to warm my body and soul.

On the eve of our second night, I was left to entertain myself for the evening. For the time being, I sensed my own journey was more of a solo one and I needed to fully embrace the alone time. On the third night of consistent downpour, Eva returned to our camp, to the inconvenient and cold reality that most of our belongings were drenched. We were both continuously sniffling and coughing. The ongoing challenge of not being able to warm up was wearing us down. We concluded that the Healing Fields festival was the last thing from healing. We decided it was best to bail so that we could fully recover and regroup for The Big Green festival, which began in only a few more days. The Big Green was the second largest festival in England and it ran fully on solar and reusable energy. Over 10,000 people gathered to display their eco-friendly, sustainable lifestyle options. It was the festival of the year and it was simply not an option to be missed.

We woke up the following morning, both totally relieved to know we were leaving as soon as we packed up our drenched gear. Once everything was ready to go, I set out to the Lost Horizons Café for my morning tea and was fortunate to connect with a delightful brother named Gavin who shared my passion for sacred theatre and expressive arts. Gavin taught music and video to young people in London. He generously offered to be our knight, and escort Eva and I out of this muddy festival. We agreed to meet at the entrance gate in a half hour since the rain did not look as if it would ever let up. This time, Eva and I were headed to our friend Simon's other home in the country, south of England, where he had invited us to stay and recuperate before The Big Green festival. Eva and I reconvened, grabbed our stuff and headed to the welcome tent to meet Gavin.

The cold and rain had worn me down and dampened my spirits. I was grateful to be warmed up momentarily by a beautiful rugged Scotsman at the exit gate who handed me a bottle of whiskey. I took a large swig directly from the bottle. *Magic!* It took the edge off the bone-gnawing chill while considerably lightening my mood. *No wonder they call it spirits here in the UK.*

Around one o'clock, Eva and I were sharing the front seat of Gavin's large cargo van, heading towards warmer and dryer horizons. We stopped in Glastonbury for dinner and to pick up our additional baggage from Saint Michael's Cottage. The sun peaked out through the heavy grey clouds and lovingly offered us a beautiful rainbow as a consolation prize for getting out of the pouring piss pot.

I was back in my comfort zone and dinner and wine tasted absolutely delicious. I basked in the restaurant's charming candlelit ambiance, feeling beyond relieved to be out of the cold. Towards the end of our sumptuous gourmet meal and just as the wine had loosened my heart, Eva's not-so-subtle flirtations began to work their magic. I had a dawning suspicion that I might be tossed aside by the end of the evening, feeling once again left out in the cold. I began to dread that this would be a repetitive theme throughout our travels. The pangs of feeling outcast and estranged surged through my veins along with the sinking feeling of my insecurity and shadows of rejection.

It was nearly 9pm by the time Gavin dropped us off at Simon's country home just outside of Brighton. By this time, I had faded as predicted into the background of Eva and Gavin's lively flirtatious banter.

The insurance settlement for the fire at Saint Michael's Cottage had compensated Simon with a lovely five-bedroom home that sat across some green pastures and spacious paddocks for keeping horses. In the light of the moon, I spotted two majestic white horses, reminding me of Jarusha's words: *'When you see white horses, the grace of the Goddess is with you.'* With a silent sigh of relief, I beamed the beautiful horses my love and let them know how much I appreciated their presence.

Inside the house, Simon was buzzing around the kitchen like a bumblebee high on super foods. He was in mad preparation for a massive raw food, supernatural dance party to be held in a large circus tent at The Big Green gathering the following day. This was the first we had seen of our rock star host since we all met at Jah Levi's party in the Bay Area. Simon was a bright-eyed, cheery man who seemed to have endless energy. As a Druid priest and Earth guardian, he was famous for gifting his global community with shamanic healing, unstoppable dance beats and vibrant living foods. He attributed his fireball presence and unstoppable life force to his diet of raw super foods and plenty of all-night dance parties.

Simon warmly welcomed us into his country home and generously offered up his bedroom for us to recuperate in. I gratefully settled in while Eva and Gavin lingered in the hallway and exchanged heated caresses. I sensed that they were absorbed in negotiating all the tantalising potentials of what might come next.

Still bone-chilled from our excursion, I was beyond grateful for the comforts of a warm bed. I reflected on how spoiled I had become living in my plush Marin community house – complete with hot tub and two fireplaces. *Thank God for this!* I consoled myself and then collapsed on the bed and wrapped myself up in a heavy wool blanket.

Before long, Eva pounced on the bed and sweetly proclaimed, 'Ambe´, I'm going to cuddle up with Gavin in his van tonight. Something wildly delicious is going on between us that I feel compelled to explore! You don't mind, do you, luv?'

'Oh, no, of course not. Have fun.' I said, mustering up a half-smile. After Eva left, I curled up into a fetal position and became surprisingly aware of an upsurge of unsettling envy, bitterness and resentment that was swelling up from my belly. A wave of carefully suppressed emotions rushed up to the surface, threatening to take me down and rob me of my joy-light. Deep down, I had no desire to project my insecurities upon Eva's fairy-like flow. I was wise enough to see that a dark and bittersweet mirror was being held up for me to see, illuminating all of the dis-owned and denied parts of myself that I had cast out as being unworthy of love. At the time, I was reluctant to face these unwanted guests simply because I was ashamed of them.

I tried to justify my angst by convincing myself that it was my genuine concern for Eva's safety and well-being that had me feeling so unsettled. *After all, you never know what's out there lurking under the sheets these days.*

Suddenly, like a strong gust of wind, Eva reappeared in the room, grabbed her toothbrush, kissed me on the cheek and blew out of the room as quickly as she came. Her bright energy made me sad and contracted in contrast. I curled up in a tight ball on Simon's bed, letting out a heavy sigh. I prayed that this desolate place inside of me would soon release its encroaching grip. I lay there, considering whether it might be better to travel on my own rather than be eclipsed in the shadows as Eva's incredible shrinking sidekick.

Assessing my little to no options, I chose to, quite literally, 'grin and bear it' while making a strong resolution to rise rather than succumb to my insidious pity party. Instead, I chose to accept and bless my sister's choices while staying true to my own feelings. *After all,* I consoled myself, *there is a larger purpose for traveling to these mythic lands in the first place.*

I sat in the silence of my own company and reminded myself to create deeper roots inside myself and not be so easily swayed by what other people were up to. As a highly sensitive empath, I tended to pick up the larger unresolved energies playing out around me and allow them to take me for a ride. This time, I was smart enough to detect that I would be utterly lost in these Grail lands if I didn't use these circumstances as an opportunity to up my dose of sovereign self-care. Little did I know at the time how many more opportunities I would have to practice staying true to myself while expanding into greater acceptance and love, no matter what was playing out around me.

That solitary night, I dreamt I was in the last stages of pregnancy. The father appeared to be a mysterious dark spirit, and yet I felt quite happy about giving birth to his starchild and leave him behind. My challenge in the dream was to accept being a single mama through integrating the dark and the light within me. Then the dream suddenly shifted and I was hanging from a trapeze with a bottomless black void beneath me. I had swung from one trapeze and had barely managed to catch the next, my raw fingertips gripping tightly as I hung suspended over the bottomless black hole. It took everything I had to hold on and not drop into the abyss. Suddenly, some of my friends appeared out of nowhere and lifted me up to the platform on the other side. I awoke from the dream feeling relieved to have landed on safe ground and elated to be pregnant in spite of the child's troubled and mysterious dark father. I simply felt happy to be alive and grateful that somehow, I had made it to the other side, thanks to a little help from my friends. *Yeah, I get by with a little help from my friends.*

CHAPTER EIGHT

THE MYTHIC CALL

Once upon a time, a galactic council was called and a mythic call was sent out to countless light beings: the children of the Sun, the angelic winged ones, the Sun runners, the rainbow warriors, and other luminous ones from many star systems. This great circle of light beings gathered from far and wide. At the appointed nexus, the Love of the Spinning Galaxies, the Great Spirit, entered, gracing them all with celestial light and the following words.

'You are invited to incarnate upon a world where a great transformation will take place,' began the Love of the Spinning Galaxies. 'You who respond to this call will go to a place of planetary evolution where the illusions of fear and separation are strong teachers. I am calling those with the needed talents and gifts to act as my emissaries there, to lift and transform the frequencies of planet Earth, simply by embodying and anchoring love's presence there. In this myth, you will be the creators of a new reality, the reality of the golden octave.'

The Love of the Spinning Galaxies continued: 'On other journeys, each of you has proven to be a 'feeling navigator,' able to awaken your consciousness and align your heart to the promptings of pure love and compassionate service. As Sun runners and torch bearers, you have already demonstrated that you will hold the light high. And so I invite you to incarnate en masse among the tribes of Earth to assist Gaia and all her children in their transformation.'

'It is part of the plan that you will be veiled in forgetting,' the Mystery of the Spinning Galaxies went on. 'However, as you remember the feeling of childlike innocence and trust, you will become the harmonic leavening

in this cycle of initiation for Earth. You will incarnate strategically, often in some of the most vibrationally dense areas on the planet. To some, this illusion of separation from love may create feelings of hopelessness, lack of support, and alienation. But by embracing your humanness, your love will transform the depths of duality, and your light will quicken the many.

'Your participation on this quest is purely voluntary; however, this transformational shift on Earth is very rare and precious. Should you choose to accept this mission, you will have the opportunity to catalyze and synthesize all that you have been during many incarnations, receiving a rarely offered quantum leap in consciousness. It is up to you to choose how you will dance with Terra Gaia and her children as she completes her ceremony of light.'

So spoke the Creator, the Light of the Spinning Galaxies. And so it was that the luminous beings who formed the countless alliances, federations, and councils of the faithful of the stars chose to incarnate on planet Earth to assist in this crucial event, the awakening of the planetary dream. There was even a fail-safe process built into the plan to awaken these beings from the illusion of separation and the veil of forgetfulness that is so rife upon Earth. The luminous ones who would journey to Gaia's assistance agreed to spark each other's remembrance. Thus, these starseeded ones were encoded in many ways with sounds, colors, lights, images, words, and symbols—a vibrational resonance that would assist them in remembering their commitment to the light. It was agreed that these coded clues would appear everywhere: in visionary art and music, in penetrating looks, in speech and feelings—all creating a deep yearning to awaken and become the embodiment of love.

So it is that you, the children of the Sun, are now being bathed in the waters of remembrance, prepared as rainbow warriors to fulfill the promise of the new and ancient myth. By simply anchoring love's presence on Earth, you lovingly draw down the mantle of the gods, sending waves of healing and love throughout Gaia's eagerly receptive body. As you emerge in this time, your gifts awaken and empower others. By utilizing the tools of laughter, song, dance, humor, joy, trust, and love, you are creating the powerful surge of transformation that will transmute the limitations of the old myth of duality and separation, birthing the miracle of unity and peace on Earth.

Utilize your gifts on behalf of Gaia. In a supernova of consciousness, Gaia and her children will ascend in robes of light, forming a luminous light body of love, to be reborn among the stars! The mythic call has been sounded. The great quest has begun. Awaken, rainbow warriors, Sun runners, luminous beings from the galactic alliances, federations, and councils! Ancient Skywalkers, newly formed in this moment, stand in the beauty and power of your true identity as love's gift to Gaia. Set aside self-doubt. You are the Divine child of the Sun! Go where your heart draws you to share your great gifts. Surrender to the magic and the light. The miracle will be manifested on Earth. Remember, we dance and sing here for the One Heart.

– Ariel Spilsbury, *The Mayan Oracle*

In the bright morning light, the ultra-groovy beats of drum and bass vibrated the paper-thin walls. Still half asleep, I rolled out of Simon's comfy bed and shuffled to the kitchen looking exceedingly rough and tumbled. The busy superhero cast of characters buzzing around the kitchen had grown by three more.

'Good morning, luv! Did you sleep well?' Simon greeted me with a smile that made him look as if he was still high on bee pollen. 'Allow me to introduce you to your supernatural friends and ground crew. Meet Labyrinth.'

'Hello, Labyrinth,' I said.

'Welcome, Sister.'

Labyrinth was a radiant, robust and blue-eyed babe, with long blond dreadlocks piled into a ponytail on top of his head. The first thing I noticed about him was the large tattoo on his back that spelled out 'alchemy' in beautifully scripted letters. Tattooed over his heart was the same sacred geometry Shekinah dove we had encountered at the ashram in Glastonbury. In further conversation, I learned that Labyrinth was a devoted raw foodie who prided himself on knowing the location of each and every natural hot spring in England. He boasted that he often frequented them to perform bathing rituals and that he had even demonstrated one of his infamous bathing rituals on BBC television last year. His tattoos of alchemy and the dove lit up like huge neon lights being broadcasted directly from the Great Mother saying, 'Pay attention, dear child! Sometimes the greatest signposts can be tattooed on someone's chest.'

Simon went on to introduce the rest of his friends. Next was the tall and lanky Malcolm from Scotland. Once a successful lawyer and scholar, he was now a devoted dad, raw food advocate, and passionate Ashtanga yoga teacher who proudly boasted that Woody Harrison was one of his students. Then there was Jai, Malcolm's eleven-year-old son, who mostly lingered in the background, picking up after his hyperactive father. I was told we would soon meet up with a handful of other crewmembers at the festival.

My heart warmly opened to all of them as I watched them loading up their converted fire truck with copious amounts of raw food supplies, kitchen accessories, a large circus tent, DJ equipment, lights and an ultra-wicked sound system.

Simon shouted out from the front cabin of the fire truck while I lingered on the front doorsteps with a cup of tea in hand. 'You and Eva make yourselves at home! We have to head off early to the festival site to set up the supernatural raw food kitchen. We'll see you lovely goddesses at The Big Green in a few days! Ciao for now,' shouted Simon.

I nodded and waved as the crew got the last of their gear loaded onto the trucks and started the large engine in preparation for takeoff. Gavin had left early that morning, and Eva and I spent the day doing laundry and handling some last-minute logistics. In truth, I was totally relieved to have some quiet downtime to recuperate from the not so very Healing Fields festival. *Time to catch our breath and get prepared for the next big shindig!*

The house was eerily quiet after the busy bee lads left. The rainy, gloomy weather had a way of creeping in and threatening to create a similar gloominess inside me. Bottom line was that I was coming down with a mild case of melancholy and longed for the familiar comforts of my Bay Area home. I had to remind myself why I was here in the first place. *I must be totally insane to leave everything I know behind in search of a mysterious statue of a woman holding a flower in her hand!* My thoughts whirled around like trash getting caught in a cyclone. I recalled that my quest had made absolutely no sense to the rest of my family – and it was making little sense to me right now. However, the Pyrenees Mountains of Southern France continued to magnetically draw me in. Wafting between the soggy weather and my gloomy thoughts, I fantasised about purple and blue jagged mountains surrounded with lush green natural hot springs.

That day, an indescribable gloominess followed me around the house like a dark cloud threatening to burst into a torrential downpour of tears. *Have I simply come down with a case of SAD attributed to the gloomy English weather?* I pondered while recollecting Jahrusha's forewarning that this journey would demand everything of me. I would have to muster my highest faith and trust that I would be lead to the promise of my true beloved, whom I was secretly longing to meet. All the while the rain continued to piss down in a very unpromising manner that no amount of English tea and biscuits could alleviate.

That night, I lay in bed with Eva and felt the grace of Divine Mother waft into the room while relishing the warmth of our tender and familiar friendship. 'Will you do an Akashic reading and shed some light on our journey and what is on the horizon for us?' Eva tenderly asked in that oh so familiar best-friendish tone of voice that soothed my soul.

I was grateful for the invitation and opportunity to tune into a higher frequency and resonance with my beloved sister, especially after the inner emotional turmoil from the night before. Despite all my well wishes, I was left with an undisclosed feeling of guilt for not feeling happier for my dear friend who was having a hayday in the realms of endless flirtations with foxy foreign men.

So I dropped into meditation and this was what the hidden voice conveyed:

'Let go, beloveds. Sing to the mystery. Be willing to release the known and step into the currents of your unfolding destiny. Do not cling to where you have been. Be willing to be in Love's presence wherever you are and to trust the divine plan as each new waking moment unfolds and reveals itself in ways that are aligned with your deepest soul's calling.

'There is a new myth unfolding and you are each a part of the weaving of a prophecy that began many ages ago across many continents and

lands. Lady Alchemia is moving in to teach you the ways of transforming the lead in your life into gold. She brings to you the ancient stories of the awakening Goddess and the re-emergence of the Feminine Christ as revealed through the legacy of Isis, Mother Mary, Mary Magdalene and the Red Queen Sophia, all of whom yearn to be embraced and remembered as an aspect of yourself.

'The dove has taken her final flight to meet the eagle and restore a long, broken alliance. You are embarking on a journey of Sacred Union wrapped in a maze of encounters born of grace and synchronicity. The twin serpents have risen! They are in an inseparable dance of rising to be crowned in the oneness of Sacred Union. Be fully present for all that is unfolding. Even in your restless and impatient heart, know that you are fully guided as you return to the places from long ago. These are places of remembrance, homecoming and devotional prayer. You will be accompanied by an entourage of unseen ascended masters and celestial guides. Upon returning to these familiar dwelling places, you will be reunited with an ancient friend and beloved. Your reunion will cause a shift in the dance of light and darkness and help to calm the destructive violence felt between the poles. For countless hours, the Sun and Moon have danced apart. Now they reunite to restore the balance between the Masculine and Feminine, the inner and the outer and thus heal the insidious illusion of separation and heartache.

'The time is now for the Sacred Marriage to commence. A Christ child of unprecedented love-light, innocence and beauty will be born to the Earth Mother. We are at the threshold of ushering in the New Earth and a brand-new humanity that is born from each being stepping into the light of their authentic Self. Sing the return of innocence into existence – it will settle our restless mother and beguiled father. Beloved one, the time is now to meet me in that place beyond all right and wrong doing. Together, we shall dissolve the last traces of separation and fear. The three-fold awakened heart of love, power and innocence will live again, and golden showers will illuminate all dark corners of our beloved Earth Mother Gaia and Father Sun. Go to the inception place from which this story was born. The time for triumphant grace is upon you. Set the white mare free to reclaim her wisdom and power to run wild once again. You will return home to illuminate a new way of relationship rooted in the trinitised field of mutual sovereignty, respect and celebrated diversity. May trust and *faith be your compass and may you always remember the way through is to go within and be grateful for each and every experience.'*

These wise and comforting words rang true for both Eva and I. They powerfully called me out of the dark, misty forest of amnesia. A pod of etheric dolphins and a golden luminous child appeared before me, beckoning me to meet myself in joyous innocence and leave behind all fears. I then felt and saw Jahrusha. He appeared to me as both a wise elder and innocent child. With a mischievous twinkle in his eye, he was assisting me to map the way to my own crucifixion and, Goddess willing, eventual resurrection.

That night, I barely slept a wink. *Why?* Because I was mystically aroused, mythically turned on and cosmically over stimulated. The pilot light of Christ Consciousness was turned on and along with it, my inner fire burned with a hot, fiery passion. My identity and everything I knew myself to be was slowly disintegrating, making way for someone, something and someplace totally unknown to reveal itself. For now, it felt miles away and simultaneously as close as my very own breath.

CHAPTER NINE

MAGIC & SYNCHRONICITY

Magic sings the tune of serendipity, synchronicity, and synergy. Magic happens due to felicitous combinations of energies, timing, people, and placement. Magic is the interactive relatedness of the creation. It is the pattern that connects. Magic requires more than one element to precipitate. Synchronicity, serendipity and synergy are some means by which the elements arrive at the same moment so that magic can happen.

Doubt exists only in the mind. Magic exists in the heart. When you experience in your heart that all things are possible here and now, suddenly doubt disappears, and magic appears. Recognize that you live in a limitless reality of creational possibilities. Also recognize that doubt obscures those possibilities from your awareness. Magic puts you in resonance with the creational matrix from which all form emanates. You are a creator. You have the power of the creator within you. Magic reminds you of that fact.

When you perceive that YOU are the magic, Heaven will celebrate. Magic is not outside of you. It is an on-going process within you. As you expand into an ever-greater love, you will perceive more within you that can be offered to others as magical expressions of your divinity. If you want to expand into greater love, simplify. Stop thinking and enter into the direct perception of what is. Recognize the miraculous that is everywhere around you; your heart will flood with love and gratitude. Gratitude is generative. More magic will manifest within you when you are appreciative.

Magic dances only in the present tense. Live life with the intensity of a dying person or a small child. There is nothing but this moment. Live in it.

Inhabit your life. Don't wait. Throw away your thermometer, holey socks, and leftovers. Throw caution to the wind. Dance life with a rose in your teeth and the passion of flamenco blaring in the background. Magic will have no choice but to dance with you, because...then, you are not boring God! Your next move cannot be predicted. You are a free radical electron in the body of God. You might do something novel, astonishing, and miraculous that will tickle the Creator. Where else would magic rather play?

– Ariel Spilsbury, *The Thirteen Moon Oracle*

Eva and I spent the following day cleaning the house from the cyclone that hit it just before the lads took off for the festival. Restoring some semblance of order and cleanliness helped me to ground my restless mind. Simmering just below the sweet surface of my present dynamic with Eva lurked an ever-encroaching bitterness. No matter how I reasoned with it, this energy refused to withdraw its gnawing tug on my heartstrings. Clearly, energies on a larger subconscious level were being stirred up, begging to be seen, felt and eventually healed.

I sat holding the mop while daydreaming about the time of chivalrous knights, exalted kingdoms and princesses. Although I could not make out the exact details, I sensed an ancient and unresolved wound festering between Eva and I. Seeded lifetimes ago, perhaps amongst these very lands, I was being beckoned to revisit it. I sensed it had something to do with a painful betrayal of our sisterhood now seeping through into this lifetime. It oozed its way in between our loving smiles, gradually eroding at our open hearts, threatening to tear us apart.

At the time, I was unclear and confused about what was actually happening and I decided to give us some space in order to manage the intensity of my crazy, irrational, erupting emotions. I knew deep down that I was responsible for creating this inexplicable encroaching tension between us.

The Big Green festival started the following day and we still had no idea how we were going to get there. Eva suggested that I go to Infinity Health food store and ask around for a ride. Happy and relieved to get some time on my own, I took the public bus while she opted to complete some last-minute errands in town on her own. There was a light misty drizzle threatening to give way to being yet another full-blown storm. *Better leave now before getting caught in the middle of another downpour.*

I arrived at the quaint health food store feeling like Inspector Clouseau from the cartoon, *The Pink Panther*. I sheepishly scanned the store for potential festival goers. The only likely candidate had just left the store and was getting on her bike.

I set my kombucha drink aside and briskly followed her outside. Just as she was cycling away, I mustered my courage and boldly flagged her down. 'Excuse me. Excuse me!' I loudly called after her. 'You wouldn't by any chance be heading over to The Big Green festival tomorrow, would you?'

I was surprised at first that she actually stopped her bike abruptly, looked back at me and replied with a grin, 'Why yes, I actually, I am.'

'Wow, fantastic. My friend and I are looking for a ride... You don't have any extra room by chance?'

She smiled more broadly and said, 'As a matter of fact, our two passengers pulled out today. I think we could probably squeeze you into my girlfriend's van. What's your name, sister?'

'Ambeʹ,' I replied.

'Ambeʹ from the Bay Area, Ambeʹ?' she responded in surprise.

'Yes,' I said.

'No way! I've actually heard about you from my girlfriend. She tried to contact you in the States and could not track you down. We've heard wonderful things about your work and she wanted to see if she could get in on a training with you.'

Wow, I thought to myself, feeling surprised and even a little flattered that I had been discovered all the way over here in the UK. *What are the chances of arriving here precisely at this moment, asking a random person for a ride and discovering she was friends with the one person from England who was trying to make contact with me in America?* Once again, I was astounded by the over the top synchronicity and precise timing of it all! Bubbling from our serendipitous meeting, we stood on the sidewalk and exchanged numbers.

'I'm so excited to tell my girlfriend that I met you! I'm sure she will be thrilled to share a ride. I'll ring you later to confirm.' My new friend called Sophie got back on her bicycle and disappeared in the mist.

With my mission now accomplished in the most serendipitous way, I caught the first bus back to Simon's house and found Eva riding on the upper deck while paging through a local fashion magazine. I was grateful to see her and share a giggle about the good news of arranging our potential ride with kindred sisters to The Big Green festival.

As soon as we arrived back at Simon's home, we began to feverishly pack our things in preparation for another go at an English festival experience. Our new friends called to confirm that they would pick us up the following day at noon. We were grateful to have a whole night to psych ourselves up as the storm clouds continued to gather above and within us.

Please, dear weather Goddess, I pleaded from my heart, *make the storm pass quickly so we don't have to endure yet another cold and wet festival in the bone-chilling English countryside!*

CHAPTER TEN

SACRED SLUDGE

Beliefs have the power to create and the power to destroy.
Human beings have the awesome ability to take any experience
of their lives and create a meaning that disempowers them
or one that can literally save their lives.

– Tony Robbins

On the initial days after the birth of this planet, the dazzling sun shone upon it with a multitude of colors streaming from the original twelve sacred rays of the Primal Creator. Each ray carried its own unique vibration, sound, and color. As they danced together, they whirled and twirled glorious ethereal art and music beyond our imagination. As the energies matured, the elements manifested as fire, water, earth, and air. Nature became the proliferation we're accustomed to today. Fabulous beings of light walked upon this earth embodying an amalgamation of all the twelve sacred rays. However, according to the divine plan, as the density of the planet increased, human consciousness decreased. Some of the higher more refined vibrations were no longer sustainable in this dense environment. So one by one, many of these rays disappeared from human perception, but continued to hold their sacred space for the eventual planetary ascension as we progressed through the natural cosmic cycle.

– Sharon Lyn Shepard, *Return of the Rainbow Tribes*

In truth, I was growing more and more restless as we waited for our scheduled 12pm ride to arrive, which actually didn't end up arriving until 3:45 pm. *Never mind!* We were prepared to go with the flow and grateful to have manifested a ride, although praying we would get to the festival before sundown to set up our tent. It wasn't looking good. Our new friend Sophie's twenty-three-year-old van drove as fast as it could while sputtering exhaust from its shotty muffler. We were all a little anxious about our tardiness and distracted ourselves with stories of world travel, Temple Arts and our unique healing journeys.

By the time we arrived, the festival fields were completely flooded and the parking lot was overflowing with soggy latecomers. We were all extremely anxious to set up camp before sundown, so we hugged abruptly and set out in opposite directions down the muddy road. Eva and I were now on our own, lugging our excessive baggage, down, down, down into the oh-so-familiar muddy trenches.

The festival was massive! It sprawled out as far as I could see in every direction. A brother in a yellow rain suit and dripping wet hat pointed us in the direction of where the 'people' camped. He said apologetically, 'They were carting people in with horse and buggy up until a half hour ago, but at this late hour, you'll need to hoof it.' We smiled and thanked him. Then we mustered up our deepest gumption to make the long hike in. The campground seemed miles away as we walked as briskly as possible through the muddy sludge. After the first ten minutes of traipsing through the mud, we were exhausted and we hadn't even made a dent on the distance we still had to go.

A small hut with twinkly Christmas lights flashed a sign that said House of Chai lured us in. We welcomed the layover, knowing that it could very well be an all-night endeavor trying to find our supernatural friends and set up camp.

OK, Ambe´, I coached myself. *Remember, this is supposed to be about having fun. It's time to lighten up and enjoy the ride!* I muttered affirmations under my breath such as, 'You got this', while simultaneously feeling grateful for the super intense thigh workout.

After a good thirty minutes of barely keeping up with Eva, we reached the House of Chai and set our ridiculously heavy bags down against the wooden post that held up the lopsided canopy. Eva and I were quick to stand in line and order a couple of chais along with a plate of organic Indian food to share between us. While waiting in the queue and getting intoxicated by the aromas coming from the tiny kitchen, I received a mysterious tap on the shoulder from someone behind me. I turned around and gasped with excited surprise. 'Sister!' It was Nicola, our yogini hostess who warmly welcomed us to Saint Michael's Cottage! I was completely delighted to meet a familiar face amongst the large sea of soggy vendors and festival troopers.

The three of us joyously greeted one another with girlish squeals and burly bear hugs.

'Blimey, I haven't left our camp once for three whole days, that is, until I heard a very persistent inner voice demanding that I take a break and go have a chai,' Nicola said. 'And voila, here you are. Wow! What divine timing. Supernatural camp is just across the field.' Nicola pointed to a large white circus tent only footsteps away. 'Let's have our chai and then I'll walk you over to our basecamp. We've been working like maniacs since we arrived to get things set up in time. You should see it. It looks bloody amazing!' she proudly boasted in her super cool North London accent.

Once again, I stood there stunned. In a sea of several thousand beings, Nicola found us exactly at the right place and precisely in the right moment in time. I took another moment to pause and appreciate how magic and synchronicity had found us once again. This mysterious phenomenon served to massage my faith muscles along with my perception that all matters of miracles happen when I stay open. *All things are being divinely guided for the greater good of all. All I need to do is trust and let the go!*

The warm plate of Indian food and the cup of hot chai were beyond delicious. I was revived just enough to lug my tired body and my bulging baggage over to the campsite. The three of us arrived just as the very last traces of daylight were visible. As we entered the buzzing hive, I heard ShimShai's heart-melting, angelic voice singing over the sound system. His prophetic lyrics and soul-infused song were a wonderful welcome home to our new supernatural basecamp. The music lit a flame within me that warmed me to the core. It was as if ShimShai was singing directly to me: 'Yehoshua, carry I along, Miriam sing out thy song in a strange land.'

Simon, Malcolm, Labyrinth and other members of the supernatural crew encircled us like a pack of panting, worn-out wolf pups that had been playing in the mud all day. They looked exhausted but victorious. They had just set up the large canvas dome in the pouring rain, which had to be dangerously challenging.

The crew was covered in mud from head to toe, their hair going off in every direction, with traces of green smoothie creating crooked green moustaches on each of their weathered faces. I was amazed they were still standing, let alone beaming smiles after setting up the big top in such horrific conditions. Simon reminded me, 'My dear, it's the English way to persevere for a great party... regardless of the weather. Nothing can stop us from serving up our raw coconut-mango pies and wicked beats!'

'Wow, that's passion! I'm sooo impressed.' I felt happy and honoured to be amongst this motley crew of raw foodies and supernatural heroes.

With the help of a couple of borrowed headlamps, we managed to set up our tiny green tent and stacked our bulging backpacks inside with the hope of keeping them as dry as possible. Eva and I were overjoyed to be settling into our new abode. It was clearly a bump up from our last outdoor camping fiasco – celebratory voices, drumming and flute filled the air from neighbouring camps. Campfire smoke mixed with mouthwatering aromas drifted into our tent from the nearby cafés. We could feel the myriad of mythic fairy kin gathered around hundreds of tiny fires, warming their bones and raising their spirits with story and song.

The grounds were an impressive twenty acres in diameter. They were sectioned off in seven different theme camps: Healing Arts and Divination, Earth Energy, Circus Arts, Permaculture, Crafts and Cottage Industry, and Family/Kid's camp. Each camp showcased world-class musicians, performers, speakers and presentations that showcased from sunrise to sundown. Attracting over fifteen thousand people and growing, The Big Green felt like a mini eco-friendly Burning Man. Our Supernatural Raw Food camp was located on the outer edge of the Family and Kid's camp, conveniently just metres away from our friends at the Lost Horizon

Sauna and Café! I was overjoyed to have familiar faces and a place to warm myself up throughout the course of the festival.

Despite my fatigue and the ongoing drizzle, I decided to venture out for a wander to quench my curiosity. A small excursion felt doable even for my damp and weary body. I set out to the nearest fire across the field, carefully avoiding large potholes and puddles of slippery red sludge. *One wrong move and I could be flat on my face.* I giggled. My steps were more like long slides as if I was cross-country skiing on thick, lumpy mud. I felt like Wonder Woman when I managed to make it to the neighbouring fire without wiping out in the muddy sludge that was becoming more and more like dubious quicksand. Yet another cup of delicious warm chai was my reward for getting to the campfire without falling flat on my face.

After getting myself another hot chai, I struck up a conversation with a man from Wales who made and collected drums from around the world. He charmed me with his thick accent, flirtatious smile and English mannerisms. We chatted about global warming and the dramatic Earth shifts encroaching upon our ill-prepared world. It didn't take long before my body shivered, reminding me of my sheer exhaustion. I politely excused myself, swallowed back the last sip of my gritty chai and headed back to base camp. *Here I go. I have five whole days to romp around this massive sprawl of mud, mirth and mythical magic, and discover why on Earth I am here.*

It turned out that Mother Nature was not going to let me get home without being baptised by her earthly embrace. Halfway across the field, one of the muddy potholes sucked up my right foot along with my shoe into her deep, dark, sludgy abyss. As I went to take my next step, I absolutely could not pull my foot out of the bloody hole. I jiggled, I wriggled and even giggled; and still my foot – along with my shoe – was sucked into the sludge by a wet, gooey, earthly suction cup that reminded me of being pulled into the vortex of the Bermuda Triangle. I had no other choice but to surrender my newly purchased shoe into the hole in order to liberate my right foot, which I absolutely could not go home without! Half-laughing, half-crying, half-freezing, I hobbled the rest of the way home to my tiny green tent – one shoe on and the other shoe gone, gone to the great beyond. *Phew, I made it!* I peeled off my muddy clothes and sheepishly crawled into my sleeping bag, passing out in a bone-chilling heap.

Mother Gaia poured down relentlessly for three more days. It was like being in a looping déjà vu. Thousands of people were now collectively being initiated into something way beyond the mere challenge of staying warm and dry. *Was this extreme weather a preview of what was to come?* Fifteen thousand festival goers were being simultaneously sucked down into the earth by what was now being referred to as the 'Kali sludge'. As the sound of the rain pounded relentlessly upon Gaia's belly, I could hear her calling her children to descend down into her bowels and listen – listen as if our lives counted on hearing what she had to say.

I will listen, dear Mother. I will come down from my mind-looping distractions into my heart and be present with you. I am here now, in the wilderness, the only place to truly be alive.

I squatted under a random tree and became silent as I heard these words speak to me from beyond the veil of pissing rain. '*This downpour is a cleansing of humanity's collective pain body. Humanities avoidance of feeling one's sequestered shame, guilt and fear has created much heaviness upon my body. Your despair cries out to be felt, honoured and healed. That which lies heavy upon your heart also lies heavy upon mine. This rain is the tears of your ancestors along with your denied self crying out to be heard, felt, forgiven and set free by your love and compassion.*

'*You have thought yourself to be separate from your Source and from each other. In so doing, you have mistaken one another as the enemy and disconnected from your own true nature. I bring you my torrential tears so that you may release your own. Do not be afraid of the sorrow and anguish now rising from the basement of your unconscious. Listen to the crying out of your soul while I cleanse all that has been buried deep within your cellular memory, weighing heavy on your body and this world. My beloved child, the time has come to free your heart and be the causeless joy that you were born to embody. Are you willing to feel all that you have been once unwilling to feel? Are you willing to open to the core fracture that has kept you exiled and outcast from your wild belonging? I am the teardrops of Gaia, and I offer you the gift of release and redemption.*'

Yes Mother, I will listen. From that moment on, I made a choice to stop whinging about the weather and instead, took time to listen to her daily through being present with my body, my breath and the precious community that surrounded me. Each moment became a practice of becoming silent in order to hear Gaia's tiny whispers... until I could feel her living and breathing inside of me, as me and through me.

This 'prepared for anything' eclectic wild tribe seemed to have gotten this Earth Mama's memo along with me. Individually and collectively, I observed the people around me rising to the opportunity of facing the harsh weather conditions with a spirit of humility, generosity, cooperation and endless service. All the while, we made it a practice to be attentive and kind to one another in what some would call 'horrendous outdoor living conditions'. As the rain relentlessly poured down, the sensitivity to the needs of one's neighbors grew bolder and brighter by the day, until at last, there was a collective feeling of *there is no other!*

Navigating this chilling experience in a pair of sandals meant for the French Riviera gave me a wicked case of Welly boot envy. On the third night, I decided to brave the cold weather and venture out to enjoy some of the evening's entertainment. Surprise, surprise, once again, my sandals were pulled into the sludgy abyss and I was reduced to bare feet and the cold, cold earth. *Brrrrrr!* The chill of the sopping red mud seeped into my bones while my inner thermostat plummeted down, down to my womb and the womb of the Earth. *How can I stoke this fire before it goes out altogether,* I cried out to the moon and the stars.

I managed to make it to a large circus tent where there was a heart-thumping, booty-bumping, gypsy-gyrating, go-go dancing, full-fledged, shake-your-booty dance party going on. Not wanting to miss out on the fun, I did my best to get into it, but all too soon, the relentless chill throbbing in my body became much stronger than the hot, pulsating bodies that surrounded me. I surrendered to the fact that I wasn't getting any warmer, and so I humbly bailed and sprinted over to the Lost Horizons Café. I could not help but prefer the warmth of a hot sauna over the seductive thrill of hundreds of gyrating bodies.

Since most people were at the thumpin' dance party, I was relieved to find no one in line for the sauna. With teeth chattering, I undressed with lightning speed, exposing my head to toe goose-bumped skin. I stacked my clothes in a little cubby hole in the co-ed dressing tent, which was merely a canopy held up by four wooden tepee poles. In a shivering flurry, I entered the sauna as if my life depended on it. *Ahhh,* the dry heat seeped into my naked flesh, serving to thaw and revive me. Before long, I joined in on the chanting of heart songs with a handful of other naked and anonymous bodies until I felt revitalised enough to face the cold night air. *Earth, my body; water, my blood; air, my heart' and fire, my spirit. Heya heya heya heya heya heya ho. Heya heya heya heya heya hoooo.*

As I was redressing, my eyes glimpsed a mesmerizing man wrapped in a sheepskin. His low baggy trousers and oversized, furry white hat gave him the look of a Muppet, mystic, and yogi all mixed in one. My heart was warmed by his lighthearted and cartoon-like mannerisms, and I was curious to know who this dashing character could be. Truth be told, I was a sucker for a man who looked like a galactic Muppet. *Pity,* I thought, since I saw that he was undressing for the sauna while I was now getting ready to leave. Best I could do was to catch his sparkly eyes and offer him a warm smile. I then scurried off to the tepee to sit next to the warm fire. Around half an hour passed while my desire to meet the majestic Mad Hatter lingered on. I restrained myself from going back into the sauna to see if he was still around. Within moments, he appeared and then squatted down next to me, placing his hands in front of the flames to warm them.

'Hiya, I'm Kailash,' he introduced himself as if we had a pre-destined date to meet precisely in that moment of time. 'I'm from the island of Jersey. Jersey, Europe, that is. Not to be confused with Jersey, New York,' he said lightheartedly. 'Who are you?'

'Ambe'. I'm from California, not to be confused with New Jersey. What kind of name is Kailash?' I said, inwardly swooning. His heartwarming smile was like a Fourth of July sparkler making my cells stand up in red-hot alert.

'I got my name in India when I became a Sanyasan, but now I live in Barcelona and teach English and offer energy healing to the local people.'

We sat talking by the fire until Phil, one of the Lost Horizon's crew, politely asked us to leave because they were shutting down for the night. Since we were so enthralled by one another's company, Kailash suggested we venture out to find another fire and continue our sharing.

'Yes, let's do it' I said, overriding the reality that I was still without shoes and proper storm attire. I must have been mad to expose myself once again to the downpour of cold rain. Kailash wrapped his body around mine to help lessen the chill. I suddenly melted as I realised how long it had been since I felt the special warmth of male companionship. I decided to endure the cold for a little while longer and get to know my new friend. Like two lost wolverines, we wandered the fields, looking for a warm den to hide out in. Apart from the full-on rave, it appeared that most of the festival people were tucked in for the evening. Kailash politely invited me to go back to his nearby tent in the Healing Fields. At this point, I craved the warmth so badly that I gratefully accepted – out of cold desperation and some obvious chemistry going on between us.

After a mad dash, we made it back to his tent, soaked from head to toe.

'Here,' he said, handing me a pair of Thai wrap-around pants and a long-sleeved white cotton T-shirt. 'Put these on.'

'Thank you.' I gratefully accepted his clothing while awkwardly aware of the intimate atmosphere I found myself in. Our rainy, 'two o'clock in the morning' stroll had left me both elated and exhausted. Kailash invited me to share his small one-person sleeping bag. We only had a small sheepskin protecting us from the cold ground beneath us. I gladly made myself at home and cuddled into his warm body. Eventually, our lips found one another, stoking that fire that melted us together in a pool of warm communion. We drifted in and out of sleep and sumptuous kisses, while simultaneously avoiding any kind of extreme movement that would derail either of us from his tiny sleeping bag. My body, heart and spirit oscillated throughout the night into the morning hours, alternately expressing one of two things – *brrr, hmm, brrr, hmm.*

Despite the allure of my deliciously cozy companion, by sunrise, I was still freezing my bum off. Out of pure survival instinct, I got up, gathered my wet clothes, kissed my friend's luscious Jersey lips goodbye and made a mad dash for home base. I galloped like a wild mare across the fields in the rain, with only one golden carrot in sight – I envisioned myself buried under multiple layers of warm blankets in the hope of reviving myself from near hypothermia.

When I arrived at our tent, Eva was nowhere to be seen. I presumed she had also found a special little someone to snuggle up with throughout the cold, rainy night. Never mind, I was getting used to her spending evenings out and I was glad for the extra space in our tent to recuperate from my snuggly escapade. I piled on as many clothes as I had, buried myself under the mountain of blankets until I passed out with a silly grin on my face.

Five hours later, I woke up midmorning to the sound of a distant saxophone. I could feel the magnetic pull of the new day and – yes, oh yes, the S-U-N! I could hardly believe it. After days of endless downpour and muddy everything, Grandfather Sun was making his debut appearance! With the excitement of a six-year-old heading to her own birthday party, I put on a mish-mash of my most colourful festival clothing. Still barefooted, I ran to the Healing Field. I was beyond grateful to feel the midmorning sun showering upon my body and upon the land.

Wow! I swooned with delight as I approached the large open field, which was filled with many constellations of bustling, glistening, rainbow star beings. The entire festival population was out to shimmer, shine and celebrate the return of the sun by dawning their finest full-feathered regalia. I stood back for a moment and took in the vast array of promenading, multicoloured, mythic dream characters. Everyone had come out to play: jugglers, minstrels, bards, fire dancers, fairies and freaky styley fungineers. A parade of mythic circus performers towered above me on stilts. They wove themselves amongst the young mamas carrying their glittery, face-painted babies upon their hips. I meandered through clusters of picnicking friends and various artisans who sat upon the shimmering grass in neat little rows displaying their sacred wares, procured from exotic travels from around the world. As I approached the centre of the large meadow, I enjoyed watching the star-dusted fairies wearing wings of all shapes and sizes, the precocious pixies hula hooping topless in the sunshine. The elven kin congregated together, looking ever so regal in their dapper waistcoats with brightly coloured feathers protruding from their top hats. There were wizard folk too, walking with their magical staffs adorned with crystals, feathers and amulets. Belly dancers made jingly sounds when they passed by, proudly parading their bare bellies, hennaed hands and layered skirts swirling from their womanly hips.

I swooned inside at the glorious sight of this Rainbow family, here to celebrate and honour the supernatural beauty that emanated from each and every unique being. Here was a tribe that celebrated creative expression and the outlandish gifts of the unhinged imagination. *This was how it was all meant to be...unity in diversity...the fully awakened splendor of Heaven on Earth!*

The collective energy was beyond dazzling and I was brimming with gratitude to have made it through the rain. The entire community was out to joyously celebrate a rebirth of unity consciousness and honour the magnificent return of the *sun*. It was as if rainbow flames blazed from every newborn heart and sweetly humbled smile. I looked around for Eva, wondering what marvelous new adventure had swept her up and away. I imagined her frolicking amongst the ecstatic crowd with a beautiful man wrapped around each of her elegant long arms. Drunk on the immense beauty of it all, I reminded myself of my top-priority mission for the day. *Shoes. I needed to find a pair of warm shoes!*

Off I went to peruse the various blankets piled high with second-hand clothing for sale and barter. Before I could say *lickety split*, my shoes jumped out to me from amongst six other pairs displayed in a neat row upon the moist grass. Based on their musty, waxy surface, they appeared to have last been seen taking out for a stroll somewhere in the early eighties. My first impression of these one-of-a-kind ankle boots was hilarious. *Oh my goddess, those are the tackiest-looking shoes I ever did see. I can't believe we ever wore shoes like that!* They were black, pointy-toed, ankle-high boots that zipped up in the back heel and had a red and gold leather flame appliqued onto each side. I tipped my head quizzically while trying to see them from a new perspective. *Okay cool, they could be a Fairy Queen disco boots with extra support for spontaneous adventures traipsing through the fields.*

Perfect! These will do just fine, I thought, adjusting my attitude to fit the opportunity at hand. *There is no way in hell I am going to spend another freezing night gallivanting around in bare-naked feet.* I slipped the boots on with a Prince Charming flare and found they fit perfectly. 'It's my lucky day,' I announced, grinning from the inside out. 'They fit like a dream!' For a mere three pounds, I had restored myself to disco Fairy Queen status. These orphaned, leather boots had waited two whole decades to be resurrected and placed onto my eager feet. I would be the lucky one to take them out for yet another spin on the dance floor. Life was definitely looking brighter. I strolled through the dewy grass meadow with a newfound spring in my step and a bedazzling twinkle in my toes.

CHAPTER ELEVEN

THREE ANGELS

Myth can be defined as the 'larger than life' archetypal patterns of awareness that we came encoded to dance with and evolve through. Archetypes are large mythic containers of consciousness that as Jung defines it, 'form constants that exist in and define a field of consciousness that transcend time, space and the individual.' Archetypes are the structures through which the Mythic dimensions of Self, play themselves out. One of the primary functions archetypes serve is to assist us in looking at our lives from a much larger, more mythic and spiritually expansive perspective than our ordinary day to day view of the Self. In virtually all cultures archetypes rise from the collective unconscious, in a multiplicity of cultural masks, especially in the dream life, making their presence known and felt as reminders that we are more than we seem in daily life, that life can be lived mythically. So what is a heroine? The heroine knows SHE IS THE ONE who makes a pivotal difference in the cosmic play on Earth. This heroine knows she is always at choice no matter what her circumstance. This heroine lives from authentic essence rather than simply accepting cultural expectations. This heroine has super human powers because she has clarity of focus and laser intent. The heroine lives daily life as a Myth by recognizing that everything is connected by pattern, symbol and thus by meaning. Begin to recognize those signs and signals in the synchronicities in your life. In living mythically, life becomes a joyful adventure. To move gracefully into the Mythic dimensions of Self there is one simple invective: move toward joy and beauty and away from disharmony. Enjoy the adventure of the journey.

– Ariel Spilsbury, *The Alchemy of Ecstasy*

We need not risk the adventure alone; for the heroes of all time have gone before us: the labyrinth is thoroughly known: we have only to follow the thread of the hero-path. And where we had thought to travel outward, we shall come to the center of our own existence: where we had thought to be alone, we shall be one with all the world.

– Joseph Campbell, *Hero with a Thousand Faces*

The various camps were buzzing with energy. Tonight was the night we were going to ride the star-dusted rainbow serpent into a brand-new harmonic reality. The indigenous elders were gathering in tepees for Sacred Ceremony in preparation for the evening. Meanwhile, the ground crew was immersed in preparing fresh juices, raw pies, nori rolls, nut pates, rainbow salads and raw treats made from exotic durian fruit imported all the way from Thailand. The DJs were tuning up their sound systems while the circus crew was busily adorning themselves in body paint, glitter and their amazing costumes. The Lost Horizon Café was chopping extra wood for the sauna and bringing out their finest large crystals for the goddess altar. Tonight would be the big night where all the diverse camps and tribes would gather and celebrate together as one unified family.

That evening, a divine manna promising miracles permeated the air. I set out early and had dinner with Christophe. He had been my neighbour in the small village of Dharamsala, India, where I once lived and studied Tibetan Buddhism three years ago. After dinner, I went for a wander and serendipitously ran into Michael, who was yet another dear friend from that same community. I discovered him brewing a large pot of chai in a tepee decorated with a colourful painted unicorn. Michael was a tall, dark, Gypsy-like man who wore an off-white dhoti cloth wrapped loosely around his thin waist, combined with a thick wool pullover sweater. He looked like the Indian deity Shiva with his two golden hoop earrings and long black hair bundled on the top of his head in a sloppy topknot.

As I peered into the entrance of the tepee, Michael saw me and beckoned me to come in with a warm hospitable smile. 'Ambe', come and sit down, my friend. It's amazing to see you here. How have you been, sister?'

'Namaste, Michael,' I responded with a cheeky tone, reminding him of our endless nights singing under the stars and around the fire in India.

I stood on my tiptoes to exchange a warm hug while soaking up the timeless bond forged from sharing a potent chapter of our lives as nomadic spiritual travellers.

Apart from being a master at making chai, Michael was now the proud owner of a handmade tepee company, a loving husband, father of three with a fourth baby on the way. I joined him in the tepee as he introduced me to a woman in a turquoise velvet hooded cape named Kiala. She was a High Priestess and energy healer from his hometown in Glastonbury. I placed the tips of my fingers to my heart to greet her. As High Priestess, her radiant presence was warmly familiar, a lineage we both shared over countless lifetimes.

Michael sat regally in his place of honour, surrounded by a plethora of jars and old tins filled with exotic herbs and spices. He prepared his special blend of chai for the evening with the nobility of a king and the attentive finesse of a Himalayan yogi. While waiting for the large blackened pot of simmering water to reach its perfect boiling temperature, Michael passed around a thickly rolled herbal cigarette. After partaking in a silent ritual, we shared stories and began to reminisce about our transformational time together in India. Tucked away in the hills of Dharamcot, the towering village just above Mcloud Gang, Dharamsala, twelve of us had spontaneously converged from around the world. We lived as one tribal community in a shared home tucked away on the hillside below the towering Himalayas. Individually and together, we went deep into our spiritual practices to heal our bodies, hearts and minds. Our collective sadhana was transformative, amplified by the Tibetan Rinpoches, who held regular pujas in the surrounding monasteries. The presence of the His Holiness, the Dalai Lama, cast an aura of immense blessing around us and the neighbouring village. We lived together in bliss, practicing our Bodhisattvas vows, whilst the Buddha, banoffee pie and weekly blessings from His Holiness bestowed their special kind of magic on us all.

While sipping slowly on Michael's spicy brew of chai, Michael spoke of his connection to the land that sits above the White Spring in Glastonbury. 'The White Spring gushes out from the bottom of a sacred hill called the Tor,' he began. 'Adjacent to it is the Chalice Well garden, where the Red Spring flows. Long ago, the White and Red waters came together at the base of the hill in an alchemical mingling of red and white, Divine Feminine and Divine Masculine. Many believe there is a portal from the land above the White Spring that leads into the Tor and its ancient initiation caves, which exist in the parallel world of Avalon. The water from the Red Spring in the Chalice Well garden is full of iron salts that give it a reddish colour. It used to be called the Red Spring, and the Blood Spring before that, so here is the alchemical symbolism of the Masculine energies at the Chalice Well. The White Spring is full of calcium salts, which give it a creamy-white precipitate if you leave it standing – this reflects back to the alchemical symbolism of the Feminine power.'

I was fascinated and focused on Michael with hawk-like precision as he went on to mesmerize me with his every word.

'Alchemists produce red and white elixirs through the process of purification. Gold was produced through the 'alchemical wedding' or the union of opposites. This the alchemists believed created the Holy Grail, the waters of everlasting life. So although the springs appear to be separate, they rise from the same source, from the axis mundi which conjoins the above with the below...Heaven and Earth.'

Kiala went on to share, 'There is so much powerful history connected with this land. I am always learning something new. Most recently, I heard that Yeshua's mother Mary, Mary Magdalene, Anna and her extended Essene family would make pilgrimages here and closely resided with the Druids and priestesses of Avalon where they would undergo spiritual initiations and broaden their mystery school studies.'

Michael leaned in closer to me over the fire, his dark eyes piercing mine with shooting starlight. In a voice a little louder than a whisper, he murmured. 'As you are well aware, many hidden truths come to the surface when one has the ears to hear and the eyes to see through the veils of 3D reality.'

He went on to say, 'Glastonbury is a powerful place to live, although the energies can be unpredictable and at times intense. Nonetheless, my family and I feel quite honoured to be one of the designated Earth guardians to the gateway to Avalon. From time to time, Avalon shimmers under the light of the full moon, calling to us from beyond the veil. Mostly, the spirit of Avalon lives on in the memory of the Priestess. Like you, dear Ambe´ and Kiala, many are drawn back here to remember and reclaim they're priestess lineage and continue their missions, conceived and set into motion lifetimes ago. Thank you for dedicating your lives to serving the way of the heart.'

As Michael spoke, I felt goose bumps ripple through my body and a strong remembrance of an ancient promise that I made as a priestess in Avalon. I couldn't recall its exact words, but the feeling to be here for the Earth and the rising of the Divine Feminine and Masculine was clear as the starry night sky. Reuniting with Michael and learning of his guardianship was an auspicious touchstone for my continued journey into remembering the true meaning of the Holy Grail. I left the tepee basking in the afterglow of our reunion. Hearing stories that felt familiar was beginning to awaken my soul's connection to these mythic lands. I walked across the field with my head tilted up, taking in the twinkling stars as if they held the answers to so many of my unanswered questions. *I wonder what the rest of the evening has in store for me,* I pondered as I headed to the Lost Horizon Café.

Just as I settled myself on the Earth in front of a small wooden table, a young man approached me, wearing a large string of thick rudra beads. I chuckled to myself as I observed a kind of Avalon-meets-India theme unfolding. He acknowledged me with his electric blue eyes and gave me a precocious elven smile, which seemed to reach all the way to his pointed ears. I smiled back and introduced myself. 'Hello, I'm Ambe´.'

'Hello, I'm Gabriel from Wales. May I sit with you?'

'Yes, of course, sit down,' I said while admiring his very enchanting accent. 'So what are you up to in life?' I questioned him inquisitively.

'I have a company that introduces people to eco-alternatives for consumption. We aim to produce and educate people to use alternative resources other than trees. You see, I love the forests, so I'm doing what I love,' he added while gifting me with another heart-warming smile.

'Oh, I'm sure Gaia is extremely grateful for your contribution in making us all a little more sustainable and conscientious.' I pointed to the thick seed-like rudra beads glowing from his neck. 'Where did you get those? They feel alive with an ancient spirit.'

'Ah yes,' he said, his hand rubbed one of the beads between his index finger and thumb. 'They're from Nepal where I frequently travel.'

In that very moment, our eyes met and I flashed back to another lifetime. We were in an ancient temple in India and I was dancing for God...and for him. I was encircled by twelve glowing candles with an array of colourful rose petals sprinkled between each one of them. The warm summer breeze gracefully blew through my ruby red and gold silk sari that moved in synch with my fluid dancing limbs. The stars felt alive and the night was sanctified by an unnamable mystical presence. I danced under a canopy of starlight in ecstatic communion with and for the Beloved. There was no I, there was no other, only a blissful transcendent union with all of existence.

Gabriel and I held each other's gaze, transfixed in a moment of awe and wonder. Like a full moon, lunar eclipse, this old/new friend's inner light was fully aglow, not dimmed and glazed over, the way most humans are these days. I felt pleasantly intoxicated by the memory of myself as a Sacred Temple dancer and my heart leaped as I realised I was in the presence of the archetypal embodiment of Krishna, the Indian Lord of Dance, Lord of Love and Devotion. I sensed that our timeless communion also transfixed Gabriel, as we simultaneously recalled one another from another place and time...a time when everything and everyone was revered as one with the cosmic dance of god/goddess.

'Who are you and where are you from?' he asked while holding the intensity of our gaze.

I had to think about it. 'I don't know,' I whispered under my breath. 'I am Ambe´ from the Bay Area, California,' I muttered.

Our eyes locked once again. In a timeless gaze, we travelled even further back to that place that has no name and where only silence remained.

A tap on his shoulder brought him back to the here and now. A friend of his had come by to remind him of his rendezvous with another. He stood up quite abruptly, paused and then smiled warmly down at me. He took off his rudra beads and placed them around my neck. Then he leaned down and tenderly kissed my cheek and said, 'These are for you, star dancer. Blessings on your journey.'

My body was filled with honey-like nectar, overflowing in gratitude for Gabriel's beyond generous offering. *Beloved Elven King from Avalon, Archangel Gabriel, won't you stay and skydance for just a little longer?* By the end of that thought, Gabriel had disappeared. *Poof! Gone, gone, gone beyond.* Just like that. He was nowhere in sight and yet I now walked with his divine essence wrapped around my neck in the form of a long string of prayer beads that were impossible to miss.

I stood up and walked into the starry night to see where the gentle wind would blow me next. I was guided toward the field of Divination Arts to the Mayan Tortuga tent, which sat across from the Lemurian Dream Temple, home to one of the Crystal skulls. I wanted to see what the Mayan Thirteen Moon Calendar family was up to in this part of the world. The walk alone under the crystal clear sky gave me some time to integrate the enormous gift of the rudra beads that Gabriel had just gifted me with.

When I arrived at the Mayan tent, I recognised a Chilean brother, Raphael. I had already crossed paths with him twice that day and felt magnetically drawn into his warmth. Each time I bumped into him, I felt that familiar spark of a kindred heart coupled with a vibrational surge up my spine. Now he was sitting in the Tortuga tent, strumming his guitar with his eyes closed, deeply entranced in his own inner melodic world. I sat quietly down next to him so as not to disturb him. Sensing my presence, he opened his eyes and greeted me with a deep and silent smile that warmed me to the core.

Wow, I thought, feeling deeply moved. *I have found myself in the grace and company of yet another beloved angelic star brother.* Like Michael and Gabriel, I sensed he was awake, and travelled between worlds into higher dimensional realms that exist beyond ordinary reality. Raphael was not only a wildly divine star brother; he was a gentle Earth guardian and loyal emissary of Gaia Sophia.

'Hermosa, would you like to sit and meditate with me?'

'I would love nothing more, dear brother.'

I entered into his sacred space with a deep reverence for his unseen world. Upon locking gazes and unifying our breath, his energy body began to entwine with mine. Our heart light braided as we soared into the higher dimensions and sky danced together in cosmic realms of sublime beauty. We travelled into the centre of the Earth where I joined him in paying homage to the thirteen Grandmothers, who keep the crystalline womb fire lit and protected for Mother Gaia. We travelled inter-dimensionally through roots and vine, rainforest and jungle to meet the guardian spirits of his ancestral land and feel the vibrancy of his shamanic lineage. We then journeyed through the Gaian and galactic ley lines and shared ancient future codes of the awakening of Universal Christ Consciousness. I felt beyond blessed to get a glimpse into this bioluminescent realm that resembled the Na'vi landscapes depicted in the movie *Avatar*.

When we reemerged from our shamanic journey into the inner Earth, we gazed into each other's earthen brown eyes with our wide-open hearts. His face shape-shifted into a jaguar and then into multiple other beings, showing me the many faces of the Amazonian Masculine Christ. I reached out and lightly touched his heart and whispered, 'Beloved Raphael, hermano d'estrellas, gentle shaman, keeper of the galactic star codes, fierce protector of Gaia's heart-womb, Earth guardian – portal opener, thank you, Beloved, for your willingness to share so transparently with me and allowing me to see and be seen by you. Inlak'ech, I am another one of you.'

He nodded with a fierce gentleness so vast that it gave me the strength to be the sensitive soul that I am on behalf of all my relations. He then placed his palms together to rest on his chest and beamed his star-dusted love out to me before I bowed in gratitude and left the tent. What a gift to fly with this radiant condor and golden childlike man from Chile.

Although brief, each encounter that evening was a timeless transmission and angelic blessing from the Divine Masculine that would continue to unfold over time. I looked up in awe at the night sky, blanketed with billions of stars twinkling back at me. As I gazed upon the Milky Way, I thanked the universe for giving me these precious encounters, each one of them reflecting an aspect of my awakened Masculine, devoted to living a life in noble truth, in service to Gaia and the rising of the Divine Feminine *and* Masculine restored to living in harmony and sacred balance.

The night was still young, so I headed back to the Lost Horizons Café for my evening ritual sauna only to find that it was closed for the night. Like a mermaid who had ventured out onto land for too long, I needed to get into water and wash away some of the muddy red sludge that clung to my hair and skin. Luckily, Lost Horizons provided an outside shower beautifully positioned just next to the goddess altar that shimmered by candlelight with an array of impressive large crystals. It didn't matter to me anymore that the night air was crisp and that there was only cold water. I needed to feel the raw bareness of my skin being baptised by water. This was my way of turning the page after an exceedingly long and arduous beginning to my journey, and make way for a more relaxed and trusting version of myself to emerge.

In the brisk night air, I quickly removed the layers of my clothing as if undressing my illusions and exposed my body to the raw naked truth. My disco fairy boots were the last to go. I dove boldly into the fountain of freezing water and invited it to wash away every muddy thought form of remaining small, victimised and afraid to simply be who I am, uncensored and unapologetic. Under a canopy of bright, twinkling stars, I used this invigorating shower to wash away the veils that had kept me floundering in countless lies of insufficiency. The brisk water served as a wake-up call to raise my vibration higher than all of my doubts, fears and insidious insecurities. Standing naked was my way of experiencing a deeper truth.

I am one with the stars above and the mud wedged between my toes. In this naked presence, all matters of possibilities will be born, I whispered under my chattering teeth.

With the moon as my witness, I declared to the night sky, 'I, Ambe´, surrender to my divine presence, willing to be all the way here, now! I choose to fully embrace this messy and uncertain future along with all of its vulnerable, brave, wild, fumbling, courageous, fierce, compassionate moments that I have left to give myself fully to this world. I trust this mysterious darkness while simultaneously living in and as the luminous light. I say 'yes' to life in all of its perfect imperfection and choose to see the undivided beauty in all things, one blessed breath at a time! To this mystery, I thee wed, for better or for worse, in sickness and in health, I will be here, for the one in the many and the many in the one, eternally blessed!' With a joyous squeal of aliveness, I turned off the tap and dried off my shivering, goose-bumped nakedness in lightning speed.

I felt revivified, open to the mystery of the moment and was called to return to the Supernatural camp to check out what was happening on the home front. *Wowza! Was it ever booming.* Fully adorned bodies were flying high on cacao elixirs and raw mango pie! A pod of pulsating humans danced to the beat of the thumping drum and bass. My whole being was vibrating with joy light, as I soaked in the waves of love mana bursting forth from a cacophony of sound, frequency and shining hearts. The best way to ease myself into this Bhakti boogie wonderland was to go behind one of the tables and serve up some raw delights. My friends and I reveled in silent awe at the gift of having survived and made it thus far. Being alive to participate in co-creating these conscious celebrations was nothing short of miraculous. Here we were, dancing in an exotic garden, each a unique and perfumed flower, embodying a facet of the whole, here to bless and be blessed with the power to co-create a New Earth, one that dances together in Oneness and mouthwatering beauty.

At last, I was ready to leap into the dancing flames and make the kind of steam that lifts the dark clouds and turns them into rainbow light. I entered the sea of sweaty bodies with the spirit of throwing myself into life while holding nothing back. Whenever I needed to take a breather, I delighted in nourishing people with living foods, prepared with a cacophony of loving hands and ecstatic hearts. I savoured the immense beauty of this universal, rainbow rockin', beat boppin', wildly divine tribe of pioneering Passionistas, who embodied the audacity to follow their joy and create their life to the beat of their inner drum. In my eyes, each person was a living superhero and I felt incredibly honoured to be a part of this global tapestry of radiant star beings. With my heart ablaze, I danced into the morning hours until the sky filled with wispy brush strokes of orange, yellow, hot pink and gold. The morning light welcomed me into a new day, blooming with what it meant to be alive and thrive amongst a hive of passionate and fiercely dedicated beings.

The festival was a condensed and amplified way to practice staying awake together – conscious of the impact our everyday choices have on each other, the whole and for generations to come. We sensed that our capacity to work and create together in flow state was our greatest power to transform a world mired in divisiveness. And as each freely contributed their unique gifts into the melting pot of our sovereign togetherness, our highest potential became liberated – alive and brimming with the power to actualize Heaven on Earth. There was nothing more gratifying to my wandering soul then to share with others in the responsibility of stewarding our Earth Mother in the knowing that each has the power to profoundly shift the whole of creation.

And just like the Buddha and so many awakened masters modeled before us, we must check ourselves and our motivations relentlessly while yielding our power with humility, wisdom and compassion for the benefit of this one precious life and all sentient beings. *Om Mani Padme Hum!*

CHAPTER TWELVE

IMAGINE THAT!

Synchronicity is the soul's 'crumb trail' that links seemingly unrelated, quantum, causal events in time space. Every synchronicity is a message from the quantum, archetypal dimensions of your being, that when listened to, direct the course of the soul's evolutionary coding. When you live your life with an appreciation of seeming coincidences and their meaning, you connect with the underlying quantum field of infinite possibilities. Generally, the more you pay attention to synchronicity, the more it happens. By applying attention and intention to these synchronicities that arise from the quantum level, you can create specific outcomes in your life. Attention activates the energy field and intention activates the information field, which causes transformation. Everything that happens in the universe starts with intention. Intent has within it the mechanisms for its own fulfilment. The seed contains all the information it needs to blossom in fulfilment. Learning how you can consciously direct the infinite potential of the quantum realms is the nature of what I call magic and miracles; to tap into that vast potential, nurture synchronicity. That is, you might consider applying the theory of quantum physics to making your transition into the 'Wonderland' that we now approach on Earth, a joyful and ecstatically fulfilling ride!

– Ariel Spilsbury

As you travel the path of the heart, the pure activity of love will always be alive inside you. But it will never diminish the arising of very alive states of vulnerability, or contract the vivid luminosity of your emotional spectrum. For these are the portals through which love will reach you, dissolving old dreams and grinding everything that is less than whole to dust, so that you may be crafted as a translucent vessel in which new forms of creativity may enter and play.

– Matt Licata

Today's ascension process that brings about global patterns of coherency or unity does not require going behind cloistered walls or taking prolonged sanctuary with master teachers, as we did in the old paradigm. Mother Earth and your life is your empowerment school. You have all kinds of support available to help you attain your Self-mastery.

– Claire Heartsong, *Anna, Grandmother of Jesus*

The next morning, my dear brother James from the Lost Horizons Café asked me if I would do a healing session with him. He was a painter and musician from Queensland, Australia. His strong physique and carved features emanated a subtle and undeniable Christ-like demeanour. I had met him while admiring his painting of a Goddess dressed in a deep royal blue gown. She stood poised, full of wisdom with an owl perched on her shoulder and surrounded by peacocks. I was mesmerised by the painting, and spent hours looking at it, attempting to understand why the cobalt-blue figure felt so familiar to me. Perhaps, like so many of the unexpected encounters on the journey, it offered me a mysterious clue into remembering a deeper aspect of myself and the many faces of the Goddess that lived within me.

Over the course of the festival, James and I had developed a silent kinship based on an unspoken sensitivity to the depth of our feeling bodies. It seemed both of us understood the subtle heartache and joy of being highly sensitive and empathic beings. I recognised his soul and sensed that there was a higher purpose for us to explore and so I was more than happy to offer him a healing session.

Later that afternoon we sat under an ancient tree and I offered him an Akashic reading. In our session, I sensed persistent internal judgment and critical thinking was draining his power and life force. Essentially, his masculine side became dominant by staying in the mental planes, refusing to allow his feminine essence to flow freely. Therefore, he was not allowing himself to be vulnerable and responsive to the urges of his deep heart and wildly creative nature.

'We can unify the feminine heart and masculine mind in such a way that neither dominates nor entraps, but instead each becomes a conscious an attracting force that heals and balances the other.'

Something in him relaxed with those words. He was able to forgive himself for suppressing his true feelings and squelching his creative heart's fire. His vulnerability was so refreshing as he revealed that he spent most of his moments feeling sad and depressed, likely symptoms of his suppressed creative fire. I saw the matching parts of him that were mirrored back to me and made sure I gave myself a hearty dose of the same forgiveness medicine. We resolved together to make more space for our instinctual feminine side and stay open to our wild heart's desires.

'Let's support one another to stay out of our heads and get more into our hearts. Shall we?'

James and I felt relieved and grateful to be seen, supported and embraced while soaking up the authentic intimacy and connection we shared. Into–me–I–see, into–we–I–see, together we rise and set our golden hearts free.

The rest of the day flowed beautifully. I enjoyed taking time to eat a fresh salad while soaking up the rays of the midday sun. We were on our last full festival day, so after lunch, I exchanged contact details with new friends before we each went our separate ways. Later in the afternoon, I went looking for my snuggle buddy Kailash to say farewell. It didn't take long before I found him under a large oak tree surrounded by frolicking barefoot children. He appeared to be playing an elaborate game of make believe. His hands were filled with a mixture of honey, oats, dates, cocoa and all the wholesome makings of the best bliss balls one could ever imagine. He warmly beckoned me to join him.

We lay lazily together on the grass, staring up at the passing clouds. It felt good to openly share about our festival experiences while exploring the possibility of deepening our connection at a later time.

'Come for a visit in Barcelona. I would love to show you the beauty of this town,' he said warmly, open to all matters of possibility. I was grateful for his affectionate friendship and the magic we exchanged on one of the coldest nights of my life.

We soaked in the silent wonder of our special time together. Life was fleeting and we were grateful for the honour of touching one another's lives, even if it was for a brief moment in eternity. Kailash and I stood up to face the last of the afternoon sun, taking in its brilliant warmth as it glistened through the surrounding trees. I held onto his sticky, gooey hand as we looked out across the fields and took in the dazzling beauty of it all. The white tops of the circus tents were towering over the midday bustle as our beautiful star family fed their kids, broke down camp and exchanged their last glimpses and soul gifts. I was filled with gratitude for what was shared in honour of Mother Gaia, Father Sun and generations to come. We silently sent out a prayer of gratitude to our star family and for all the potent heart medicine exchanged in the visible and invisible realms.

'Thank you, shining ones, for inspiring me to grow and to know that all things are possible when our hearts stay open to the magic and wonder of it all! May we forever walk in beauty on behalf of all beings and generations to come. Aho!'

With that, I bid Kailash a warm farewell. We locked gazes, then embraced, taking several full-bodied breaths pressed together as if to reinforce our journeys to come. We silently exchanged our gratitude for meeting and the opportunity to share warmth and sumptuous caresses during our enchanting evening together. 'Bye for now, beloved Muppet lover.'

As I walked back to my tent, I acknowledged that each and every being at the festival had touched my life in some visible or invisible way. I felt into the sublime sacredness of every unique connection – likened to a sparkling dewdrop shimmering on a giant luminous spider web. We are each a golden thread woven into an interconnected, super-conductive tapestry of Universal Love, Beauty Intelligence. My heart expanded to include the entire planet as I sent waves of light out to shower each and every life form, imagining every life particle receiving exactly what they needed to blossom into their highest divine destiny.

The Big Green festival not only fueled me with a dose of big Love for my journey, it gave me the gift of appreciating that our greatest resource is to be grounded to the Earth and plugged into our sovereign source of power, pleasure and love so that we may enjoy the fruits of community in a way that nourishes all beings everywhere. Before long, I would find this awareness tested beyond all measure.

By the time I returned to camp, I found the Supernatural crew in full production for the after party entertainment. Our crew decided to stay on for a couple more days until all of the coconuts and fresh fruit had been completely devoured. I decided to hang out with them and help prepare the delicious raw treats for the evening's festivities. I delighted in the excitement of our ravenous patrons, some of whom were only just discovering the nectar of being nourished by raw, living foods for the very first time.

For my last night, I devoted myself to savouring the company of my enchanting sisters. Around sundown, I guided our little posse in a birthday ritual for a lovely priestess from Glastonbury. After lavishing one another in mutual adoration and much-shared laughter, a mutual thirst for hot chai kicked in. The five of us ventured out under the moonlight to manifest a round of hot chais to quench the goddesses thirst for something warm, sweet and creamy. Arm in arm, we pranced like ponies into the clear, starry night, sharing stories and laughing boisterously until our bellies ached. We thought for sure we'd get lucky at the neighbouring café called The Mad Hatter, but Sunbird, the proprietor, appeared to be closing up for the night. We lingered for a moment to admire his dapper purple velvet waistcoat and large velvet top hat. Our Shakti pod showered him with our pleading eyes and then sweetly asked him for a round of hot chais.

'Sorry, luvs, I'm afraid the last of the chai ran dry about an hour ago,' Sunbird said apologetically.

'Ahhhh!' We collectively agreed not to get disheartened and instead decided on the next best thing; we would take in the warmth at his glowing campfire.

'Maybe some chai will magically appear,' Lucinda suggested.

'Let's offer a spontaneous prayer to the Chai goddess to work her special magic and produce some evening refreshments for us all,' Eva chimed in.

As the impatient one in the bunch, I decided why wait – so I pulled out my imaginary teapot, cups, saucers, honey and cream. 'Won't you join me for a tea party?' I asked in my best English accent. 'After all, we are honourary guests at The Mad Hatter's fire!' I proceeded to pass out the imaginary teacups and saucers. There was a momentary silence. The women had to register the utter foolishness of what I was conjuring and decide if they wanted to play along. After a long bewildered silence, they collectively chimed in with a barrage of bird like responses. I was relieved and delighted that our chai had managed to find its way to our circle after all.

'Oh, yes, I'll have some!'

'Why not?'

'Jolly good idea!'

I politely invited the two brothers sitting at the fire to join us and they accepted quite naturally. I poured the imaginary tea into each cup and then passed along the cream and honey to follow. At first, everyone was a bit tentative as they brought their lips to their make-believe cups to take their first sip. And then the pure delight rolled in like a wave of syrupy warmth, enveloping us all in a most pleasant surprise.

'Oh, my, this is sooooo delicious,' Eva said, tasting each sip as if it was prepared especially for her Royal Highness.

'Would anyone care for a biscuit?' Lucinda held out a plate of imaginary cookies, feeling over the moon about conjuring up the complimentary refreshments.

'Oh, yes,' we all replied in unison, reaching for a mouthwatering biscuit as she passed them around.

'I'd prefer a coconut!' One of the brothers gestured as if making one magically appear in his large sooty hands. He then took a long large gulp. 'A round of coconuts from the sky for all!' He gestured like a great king gifting his most loyal subjects.

I was utterly astounded by how life-like and delicious the tea, biscuits and coconuts tasted. We soon went on to feeding one another bites of our triple-layered chocolate cake, raw mango pie and freshly picked strawberries. Then washed it all down with fresh coconuts and steamy hot chai. One of the sisters then suddenly boasted, 'All of this imaginary feasting is genuinely making me famished. I'm so hungry I could eat a beet root!'

Low and behold, before any of us had a chance to respond to this outlandish statement, a young man pulling a red wagon stopped in front of us and asked us quite innocently, 'Excuse me, would anyone care for the rest of my beet root?' Apparently, he was attempting to get rid of the last of his fresh vegetables before setting off in the morning.

Our jaws simultaneously dropped open in disbelief. Then we burst into a cacophony of contagious laughter, totally amazed at the way our sister's outlandish desire for beet root manifested before our very own eyes.

This random episode was a clear affirmation of the morphogenetic field that allows for instantaneous manifestation through sacred resonance, vibrating back our thoughts, feelings and frequencies. As we humans master the art of opening, listening with all of our senses, we become receptive and available to the invisible networks of matching intent and vibration to coincide with our desires. Since the Universe is always creating on our behalf and knows only infinite possibility, the more we learn to align with our desires by feeling as if they are already here, the more they become manifest reality. As instruments of the Divine, there is no limit to the miracles we can create simply by staying open in coherent resonance and knowing that all things are possible!

This evolutionary cycle marks the beginning of embodied balanced harmonics between the conscious Masculine and conscious Feminine. It is the divine union of polarities, to bring Heaven on Earth. The Mayans and wisdom cultures throughout the world say that humanity is literally running out of linear time. Consider time to be a progression of events produced by the polarized thought projections coming from the fracture of the mind. We are now entering a time of healing these cracks in our perception and unifying apparent opposites such as the heart and the mind. This coherent union of opposites is found in all of nature, harmonizing every singularity with the unified field of the Divine. As we align with living in 'now' time, our thoughts ripen instantaneously to create our 'thought done' reality. It becomes vital for us to realize the immense responsibility of our thoughts as they ripple into the collective and return to us, literally in no time! This zero point reality is likened to a magical blank canvas, where time becomes art and we are each free to create endless beauty that uplifts and enlivens the whole.

Lucinda graciously took the beets from our brother with the wagon full of veggies and passed them around. We nibbled on them around the fire, silently reveling in the magical intention that collectively produced them. In turn, the red beetroot was absolutely delicious, making our teeth and our mouths bright cherry red, while perfectly complementing our feast of imaginary delights!

On the last day of the Big Green festival, I couldn't help but feel a mixture of melancholy and triumph. I was sad to leave and yet felt triumphant to have made it through the English weather while having a good dose of poignant playtime! My moral and inner fire was now well replenished and ready for our next grand adventure.

The time had now come for Eva and I to make our way back to London. We were booked to catch a flight to Perpignan, France, the following morning. By midday, we were packed up and had returned the tent back to Stella. We said our goodbyes and stood outside the Supernatural camp preparing for our long walk to the parking lot to meet our ride to London. Truthfully, we were dreading the long hike with the burden of our heavy gear until Uriel pulled up in his chariot jeep to say goodbye. 'Hop in, Goddesses. I'll give you a lift to the parking lot!' He gestured for us to load the gear in the back, and we were off and running in no time. We passed the Gypsy camp on the way out; it was a sight out of a Felinni film. Painted horse-drawn carriages were parked in a half circle with horses tied up to trees, nibbling on the scrawny grass. A gaggle of kids coated in dirt played amongst themselves. I admired their unruly dreadlocked hair laced with feathers and coloured ribbons and raggle-taggled clothing that blended perfectly with their colourful carriages. These were real Gypsy folk who travelled and lived throughout Europe in their horse-drawn, hand-built caravans. Though they tended to be marginalised in 'everyday society', they radiated a mixture of pride and freedom that stood out amongst the other camps.

As we neared the exit gate, I felt profoundly grateful for the friendships I had rekindled during my time at the festival. Eva and I managed to find a ride to London with some friends on a reconverted school bus. Uriel dropped us off right in front of the accordion door. We hopped on, took our place in one of the bench seats and zoomed out of the dusty parking lot with a roar.

Before long, we were humming along on the super highway and passed the time reciting poetry and singing heart songs. Eva made up a very clever poem about the resurrection of the Elven King and Queen, who came to release themselves from the curse of their exile through radical forgiveness. Our hosts were highly entertained and impressed. The truth was, Eva was utterly enchanting to mostly everyone who was fortunate enough to be caught in her magical web and delighted by her whimsical musings.

At dusk, we were dropped off on the outskirts of London, where one of our supernatural friends, Julia, had generously offered to put us up for the night. It was amazing to feel how cared for we were, every step of the way. After one more sleep, we'd be in France early the following morning.

Julia's tiny flat was in a sketchy part of the outskirts of the city and made quite the contrast to Simon's posh country home. Nonetheless, we were beyond grateful to have a dry bed, warm bath and organise ourselves for Ambe´ and Eva's further Adventures in Wonderland.

CHAPTER THIRTEEN

KUNDALĪNI RISING

*Love opens the doors into everything, as far as I can see,
including and perhaps most of all, the door into one's own secret,
and often terrible and frightening, real self.*

– May Sarton

*An initiation is that inner-directed experience that takes you over
the threshold of irreversible change. In the initiations of resurrection
and ascension, your former linked identity transforms into a more
expansive awareness of inherent potential.*

– Claire Heartsong, *Anna, Grandmother of Jesus*

Upon arriving in Foix, we were greeted with a waft of velvety, warm French air. I felt like I could breathe again. The first thing I saw when we arrived outside the quaint little train station were fields of multi-coloured wild flowers, cheerfully scattered throughout the rolling green hills. For a brief moment, I imagined them waving at me as if to say, 'Bonjour, mademoiselle. Welcome to France!' The bright blue sky was a huge contrast to the gloomy grey weather of England and my spirits felt instantaneously lifted. We walked with our backpacks towards a cobblestone lane lined with quaint little shops all tightly wedged together. The smell of French coffee and freshly baked pastry wafted through the air. Towering just beyond the green rolling hills was a landscape of jagged purple and brown mountains that stretched to the sky.

Eva and I took a long pause to take in the landscape complete with medieval castle on the adjacent hillside. Then we bolted to the local laundromat and unpacked our disheveled belongings as quickly as possible. I shoved my soiled laundry into the large machines as if to wash away any residual evidence of prior hardships. While waiting for our wash to complete, we each took a turn exploring the local shops and outdoor market. When Eva returned from her jaunt, she was not alone. She had found our friend Tomas, whom I had recently met at the Health and Harmony Festival in California. Tomas and I had emailed each other and arranged to rendezvous in Foix and then carry on together to the Rainbow Gathering thirty kilometers North of Foix. His full head of strawberry blonde dreadlocks, piercing green eyes and light freckled skin made Tomas stand out in any crowd. Born and raised in Virginia, he talked with an ever so slight Southern twang. He was well travelled and versed in all the worldly, cosmic and shamanic ways. His paintings were stories of the awakening of the Cosmic Christ depicted in colours, symbols and multi-layered sacred geometries. They depicted what one might see and experience on a really profound and insightful shamanic journey. We got reacquainted while sitting on the washing machines. Tomas had just completed his visionary painting course in Cadeques, on the East coast of Spain. The name still gave me magical shivers.

'Tomas, would you do us the honour of sharing what you've been working on?' I was very excited to see his latest painting.

He pulled out a plastic shopping bag, casually removed the loose tie that held the carefully rolled up canvas to unveil his work in progress. Once again, my mouth dropped and my eyes grew larger as I took in the composition of images that were only partially filled in with light washes of colour. In the centre were two inter-connected chalices that framed a luminous three-dimensional, six-pointed Star Tetrahedron. I had instant chills as I recognised the various symbols and light codes woven throughout his painting as visual records of my Christos Sophia bloodline. The painting was like a pictorial map of my soul – an alchemical portrait of Divine Sacred Union.

I needed time alone to digest the significance of Tomas's prophetic painting, so I volunteered to scout out a hotel while our laundry dried. Even though the town was supposedly 'booked solid', I managed to find a modest room for the three of us. It was in a local hotel built to accommodate large groups of outdoor recreational travelers who came to Foix to climb the neighbouring mountains. The hotel would be perfect for a few nights before setting out for the Rainbow Gathering nestled in the Northwest Pyrenees Mountains.

That evening, the three of us got reacquainted over some local red wine, freshly baked baguettes and garden salad smothered in fresh herbs and balsamic vinaigrette. *Oh la la!* The three of us swooned with delight as we took in the mouthwatering tastes, intoxicating smells and sublime togetherness. *Viva la France!*

Over the next three days, I awoke each morning drenched in sweat. I reflected on my all-consuming lucid dreaming with a mixture of awe and curiosity. I had a strong feeling of being worked on by a team of celestial Light beings who were giving me cellular and energetic frequency upgrades. I referred to their presence as the Ones with No Names. I sensed that they knew more of what lay ahead for me than I did and that they were helping me to strengthen and prepare my subtle body for what was to come. Each night, I underwent an epic immersion into unlocking the records archived within my DNA. Each morning, I awoke with my sheets drenched and recalled the multi-dimensional vignettes of my dreamtime. I time travelled in and out of parallel realities and simultaneous lifetimes, sometimes repairing, sometimes clearing, and sometimes integrating the new codes of light.

8 August 2003, Lions Gate, Foix

What I am coming to remember is that Gaia Sophia is the conscious life force animating from within me and all of nature. She has returned to reclaim all of her children that have been entrapped within the false dark and false light hosting cycle. This Solar gateway is supporting the transfiguration of the parts of one's consciousness that have become enslaved and entrapped within this false matrix. That is until now, when humanity is undergoing a metamorphosis, waking up and being activated by the plasmic diamond sun that illuminates the truth of who we really are by shining light into the unconscious, bringing forth unhealed genetic wounding that has been carried through our Christos Sophionic bloodline.

Sophia's loving presence permeates both darkness and the light. When I am in silence, I can sense her in the subtlest of realms. Her frequency pulsates within the black light of emptiness, or as a subtle murmur in my heart-womb. When I rest in that place between sleeping and waking, I feel her radiant hues of aquamarine light, rainbow opalescent and gold, bathing me in a blissful diamond light. Her incandescent frequency comes from beyond this Earthly plane...a place that knows no separation, where wild innocence reigns. When I feel restless or anxious, *She* is there, consoling me with her fierce, unwavering presence. Relaxing into her, she tenderly unwinds the tightly woven energy in my sacrum, enticing me to unfurl like a blooming star being kissed by the sun. As her serpentine waves pulsate up my spinal pathway, the energy gullies and swirls into each chakra until it fountains at my crown. Then along with my breath, the energy returns to pool in my heart-womb, where the journey begins again, repeating itself with fluid, sensual coherence. Inside this Sacred Union, I am bathed in a toroidal fountain of golden-pink, sparkly love nectar. Every atom of my being is profoundly nourished in grace as my light body dances with Hers. Wow!

On the third morning of energetic upgrades, I awoke to find myself surrounded by a pod of etheric dolphins. They were encircling me in a playful dance, as if to welcome me home to the inner sanctums of my crystalline nature and cosmic heart. The back of my neck released from constriction and ancient paradigms of control. The right side of my heart was stretched open and expanded as if to be made a pocket for god/goddess to rest inside. Feeling sublimely gifted by the energetic presence and support of Christos Sophia and my Family of Light, I experienced my soul braiding with my cells returning me into plasmic light.. Within each undulating breath, the molecules of my being felt to shimmer as if they were individually coated in incandescent stardust. As my heart pounded under this waterfall of grace, I dared not to interpret what was happening to me, as I knew it to be beyond what I could comprehend with my ordinary mind. All that I knew was that I was being given a precious jewel of remembrance, a gift of reunion with the 'I AM' who exists before there was a me.

CHAPTER FOURTEEN

FELINE TENDENCIES

A Sister Goddess knows that every single step in her story line has been created by her and for her. She knows that she is no one's victim. She has rejected the cultural pull toward commiseration and victimhood. She replaces these habits with the unshakable sense that she, herself, has called in every circumstance in her life for the purpose of taking her higher. She remembers that, through rupture, the Goddess is remaking her into the woman she was born to become. She knows, deep inside herself, that there is an inherent perfection to everything and everyone. She lives in the truth that every moment is a gift and a chance to go higher.

– Regena Thomashauer, *Pussy: A Reclamation*

The longing for love draws to you all that your soul requires to be met by the presence of your own love. Through this sacred gnosis, may you know that love was never separate from you. Everything now becomes fuel for you to embody the perfect, unique divine expression of all that you are…a beacon of love… for loves sake.

– Nicola Povey

Despite my highest desire and intention to be patient and accepting, the persistent irritation with my travelling companion Eva continued to percolate within me. No matter what I tried to do to calm and centre myself, I felt our unnerving dynamic gritting at my nerves. The womanly part of me felt like I was in a pressure cooker that simmered in an uncomfortable silent tension. As I investigated deeper into my trigger, I became aware of an ancient lifetime bleeding through into the present one, like two different stories that left off at the same exact place. During one of my morning meditations, I was able to get a glimpse into a parallel lifetime, and this was what I saw: Eva and I had been close sisters in a family of great stature and nobility. She had cast me out of her life over a suitor that we mutually had great admiration and love. Consequently, we experienced a heart-wrenching fallout that led to a most devastating outcome. I ended up dying from a lonely and bitter heart, never able to forgive the sense of betrayal I felt from the two people I had loved the most casting me out from their love. *Woe is me!*

Even though I recognised the opportunity to resolve an ancient timeline, the dynamic tension between Eva and I continued to fester and gnaw at the sacred core of our sisterhood. I struggled on how to understand and reconcile the situation, especially since many of my symptoms were surfacing from unresolved timelines and lifetimes. I felt frozen and confused since the past, present and future were all blending together. Waves of uncomfortable emotions simmered to the surface to be felt all the way through. Like uninvited guests, I had no way to reference or explain their origin. All I knew was that I had to do something to clear the air and move out of feeling like a victim to my circumstances. I decided to get very pragmatic and create space to feel the situation from a place of 'what was real now.' In truth, a barrage of unsavory feelings were coming up to haunt me: rejection, abandonment, jealousy, envy and even awe!

I would observe with amazement as Eva broadcasted her desire through the quantum field through a pheromonal circuit that most magically entranced her prey. I was both repelled and utterly fascinated by her captivating finesse to bedazzle and enchant with her womanly beauty and charm. The more I witnessed the temptress in her, the more exasperated I became. I was both repulsed and astounded by her remarkable power to create endless romantic liasons for the sake her own pleasure and enjoyment.

Bottom line – I felt excluded and eclipsed in the company of Eva when she was entertaining her new and exciting friends and there was nobody to blame but myself. *Where and when had I disconnected from my Feminine power?* I concluded, perhaps Eva's version of Feminine energy was not for me to adopt or compare myself to. My version had its own unique way of expressing itself, one that honored my unique sensitivity to sharing energy from a place of inclusivity. Because when you have an ancient childlike heart like mine one must feel deeply but go lightly while being sensitive to others.

Clearly I had some work to do in this area of my life. I was being initiated into a deeper embodiment of my feminine Shakti force which called me to descend into my womb and confront my hidden shame and tenacious insecurities. It was time for me to acknowledge that my feelings were leading me to discover a flavor of intimacy that was not propelled by seduction - but the instinctual wisdom of how to trace and ride the waves of true authentic connection that was rooted in deep respect for all.

Jahrusha's premonition and warning was coming to bear light. I was well aware that it was all being perfectly orchestrated, complete with invaluable soul lessons that would reveal themselves on the journey to come. I was being called into the mysteries of my Feminine essence in relationship to pleasure and sexual passion – all of which were beginning to simmer within the wellspring of my awakening womb.

I stood in the middle of a small bridge that conjoined two sides of a canal and put out a prayer request to the Great Mother, asking for clarity and resolve in my predicament, and this is what I heard:

'My dear heart, all disappointments point to where you are denying and disowning your own power, passion and highest potential. Whenever one makes the 'other' the so-called 'problem', be assured that you are being invited to step into greater self-responsibility while showing up to embrace your own deepest wounds and desires.

'Try to understand that when an outside person is not loving you in the way you prefer to be loved, it is often a reflection of those parts of you where you are not loving yourself. Use this time as an opportunity to call back your power and projections and to love yourself more instead of less, especially those unseemly parts that you tend to judge in others! Then shift your focus and awareness from what others are choosing and doing to focusing on the flavour of love that you would most like to experience

for yourself. As a highly sensitive empath, you have a tendency to feel you have to match everyone else's experience. This is not so! When under the influence of another's powerful energy, lean in and love yourself more as the answer to all that avails you. When you take full responsibility for being the Love rather than seeking it from outside of you, you can relax into the feeling of enjoying oneself rather than needing to change another. At which point you will soon discover that disappointment is never worth the happiness you are missing out on!

'Now can you forgive yourself and forgive all others for not loving you in the way that you desire to be loved?'

Yes, I responded inwardly, feeling the Divine Mother's support as the solid ground beneath my feet again.

The following morning, Eva, Tomas and I made our final travel preparations for the Rainbow Gathering in the Pyrenees Mountains, which included picking up a rental car from Perpignan Airport. Moment by moment and breath by breath, I entrained myself to move to the rhythm of my own deepest truth while slow dancing with my raw and tender heart. It was only a matter of time before my solo journey would open up before me. For now, I was being given the golden opportunity to stay centred and build the soul stamina to not be influenced by the choices of others. I was being initiated into Love's infinite ways of growing one's soul as a full-time student of life's spiritual boot camp/mystery school. I had no other choice than to respect the rite for each to create their own beautiful messy reality, just as I had the rite to create mine. I heard a small still voice cheering me on. *Keep swimming dear one, practice staying in your own lane! If diversity is the spice of life, then divine sovereignty is the mother of all spices. When distinctly honoured, each ingredient enhances all other ingredients, bringing supreme satisfaction to the insatiable hunger to know and recognise oneself in the other. This gnosis is the Grail of becoming One with All.*

CHAPTER FIFTEEN

UNDER THE RAINBOW

Dear One. Have mercy on your tender and wounded parts. Have mercy for the countless ways you sought protection from the heartaches of this life. Have mercy for all of the characters that play their perfect part to bring you to this moment. You have reached the threshold of these burdens that have weighed you endlessly down. The heart of hearts calls out to you now. The flame of this holy fire purifies your essence, bringing love and liberation. With equal measure for your sacred wound, this winged grace of divine love, tenderly anoints you. Illumined with clarity, insight and deep compassion for the human heart, walk on, beloved, walk on. You are free to be free.

– Nicola Povey

CATHAR CREED

It has no membership, save those who know they belong. It has no rivals because it is non-competitive. It has no ambition – it seeks only to serve. It knows no boundaries, for nationalisms are unloving. It is not of itself because it seeks to enrich all groups and religions. It acknowledges all great teachers of all the ages who have shown the truth of love. Those who participate practice the truth of love in all their being. There is no walk of life or nationality that is a barrier. Those who are, know. It seeks not to teach, but to be, and by being, enriched. It recognizes that the way we are may be the way of those around us because we are that way. It recognizes the whole planet as a being of which we are a part of. It recognizes that the time has come for the supreme transmutation, the ultimate alchemical act of conscious change of the ego to voluntary return to the whole. It does not proclaim itself with a loud voice but in the subtle realms of loving. It salutes all those in the past who have blazoned the path but have paid the price. It admits no hierarchy or structure, for no one is greater than another. Its members shall know each other by their deeds and being, and by their eyes and by no other outward sign, save the fraternal embrace. Each one will dedicate their life to the silent loving of their neighbour and environment, and the planet will carry out their task, however exalted or humble. It recognizes the supremacy of the great idea, which may only be accomplished if the human race practices the supremacy of love. It has no reward to offer, either here or in the hereafter, save that of the ineffable joy of being and loving. Each shall seek to advance the cause of understanding, doing good by stealth and teaching only by example. They shall heal their neighbour, their community, our planet and living beings in whatever form they take. They shall know no fear and feel no shame and their witness shall prevail over all odds. It has no secret, no arcanum, no initiation, save that of true understanding of the power of love and that, if we want it to be so, the world will change, but only if we change. All who belong, belong; they belong to the Church of Love.

Tomas, Eva and I headed north towards the beautiful spa town of Aix De Thermos in our olive-green Renault rental car. We set out from Foix to find the small mountainous road that would lead us to the remote Rainbow Gathering in the French Pyrenees. On the way, we stopped in the beautiful town of Ax les Thermes to pick up some seasonal fruits, a tarp, and some fresh croissants. The delightful little town was buzzing with tourists from Provence out for a weekend holiday. The bustling outdoor cafés vibrated with festivity as glasses clanked through cloudy cigarette smoke wafting through the crisp air. Although none of us drank at midday, we felt the allure of sipping on a special beverage while chatting the day away with friends and family. Instead, we strolled past the cafés toward the town square and took a moment to dip our feet in the fountain, infamous for its healing thermal water. After our dip, we crossed the road to a large provincial cathedral with stained glass windows, whose colours were more brightened by the midday sun.

Like two luxuriating cats, Tomas and Eva opted to recline outside on the steps and soak in the sunshine, while I wandered into the dimly lit church. As I quietly sat down on one of the wooden benches, I observed a group of elderly women wearing black lace veils, chanting Hail Mary's in perfect unison. They were unwaveringly devoted to their rosaries and the words of the prayer, which rolled off their tongues in a repetitive drone. I felt honoured to witness a lineage of women who faithfully kept up this tradition over the course of countless generations. They recited their prayers in a way that reminded me of how one would read off a cake recipe to a friend. I admired how Mother Mary united these women in their devotion and yet remained corious as to why religion encourages their subjects to be 'God fearing'. *Wasn't God the opposite of fear?*

My eyes scanned the white stucco walls of the old church and observed the many renditions of Mother Mary holding the Christ child. Despite having no Catholic background, at least in this lifetime, I felt noticeably comforted in the presence of her Feminine spirit. In my own mysterious way, I knew I belonged here with this flock of praying women as we paid homage to Madre Maria, who felt to be closer to me than ever before.

I put my palms together, simulating the elders who were nestled closely together in two adjacent wooden benches and whispered ever so quietly, 'Remember me, Mere? You came to me in a vision at Gaia's Grove and showed me how once upon a time, I too was a part of your family. I am here now, Mother. I'm not quite sure why, but I am – here now. In truth, I feel a little lost at the moment. Please light the way for me. Show me how to best serve this precious human life.'

I left the church as quietly as I came in. Eva and Tomas were stretched out like cats, lounging on the warm, white marble steps. The sun shined upon their blissful, bright-eyed faces as they smiled to me.

'Ready, Ambe´?' Eva asked.

'Yes. As ready as I'll ever be,' I murmured to myself, still totally uncertain as to where this journey was actually taking me.

We didn't get very far along the road before a hitchhiking hippy sprung in front of our car waving his arms in the air and then practically forced himself into our vehicle. 'I've hitched all the way from Czechoslovakia to attend dis Rainbow Gathering,' he boasted in his thick accent and broken English. Ironically, his behavior was extremely aggressive in making sure that he actually got there. Since we were headed to the festival of 'peace and love', Tomas felt beholden to squeeze him in amongst our bulging luggage.

An eerie somberness filled the air. Very little was spoken as we wound up the narrow roads sprinkled with tiny villages nestled into the side of the mountain. The number of dreadlocked hippies hanging out on the side of the road substantially increased as we climbed higher in altitude. We descended and ascended twice again before arriving at a large outdoor market. This was the last place to gather last-minute supplies and finalise our directions. We soon discovered that we had driven passed the road into basecamp. Not wanting to overshoot our destination again, we ended up following a van full of Israelis for another sixteen kilometres over a gravel road until we arrived at a massive dirt parking lot overflowing with colourful caravans.

'Country roads, take me home, to the place where I belong: West Virginia, mountain momma, take me home, country roads,' Tomas sang aloud, bringing levity to the heavy cloud of silence with a dose of his lighthearted Virginian twang.

After what felt like hours of driving up desolate winding roads, we finally arrived and parked in the dusty parking lot. One by one, we unloaded our stuff in preparation for the half-hour hike up the mountain. As I tightened my large backpack around my waist, I was reminded of trekking in the Himalayan Mountains of Nepal. I felt fairly strong and I was prepared to tough it out once again. After all, the glorious sun was shining, I was warm and I wasn't hiking through miles of mud, rain and sludge. All conditions were now in my favour. We were excited to meet our European Rainbow family in these purple majestic mountains under the light of a super moon.

I seemed to be the only one panting when we finally arrived at the top of the hill. The path had opened up to a large meadow the size of several football fields. What an amazing vision it was! Thousands of people were gathered in an enormous circle. We soon found that they were waiting for dinner to be distributed by a team of people carrying large white buckets containing Indian dal, rice and salad. While waiting for food, they passed the time singing heartsongs and exchanging stories in broken English. Children frolicked in the grass and people of all ages reclined on the field as naturally as they would in their own living rooms. I stopped to take in the rarified beauty of the massive circle. It felt good to be amongst tribe, Star family and for the time being, my home. Just as the evening sun began to set behind the surrounding mountains, we continued to walk on the outer edge of the circle, our hearts beating and beaming with a rarified kind of love. I felt such gratitude to be a part of this global mélange – where people gathered to celebrate the bounties of Earth Mother, in harmony and respect for each other and all that makes us human *and* divine.

People called out to us as we walked by. 'Welcome home, brother! Welcome home, sister!' We beamed our heart smiles as we walked on past, holding our focus to find a campsite for the night before it got too dark.

'Let's set our things down here and join the circle for food before setting up camp,' Tomas suggested. Happily, we all agreed to take a break and enjoy the first meal of the gathering. Tomas borrowed a couple of Frisbees for us to eat out of and provided us with some broken sticks to use as makeshift spoons. Before long, we were gobbling down our rice and dal, grateful for the well-needed sustenance. Even though it was far from gourmet, I so appreciated the love and energy that went into preparing the food for thousands of hungry bellies and grateful mouths.

'Quick!' said Tomas. 'It is near sundown – we'd better find us a camping spot before it gets too dark.' He pointed to the other end of the huge circle. 'I think there is a path over there leading to the camp sites.'

By the time we had circumambulated the large circle, our bodies felt wiped out from the hike. We took the first spot we saw, agreeing that we would scout out something more preferable the following morning. After setting up camp, our excited curiosity lured us out on an evening walk before bedtime. We strolled only a few yards up the main path before coming across two cloaked figures huddling around a small fire.

'Hello,' I said. 'My name is Ambe´.'

The woman leaned in closer. 'Ambe´? Oh my goodness, really? Didn't I share a room next door to you in Dharamsala, India, years ago?'

'Wow. Yes! Of course!' I responded as I recognised my dear Australian sister Angelina, wearing a dark purple velvet cape that hung loosely over her vibrant green eyes. She beamed at me, full of life, looking brighter and more beautiful than ever.

'This is my partner, Lotus,' she said, introducing the man next to her, who wore an almost identical green cloak that also hung over his large brown eyes.

Angelina was travelling with Lotus while offering street performance with a circus troupe in Prague. They had decided to make one last stop at the Rainbow Gathering before returning to their hometown in Perth, Australia. I always admired Angelina for her joyous effervescence and her appetite for mythic travel and spiritual adventures.

After introductions all around, I said in awe, 'Wow, what an amazing synchronicity to be here in the middle of nowhere – and the first person I run into is yet another friend from our India pilgrimage in Dharamsala. Imagine that!'

Seeing Angelina brought me back to the time I lived in the community in India. We had become a tight little tribe, spending countless nights together, singing and playing devotional Indian heart songs by the fire until sunrise. More importantly, this had been a time of initiation into all forms and expressions of love. In fact, the last time I was head over heels in love with a man was during the time I spent living just below Angelina's little house in India.

It wasn't long before Angelina asked me about him and how he was doing. I felt a twinge in my heart as I remembered this great love of mine like long-forgotten wings. It had ended in such a bittersweet way. At the time, we did not have the right circumstances for our love to bloom beyond our intense communion in India. We parted ways, never to see each other again. I was reminded of a hole in my heart for never getting to fulfill my desire to create a life with this great love of mine. Our life circumstances, including his children, had determined our short destiny together. I couldn't help but wonder if I would find my true beloved this time around. I had longed for someone who was free to love me as I loved him.

The four of us walked up the path to a beautiful vista overlooking the neighbouring valley. We relaxed into the comfort of being together as reunited soul family. As the last light faded, we sat perched under the starry night sky and spoke about our lives. It seemed each one of us was experiencing a unique version of going through the contractions that proceed a spiritual rebirth.

'These contractions are the Divine's way of clearing out whatever has blocked our soul essence from shining through our organic true nature. If we are to fulfill our soul purpose and birth our true essence into an emerging new world we must allow these contractions to purify all that remains false within us. Earth is also experiencing her own version of rebirth, throwing off all that is toxic to her pristine nature. This evolutionary cycle can make us feel as if our world is shaking and that we are in an existential crisis. Luckily, all crisis tends to proceed creation, birthing us into something entirely brand new and even greater than we can imagine,' I shared while noticing in that moment I felt more like a caterpillar being devoured by her own flesh.

At the time, I really had no clue as to who and what I was becoming. I had to go on trusting and have faith that somewhere gestating within me was a monarch butterfly destined to be hatched.

Our little tribe huddled together in humble awareness that these planetary birth contractions were propelling each one of us to die to all we once knew ourselves to be, and dissolve all outlived identities. We shared the urge to let it all go while attuning and being guided by the tiniest whispers of one's own true heart. This is in essence was all that we had to ensure a healthy and Goddess-willing ecstatic birth of the butterfly we each were in the process of birthing into being.

That night, Eva, Tomas and I passed out on top of our brand-new tarp, spooning one another in order to stay warm under the light of the full moon. By dawn, we were stirred awake by the sound of clinking pans and the high-pitched shrills of small children playing around the morning fire. Our sleeping bags were covered in a blanket of dewdrops, some of which had tiny fractal rainbows glistening inside of them.

After breakfast, Eva, Tomas and I decided to go our own ways and explore the various clusters of people scattered throughout the mountainside. I felt strangely invisible as I wandered through the campsites and absorbed the overall vibe of the gathering. Admittedly, I had anticipated finding loads of gregarious people to welcome me into their camps, share stories, yummy treats and heart songs – just like the Rainbow Gatherings I had attended back in the U.S. Much to my surprise, I was met by an entirely different vibe. In fact, my experience did not resemble anything like the overly friendly hippy folk you find back at home. Instead, I found people to be highly reserved and extremely insular, staying cloistered within their social bubbles and family clans. *Was this simply the European way?* I wondered, still open to finding my groove amongst the cool and contained parties in which I was clearly not invited.

As I wandered through the various pathways blanketed in pine needles, I began to feel a dark cloud of morose encroaching upon me. Before long, I stumbled upon a camp that was openly serving chai to the insiders and the outsiders. Feeling the irony along with a pleasant surprise, I perched myself under the dusty canopy to enjoy a 'cuppa' and hopefully meet some new friends. Looking round, I observed the small clusters of people smoking hand-rolled cigarettes and having conversations in their native tongues. A man strummed an old guitar while another joined in on his wooden flute. Even amongst the beautiful music, I sensed a mysterious somberness shared amongst my European brothers and sisters. It lingered just below the surface of their stoic warrior facades.

There was a chilling resignation and undeniable hopelessness that permeated the mountain air. I got the feeling that people generally felt entrapped inside a prison that no one had the courage to name or speak of. It was a prison of helpless despair and all that was yet to be fully grieved and forgiven.

While quietly sipping tea, I reflected on some of the things I had in common with my European Rainbow tribe. For one, I sensed the collective pangs of feeling exiled from a world that undervalued the kind of people who put the Earth first over personal gain. The ones who were brave enough to live according to their conscience rather than be shepherded by the status quo.

There was also the disadvantages of 'tribal consciousness' to be considered. Being beholden to a tribe of people could easily become another version of imprisonment – a kind that validates righteous indignation and justified judgment, creating even more separation. The Rainbow tribe may have prided itself on living a more sustainable lifestyle in harmony with Mother Nature, yet many were still entrapped in the prison of blame, lack and victim consciousness. It wasn't enough to wear natural clothing, do yoga and drink chai for breakfast. Our realisation of Oneness was not enough, we were being called to exemplify true equality with all our relations, actions and endeavours.

As long as we perceived ourselves as being separate from each other and the mainstream world – seeing through the eyes of us and them, right and wrong, good and evil, good guys and bad guys, and so forth – we would be trapped in defending and protecting ourselves from the so-called wrongs of the world, getting caught in the trap of false superiority and the need to 'be right'. Each and every being has the rite to be exactly where they're at. It's our job to embody, educate and model compelling solutions without the need to undermine anyone or anything else in the process. I recognised that I had much in common with this tribe of misfits living on the fringe of society, questioning our sense of belonging in a world that valued consumption over caring for life on Earth.

I wanted to investigate a little more deeply the origin of this pervasive dark cloud that permeated the air. Whatever was weighing this tribe down had become their 'normal' vibrational set point. I could feel that something important was being hidden. It hovered around my brothers and sisters as a cloud of thick ganja smoke, which served to mask a silent collective heartbreak. Before long, I noticed a young man with deep brown eyes and a stubbly complexion sitting beside me. He was rolling a cigarette and sipped his chai from a coconut shell. I decided to break the ice and say hello.

'*Bonjour,*' I said. Then I added, 'Do you speak English?'

'Yes, of course,' he replied.

'I was wondering if I can ask you some questions about the land here.'

'Sure, why not.'

'Where are you from?' I asked.

'Actually, I'm Spanish but I was raised here in France. So I am French and Spanish mixed.'

'Well, I was wondering why I feel this land to be so melancholy. People seem kind of sad in an unspoken kind of way.' I looked at him. 'Do you know what I mean?'

'*Mais oui!* Oh, yes, I know what you mean.' He took a long drag off his rolly, then began to speak in a slow, pensive manner. 'I guess people have given up in a way. You see, a long time ago, this land was very different from the way it is today.'

'Really? How so?' I said, curious and relaxing into his presence a little more.

'A long time ago, this land and its people were spiritually flourishing in harmony with nature and the cosmos. Our wide-open hearts were flourishing in love with each other and our connection with spirit. This was the land of the Cathars. It's only now that some of us are beginning to return to the land of our ancestors and take up residence again.'

'Cathars? Who are they?'

'Some say they are the direct descendants of the Christ and Magdalene bloodline.'

My ears perked up as I adjusted my body to sit a little closer, urging him to continue.

He took a sip of chai with a faraway look in his eyes. 'They honoured the Earth and the mystery school teachings brought forth by Mary Magdalene and her Beloved Yeshua. They say the Master himself also carried on the teachings in this land, after his resurrection. *Oui,* the Cathars were the descendants of Mary and Yeshua, and the mystical, Earth-loving peoples of this region. They were considered to be the 'lovers of the world' and valued the sanctity of life through abiding in loving kindness and compassion for all beings. Nature, animals and humans were held as sacred, much like other indigenous cultures throughout the world. They were great scholars, artists, healers, free thinkers and mystics of their time.'

His eyes met mine with a polite smile mixed with heartbreak and pain. 'They were not so different from our Rainbow family, eh? Like many of us, they valued love above all and lived in deep reverence for life, nature and spirit. But they were called heretics by the Roman Church and therefore considered a threat, even though they had existed here for more than a thousand years. Do you know of the Albigensian Crusade?'

I shook my head no.

'Well, this inquisition was instigated to wipe them all out because they still held true to The Book of Love, which contained the original teachings of Yeshua and Mary. At one time their descendants had much land and power and that also didn't sit well with the church. 'Mostly all of them were tragically massacred, thousands upon thousands – burned alive – at Montségur, their last stronghold. But somewhere, their treasure still exists.'

He sighed deeply, filled with defeat. He reached for his packet of rolling tobacco and began rolling another cigarette. 'And still some Cathars remain. Perhaps now, at this time in history, it is safe for us to be open about it. But for a very long time nobody dared to speak, in fear of the repercussions. I feel many of us have returned to these lands, seeking what was once lost. We wander in a kind of hopeless despair while seeking for the place we are welcomed and belong. For those who still carry the memory, we will not settle until we find a way to live in harmony with Tierra Madre, the spirit of true love and purity of heart.'

Tomas and Eva had wandered up to sit next to me and listen in on this beautiful brother's story. Afterwards, we sat in silence, feeling the profundity of his words – both the sadness and the ray of new possibility. I wondered about the 'treasure' of the Cathars. Was it literally a treasure, or something more metaphysical? Tomas broke out his paints and canvas and began to paint.

After this enlightening conversation, I felt into my own lingering sadness and despair. The brother's story seemed to explain why I was picking up on so much heartache as I walked this sacred land. Was I once a Cathar? *Was I one who, in spirit, or even in blood, had been called back to remember my bloodline lineage, also known as the Sangraal?* My body shuddered as an ancient archive buried within my DNA opened along with the first page of the Book of Love, a story of Universal Christ Consciousness that felt to be archived somewhere deep inside of me.

I gazed into my brother Miguel's dark brown eyes. They reached straight back to this mystical time. Although many of us still carried the blood scars from being burned alive and banished from our spiritual roots, I felt a glimmer of hope that I too, had returned to remember my place within this royal bloodline where *Love* is *All* and *All* is *Love*.

CHAPTER SIXTEEN

COLD, COLD WATER

Who are these ancestors and what are they saying about loving the world, serving the world, transforming the world? Finding the answer requires that you turn your eyes and ears inward and really listen to your authentic self and let your spirit open up. What you will hear is your own authentic and unique destiny. When you do this, you unleash the incredible power, love and compassion of the ancestors, whose longing lives within you.

– Andrew Harvey, An Evolutionary Vison of Relationships

As recorded in the ancient scrolls, the omnipotent omniscient omnipresent God, in order to experience the infinite facets of life, made a decision to divide into what we have come to know as the female and male aspects of Mother/Father God. The original divine plan for the division into masculine and feminine aspects was purposefully created to expand the experience of creative expression. With this division, each aspect of the polarities of yin and yang holds within it the seed of the other as a reminder of our wholeness through all dimensions, throughout all eternity. Therefore, there has never truly been a separation.

The separation that we've been experiencing, is an erroneous perception of the separation from God that's been perpetrated by humanity. At our core, in our heart space, we are all whole and complete. Unfortunately, many religions have taught that as humans we are flawed in our nature causing enormous destruction to the human psyche. The memory of these wounds are carried within us, thus we lost our sense of divinity. As a result, we now live in a world of imbalanced duality in fear of acknowledging our own God Self as sovereign creators.

– Sharon Lyn Shepard

The nights were getting colder. Once again, keeping warm was an ongoing challenge. Bottom line, I was hungry, tired and getting grimier by the day. Even though I was amongst my so-called soul tribe, the feeling of loneliness was eroding my heart, making a canyon so deep, I questioned if I would ever make my way out of it. I had not felt so outcast and out of sorts since I was a young girl and was plagued by my nightly visions of global destruction.

Even though my surroundings were glistening in natural beauty, I felt like a stranger walking in a strange land. I began to doubt everything about my life, including where my next meal would come from. A gloomy melancholy continued to gnaw at my heart. All I could do was pray for a miraculous return of my *joie de vivre*. Was I picking up the feelings of the collective pain of the Cathar massacres? Was I feeling the devastation of mass heartbreak and betrayal? Or perhaps I was feeling exiled, from my own true source of love and belonging? *Hmm.*

On the fourth day of 'toughing it out', I realised I actually had a choice. I could simply pack up and leave the gathering! *Simple as that!* I desperately wanted to go someplace where I could breathe clean air and soak in a fresh water hotspring. I began to devise my escape plan. First, I would search for some food. I hadn't eaten anything for twenty-four hours and I needed some sustenance to think straight. I wandered up the dirt road where the Hare Krishna's were preparing their afternoon meal. *What a brilliant idea. My good ol' Bhakti buddies will feed me and then I'll take off from there!* I sighed with a combination of relief and divine irony. In that moment, the Hari Krishna's felt like my most loyal and familiar friends. I sat upon the Earth amongst a sea of hungry mouths and wept pathetically as they dolloped dal, rice and colourful crackers onto my day-glow, lime green Frisbee. Every ounce of my being cried out for mercy. With a humble presence and an eager rumble in the pit of my belly, I received the strange-looking orange, purple and green food. *Thank you, Krishna, for nourishing my body and soul on this strange and beautiful day.* Tears rolled down my cheek as I sang softly, 'Hare Krishna, Hare Krishna, Krishna, Krishna, Hare, Hare,' just like they did in the airports while chiming their finger bells. I savoured every bite while observing the divine irony and absurdity of it all.

After lunch, I felt stronger *and* braver, due to the combination of releasing some tears and a quieted belly. I resolved to travel alone for a few days and then come back to fetch Eva and Tomas at the end of the gathering. Even though I rekindled a fondness for my Krishna friends, I knew that I would be way better off lounging in some hotsprings somewhere nearby. I fantasised about floating in the thermals while sipping sparkling lemon water rather than dragging myself through another day of morose, melancholy and martyrdom. With strong resolve, I quickly returned to my camp, packed up my things and told Eva that I would be back in a few days to fetch her.

Eva was totally surprised and urged me to stay. 'But Ambe´, I finally met some of our soul family up on the West side of the mountain ridge! Come join us for dinner tonight. I know you'll feel better once you connect with some of our star tribe!'

Every part of me wanted to leave then and there, but I decided to make one last go of it and head out first thing in the morning. I passed the rest of the day under a large canvas tarp, sharing chai and heart songs. My weary heart was eased just enough to tough it out for another night. Perhaps Eva's invitation to join her that evening with her new friends would turn the tides for me.

Around twilight, I returned to our campsite with Eva where we changed into our warmest clothes for the evening. We silently walked through a maze of old growth trees to get to her new friends' campsite. Around twenty minutes later, after meandering through small footpaths that led us up the mountain ridge, we came to a fire circle overlooking a beautiful vista. The majestic purple mountains towered over a steep drop into a neighbouring valley. I soaked in the stunning beauty of the land from this new vantage point. *What a breathtaking view! Sometimes the only thing one can do to raise one's own vibration is to go higher ground.*

I marveled at how Gaia Sophia loved a good game of hide and seek. She's always there, enticing me to uncover my deepest truth and discover that the source of fulfillment lives within me.

A confluence of people sat around the flickering fire, passing around a plate of boiled eggs. Everyone seemed quite comfortable and at home with one another. Eva greeted the circle with her effervescent smile and sparkling hazel blue eyes. She gleefully introduced me to her new group of friends one by one. I looked around the fire and was pleasantly surprised to find that I had already met some of these people on prior sacred-site journeys! Soul family could be found in all manner of unexpected places and situations. I started to lighten up and feel more relaxed in my new surroundings amongst these kindred hearts.

A well-built man with huge, smiling emerald-green eyes and long thick dreadlocks approached me. 'Hello, luv.' He introduced himself with a warm hug. 'I'm Sparrow, like the bird.' He wore a forest green punomo stone around his neck that was gifted to him from a Māori wisdom keeper while travelling in New Zealand. I instantly sensed his awakened presence and was intrigued and charmed by his refreshingly warm, open and congenial heart. He reminded me of a mythical pirate. From the look of his clear emerald eyes, heavily creased forehead and tattooed torso, he had a tale or two to tell of timeless treasures both lost and found.

Sparrow and I soon discovered that we had both spent time living in India, and we shared passionately about our rich adventures there. His genuine authentic warmth made it easy to connect and confide in him. I instantly warmed to him and felt delighted to finally be speaking to someone who saw and appreciated me simply for being me.

Just as the conversation was beginning to deepen and go to the next level of getting to know one another, Eva swooped in like an exotic bird and perched herself on the log before us. Sparrow's attention and gaze was immediately drawn to her tantalising sparkle. They locked eyes like two jaguars rendezvousing in the night. The inevitable shooting stars and fireworks began, while I, like a dying star, faded into the blur of the night. I looked to the fire where a spliff was now being passed around. In that moment, I preferred to go to bed early. I was being called to feel what was real rather than lose myself in the allure of the tribal field. I swiftly thanked everyone for the warm welcome and rapidly excused myself from the campfire.

Enough! I have definitely had enough! Feeling deflated, humiliated and more alienated than ever, I sobbed my way down the windy, wooded path and collapsed on top of my damp sleeping bag.

Eva did not come back to the tent that night. I saw her in the late morning. Her hair was matted and tousled, her eyes bloodshot, her clothes tattered and covered in tiny twigs and branches that clung to her clothes from rolling around on the forest floor. She had a wild look blazing from her hazel blue eyes.

'Hiya, Eva,' I said. 'I've been feeling you all morning and I would love it if we could have a little heart to heart chat.' I realised that the time had come to be totally transparent, clear the air and reveal to her what I was feeling.

She looked surprised but willing. 'Sure, Ambé. What's up, luv?'

I took several deep breaths, which helped me to find my centre beyond my shame for not being able to fully accept my dearest friend just as she was. Finally, I mustered up the courage to share my deep heart. 'I'm not sure if you are even aware of what I've been going through,' I said sheepishly.

She shook her head as if she didn't have a clue.

We sat down next to our tent and had a long-overdue, deep and painfully honest conversation about the challenges that our dynamic was bringing up for us in our friendship. Like a dam that finally came tumbling down, I allowed my raw truth to at last flow out of me – no matter how mixed up with my own emotional wounding it was. Communication was our only way through this menagery of swallowed-back feelings.

'I feel that I have lost trust in our capacity to be together in social situations in a way that includes and cares for both our hearts,' I said. 'In truth, I would rather be alone than feel as if I'm being tossed aside for the next best thing on the menu!'

Her eyes widened in surprise, but she kept listening.

'I treasure our sisterhood and at the same time realise that we have different intentions for being here on this journey.'

Eva's words came out in a rush. 'I hear you, Ambé´, and I am truly sorry that it has been so challenging for you! I guess I've been searching too, in my own way. And now, I finally feel that I have met the man of my dreams! I felt such a strong instant connection and bond with him at the fire last night that there was only one thing for me to do. I'm sorry you felt excluded. I just had to go for it! I guess I wasn't paying much attention to you. I'm truly sorry luv. Sparrow and I have fallen, I mean, risen in love! I believe I have truly met my beloved soul mate! And guess what? He has decided to follow me to the Bay Area so that we can be together! I hope you can be happy for me. I'm totally head over heels in love with him!'

Wowza, that was super-duper quick, I thought, inwardly questioning the whole soul mate trip and whether it was all one big, highly over-rated, projection of our instinctual urge for procreation. I then quickly shifted my attitude to honour the undeniable spirit of Eros, as irrational as it was. After all, Eros was also a god of sorts whose power to unite lovers has existed for as long as man and woman have.

After getting it all out on the table, I found it way easier to adjust my attitude and go back to being a supportive and caring friend. In truth, I missed our special closeness and wanted to celebrate her along with her newfound swash-buckling heartthrob. I shook off the remains of any hurt feelings. After all, if I felt sovereign and whole from within my own being, I would most likely not be triggered by her behavior in the first place.

As uncomfortable as it was, I felt gratitude for the lesson and took Evas hand and squeezed it tightly. 'I'm truly happy for you, darlin'. I wish you all the best with Sparrow. I only ask that you look after yourself in all of this. I care for you, our friendship *and* your well-being! I'm going to take off and travel for a few days. I'll be back to fetch you and Tomas. Take good care of your beautiful self and have an amazing time with your new love. He seems to be an exotic and genuine jewel.'

She nodded. 'I will. And thank you for taking care of our heart space. It means a lot to me.'

'I'm really happy we had a chance to clear things up. *Au revoir* for now, dear sister. I love you, darln'.'

She threw her arms around me and gave me a fierce lioness hug. 'Ciao for now, sweet Ambe´! I'm super grateful for our sisterhood and truly hope you find what you are looking for.'

I smiled warmly and looked deep into her eyes, past all that had transpired between us. After a drawn out hug, I threw my large backpack on my shoulders and headed for the long and winding path down to the parking lot.

Midway down the hill, I ran into my friend, Sahrah, from the Mystic Family Circus community. I was grateful to have found a sister from the Bay Area to talk to on the way down the hill. She shared that she was also going through a similar ordeal of feeling oddly estranged and disconnected. I invited her to walk with me for a while. We made a small detour to the shower stalls and scrubbed off the residue of three very long days and nights. Although the water was quite chilly, it felt incredible to wash off the layer of dirt that had formed a second skin! Feeling alive and refreshed, we carefully traipsed through the muddy puddles and resumed the long walk down to the parking lot. Sahrah accompanied me as we shared in some soul-nourishing giggles and reminisced about the good ol' days in San Francisco, our love for the creative culture, cherished friends and our mutual calling to leave it all behind.

'The enrichment that comes from exploring new lands and cultures is a lifestyle for those of us who identify more with being universal citizens rather than rooted to one place,' I said, as if to smooth out my present predicament of feeling uprooted and displaced.

She lightened my heart by reminding me of the Ambe´ she knew back home, saying, 'It's easy to forget who we really are when we are so empathic and find ourselves lost in a forest of foreigners, *mais non mademoiselle?*'.

When we finally got down to the rental car, we were both totally stunned by what we saw. All four tires on the Renault were completely flattened to the ground! Somebody had let out all of the air! I looked around to see if any other tires had been flattened. Nope, only my poor little rental car!

Wow, how could this happen? I thought to myself, feeling totally baffled and bewildered.

My jaw dropped as open I turned to Sahrah in shock. 'This trip is turning out to be a comedy of errors!'

'I'm not quite sure what you should do about this,' she said, shrugging her shoulders and looking as stunned and bewildered as I was.

We stood there for a moment, staring at the deflated rental car in disbelief. I imagined blowing every tire up with a bicycle pump and then hauling my ass out of there. But I didn't have a bicycle pump and so resigned to the only option I could think of. 'I guess I have to go back up to the gathering, find Tomas, and ask him to help sort out this totally bizarre escapade.'

Sahrah nodded, then added, '*Mon Dieu!*'

'*Merde* is more like it,' I muttered. *Shiiit!* Naturally, I was terribly reluctant to go all the way back up to the gathering. The thought of it turned my stomach, yet clearly, there was no way out without my wheels. So Sahrah and I hiked a mile and a half back up the steep forest path. *How on earth did all four tires manage to get deflated and no one else's?* I replayed the scenario over and over again, attempting to make rhyme or reason out of the whole shenanigan.

When we finally got back up to the main circle, Sahrah gave me a long hug as if to re-inflate my morale, and then wished me luck. Luckily, Tomas was quite easy to find. He was perched in his favourite spot, painting under the canopy where he had been hanging out for the last few days. The painting was coming alive in brilliant iridescent colours and intricate geometries. He was revealing yet another layer of the alchemy encoded within these Cathar lands. I stood there for a long moment, mesmerised by the painting and then suddenly heard the hidden voice whisper, *Be patient, dear child. All is unfolding in divine and perfect order. This too shall pass and you will be on your way once again.* I took a deep breath and let it out with a loud sigh before I explained to Tomas what I had just discovered in the parking lot.

He flashed me with a gallant knight-like smile. 'We just need to find someone with an air compressor to pump up the tires. With all the RVs and school buses around, that should be fairly easy. No worries, I needed to take a break from the painting anyway. It's been consuming me all day.'

As long as that painting is still going, I can keep going too. I just need to keep the faith, and trust that all is unfolding in divine and perfect order,

I consoled myself, as Tomas and I traipsed back down the winding trail and searched the parking lot for someone with a tire pump. Since it was midday, we soon discovered that most people were up at the gathering to get lunch. We had no luck rounding up a compressor. I bowed to the inevitable as we agreed to try again the following morning when people were closer to their caravans after waking up.

I was utterly exhausted by the time I made it back up to our camp and dropped my backpack down by the side of our tent. Eva was there. She looked up, surprised to find me back at the campsite. She had been gathering her things to move up to Sparrow's camp.

'Why are you back, sweetie? I thought you were off to travel for a few days. Whoa, you look bloody knackered! By the way, I'm moving in with Sparrow,' she said, grinning up to her ears.

I told her how all four tires had been deflated on the rental car, and that I had traipsed up and down the mountain to the parking lot four times that afternoon, to no avail. 'So Tomas and I decided we have to wait till the morning to find someone to help us inflate the tires again.'

'Whoa! Well, might as well make the best of being here. Why don't you come back up to the fire with me tonight? My friends are preparing a lovely Sabbath meal. It's going to be a very special night, you know. Please join us! Maybe there's a really good reason for you to stay,' she said, trying to console me.

At first, I was reluctant to accept her gracious invitation. 'Well, I could use the warmth of a fire and the comfort of a meal. And in truth, I feel way better after the heart-to-heart clearing we had,' I reasoned.

Eva's invitation certainly sounded like a way better option than spending my evening cold, hungry and alone in a tent. I decided to leave my disgruntled attitude behind and make a fresh start. A wave of raw vulnerability rushed in, pooling in my belly. I felt pregnant with a flock of butterflies. After letting out a long sigh, I recommitted to holding my tender heart in the arms of radical self-love – come what may. 'All right then, I'm in!' and then unzipped the tent to change into something to keep me warm throughout the chilly night.

CHAPTER SEVENTEEN

FULL MOON MERKABA

As many of the ancient prophecies predicted, the day would come when all the rainbow tribes would once again reunite and dance together transcending the illusions of separation and duality. These harmonizing vibrations will reunite all twelve sacred rays in a new golden age. Thus, we shall walk together in our diversity and uniqueness on the sacred path of peace across all cultural boundaries, laying down our weapons, living in harmlessness in balance with all beings, and living side by side to enhance life.

This spiral was destined to reverse itself at the appointed time to initiate the integration of all aspects of our GodSelf. The rainbow tribes are gathering once again. It is time to birth the new reality that has been written in the prophecies passed down through eons of time. This is the precipice upon which we now stand as the Universe fully opens to us once again.

The journey has been a long one, much longer than any of us would have liked it to be. However, this tear in the fabric of the web of the collective coupled with the diminishment of pure Love has always been part of the divine plan as a way to increase our experience of Love. Our separation from Love in the form of duality has been a powerful teaching, for the only way to truly know Love is to separate ourselves from it.

As the original wound of separation is rising to the surface within each of us, mass consciousness continues to cycle through its play-back via extreme polarities. Attempting to fix what appears to be the problem only exacerbates it. Instead, by finding harmony amidst the flux of duality we find the core of our GodSelf, free of any separation. Herein we find Love for our self with all its human foibles, Love beyond our human bounds for all our brothers and sisters, and Love for all sentient beings.

Herein, we find peace with All-That-Is and we rise sovereign and free as creators of a new reality.

– Sharon Lyn Shepard

Compared to the lifespan of the universe,
our lives begin and end in a single day.
'Everyone we meet and every choice we make is part of our story.
A million futures lie before us. Which one will come true?'

– Nicola Yoon, The Sun Is Also a Star

Just before sundown, Eva and I walked to the upper fire together in raw and humble silence. Even though I felt waves of trepidation wash through me, I was intent on having a whole new experience that evening. I wore my warmest attire of black cotton leggings and a green and gold, hand-knitted, fairy dress, which I had picked up at the Big Green festival along with my funky ol' disco boots. The golden sun was just setting over the mountain and the air felt lighter than it had for days.

Upon arriving at the fire, I sat down on the welcoming Earth. I proceeded to smile warmly at the familiar faces and then dropped into a quiet meditative space. After a few moments of grounding my energy, I became aware that the man sitting next to me at the fire had joined me in my discreet meditation. We seemed to open our eyes simultaneously.

He turned to me and announced himself, 'Hello, my name is Aiden.'

The first thing I noticed was that he wore a white knitted cap and a T-shirt with a print of two leaping dolphins that said 'Dolphin Telepathic Society'. I was delighted to see his T-shirt since the dolphins always signified to me that I was on my highest path.

'Hi, I'm Ambeˊ.'

'I'm going to be a father soon,' he said matter-of-factly.

'Oh, wow, how wonderful for you! You must be so excited to be a papa,' I said, a little uncertain as to why he chose to open the conversation in that way.

'Yeah, it'll be good fun, that is, I hope so.'

I noticed his mixed emotions on the matter and decided to change the subject. 'What are you up to in the world, Aiden?'

'I am a healer of sorts. I go around to sacred sites, say a few mantras and dance around on the earth to rebalance the discordant energies,' he said with an air of slight cheekiness. 'I also facilitate spiritual workshops.'

I could sense he was making light of his vocation. I immediately recognised that we both shared the path of being a planetary healers, grid and Lightworkers. My heart began to beat a little faster. 'How interesting. That's what I'm up to as well! I've actually been sent on a rather mysterious mission to explore this area and its relationship to Yeshua, Mary Magdalene and the Grail Mysteries.'

'Oh really?' He spoke, dragging out the word as if to indicate the coincidence. 'That's wonderful. I know a lot about the sacred sites around here. I'm also connected with quite a few of the local Grail family. I can introduce you to them if you like,' he said, with an aire of hospitality.

'Wow, that's super kind of you!' My heart began to race involuntarily. I turned to him impulsively. I asked, 'Would you like to walk up to the ridge and watch the sun set over the mountain?'

He paused, hesitated slightly and then said, 'Yes, why not.'

I felt a sense of relief and excitement to have finally met a friend who understood something about the history and spiritual lore of the land. We walked up the mountain to stand at the edge of the mountain ridge and face the setting sun. This was the same place where I had done ceremony two evenings ago with Eva and Tomas. Here, through sacred vision, I received a vivid vision of White Buffalo Calf Woman presiding over the Rainbow Gathering. Her outstretched arms and massive shimmering rainbow wings embraced the entire valley within them. She was the epiphany of the Cosmic Earth Mother. Her radiant heart-light bestowed blessings upon all her precious Rainbow children and creatures of the land. We walked to the exact spot where I had put out a powerful prayer for the split between the Divine Masculine and Feminine to be brought into harmony, restored to peace and end all wars within and without.

As we approached the ridge, I spotted Eva and Sparrow standing on a fallen tree log, entwined together while sharing a long passionate kiss. Ironically, I noticed that I was not in the least bit triggered by what I saw. I was more preoccupied with a painful throbbing in my head, which I noticed was growing in intensity while being in the company of my new friend.

'Hello,' Eva shouted out to us. 'Come join us for a sunset prayer!'

The tree stump was large enough for the four of us to stand upon. I looked out over the vast mountainous vista that dropped into a valley and whispered, 'What a breathtaking view.'

'Whoa, I'm having a déjà vu. It's as if the four of us have stood here together in some prior lifetime,' Aiden said. 'Look, see this spiral carved on the top of this trunk? I carved it this afternoon. On some level, I must have known that we would all be up here offering up our prayers tonight.'

I too felt the timeless connection as the four of us grounded and opened to Great Spirit and the higher dimensions. Toning sounds and sonic prayers poured through us, echoing into the valley below. We each shared a mutual desire to forgive and release all that had transpired on this land and to heal the karmic pain that had carried over into the present generations. Of course, our prayers meant we also had to release our own pain and forgive ourselves, to truly honour this once-in-a lifetime moment. The gift of getting to do this for humanity amazed and humbled me. I allowed myself to gently release my frustration from the day, while tenderly opening to the magic and grace of what was unfolding before me now. The tight grip on my heart began to soften as I gazed at the pink, orange and purple light of the setting sun. If my tires had not been mysteriously deflated, I would not be here to enjoy this beautiful sunset with my new friends. I inwardly acknowledged feeling the awe and wonder of it all.

After the sun disappeared behind the mountain, the four of us traipsed back to the fire to join with the others. Within seconds of our arrival, a young brother quite spontaneously belted out an Indian bhajan song called 'Gopala', which happened to hold a very sentimental place in my heart from my days living in India. It wasn't long before I released an avalanche of withheld tears. I began to sob and sob as discreetly as I could possibly manage. The torrential downpour of tears seemed to go back to the first memory prior to my birth, the very inception of my soul.

I was grateful that the others were engrossed in the singing circle, giving me the space to go through whatever I needed, without interfering or judging. I lay back onto the cool earth and gave way to the cleansing release. My tears poured out not only for myself, but for the descendants of this land, my ancestors and for all my relations. After nearly half an hour of lying back on the earth, I heard Eva's melodic, sweet voice singing the sacred chant, 'Jai Ambe.' Her angelic voice lured me up from the ground. I joined the circle, dusted off the twigs and leaves that had stuck to my dress, and began to sway in unison with the bhajan and the flames that danced before me. Everyone sang out with full-hearted devotion until the whole circle was unified in one beautiful, all-out chant devoted to Jagadambe, Divine Mother of the Universe.

Sometimes, one has to let it all go to realize what was there all along. A light went on as I realised no one 'out there' was doing anything to me to keep me feeling separate and alone. My experience was coming from inside of me, and the meaning I ascribed to what I was feeling. *What a revelation and what a relief!* I was being given the golden opportunity to shift my reality from victim to victorious. In that moment, by the warm glowing fire, surrounded by friends from around the globe while chanting the Divine Mother's sacred name, I made a conscious choice to self-select myself into the circle of life– *as if it could ever be any other way!*

Within the split second of joining in, my gaze met Aiden's from across the fire circle. All at once, time and space collided with eternity. It felt like a laser beam of light crossed eternity to find my soul sitting across the fire. Once again, I fell back onto the cool earth. This time I needed to integrate what just shot through my heart like a thunder bolt in one fleeting glance. I was overtaken by what felt like countless timelines converging all into a singular glance. All I could do was laugh and sob all at once. These were tears of release, joy and surrender. I was struck by the divine irony of how life seems to happen when we give up control and fully release our tight grasp on reality. All the energy it had taken me to resist and stay separate popped like a hot-air balloon being punctured by a tiny pin. Destiny had finally made its way to meet me and I went from nothing to everything in a blink of an eye.

Aiden came over to lie next to me. I turned my head to look at him through my glassy wet eyes in absolute raw, open vulnerability. My throbbing head was about to split into a million pieces.

'May I offer you some healing?' Aiden asked politely.

'Yes, please. Let's move back away from the fire so as not to disturb the others, okay?'

'Of course,' he said.

We quietly inched our way back several yards from the circle and lay back on the forest floor. His large hands waved around my energy centres. He told me that he was assisting me to release some old stuck energy connected to a child spirit that was still lingering in my womb space. He described a stillborn whose spirit had not been fully cleared from my womb. With my permission, he released the unborn child along with my headache.

'Interesting, a stillbirth,' he said. 'Quite a lot of creative potential you have been holding on to.'

Feeling impressed by my new friend's healing finesse, I celebrated my newly liberated and spacious womb by sticking my legs in the air and shaking them like an animal released from a cage. Aiden joined me, putting his long legs in the air alongside my own and waving them about. We gazed up at the canopy of stars twinkling above us while delighting in the freedom and space to begin anew.

'Ah, I'm free at last, free at last...to play, that is! That's what I love – to play and share in the miracle of life's endless wonders instead of being buried underneath them. What a blessing! Thank you for that healing, Aiden. I am feeling much better now,' I said while wriggling my toes to the sky.

Aiden grabbed my hand and lured me towards the beckoning full moon rising in the distance. Soon, we picked up the pace and naturally began to frolic and dance through the forest like two ancient elven-fairy friends. We were both enamoured with the sheer miracle of our lives colliding within this blink of moonlit eternity.

'Greetings, my Lady. I am Sir Arthur, King of Camelot, and I am thrilled to make your acquaintance, that is, once again.' Aiden had re-introduced himself with a strong English accent born of high nobility. He then offered me a gregarious grin and chivalrous bow. His aquamarine eyes sparkled brightly under the light of the full moon.

He truly embodied the King Arthur archetype, an energy that I had long dreamt of becoming reacquainted with in this lifetime. I was flooded with a familiar joy as we danced upon the forest floor like king and queen, two mythic lovers, sun and moon, carefree and innocent, in a playful abandon under a canopy of shimmering starlight.

'Please don't take this personally,' he said, pulling me gallantly toward him and holding me close to his well-toned chest. As his body pressed into mine, it felt cosmically romantic, spiritually arousing, mythically erotic and mysteriously prophetic. We melted into a timeless tantric swoon that dissolved my being into pure, pristine, bliss-filled presence. My body trembled in sensual delight as my spirit soared like a golden hawk. In my heightened state, it was clear that this was not the first time our souls had skydanced together in this way. The waking dream, déjà vu went on and on as we continued our mythic dance through the forest under the glorious light of the milky white moon. And then, coming down to Earth, I lovingly reminded myself, *'Ambe´, you are not to take this personally!' What on Earth does he actually mean by that?* I inwardly pondered what felt like a Zen koan to me.

Our forest dance changed into a meander. We came to an open clearing where I became aware of three very bright stars in the shape of a triangle beaming above our heads. While looking up toward them, I saw a star tetrahedron descend in a shaft of golden white light and anchor all around us. In a flash, I remembered a recent lucid dream! I had dreamt that I was embracing a beautiful soul mate companion under the light of a full moon while a star tetrahedron came down from above, activating our DNA and braiding our light bodies with our divine essence. *Oh my goodness, I must be dreaming awake...because that just happened!*

In that moment, I knew that these two distant stars had just collided and my meeting with Aiden was the destiny appointment that my soul was anticipating. My heart-womb was on fire, confirming my knowingness that this was the cosmic meeting that Jahrusha had foreseen for me during our sacred counsel at Gaia's Grove. Once more, I had a full-body knowingness that I was in for quite the wild ride, one that could easily be the end of all I once knew myself to be.

Aiden and I continued our mythic frolic over to the open meadow where the glow of the full moon lit up the surrounding trees. We sat down on a fallen old growth tree to get a direct view of the moon as she hovered low in the sky. There was a misty rainbow ring around her. We gazed in silence then simultaneously became aware of that we had front-row seats to a magnificent lunar eclipse.

'*Que bella luna,*' Aiden uttered quite romantically.

I swooned with the sound of these three words, agreeing whole heartedly. 'What a beautiful moon. So what is the nature of your relationship with the mama of your child to be?' I blurted out as if to scope out what was down the rabbit hole before entering in.

'We're not together romantically anymore, so we have an open arrangement and I am free to explore relationship with whomever I wish.' Interestingly enough, he then proceeded to complain of an upset belly.

I sat in silence for a few moments. I wanted to feel into being in integrity with our connection as it felt powerfully intimate in its own unique way. I knew without a doubt that I had a destiny appointment with this ancient new friend. I was not about to go any further with a man who was on the threshold of fatherhood unless I was absolutely clear that this was an integral part of our mutual soul's growth and evolution. I asked the Divine to show me the best way to proceed while staying in full integrity and respect for all beings involved. I imagined a crossroads where I could go back to the fire alone or stay present with Aiden. I was then shown that this was a pre-destined appointment and that my highest soul growth was to stay open to what wanted to unfold as it unfolded.

'May I reciprocate your healing on me by offering you an internal organ massage to help soothe your upset belly? Chi Nei

Tsang massage is one of my specialties. Perhaps I can relieve some of your discomfort.'

'Well, yes. That sounds like it could be very helpful. My tent is set up just nearby. Shall we go there for the healing?'

'Sounds good,' I said, as all the possible implications flashed through my mind in a heartbeat.

After a short walk through the forest, we settled into Aiden's blue tent. It was just large enough for two, so I could work comfortably by his side. I began my session with a centering prayer. Within moments of touching Aiden's belly, I felt massive waves of blocked energy ripple through his fascia, muscles and bones. I placed one hand on his belly and another on his heart. I invited Aiden to breathe into my hands while guiding his breath to smooth out any places of remaining tension throughout his body. A massive blockage of constricted energy released and cleared from his solar plexus. When I sensed the energy had integrated and the session was complete, I asked if I could lie down and breathe with him for a little while.

I silently lay next to him and began to breathe a series of long deep cleansing breathes. Little did I know that synchronised breathing would be the magic key to unlock a storehouse of memory. Our connection felt to go back to beginingless time! As we telepathically linked in, our souls skydanced, releasing a cache of lucid images that were intertwined on an ancient grape vine. With the rising and falling of each breath, a time capsule opened where past and future memories unraveled from my DNA like an epic movie that had no beginning and no end.

After what seemed like hours of energetic intermingling and telepathic conversing, Aiden broke the silence and shared some of his perceptions aloud while I remained suspended in awe. I was way too engaged in our re-union to find words for what I was seeing and feeling. Likened to my prior medicine journey at the Grove, I experienced a holographic overview of my divine soul codes manifesting throughout various incarnations over my many spiritual lineages. To add to the wonder, a choir of fully unified angelic voices serenaded us from a nearby fire. They sang chants to the Divine Universal Mother, Jagadambe, until the crack of dawn.

Honestly, it felt as if they were serenading my soul. Like a choir of celestial angels, they were marking this undeniable, lucid destiny appointment with fate.

'*Hey Amba, hey Amba, hey Amba bol, ishwara satachita ananda bol... Jagadambe Jai Jai Ma, Jagadambe Jai Jai Ma... Jai Ambe Jagadambe, Matabhavani Jai Ambe.*'

It was as if the whole universe conspired to reunite our souls in order to fulfil a hidden purpose yet to be revealed. I felt consumed with gratitude and simultaneously full of mysterious trepidation. As I lay there, entranced and mesmerised by the devotional singing wafting into our tent, I continued to synchronise my breathing with Aiden's. In a spark of knowingness, I embraced the reality that my life would never be the same again. By dawn, I finally drifted off to sleep, pondering the question as if I was Sleeping Beauty: *who on Earth is this dazzling prince – awakener of my soul whose memory goes back as far as I can imagine.*

The following morning, Aiden and I had both received guidance to leave the gathering together. We agreed to head off to some of the Mary Magdalene sites woven throughout the mountains of the French Pyrenees. I reminded Eva, who was now in the full bloom of her honeymoon, that I would return for her in a few days. She was more than happy to nest with her new Rainbow beau. Just a little after midday, Aiden and I had packed up our things and headed out in Aiden's car towards Rennes Le Chateau. We planned to stop at the sacred sites as we wandered toward Limoux, where a dear friend of his from America had opened a healing center called La Maison Lumiere which translates to, The Light House. I sent out a silent prayer, 'Please beloved God/Goddess, let there be light!'

CHAPTER EIGHTEEN

LIFE-GIVING WATERS

The truth rises like the morning sun
birthing dew drops into misty veils
that enchant us all into looking
beyond the mind's eyes of dual limitation
and into the wonder of boundless vastness
dropping duality
embracing everything with possibility
A heart-centred reality
where the mind can intertwine with the heart
and dream into a limitless potentiality.
A dream where our wings will take us
damsely dancing like dragonflies on the
softness of warm ocean breezes.

– Alice O. Howell, *The Dove in the Stone*

I was dead; I became alive.
I was tears; I became laughter
The power of love arrived
And made me everlasting power!
I have seen everything.
I have no fear
I have the heart of the lion!
I shine like Venus.

– Jelaluddin Rumi

'**F**irst things first,' Aiden said. 'To Les Thermals!'

I whole heartedly agreed, adding, '*Laisse aller aux sources chaudes!*'

You can only imagine how relieved I was to be driving out of the Rainbow Gathering and over the mountains, leaving a cloud of dust behind. Aiden and I sought out the first nearby town that had hot springs. By mid-afternoon, we found one of the more upscale commercial thermal baths called St Tomas. 'I can hardly wait to get into those life-giving waters!'

After around forty minutes of winding roads and light conversation, we pulled into the parking lot of Les Thermals. Aiden and I parted ways to undress in our designated dressing rooms where luxurious white spa robes awaited us.

As I descended into the warm pool, every tight muscle melted and the whole of my body tingled in bliss-light. I savoured the feeling as all the prior pain of separation washed away, as if it never existed.

Ah, what a relief! This is quite a blessing after four nights in the woods. Perhaps I'm more cut out for a spa vacation rather than a festival camping trip, I mused with a smile. *Like never before, all that I am is here now.*

Undeniably, I felt more like myself than I had throughout this whole bone-chilling journey. My inner dolphin was elated to be back in the warm waters where she could frolic and play freely without all the grunge that comes along with camping in the woods.

Aiden approached me in the pools and reached out to cradle my body. He held my head and the small of my back while I floated weightlessly, gazing into the vast blue sky. The sun danced on the surface of my body. Along with the water's warm sensual embrace, I was captivated by Aiden's tender presence that relaxed me in all those womanly ways. I allowed myself to completely surrender into his muscular arms after what felt like lifetimes of longing. As I looked up to the billowing white clouds floating by, my body melted into pure bliss light.

Aiden's soothing voice put me into a blissful trance as he channeled the following words: 'Ambe´, you are here to step into the power, beauty and remembrance of the Goddess. Encoded within you are the wisdom codes of the Feminine Christ that will awaken and bring you into a new way of living in balance with the Sacred Feminine and Masculine. There are many masters and celestial beings here to guide your way. Each one will assist you to come into a greater aspect of your divine essence and embodiment. You can feel safely protected in this unfolding, entrusting the Divine Mother and Father God are with you every step of your way. May this time of awakening be a blessing to all who have walked before you and for all whose lives will be touched by this Sacred Union. It is with great honour that we meet you here at this time as you remember the truth and beauty of who you are.'

Like the birds that encircled us, our spirits soared high as our heart wings unfurled with the ripeness of being together. If it wasn't for the sun that was descending from behind the mountain, I would have floated in those warm waters forever. Instead, we both knew it was time to conclude our water ritual and set out to find a room for the night before it got too dark.

Feeling sublimely relaxed and rejuvenated, we headed toward the only hotel in the region, about two miles back from Les Thermals. Built in the late 1800s, the two-story lodge towered precariously over the edge of a very steep mountainous cliff. Upon entering the lobby, we found the hotel to be totally deserted, as if we were the only guests to drop by in a hundred years. The ghostly man behind the counter handed us one of those old fashion, metal keys and pointed up to the ceiling, suggesting that our room was just above the bar. As we carefully ascended the rickety steps, I imagined that one false move and the lopsided hotel could topple over, rolling down the mile-long ravine and taking us along with it.

The air in the hallway was musty and smelled like old stale Gitanes cigarettes. Aiden opened our chamber door with the large antique key. The first thing I noticed was the patchy floral wallpaper that appeared to be a few hundred years old. I couldn't help but imagine myself as an elegant French woman from the 1800s. First, I would remove my large floral hat that tied at the neck by a long crimson ribbon and hang it on the standing wooden rack. I would then slowly untie the layers of skirts and petticoats to reveal my tightly laced corset, starched white cotton bloomers, and laced-up black ankle boots.

It didn't matter that our room had wallpaper peeling off the walls or that the mattress had springs poking up from underneath. I was completely enchanted by the majestic purple mountains towering just outside our tiny window. I opened the shutters to let the last rays of the setting sun stream through, filling our room with a delicious golden shower. Twilight was always the most magical time of the day for me. It felt like anything and everything was possible. My heart was glowing with the same light pouring through the old wooden shutters.

While Aiden showered, I prepared an array of fresh veggies that we had picked up from the local supermarché on the way to the hotel. Dinner tonight would be a salad of garden-fresh leafy greens, tomato, cucumber, red pepper, freshly baked bread, goat cheese and a bottle of local red wine.

By the time I finished my shower, the moon had risen to light up the mountains and beckoned me to stick my head out our little window to greet her. I could see the edge of the cliff that the rickety old hotel was perched upon. Just below was a steep ravine that looked to drop for miles down with no apparent bottom. A feeling of exhilaration and fear washed through me all at once. In some bizarre and timeless way, I felt welcomed home by the warm soft breeze that caressed my face, as if I knew this land intimately. The familiar scent of blooming jasmine, the mountain air, the special way the stars shimmered in the cobalt sky all seemed to whisper, 'Welcome home, bright one. We're so glad to find you here.'

I felt at home in the Pyrenees after what felt like an eternity of wandering in exile.

Over dinner and a delicious bottle of regional red wine, Aiden and I shared about our lives and soon discovered that we had many of the same life experiences. The more we talked, the more I became filled with wonder and awe. It was as if my innermost heart began to thaw after a long, deep freeze. In truth, I had never encountered another human being with whom I felt so much affinity and resonance. His soul mirrored mine in a way I had never experienced with another before. He was reflecting back to me a depth of awakened presence that was full of passion, adventure that drew out my most authentic nature. I began to sense that I was in the presence of someone very significant, a being that I felt more alive and myself with than anyone I had ever known before. Yet at the same time, he remained distant, held back and strangely mysterious for reasons I was yet to fully comprehend.

After we polished off the last drop of wine, a series of yawns came over us, making it apparent that we could both use a good night's sleep. 'Why don't we go to bed so we can get a fresh start in the morning?' Aiden suggested while I yawned some more in agreement.

We disrobed into our undergarments and slipped into the squeaky double bed. I sensed if we weren't careful, the bed could easily collapse and fall through the floorboards. My heart raced uncontrollably as we settled in. Aiden lay by my side in a hauntingly still silence and then very slowly he reached for my hand and placed it on his bare chest to rest. For now, that was as much as our bodies would touch. I drifted off recalling one of my favorite poems entitled, 'Love Song' by Rainer Maria Rilke.

How can I keep my soul in me
so that it doesn't touch your soul?
How can I raise it high enough, past you, to other things?
I would like to shelter it, among remote
lost objects, in some dark and silent place
that doesn't resonate when your depths resound.
Yet everything that touches us, me and you,
takes us together like a violin's bow,
which draws ONE voice out of two separate strings.

CHAPTER NINETEEN

THE FAIRY QUEEN

The Celtic archetype of the Green Man represents the open, sensitive, vulnerable, artistic aspect of male consciousness that has been so repressed in Western culture. In Celtic Lore, the Stag King and the Green Man combine to form a complete picture of male consciousness. The Green Man is depicted as the champion of innocence, the Goddess and the natural world. He is the gentle keeper of the Sacred Garden of Earth. He is the singer of the Mysteries, celebrant of the Goddess, inebriant of the God. He honours and communes with all life equally. His sensitivity is the hallmark of the return to balance internally and externally that is so desperately needed now on Earth.

– Ariel Spilsbury

The pituitary is the kingly gland that rules our threefold mental, emotional and physical being. When stimulated by the down pouring fire of spirit, it discharges elixirs into the blood stream. This is the elixir of life, the healing promised to those who find the Grail. These elixirs purify the blood. The blood will carry them to stimulate all other glands in the endocrine system. The secretion of those elixirs signals the endocrine system to set in motion a process that will open the chakras and raise the kundalini.

The greatly increased activity of the pituitary gland begins the opening of the alta major chakra. The carotid gland governs the condition of the alta major, which rules the spine. During the process of initiation, the alta major projects the fire of down-pouring spirit into the channel situated on the right hand side of the spine known as Pingala. As the fire of illumination penetrates deeper into the chakras, the psychic refuse of our ancestral lives is gradually discharged upwards, flowing up the channel on the left hand side of the spine known as Ida.

The alta major is the gateway to the emotional astral world. It is the back door to the unconscious. The next chakra that will open is the solar plexus, which is the seat of emotion. When the fire of illumination penetrates the solar plexus, our emotions are raised into the heart. They pierce the heart from below, rupturing the hearts etheric web.

The heart now begins its full awakening. Acting as a magnet, it begins the slow and painful turn of direction that will draw primal energy of the lower chakras up into consciousness. All the energy of the lower worlds must be transmuted through the heart.

– Niamh Clune, *The Coming of the Feminine Christ*

Aiden and I awoke early the next morning and set out toward his friend's home in the quaint village of Limoux. Feeling refreshed, we rolled the windows down to let in the warm breeze. It blew through our hair and lifted our spirits as we zoomed along the steep, winding mountainous road. As soon as we spotted an arrow pointing to a medieval village, our little blue car swerved off to the side of the road as if it had a mind of its own. Feeling magnetically drawn, we decided to explore a little and grab a bite to eat for lunch.

The village immediately captivated us. 'Wow, I feel like I'm a time traveler who has just been transported to a place where I had once lived centuries ago,' I said, astounded by what I saw.

The tiny cobblestone lanes were lined with crooked shops displaying all manner of accoutrements that reflected the history of times long ago. Each shop window was lit up with its own specialty item. One had swords, each one unique because of their intricately engraved handles. Another window displayed a variety of golden chalices ornamented with finely embedded jewels. There was a shop especially for hand-sewn leather satchels, an archery shop full of bows and arrows, and a craft shop with handmade beeswax candles of all shapes and sizes. There was even a shop with life-like statues of unicorns, dragons, wizards, fairies, and Knight Templars.

Altogether, the shops in this medieval village told a story about a time when battles were fought between opposing kingdoms – while magic and sorcery were used as weapons to fight battles based on whose god was the lesser of two evils.

Being a lush for pretty things, I was drawn into a corner shop that specialised in goddess clothing and exotic imports from India. Aiden and I entered the quaint boutique, and I immediately fell in love with a silk wrap-around skirt. It's intricate floral motif were the colours of an East Indian sunset, glowing in hot pink, tangy orange and ruby red.

'Hello! Er, *bonjour*,' I said, introducing myself to the elderly shopkeeper who had a face like a Basset hound, all droopy eyed and sagging at the chin.

'Bonjour, *mademoiselle, monsieur*,' she replied. And then whined, 'It is so very, very dry here and such unusual weather for this time of the year. *Ne'cest pas?* In all my years I've never seen anything quite like it.' She spoke as if she was complaining to a couple of old family friends she had known for years.

'*Mai we*,' I said.

Aiden nodded empathetically.

'*Mon Dieu*, it's so unpredictable and unstable here, just like the world right now. You know what I mean? I'm actually scared. From one moment to the other, I don't know what's going to happen to me, or my village. I just wish we could get some rain,' she added quite desperately.

'Well, that's why we've come today, Madame. We've come to bring you rain as an offering of our love and gratitude for this land and its people,' I replied, sincerely wishing that the rain would come and relieve this woman of her strife and her worry. I purchased the flowing skirt and added, 'I wish that all your prayers come true, Madame. *Merci beaucoup. Au revoir!*'

Aiden and I carried on with our window-shopping adventure, fully mesmerized by the affinity and familiarity of all the mythic symbolism on display. Each storefront took us further into its history, complete with magical lore.

Each shop depicted a part of history when gallant knights defended their kingdoms and their lands in the name of Jesus

Christ. Countless religious bloody battles were fought in his name to gain power over people and control how they lived, worshiped and ultimately paid taxes.

I felt that there was much more to this historic tale that remained hidden beneath the surface, as if a very dark secret of what really happened was silenced and buried long ago... along with the joy of life. Whatever it was, it felt like a curse that had kept this village frozen in time, caught in a looping story that could not move on until there was resolve and ultimately a much happier ending. Typical to those in power, the historical accounts 'of what actually happened' were buried long ago and by now nearly forgotten.

Whatever it was, it festered deep within the basement of my unconscious, bubbling to the surface to be known. I resolved to uncover whatever it was, in the hopes that if I did, it might just bring back the rain, a symbol of new life and healing from all that was once severed from love, dignity and honour.

In the centre of the village square was a beautiful old cathedral made of ancient grey stones. Aiden and I entered quietly, uncertain of what we would find. I was drawn to a larger than life wooden carving of a reclining Yeshua. He looked strangely alive, lying on top of his tomb with his muscular arms crossed over his heart. I knelt before him and wept while silently dialoguing with his essence.

I'm so sorry, beloved, so much blood has been shed in your name. How far we've wandered from your teachings of loving kindness for all beings. At times, I feel this world is getting darker, lost in the illusion of fear, greed and separation. When did life become more like a prison rather than a beautiful celebration of the gift of life? Thank you for always reminding me of the truth and light that I am. This is why I am here...to remember what Love is and what Love can and will be.

Tears streamed down my face as I confided in Yeshua as if he was my brother, my beloved and my very best friend. I recollected the visitation from my Family of Light and how they showed me that I had walked with this soul family throughout countless lifetimes. There would be moments when the personality of Ambe´ would fade away and I would be transported to a time when the family was gathered around that sacred fire. We shared heart songs and spoke of times to come. I was participating in a narrative that was as alive today as it was thousands of years ago when we walked the Earth together as one. And then there were times, I experienced his essence through the eyes and heart of his beloved, someone who knew his most vulnerable moments in as much as his wholly divine presence. The completeness of what we shared blossomed alive inside of me as if there was no gap in time. The presence of Yeshua stretched my heart wide open and enveloped me in his loving embrace.

I heard his wise and gentle voice counsel me from beyond the veil. *'Dearest one, once upon a time, first man and first woman sat together under the Tree of Life and offered their pledge to live in Oneness with all beings. As their Starseed descendant, you have travelled long and far on this earthly plane, honouring the sacred promise to leave no one behind. In truth, in your altruism, you have become somewhat lost and distanced from your Self. To know me is to know yourself! When you perceive fear and separation as real, when you grasp for someone or something outside to complete you, you sever the bond of the unified heart. It is time to come home to your true Self Beloved – to be fully human and divine!*

'When you allow yourself to love all of you, you become a lover of the world. Stand strong, rooted in the centre, and surrender the last traces of unworthiness. Stay true to living in alignment with your highest truth so that no poison may taint nor tarnish you. Be resolute so that you may lead and be lead with the gentleness of a lamb and the fierce nobility of a lion. As you nourish yourself with the light of the Divine you shine light into the darkness and become the Wayshower through embodying the way.

I remained kneeling by Yeshua's reclining, life-like body. Still vibrating with his potent transmission, I recollected some of his most famous parables before getting up to see where Aiden was.

'Cast off your wearisome burdens of guilt, false pride and self-loathing. Come to the fountain of your own light and know the peace that passes all understanding. For here with me you may drink and find refreshment, until you find your way to Father-Mother's eternal spring.'

When the energy settled, I walked towards the front of the church. Aiden and I met somewhere in the middle of the nave. We held hands, remaining silent as we looked up at a statue of

Mother Mary holding the Christ child. I leaned into his shoulder and whispered, 'Even though you and I are not necessarily the religious types, I sense we are being guided by a stream of higher consciousness far greater than we could ever conjure with our own imagination. I am so grateful for all of the spiritual transmissions I am experiencing. How about you?'

'Yeah, yeah, for sure,' Aiden added unconvincingly as I detected his mind lingered elsewhere.

We proceeded to walk outside and greet the warm sun, from which we shared a moment of unabashed worship. Suddenly ravenous, our bellies led us to a nearby outdoor café. Rows of white plastic chairs, tables and umbrellas lined the square. We found a table amongst clanking glasses and wafts of strong cigarette smoke. Surrounding us were dozens of tourists smoking, drinking Coca-Cola and eating sandwiches made with thick French baguettes. Aiden ordered a couple of *Nicoise* salads, some chips and a pitcher of lemon water for us to share.

I began to notice an uncomfortable silence growing between us. A wall was forming with a sign that said 'forbidden to trespass'. I sensed something was deeply troubling Aiden, yet I was reluctant to pry too much, especially since I felt no invitation from him to do so. Instead, I chose to give him space and as per his initial request, do my very best not to 'take anything personally'.

After lunch, we headed back to the car and were astonished at how time seemed to fly, as it was already 3.33pm! Within seconds of driving away from the village, we experienced a miracle. Much to our surprise, it began not only to rain but also to hail! Yes, the weather went from beaming sunshine to large pellets of rain and hail coming from goddess only knows where.

'*Mon Dieu*, it's raining!' I exclaimed. Our prayers for the disheartened shopkeeper had actualised before our very eyes! We sat in the car, grinning from head to toe. It was such a wonderful feeling knowing that our shopkeeper friend was probably sharing the same amazement with this unexpected downpour of grace. *Blessed be these life-giving waters!*

We drove off in the pouring rain, that is, until we spotted our first double rainbow just a few miles down the road. We were headed toward Limoux, via a stopover in Rennes Le Chateau, enigmatic home of many of the renowned Grail mysteries. Around six kilometres down the winding mountain road, I began to feel the base of my spine tingle and flutter and then suddenly convulse with rushes of erupting energy. This sudden surge of kundalini was a sign that my subtle energy body was opening to accommodate the new downpour of frequency. I paid extra close attention as the energy amplified until I literally about to burst out of my skin. We drove around a bend, and Aiden spotted an alcove barely visible amongst the surrounding foliage. Unable to ignore his convulsing passenger, he promptly pulled over to the side of the road and looked at me to try to assess if this was a good convulsion or a bout of food poisoning.

We got out of the car, grabbed hands and walked into a wooded area full of overgrown ferns and emerald green foliage. After a few minutes of walking, I felt a dramatic shift in the energy of the landscape. Everything began to appear brighter, clearer and more sparkling, the way things look in technicolor. We stopped in front of a beautiful, bubbling brook. Three tiny waterfalls converged into one and then flowed into a larger stream. I sensed we were in a very special earth temple, rarely visited by humans. We became very quiet.

'Shh, listen. Do you hear what I here?'

All we could hear was the trickling stream making contact with the water's surface from the three converging waterfalls and a rustling in the leaves.

I sat down by the spring to meditate. The Akashic records revealed to me that the surrounding land was once inhabited by Fairies, along with a wide variety of other inner earth elemental beings. I saw that they were presently being held frozen in time by an evil curse cast by the overlord of this valley. He insisted on governing through hatred and tyranny. In confirmation of this awareness, the energy in my spine intensified and I began to stretch, yawn and open my chakras in an attempt to distribute some of the jolts of kundalini loosening from my sacrum.

Aiden and I joined hands above our heads to form a bridge while walking our legs out to stretch out our lower backs. Within only a few moments of connecting our bodies, we were joined by two other beings that began to spontaneously animate and express through us. I took a moment to check in and verify that the origin of these beings was purposeful, clear and respectful. When permission was granted, a radiant woman of great nobility merged with my subtle body and filled me with the most delicious, succulent, golden, nectar-like frequency. She wore a ruby-red velvet cloak with golden trim around a large oversized hood. Her shimmering effervescent wings were tucked neatly inside her cloak. An intense blend of heart light mixed with the energetic presence of every wild species of her natural queendom danced with her radiant presence. She embodied the intelligence of the mineral kingdom, the heart light of the Devic realms, the instinctual love of the animals, and the fierce presence of all mothers who would do anything to protect her children. I became one with her – the very heart and soul of nature. I savoured her ever so subtle, succulent, honey-like nectar that coursed through my veins, the life blood that animates all of nature. My whole being began to vibrate and glow with an effervescent joy that was likened to being orgasmic...except it was Gaia-gasmic.

Aiden also felt a presence come through him whom he described as the strong yet gentle, protective energy of the Green Man, otherwise known as Pan. As we opened to the energies and entrusted ourselves to their presence, they began to move through us until we became comfortable speaking on their behalf. Aiden opened the dialogue by saying, 'There was once a great Kingdom here, likened to Camelot.'

As he said that, I instantly became aware of an inner Earth civilisation of Light that coexisted in a parallel dimension with this one. The beings of the inner Earth realms carry the vibrational codes of magic married with innocence. They know how to live in harmony, respect and sovereignty with each other, nature and the cosmos. My awareness expanded to welcome in the presence of an extremely high frequency being.

'I am the Queen of the Fairies,' she introduced herself in a voice that vibrated with loving kindness, nobility and a pristine diamond-like clarity. 'I have come for the purpose of summoning my family from their slumber and into the wonder of fulfilling their highest destiny. Each must play their part in enchanting the world into remembering our true nature as magical creator beings. The misty veils are now lifting and many are remembering their ancient oath to join with the inner Earth and the soul of nature.

'Come out from your hiding, dear ones. It is time to fly with the winged ones, frolic with the animals and hum with the insects once again! Let us reclaim our sacred passion to weave the golden web with our childlike wonder, wild innocence and sumptuous beauty. This world has been mired, polluted and dulled for far too long. It's time to spruce up our sparkle and re-pollinate the hearts of the people so that they may bloom to the tune of our wild grace. Join me in lavishly sprinkling our magical stardust upon the Earth's broken hearted so that we may flourish and thrive in joyous co-creation. Come now, beloveds, won't you dive into the jeweled waters and drink from the sundrenched honeysuckles with me?' The Fairy Queen passionately beckoned her once-banished family to return to nature's playground amongst the glistening streams, succulent roots and majestic treetops.

Aiden embodied the essence of the Green Man. We swayed together to a symphony of bird songs mingling with the rustling of leaves. The Green Man exuded the noble pride of the Elven King while assisting me to ground the hummingbird thunder of my love-bursting heart. We witnessed countless Inner Earth beings begin to rumble and stir. One by one, they emerged from their long frozen slumber, rising from the seclusion caused from the rape, pillage and massacre that had once desecrated their beloved kin and sacred earth temples.

Now the fairy kin gathered round us in exuberant celebration. Their joy filled us from head to toe in a cascade of incandescent, sparkly fairy light. The Green Man and the Fairy Queen spoke in the timeless language of light, while iridescent rainbow orbs danced along the water and bounced in the golden sunlight streaming through the emerald trees. I, as Ambe´, remained present and aware, bearing witness to this wondrous festivity. Aiden and I were overcome with tears of joy, laughter and ever so grateful to be a part of this beauteous reunion and homecoming. What a precious gift it was to get to feel our own archetypal codes of light embodied within the Fairy Queen and Elven King. I kneeled by the triple waterfall with tears of gratitude streaming down my cheek.

'Thank you, dear ones, for your passionate presence and for your courage to return and be a part of restoring the magic to this once desolate land. I am at your humble service.'

Aiden and I held hands and went on to telepathically communicate with them from the depths of our hearts. 'Thank you for assisting us to open all of our senses to the wondrous gifts of the invisible realms. So much of the Earth is being raped and desecrated by unconscious greed. It is mind-blowing to fathom that we are the only species that destroy its own home when we can be celebrating the glory of life with one another. I know we are on the brink of no return, and yet there is great hope in the knowing that you have not given up on us and you are here with us now! For the sake of all beings, I pray we humans wake up in time.'

Aiden took out a few ripe nectarines from his backpack and set them on the bank of the creek as an offering of our gratitude, and then handed one to me. I bit into the plump and juicy ball of golden nectar and allowed the succulent juices to drip down my face. There was no better way to consecrate the moment. We threw the pits into the forest, knowing that they would make a welcome addition to any new fairy home. Thank you, precious kin, for always being a wild light in this world that can never be extinguished.

Holding hands, we walked back to the car, brimming with joy from our spontaneous encounter with these magical beings. Upon getting into the passenger seat, I sat down on my sunglasses and shattered them. With an air of all-knowingness, Aiden pronounced, 'I guess it's time to see the world with brand-new eyes.'

Just as he said that, we both looked to the right of the car and saw a large human eye painted on a five-foot round boulder protruding from the side of the road. Once again, we looked at each other astounded by what we saw.

'Do you ever feel like you are in a waking dream?'

'It's more like dreaming awake to me!' Aiden replied.

I rolled down my window to let the warm breeze flow through my hair as we proceeded down the road. 'Hmmm, do you feel what I feel? I sense we are not alone.' I looked behind me and then began to giggle. I could feel the clear presence of two mischievous fairy kin hitching a ride with us in the back seat. Aiden played it cool, as if it was the most ordinary thing in the world to pick up a couple of hitchhiking fairies. He kept his eyes on the road, but I could tell he sensed their presence too by the grin on his face. We shared a heart-melting smile that bridged lifetimes and worlds.

However, we did not get more than a few kilometres down the mountain before I felt a strong quivering of kundalini begin to percolate in the base of my spine once again. I was hesitant to say anything and delay our journey to Limoux once more, but eventually, I felt I might burst if I didn't. In truth, this was all very exciting to me. I relished being in the French Pyrenees while having spontaneous Earth-healing adventures with my ancient new friend. Being with him was like having the best of all worlds. Planetary service, Gaian Tantra, sacred-site excursions, delicious conscious companionship – this recipe of relating was something I had longed for, for ages. And yet, I continued to sense that my growing feelings of fondness were better kept to myself. I flashed back to the Rainbow Gathering when Aiden pulled my body close to his and said, 'Please do not take this personally.' *Really, Mother? Really? Is this some kind of cosmic joke?*

Now familiar with my bodily symptoms, Aiden pulled over to the side of the road. While the kundalini energy continued to surge up my spine, I scanned my surroundings to see what was lighting up. I looked to the right and saw an elegant manor house. It seemed to call out to me amongst the other historical homes of this region. It had red wooden shutters and a large archway made of ancient stones entwined with green wisteria. As I observed the house more closely, a wave of goddess bumps washed over my skin. Aiden also picked up on the energy and slowly pulled up closer to the mysterious house, which appeared to be uninhabited. We sat in the car, closed our eyes and listened to what was being asked for. The house beckoned to me to come out and explore it further. Even though I knew that we'd be trespassing, Aiden and I chose to accept the calling of our next assignment together.

I walked around to the backyard, where there was a beautiful well and spacious garden. A rope swing hung perfectly between two ancient elm trees. In a strange way, the garden felt to be inhabited by its former occupants from long ago. As I turned back to face the house, I noticed the back steps leading to the upper floor. The house felt to be frozen in time, just as the fairy queendom had been for centuries and perhaps just like me. Feeling drawn in, I walked up the stairs to have a look inside the deserted rooms. Expecting the door to be locked, I turned the handle and was surprised that it opened. There was nothing but two antique wooden chairs and an old dusty mattress. It was strange to come across a dwelling in modern times that remained untouched for what seemed to be decades. I was curious as to why. As if by silent invitation, I went into the dusty room and sat down on an old wooden chair. I closed my eyes, dropped into meditation and listened to the story emanating from the ancient stonewall. I saw a man in his late thirties wearing provincial clothing from around the early 1800s. He sat at a kitchen table made of thick ebony wood. His head was bent down and rested in his arms. He felt to be devastated and frozen in despair. I silently made a prayer to open and attune to the Akashic records *Maybe I could assist in some way.*

I was shown that this ghost of a man was the governing lord who once presided over this region with a harsh and tyrannical hand. I looked further into his disposition and came to understand that he was gutted by the loss of his beloved wife and child, both of whom had died in childbirth. He blamed himself and God for his unbearable loss. He managed to carry on with life as a miserable widowed man who blamed everything and everyone for his loss. Each year, he grew increasingly bitter, angry and outraged. He became known throughout this land for his cruel governance and tyrannical hand.

I heard his voice loud and clear, as if he had come to life simply by me putting my attention on him. *If I must live in misery, then I will ensure everyone else lives in misery as well!* This man held desperately to the perception that God had unfairly punished him, so his perverse pleasure was to unfairly punish others. Eventually, he took to the bottle, his health declined and he died in this very desolate place, face down on the wooden table.

I saw how his spirit had refused to let go after his death and he remained there, imprisoned within his self-imposed hell realm.

Aiden sat quietly on the other wooden chair and joined me in meditation. He agreed that it would be best to assist the governing lord to transition to the other side where he could release himself from the burden of guilt and shame. We asked for permission to communicate with his spirit on a soul level. Once that was granted, we proceeded to convey to him that nobody was to blame for the loss of his wife and child. We telepathically reminded him that each soul makes its choices according to what is here to experience, learn, transcend, and evolve for the one. The healing began once he could feel, see and understand that he had been punishing himself and others through staying in a state of misery.

His head lifted from the table, groggy yet open to this new perception. He had gotten the message and was able to see his self-imposed prison in a new light. We witnessed the shift as a frequency of mercy and compassion permeated the room. The last piece was to hold the space for him to forgive himself and everyone he had brutally lashed out on in response to his loss. The musty room and the heavy cloud lifted as we guided him into the light and into the loving arms of his wife and child who were there to lovingly greet him. As he transitioned, the house brightened with sunlight. Aiden and I smiled to one another, sensing that this enchanting home was now clear and free to serve as a loving sanctuary for the next people to come.

I took a moment to reflect on my childhood; dad's unpredictable outbursts of rage were terrifying to me. They were often accompanied by inappropriate and invasive behaviour. Humiliation, sexual objectification and pontification of his laws were meant to be beared and unchallenged on a daily basis. Just like the overlord we set free, my father ruled his castle with a harsh and tyrannical hand. He used to refer to himself as the 'King', which was actually true, as our last name 'Ray' actually means 'king'. He would saunter into a room and the air would grow heavy and thick, reeking of booze and cigarettes. 'I'm the head of this household,' he would boast with an air of threatening superiority. 'If you want to live under my roof, you better listen to me, or else!' I was intimidated and would often shrink and shut down in his presence.

No wonder a sensitive little child like me had chosen to hide deep within herself, until she felt safe enough to come out. I observed the parts of me that remained frozen in time, a survival response to my father's unpredictable and narcissistic outbursts. Eventually, I forgot about these frozen parts of me suspended in time. I felt into my inner child calling forth a more conscious love, the kind that would melt her trauma and free her winged heart.

There was no accident that I was drawn into this desolate home. In seeing this man, I was being given an opportunity to see my father through compassionate eyes. *Perhaps my father had also suffered an unbearable loss. Victims tend to victimise and so the cycle repeats itself, creating generational trauma that stays stuck in the body, costing us nothing less than our capacity to manifest our dreams. That is, until we become aware, address the traumas and set ourselves and the perpetrators free.*

Thank goodness, by the age of ten, my mother had the sense to send me to a transformational workshop called, The Children's Seminar. I remember learning my first creative visualisation. I was to imagine stroking a little puppy dog in my lap. As I absolutely love animals, I took to this methodology immediately. It became so real to me that my whole body filled up with a warm, mushy glow. The facilitator's words still resonated in my mind as if it was yesterday.

'You can change your fear-based emotions by first changing your thoughts. Your thoughts are what create your reality. What you focus on is what you create. First, you must realise that you are the one creating all of those scary thoughts. So if you are the one creating them, you can magically un-create them! Every time you have a scary thought, imagine holding and loving yourself in the same way you would hold a little kitten. You change your outside world by changing your inside world. This magical quality lies within you! No one else has the power to alter the course of your life better than you do! And no one can love you in the way you can love you. When you really get that, you will understand that the universe is reflective and mirrors back to you whatever you are feeling inside. Like creates like. What you perceive and feel is what you tend to get!'

I have always been grateful for those initial lessons on how to create my reality by becoming aware of the power of my thoughts, feelings and perceptions. Yoga and meditation had given me the tools to come into my body and become aware of the parts of me that called out for my love and integration. Yet in that moment of quietude, I noticed there was a part of my nervous system, wired from early on, to fight or stay frozen in order to survive. Seeking validation and people pleasing were some of my ways of compensating for the parts of my power that recoiled in the face of Masculine authority.

It's time to take a stand, speak my truth and trust my inner cues rather than override or diminish them, I affirmed, determined to create disconfirming evidence that it was now safe to be fully in my Feminine power.

I opened my eyes from the clearing meditation at the same exact moment Aiden did. We smiled at one another warmly, knowing that liberating one tormented being also liberated the parts of us that remained immobilized from unresolved traumas buried over time.

After all, when one is set free, we all get a little freer. Voila!

CHAPTER TWENTY

SHIVA & SHAKTI

Shakti is the serpentine upsurge that opens our spine to receive the glory of God in our bones. Her moist elixir teases the obstacles out of our way, by hinting of the promised land in our midst. She brings a shimmering ecstasy to our dry and parched deserts, as our hips and breasts fill with life as we hopelessly attempt to contain her. Ha! What a Divine joke. Shakti is free to roam and wander, dancing delightfully through our stiff and awkward humanness. She is hunting for Shiva. Earnestly roaming for that fully awakened and realized, I Am. Their thirst and hunger to unite in our body will render us...gone. Let us surrender to her irrigation of our flesh, permitting her wild fancies and joining with her as the purser of Divine presence. For this process is the pathway to Divine union.

– Anaiya Sophia

THE LIGHT *and the* DARK RIVERS

The Dark River, as she flows, will open us to gnosis, revelation and wild ecstatic freedom. The Dark River is the fierce feminine, sacred outrage and most needed expression on this Earth at this time. She is unapologetic, brazen, bold, vastly intelligent, initiatory and mesmerising. But she does not harm, misrepresent, endanger, misinform, manipulate or coerce the self, or others. She lives outside of rule and order. Her outwardly action is the shattering of lies, denials and illusion. Her inward action is initiation, revelation and authentic gnosis.

The Light River emerges from our sacred origins. She is exquisite tenderness, the sacred heart, purity and virgin light-power. The Light River is not passive, weak, naïve or ineffective. The Light River's true strength flows within her purity, her absolute irrevocable union with what sustains, sources and births at the most incandescent levels – that is her virtue; her faith and knowingness of her own true nobility and elegance. She is graceful, dignified, compassionate, empathic, sacredly connected with all life, at peace and filled with devotional bliss.

Her touch, her glance, her voice, her body soothes, softens, eases and heals. Like the sweetest honey, the most refreshing spring water, she brings us new life, faith and a restored vigour to join with life more than ever before. The Light Goddess holds open the door to our pure vulnerability and quiet humility, and encourages us to earnestly reach for them.

The Light River beckons our soul, as she pours us into the secret Rumi heart, bringing us into contact with our unspeakable purity and worship as we drown in devotion at what we find there. The Dark River loosens up our mind, shakes off our mask, vivifies our sacred purpose and makes real our soul memories and your reason for being here.

So, when we imagine the authentic coming together of these two... their fusion births us into an entirely whole and new reality. Her outwardly action is the comforting of the soul, healing of all wounds and the restoration of harmony on Earth. Her inward action is gentle guidance towards the heart, the softening of all that is rigid within and the restorer of trust, innocence and immaculate sovereignty. As the two rivers come into contact and merge in the psyche, the long awaited union explodes the body, heart, mind into a third and currently unknown new being. Woman must unite her rivers and reveal the deeper truths to man through love. By harnessing her full range of sovereign expression, She will reveal the Way of Truth.

– Anaiya Sophia

The sun was slowly descending behind the mountains. Aiden and I continued down the road in silent awe. This simple two-and-a-half-hour trip had transformed into a timeless saga. Each event highlighted a larger archetypal theme that reflected aspects of our sojourn that traversed lifetimes. Our basic human needs were kicking in and we were ready to have some time to integrate the enormity of what we were each experiencing.

'How 'bout we take a bit of a break and relax our minds and voices?' Aiden encouraged in his thick Australian accent.

I agreed and took a long, deep breath, relaxing my back in my seat for the rest of the ride. Suddenly, I felt more like a nuisance than a close friend. Perhaps it was his hunger that was inching its way between us. Just as I closed my eyes and began to drift off, Aiden swerved the car to the side of the road and came to a screeching halt that sent me and the hitchhiking fairies flying forward in our seats. Aiden looked behind him, mesmerised by a sixteen-foot rock towering above the tree line. It was shaped like a Shiva lingam, the tantric Indian word for 'phallus'. It stood larger than life, beaming straight into the Heavens. With one glance, we mutually decided that this towering rock was worth a brief excursion. We got out of the car and scurried down the steep terrain to where the lingam rock overlooked the simple homes nestled into the surrounding hillside. Its presence was undeniably powerful.

When we reached the base of the erect stone, we discovered a large curvaceous rock in the sensual shape of a yoni anchored right next to it. Like Stonehenge or the Giza pyramids, they appeared to be placed there by some invisible force of nature. I put my hand on the yoni rock and sensed an aliveness that pulsated in synch with my womb. Likened to the most impressive tantric sites in India that paid homage to the Divine Masculine God, Shiva, and Divine Feminine Goddess, Shakti, this site was just as potent and alive. Quite naturally, Aiden and I calmed our excitement and grounded into empty presence to listen. This time, it was my turn to stay grounded while Aiden attuned to the Akash and opened up to the records connected to these ancient stone temples.

'Hmmm, I'm picking up on an extremely dark energy,' Aiden said with curiosity and surprise. With eyes closed and furrowed brow he continued to share, 'I feel the volatile oppression of women steeped in a long history of moral, religious, political and patriarchal domination. Not long ago, the men of the neighbouring village misused their energy against the women of the village. Rape, abuse, enslavement, desecration took place at an overwhelming magnitude that is unbearable for me to fully comprehend or feel in this moment. All I know is that the men's primary sense of 'duty' was to violate the women as a means to dominate, oppress and overpower them. The patriarchal energy still overlays this village and I'm sure many places in this world, like a heavy cloud of darkness. It keeps the people stuck in a kind of unspoken shame where they remain victims of unspeakable crimes passed on generation after generation. Although this energy is quite heavy, it is also very ready to be shifted. Shall we give it a go, Bella?'

He stopped with an expression of pain that made his eyes squint up towards his forehead. Then he took a deep breath, relaxed his furrowed brow and turned to face me. 'Ambe´, will you join me in clearing these timelines of sexual misery from this valley?'

'Yes, of course,' I said as my heart leaped into service. I reflected on the insidious erosion of body, mind and soul through sexual trauma, inequality and domination embedded within the various cultures and countries of the world. I wondered for how long men, women and children have been bullied into giving their sexual power over in exchange for their illusive safety, survival and belonging. We are only just waking up from thousands of years of unfathomable human, child, animal and environmental domination and abuse. These transgressions need to be brought into accountability and healed as they violate the fundamental right for each and every being to exist as sovereign and free.

'I am as ready as I'll ever be,' I said to Aiden while taking a moment to ground my energy, clear my chakras and call upon the Council of Light to assist us in this clearing. I then consciously connected with the feeling of being whole, empowered and strong, while standing in the fullness of my divine sovereign presence. I was more than ready to take a stand for all women, and all sentient beings throughout all lands, cultures and ethnicities.

Aiden stood next to me and reached for my hand. Together, we came into a frequency of fierce love and compassion while comprehending that this traumatic history was still alive inside the both us, as shadows lingering upon the timelines of our soul. I went on to offer this decree.

'I call upon the energies of the Christos Sophia, Solar Feminine and Solar Masculine to assist us in cleansing and clearing all violations and transgressions between man, woman and child. May all patterns and realities of injustice, conflict, war, scarcity, persecution, torture, rape along with all hurt, sorrow, pain and tragedy, misuse of power, lies, deception, and issues of control be cleared from all layers and dimensions of myself, Aiden and the memory of this land, its peoples and energetic field and throughout all timelines, spaces and dimensions. May all transgressions and crimes on humanity be released and returned to their source of origin once and for all. And may this miasma of misuse of power and will be transmuted completely and healed to completion now.

'May we come to forgive our self and each other for every trespass and violation that has ever caused harm to our self or another. May we come to take full responsibility for all of our choices, actions and creations. May we call into balance the conscious harmonious union of the Divine Masculine and Divine Feminine. May we trust our innate innocence as our greatest power and come to know mutual respect, honour and dignity as the highest expressions of love. May each and every being – man, woman and child– tap into their innate wholeness and awakened compassion to live in reverence for the sanctity of each and every life form. *So be it* and *so it is!*'

We silently held the energetic field for several moments while observing the collective pain body of the neighbouring village magically vaporise like a heavy fog being lifted from the valley and merge with the clear blue sky. The air brightened as we each recognised our painful history and cellular memories of abuse and oppression loosening its grip. When we sensed the energetic completion, we turned to each other and brought our lips together in a most tender and sweet kiss. Our mouths lingered upon the other's as if they held their own sacred prayer. In that sensual kiss, my heart expanded into a burst of gratitude that included the surrounding land and all the beings that inhabited it.

Waves upon waves of nectarous warmth coursed through my body. Like a magical love elixir, the more time I shared with Aiden, the more he got under my skin. As I vibrated in this powerful bloom of evolutionary love, I had to remind myself, once again, of the request Aiden had made back at the Rainbow Gathering as he drew me close into his chest. 'Now, try not to take this too personally,' he said, pulling me ever so closer so that our hearts pressed together and pounded as one. Admittedly, his request was becoming increasingly challenging to manage. I couldn't help but to be delighted to have found a kindred companion to love, serve and remember with. Being in his presence seemed to activate and quicken the best parts of me. And yet a dark, unnamable shadow continued to hover around me, threatening to pounce and put out my sparkle. I felt bewildered as to why I would attract someone I resonated so fully with while simultaneously he was unavailable to reciprocate. What I had failed to fully comprehend at that time was that Aiden may have been the catalyst, but he was not the maker of these ecstatic feelings – I was.

While Aiden headed back to the car, I remained at the site just long enough to give myself a laser coaching session. *Ambe´ darlin', do your best not to make romantic spinoffs out of the spark of love that's growing inside of you. You must learn to harness this fire!* I knew that there would come a time, with the right person, that my fire would be celebrated and welcomed. For now, I was being tested not to 'make something' out of my experience because as soon as I did, I would begin to kill it off, and that was the absolute last thing I wanted to do.

As we settled back into the car, our exhaustion and overwhelm became more apparent than ever. We needed replenishment, and we needed it quick. Our happy traveler moods began to shift into cranky irritability mixed with severe dehydration. In the silence between us, I sensed that Aiden was picking up on my growing amorous feelings for him, especially after our kiss. I could sense his growing agitation along with an increasing edge of irritability. Maybe he felt pressured. I could understand. I looked at him warmly and he met my eyes with an icy cold response. And then, it happened. We hit a land mine, and without any warning whatsoever, he quite unexpectedly blurted out, 'Oh, no no no. Don't you try that womanly magic stuff on me, lady!'

My heart instantly nose-dived into the pit of my belly. *Uh-oh*, I thought. *Lady? Was I just some random lady in his eyes?* We were now entering the dangerous and murky waters of our own unconscious man-woman relationship wounds, which typically erupt as the dance of intimacy deepens. *Here we go. Fasten your seatbelt*, I said to myself, apprehending what might come next. My inner child felt shattered. Her vulnerable openness had been painfully misunderstood and met by callous cynicism and blatant mistrust.

For the next ten kilometres, the car was silent and the tension between us escalated into a simmering heat. My warm, tingly feeling shifted into a hollow ache that grew like a pesky tumour in the centre of my heart. With every kilometre, my throat swelled larger and the base of my spine began to throb with painful, raw heat.

Suddenly, I burst out in a strong yet wobbly voice, 'I am not that womanly magic stuff! I am me! I am a woman who feels from the depths of her heart and cherishes the precious gift of getting to share it with another...with you. So you can take back your wounded projections that only serve to stereotype and condemn me to some impenetrable place outside of your heart! I have the right to feel what I feel, regardless if it coincides with your feelings!'

I took a shaky breath. The toad in my throat was shrinking, but I had more to say. 'The truth is, Aiden, I am experiencing an undeniable attraction to you that feels to go back lifetimes. I don't feel the need to reduce our meeting to some arbitrary coincidence. In my mind, it's a miracle that I met you, so why bereave me for genuinely feeling moved to explore and grow our connection? We clearly have a soul contract to come together for a deep and transformative reason. Otherwise, we wouldn't be here together now!'

All I got back was a deafening silence, so I continued on with my rant, 'The last thing I want to create is more of the old man-woman story. Been there, done that! I want to explore a kind of love that takes full responsibility for one's experience and feels safe enough to listen to your deep heart and safely witness your pain. One that let's me in to feel your experience while I make sure that I am nothing like the past that hurt you. Allow me to show you how safe and honoured you can be in my presence, and let me help erase the pain and the hardship through modeling something new. I believe that the best use of being together is to practice loving ourselves and one another more than our violent human past ever did!' I said, disbelieving the boldness of my words as they came spilling out of my heart.

I took a long deep breath, as I was aware that my rant was more likened to a declaration for the Beloved, the Masculine part of me that I had neglected for so long. 'I am committed to creating a brand new kind of man woman relationship, one that reflects kindness, authenticity, transparency and deep mutual respect – one that shares a passion for service, justice, peace and enlivening the world with our shared heart flame. This larger love requires a willingness to be open and bare our wounds as the Divine's way of getting in and saying, 'This too is love. It's all love!"

I came back to focusing on Aiden and continued, 'Even though I'm unclear as to what our soul contract is really about, my heart knows to honour our connection as the powerful medicine that it is, not just for us, but for the greater healing of the Divine Feminine and Masculine in all. So this is why I am choosing to fully show up here and make the most of the moments we have.'

Relieved for speaking my deep heart, coupled with the feeling of overwhelming vulnerability, I looked at Aiden and awaited his response.

He took a deep breath, puffed up his cheeks and blew out the air in a long exasperated sigh that essentially communicated he was not really up to exposing any more of himself to me. I could sense that he heard me, but he was very reluctant to soften and share his whole truth. 'Honestly, I have a deep mistrust for women in general.'

We were caught in the shadows of intimacy, where any grasping or projecting onto the other only served to aggravate the scars of old relationship wounds. Radical honesty and heart-centred communication was our only way out of our emotional grid lock.

In that moment, we had a choice. We could stay open or close our hearts down. I chose to keep my heart open while the schism between us seemed to grow from a crack to a canyon.

Aiden let out yet another long deep sigh and said, 'In truth, I feel pressured by the vision you had before meeting me. I don't want to play a part in fulfilling you're so called, 'prophetic vision', no matter how real it is for you.'

'My vision?' I was surprised. I had only casually spoken to him the night before about what Jahrusha had predicted about our prophetic meeting. Suddenly, I got it. Naturally, he didn't like being cast in a role in my 'movie'. In fact, he hadn't necessarily even agreed to play a part in it. In essence, this was his way of letting me know that he felt that I was 'projecting' on him and this was not serving to cultivate openness and trust between us. *Fair enough!* I thought, aware that our two versions of reality had collided midair. Was this so-called projection going both ways?

From the moment we met, I was extremely conscientious not to 'overlay' my vision or version of reality onto him. I had foreseen that this misunderstanding could interfere with the higher purpose of our coming together. Aiden couldn't help but oscillate between drawing me in closer and then pushing me away. We were living in the shadows casted by our own fears of intimacy that led us to painfully withdraw from one another.

'I get it!' I said empathetically. 'I can understand your trepidation about being cast as yet another woman's Prince Charming in order to fulfil her fairytale fantasy of happily ever after,' I said, even though I knew our dynamic was more about being vulnerable and our capacity to open to love in present time.

Honestly, we were ensnarled in a sticky web that had managed to entangle itself over countless lifetimes. I sat there, baffled by the biggest irony of all. How was it that Aiden could proclaim to be in service to healing the wounded Feminine while simultaneously be so reluctant to open up and look beyond the surface of his own wounded Masculine? I was now discovering that when it came down to addressing his up close and personal stuff, I would be met with a stingy resistance. How would we ever grow beyond our past without the mutual willingness to expose what lies beneath the surface of our protective and defensive layers?

I looked at Aiden intently and saw that he was attempting to hold back his tears. I wanted to reach out and hold his hand, but instead, I held back and said, 'I'm truly sorry for whatever I did to you to fracture your trust in the Feminine.'

I swallowed back my tears and stepped into his shoes. *No wonder he did not trust women.* I imagined him being the receptacle of countless women seducing him in order to fulfil their selfish desires and agendas. This underhanded manipulation was not love. It served only to highlight their lack of integrity and wholeness. The brothers were not the only ones affected by this version of misguided 'love'. The sacred sisterhood is only now recovering. We are rising out of a long painful history of mistrust, petty competition and undermining one another for personal gain. I know, I only just experienced these ancient wounds with Eva. I silently pondered my part in the making of 'her story' and inwardly asked myself, *Where, why and when did I split off from my source of love and power?*

I turned to Aiden and chose to be fully transparent. 'Aiden, I acknowledge how painful it is to be deceived by someone you trust and love. This is not the woman I am or choose to be. I am learning that the source of my love, wholeness and fulfilment is found within me. I know beyond all else that anything I am looking at is equal to what I am standing in!' I drifted off for a moment and imagined a world that loved from a whole and complete place rather than pursuing something that felt to be missing from within.

I reached out to give Aiden's hand a squeeze. The last thing I desired was for Aiden to close himself off to our connection because I was laying some kind of 'womanly trip' on him. I felt caught in some kind of cosmic riddle and spiritual conundrum. *How was I to be honest and honour my own authentic feelings for Aiden without involving him in some way?* The terrain was slippery to navigate, likened to the sludge I traversed back at the Big Green festival when I had to do everything in my power not to get sucked into the muddy abyss or fall flat on my face. I had owned my part and that was all I could do at the time.

By the time we pulled into Rennes Le Chateau, Aiden and I were inflamed with emotion and both virtually in tears. The energy was encapsulated in a chasm so deep, it was like being trapped at the bottom of the Grand Canyon with no apparent way out. We were at a stalemate. Even with my empathic overtures to find a common ground, the air was thick with an aura of unresolved emotional pain. How did we manage to lose the magic of our day and the preciousness of the moment together? I felt a cold rejection wash through my bones, alluring me to retreat into my safe cocoon where I could isolate. Thank heavens, I was able to stay fully present in my body and trust that all was unfolding according to our highest soul growth and evolution.

I was well aware that at the root of all relationship 'problems' lives the seed of one's unconscious, unresolved, separation from Source. Furthermore, every relationship plays a pre-determined role to trigger and mirror back to us the disowned and judged parts of our Self that were created to conceal our most fragile of childhood wounds. Until we are each willing to embrace our own shadow and all that was once outcast within oneself, we will continue to project and blame the 'other' for not fulfilling what is crying out to be loved within us.

Even though some grown-up part of me recognised the higher truth that permeated the space between us, I could not find the words at the time to express it. The wounded child in me remained frozen in time and felt powerless to change my dynamic with Aiden. All that was left for me to do was to love myself more while continuing to examine my relationship to the wounded Masculine and Feminine that resided within me.

When we arrived at the church, the sun was setting in bright pink, orange and violet over the beautiful green valley of Rennes La Chateau. Many believe that the church sat upon an ancient Isis temple and that Mary Magdalene was buried there, along with the relics of Christ. In the distance, I could see Mount Bugarach, the sacred mountain of this mysterious Languedoc Valley. The mountain called out to me as if it longed to be reunited with my soul. I silently vowed to return to her soon.

We sat on a stone ledge that looked out upon the Languedoc Valley and surrounding mountains. I took a moment to breathe into my constricted heart while drinking in the magnificent surroundings. I scanned my memories for the original tear of sacred trust between man and woman. Images of rape, torture and abuse flashed through my mind from all the times my spirit had been persecuted by the patriarchy. Over countless lifetimes of being broken down, my covenant with my Divine Beloved was transferred onto 'man' who, over time, usurped the power to fulfil my longing for wholeness. Like countless women, we were taught to acquiesce and give over our power in order to survive. This was an unnatural program where the Masculine was now cast as protector and destroyer, rapist and redeemer, keeper and betrayer. Over time, I had been pressured and conditioned by family, culture and society that securing a man's love was the greatest attainment there was for a woman. *Not!*

I then took my time to feel into the special love that Mary and Yeshua had for one another. It was a love rooted in respect, sovereignty and sacred mutuality. They cherished one another as God and Goddess, while fully embracing their humanity and serving something larger than their privatised relationship. I prayed to Mary for an answer to what love would do now.

In that moment, I glimpsed the deeper alchemy of Yeshua and Magdalene's sacred contract to be with one another. They had come together to forge a pathway of Sacred Union through the tender human pathways of intimate relationship. In time, their love would serve as an evolutionary template for all beings to aspire to.

I sensed Aiden and my potential to do the same, to cast off the demons of our wounded past so that we might glimpse a higher love on behalf of all beings. I brought my attention back to the painful reality of the moment. I looked over to Aiden, who was sitting on the edge of the cobblestone wall perched high above the steep valley below. I could feel the frustration steaming off his pain body. His energy body remained cool and aloof and the temptation to polarise was intensely present. In that moment, I chose to stand in *his* shoes and widen my empathy and compassion instead of closing and shutting down.

I walked over to Aiden and looked straight into his distraught, crystal blue eyes. I stretched my heart open to feel what he was feeling. I could barely speak and yet mustered the strength and courage to share these words.

'On behalf of myself and all women, I wish to apologise for ever believing that you or the Masculine are the source of completing me. Please forgive me for ever physically, emotionally or energetically disrespecting your sovereignty and freedom. I now call back all energy that has ever been projected upon you and all that has been out of alignment with the Divine law of Love, Sovereignty and Oneness.' I took a moment to offer the Feminine the same prayer. 'So be it and so it is!'

Aiden sat there, soaking in my words in a long and silent pause. Based on the energy substantially lightening between us, I felt my apologetic decree had landed in some place deep inside of him. 'Thank you, Bella. I'm starving. Shall we go have some dinner?'

It's true the heart of man lies in his stomach and with that, we bid the day's sun goodbye and walked over to Rennes la Chateau's enchanting garden restaurant. It was lit with twinkly lights that hung from the branches of the surrounding trees. The pink, blue and golden twilight sky magnified the undeniable warmth and beauty of the French countryside. I continued to gaze out at the mountain as if they held the answer to all that remained hidden and disheartening. Aiden and I grappled with releasing the tension between us so that we could absorb the beauty of our surroundings and open to the gift of enjoying our precious time together.

After several awkward moments of silence, Aiden finally gave in and chivalrously suggested, 'Why don't we set down our weapons for the evening and enjoy our salads and wine?'

Feeling more like a peacekeeper than a soldier, I let out a deep sigh, nodded in agreement and offered him a warm smile. With each bite of my delicately dressed *Nicoise* salad and freshly baked bread dripping in olive oil, I gave myself over to gratitude for the simple and sensual pleasures that began to soften our constricted hearts. The presence of Mary Magdalene wafted in the warm breeze as if to say, *'Lighten up, beloveds. Allow your pleasure to serve as a healing balm to your troublesome hearts. After all, pleasure is the Divine's most direct way of opening up a stubborn heart.'*

I found comfort in the knowing that we were dining in a sacred site, dedicated to the champions of unconditional love. For now, the closest we would get to that love was to call a truce and remain open to one another even when every other part of our being wanted to find safety in closing. I marveled at our dynamic tension with a mixture of wonder, despair, and admiration. I was strengthening my commitment to stay in the fire of love whether it presents in shadow or in light.

CHAPTER TWENTY-ONE

THE LIGHT HOUSE

The Grail, or chalice that is kept in the Grail castle, represents the open heart and the state of union with God. The Grail represents the Feminine principle, and the body, or 'golden bowl' that is the container for God's love. You, the Parsifal's of your own time, must find the chalice. Open your hearts and purify them. Confront the demons that lurk in the shadows. Know yourselves. This is the way to unity with each other and the world. Awaken the compassionate man who sleeps at the heart of the Feminine world. This is the power of the chalice. The chalice is within.

– Niamh Clune, *The Coming of the Feminine Christ*

Sovereignty is about fully inhabiting oneself so that we may know our place within the whole. Sovereignty allows more focused light to move through you unhindered, without the blur or muddiness of other thought forms that are not coherently aligned with your own truth based on social/culture constructs and other people's beliefs and agendas influencing you. You stand as the quintessential truth of your own unique being, the fullness of your potential realised, from which you can give your presence that much more coherently in the world. You do not isolate from this world when you become sovereign, you co-create with this world that much more effectively as a prism of your own divine presence functioning within the whole, governed by your unconditional love that needs nothing from anyone else and truly operates from selflessness.

– Amoraea

By the time we finished our supper, it was well after eight and we were physically and emotionally exhausted from our full-blown day. We drove on to Limoux, where Aiden's friend Gaianna had converted her home to a centre for healing. When we arrived, the house was full of spiritual travelers. Aiden and I sat quietly, observing the heated conversation before we introduced ourselves to the group. As I listened to the opinionated banter around clanking glasses, I recognised the tendency for pilgrims to seek the Grail as if it was an object, hidden in some part of history, that dwells in the past. *The ancients may have left us clues, but the keys to our quest are embedded in our everyday lives — the ultimate mystery school that initiates us into discovering that which we seek is hiding in plain sight.*

Upon meeting Gaianna, I discovered that we came from the same town in Marin County, which was known for its health-conscious, spiritual and eclectic yoga culture. Gaianna had a regal air about her. She was tall and wore her hair in two long silvery-white braids that cascaded over her delicate shoulders. Dressed in natural, white flowing clothing, her blue eyes sparkled with the light of a living Goddess. There was no doubt that she was the living embodiment of a modern-day Grail priestess. I was extremely grateful to be in the presence of a friend who was both a wise elder and a kindred companion of the Grail mysteries.

By the time we got settled into La Maison Lumiere, I was beyond exhausted. I politely excused myself, showered and then put myself to bed on a futon in the reading room upstairs. Tomorrow was a new day and I was looking forward to having a fresh start. Aiden went to bed in the adjacent room that was more like a loft overlooking the living room. That night, my mind was restless as it reeled through endless possibilities and sought answers to impossible questions. I lay in bed as question after question crashed down like waves upon my restless heart. Multiple stories of the Beloved unraveled from the archives of my soul.

Which one was fantasy? Which one could I trust? Which one would lead me to the Grail? Which one was my death, which one my rebirth? Which one was I to follow? Which truth was large enough to transcend and include all of it?

The following morning, I discovered that Aiden had spent the night tossing and turning with a high fever that burned like a wildfire. I spent the day looking after him. With a joyous heart, I gave him a massage, rebalanced his chakras, made him some yummy soup and helped to nurture him back to health in the best way I knew how. I was happy to look after him. It came naturally to me and I enjoyed a dose of domestic bliss. In his physically weak state, his heart had softened and he did not resist my nurturing presence. I recollected a story I once read, in which Yeshua and Magdalene served one another to clear the demons of illusion entwined within each of the seven chakras, also known as the seven seals. I strongly felt that Aiden and I were brought together to serve in a simular way – to clear the karmic knots and liberate the ancient wounds ready to be forgiven, transmuted and released from our body temples.

Even though Aiden admitted to feeling some relief, I rarely saw him over the next couple of days. His fever burned all through the following day and night while his rage and resentment only intensified. His symptoms grew worse as he continued to blame 'women' and 'the messed up world' for his condition. Not fully comprehending the deep reasons behind his cold aloofness, I surmised that the best way to serve him was by respecting the space he required in order to recover. I did my best to bypass the sensation that his anger and blame was silently being projected onto me.

While Aiden remained hidden away in his loft/cave, I occupied myself with yoga, prayers, journal writing, meditation and long walks in the neighboring forest. My nights were restless. I fell asleep replaying the spiritual visions I received from my journey back at Gaia's Grove as well as the messages from my vision council with Jahrusha. I sought a sudden epiphany that would magically set me free from the unresolvable riddle of my womanly predicament. On top of everything else, the high frequencies of this Magdalene land were activating memories of something set into motion from a parallel lifetime. Whatever it was, it encouraged me to stay present with the process and trust that I was being lead to an unforeseen treasure.

On the third night, I lay in bed and went into a deep meditation where symbols of Heiros Gamos flooded my consciousness. I saw majestic mountains, planetary birthing, Starseed babies, golden dolphins, crystalline DNA, star tetrahedrons, rainbow diamond light grids, new paradigms of love and a white sacred dove perched upon the screen of my mind's eye. Divine Mother, Divine Father, Divine Child, Divine Lover, the Sacred Marriage, a golden chalice and a most majestic, winged white horse flooded my consciousness. I was bathed in Divine Mother's Love, that same rarified frequency that enveloped me back at Gaia's Grove. I knew deep down that these symbols encoded within my crystalline DNA and seeded within my psyche had been poised to awaken for this exact timeline in my life. If I could learn to trust and remain open, these experiences would imminently guide me home to my soul's deepest calling. I fell asleep with a prayer in my heart. *Dear Father Mother God, as I awaken and evolve, may I be a living embodiment and example of conscious love to all those around me, opposite to the traumatic memories that I may hold in my cellular body. And when anyone is triggered by what I seem to represent, may they experience the most conscious example of compassion, tolerance and respect so as to heal the past and open the way for a Love large enough to embrace it all. So be it and so it is!*

Three tumultuous evenings had passed before Aiden reappeared for breakfast looking rather disheveled, weak and full of self-pity. I noticed that he continued to be closed and guarded towards me. I held my centre, all the while knowing that Aiden and I were not complete with the sacred contract that brought our souls together in the first place. The compelling option of renting a car and setting out on my own lingered in the back of my mind. My escape plan helped me to hold my ground and give Aiden the space to choose his path and direction without interfering or influencing him. I watched him curiously as he gobbled down his bowl of muesli and glass of OJ – as if each bite might magically reveal the answers to our unending questions. As we ate in an eerie silence, I was grateful for the occasional glance that reminded me of an enduring bond strong enough to endure all of our present confusion.

Finally, I mustered up the courage to ask him the only relevant question. 'I will be leaving in a few days, Aiden. I would like to know if you will you be travelling on with me so that I can make my necessary arrangements.'

Aiden gazed deeply into the bottom of his cereal bowl as if to retrieve the answer to my question. After what felt like an eternity, he lifted his head and with his piercing blue eyes, looked deeply into mine and said, 'We've only just begun, dear Bella.' He coughed like he was trying to get a little more breath into his restricted lungs and then offered me a ghost of a smile.

I said nothing, only smiled inside. My heart grew brighter in the knowing that we still had time to fulfil our sacred contract together.

CHAPTER TWENTY-TWO

FALLING SLOWLY

The soul speaks in symbols. Its quiet call out of the darkness needs to be heard. But it can only be heard with our hearts. The heart translates the language of symbols. The heart feels their meaning. If the language of symbols is not heard with the heart, the images expressed by the Soul remain as lifeless things, and their power to transform us is lost. The soul's life then passes unnoticed back into the world of shadows.

– Author unknown

Everybody wants to let go. But how do you let go if you don't hold things, if you don't touch things in full consciousness, with a totally open heart? In Tantra, the first thing is having the experience of touch, of profound contact with things, with the universe without mental commotion. Everything begins there: touching the universe deeply. If you let go before touching deeply, that can bring on severe mental turmoil. Many beginning yogis make this mistake. They let go before taking hold. They lose contact with reality. The heart is never opened. They enter into a sterile void and remain imprisoned there. When you touch deeply, you no longer need to let go. That occurs naturally. The world is passed through in full consciousness. There is no other way, not a single detour or shortcut. When you hold something with all your consciousness, like the newborn that grabs your finger, it is enough to open your hand. Why is it that the newborn has so much strength? Because his whole being takes part in the movement that results in seizing your finger. In this instant, he is so strong that you are in his power. Tantrism is agreeing to live out this power.

– Daniel Odier, *Tantric Quest*

Gaianna and I had the pleasure of getting to know one another during the last few days of my stay at La Maison Lumiere. While residing in her guest room/library, I came across a book that magically leapt off the bookshelf into my arms called, *Anna, Grandmother of Jesus* by Claire Heartsong. The book is a living record of the story of Mary Magdalene and Yeshua's relationship and family of Christ as told by Yeshua's beloved grandmother, Anna. It gave a vital account of the alchemical initiations and personal life stories of Yeshua and Mary according to the intimate recollection, recounted by Mother Mary's birth mother, Anna. This book was clearly an invaluable roadmap for my journey ahead and so I asked Gaianna if she would mind lending it to me.

'Oh yes, beloved, this is a must read for the road ahead. Here, take it as my gift to you. The only condition is that you must pass it on to just the right person,' she said, pressing the book to her heart before placing it in my hands.

It was now one day after I had agreed to return to the Rainbow Gathering to pick up Eva. Unfortunately, I had also agreed to drive her to Barcelona so she could catch her flight back to the U.S. I felt enormous resistance to part ways with Aiden while there was still a great deal of unresolved energy that lingered between us. After all, I hadn't travelled over countless lifetimes to find him, just so I could leave him because I promised my friend a lift to the airport. Or did I?

Aiden and I acknowledged that we had been brought together for a reason...a reason that was yet to be revealed. We knew whatever it was, it would take us far beyond what we could possibly foresee in the present moment. We decided to trust the process and surrender to this mutual higher calling. Reluctantly, Aiden agreed to give me a ride back to the gathering to reunite with Eva and chauffeur her to Barcelona as promised. Little did I know at the time the vast distance I would have to travel before I would be back by Aiden's side once again.

After breakfast, we drove across the Pyrenees mountain range. Aiden broke the silence by clearing his throat with a firm yet shaky voice and said, 'Can we keep the conversation light for the duration of the ride? I still feel a little weak and want to conserve my energy.'

I swallowed back my umpteen questions and sheepishly acquiesced. Our ride together was pleasant enough. We munched on the juiciest, freshly picked plums as we retraced our way back through the green winding roads. Eventually we pulled into the lower parking lot of the Rainbow Gathering. As I got out of the car, I thanked Aiden for the potent beauty of our shared time together and wished him ease and grace in his continued recovery.

'So you are going to drop Eva off in Barcelona, then drive all the way back to Gaianna's in three days. Right?' he questioned. Neither of us could disguise the vulnerability that was coming up for the both of us.

'Yes, and when I return we'll get to travel on together and visit some of the sacred Magdalene sights in the surrounding area. I'm super exited to visit the mountain with you. So feel better soon. We have a journey ahead of us, dear one.' My words tapered off towards the end of my sentence.

I could hardly say goodbye, let alone breathe. 'See you in a few days, Aiden. I'll return as quickly as I possibly can.' I clearly had no clue as to how long this 450-mile round trip would actually take me. My stomach ached. Perhaps it was because my heart had sunk to the bottom of my belly. I couldn't help but feel that I was going in the opposite direction from where I was truly meant to be.

I sensed that Aiden was just as shaken by my abrupt departure as I was. The whole timing of this poorly timed interlude felt like a massive test. In letting go, we were forced to trust that all that needed to transpire between us was in fate's hands, both together – and apart.

To top that off, I was scheduled to meet up with my ex-partner, Murray, in England in ten days! This meant that after the drive to Barcelona and back, Aiden and I would have less than a full week to fulfil our destiny appointment together. As usual, I had no other choice than to let go and allow the greater plan to unfold.

When I returned to the camp where our tent had been pitched, everything looked dirty and discombobulated. Tomas and Eva were nowhere in sight, so I hiked to the upper camp where we had first met Sparrow. Sure enough, when I arrived, they were all hanging out around the fire, sipping chai and chatting away. It was quite a wildly domestic scene. Eva had that tussled, fresh-out-of-bed look that oozed a womanly shine from every pore of her being, as if to say, 'It's true, I've been loved opened by God – body, heart and soul! *Roarr!*'

'Ambe´!' Eva was so happy to see me and leapt into my arms.

'So what are you up to?' I asked, secretly hoping she was ready to pack up and go immediately!

'Well,' she replied, 'I'm having the best time ever! Tonight, there is a ceremony on the other ridge. Tomas and I have already decided to stay and attend it.' She grabbed my hand. 'You must come too, Ambe´! You are so meant to be there with us.'

I felt her resistance pulling on my energy, but my focus was fixed. It had dawned on me that Barcelona was a full two-day drive, and we would need to stop over and sleep somewhere to break up the long ride.

'Look, Eva, I really need to get back to Aiden as soon as possible. You and I had an agreement that I'd pick you up yesterday. Please, honey, we need to set off for Barcelona right away.'

She stood there looking dumbfounded. This meant she would have to part ways with her lover sooner than later. We were *both* being tested to let go, big time!

At last, after some strong persuasion, Eva agreed to leave with me that day. While Tomas would go on his own way to procure special paint pigments at a nearby village. Eva went on to offer Sparrow a long-drawn-out goodbye kiss. Luckily, he would be meeting up with her in America in less than a month. I helped her pack up and we set out in the late afternoon, taking the pine needles and musky smell of the campfire along for the ride.

CHAPTER TWENTY-THREE

BARCELONA OR BUST

As you know, you are living inside of a dream, a hologram, and a reality that comes from your own expectations, your own cultural beliefs. For a long time, you have been programmed that it is the only reality that exists. The program took you into so much separation on the outside, but also so much separation within yourself. Now is the time to harness all that you have learned in this lifetime, and all other lifetimes. Use that awareness and power within yourself to open a new consciousness that has not been on this planet for thousands of years, a way of living through freedom... You know how to do this... It will happen naturally, for you are nature. Just don't resist, and stay awake in the dream.

– Author Unknown

What the caterpillar calls the end of the world the master calls a butterfly.

– Richard Bach

With the help of an unfolded map that took up half of our front seat, Eva and I managed to navigate our way out of France into the neighbouring country of Spain. I was extremely anxious and found it challenging to be fully present with her. Everything inside of me screamed out that I was going in the wrong direction and I felt utterly powerless to change it. *I have just travelled miles upon miles to meet the most profound soul mirror of my life and now I'm driving away from him. I must be totally insane! If I am the source of my power and love, why do I feel so bloody out of control?*

Eva and I decided to break up the drive by stopping in Cadeques. This was the famous coastal village where Salvador Dali once lived and where Tomas had taken his visionary art course. It made sense, according to our map, that indicated that Cadeques was just a small detour from the direct route to Barcelona. Needless to say, by the time we navigated our way through the winding mountainous roads that hugged the coastline, we had taken a five-hour diversion. Not to mention the traffic accident that held us up an additional two hours, just as we were approaching the town. I tried to stay calm and composed and not drive us off a cliff, just like in the movie, *Thelma and Louise*. However, the more I attempted to keep my cool, the more an undeniable pressure built up, threatening to erupt and spew hot lava all over Eva, the car and my entire reality.

At last, the accident cleared up, traffic moved on, and we pulled into the little seaside town a little after 11pm. We proceeded to drive in circles, looking for a room to stay for the night. After several attempts to locate an affordable vacancy in this high-class tourist destination, we spotted an arrow with a picture of a tent that pointed to a campground. With great hope, we zoomed up the steep hill while mustering our last little bit of energy, knowing we still had to set up our tent.

An elderly Spanish man sat on a stool in front of a small office. A sea of neatly parked recreational vehicles loomed behind his frail body. He took long puffs off his hand-rolled cigarette and then a long swig out of a wine bottle. 'Hola,' he sang out in a drunken swagger. It didn't take long to discover that he didn't speak a word of English. I managed to mime to him that we wanted a space to camp for the night. He nodded to me with his large, toothless smile and pointed us to drive to the last row of campers, caravans and tents.

At around midnight, our tiny green tent was set up, nestled in a tiny corner of pavement backed up into a cement wall. We laid our sleeping bags out along with our withering bodies and crawled into our tent. We both let out a pleasurable sigh of gratitude and relief to have finally found a place to lie our weary bones down for the night.

Within five minutes, Eva was asleep. I could tell by her purr at the end of her exhale. While I, like a deer in the headlights, lay there with my eyes wide open, staring blankly at the stitching on the ceiling of our tent. My heart wouldn't stop racing and it took me over an hour to calm myself down enough to sleep. Just as I was about to nod off, a huge burst of torrential rain came pouring down. The campground was getting soaked and so was our luggage, which we had tucked neatly against the concrete wall outside. Eva lay motionless as the rain hammered down, making thunderous sounds on the roof. With a grunt of frustration, I wriggled out of my sleeping bag and squirmed out of the tent to throw our soaked luggage into the trunk of the rental car. My thunderous heart was pounding in my chest from the sudden rush of adrenaline and getting soaked by the torrential downpour of cool rain.

I bolted back into the tent, dripping wet from head to toe. I had to strip down to my cold, wet skin and dry myself off with Eva's hoodie. As I inched my way back inside my sleeping bag, all I could feel was my heart thumping with intense ferocity. It felt like it was going to leap right out of my chest and wake Eva up.

My mind recollected vignettes of all that had just transpired between Aiden and I throughout our time together in the French Pyrenees. Then it struck me, like the lightning that was presently breaking open the sky. *Oh, my goodness! Am I in love with this dangerously dazzling, cosmically complex, mysteriously cool, irresistibly warm, enticingly charismatic, Christ-hearted companion from way down under?*

I took a deep breath as if to simultaneously console and congratulate myself all at once. *I am head over heels in love with a man I've only just met and yet feels to be a part of me for as long as my soul can remember!*

This confession brought me into a state of simultaneous shock, dread and awe. An overly rational voice reminded me that my love would not be reciprocated in full.

Rationalise all you want, I thought. *There is no escaping the madness of my bursting heart.* Nevertheless, I couldn't help but wonder what our last week together would hold for us. I tossed and turned along with the Spanish wind that blew through the trees, until at last, I drifted to sleep to the tune of the great poet Rumi.

Love is a madman,
working his wild schemes, tearing off his clothes,
running through the mountains, drinking poison,
and now quietly choosing annihilation.

The following morning, I got up with the sun and headed to the washing machines to put our soaked clothing into the public dryers. Eva was still sound asleep in the tent, but with my tumultuous heart, I couldn't sleep any longer. If I projected into the future with Aiden, I would surely go mad. I was already well on my way. I needed to find my centre. Being in full respect for Aiden's truth and sovereignty was paramount for me. I was wise enough to know at the time that love is not something to grab hold onto. Love is to be honoured and upheld as a gift rather than a 'something' or 'someone' to be possessed.

I resolved to stay calm and breathe deeply whenever possible. Being fully present in the here and now was the only way I was going to get through the next few days. The future would have to take care of itself. The realisation that I was in love with Aiden felt immature, dangerous, beautiful and confusing all at once. In truth, I had no inkling of what would unfold when I returned to La Maison Lumiere.

Best not to get your hopes up and expect him to welcome you home with a waterfall of warm kisses and declare you the love of his life. After all, the man is about to begin a whole new chapter of his life! Listen up, Ambe´, you must resist the urge to make these powerful feelings mean anything! Whatever love you are feeling for him, feel it, honour it and then let him go! I repeated this mantra over and over to myself to make extra sure I got the message in all of my womanly places.

Love is a madman because no matter what my head knew to be true, my heart would simply not listen. And as for my body, all that she knew was a warm, nectarous glow that nourished my being beyond all reason and rationale.

When Eva finally woke up, we decided to go for breakfast in this stylish seaside café that hugged the Spanish coastline. These days, it was visited by hundreds of fashionable weekend holidayers. In Cadeques, one lounged at outdoor seaside cafés next to super models and movie stars – the wannabe famous as well as the famous ones that are followed by the paparazzi working for European tabloid magazines.

After coffee, I wandered off to the outdoor marketplace while Eva went to call Sparrow. The seaside marche was lined with fresh fruit and vegetable stalls, clothing and more importantly, shoes galore! I purchased the first pair of comfortable walking shoes that I could find. Three stalls later, I bought a second pair, just in case I lost my first pair again. I also found a beautiful violet silk sarong and a flowing white goddess-like skirt. Nothing like a wardrobe upgrade to smooth out the singes of unrequited love.

Aware of the time, I retrieved our rental car and headed back to fetch Eva at the campsite. Gratefully, she was all packed and ready to roll. We headed back into the hills toward Barcelona, determined to make it with no further delays. Miraculously, I managed to drive us straight into the heart of Barcelona in a record speed of two hours and forty-five minutes. To top it off, I parked only minutes away from Café Organica, where Eva was to meet up with an old friend from the Bay Area and then head off to the airport the following morning.

Upon entering the restaurant, Eva and I grinned at one another as we heard the sound of ShimShai's voice singing over the sound system. His prophetic lyrics and melodic tones filled our hearts, reminding us of our original purpose for setting out on this journey together. 'Yehoshua, carry I along ... Miriam oh, ho, sing I thy song in a strange land.'

Once again, ShimShai was my beacon of golden light, always there to welcome me into the next unfolding chapter of this heart wrenching, roller coaster of a Grail ride.

Traverse this labyrinth and you will arrive at the source of the longest river, the source of the hidden waterfall. A wise and tender voice consoled the unsettled parts of me that were doing their best not to totally freak out.

Eva and I feasted on raw organic salad sprinkled with toasted sunflower seeds and dripping in tahini dressing. *Yum!* My native California taste buds were bursting in bliss. Organic salad to a girl from California is what fish 'n chips are to an Englishman or tapas, red wine and olives are to a Spaniard. I was proud and delighted to fill my plate with nature's finest raw grub. As I devoured my salad, I offered up a prayer. *Thank you, thank you, thank you, Great Mother, for helping us to arrive here in Barcelona safe and sound. You are so much more than any travel guidebook could ever be!*

After our deliciously nourishing lunch, Eva and I parted ways, still a little bruised by what had transpired, yet determined to stay open to the love that was larger than anything that could tear us apart. Both of us knew that on a soul level, we had served one another perfectly by playing the perfect roles to trigger and heal the unconscious wounds of our sacred sisterhood. We knew that our friendship would endure and that in some mysterious way, this shared experience had been a necessary initiation for the both of us. With our tender hearts racing, we silently acknowledged that our faerie-unicorn friendship could and would endure the bumps along the way and with time, all would be clarified for both of us.

'Who would have known that a couple of charismatic Aussie men would steal our hopelessly romantic hearts away?' Eva whispered in my ear as she hugged me goodbye. We shared one last giggle by the outrageous synchronicity.

It was way later on my journey that I became aware that my dynamic with Eva reflected the archetypal split of Lilith and Eve that festered deep within my psyche. It beckoned me to reconcile my pure heart with my primordial sexual nature. Our relationship also reminded me of another sisterly dynamic. One that *Anna, Grandmother of Jesus* describes in the relationship between Mariam and young Mary Magdalene, both cousins and closest confidants in the following passage:

> Mariam understood her cousin to be more like herself than anyone else that she knew. The essential difference between them was that young Mary did not hesitate when there was an opportunity to be an active reformer of the outer world, while Mariam preferred to invisibly harmonize discord on the inner planes.
>
> When Mary was ill, Mariam resolved...in time to support her cousin with every ounce of strength

she had. Young Mary found a loyal friend from whom she could open her aching heart. And so it was that these two began to truly know each other. They found solace by bringing healing balm to one another's broken hearts. However, there continued to be a barb of jealousy over their mutual love of Yeshua and their suppressed fantasy that he would someday choose one over the other in marriage. Although this thorn continued to test them through...their early years, they opened their hearts to each other as only soulmates can once they see through the veil of distrust.

Mariam discovered that her cousin's trials and dreams were just like her own. So these two bonded and healed as they emptied their hearts out to each other....

Both of these woman shared a growing sensitivity to the ways of spirit. They searched deep within themselves and found a profound, abiding love for the One God/Goddess.

They knew their purpose was to restore life to that which was dead within the minds, bodies, souls and outer institutions of mankind. Claiming the prize of self-mastery was the pearl of great price they both sought. Thus, embracing, balancing and unifying the polarities within themselves became the goal of these two young women, who found in each other a perfect mirror. They also knew that their lives were integrally entwined with their cousin, Yeshua. He became their constant guiding star and the mystery they both desired to unveil.

In future years, Young Mary would become Yeshua's beloved consort. Mariam, his adopted sister whom he called Mary Grace, continued to be his loyal friend and confidante.

– Claire Heartsong,
Anna, Grandmother of Jesus

I returned to my lucky parking place, accompanied by a tall takeaway cup of Yerba Mate tea. Eagerly, I headed north, out of the city, and soon discovered that getting out of this city was not as easy as getting into it. With my heart racing in anticipation to get back to Aiden, I spent the first hour getting lost in a seaside town, until I finally discovered I had just driven over thirty miles in the wrong direction! My love-struck heart pounded with a mixture of panic and excited anticipation.

I surrender! Thankfully, that was all it took to put me back on track and I resumed a steady 100 kilometres an hour until I was forced to slow down at the toll road. After over a hundred-dollars-worth of road tolls, I crossed the Spanish border and found myself in the now familiar territory of Perpignan, France. Perpignan was only two hours from La Maison Lumiere in Limoux. I made one brief stop for some fresh mangos, jasmine tea and dark chocolate as an offering for my return. My body ached, my heart yearned and my mind raced along with my rental car. Most significantly, my spirit braced herself for the inevitable ride of her life. *Vroom, vroom, vroom! There is no going back now.*

THE GUEST HOUSE

THE GUEST HOUSE

Being human is a guest house.
Every morning a new arrival.
A joy, a depression, a meanness,
some momentary awareness comes
As an unexpected visitor.
Welcome and entertain them all!
Even if they're a crowd of sorrows,
who violently sweep your house
empty of its furniture,
still treat each guest honourably.
He may be clearing you out
for some new delight.
The dark thought, the shame, the malice,
meet them at the door laughing,
and invite them in.
Be grateful for whoever comes,
because each has been sent
as a guide from beyond.

– Jelaluddin Rumi

The Feminine principle is the receptive. It is water, Soul, being, caring and feeling. It is that which gives meaning and value to things. Vulnerability is a truth. It is seen as weakness instead of strength. The Feminine principle is not ambitious. It is therefore seen as serving no useful purpose. The Feminine measures life by how it feels and how others feel. It experiences rather than analyses. It is the inner nurturer and would nourish us if we allowed it. We wound our Feminine by not listening to our feelings. We do not trust them. We rationalise or deny them completely. Our Feminine side is treated as if it were a silly goose.

– Niamh Clune, *The Coming of the Feminine Christ*

A combination of nervous and giddy describes how I felt when I pulled into the driveway of La Maison Lumiere. I had made it back to Aiden in just under sixteen hours. Honestly, I had no clue as to what I might find when I opened that car door. I sat in the driver's seat and took a moment to centre myself and muster up the courage to face my fatal attraction for better or for worse. But first, I gave my body a good stretch and shook out some of the road fatigue.

By the time I turned around, Aiden was at the top of the driveway wearing long khaki shorts, a black T-shirt and a warm welcoming smile. I felt empowered as I walked toward him but also a little raw and vulnerable. He held out his arms and my weary body melted into him. We walked back to the house together, mutually relieved that I had returned safely from my cross-country shuttle service to Barcelona.

Aiden brewed a pot of jasmine tea. I handed him the mangos and dark chocolate as a peace offering. While we relaxed, I shared with him a little about my journey and the beauty of Cadeques.

Oddly enough, his voice held an accusatory tone. 'I've had a strong fever for two days and I've hardly eaten or slept. I feel like I've literally been on my deathbed. I have never felt so ill in my life.'

I rushed in with deep compassion. 'Aiden, I'm truly sorry you are having such a rough go of it! I'd be glad to offer you some bodywork if that would help.'

Aiden shrugged weakly. 'Thanks. I'd love that.'

Over the course of the day, I gave him a long deep massage and energy body clearing. I made soup, changed his sheets, did laundry and other chores to be of service to him and Gaianna. It was a joy to be of service to the people I loved.

Aiden remained in his man cave for another two days. He came out for brief intervals to get food and water. During our sparse conversations, he remained cold and aloof. Even though I gave him plenty of space, his 'poor ol' me' attitude ensured that I suffered along with him. I began to suspect that he really did covertly blame me for his illness. I felt frustrated and hurt; he had become even more closed to me than he was before I left for Barcelona.

When I could stand it no more, I decided to take the bull by the horns and confront him directly. I marched into his room, firmly closed the door behind me and took a deep breath.

'Okay, Aiden, I need to know – what is it that you are really feeling? What's going on with you? I would love to understand what on Earth is making you so darn cold hearted.' My voice trailed away as I awaited his response.

He looked back at me despondently, searching for his words. I sensed that there was something deep within him that was resisting being fully transparent. 'You are so beautiful,' was all he could say. It was slow in coming, but over the next few days, my direct confrontation eventually opened up a series of deep conversations between us.

Up until this time, I had only shared with Aiden a glimpse of what had led up to our meeting. Aware of the enormity of 'my story', I tried my best to keep it to myself. After all, it was my story, not his, and I wanted to respect his space and sovereignty. No matter how pre-destined I felt our meeting was, I knew he had to make his own choices and meet me according to his authentic truth. I concluded that total transparency was the only way out of this dark and nameless cloud that loomed over us. I had to tell Aiden everything that had led me to find him sitting at that fire under the full moon in the mountains of the French Pyrenees.

We sat at the small kitchen table clutching our jasmine tea as if it was the only secure thing we could hold on to between us. It was time for the big reveal and lay all of my cards out on the table. Mustering my courage, I shared about the ceremony, Jahrusha's vision and the series of events that led up to meeting him. It felt risky and vulnerable, but it was the only way to clear the air and rise from the funk of all that remained unspoken.

'Aiden, a well-entrusted intuitive described you as a beloved soul-mirror who would in truth be more like a friend than a lover. You were also described as someone who had a likeness to King Arthur and who works on many levels with energy and the spirit of the land. I was told that the dolphins would lead me to you and when they did, a star tetrahedron would open and descend from the sky and bless our reunion. I was told I would meet my king and that he would be one of a long line of Priests coming from the Melchizedek Order. I have experienced countless synchronicities since meeting you, and everything within me tells me that this person foretold is *you*! And now that I have met you, the strength of our connection is undeniable. So what am I to do, disregard everything I'm feeling and pretend that none of it is happening?'

I waited silently for his response. As I watched his face, I prepared myself to accept whatever his truth was. Even though I intellectually knew that with every person we meet, there are billions of possibilities and parallel realities that could be acted upon according to free will. I had put my truth and my heart out on the table. The rest was entirely up to him.

Aiden paused for a long and heavy moment. And then he exhaled like an exasperated bull. His face contorted as he tried to compose himself. I felt the wave of blood-curdling anger percolating from deep inside of him. I sensed his overwhelm – a mixture of fear, mistrust and plain old reluctance to feel deeply into an ancient festering wound that called out for his love. In that moment, Aiden made the choice to cling to his 'story' of being misled and beguiled by the Feminine, while clinging desperately to the pent-up emotions that went along with it.

I could relate. I too had experienced my fare share of being swept up in a web of deception by the Masculine. And yet, I was aware enough to know that we were being given an opportunity to flip the script and that this was exactly what I intended to do with or without him.

'My intention is to heal the trauma of the past and create a new narrative, one of forgiveness, love and mutual understanding rather than splitting further off into the allure of greater separation.'

The heat of vulnerability tore through my flesh while I waited for his response. I did my best to remain centred and breathe through it all. In the uncomfortable silence, I reminded myself that I had appeared just as he was gearing up to begin a whole new life as a father. I really had no idea what was happening in his larger world.

'Look, Ambe´, I...um...I have a long history of mistrusting the dark side of the Feminine.'

'Uh-huh.' I nodded with curious and compassionate eyes.

He rushed on, 'I do have genuine feelings for you. I love who you are and find you to be a very special and beautiful woman, inside and out. I just...' He fell silent.

I could sense his turmoil around our dilemma. Deep inside, his little boy felt as vulnerable and confused as my little girl did.

Aiden got up from the table and paced around the room. He poured us a fresh cup of tea and brought the chocolate over as if it held the magic key to resolving our differences. After he broke off a piece of chocolate and popped it into his mouth, he seemed to regain his composure. He said nothing. Instead, he took my arm, led me upstairs to the sitting room, sat me down on the couch next to him and began to share his current perspective on intimate man-woman relationship.

'The old paradigm for intimate relationship is clearly changing into something entirely brand new. I will no longer be possessed or owned under the framework of traditional ways of coupling, which are full of projected needs, expectations and conditions on love. I am a free and sovereign man and will not be entrapped or confined by another! I must be able to do what I want, with whom I want, whenever I want.'

He practically glared at me as he continued, 'I am a friend. I believe that friendship is the highest path and is to be honoured above all other forms of relating. Within friendship is an understanding to work things out and come back together stronger. Friendship has a field of inclusiveness rather than exclusiveness. It gives space and room for each individual to grow and evolve according to their own authentic sovereign truth and free will. My little boy chooses his friends carefully and when he does, he chooses them for life and they become more important than any other kind of relationship.'

He turned to me and said warmly, 'You are my friend, Ambe´'. That is who you are to me. In this way, we can love one another unconditionally with no strings attached.'

Blinking back my tears, I allowed Aiden's words to settle into my heart. I was grateful for his sincerity and his willingness to offer me his deep heart. In truth, I felt in resonance with mostly everything he had shared. Indeed, there was great wisdom in honouring friendship as the foundation and bedrock of intimate relationship, and yet within all truths, their lies paradox. *Doesn't commitment allow for the greatest freedom and friendship?* I inwardly questioned.

I attempted to share my paradigm of relationship, though I had little experience of what it actually was at the time. 'For me, my relationship with my divine Self is at the core of all other relationships! And it's true, friendship is at the heart of all authentic relating. Once that's anchored, the deep vulnerable river of intimacy can provide a safe place to learn and grow the love, in all of our messy humanity and pristine divinity. Committing to an integral partnership provides a sacred crucible to explore all the places within ourselves where we have placed conditions on our love, until that love expands large enough to include all beings within its benevolent embrace.' I continued, 'and, yes, when a whole man and a whole woman unite in partnership, there is an enduring respect for the freedom and sovereignty of the other. The relationship becomes a conduit to serve the combined essence of each individual. This sacred third is the child of their highest divine and creative potential, whose very purpose is to enliven and bless the world with their unique recipe of evolutionary love.'

I paused and acknowledged that the love story I yearned for was encoded in every cell of my being. I could integrate both our perspectives – an embodied intimacy grounded in friendship that was not privatised but intended to serve to enliven and bless the whole of the world. I took a deep breath while giving space for the silence to speak all that I could not find the words to express.

Aiden looked down at his hands. I could feel extreme pain in his voice as he spoke.

'Ambe´', I've never been confident in the realms of personal relationship. I have always found that intimate relationships are messy and have led to great suffering and disappointment for both people involved. Therefore, I have resolved to focus more on the non-personal. I would say this is where I naturally excel. This human love thing is just not my cuppa tea! I am a visionary man and I prefer to exist in the realms of spirit.'

He looked up at me. 'Maybe one day someone will come along and teach me a healthy way of humanly relating in intimacy. Maybe then, I could restore my desire and capacity to show up there. But so far, I have not found a person who is capable of modelling such a way... who knows, maybe this is who you could be to me.' He looked at me with his bright blue, husky dog eyes and offered me the first warm smile I had seen in days.

Right then, I noticed the fairytale princess in me wanting to leap into his arms, cover his face in kisses, and say, '*Yes, oh yes, I would love to be that special person!*' But then, I caught myself, not wanting to leap so easily into a relationship of coldness and withdrawal. *Was I really the kind of woman who would give her power away so readily? Had I become so love struck that I was blinded by the undeniable chemistry and magnetic attraction I felt for this man? Was I lacking in all matters of discernment? Or perhaps, I could be 'the one' to restore his faith in true love? After all, I was an excellent healer. How could I ever resist such a compelling invitation? Whoaaa Nellie...hold your wild horses!*

I opened my mouth, unsure of what foolish words were going to come tumbling out next. Then I gazed into Aiden's eyes and saw that despite what he had just said about me potentially being the 'one', he was committed to staying on the cool side of friendship. I swallowed back my feelings like a large bitter pill along with my desire for a partner who could meet me, just as I am.

After our truth pow wow, Aiden retired to his safe man cave, resolved to remain distant and aloof. I retired to the guest room feeling more bewildered and perplexed than ever. I sat by the window and looked as far out as I could into the night sky while I pondered these questions: *why did I feel so compelled to give my heart to this mysterious man who offered me breadcrumbs in return? When did I start believing that my feelings did not matter? When did I first learn to undervalue and abandon myself for the sake of caring more for the illusive promise of love rather than the real deal?*

I was straddling one of the greatest paradoxes of my life. My heart and my head were sumo wrestling and there was no truce in sight. I stared out the French windows and looked up at the Venus star twinkling amongst the canopy of stars. *Please give me courage and strength to know what love is and can be.* I inwardly pleaded.

Then I heard the hidden voice lovingly prompt me, *Change your flight to Brighton and push back your travel plans with Murray. You will most certainly need at least another week to bring this initiation of the heart all the way through.*

That night, as I fell asleep, I recollected one of my Taoist teachers lecturing the class about the nature of emotions.

'*Emotions are like little children and most of the time are completely irrational. As soon as you try to analyze, control, deny or contain them, they fight back even harder. Emotions need to be gently and tenderly escorted into the realm of feelings where they can be metabolized, digested, integrated and eventually fully embraced. Unexpressed emotions can fester inside of us, blocking the life-force energy from flowing freely. Your emotions deserve your love, time and attention. Do not deny them. Embrace them as your very own children crying out for your love. As you tenderly meet every emotion with welcome curiosity, they will lead you to a wellspring of untapped creativity and unleash your power, passion and soul purpose.*'

CHAPTER TWENTY-FIVE

THE ENTOURAGE

Traveling the path of love is simple, but 'simple' is not synonymous with 'easy.' The very dynamic self-narratives, limiting beliefs, schemas, templates, internal working models and attachment styles – whatever our orientation – are cellularly embedded. While they are not who you ultimately are, their appearance is vivid and colorful – and as guests of your miracle nervous system – deserving of your care and attention.

We are human beings with sensitive, beautiful, gorgeous brains, hearts, psyches and organs – what a raging eruption of grace that is. We hear compelling stories about how if we learn how to 'be happy all the time,' manifest everything we want, and discover 'secrets' about how to change our lives through thinking that these archaic organizing principles will yield: the charismatic new teacher, the right 'five steps,' the latest powerful technique (no, really, this one is IT!) – that somehow the 'good other' will arrive and dismantle it all, landing us in unending bliss, with no more vulnerability and risk of heartbreak, happy all the time, somehow magically resolving the wild, groundless terrain of love.

But there is no resolution to love. There is no reference point to rest and take refuge in. There is no fixed state. There is no 'secret.' For love is alive, and a firestorm of unprecedented creativity. There is no technique that will ever touch the wild majesty that you are – that is this tender, raw, beating human heart.

What you are need not be 'healed,' but held. There is no magical solution waiting for you around the corner. Burn this dream world up and start exactly where you are. Send kind awareness into your body, your heart, and your psyche...and listen...and see. Each and every experience you are having is valid. It is all path. Set aside the ancient activity of abandoning your experience – as was likely done to you as a little one – and see what has always been here. Based on the illuminating realities of neuroplasticity and the clear seeing of emptiness-luminosity, the narrative of 'me' can be re-told, the brain and nervous system can be re-shaped, and the cells of the psyche and heart can be re-arranged. Of course, it is love, which is the re-arranger. If you will slow way down and make an unconditional commitment to infusing your present experience with space and kindness – and finally attune to what is here – new grooves will form and deepen – golden pathways of awareness, sensitivity, empathy, attunement and compassion. It is inside these pathways that the Beloved will be there, welcoming you back home into the mandala where you have always been together, where you have actually never left, where you will be crafted as a vessel to carry love into this world.

– Matt Licata

Lose your head!
Not a single thread that has a head
Can go through the eye of the needle.

– Jelaluddin Rumi

The Divine Mother's voice consoled me throughout the night. *'Trust yourself, dear one, and most of all, trust your feelings. Do not project them onto others, but embrace them as the voice of your soul's light loving you just the way you are. Tenderly call back the parts of you that you have banished from your own self-acceptance and love. Allow your raw vulnerability to blaze the way for your authentic self to shine through.'*

Yes, yes, I can do that. I will honour my feelings and be true to myself, I affirmed inwardly.

By morning I was clear on one thing: whatever Aiden and I were playing out could not be understood with the ordinary mind. We were illuminating an ancient story between the wounded Feminine and Masculine, and these Grail lands held the keys and codes to resolving it. I had no choice other than to surrender my heart to what was unfolding and commit fully to unravelling this mysterious rift between man and woman whose origins began eons ago.

As I became more aware of my fractured identity, I was resolved to embrace these exiled and abandoned parts of myself being stirred up in the flames of love. Especially the neglected little girl who cried out for her missing mother and father's love. She beckoned me from beyond the veil to rescue her and bring her safe passage all the way home – once and for *all*.

> *This little piggy went to market,*
> *This little piggy stayed home,*
> *This little piggy had roast beef,*
> *This little piggy had none.*
> *This little piggy went...*
> *Wee, wee, wee,*
> *all the way home!*
>
> – Mother Goose, *This Little Piggy*

After breakfast, Gaianna and I went for a long walk in the nearby forest. I skipped on the earth, feeling the strength and support of my new shoes on the thick forest floor. The fresh morning breeze was a welcomed relief from the unspoken tension that filled the air back at La Maison Lumiere.

'Nature is my most loyal and enduring friend of all,' I pronounced to Gaianna, who was caught up in her a blissful morning daydream. I soaked up the blessings of the sunlight dancing upon the emerald leaves while admiring nature's infinite shapes and patterns. Gaianna pointed out some of her most enchanting forest alcoves, where I saw flittering fairies weaving in and out of the morning light. We felt fully at home in Gaia's shimmering wonderland. The rustling of tiny critters and darting dragonflies were just a few of the infinitesimal ways she enjoyed flirting with us that morning. I could hear her gentle voice whisper to me, *'Just like nature, you must remember how to bend with the wind, flow with the streams and know when it is time to stay rooted at the core while letting go of your autumn leaves.'*

Gaianna took my hand and led me to her favourite tree, which she introduced as the Golden Harp tree. Its thick, curvaceous branches grew horizontally in the shape of a beautiful harp. We sat down upon the warm nurturing earth and leaned on her as we took turns confiding in one another as sisters do.

'I feel caught in the paradox of my burning desire to be met in true intimate relationship, while simultaneously aspiring to be fulfilled within my own sovereignty. Luckily, I rather like my own company.' Gianna added.

'I know what you mean. Such a paradox this man-woman love stuff is, while it's effortless to love you and your company too!' I said, beaming with the bittersweet irony of life and what it required of us to show up for. I felt full of gratitude for this beautiful, wise and generous woman who resembled Mother Mary and who chose to lovingly join with me in the ways of the sacred heart.

When we returned from our walk, relaxed and replenished, we found Aiden in the kitchen slurping down a bowl of cereal. This was a very good sign that his health was returning.

'Good morning, ladies. I'm feeling stronger today, but still a little weak,' Aiden announced to us with the promise of hope in his voice.

Gaianna and I looked to one another and shared one of those sisterly smiles that encompassed everything and nothing all at once. After all, any news was good news!

After tea, Aiden and I went upstairs to talk about what sacred sites of this particular region we were being called to visit. We agreed that the neighbouring Mt Bugarach would be our next outing.

'Let's do a deeper check-in, shall we, Bella?' Aiden suggested while turning to face me in lotus position. We closed our eyes, took a few deep breaths, grounded and then opened up to our inner guidance.

Just as I completed clearing my chakras and steadied my breathing, Aiden let out a huge gasp and said, 'Whoa!' as if he had seen a giant ghost.

'What is it?' I asked.

'Whoa,' he repeated. 'I have never seen anything quite like this before. The room is full to the brim!'

'Oh yeah, full to the brim with what?' I said curiously.

'Not what – who,' Aiden burst out. 'Everyone imaginable! Everyone you have ever worked with from beginning-less time is here now, surrounding you. You got Tibetan masters, Hindu deities,

Archangels, Mayan shamans, Egyptian priests and priestesses, Indian chiefs, Sadhus, elemental spirits, masters of all tribes and lineages – you name it, they are all frickin' here!'

In a clear and direct voice, Aiden asked the beings, 'Why are you all here?'

He spoke aloud as they answered, 'Your friend Ambe´ is a very special being of Light, here to serve Mother Gaia in the birthing of a divine new humanity. We are here to protect and guide her on her way.'

'Well, well, well,' Aiden said with a tone of personal pride. 'Not only are they here, but some of them are actually ganging up on me! They are pushing up against me with all their might and threatening me by extending an aggressive, energetic force field. They are attempting to protect you from me!'

'Why are they protecting me from you?' I asked with a mixture of surprise and naivety.

'There is a very burly Ganesh figure in front of all the others which is being especially bullyish. I must make my energy big, burly and strong like his and meet his intimidating energy with my own. 'Back off, or else I'll retaliate and it won't be very pleasant for either of us. What are you protecting Ambe´ from?" Aiden inquired.

'Ambe´ is going to love you and then you are going to hurt her in a big way,' Aiden reported back to me, as if he was talking about some other guy in the room.

I took in his words, half believing them and half brushing them off. I didn't want to believe that Aiden could or would hurt me intentionally. I loved Ganesha and I loved Aiden! Tomorrow we would be setting off to the sacred sites together to continue our energy work.

How could this be? These disembodied entities are not going to interfere with my life and tell me whom I can and cannot love. I mean, really, who do they think they are, trying to run my love life? I reacted in my best attempt to be a badass. *I mean, really, I'm not about to let anyone get in the way of my so-called affairs,* I thought, reminding myself who was really the boss. *After all, I know how to take care of myself, don't I?*

Aiden then went on to report, 'I now see a large cobra head with two fanged teeth and three white stripes painted on its forehead. He's hovering above your crown, giving me a fierce and terrifying glare.'

Aiden demanded boldly, 'Identify yourself!' He went on to report that it shape-shifted into the fierce warrior aspect of Shiva, who warned him of the consequences of messing with me and then turned back into a snake.

Aiden was getting a little cocky while enjoying the challenge and competition. He kind of reminded me of Buzz Lightyear from the movie *Toy Story*.

'I'll have to get as big as that energy and once again match it by letting it know it better back off, or else.' He continued to keep me informed, describing the encounter, like a sports broadcaster. He described his experience like getting into a brawl with some heavies where each tried to intimidate and outdo the other. The only thing I could do at the time was sit there and witness the absurdities that were being revealed to me, play by play.

'The only way to avert them is to become exactly like them,' Aiden said, impressed with himself as he discovered something brand new in the energy realms.

I was dumbfounded by the insanity of the situation. All I could do was continue to sit there in lotus position and pay attention to each intriguing detail. Honestly, I felt nothing of the intense inner battle that Aiden was participating in – and why on earth my entourage would put up such a fuss in the first place.

In truth, I regret politely discarding the protection of my spiritual entourage. At the time, acknowledging it as real would mean I'd have to admit that Aiden was actually endangering me! *What kind of ridiculous divine setup would that be?* I was simply unwilling to see it that way, despite the battle raging around me. As I witnessed this peculiar interplay, I made the choice to partially override my entourage's attempts to protect me from Aiden! *After all, why on earth would I come all the way to Europe, close down my healing practice, give up my beautiful home and spend every last penny I have to meet the man of my dreams – only to have him be the one to hurt me? That's ridiculous and makes absolutely no sense at all!*

I took a long silent pause to go within. After considering my options, I came out of the meditation with the feeling that I had no other option other than to show up for whatever this was. Bottom line – I was going to choose love anyways. After all, trying to hold back love was like trying to hold back the Niagara Falls. The problem was, I really had no comprehension of what *real* love was at the time.

'I can protect myself, thank you very much! And by the way, I'm the one in charge here!' I mumbled as my best attempt to mimic Aiden's puffed up demeanor. *I will just have to be stronger than all of these invisible forces which insist on interfering with my love life! I mean, really, who do they think they are?*

After a long moment of silence, Aiden gasped and let out a large sigh of relief.

'Ah, now that's better. I sent them all off. I should be feeling much better now. I just needed to be a man and show them whose boss around here. I guess in my sickness, I've been a little weak and unable to meet these confrontational energies. Whoa, I now understand that much of the pressure that I presumed was coming from you was in fact coming from your fierce entourage of protectors and guides!' He reached for my hand tenderly. 'We can now get on with it, luv, you and I, our travels and all the magical adventures yet to come.' He flashed me a warm and endearing heroic smile.

Yep, Aiden Buzz Lightyear to the rescue!

Funnily enough, Aiden carried on for the rest of the day as if everything was normal again. He eagerly proceeded to map out our travel itinerary while humming a tune with a mixed aura of manly pride and massive relief.

I resigned myself to the moment and decided to trust that our coming together served a higher purpose. Despite everything, when I was in the presence of Aiden, I felt more alive than ever before. I told myself that it would be better to trust that destiny brought us together for a reason rather than abort the mission midway. Even though a wiser part of me questioned whether it was the best idea to carry on with him, I chose to surrender to each precious moment and enjoy the ride for all that it was and all it would be.

The rest of the day was spent making flight arrangements to extend my trip as I was guided to do. As it turned out, my workshop in Brighton had been cancelled and it worked out much better for Murray to meet up with me a week later anyway. The Universe aligned with our plans and I was filled with renewed faith that life... well life would keep giving me exactly what I needed to fulfill my highest destiny.

CHAPTER TWENTY-SIX

BRIDGE TO INFINITY

TRUST

If you trust, only then can you drop knowledge,
Only then can you put your mind aside.
And with trust, something immense opens up.
Then this life is no longer ordinary life.
It becomes overflowing
When the heart is innocent and the walls have disappeared,
You are bridged with infinity
And you are not deceived.
There is nothing that can be taken away from you.
That which can be taken away from you,
Is not worth keeping
You cannot lose real treasure.
Trust life.

– Osho

The logical mind runs away from drowning.
Lovers accept drowning
In the sea as their destiny.
The logical mind finds consolation
reaching a level of comfort in life.
Lovers are focused beyond their own comfort.

– Jelaluddin Rumi

After a delicious and nurturing dinner, Aiden and I retired upstairs to get some well-needed rest from our endless stream of emotional mayhem. We decided to watch a movie and indulge in somebody else's drama for a change. Aiden chose a movie starring Robin Williams called, *What Dreams May Come.* I cosied up close to his warm body on the couch. It felt delicious to take some time to enjoy a normal activity, like two ordinary human beings. Yeah, right! Before long, my heart felt like it was going to burst out of my skin, splatter all over the white futon couch. Not wanting to make an emotional mess, I excused myself and went to the bathroom, where I nearly passed out before I even got to the door. I took some deep breaths, regained my composure and sternly reminded myself that it was only a movie, before returning to our cozy nest.

The movie obviously triggered a trauma buried deep within my pain body. The female character was locked in the hell realms after the loss of her two beloved children. They were tragically killed in an automobile accident. The beautiful woman, once blissfully in love, was now imprisoned by her perpetual state of blame and shame – otherwise known as purgatory. The storyline conveys how our unhealed traumas can get lodged in our nervous system, keeping us locked safely in our frozen cages as the best way to feel safe and survive the unbearable. We feel helpless, cut off from our love and power to shift our experience. Perhaps this is the true meaning of 'living in hell'.

The story goes on to illuminate how our subconscious beliefs create our moment-to-moment reality and get reflected on the outer, creating how we experience our lives. Humans have the innate power to free themselves by waking up and taking back the reigns of our perception. We must learn to trust that life gives us countless opportunities to wake up from our nightmares and grow beyond our limitations, no matter how painful they may appear to be. Some refer to this theory as syntropy, the benevolent force of the Universe that is always moving us toward greater harmony, love and coherence with our divine nature. By taking responsibility, we come to see that everything is serving a function and we have the power to assign a new meaning to that function that is life affirming. In order to walk free from the prison of our fractured mind and create Heaven on Earth, we must heal our traumatic experiences and hence redeem the super powers embedded within our core wounds.

After the movie, I rolled onto my side, pulled a pillow over my head and gave way to a flood of tears whose origin seemed to go all the way back to the beginning of time. I sobbed and sobbed, oblivious to anything other than a torrential downpour of sorrow and despair. I cried for the Earth, for nature, the animals, the children and the whole collective sea of a drowning humanity caught in the prison of seeing themselves as separate from the whole.

I was tapping into the collective wound, feeling lifetimes of miscarried hopes and dreams. I felt into the literal and creative children that never made it past the birth canal to grow into their full maturity. Tears continued to pour down my cheeks like the rain pouring down outside the window. Aiden sat beside me, supporting me to feel fully into the bottom of my grief and be lovingly witnessed in it. I was grateful that he was there to hold sacred space for me. All that was missing was the sad violins. I knew then that the bravest thing for me to do was to tenderly feel all of it, right down to the marrow of my quivering bones.

After some time, Aiden said goodnight and left me to fall asleep in a puddle of my own tears. I honestly did not know how much more my heart could take. I knew I had to trust that everything was unfolding for me rather than against me. It always came down to that.

Feel everything while remaining open, or be sentenced to a life in hell just like the beautiful mother who prematurely lost her children in the film. She remained trapped in the purgatory of her mind until she could see past her victimhood into the underlying truth, that the one thing that cannot ever be taken is our power of choice to love and create beauty out of all we experience in both shadow and light.

In the morning, I crossed the great hallway divide and cuddled up next to Aiden in his bed. 'Aiden, I only have a very short time before I must return to England. Saintes-Maries-de-la-Mer is calling out to me to come before leaving France. Would you like to join me?' Somehow, in daring to ask him this, I felt as if I was putting my entire life on the line.

He lay on his back in silence for a very long minute. I could feel he was checking in with his spirit guides. Finally, he answered, 'Yes, Bella, I will come along.' Then he softly mumbled, 'You know, your love is a beautiful thing.'

We set off later that morning, clutching our morning tea while hugging the crest of the mountainous roads. Mount Bugarach is a majestic, eggplant-coloured mountain. I had seen it twice before from a distance and each time, it called out to me like a long lost love. Its magnetism and undeniable power reminded me of what it felt like to be in the majestic presence of Mount Shasta. The day had finally come for Aiden and I to do what we did best together – our sacred Earthwork.

The Grail family and people of the region described Mount Bugarach to be an etheric city of light, an inverted pyramid linked to Egypt and other sacred sites of the world. They believed that Yeshua and Mary resided nearby, and accessed a portal that led to higher-dimensional worlds, where the ancient and the new, past and the future danced together as one.

After several winding hillside roads, we arrived at the base of the mountain. I gathered some leftover bread, cheese and cucumbers for a picnic. We set out and walked along the riverbed that lay at the base of the mountain. We chose a spot where we could get the best view of the mountain and laid a blanket down to have a picnic before going into meditation. After enjoying our delicious sandwiches in silence, Aiden and I lay back on the grassy slope to attune to the surrounding energies of the Earth and sacred mountain.

Within moments, I felt myself drift into a vivid parallel reality in Egypt. In my vision, I lay with my beloved on the banks of the River Nile, hidden amongst long golden reeds of grass. We bathed in the bliss of our entwined bodies and relished in the silent communion of our braided souls. I remembered this time as if it was just yesterday, tasting the lingering sweet meats on my tongue and inhaling the musky perfume on my beloved's warm brown skin. In love's tender embrace, we dreamt of a time on Earth when humanity would be free from the needless suffering and war. Life would flourish in joy, innocence, wonder and reverence for the sanctity of all life. We sensed the inevitability of our prayer and yet knew that our human family still had much to learn before crossing the vast sea of pain and separation to land upon the shore of a harmonic New Earth.

My awareness shifted to my womb space. It suddenly began to shudder and vibrate. Then it filled with the golden light pulsation of an etheric child whose origins were from another dimension. The inner voice went on to guide me, '*Be still and feel your innermost heart-womb. The time of planetary birth is upon you. The child that glows within your womb is an aspect of your Self who has come from beyond to inoculate this Earth with your Love Divine. Your higher purpose is to birth your Christic being, born from the Inner Marriage to Self, Source and Divinity.*

'*Humanity is in the final hours of playing out the destructive forces of good and evil. 'Armageddon' is a false construct, an unnatural program that is in its final days as individuals reclaim their sovereignty born of divine innocence. This sacred mountain holds the key codes of remembrance that will support you on your journey. You are here to lay the foundation for a new generation of crystalline light beings to flourish in peace and harmony upon the garden of the New Earth.*

Gestating within you are the seeds to embody and express your highest divine human potential. As they ripen, you will come to realise that you have always been whole and complete unto yourself. Until then, release all that no longer serves you. You are being initiated into the rite of the Inner Marriage. Prepare to give birth to a child of the Sun, the Christos Sophia.'

I gently came out of trance and was reminded of where I was. I glanced at Aiden's profile. Streams of sunlight piercing the clouds lit up his face. I turned over on my side and wrapped my arms around his robust torso. Golden light streamed through the clouds and bounced like honey nectar off his strong muscular neck and kingly profile.

What an amazing gift it is to cross paths with you now, after so many lifetimes of travelling apart, I thought. Goosebumps covered my body as I allowed myself to feel and remember our ancient/new love. *I know you as myself, my brother, my lover, my child, my king. I know you from a time before time, an unsolvable riddle, and a relentless and unceasing ache of longing pulsating in the marrow of my bones.* And with this remembrance, Aiden's body shuddered exactly in synch with mine.

He then sat up abruptly and suggested we move to another part of the mountain to go deeper into our meditation. So we returned to the car and drove a little further up the mountain. We walked onto a large plateau overlooking a steep ravine. Below us was a valley lush with emerald foliage and small waterfalls gushing forth from the rocky terrain. We turned to face the central axis point of Mount Bugarach. Here it appeared to be split into two distinct mountains, creating a heart shape. I could see directly into the centre of the mountain's heart cavity. Following our inner guidance, we sat down in lotus position on the dusty plateau, faced each other, closed our eyes and once again attuned to the energies of our magnificent surroundings.

What I saw next came as a surprise to the both of us! I saw hundreds of tiny etheric daggers lodged into the back of Aiden's heart – all lit up like one of those game boards at a carnival. I was clear that whatever we were becoming aware of for each other, we were also becoming aware of for the One. As I felt into the origin of each dagger, I saw that each one represented a wound of love and its complementary remedy: denial/embrace, betrayal/trust, judgment/forgiveness, separation/surrender, abandonment/reunion. Each wound was intrinsically designed to catalyse the soul to retrieve the gift that lay within. I mustered up my inner strength in the knowing that delving into the inception point of our sacred wounds is the pathway back to thriving in original innocence. This was the way to liberate us from the tyranny of the past and come into Sacred Union with the gift of pure presence.

I grounded my energy into the earth and held space for strong neutrality, while tracing the lines of sharp, shard-like energy back to their inception points to see if I could assist in identifying their origin. I saw a stream of events and incidents where Aiden had experienced abuse or had violated another within his ancestral family bloodline. I followed the visual clues with great reverence and compassion. I knew beyond a shadow of a doubt that what I saw in him was also within me.

I saw a scared and wounded little child shrinking in terror from a hysterical mother and emotionally disconnected father. I saw a mother painfully haunted by her own terror caused from her hostile and tyrannical father. I saw a narcissistic father, fully absorbed in his own desires, unable to have empathy and compassion for the ones closest to him. And then I saw Aiden and I, running both towards and away from love, torn by our strong desire for authentic intimacy coupled with our fear of its destructive power. The cycles of abuse within the culture of humanity seemed to go as far back as I could see and remember. The lucid visions went on.

I saw a barren woman loathing herself and despising her partner for allowing him to prey upon her. Her desperate need for love and validation allowed him to suck the life force out of her in order to fulfill his own insatiable hunger. I saw how the man grew enraged at the woman as he was expected to be everything the woman had projected onto him, making him her source of self-worth. And I saw how that very same man raped her again and again due to his disconnection from his Feminine heart, causing him to dominate, possess and overpower her.

In essence, I saw myself and him caught within this endless cycle of ancestral trauma passed on through the generations. It seemingly went all the way back to the cataclysm that had humanity come to believe that we were being punished, cast out and abandoned by our Creator – what some refer to as the fall from grace. Yet this destructive force has served a hidden function. We humans continue to transcend and prevail, surviving one atrocity after another, until we can come to embrace the complexity of all that we are, in darkness and in light without turning away. And as we confront what was once denied, we uncover the true light of our soul.

The last of the daggers dissolved as we acknowledged, forgave, released and filled in the now vacant energy with the love, wisdom and compassion that we're made of. Through each and every experience, we are given an opportunity to embrace what was once denied through reclaiming the quality that redeems us.

Feeling lighter, Aiden and I stood up and grounded back into our surroundings. We stretched, toned and took several deep breaths of cool mountain air that assisted us to integrate the intense energetic clearing. We invoked the guardians of the mountain, Yeshua and Mary, and called upon the Divine Mother and Father, who embraced us with a warm shower of radiant golden sunlight. We sensed we were not quite complete and so we faced the mountain and dropped back into our seated meditation.

My awareness was transported into a majestic Temple of Light with high ceilings and jewelled tiled walls in the shape of six-pointed stars all perfectly interlaced with one another. I envisioned sitting to the left of Aiden upon a golden throne laden with emeralds, diamonds and rubies. Together, we made a triangle. The apex of the triangle was directly in front of us and was connected to a downward-facing triangle that conjoined, forming a star tetrahedron. Nestled within the centre of the intertwined triangles was a beautiful unborn child. He/she was curled up peacefully in fetal position, blissfully sleeping within a glowing translucent embryo. I remained transfixed on this sleeping child while listening to the following message being transmitted from within my innermost heart-womb.

'I live inside of you and have always been with you. Through tenderly witnessing, forgiving and releasing all that has once been held separate from me, your birth chrysalis becomes transparent, the inner and the outer become one and original innocence is reborn. This is the promise of the Heiros Gamos...to make your heartbeat match the heartbeat of creation.'

I felt into the presence of a golden etheric child that gestated within my heart-womb and listened to her tiniest whisper, *'Will you give life to me so that I may give life to all?'*

With a wide-open heart, I said a resounding, full-bodied, 'Yes!' At that very same moment, I was given a vision of the same radiant child nestled within the trunk of the Tree of Life. The majestic tree roots reached deep into Mother Gaia and its green leafy branches were abundant with hundreds of shimmering emerald and golden leaves that glistened from the sun. I followed the burly roots that grew down into the crystalline core of the earth and simultaneously grew up into the centre of the sun. The Tree of Life was a toroidal fountain of eternal life, where all is connected as One.

My vision transported me into a sea of crystalline aqua-marine water, shimmering with orbs of opalescent light. I was shown a crystal pyramid that was the centre point of an underwater nursery. I saw hundreds of unborn babies nestled inside their translucent bubble embryo. They slept in fetal position while blissfully dreaming, until it was their moment to slide into this world as the next wave of awakened children.

While each adorable baby gestated in their luminous cocoon, they were connected through a pearlescent umbilical cord to a dolphin. Each encircling dolphin served as a loving and attentive nanny. I could hear their high-pitched squeals, whistles and clicks as they joyously swam around the future souls resting peacefully within their protected embryonic light bubbles. The golden dolphins telepathically communicated to the unborn children through sonic pulsations of sound and light. I saw that the dolphins were also connected to the heart-womb of Gaia and the aurora diamond light grids of the New Earth. Each was a playful and joyous guardian, ensuring that each gestating child was nourished with the highest frequencies and vibrations of love, life and joy.

These new children looked distinctly different from the babies I was accustomed to seeing. Their heads were oval around the top and their ears were large and came to a point at the tips. The corners of their mouths naturally turned upward as if they had a permanent inner smile. It appeared that all their senses were enlivened in ways that I was yet to fully comprehend. Clearly, they were awakened heart beings, oscillating in a warm golden glowing presence, beaming unconditional love while remaining connected to an unbroken circuit to their Source, Self and Divinity. Their gregarious grins and large almond eyes reflected how at home they were inside their own skin that glowed with a translucent, milky white luminescence. They were fully integrated with the higher and lower dimensions and could flourish in both shadow and light. As each unborn being lay resting in lucid awareness, they emanated a divine sparkle that radiated from their tiny hearts, beating in harmony with the one shared heart.

Like their golden dolphin friends, these babies communicated telepathically through generating sonar pulses, clear pictures, harmonic sound waves and an endless variety of feeling frequencies born from their innocence and perpetual state of wonder and awe.

I delighted in watching the dolphins vibrationally entertain and nurture the children until their time came to enter this realm and seed the planet with their divine specialties, soul gifts and unique personas. The Cosmic Mama chimed in and whispered to me as if not to awaken the sleeping babes.

'They are coming to live in joyous communion with life while tenderly nurturing the gardens of the New Earth in all of her infinite creative expressions. You, dear one, are one of their dolphin mamas who took on a human form. In this life, you happened to come a little earlier to prepare the way and assist them to feel at home when it's their time to be born. It is of the highest importance that you release all density and undergo your own metamorphosis. You are being prepared along with countless others to receive these new children who will feel comfort, affinity and at home in your glowing presence.

'Many of these new beings have already arrived and are demonstrating remarkable creative capacities. They have boundless compassion, uninhibited affection, playful loving-kindness, heightened sensitivity, extra-sensory perception and brilliant supernatural powers that flow effortlessly through them. These new star blossoms are born from wholeness, unified with their Creator and belong to the whole of existence. They kindly request that each and every being, make it top priority to give birth to our divine Self. This will assist them greatly to feel at home as they develop their specialties and grow into being the guardians and gardeners of the New Earth.'

I felt Aiden's hand warmly squeeze mine and startle me out of my meditation. I had nearly forgotten that he sat next to me, holding my hand the entire time as I was receiving these mind-blowing visions. We looked into each other's eyes that were portals into eternity. In a flash, I saw that just like me, he was once a dolphin too.

Just as all of me landed back into to our Earthly dimension, a random vehicle pulled up onto the plateau where we were perched. Out came two elderly couples to take in the view of the mountain. Aiden and I took another moment to look into one another's eyes and honour the profound journey we had just emerged from. We burst out into laughter, feeling amused by the tourists' boisterous outbursts and carefree mannerisms. They frolicked as young lovers would, except for them, this could very well be their second or even third honeymoon.

Aiden grabbed my hand, helped me stand up to stretch and then said, 'Come on, Bella. Let's go to the Goddess Spring and share our experiences there.'

We offered a closing prayer to the mountain and thanked the Council of Light that assisted us to see and feel beyond the ordinary world. We then scampered over the edge of the plateau, straight down the ravine and entered another world of lush emerald green plant life. A jungle ecosystem emerged from the underbelly of this sacred mountain. Moss, fern and flower grew in wild abandon among the meandering trickles of water that poured into larger pools surrounded by moss-covered rocks. I was in awe of the hidden paradise that existed in the valley of this mountain. We walked over the variety of shapely rocks for less than fifteen minutes until a beautiful pool fed by a miniature waterfall opened up before us. I stumbled and nearly tripped, as I do when I get ungrounded by the overwhelming beauty of nature's magnificent playground.

Aiden took notice. He reached for a stick, broke it in half over his knee and handed it to me. He then did the same for himself. I was overjoyed to have such a practical tool at my side. It was well suited for someone like me, who frequently embarked upon walks in nature to explore what exists between the worlds. Although I immediately felt more supported, I was still a little ungrounded from the energies of the mountain. The magnitude of the visual and energetic transmissions continued to integrate as we walked.

After some time hiking in silence, we chose two giant rocks to perch ourselves upon. It was time to share about what had happened for us in our meditative journeys. Aiden chose to share first about what he called the opposing forces that made themselves known.

'It seems with every move we make as Lightworkers, it's matched with a counter move by opposing forces bearing malevolent agendas. It's just like a cosmic chess game,' Aiden commented.

'Are you referring to a phenomenon that lives outside of our self?' I inquired curiously. I was trying to relate because in that moment, I was being bathed in Mother Nature's sublime beauty.

'Ambe´, are you so naïve that you are unaware of the dark agendas and malevolent forces that are playing full out at this time on our planet? They are like parasites that feed off the emotional density of humanity's fear.'

I flashed upon my encounters with dark energies throughout my life. I honed in on the part of me that was reluctant to admit that they actually existed and had any power over me. Admitting to evil was to face the devastation that my soul had endured throughout countless lifetimes. And so, I created my naivety as a way to keep my innate goodness alive. To feel the rape and pillage that my soul had endured would kill off any last hope of getting my 'happily ever after'. Hence, I learned to preserve what remained of the light by falling in love with the fantasy, rather than facing the grim reality.

I was aware that my dark thoughts were like magnets that could attract and amplify these so-called dark agendas. Maybe the 'dark side' represented the unconscious parts of me that cried out for more love instead of less. I continued to contemplate this mystery. Perhaps, it was my naivety that attracted these energies to me, prompting me to stand in my strength and claim my true sovereign power.

I lay back on the rocks and invited my body to mold to their shape. My eyes gently closed to contemplate the mystery of the so-called darkness. I was shown a perspective that allowed me to make some sense of it all, at least, for the time being.

Approximately 300,000 years ago, an event took place that affected a great deal of humanity. Before the event, humans existed in a field of unity and diversity, celebrating the uniqueness of each individual life form. Ecstatic states were revered and celebrated from the blending of unique and individuated expressions of the Creator.

At some point, a malevolent force came through a crack in our universe and a dark race of beings bred with the humans, creating polarity. The Higher Councils of Light remained present, but chose a more passive role given the law of free will. This fundamentally created a profound mistrust in 'the Light'. Many beings made the choice to side with the 'dark side' as the 'safer' option to prevent a reoccurring attack. Humanity still believed in the goodness of the Light, but mistrusted it to take care of their needs on a survival level. Perhaps that's what it means to 'make a deal with the devil'.

As hybrids, humanity carried on living in both worlds. Not feeling we fully belonged to either, and susceptible to being harmed by both sides, a kind of a lose-lose situation. Outsourcing our power and love became the only way we believed we could survive as we spun out from our centre rather than delving into our source. For some, living half-heartedly, in a kind of limbo, with one foot in both worlds became the norm – a kind of pseudo second nature.

After the inbreeding occurred, many made vows to remain enslaved to the false dark, all the while preserving the light. As life carried on, some beings evolved from the bottom up, others from the top down, experiencing earthly density as a most foreign and alienating experience.

To cope with the atrocities of the 'false dark', we needed to create an unconscious – a place to store our guilt for genetically being born out of darkness while simultaneously believing in our light. To manage this menagerie, we went on to create judgment as a way to deflect our own denied Self. The state of perpetual judgment only furthered our perception of being cut off and separate. To compensate for the split we took up residence in the 'false light' and 'false dark'. *Ah, this is why so many of us have felt somewhat alienated here, searching for that elusive place where we truly belong. That is, until now.*

It's a new dawn and humanity is at last waking up, recognising that the darkness serves a function as much as the light. As we come to accept that we are made up of everything, we access the courage to open the basement of our unconscious, clean out all that junk DNA, and integrate what was once outcast and denied. The more we embody our core essence, the less we need to fall back on judgment and blame to shield us from our unconscious. Instead, we begin to heal the fracture through loving all that we are, more than the past ever has!

All of these dark forces are getting us to choose the reality and paradigm we want to live in this lifetime. Instead of separating to survive, we practice discernment and create clear boundaries so that we can open more to include rather than having to control and contract.

Like the arborous snake that comes full circle to meet its tail, the journey is one of returning over and over again to our natural state of pristine innocence – that place of feeling our inherent preciousness and beauty, and at last remember ourselves as whole and complete beings. I felt humbled by what I was growing into and more inspired than ever to inhabit the fullness of my being in service to the One.

Eventually my consciousness drifted back to my surroundings. I felt so grateful to be in this stunning natural playground and in the company of my dashing travel companion. I loved the feeling of my whole being opening and expanding in his presence. I was getting to enjoy parts of myself that had remained unmet and un-reflected until I met Aiden. As mysterious as it was, I simply came alive when I was with him. I wanted to tell him how I felt, but he was still very enrolled in talking about the 'dark side'. Apparently, the warrior in him still got off on a good energetic battle in the realms of good and evil.

Before long, I noticed my body ached from the intensity of the meditations and massive clearings. I took a moment to feel deeply into what kind of support would best replenish me. I envisioned myself under a warm waterfall. 'All I need now is a waterfall to soak under and then I'll feel this day to be magnificently complete!'

Aiden grinned and replied, 'Come on, Bella. I know just the place for us. We better get going if we want to arrive before sundown.'

We leapt up, grabbed our walking sticks, and buoyantly skipped over the rocks through the thick foliage and up the face of the mountain ravine.

My heart swooned as I whispered under my breath, 'How joyous it is to play in Sophia's garden with this magical Elven King!'

CHAPTER TWENTY-SEVEN

THE HIDDEN WATERFALL

Unveiling the mysteries through her heart
her every move her every breath
Pulsating with passion, undulating in ecstasy
She devotes her being to the awakening
of every cell of every inch of her body
for she knows these molecules are the keys
the keys to the ultimate liberation
and when they unlock their codes
she is the connection to the infinite ...
for within her is the Earth, the sun, the moon
and all of existence... she is the key
she is the portal of Divinity.

– Eve-Olution

Huffing and puffing with walking sticks in hand, we made our way up the side of the wooded ravine to the road. The tourists were long gone and the sun nearly setting. We entered our rental car and settled into our ride to the hidden waterfall.

For some strange reason, Aiden chose to put on a heavy-metal rock 'n roll CD and turned the volume way up. I sat quietly, observing the downshift in our energies while sensing something was way off kilter. Suddenly, I felt a wave of nausea course through my blood. I became aware of two energetic hooks attached to my ovaries. As the car drove forward, the hooks pulled me backwards. I stayed quiet and observed for a little longer. When it dawned on me that I was being interfered with by some kind of external energies, I turned down the music and mentioned to Aiden what I was experiencing.

He tuned in with me and then affirmed in his swanky Aussie accent, 'Seems like we've brought along some pesky hitchhikers whose job is to intimidate and put some fear into us.' He then abruptly swerved to the side of the road, bringing the car to a screeching halt.

'I recommend we let these uninvited hitchhikers know that their purpose would be better served elsewhere. Don't you agree, luv?' He puffed himself up and put on his ultra-tough guy voice, the same one he had used to spar with my entourage back at La Maison Lumiere. 'Thanks for coming, guys, and doing your part in our divine play. I acknowledge your presence and now highly suggest that you leave *now*!'

The energies were tenacious and somewhat threatening. I was beginning to feel like my life-force energy was being drained from the back of my kidneys. I knew I was being called to stay neutral rather than go into some helpless damsel-in-distress mode.

Aiden suggested I grow my energy body super big, and then with great clarity and assertiveness, command that any and all energies that are not in the highest light and love leave now! I was immediately on it... and grounded my energy into the Earth, connected to my breath and attuned to my core pillar of Light. I saw how I had unconsciously invited them in when I became ungrounded and tripped and fell. With fierce love in my heart, I filled up my bio-energetic field with an intense ultra-violet and golden light. I proceeded to raise my frequency, by sending them apprecition for showing me where I made myself susceptible through not fully inhabiting my sovereign power and authentic Self. Feeling grateful for yet another lesson in energetic bounderies, I commanded them to leave my body, space, aura and hologram, and return to their origin and Source. I fortified my auric field by focusing on a shimmering diamond light filling me from the tiniest cell and expanding all the way out to form a luminous cocoon that surrounded my entire being. Aiden joined me in the clearing and within a blink of an eye, we felt the pesky energies pop off like leeches and *poof* – instantly disappear from our space.

'Are you OK?' Aiden asked, looking at me with an air of chivalry mixed with gentlemanly concern.

I nodded my head. 'Yes, I think so. I guess those gremlins are more like teachers, showing us where our energy is unclaimed.'

Oddly enough, he turned the music up really loud as we drove on to the small town of Rennes Le Baines, a provincial village known for its natural hot springs. From what I had read, this was a place where Mary and Yeshua had once resided together. By the time we arrived and parked, we were exhausted and ready for a long refreshing soak. Aiden got out of the car and began to walk ahead as I followed close behind.

Nightfall had come upon us and it was hard to see where we were going because the moon hadn't quite risen yet. I looked up as I walked along the wide woodsy path, taking in the majesty of the gently swaying tree tops. Trillions of twinkling stars formed a glistening canopy over our heads. Around ten minutes later, we arrived at a natural pool that formed under a bridge. Warm water gushed out from a small spout that protruded from the rocky terrain onto a mosaic of tiny rocks. We removed our clothes in silent awe of the surrounding beauty. Aiden took my hand and walked me into the clear stream. I squatted on top of a rock so I could get my whole body submerged under the refreshing waterfall. Every cell of my being tingled in ecstatic gratitude as I let go into the embrace and surrendered my fatigue into Gaia's natural wonder.

I looked over at Aiden squatting next to me on the rock, and saw how his energy lightened in the living waters. We gave ourselves entirely to the waterfall as it cascaded over our naked bodies, blessing us both with pure liquid mana, from Heaven. Before I knew it, my gratitude grew into joy. Wave upon wave of pleasure flooded my being in a nectarous bliss that was beyond anything I had ever felt before. I was in my wild divine Heaven!

I was totally surprised when Aiden leaned into me and passionately kissed me with full body presence. In that timeless moment, I felt his being dissolve into golden light as he released himself to the sensation of our mouths joining as one. An intense heart light flowed between us, bringing us into an ecstatic union with the earth, water, fire and air and what felt to be all of the stars in the universe. All prior resistance melted as we opened to one another, and at last, offered our first undefended hello, mouth-to-mouth and soul-to-soul.

And then the kiss ended. We were both a little startled to have tasted the sublime joy of skydancing together. Almost instantly, I felt a part of Aiden bolt straight into his head, tense up and withdraw like an animal in fear. By kissing me, he had lost control and I could tell that terrified him more than anything else. I, on the other hand, yearned to entwine our wings, wet from the wonder of our hidden waterfall. But it was not to be. We slipped off the rock, dressed quickly and drove back home to La Maison Lumiere in a deafening silence.

That night, I slept outside in Gaianna's backyard under a canopy of glistening stars. Aiden snuggled up with me for a few blissful moments and then returned to his private man cave to sleep. I could feel the turmoil growing like a wild beast inside of him and inside of me for that matter. There was nothing I could do or say to lessen his internal battle. In truth, I knew very little about this irresistible man who was slowly turning my insides upside down. Before falling to sleep, I wrestled with my ignited passion that lit an unruly wildfire within my heart-womb. I felt a natural upsurge and longing to snuggle in closer, full body, heart and soul. As I lay there, staring up at the stars, I came to accept the impossibility of our being physically together while simultaneously noticing my insane longing. I practiced circulating my microcosmic orbit through my body and then bringing my sexual fire to pool in my heart as greater self-love. I felt like a circus performer walking a dangerous tight rope that connects two ends of creation – the primordial body with the eternal light of the Divine.

CHAPTER TWENTY-EIGHT

TRUTH CLUB

Deep in the woods of bewilderment, in the misty veils of the astral world, desire runs quickly after the beautiful, shimmering things that live there. They are the glamours that play hide and seek with desire. Shining will of the wisps of illusion, they disappear as soon as desire approaches them. Desire never sees the true form of that which it pursues.

– Niamh Clune, *The Coming of the Feminine Christ*

If love leads me to a musky thick wine it must be what I need. Not an austere hypocrisy. If everyone in the world advised against my loving... still I would. One lives in the Zikr circle so that the One knot in the Beloved's hair will be undone.

– Hafiz

On the following morning, while sipping our morning tea, Gaianna reminded us that she had scheduled haircuts for us in the village of Rennes Le Baines. She then leaned over the table and whispered in a cheeky voice, 'And this evening I'm bringing home a special surprise for you, *mon cherie!*'

I kissed her cheek as butterflies flittered about in my belly in anticipation. I was beyond grateful for the sisterly kindness. In just two more days, I would be on my way to the seaside town where allegedly Mary Magdalene had arrived on a boat with her extended family from the Middle East. At this stage, I was unclear whether

Aiden would continue on to Saintes-Maries with me or not. With or without him, a surge of excitement coursed through my bones when I felt into what lay on the horizon for me.

My love for Aiden grew stronger by the day. Like an encroaching tidal wave, I felt the warning signals flare up in my emotional body, which I both welcomed and simultaneously tried my best to divert. My body would occasionally set off an alarm: 'Warning! Warning! Red alert! A class five tsunami is approaching with a magnitude of total mass destruction, wiping out huge portions of the heart, destroying the ego and leveling out the soul completely!'

How do I love someone who is choosing not to love me back in the same way? And how can I love myself enough to stand in the fire of love without being burned to the ground?

I remembered the words of the protective cobra in my aura. '*We are protecting her because she will love you and you will hurt her.*' A part of me could not believe this was actually happening. The 'I' that I knew myself to be was being cooked, simmering on a low fire of unrequited love, soon to come to a raging boil!

The stark realisation of my predicament became even clearer upon arriving at Caitlin, the hairdressers house in Rennes Le Baines. Caitlin was a very attractive, red-headed, Irish woman in her early thirties. Recently divorced, she now lived in the village with her young son Timothy.

When we walked into her quaint little house overlooking the river, the first thing she asked in her thick Irish accent was, 'So how long have you two been together?'

My heart skipped a beat. Aiden closed down in dead silence.

'Uh...um,' I stuttered, 'well...we are not actually together. We are more like friends.' It took a lot for me to say those words when inwardly my heart ached for Aiden to meet my love in that special way.

'Why don't you two go out for a cuppa while I get my highlights touched up. When you return, Aiden can go next and then Ambe´ will have some time to relax at the river,' Gaianna thoughtfully suggested.

Once again, Aiden and I set out in an uncomfortable silence that I was growing accustomed to. We walked into the town square café and ordered a pot of Earl Grey tea. My awkwardness was noticeable as I attempted to remain in my centre instead of match his aloofness. It seemed the more I held back my affection, the more my body reared up like some kind of wild animal. My throat was tight and swollen. Our conversation was sparse, with a few insignificant words sprinkled here and there over frequent sips of tea and awkward wandering eyes.

After tea, we walked back to the quaint house to find Gaianna's head covered in dangling foils filled with bleach. I felt my heart experiencing the same – becoming stripped of all its original lustre and colour. Aiden settled himself in Caitlin's hospitable hands. I noticed she was smitten and especially excited to cut a dashing man's hair. I passed the time with a walk to the river, where I observed a handful of children diving off the bridge into the flowing current. I imagined jumping in and allowing the current to take me far away from this infuriating love sickness. More determined than ever, I sought to gain some emotional composure before returning to Caitlin's house to get my haircut.

When I returned, Gaianna looked at me with loving concern. Women have a keen way of sniffing out a pale face and tumultuous heart. She intuited my predicament right off the bat and asked, 'Are you OK, love? You look so pale as if you've just seen a ghost.'

Right then and there, I nearly broke down in tears as I confided in her while Aiden was still upstairs getting his finishing touches. Thankfully, I was able to let out some of the pressure from my bursting heart before he reappeared.

As he came downstairs with Caitlin, I overheard her say, 'Please come by anytime and visit me! I'd love to have ye over for a cuppa.' She said with a thick Irish accent and a beguiling smile.

Aiden lavished her in one of his Prince Charming smiles and then praised her skill as he showed off his dapper new haircut. Gaianna and I smiled at him with admiration, though my smile shimmered through damp eyes.

I went upstairs and as Caitlin settled me into the chair, she said, 'Lovely man, that Aiden.' It was obvious that she had also been struck by Aiden's lightning sparkle and irresistible charm. I empathically felt that Caitlin and I shared in that oh so familiar longing to be swept up by our very own Prince Charming.

'Yes, he's a rare one indeed,' I agreed.

'Too bad he's just a friend, eh? Maybe something more romantic will happen between the two of you! I wouldn't mind it myself,' she giggled.

I nodded politely and mustered a half smile. *Good luck with that.* I commented inwardly. As Caitlin trimmed my hair, we shared the silent story of two women who pined for a love that continued to elude them while living in the secret wondering: *are we not good enough, pretty enough, wise enough, womanly enough, or plain ol' enough for our heart's desires to be met with a man's affections?* Caitlin gave me the gift of seeing how easy it was to slip into a state of deficiency rather than abide in a state of fullness. It really all boiled down to how much I valued and loved myself. Right then and there, I resolved to change the deep-seated belief that I needed a man to complete me.

Come what may... I am worthy, I am whole and I am complete! So be it and so it is!

After my haircut, we walked down the old wooden staircase to the kitchen. It became glaringly apparent to all of us that Caitlin's house desperately needed an energetic clearing. The old dwelling felt as if it was still occupied by a prior tenant who refused to move on. I was finding this to be a common phenomenon in houses that old. Aiden and I were happy to oblige her by doing a complimentary house clearing and blessing, and get back to doing what we did best together. Caitlin was so grateful that she decided to give us our haircuts on the house. With beaming hearts, we returned her kindness with a round of hugs and thanked her for her Irish hospitality. We then headed back to the parking lot and hugged Gaianna goodbye.

'We'll catch up with you later in the evening for dinner. We're heading off to the Goddess spring.'

Gaianna shared a private smile with Aiden as if to telepathically say, *'Go easy on her. Her heart is like a butterfly's wings. Rub them the wrong way and they lose their illustrious glow.'*

CHAPTER TWENTY-NINE

GODDESS SPRINGS

Everything in the garden
Is granted the right
From the Divine Court
To appear for our delight.
Everything is here
To make the earth green and alive
As a haven for our life.
What remains
Buried in the soil
Will always endeavor to reach out.
No one truly alive
Can ever be pawned
To a prison or a tomb.

– Jelaluddin Rumi

THE MAGDALENE MANIFESTO

Magdalene is a wild, wild woman – whirling with Shakti, passion and the primordial forces of creation. She is soft. She is powerful. She is soft power. We so often connect to the soft, loving side of this feminine energy, but we forget, leave out or deliberately avoid her enraptured, wild side. Magdalene is also an enchantress, in its truest sense, pulsing with a sensual, magnetic energy. She is the Lady in Red, full of passion, power, ecstatic Womb Enlightenment, wisdom, fierce devotion. She sings the Song of Songs with joyful abandon.

She comes bearing a gift – the sensual serpent of life, wild, free, radical, ecstatic. When we have had our pure sensual energy, our Grail Light, stolen, used, abused or crushed, the light of the Feminine Soul of the World dims. We lose our 'life force', our Christ force. The Feminine Christ returns to anoint us once again in the magical balm and elixir of our sacred sensual energy, the primal living liquid light. This dynamic, Wild Feminine is not limited to the story of one person or Priestess – it is a living, vibrant frequency within everyone, calling to be remembered and embodied. Magdalene means 'Magic Doorway', at its deepest levels it is a frequency of Womb Consciousness beckoning us within.

– Azra Bertrand, MD and Seren Bertrand,
Womb Awakening

The more I honoured my feelings, the more my inner radiance began to shine through. I practiced staying out of my head and opening to trust the perfection of each unfolding moment. Clearly, I was not getting what I wanted, but I was getting exactly what I needed to descend even further into the well of abiding self love.

Meanwhile, I was off on yet another adventure with my dear 'ol' friend', Sir Aiden Arthur! *Why waste a precious moment?* I thought. However insane, I was determined to follow the way of the heart as my only real choice. There was plenty of time left in the day to explore more of the surrounding sites and get a bite to eat. We found a small market and grabbed what they had left: a day-old baguette, cucumber, fresh goat cheese and an extremely ripe avocado. Quietly anticipating what may come next, we walked to the car with our little picnic in hand while soaking in the beauty of the day.

'The Goddess Springs is a very rare and special place,' Aiden said. 'We can have a picnic by the lovely little waterfall.'

I smiled shyly. 'Sounds amazing!'

As we drove through the village, I commented, 'How odd it is not to see any people out on the streets. It practically looks like a ghost town.'

However, just as I completed my sentence, we rounded a corner and a festive scene emerged from out of nowhere. Voila, the street was lined with café style tables and chairs. People relaxed in the afternoon sun, sipping wine and nibbling on tradicional French delicacies. A full-fledged orchestra played on a bandstand adorned with bright banners in the colours of the French flag.

We giggled our way out of town and soon found a good spot to park the car for our Goddess Springs excursion. With picnic food and a few sarongs in hand, we headed down the wooded path that led us into a forest of thick emerald fauna. Around twenty minutes later, we reached the magnificent water temple.

'Oh my goddess, this place is even more magnificent than the last,' I exclaimed.

Aiden nodded, looking around and soaking up the beauty along with me.

A large thermal spring poured into a yoni shaped rock with a curvaceous serpentine crack down the middle. The water streamed out into an emerald-green shimmering pool. The pool was nestled in the most vibrant array of moss, vines and tree roots growing around the cavernous curves of the sacred rock formation.

'Oh, I can see why they call this place Goddess Springs,' I said as electric love tingles pulsed through my body. Nature is my ultimate tantric partner, and her majestic presence fulfills me like no other. Except here I was with Aiden, feeling turned on by the radiant beauty of it all. Fleetingly, I wondered if we might share another supernatural kiss in paradise.

Just above the outer circumference of the emerald pool was a soft, moss-covered plateau perfect for picnicking and lounging upon after soaking. We set our things down and felt the potency of the hot sun dancing upon the surface of the water. I began my bathing ritual by first lying face down on the mossy carpet and attuning my heart-womb to Gaia's womb. Every cell of my being began to stir and open with the womb of the Earth Mother. Gaia was alive and vibrating in a way I had never felt her before. The raw, primordial surge of Shakti pulsed inside every molecule of my being, quickening me, my bones, until they began to vibrate. The sleeping serpent was awakening within me. Her erotic energy meandered through my flesh, making my skin shimmer with aliveness. I lay on the earth and went into circular breathing as the coiled kundalini serpent stirred awake and slithered up my spine in oscillating waves of nectarous warmth. Her currents washed through my being in pleasurable undulating waves. I took a few moments to breathe deeply into my belly, as the energy coursed through me like streams of golden nectar. This energy was a gift from Mother Gaia to bless my being with the healing elixir of pleasure. I spread the sacred fire through my body and then offered it up to Father Sun for the healing of Mother Earth.

When I looked around for Aiden, I saw that he was sitting on a large boulder, staring into the pool. His energy was pulled way back, tightly contracted into himself. Before getting up, I stretched my limbs while contemplating how conditioned I had become to offer up this special kind of erotic energy to a man, as if it was never mine to enjoy in the first place. I affirmed: this surge of feminine life-force is a natural gift from the Goddess that can be cultivated and enjoyed for one's pleasure, health, awakening, creative expression and dedicated as a blessing for all. With that, I walked to the spring to immerse myself in the warm and welcoming waters.

Feeling vulnerable and exposed, I undressed slowly behind a tree. As I entered the pool, I felt like an honourary guest. The water was so clear and pristine. I could sense the water devas, undines and elementals joyously welcoming me into their sacred Earth Temple. As always, the water enveloped me, sensually coaxing me to release any residual turmoil that lingered in my heart. I experienced the blessing of pure love reciprocity, a contrast to the coolness emanating from Aiden's distant demeanour.

I sat under the fountain of the spring and offered myself to the spirit of these living waters. While imagining myself to be a sprite, I danced a water ballet and hummed a melody. My audience was the glistening sunlight bouncing on the surface of the water. Aiden and my gaze collided in midair. My warm smile assured him that he was safe to come in and enjoy the spring. *I promise, you won't be pounced upon by a water nymph.*

'Are you coming in?' I called out to him. Aiden remained firmly perched on his rock, his brow furrowed and arms tightly crossed around his chest, essentially ignoring my invitation.

Uncomfortably aware, I continued to swirl in the water, reclaiming my bliss while washing off his apparent rejection. Yet despite my best efforts, I felt it creep into my blood and spread like black ink released into the crystalline pool. Everything in my heart told me that he too yearned to relax and enjoy the bliss and beauty of the moment. I was confused by his choices as I felt the sting of rejection course through my veins.

I sent Aiden a telepathic message. *Come in, dear one. The water is pure mana from Heaven!* Not long after, he softened his rigid posture, undressed and joined me in the spring. He maintained his distance by staying at the edges, while I frolicked and played like a giddy mermaid in the centre. Our eyes darted to avoid one another's direct gaze. When his eyes would accidentally catch mine, he offered me a cool and calculated glare. I could feel the unspoken tension between us. He held onto a vine as if for dear life, while I splashed and frolicked about on my own.

Finally, when I could take the austere silence no longer, I broke the ice and asked him flat out, 'Aiden, thank you for bringing me here. I feel as if I'm in paradise! May I ask, what's keeping you from enjoying this magnificent spring?'

'I'm still regaining my strength from being ill,' he replied, as if he had rehearsed his answer all along.

'Oh, I see.'

Despite my highest knowing in that moment, I was unable to comprehend why my cosmic playmate was choosing to close off to me. For a split moment, I slid back into that dangerous default program. *Something must be wrong with me?* I sighed. I knew better than to indulge in that slippery slope of doubt and insecurity, yet I felt washed in rejection. *It's my fault. I must simply be...unlovable!*

Before I went any further, I reeled myself in, like a stern parent grabbing a rebellious child who was about to drive her tricycle over a cliff. *Come back, dear Ambe'. You are not to blame for Aiden's mysterious moods. Feel it! But once you go down that rabbit hole, it won't be easy to crawl your way out of it! Yes, you're responsible for creating your reality...and yet some things are simply not yours to take on! As a highly sensitive being, it is time you practised some discerning boundaries around what is yours to take on...and what is not!*

The crazy thing about our time in the pool was that the more Aiden retracted his energy, the more mine seemed to bubble up! I felt overtaken by my Shakti energy that was activated in his presence, amplified by the potency of these luscious lands. Despite the cooling water, I burned in an inferno that spread uncontrollably throughout my entire body. I observed the utter madness of my predicament and once again felt that there was absolutely no other way than to, 'burn, baby, burn' and know that everything was invariably alchemising my being. Breath by breath, I was being called to surrender my need for Aiden's engagement with me. Instead, I was encouraged to cultivate my enoughness and be warmly OK with enjoying my own company...on my own terms. The Magdalene energies of these lands were clearly initiating me into their awakened womb mysteries and my capacity to move further into my sovereignty. It was more than enough to share this experience with the Goddess whose generosity gushed forth with immaculate beauty.

I lingered in the healing waters until I could summon the courage to return to the grassy terrace where Aiden had built a small fire. Wrapped in my sarong, I came to squat in front of the dancing flames, my heart racing, my womb throbbing and my mind reeling. I called upon my guides and guardians of Light to assist me in transmuting this relentless inferno that burned in my heart-womb.

There is no need to suppress, squelch or change who you are, I advised myself. *Instead, allow the fire to consume all shame and come to know the primal and the Divine are one and the same.*

Eventually, Aiden cleared his throat and said, 'I suggest we go soon, Bella. We have dinner plans tonight with Gaianna.'

'Thank you for creating this beautiful fire,' I said while standing up to gather my things. Before leaving, I kneeled at the bank of the Goddess Spring, place my forehead on the mossy ground and said a silent farewell to the most beautiful Earth Temple I had ever encountered. I prayed, to one day return to this jewelled fountain where the Goddess infused my body with pure sunlight on water.

As we drove home to La Maison Lumiere, it didn't take long for my inner fire to sputter and grow dim. I simply could not bring myself to understand the discrepancy that oscillated between Aiden and I. *Perhaps Aiden was 'the one', but more importantly I questioned, 'the one' for what?*

CHAPTER THIRTY

WHITE BUFFALO CALF WOMAN

The secrets of initiation are difficult to reveal. When the soul begins to overlight and take control of the personality, it brings us to a point of spiritual crisis. The crisis is one of longing for something lost, perhaps never yet experienced. We can resist the longing. We can hide from the aching emptiness that has been stirred. Or we can accept it and pass through the inevitable disruption that follows in its wake.

So often, when disruptive, painful events happen in our lives, they are ignored. However, these are rites of passage – times when it is possible to reach far enough down into Self to extract the deeper meaning of loss, grief, rejection, abandonment and desperation.

– Author unknown

While it may seem that your greatest fear is coming to terms with the belief that something is wrong with you, that you are not enough, or that you are unlovable as you are, what if it were just the opposite? What if you came face-to-face with the raging truth that you are not the unlovable one, that there is nothing wrong with you and never has been, and that you are so much more than 'enough'? What sort of primordial fear might be unleashed in the full embodiment of this truth? What would have to change? What if you could no longer delay full, embodied, conscious participation in this miracle world while you 'wait' for your past to be 'resolved', for all of your wounds to be healed, until you awaken into some 'permanent' state of invulnerability and safety from heartbreak, until you always feel 'happy', until you find your 'soulmate', manifest your 'life's purpose' or 'complete' some mythical spiritual journey? What if you could truly no longer blame yourself, your parents, your partner, your kids, your boss, or anyone or anything for your unhappiness and dissatisfaction?

Let us love ourselves — and all beings everywhere — by taking a moment to contemplate what it is that is truly motivating us to act the way we do. We can honour the protective function these identities have provided while finally releasing them from the burden of protecting us any longer. We can touch them for a moment and then let them dissolve back into the vast space of awareness, releasing them from the burden of providing shelter from the uncompromising, relentless, unresolvable, groundless reality of love.

Yes, as a result of releasing these ones, we may be asked to stay embodied to surging waves of feeling and sensation that these narratives have protected and numbed us from — including loneliness, fear, panic, and anxiety. But that is fine. Everything is welcome here. It is all path. We can contain all of it in the majesty that we are. Your commitment to staying close with your vulnerability is the doorway into the aliveness you are longing for. It is so full-spectrum in the vastness of your heart. May we no longer postpone full engagement with this precious human life, until our 'sense of self' or our outer circumstances have magically configured into the way we think they should be. For it will all be gone before we know it.

This life is here, now, but appears to be hidden or just out of reach. The veil which has separated us from aliveness is translucent and is only ever parted through your commitment to staying fully embodied to very vivid states of vulnerability, and to sending your kind presence into the core of all form as it arises in the majesty of now. You cannot feel alive unless you are willing to practice intimacy with your sacred vulnerability, for these two energies are one, and mutually co-arise in the vastness of what you are.

— Matt Licata

W hen we returned to Gaianna's, it was late afternoon and the last of the golden sunlight slanted through the clouds. Aiden parked the car. I looked at him, searching his eyes. For a brief moment, the deeper connection flared. He lowered his gaze abruptly and said gruffly, 'I've got some email to attend to. Dinner is at eight.

I'll see you then.' He then kissed me on the cheek, slipped out of the car and disappeared into the house.

Gaianna invited us to dinner at the local French-Indian restaurant to celebrate our last night together. Café De Limoux was the one and only restaurant in this tiny provincial village, so it felt like we would be dining at the Royal Palace! I didn't feel especially festive, but there was still some time to give myself a well-needed attitude adjustment.

Prior to bathing and dressing for dinner, Gaianna invited me upstairs to see the surprise she had brought home for me. We held hands as I followed her into the guest room. 'What's this?' I said, pointing to a large painting covered in cloth and leaning against the white stucco wall.

With an air of revealing a great masterpiece, Gaianna turned the painting around and pulled off the muslin cloth. My mouth dropped and my eyes filled with tears. Standing in her majestic beauty was White Buffalo Calf Woman, wrapped in a white dear hide. A single eagle feather protruded from her ebony braided hair. Surrounded by luminous rainbow clouds, she held her sacred chanupa pipe.

I recalled the myth around White Buffalo Calf Woman introducing the chanupa, as retold by Black Elk. Holding the pipe up with its stem to the Heavens, she said, *'With this sacred pipe, you will walk upon the Earth. For the Earth is your Grandmother and Mother, and she is sacred. Every step that is taken upon her is a living prayer. The bowl of the pipe is red stone: it is the womb of the Earth. Carved in the stone and facing the centre is the buffalo calf, who represents all the four-leggeds who live upon your Mother. The stem of the pipe is of wood, and this represents all that grows upon the Earth.'*

White Buffalo Calf Woman's truth-filled eyes pierced my heart. Her life-like presence was like a soothing medicine balm to my tender heart. Her Beauty Way blessings filled the room in a shower of iridescent rainbow love-light.

'Oh, Gaianna! It feels like my best friend has travelled all the way from America to remind me of who I really am!' My eyes pooled with tears of gratitude. I had so much reverence for this emissary of the Divine Mother. She represented the way of the heart and what it is to live in harmony and respect with the Earth and all her relations.

'I knew you would love her,' Gaianna said, giving me a hug. 'I'll let you two catch up! We still have some time before we need to go to dinner.' She left the room, closing the door quietly behind her.

I stared at the beautiful painting, mesmerised by the life-like frequency that filled the room. From time to time, I had felt her unmistakable presence.

How curious, I thought. *White Buffalo Calf Woman has appeared to me once again in these far off lands.* She wore knee-high moccasins and a long white robe with tassels hanging from the sleeves. The first I saw her, she was hovering in the clear blue sky over the majestic Pyrenees Mountains. Her arms outreached in a gesture of offering blessings to the Earth while smiling upon all her relations. Her presence was so large that it blanketed the entire Rainbow Gathering with golden heart-light. She is the Native Indian's emissary of the Divine Mother Sophia, a pure embodiment of grace, fierce love and compassion. She serves the planetary awakening along with countless others who have come to starseed the planet and embody the Beauty Way.

I gazed deep into her chocolate brown eyes and remembered that the Languedoc region of Southern France had experienced mass genocide likened to the massacres of the Native Indian people. In the eleventh century, the Inquisition attempted to destroy all the Cathars, descendants and carriers of the Christ-Magdalene teachings, and finally burned most of them at Montsegur in 1244. White Buffalo Calf Woman's own Native people had undergone their own traumatic massacre. I saw that she, Tara, Mother Mary, Isis, Shakti, Mary Magdalene and Quan Yin were the same face of the Goddess, appearing in different forms and at different places. Each held the keys to radical forgiveness, compassion and the ability to heal our broken bloodlines. Each carried the star-seeded codes of the Feminine Christ, here to assist humanity to remember our true origin and regenerate the evolutionary spiral of life, referred to in the Native American tradition as the Sacred Hoop.

I dropped to my knees before the painting and wept with compassion as I felt the pain of the various desecrated races and tribes throughout the world. At some point or another, each and every being has experienced the trauma of being betrayed, exiled, and cast out from our true origin and sense of wild belonging. I sobbed in a blend of sadness, compassion and joy all at once. I then began to vibrate with love as I went into an energetic communion with the over-soul of White Buffalo Calf Woman whose spirit was emanating from the painting. I listened to her words being spoken through and as me.

'My dear sister of the Starfire, keeper of the white feather and sacred pipe, blessings and love from the central fire and the Galactic Council of Light. I have come with a gentle reminder for you to trust the ground that you walk upon. Your vision quest will lead you home to the source of the sacred spring that will serve to replenish this barren Earth. You are here to lay a path of starlight through becoming pure of heart like the sacred springs that weave through this land. Water is life! Go to them often, offer prayers for all your relations to live in harmony and restore the sacred balance, such that we may honour Creator for the gift of life.

'You are in the cycle of your Sun Dance and are invited to offer up your suffering to Great Spirit and alchemise it for the whole. Know that your tears are one with the tears of your ancestors that surround you now. They are felt and shared by all peoples who have been exiled from their land and seek a home upon the belly of this Earthstar – a place where we may flourish as One people in unison with Great Spirit, Wankantanka.

'You are here as a Wayshower, here to wed the Divine and become one with your soul star. As Gaia's daughter, you are being called forth to shine your wisdom-light and blaze your fierce compassion upon this Earth that is, like you, presently being reborn into her next expression. Find the courage to put aside your fear and stand strong in your truth even when it appears that you are alone in doing so. Earth Mother is going through massive changes, where the loss of precious life can seem unjust and unfathomable. As the fires ravage her body, be brave enough to feel her birth contractions and embody her inflow of energy and power. Even when the ground may be quaking and crumbling below you, life is offering you an opportunity to root and rise from the centre of the centre – the zero point that connects us all to the heart of the One.

'Do not be fooled or dismayed by the naysayers along the way who purposefully undermine you, testing your faith and convictions. They

are here to strengthen and deepen your bond with yourself as Creator. Remember, dear one, the only place for truth to be birthed is when you embody the Solar Feminine, which will raise you into the purity of the awakened heart.

'Through the re-balancing of the Divine Feminine and Divine Masculine within, you activate and embody a toroidal field that naturally invites all beings to return to the fountain of life. Keep the chalice of your heart-womb nourished and open – for only in your receptive presence can Great Spirit make Herself known through you, in you and as you. Be still, commune with nature, look to Grandfather Sun for guidance and know that the home you seek exists within you. As you walk upon the Earth's body as a carrier of the Sacred Peace Pipe, a symbol of everlasting wholeness. Be grateful for everything in shadow and in light.

'Until we meet again, follow the sun, flow like the water, walk in beauty and honour the invisible spirit that animates all of creation. I will always be near, walking beside you, and smiling inside you. We are woven from the same tapestry of starlight, and together, we weave a rainbow bridge that joins Heaven and Earth. Know that yours prayers have been heard and carried on the wings of our beloved Bird Tribe. Their songs call for each to remember our souls' song that comprises the song of the Universe. May you always be sheltered in robes of rainbow starlight and remember that – we are in ALL ways ONE. Aho, Mitakuye Oyasin.'

I was deep in meditation with tears streaming down my cheek when Gaianna gently put her hand on my shoulder and whispered, 'Our dinner reservation is in thirty minutes, dear. You best get ready to go soon.'

I looked up at her with shining eyes, filled with pools of water. 'Thank you for this precious gift, beloved sister.'

She winked at me. 'I figured White Buffalo Calf Woman had a message for you. I hope she has helped to lighten your heart, *mon cherie*. I'll see you after you get dressed.'

Moments later, our little tribe convened downstairs and walked in silence out into the warm balmy night. Our path led through the narrow stone roads. Aiden stayed slightly back. His body language indicated that he had not quite shaken off his inner turmoil. When we arrived at the café, our hosts were there to greet us with warm smiles. They escorted us to our beautifully prepared, candlelit table as their honourary and only guests thus far.

Aiden's mysterious silence added to the awkward formality of the meal. I wondered whether he was going to announce that he had in fact changed his mind about accompanying me to Saintes-Maries-de-la-Mer.

Oh well, no matter, I thought with an air of resignation and determination all at once. *My journey will carry on with or without you.*

I decided to break the ice by complimenting Gaianna. 'I absolutely love your new hairdo. You are glowing in radiant beauty.'

Aiden still said nothing. I wasn't sure he had even heard us. He buttered his bread intently, his mind somewhere else, off in the distance.

Our hostess came by and placed a ruby carafe of red wine on the table, along with three sparkling clean glasses. 'We have a local favourite for you tonight, *mes amis*! See the beautiful colour, eh?' She poured out the wine and had us sniff the unique bouquet. Then with a flirtatious smile, she bustled back to the kitchen to oversee the next course, which her husband, the chef, was preparing with unrestrained passion and pride.

We raised our glasses and joined Gaianna as she offered a toast. 'To the gift of true friends!'

'Here, here,' seconded Aiden. Our glasses clinked softly. The wine was smooth, pungent and went down like a dream.

Then out came our beautiful salads – French butter lettuce sprinkled with toasted croutons and delicately chopped purple onions. After our glasses cheered, the uncomfortable silence returned. I held back from letting out a big sigh that would reveal my growing agitation with Aiden's hot and cold spells. Our clanking dinnerware and crunching food was the loudest conversation at the table. Even Gaianna had very little to say.

Thankfully, the fish arrived with a flourish, garnished with delicate finger potatoes and delicately braised green beans. Our beautifully prepared meal held the power to break our uncomfortable silence with a simultaneous chorus of 'Ahhhh!'

'Wow!'

'C'est tres bon!'

Our hostess laughed with delight and laid our entrees carefully on the table. For her, Heaven was here now, in this fleeting moment... the only thing any of us really have.

Our gourmet meal was the centre of attention as the succulent bouquet of fresh herbs and French Indian spices filled the space between us with the comforting presence of mouthwatering nourishment.

I glanced at Aiden between bites. He was clearly not present. In fact, it was obvious that he was somewhere far, far away. Just to be clear – everyone loved Aiden; his charm was undeniable and irresistible. Afterall, he was extremely talented, funny, caring, spiritual, brilliant, musical, full of valour and at the best of times, totally delightful to be with. So when he withdrew his energy, with little or no real explanation, it felt especially alienating to those of us closest to him. We simply missed the gift of his magical, warm presence.

Nevertheless, Gaianna and I chose to initiate light conversation throughout dinner. We seemed to be in silent agreement to mask our discomfort. The food was amazing and so we did our very best to enjoy our meal and appreciate each other's company. After all, she had generously arranged this last supper for us to be together and it was unfair to spoil it. The bright note of the evening was the joy our host and hostess took in preparing and serving our three-course dinner. Even Aiden's morose silence couldn't diminish that.

After our profuse 'thank-you's' to the owners of Café Limoux, Gaianna walked back to the house while Aiden and I went for an after-dinner stroll through the village square. Under the warm night sky, everything appeared to be so simple, so normal and so typically French. There was a bingo game happening in the community hall. A cluster of local gentlemen were outside playing chess on a rickety table. A handful of teenagers huddled around a park bench, smoking cigarettes and chuckling amongst themselves. An old couple strolled leisurely by while being tugged by their pug dog. Even Aiden and I appeared to be a happy, normal couple out for an evening stroll. I pondered how humanity has been so well trained to keep up with appearances, only to mask our true feelings buried just below the surface.

I was relieved to return to La Maison Lumiere. Aiden promptly excused himself and retreated to his loft space to read his book. I was left on my own to pace around the back garden, like a caged lioness, trapped in a self-imposed prison of bewilderment. *Why? Why? Why?* I inwardly protested and then sat down on an old wooden bench.

'This all seems like an absurdly bad, cosmic joke,' I muttered, utterly at a loss as to why I would create this circus travesty for myself. I concentrated on my breathing as the night air wafted softly around me. The only thing that felt to be holding me was the canopy of twinkling stars. I looked up to the Venus star that was shining extra brightly and began to quietly sing myself a soothing lullaby. 'Twinkle, twinkle, little star, how I wonder what you are. Up above the world so high, like a diamond in the sky. When the blazing sun is gone, when the nothing shines upon, then you show your little light, twinkle, all the night. Then the traveller in the dark, thank you for your tiny spark. She could not see which way to go, if you did not twinkle so. In the dark, blue sky you keep, and often through my curtains peep, for you never shut your eye, till the sun is in the sky. As your bright and tiny spark lights the traveller in the dark. Though I know not what you are, Twinkle, twinkle, little star.'

After a long pause, I finally glimpsed a twinkling of a clue to this bittersweet riddle. *Aha, good goddess! I see now! This has all been a big set up to mirror back to me my relationship with my Father AKA God! Oh my goddess, I'm so frickin' busted! I wonder how long I have been holding onto the crazy-ass belief that I was rejected and cast out of his heart.* To top that one off, I became painfully aware that I had been conditioned to believe that I would have to spend my entire life desperately trying to get his love, approval and attention. *If only I was good enough, lovable enough and worthy enough to gain his favour, maybe then he would notice me. Aye yaye yaye!* My father, Aiden, men – they all simply mirroring back to me my relationship with the Masculine. *Halleluiah, I'm starting to see the light.* The realisations rained down like diamonds from the sky. *What about the belief that if I just gave or sacrificed myself enough, I would eventually regain His favour and be rewarded with some kind of idealised version of safety, love and belonging? I know I was promised that! Was I not?* I stated my case as if I was standing in front of an invisible jury in Heaven who rewarded good little girls who do everything right especially the ones who are extra proficient at pleasing others in exchange for Father God's approval! *Not!* I looked up into the starry night. *So where have I gone wrong? Where have I given my source of love and power away for the promise of something more?* But most importantly, I was beginning to see how my initial relationship with my father got transferred onto the masculine face of God and this was the first relationship that was calling to be cleaned up. *Pronto!*

Venus continued to twinkle back at me. Her shimmering feminine love pierced the centre of my heart as She went on to offer me this wise transmission. *I am she who liberates the love from within your heart-womb, lifting the veil and in so doing spin the wheel of fortune. For you to regenerate your life, you must see yourself as I see you. To gain this vision, you must trust your feelings, which are the feelings of the Goddess.*

Suddenly, I burst out in a huge belly laugh at the over-the-top, ludicrous perception that I had been conditioned to believe in – not just in this life but over countless lifetimes! *First of all,* I asked myself straight up, *let's get real, shall we? Do you really believe there is some white bearded dude in the sky holding all the cards to fulfill your happily-ever-after, fairy-tale promise? Do you really believe this is how it all works? It's time to wake up and smell the blooming roses! He's not coming – nobody 'out there' is coming. Do you get it? There is no one up there, nor out there that can give to you what you are not already giving yourself. You have been dealt the hand of free will and so the outer can only meet you as far as you are meeting yourself on the inner. Capiche?*

I was beginning to see the mass programing I had been educated to believe in. A program so engrained that I was literally hard wired to feel powerless, helpless and at the whim of some invisible ol' dude that dealt the cards, pulled the strings and offered morsels of validation and approval.

'OK, let me get this straight once and for all,' I said aloud to Venus and the surrounding twinkling stars that were standing in as my jury. I took a deep breath to gain my composure as if I was about to win the ultimate court case with God himself on trial.

Then, as quickly as I asked the question, my mouth dropped open in utter astonishment. All of the conditions that I believed God had put upon me to gain his favour, I had put upon myself to gain my own favour. *No wonder I felt like I was never good enough. I was rejecting myself again and again by holding myself up to some impossible standard, an artificial measuring stick that determined whether or not I was deserving or worthy of love and acceptance.* I felt into the endless slew of self-imposed conditions I had placed upon myself and how much love I had withheld from believing that I simply did not measure up.

Once again, I was so busted! In this equation, I had related to love as if it was something to be parcelled out based on whether I measured up to some impossible yardstick. Basically, I was relating to love as a commodity, something I would either qualify or disqualify for based on conditions that were inherently designed to avail me. *This was not love; this was a sham!*

I traced the origin of this matrix programming that permeated mostly all of social consciousness – education, organised religion, the media and even the promise of romantic love. I scanned the messaging embedded in almost every storybook, film and pop song. Just like white sugar, nearly everything was laced with this artificial promise of happiness and fulfillment that would magically materialise from 'something' or 'someone' outside of our very own being.

I stood frozen while standing on the grass looking up into the midnight starry sky. *How long and for how many lifetimes have I believed that my happiness was dependent on gaining something outside of myself? And what lengths was I willing to go to secure this elusive upgrade in fortune?*

I looked up at Venus in utter disbelief of what I was coming to realise. She then lovingly conveyed to me, '*My dear, every time you make something outside of you your Source of wholeness, it is cleverly designed to betray you so as to show you that there is nothing you could possibly gain that would make you more whole.*' With this dawning of awareness, I could finally comprehend why I had never felt good or worthy enough. I had been delegating my self-worth and value to some outer authority, while neglecting to embrace and embody what was within me all along. *'All that you are or ever will be is already here now, living inside of you.'* I sat there looking up to the stars and acknowledged how cruel, harsh and judgmental I had been on myself throughout my life, all to gain the love, favour and approval of some outer authority that seemingly held the purse strings to my worthiness. All the while, I was not showing up for me when I needed me the most! *'You see, God didn't neglect you...you neglected to see that God/Goddess is you!'*

Well, enough is enough! My entire being made a radical pivot. *I am that I am and that is that!* I declared to Venus, the moon, the stars and most importantly, to my living, pulsing heart-womb...the true source of all creation!

I recollected and felt into the all-pervading Love that I communed with during the ceremony at Gaia's Grove from which was clearly inseparable from me. The magnitude of this Love had come to infuse me with the clear knowingness that we are undivided, one and the same...always have been and always will be.

'Oh, Aiden,' I whispered under my breath. 'Is this what you have come to teach me?'

At last, the precarious veils had lifted, and I was beginning to see and feel the greater purpose for my soul's pilgrimage. I felt immensely relieved to have finally discovered a new orientation to all that I was experiencing. I stood under the canopy of stars and called all the love and power that I had ever projected outside of myself home to the unconditional love that resided within my innermost being. Little did I know at the time that this would be a life long practice, one that would require a ferocious commitment and tenacity to return to again and again to the essence of who I *really* am.

Late that night, just as I was finally dozing off to sleep, Aiden tapped on my door, came into my room and told me that he had decided to travel on with me to Saintes-Maries-de-la-Mer. His energy was calm and much warmer then I had felt it in the last several days. He smiled warmly as then said good night. I felt deeply moved, especially after my epiphany with Venus under the twinkling stars. I sensed that the delicate terrain that we were traversing would one day ripple into the hearts of all who dared to cross the dark river of illusion to land on the shore of a larger Love. More inspired than ever, I sensed that this was only the beginning. In just one more sleep, Aiden and I would be on the Mediterranean Sea, where Mary Magdalene and her brethren had come to guide others in the alchemy of Sacred Union and transmit from the Book of Love.

By morning, the spirit of travel and new experiences was in the air. Our journey together would continue on to the Camargue – the majestic land of Mary Magdalene, the Black Madonna, pink flamingos, white horses, the Gypsy Kings and untamable Gypsy Queens. We were genuinely elated to set out on another magical adventure together. My heart fluttered and tingled with excitement, in the knowing I was headed to a land that held ancient memories and sacred gifts for me.

I felt braver, stronger and more committed than ever to stay grounded in the centre of my newly awakening heart. I intended to remain grateful for whatever precious moments I still had left with Aiden. *Ever since communing with the Venus star, you no longer hold the reigns on my body, nor my heart. Being with you is a golden opportunity for greater awareness and self-love, and that's more than enough!* At least that's what I told myself at the time.

Prior to setting out on my journey, I reflected on how Saintes-Maries-de-la-Mer was the only destination I actually had a name for. When friends would ask, 'Where in the world are you off to now?' I would respond France. When they asked, 'Where in France?' I replied unerringly, as if I had been there a million times before – Saintes-Maries-de-la-Mer. Each time I uttered the name, it rang a bell deep within my soul and stirred an ancient memory of someplace I would one day return to.

As I prepared for the journey, back in California, I sang a soul-stirring song by one of my favourite bands, Freedom Tribe. Freedom's song played over and over in my mind, as if it held some secret clue into my future destiny. Now that my destiny was upon me, with such a confusing mix of emotion and experience, I was less certain. Yet, I knew I had nothing but my trust and faith to carry me forward, and a glimmer of a future memory, which called me irresistibly forth. The lyrics whispered the promise of some blessed reunion, suspended in time – somewhere over the rainbow, where the river greets the sea.

WHERE *the* RIVER GREETS *the* SEA

I Walk Outside to the Leaves of Gold
Speak the Words of Time Untold
Watch the Sacred River Fold
Another Love unto the Sea
Oh How I Long for Thee
For and Beyond the Day Before
Far in the Song to the Poets Core
We Walk a Dragons Path
On the Cliff Edge
At the Edge of Time
The Movement and the Rhyme
Sanction from the Wrath
In Your Wings I Find
Long to Yearn and Learn
His Lover's Song
What Have I Done
The Earth Beats and the Wheel Spins
The Time of Truth Is Here Again
I Give to You My Timeless Friend
Water in the Desert
A Love Once in Forever Comes
As the Two Pour into One
The Moon and the Sun
Where the River Greets the Sea
This Is How I Love Thee
Forgive Me for My Uncertainty

I Am a Lone Ship on a Stormy Sea
Within Me
I Was Guided Here by Lady Fate
And the Mighty Mystery
Can You Hear Me
My Love
Eternity in the Falling Leaves
When You Are Away
The Length of the Day
Goes All the Way
Down My Road
Where the River Greets the Sea
This Is How I Love Thee
I Walk the Forest beside You
I Seek the Fruits Between
No Thing Can Take Your Love Away
No Ghost Can Break Your Bones
Long to Yearn and Learn
His Lovers Songs
If Every Drop of Water Is the Ocean
I Can Reach to You My Love
My Canyon Echoes without You
How I Long For Thee
White Buffalo Call
The Falling Leaves They Follow Me
The Eagle Wears the Setting Sun
Of What Have I Done
Where the River Greets the Sea
This Is How I Love Thee
Where the River Greets the Sea
This Is How I Know Thee
My Love
Art Thou with Me
At the Journey's End.

– Freedom

CHAPTER THIRTY-ONE

WHERE THE RIVER GREETS THE SEA

The conversation we're having here is a very human one. Inside the mandala of love, we are all naked, raw, tender and ripe. Enter here and you will be unclothed – of concept and of any remaining separation between you and 'other'. Whether that 'other' is another person or the unwanted within you, you are alive between Heaven and Earth.

You need no longer apologize for what you are. Your sensitivity and your vulnerability need not be 'fixed', nor your heartbreak 'healed'. For these are the gates to the mandala and the ways you will connect and attune to beings everywhere.

If you will slow down, open your senses and listen carefully, you will see that the Beloved has placed a longing inside you, a yearning that is unique to you, to know love as the organizing principle of this very rare and precious world. We have no idea, truly, if there will be another opportunity quite like this, some other star of love floating around out there. For a moment, let us assume there is not. Let us commit to being right here, and right now. And see what happens. We each have our way of knowing and expressing this longing, of opening our hearts, our bodies, and our nervous systems to the truth of being, to the unbearable creativity that is this human life. As Rumi reminds us, 'Let the beauty we love be what we do. There are hundreds of ways to kneel and kiss the ground.'

– Matt Licata

The little group arrived on the Mediterranean Coast in a boat with no oars after narrowly escaping death during a storm at sea. With them on the boat was a pre-adolescent child named Sarah, known as "Sarah the Egyptian." The legend assumes that Sarah was maidservant to the three Marys, Mary Magdalene, Mary Salome, and Mary Jacobi. In 1985, I read a book called "Holy Blood, Holy Grail" that suggested that Jesus and Mary Magdalene were married and that their bloodline survived in Western Europe. The word "Sangraal" had, it seems, been misunderstood. When the word was broken after the "n" (san graal) it was thought to mean "Holy Grail," but if it was broken after the "g," the word rendered "sang raal," which in Old French meant, "blood royal."

We are now faced with a legend that says that Mary Magdalene brought the "blood royal" to the coast of France in 42 A.D. One does not carry the blood royal in an alabaster ointment jar with a lid. The blood of kings is carried in the veins of a child. The "vessel" that once contained the "sang raal" was not an artifact, but rather, a woman—Mary Magdalene herself—mother of a royal offspring of the Davidic bloodline. This quest brings us back to Sarah, the adolescent refugee girl on the boat, whose name means "princess" in Hebrew. Might she not have been the forgotten child of the "sang raal"—the blood royal? Could little Sarah be the daughter of Mary Magdalene?

The importance of the Grail legend lies in its proclamation of the "Sacred Union" at the heart of the mythology—that of Christ and Magdalene—which provides a paradigm of sacred partnership for the new millennium.

– Margaret Starbird, *Mary Magdalene,*
Bearer of the Holy Grail

The road to Saintes-Maries-de-la-Mer goes through fields of tall green and gold reeds that rise from the moist marshlands surrounded by the inland rivers. The long necks of the bubblegum-pink flamingos peaked out from the tall grasses, adding a kitschy and eclectic aura to this Gypsy seaside town. As we zoomed down the long flat road to the main part of town, we saw numerous stables lining the road. Wooden signs read in French and English, 'Horseback Riding & Vacant Rooms'. The white Camargue horses are an important symbol of the history and mythical lore of this sacred land. They are said to symbolise the purity, grace and unbridled freedom of the sovereign Goddess.

I love this place, I thought, as I gazed out the car window at the wind-swept dwellings. The warm, soft air filled me with a distinct feeling of being at home for the first time since setting out on this mysterious Grail ride.

Aiden and I had the choice of entering the town of Saintes-Maries by going around the river or crossing it on a small ferry. We opted for the ferry as it felt more symbolic. After we boarded the tiny barge-like vessel, we stepped out of the car to take in the magnificent view.

Aiden insisted on snapping a picture of me leaning against the paint-chipped rail. 'I sense that this is an important moment for you, Bella. After all, this is not the first time you have arrived by boat to this seaside town,' he said, smiling warmly at me.

I smiled back into the eye of the camera. 'Where the river greets the sea...this is how I love thee,' I whispered quietly into the breeze. Even though, I longed for his heart to open and join in gratitude with mine, I was coming to accept the awkward silence that lingered between us. Perhaps in time, Aiden would open up and share his burden. Our dynamic called for patience and constant reminders not to take anything too 'personally'. Instead, I practiced using the moments we had left to deepen my connection to source, reaffirming that this was where my true love lay.

As we entered this magical dwelling place of Mary Magdalene, Mother Mary and Mary Solome, I could feel their energetic and archetypal presence awakening inside of me. The three Mary's were said to have arrived here in approximately the year of 42 on a ship without sails. Mary Magdalene was said to have preached here about what it means to be 'a true human being', someone who is fully human and fully divine.

The deserted horse stables along the road added to my feeling of estrangement from my travelling companion. *I will not settle for being one of those docile horses who hangs out in hopeless resignation, wondering when someone might notice me and take me out for a ride. Instead, I would be fearless, jump the corral fence and gallop into life with full power, presence and passion. I will take the reigns with all of my sovereign, unique, mysterious knowing intact and restore the full reclaimed memory of all that I am.*

My heart began to pound in a synchronised rhythm with the heartbeat of the Mother. As I reemerged from my little daydream, I coached myself, *No matter what happens here, stay true to You!*

As Aiden and I drove off the ferry into the main town, I became acutely aware that I was approaching an ancient and familiar home. I tried to imagine what the three Mary's must have felt as their small wooden boat anchored on the shores of the Mediterranean Sea. Mary Magdalene had left so much behind and carried only a chest filled with sacred relics and only enough to get her through the night. The true gift stood beside her, a dark, hidden princess of the royal bloodline. I knew without a doubt that the Mary's had come to mark a new era as they went on to spread the way of the awakened heart.

'*J'ai arrivé,*' I pronounced in my best rendition of a French accent. Excited to be in this charming seaside village, we parked the car and headed to the nearby boardwalk. It was comprised of interconnected alleys lined with outdoor boutiques that displayed festive pastry, colourful provincial fabrics, hand-milled lavender soap, fine wines, sausage, beeswax candles, dried fruits, local honey, olive oil and a variety of sumptuous French delicacies.

Even amidst the provincial boutiques, there was something blatantly wild and untamed about Saintes-Maries-de-la-Mer. Perhaps it was because the Gypsy folk flocked here from all over Europe to pay homage to Mary Magdalene and Yeshua's daughter, Sarah the Princess. The shops were filled with special souvenirs that symbolised the legacy of Mary Magdalene. They lined their windows with flickering lights as if they were showcasing a famous movie star. I stopped to admire a pendant shaped in an anchor with a heart in the centre. It's called, La Croix de Camargue, also known as the Guardian's Cross. The cross at the top represents faith, the anchor at the bottom represents hope and the heart in the middle represents the love that changes everything. I bought one to serve as a constant reminder to stay anchored in the heart of the Beloved.

Mary Magdalene shared her fame with the popular band, The Gypsy Kings, who originated from here. The town was also known for Flamenco guitar serenades, voluptuous tattooed women and freshly baked croissants dripping in red raspberry jam. Its world-famous Mediterranean cuisine was prepared with feisty passion to ensure its spicy succulence. This little seaside town pulsated with unapologetic passion for its patron Queen of the Stars, Saintes-Maria-Magdalena-de-la-Mer, and her cherished daughter Sarah, otherwise known as the Black Madonna.

We soon found out that the reason the town was bustling, yet simultaneously deserted, was because of a bullfight at the local arena, just a few kilometres out of town. We agreed – we definitely did not want to attend a bullfight.

Aiden shared with me that he had picked the Fox card from the Animal Medicine Oracle deck before we left Limoux. 'The fox says we must dodge invisibly through places without being seen,' he said while flashing me a fox-like grin. He then proceeded to put his dark sunglasses on and gestured for me to do the same.

'I guess we are going incognito.' I giggled as I put mine on, never questioning his real motives for lying low. We ducked into an outdoor café to order some refreshments after our long drive. I chose a salad Nicoise and Aiden picked a gourmet Mediterranean-style pizza. We shared a refreshing beer and few words while we absorbed the new energies of the town. At its centre thrived the ancient Cathedral of Mary Magdalene. The pulse of her undeniable presence circulated with the seaside breeze. Like a rarified yet familiar perfume, her essence permeated in every little nook and cranny of this eclectic seaside town. Along with her daughter Sarah, they created a community among all who gathered here to taste their living legacy. Whether for vacation or pilgrimage, our Sovereign Ladies were celebrated and adored by all.

Our waitress overheard us speaking about the Magdalene energies. 'Ah, *mais oui*, you are 'ere because of ze Lady!' She set Aiden's aromatic pizza before him. '*Oui*, it is ze truth – eef you made it 'ere, it is because of 'er!'

I smiled at her and marvelled at how much I felt at home here. There was no doubt that this was not my first visit to this familiar region – and that indeed the spirit of Magdalene had called me here once again.

After lunch, Aiden and I headed to the tourist office to inquire about accommodations for the night. The petite lady behind the counter had bright auburn hair. She sprayed it back so you could see the finely sculpted curve of her tweezed eyebrows and tightly pursed lips, stained in burnt orange lipstick.

Aiden inquired about places to stay. 'Gooday, do you know of a room for us to stay? Somewhere nearby, please.'

She tapped at her computer confidently. '*Rien, rien, rien,*' she said decisively. 'Nothing, Monsieur. Zat ees, nothing in ze town,' she reported with an exceptionally thick accent steeped in an equally thick brew of snobbish, cool confidence. 'Try just outside of town. Zere you will 'av better luck. *Au revoir.*' She turned back to her computer and with a wave of her long manicured finger, dismissed us. We were quickly reduced to just another one of her many unwelcomed nuisances of the day.

Like two scolded puppy dogs, we thanked her and then retreated to our car. As soon as we felt the warm glow of the sun, we decided to first pay homage to the beautiful sea. 'How 'bout we go for a quick dip, then we'll look for our chamber for the night?' Aiden suggested.

'Sounds lovely,' I said, never passing up a chance for a swim.

We drove along the coastal road until we could drive no further. The road simply ended and turned into a massive lot lined with RVs and trailers, full of European vacationers. The camping area was filled with overflowing bosoms and thunderous tanned thighs, protruding from skimpy spandex swimsuits. We surveyed the horizon. It was lit up with sunlight glistening on the water.

Beyond the buzz of the holiday parking lot stretched an expanse of silky white sand, that lead to the shimmering turquoise bay. The lapping shoreline beckoned me to plunge into her undulating folds, where water and wave welcomed me home to her wild embrace.

CHAPTER THIRTY-TWO

TOWARDS THE SUN

The same child with all its hurts and rejections, cries to be heard, cries for love. It roams the astral world overwhelmed, living again the denials of its parents, reliving its shock. This adult child is frozen in the reality of being unloved and will recreate the pattern of rejection in outer reality. Awakening to our denial means we must re-parent the inner child. We do this by allowing the inner child to feel its pain, to cry it out, to express what could not be expressed in childhood. All the areas where the child has been made impotent must be given recognition with our adult consciousness.

– Niamh Clune,
The Coming of the Feminine Christ

Many souls on the planet are doing the deep work of the inner alchemy. At times, this is a work that can bring us to our knees. We are being asked to allow the last projections of human desire to come up and be transmuted. The path that leads us to this 'Great Work of Transmutation' is one of great humility and understanding of the Presence within our heart. Without our recognition of the Presence, we would never come so far as this stage of the work. It is not possible to work with the Sacred Fire without these initiations of the soul.

It is meant to be known, that pain and suffering are never required, however, this sacred fire will call forth all human creations from the subconscious mind to be purified. This can feel like great suffering. These are the creations of our own projection, they are a result of our fall from the garden of the heart. When we feel the pain of this purification, it draws us deeper into our own center where we find the mysterious light of the inner and become initiated into Her true wisdom. When we can see the fallen projection of the Masculine and Feminine for what it is, we will find our true power and see that we are balanced and whole. When a woman changes, everything changes.

– Shannon Port, *Art of the Feminine*

We undressed in the car to Enya's melodic voice and lush harmonies. 'Come sail away, come sail away, come and sail on the Orinoco flow… Let me sail, let me sail, let me crash upon your shore.'

Like two children, our hearts pounded with excited anticipation as we wrapped our sarongs around our waists and locked up the car. I longed to be released from the web of emotional density that had entangled our hearts. Full of promise and hope, we made our way through the maze of suntanned campers and then galloped to the water's edge like a couple of unbridled horses. We stood for a moment in silent gratitude. As I looked out to the sea, the first thing I noticed was an adorable little girl, joyously riding upon the back of a life-sized, blow-up, Orca whale. Her tiny hands held the plastic dorsal fin as she bounced on the surface of the waves with joy and innocence. This little whale rider was not exactly what I had imagined when Jahrusha told me that a giant whale would jump from the sea, assisting me to remember my childlike innocence! *But hey, this was close enough!* I grinned down to my toes as they kneaded the warm sand beneath me, like a cat massaging the belly of its mother.

I knew that this was exactly what Jahrusha had described! His words echoed in my mind. *'Pay extra attention to the importance of this gift!'*

I consciously grounded into the crystalline core of the Earth, attuned to the sun and synchronised my breath with the incoming waves. I heard a voice whisper. *Be still and know your heart. The rise of the Solar Feminine is a seed, fertilized by Spirit so it may rise into the bridal chamber of your heart…and birth again, the supernal light of your divine nature. Every prayer is being heard, every teardrop witnessed by the Ones who love and surround you now.*

Along with the effervescent ocean spray, a wave of newfound trust washed over me. Aiden and I stood knee deep in the lapping waves as the heat of the afternoon sun covered our skin in golden sunlit kisses. Overflowing with gratitude, I turned toward the sun and offered up a prayer.

'*Thank you, Grandfather Sun, for my life, for Aiden and for bringing us to this place of such radiant beauty. With you as my sacred witness, I offer up any and all distorted patterns that cloak the light of my inner sun shining upon this world. May your wisdom light Illuminate the deepest truth beyond all illusion and set my heart and all hearts free. So be it and so it is!*'

I turned toward the crashing waves, stretched my arms high over my head, placed my hands together in prayer, then dove into the water, disappearing into a silent communion with the Mother. I held my breath under water for as long as I could, smiling inwardly into every molecule of my being. And then, like a dolphin leaping into the air, I burst out of the water and took a full-bodied breath, as if for the very first time. After what had seemed like endless wandering down dead-end streets, I had finally arrived within the temple of my very own heart. *Awww, this is what a heart of a dolphin must feel like! Sqeeel!*

Aiden vanished into the dancing folds of the waves. I was aware of the presence of my etheric dolphin friends, who were now surrounding me, leaping and spinning in joyous delight. I knew that there was still a long road ahead of me, and yet I chose to open fully to the gifts of the moment. This magical time would inevitably change into a fading memory. Just like the white puffy clouds that drifted above me, life was constantly changing into something entirely new.

Scanning the horizon, I saw Aiden's head bobbing in the distance and celebrated his joyous abandon. It was delightful to witness him let go and embody his unbridled joy. So I pretended to be a mermaid and swim out to him, and before long was frolicking in the waves beside him as the high sun bounced off our massive grins.

We bobbed and swayed in the waves, abandoning our monkey minds to the pleasure of the moment, until Aiden spontaneously began to speak. He turned to me and pierced me with his aquamarine eyes. 'I apologise, sweet goddess, for the anger and frustration that I have projected onto you. I have blamed you for my illness and the dark night of my soul. I have made you the cause of my suffering and I can see now, that you are entirely innocent in this matter. In fact, I know that it was not you who made me sick but my own demons coming up to be reckoned with. I wish to forgive you and myself, and return to a place of higher love.' His pleading blue eyes looked deep into mine and I could sense his genuine wish to forgive and be forgiven.

Quite unexpectedly, I did not know how to receive Aiden's apologetic words. *He wished to forgive me?* Part of me was astounded that he had come forward to own his part in our co-creation. The dark and dreary cloud that had hovered over us, over the last several days, was now fully exposed with the light of the sun. On one level, I felt relieved that this unnamable tension could shift into something more harmonious and enjoyable for the both of us. I longed to flush my heavy heart down the ocean sink, to let it all go and begin again.

If only it was that simple. There had been too much venomous projection exchanged between us. Even though I wished nothing more than to forgive him and move on, I found in that moment, I simply could not.

Suddenly chilled and speechless, all I could manage was to float on my back upon the churning sea. *Isn't this what you dreamed of, Ambe'?* I questioned myself. *Why can't you just dive under the waves and arise anew?*

Despite my gratitude for Aiden's confession, the little girl inside of me felt hurt and she needed him to know how it felt to be the recipient of his incessant make-wrong, perpetual blame and overt judgment. I looked at him, confused and still silent. Then I dove under the water as if to momentarily escape the confrontation. I wanted to disappear further into the water so as not risk exposing myself to the emotional turmoil bubbling to the surface. I surfaced behind Aiden.

He turned to look at me, but I remained silent as the waves joggled me. I allowed Aiden's words to linger and sink in a little deeper. As much as I wanted to forgive and let it all go, I felt frozen inside an ancient trauma. Without a word, I swam back to the shore, collapsed onto the warm sand and looked to Grandfather Sun to melt this frigid place inside of me.

Please, Grandfather Sun, I inwardly pleaded. *Help me to melt away the icy layer of protection that has formed around my heart.* Before I knew it, a massive wave of emotion swelled up inside me and crashed down upon my heavy heart, leaving me feeling utterly deflated.

Aiden staggered out of the sea looking like a golden god and collapsed onto the sand to lie down beside me. After several moments of silence, mingled with an occasional deep sigh, the dam burst. I could no longer withhold all that I had been suppressing over the course of the last several days. I turned to him and rattled off a monologue of uncensored, unresolved feelings that splattered all over us like the Exxon Valdez oil spill. This eruption of repressed emotion had been crammed into my 'I'll deal with you later' denial bank account. I felt angry and resentful that he had made me the receptacle of his anger and rage toward the Feminine. It had to eventually come out, and it did – it spewed out like a ten-foot spray from the spout of a giant killer whale.

Instead of hearing and witnessing my outpour, Aiden chose to react with his own hurt and defensive little-boy banter. I could certainly understand why. He had risked being vulnerable in his apology, only to be pummeled by the onslaught of my emotional tsunami. *Splat!* Our wounded pain bodies were now sparring, and once again, we found ourselves polarised in paradise! All the while, the radiant sun continued to tenderly kiss our naked skin as if to make it magically all better between us.

With an intense fire streaming from his sapphire eyes, Aiden turned to me and said, 'Can't you see? The light of your being is being over-shadowed by layers of frozen protection that are defending and hiding. Please allow me to help you come out of your frozen shell.'

I absorbed his words, allowing them to sink under my skin. I had barely recovered from our previous round, quite suddenly, his tone changed to loving kindness and compassion. *Was I to now trust him and expose the most vulnerable parts of me? Isn't that exactly what I was wanting from him?*

'Okay, Aiden. I admit – you see and speak the truth. I am feeling hurt, afraid and feel the need to protect and defend myself.'

I turned to Aiden, raw and blazing. 'Perhaps you too would feel enraged and upset if for thousands upon thousands of years you were made the enemy and cast out as evil for standing in the light of your Feminine wisdom and power! Or even outraged that your natural expression of love and sexuality was such a deep threat to others that it was condemned as black magic and declared a dark, poisonous force that needed to be eradicated and cleansed from the Earth. Why on Earth has the Masculine been so darn threatened by the Feminine anyway?' I looked out to sea again, breathing hard.

Aiden nodded slowly. 'I can see how this has opened up a huge wound for you – way bigger than just me. You are healing a wound that is held in the memory and collective consciousness of women. For eons the Feminine soul energy has been under the patriarchal dominance of the Masculine, creating so much pain and suffering. Essentially, we have been taught to fear and be at war with each other, and for this, I am sorry.

'The Feminine and the Masculine carry both the dark and the light side. They often get muddled and send mixed messages and hidden agendas. We must heal this split within us to know ourselves in a pure and integral way.'

'Look, Ambe´, I feel ready now to meet you and offer whatever support I can. I don't know what else to say...' he trailed off. Then he turned to me. His face appeared vulnerable and willing to expose something deeper. 'I am sorry that I hurt you.'

I could feel his sincerity and desire for reconciliation. We were fumbling through material so ancient and buried that we could not possibly name it, as its essence had been covered up for as far as the heart can see.

'Well, all right. I will stay open to this "healing" support that you wish to offer me,' I said stiffly, feeling reluctant to fully trust him. 'All I want is to move beyond all this resistance and relax into a place of softening, compassion and gratitude for being in the presence of one another.'

'Yeah. Me too. May I hold you? As a friend,' he added.

I nodded and shivered all at once.

'Lie down,' he said tenderly.

Aiden rolled over, snuggled in close to me and put his arm around my sandy waist. We held each other and breathed in silence while feeling an ocean of pain held within our cellular memory wash through us. Our mutual compassion allowed us to stay open to the moment, bypassing the reflex to defend, protect and polarise even more. Focusing on our breath, our empathy expanded to tenderly include the other.

The moment our animal bodies touched, a bonfire ignited sending sparks through my limbs. *Shazam!* Just like that, my prior resistance to Aiden and the Masculine dissolved away – replaced by a highly irrational instinct to melt into the bliss of tender entwinement.

Instead, I brought that burning fire into my heart and said, 'Thank you, Aiden. I am truly grateful for your support. I admire your courage to share your feelings and take responsibility for your part in our healing journey together.'

He drew me in closer, and I shivered with another irrational wave of electricity that rippled through my flesh.

'I truly apologise for the part that I have played in creating all of this unsavoury pain and polarity,' I said.

'And so am I,' he added.

This love stuff was like being swept through dangerous rapids that were leading me to a bottomless free fall. I felt out of control, with absolutely no capacity to change my present course. I knew more than ever that this bittersweet meeting with Aiden had ignited an alchemical fire whose sole intent was to singe every part of my illusions on love.

There's no going back now. You bought the ticket, took the plunge and now I'm in for the ride of my life. What else can I do but let go, surrender and allow this raging river to run its full course... all the way down to the sea.

I turned my body toward the setting sun and gave way to the river of tears that poured from my eyes. *I'm so very sorry,* I silently whispered to Grandfather Sun and prayed to be given the clarity and strength to trust myself along with all that I was feeling. I also prayed that through compassionately opening to understand and respect one another, we would inevitably be delivered to a more harmonious shore.

Grandfather Sun was quickly descending over the horizon. We took this as a sign to move on and find our next home for the night. The ocean of joy that had earlier enveloped us had washed away our protective layers, leaving us utterly exposed in a raw and tender vulnerability. We silently wrapped our sarongs around our sandy bodies and headed back to the car. The magnitude of our meeting was now becoming apparent. All at once, I realised that our primary purpose for coming together was to shine the light on our unconscious by healing the split of the Feminine and Masculine within us.

I looked up to Grandfather Sun. *No wonder so many choose to stay comfortably num rather than truly inhabit one's authentic freedom. It takes tremendous courage to confront one's protective layers and tenderly, tenderly embrace all that was once unbearable to feel and ultimately forgive.*

CHAPTER THIRTY-THREE

WILD WHITE HORSES

There comes a time in our spiritual journey when we are asked to let go of everything we think we are, everything we think we are good at, and everything we think we know about our Self. This time requires our complete surrender. Often times, the circumstances involved give us little choice but to let go. It may feel like we are losing everything – but on the other side of this dark tunnel is a more realised version of our Self. The things we cling to are sacrificed for something greater than we could have imagined. The Universe has a funny way of shaking things up and teaching us to trust in the enfoldment of our Divine Self. We see that the most realised beings on Earth have been simple, joyful and ready to accept the moment without fail, knowing that acceptance and faith are the keys that unlock the door of the limitless love and the power of the soul.

– Shannon Port, *Art of the Feminine*

We are designed to rupture in order to continually shed the skin that no longer fits us. Through rupture, we evolve into new iterations of ourselves. The tears of our devastation fertilise the soil of our evolution. Mostly we have been taught that rupture victimises us. But that's only because we don't know how to move our feelings through and find the radiance on the other side. Being radiantly turned on is a spiritual state. It is the golden thread that connects a woman to the meaning of her life, and to her desire. The consequence of turn-on is that a woman is plugged into her power source, connected to her Divinity. In this way, rupture becomes the key to our evolution.

– Regena Thomashauser, *Pussy: A Reclamation*

The beautiful hymns of Enya welcomed us back into our white chariot. Aiden and I put on our foxy sunglasses at the same time and shared a vulnerable grin. I could tell that neither of us was entirely clear on what had just gone down between us.

We headed back onto the long stretch of highway lined with docile white horses fenced into small square corrals. I momentarily fantasised about paying seventy-five euros to feel the freedom of galloping down a long stretch of white sandy beach. Instead, I looked out the car window, passing one desolate stable after the other and spoke this inner decree, *With all of my heart and all of my being, I, Ambe´, stand in my Divine presence and set myself free...free from all that confines my wild feminine passion and power. I call back any and all soul fractures and fragments from all lifetimes, timelines and dimensions where my spirit has been broken through trauma and abuse and or where I have traumatised or abused another. I ask that these soul fragments be cleansed, cleared and purified by the Holy Waters of the Living Grail, and returned back to me now! So be it and so it is!*

I stole a glance at Aiden, alive with the confusing mix of love and disdain that he triggered in me. Then I imagined myself as Pegasus, soaring with wide open wings, triumphant from transcending all ruptures of the heart. *I am here to live in Sacred Union with the Beloved, not as a fleeting glimmer but as the truth of who and what I am.*

We drove about three miles out of town until we saw a vacancy sign on the right-hand side of the road. Aiden turned off into the long, dusty driveway that ended at a modest, white house with a wrap-around veranda.

'I'll wait here luv, while you inquire about a room,' he said in a practical tone.

'Sure.' I got out of the car and headed to the porch where there was a lady sitting on a velvet pink chair. She was smoking one of those extra slim cigarettes held in a plastic filter. She seemed to be expecting me.

'Bonjour,' I called out. 'Er, *avez vous une chambre pour la nuit?*' I smiled to apologize for my awkward French.

The woman took a long drag off her elegant cigarette. She appeared to be in her late forties. She sat on her porch, dressed in high heels and a tight white miniskirt. Her full porcelain breasts spilt evenly out of her white designer blouse. She had meticulously stylised bleached-blond hair. Her dark lashes were accented by extra thick mascara and ebony painted eyebrows.

With a spring in her step, she stood up and walked towards me, and then fired off several rapid sentences in unintelligible French. Then she pointed further down the driveway, nodding at me with encouragement. What a full-fledged supernatural W-O-M-A-N!

Completely mesmerised by her presence, I pretended to understand every unintelligible word. It was not hard to see that life's hardships had broken her time after time. I was fascinated by how they had served to refine and strengthen her untamable spirit. She appeared to be free from the expectations of society. You could see it in her no-bullshit gaze. She lived and accepted life for what it was, entirely on her own terms. She didn't sit around in quiet desperation, wishing for some other life that may never come. She accepted that she – like life – was far from perfect. It didn't matter that her curvaceous belly bulged out of her tightly buttoned blouse. She wasn't aiming for perfection or some elusive, unattainable beauty. Her radical self-acceptance was what made her magnificent, flooding her aura with an inextinguishable light.

I continued to observe her with a mixture of fascination and envy while she gave herself fully to the pleasure of her long drags off her cigarette. This Madonna proudly displayed a lifetime of nicks and dings, while unabashedly showing off her womanly gifts. Free of self-judgment and shame, she celebrated herself just as she was, bulging cellulite and all.

This is the gift and teaching of the Black Madonna, who intentionally turns away from the light to descend into the darkness of her soul. In so doing, she shines the light of unconditional love into all of the places where we humans have a tendency to banish, judge and send into exile. These accumulated denials form a dross that dull the radiance of our soul. The Black Madonna invites us into living in a state of radical self-love and acceptance...warts and all, as they say. She shows us how to transform the ugliness in our lives into rich compost that in turn becomes the fertiliser that blossoms our soul's beauty. She is Lady Alchemia, whose specialty is to marry the sacred with the profane, infuse spirit into density and transmute the heavy lead of our lives into golden gratitude. *After all, it is the hardships that we have survived and endured that has made us into the resilient diamonds that we are.*

I spontaneously threw my arms around this voluptuous goddess, as if I had just met one of my greatest super heroines. She was a little bewildered by my unwarranted affections, then offered up a crooked smile and directed us down the road in her rapid-fire indiscernible French.

A man with a long salt-and-pepper beard pulled up next to us on his motorcycle. I noticed his entire body was covered in tattoos. I focused on his left bulging bicep. It was an anchor with a heart inside it, and the one on his back was a galloping white stallion whose wild mane went flying in the air. The woman gestured with her cigarette and they exchanged another volley of French. He planted a kiss on her cheek and then waved to us to follow him. Aiden started the car and pulled out after the motorcycle. I privately wondered if our guide was the lover or husband of the ample-bosomed, bleached-blond Lady Madonna.

We followed him until he turned off to the left and parked in front of a discreet fence just off the side of the road. Our escort opened the gate and led us onto the river front property.

Much to our surprise and delight, a gigantic white ferryboat, powered by steam was cruising by. It was brimming with excited passengers waving a gleeful hello to us. I imagined them singing, 'Row, row, row your boat gently down the stream, merrily, merrily, merrily, merrily, life is but a dream and and then offering me some unsolicited advice, *Lighten up and enjoy the ride. It will be over before you know it, and all that will remain is how much you dared to live and to love inside of this waking dream.'*

So many different realities and dimensions intersect in every moment,' I thought bemusedly as the warm-hearted Gypsy Casanova showed us into our extremely rugged, one-room bungalow, nestled at the edge of the mossy green river.

Aiden and I glanced over at each other and telepathically acknowledged we had found our home for the night.

'You leave, you pay,' Ralph said, winking as he handed us each our own key. Then he got on his bike and roared off. I envisioned him going home to embrace his buxom woman with another drawn-out, passionate kiss.

Our moods were instantaneously elevated by our quaint riverside abode. I popped open a bottle of red wine while Aiden drew open the large wooden shutters to air out the musty room. Even though the bungalow was extremely low budget in its 1970s décor, it was fully equipped with all that we needed. It had a stove, a refrigerator, a small TV and a large plaid couch that converted into a bed. The shower and toilet was more like an outhouse. It was awkwardly built to stand alone in the front yard so that when you went about your business, you would have a view of the flowing river.

We were thrilled to be home and appreciated the grace of being gifted the privacy and space to relax and enjoy our low-budget paradise, nestled on the banks of the Camargue River. As Aiden prepared our foldout bed, I went to the car to unload our groceries. Before long, we had settled into our humble abode like a couple of retired old folks on summer holiday. I prepared us a platter consisting of warm bread, goat cheese and freshly picked tomatoes for a sunset picnic.

It was nice to be away from the bustle of town. The river was calm apart from hearing the sound of lapping water as it hit the side of the dock. I looked up and admired the sliver of the moon as it began to peak out through the dusky sky. I was warmly content and also spent from our long day of travel. With our bellies well nourished, we decided to retire early.

Holy Mama, did it feel good to at last lie down. Our fold-out bed had all the attributes of a well-worn mattress complete with metal springs poking through the top of it. If you ventured too far from the natural slumps, you might get stuck by one of those rogue springs. Aiden crossed the divide and reached for my hand under the tattered beige sheets. This was his cue to begin our routine of synchronised breathing. A few full-bodied breaths, coupled with extra big sighs, was all it took for our hearts to tenderly soften, until we slipped off together into a deep sleep...full of wonder for all that had transpired and was yet to come.

CHAPTER THIRTY-FOUR

SOLAR LOGOS

Passion comes from a heart that is open, from a heart that wants to be as big as it can be. Passion comes from a heart that realizes it contains the whole world. Our love can only flourish if we come out of our personalised and privatised prison and open ourselves in service to the world, to the planet, and to the Divine. Our service is to divine love. We are, in essence, the great lovers of the world and the universe. As we rediscover and claim our essence, we open the doors wide for love.

What the Divine Mother is now birthing in all those open to her is a vision of total relationship between heart, mind, body, and soul, so that through that deep sacred relationship, we can come into the unified force field of reality, become completely embodied and present, and use that inner love to express our longing to see the world transformed by justice and to protect creation. The real thrust, purpose and meaning of relationship is to give us the fuel to take on the world, the passion to embrace the struggle for justice, the energy to keep on pouring ourselves out for the creation of a new world.

– Andrew Harvey, An Evolutionary Vision of Relationships

*By transcending the illusions of separation and duality,
we walk in harmony on the sacred path of peace, love, and joy.*

– Sharon Lyn Shepard, The Black Madonna

I rose with the morning sun and wandered outside to greet the new day. Still glazed over from sleep, I admired the current of the river, so clear on its purpose to flow to the sea. *This place is perfect for yoga and a brisk morning swim.* My practice had suffered a bit over the last few weeks while travelling so much. I wanted to take full advantage of this glorious morning while Aiden was still asleep.

Yoga is my lifeboat! I thought, as I laid out my aqua blue yoga mat along the dock of the river. While gazing out onto the current, I placed my palms over my heart and gave thanks for all the times yoga has literally saved my life *and* my bum!

About midway through my sun salutations, Aiden walked out of our bungalow wearing bright white Calvin Klein underwear and holding a bowl of muesli and yogurt. I felt besotted to be in the presence of King Arthur of the Camargue as he relaxed with his morning cereal in designer underwear! *This man truly embodies mythic royalty right down to his knickers.*

While basking in Aiden's charismatic glow, I noticed how frightfully willing I was to overlook his extreme hot and cold temperament. Instead, I chose to turn a blind eye and see him through the eyes of being an unavailable Prince Charming, who challenged me to reclaim my sovereignty.

Am I in some kind of weird, hypnotic love trance? I pondered while attempting to focus on my deep yogic breathing. I sat facing the river with both hands joined together in a prayer position at my heart. *No matter how unpredictable his moods – or mine, for that matter – I simply love how alive I feel when I'm in his presence. Oh my goddess, am I losing my mind? SOS. SOS. Abandon yoga lifeboat!*

I knew it wasn't just the designer underwear. His presence had captivated me in an indiscernible way. I dove into the cool river, as if to temporarily divert my attention from this dashing Calvin Klein king.

The current was strong, and the brisk water served as a refreshing antidote to cool the fires that burned inside me. While treading water, I watched the approaching ferryboat brimming with waving tourists. The whole scene appeared to be out of a Disney movie.

You may or may not get your Prince Charming, but I guarantee you will get your happily ever after. I consoled myself as I watched the large vessel approaching me. *Because you are the one that gets to create your happiness! The Creator endows all of her children with this majestic power. You see, no matter what King Calvin Christ chooses, or anyone else for that matter, your happily ever after is not contingent on anyone or anything outside of you. You're the writer, star and director of your own movie! Are you willing to drop the conditions you have placed on your own happiness?*

The fiercely loving voice of the Wise Mother continued to coach me. *'Call your power and energy back from all beings visible and invisible, who have syphoned, hijacked or held claim upon your sovereign being now! If he chooses love today, be grateful. If not, you know you can always choose love anyways. Know that all that you admire in him is a reflection of what is inside of you! The Solar Feminine that is rising within you does not inflate or deflate according to the whimsy of the ever-changing tides. Instead, she remains buoyantly alive through being accountable for the wisdom she carries. And when she ventures off course, her internal compass steers her to the source of love that dwells within... and that is liberation. Now go and get ready for the wonderful adventures that await you on this brand-new day.'*

After my sobering swim, Aiden and I sat by the rushing river. We listened for guidance as to where to go for the day. The Mary Magdalene Church in the centre of town called to us, along with a return visit to the sea for another glorious swim. We agreed to begin our day at the ocean and then allow the Gypsy spirit of this mythic land to guide us from there.

After completing our morning rituals, we returned to the same beach we visited the day before. The ocean, like a powerful goddess, had an irresistible magnetism. People from all over the world flock to the sea of Saintes-Maries to cleanse and heal from the weary battlefield of their human lives. Her salty elixir held the secret recipe to absolving the scars that coagulated around our most stubborn of wounds. In the crash of a single wave, one's pain and suffering could be cleansed in her merciful embrace, while joy instantaneously restored.

As I entered her refreshing folds, the water engulfed every crevice of my being and seeped into the darkness congealed around the back of my heart. The sunlight bouncing on the surface of the water was hypnotic. Before long, the sticky haze dissolved and was replaced by a feeling of blissful well-being. I floated on my back for a moment and then dove straight down into her dark blue abyss. Coming up for air, I turned to gaze directly into the centre of the sun. As I bobbled in the lapping waves, it burned the bridge of my nose. Before long I fell into a lucid state of heightened awareness.

Wave upon wave of feeling frequency scintillated through me until there was no trace of a 'me' left at all. While floating in a trance, I heard an omnipresent voice speak to me in a timeless tongue. My heart grew wings as I heard these words from this wise and familiar Father Sun.

'Child of the Sun, at one time your human consciousness was pure and pristine. You lived and embodied your primordial archetypal form and light body. You had access to all realms of creation and were not bound by poverty and lack consciousness that has become the density of your third-dimensional world. The Grail is not a thing — it is a way of being that represents the true wealth of who you are. To embody and become the Grail — you must liberate the wealth of spirit within you by remembering you are one being that split into billions of parts and that you are a part of it all. As you purify your heart and free yourself from the density of this world, that density no longer has the power to define you!

'The Solar Christ force is here to restore and regenerate humanity's fallen consciousness. Forgiveness and mass reconciliation is an essential part of healing the collective heart of humanity. Many will be called to cultivate the strength and courage to forgive all that once imprisoned the spirit, such that it may rise to rejoin the heart of Father-Mother God. Faith, along with a fierce tenacity to love the unlovable, will carry you through these winds of change. They are blowing through to cleanse the monadic heart of all that once sequestered the light of your inner sun.'

I responded in a language of light, generated from the pure feeling tone of my soul. *'Mariah ah heya, tiah Ka, doe ma saria, oh lahuana Rael tiakoa.'* Although I muttered no discernable words, my heart poured out in gratitude. *'Thank you, Father Sun, for the precious gift of your wisdom light.'* It felt as if the sun burst inside the centre of my heart, clearing out the cobwebs of doubt and fear. While floating on my back, I soaked in the gifts of these solar light codes while being held in the lapping arms of the Mother.

Feeling completely altered, I swam vigorously out to the horizon with the desire to keep going until I reached the elusive other side. Eventually, I ran out of steam and turned around to see Aiden as a mere speck in the distance. He appeared to also be communing with the Solar Logos. Intentionally choosing to remain in my own space, I swam back to the shore, collapsed onto the warm blanket of sand and breathed deeply into the base of my spine. I expanded my belly like a giant beach ball and exhaled fully, letting go into the embrace of the Earth Mother below me. It felt exhilarating to absorb the suns penetrating rays into every cell of my being as pure, crystalline light. I noticed as I plugged into my Solar Feminine power, my creative life force was ignited and charged by the intoxicating rays of the sun.

Aiden soon appeared and collapsed onto the warm sand next to me. Even though I felt the urge to roll over and smother his skin in golden sunlit kisses, I was now blissfully content to lie side by side. My chest pounded so loud that I felt I was in the centre of a massive drum circle. The beating of our thunderous hearts synchronised as we descended into a hypnotic state. It was if we were transported into the centre of the sun where we were being flooded with heiroglyphic codes of solar light.

'Saint Germain has come in to offer us some reflective words. Are you up for listening?' Then the voice of an upper-class English gentleman began to speak through Aiden.

'Yes, of course,' I responded with open curiosity.

'Hello, dear ones. Thank you for showing up in service at this time of humanity's great awakening. We would say you're coming together is fulfilling a great purpose for all, as you serve to heal the Masculine and Feminine within you. And yet, at the same time we ask you to be aware of getting lost in the illusions that ensnarl you. Personality will craft elaborate dramas to distract you from embodying your full power as sovereign masters of creating your reality. The egoic mind will cleverly invent countless scenarios to detour you from seeing the truth of your 'I am' presence. My dears, each of you has the power to create your own Heaven or hell. And each has dominion to change the channel from where you are broadcasting your consciousness at any time.

Your thoughts, frequency and vibration is what is creating your reality based on the vibrational station you are attuning to. In any given moment, you have the power to choose your manifest–station. It's as simple as that.'

'For many, the fractured mind has taken the reign over one's perception, leading one to cling to the station of helpless victimhood, unable to change the reality one is experiencing at will. What you are experiencing is the unfulfilled and separate parts of yourself that cling to the hope of 'the other' as the one to fulfill the empty places within. While appearing convincingly true, they are essentially holding your true self hostage in the illusion that what you most seek will be fulfilled by joining with another. This can be a great deterrent from the higher service that your souls have come to fulfill.

'Do not get me wrong. A great love is present here between the both of you. And we would even say your love is "quite kosher". And yet love must first be fulfilled within oneself for it to truly flourish in its highest expression with another. And so, dear ones, we ask you to listen more closely to the higher calling that has brought you together. Thank you both for listening and being here. I am honoured to be of service to you as you forge a new paradigm of love.' Aiden cleared his throat as if to signify he was now Aiden and no longer Saint Germain.

I lay in silence, absorbing Saint Germain's wise words, bemused that our love was 'kosher' even in his eyes. Even amongst our polarised perceptions, I felt such an overwhelming love for Aiden – from our highest soul purpose to the very core of my womanly being, where obviously our issues were entangled.

As I integrated the wise words of Saint Germain, my heart-womb yearned to be heard on her own terms and in her own voice. I could feel the sacred codes for evolutionary relationship scintillating within me. I sensed a new way was emerging, one that was large enough to include and bless all beings in its wake. This was what Yeshua and Magdalene were modeling as the lovers of the world. They too were in touch with this way...the way of the unified shared heart.

Even though I was yet to experience this expression of intimate love, I was moved to offer another perspective by following the somatic sensations dancing within my body. My womb held wisdom that it longed to share as the voice of the Divine Feminine! A visceral knowingness coursed through my flesh. I became aware that there is nothing in existence that is not sexual in nature and born from a joining with another. The wisdom of the body must be honoured as an equal partner to the heart and the mind!

I felt into a possibility for a loving partnership that could dance together in sovereign symbiotic union – a loving relationship that embraced the totality of our human and divine experience, bridging instinct with intent, personal and transpersonal, intuition and deliberation, highly personal and utterly transpersonal. In that moment, I could sense a possibility for a sacred relationship that was grounded and expanded enough to welcome and celebrate it all – the wilderness of our animal bodies, the tenderness of our hearts and the conscious light of our divinity. *What a sublime trinity!*

Finally, the fierce voice of my silenced womb summoned the courage to voice my truth on behalf of all silenced wombs while wave upon wave of kundalini energy rippled through my limbs.

'I am the voice of your womb and it is high time that you descend into the depths of my mystery. I invite you to dive into the black fecund of your being and know that this is where all life emerges into this world. Within me lives the spark of enlightenment, the flame of passion and inferno of endless creative life-force. My blood carries the living records of all that has been and ever will be. For too long I have been silenced, abused, denied and mistreated! Those who feared my power have judged and violated me as a way to suppress and control me. They have enslaved, raped, objectified, banished and even sold me for personal gain.'

I paused, inhaled deeply and went on. 'We must change the story! For far too long, women have suffered the wounds of being falsely accused, paralysed by the fear of the world finding out how powerful we are, especially when we come together. No longer will we hide, cloaking our innocence under a blanket of misguided guilt and shame. We will no longer tolerate the oppression of the Divine Feminine!'

I softened my tone and went on. 'I am a sacred and holy vessel, giver of all *life*! To know me is to honour the chalice of my wild innocence. I invite you to open and relax into my awakened, sensate presence, which blooms like a rose through subtlety, breath and sound. If you wish to experience the gifts of my presence, become silent, empty and free of all agenda. If you are moved to partake in the wonder of Source intelligence, surrender your need to dominate and control with your clever schemes. If you care to swim in an ocean of pure aliveness, I invite you to respectfully listen, attune and share without the need for personal gain.'

I took a long deep breath into my swollen belly and then let it out with a big sigh. Tears rolled down my cheeks. I felt relieved to have at last given voice to all that was once silenced. This voice was one with the elemental soul of nature that pulsed through the arteries of the surrounding land. I had known for quite some time that reconnecting with this primordial wisdom was an essential part of my journey, with or without Aiden by my side. This was my destiny, to blossom into a succulent rose whose radiance is drawn forth from her wild roots joining with the Solar Logos.

Aiden remained still as he lay next to me in the sand. His cool presence seemed like a forced restraint while my fire only intensified, causing my heart-womb to burn even brighter! I wisely reassessed that this was still not the moment to cover him in sun-drenched kisses. Instead, I respectfully yielded to the 'closed' sign that hung over his heart.

What is it that you need to feel held and supported, beloved? I asked myself. I needed to care for myself and stay present with my heart-womb space. I envisioned myself running into the sea and diving into the folds of Mother's curvaceous waves. Instead, I stood up, grabbed my bag and strode across the long stretch of sand, heading towards the car. Swollen with a mixture of heartache and revelation, I trampled over the hot sand, as if each step freed me from lifetimes of deceit, coupled with the heat of the moment. I sensed the part of me that was unshackling myself from an intrinsic enslavement while simultaneously walking towards a whole new way of stewarding the sovereign sanctity of the Feminine womb.

Aiden followed behind me at a brisk pace and then walked past me, kicking up the sand behind him. I could have sworn I saw sparks flying off his glistening skin. Then he turned to face me and stood with his muscular arms open wide – completely transparent, open and vulnerable. Aiden began to speak in a language of light – the same kind of sound frequency language that I had spontaneously expressed earlier while communing with Father Sun. I stood, trembling in awe and gave way to his light language that penetrated my innermost heart and sent shivers through the marrow of my bones.

With eyes ablaze, he stepped closer to me and spoke, '*Ah naya ah tu tura ba ishq ka naila ra uma sa.* I am the voice of the Solar Masculine that comes from the diamond Heart of the Sun.'

My human pain dissolved from me instantly. At last, the veil was lifted between us as he began to communicate from a place we both could decipher as higher truth. In a raw, naked presence, we met one another as two transparent light-beings who came from a place far beyond third dimensional reality. We began to exchange light-encoded sound language that transmitted the codes of the Solar Masculine and Feminine. This exquisitely beautiful vibration streamed in from the crystalline core of the central Sun, a place where my soul had longed to return. With tears of joy streaming down our sun-kissed cheeks, we gave ourselves fully to this passionate exchange that melted all perceptions that we were two separate beings. Instead, we saw each other as one being, expressing through two different bodies. All references to ordinary reality dissolved, along with the awareness of our outer environment. We were two illuminated bodies of light, meeting one another in a realm and dimension that can only be described as the monadic body of the Christos Sophia.

Aiden's entire body turned golden as he was showered in the rays of the afternoon sun. I remained standing naked, raw and in empty presence, fully transfixed and receptive to his offering. He dropped to his knees. His face and body trembled in a feverish offering of truth and love.

Then, in the full strength of his Solar Masculine presence, he offered me a most heartfelt prayer. 'Ambe´, I deeply honour you as a Solar Feminine Goddess. I recognise our timeless connection as ancient flames, children of the Great Central Sun reuniting for the purpose of reawakening the God/Goddess essence within. There is such healing, beauty and magnitude in the meeting of our souls, my dear. Please, no matter what happens, always remember the higher purpose of our joining at this time!'

Golden light continued to blaze from his luminous, sun-drenched skin. He began to move and tone in a ritual dance. His jewel-like eyes glowed, becoming pools of passion and gateways to a larger truth that existed far beyond the ordinary world. His lips, limbs and hands danced the story of Sacred Union – two hearts joining as one.

My heart-womb leapt up in recognition as Aiden transmitted the truth-light of his longing for Sacred Union from the depths of his feeling body. I stood transfixed in sacred witness as Aiden's wall of resistance came washing down, like a very complex and elaborate sand castle.

Here we were, two human souls caught in the alchemical fire of reconciling a great paradox of life: the rational mind with the feeling heart and the instinctual womb. The world around us disappeared as our living ceremony unfolded in the wide-open spaces of this public beach once frequented by Mary Magdalene and her Family of Light.

I grounded my roots deep into the Earth and absorbed Aiden's inferno of energy with full body breaths. I responded with a fluid dance of devotional mudras that spontaneously rippled through my arms and hands.

This is important. This is sacred. This prayer is for all beings everywhere, I affirmed to myself, as my surroundings were absorbed into the sun's rainbow prismatic rays. *We are here now,* I thought in awe. *Two war-torn humans, resilient, sun-drenched refugees, who have come to incarnate the fullness of their divine humanity.*

I went on to acknowledge, *I am the disease and I am the cure. I am the saviour and I am the saved. I am the villain and I am the heroine. I am my worst enemy and my own greatest friend. I am the Creator and I am Creation! And all of this suspense-filled drama is immaculately designed to shatter my protective shell and wake me from this falsity into my wildest and most glorious dream! May the fire of the sun expose all distorted perceptions and misguided notions of Self until all that remains is the pure light of awakened consciousness! I am here now, here to embody a love that flourishes in passion, pleasure and knows the precious gift of original life, love and joy. Here to shine the light for all beings to know oneself as the Beloved, here to embody the flower of Sacred Union that blossoms forth from the Grail of sovereign divinity.*

As I radiate a vibration of light in all directions, I declare this world an awakened expression of light and allow all to transform and return to the light. I am the light, the light I AM. I am the light, the light I AM. I am the light, the light I AM. Victory to the light. So be it and so it is!

My spine undulated in a dance that braided Heaven and Earth, while my arms told the story of the Father Sun making majestic love to Mother Earth. Aiden bowed in reverent respect. I stood open to welcome the solar light of the Beloved and then turned toward Aiden, alight with the power of my prayer. Again, he bowed with the air of a Sun God and then reached out and took my hand to his lips. 'Bella, I see your light. I honour your womb.'

At that moment, I let go and surrendered my life to the setting Sun and the fire burning within my heart-womb. It dawned on me that I was actually pregnant with the Sun, the very seed of Christ consciousness. And, as with all births, there are contractions that assist one to purify, open and prepare for the delivery of something far more greater than one could possibly ever imagine.

CHAPTER THIRTY-FIVE

GOLDFINGER

The return of the Feminine is the return to the wisdom heart. Not born of intellect and rationalization but of an innate intelligence, which seeks to harmonize and grow and preserve life. We can only do this by experiencing life through the heart. All of it—the pain and the ecstasy. This is being true to our own inner ecology, which relies upon the rain and the sun to grow the full potentiality of our God selves.

– Niamh Clune, *The Coming of the Feminine Christ*

Let go of thought!
Don't take it into your heart!
You are naked,
And thought is like ice.
You use thought to seek
Release from suffering and pain,
While thought is the cause of your suffering and pain.
The realm of creation
Is outside the scope of thought,
O foolish one,
See the opus, and behold the beauty!
Look in the direction from which the images flow.
See the brook that causes the wheel to turn.

– Jelaluddin Rumi

Aiden and I returned to the car and took a series of long synchronised breaths to assist us in acclimating back to the third dimensional world. Once we did, we noticed that we were beyond famished! The entire day had passed and the sun was quickly disappearing. We decided to make a brief visit to Mary Magdalene's Church and stop at the grocery store on the way back to our quaint riverside bungalow.

Upon entering our kitschy little bungalow, we looked to one another with huge grins. We couldn't help but notice the dramatic change in scenery compared to our recent date on the beach with the Solar Logos.

Aiden sat on the edge of the couch in his sporty white underwear, turned on the TV and took a long swig out of an open bottle of red wine. I stood by the one-burner stove and waited for the water to boil for tea. My heart smiled while observing the charm of this domestic setting. *The mundane moments of life can be profoundly nourishing to a woman's soul,* I mused to myself while appreciating the scenery.

Aiden switched the TV channel and I heard a loud, sultry female voice belt out from the old 1970s television. 'Goldfinger, he's the man with the Midas touch. Golden words, he will pour in your ear. But his lies can't disguise what you fear. For a golden girl knows when he's kissed her, it's the kiss of death from Mr Goldfinger!'

'Good goddess,' I gasped as I listened to the lyrics while pouring the tea. The hot water overflowed from the cup and spilled onto the small counter. I was astounded how the song was like an oracle, giving me clues into my womanly predicament. Aiden remained glued to the TV. I stood at the little table, steaming cup in hand and thought, *Whoa! I'm living out my own mythic version of a 007 film! It's complete with action-packed adventure, dangerous love, the 'mysterious enemy,' and ultimately, the looming fate of this precious Earth.* I didn't know whether to laugh, cry or catch a ride on the next passing ferryboat.

I remembered those unforgettable visions of Armageddon that haunted me in my dreams as a child. These visions planted the seeds for my 007 Light-worker mission to ripen at this very time. I wasn't going to stand on the sidelines of life as a so-called innocent bystander. As if there was such a thing. *My mission was to be on the front lines and stand by Her...with Her...and as Her.*

I handed Aiden his tea. He placed it on the side table and instead took another swig from his bottle of wine while completely absorbed by the film.

I flashed on the old game show I grew up with called, *The Price is Right,* which would have been better named, *The Price is Way Too High!* The audience sits at the edge of their seats in suspense while a random contestant chooses a door that conceals a prize that can change their entire world in a single spin of a wheel.

Hmmm, I thought to myself with an air of irony, *what door will humanity choose? Door number one: full annihilation of all sentient beings caused by misappropriated use of leadership, power, resources, war and blatant disrespect for life on Earth? Or, door number two: everyone tries to fix and change the broken systems with new and improved systems that are built on top of the old ones. Hmmm?*

I closed my eyes. *I choose door number three! This is the threshold of radical self-responsibility, where we view our global crisis as a catalyst for radical change. Where we wake up to our highest potential as interdependent, planetary custodians of life on Earth. Instead of privatising or hoarding, we synergise our gifts and optimise our unified potential. Each life-form gets to flourish as a resource for generous contribution by loving more, blessing more, giving more and showing up more for the whole. This level of self-sourcing would empower individuals to take full responsibility for the part they are playing in the larger pattern of the whole. As each of us becomes congruent with the larger pattern of ones soul, we become the change, the genesis medium that births the next octave of evolution.*

Yes, door number three ...the door of me into we. This is the door where the amnesia finally wears off and each comes to re-member that life is not happening to us – it's happening through us and as us...and ultimately for us! Yes! Door number three it is. The door where everyone is a winner!

In that moment, I glimpsed the responsibility of who I was as a conscious co-creator. I knew beyond a shadow of a doubt that this universal benevolent force expressing as conscious Love, Beauty Intelligence, is always creating on my behalf and could meet me only in and as much as I could meet myself. Like all of human life,

I stood at a crossroads and was being invited to move beyond the seductive dramas of externalised good and evil, right and wrong, and so forth. It was time to inhabit my place within the centre of it all, embracing the full spectrum of light and dark with gratitude for the inherent gift in it all. My 007 mission was to join the land of the living through the recognition that there is no power greater than the power of my own perception to see everything…especially myself through the eyes of being the love rather than being blind-sighted by the illusion of unrequited love. *Hah!*

What will it take to move beyond war and choose the way of peace? I imagined, holding the microphone up to all of humanity as the cosmic MC from the hit television show, *the Price Is Way Too High.*

My cheeky captivation with TV game shows and the Goldfinger metaphor soon subsided. I switched gears and gently asked Aiden, 'Would you like to come out and enjoy a cuppa by the river? I would love to reflect on our day and share about the powerful experiences we had.'

I received no response. Instead, Aiden chose to escape further into the TV, aimlessly changing channels as if to disengage from the raw vulnerability of his heart being blown wide open by the Solar Logos.

I so wanted to celebrate our communion with the heart of the Sun. But once again, Mr. Hot & Cold preferred to hide out in his man cave, somewhere far, far away in TV land. I gazed out of the thick wooden shutters to get a glimpse of the rising moon and then resigned myself to lie down in our lopsided bed. My heart pounded furiously under my skin.

Twenty minutes later, Aiden came to lie next to me in bed and fell asleep in approximately three point five minutes. I was sure I would wake him as my thunderous heart pounded in my chest. Finally, I couldn't contain myself any longer. The dam wore thin and I began to sob. Aiden stirred and moaned, and then with an air of irritation, gestured for me to deal with my emotions on my own. 'Go outside, *please*,' he grumbled, as if reprimanding a disruptive child.

'Of course,' I conceded. I went outside stark naked and sat at the riverbank to offer my tears to the light of the beautiful full moon. This was Mary's moon. I could tell by the iridescent light dancing on the water that was always a sign of her presence. The paradox of my experiences dumbfounded me. Even amongst my glimpses of higher truth and enlightened epiphanies, there was no escaping this avalanche of erupting emotion. It was true, I thought as I sensed a larger pattern unfolding. My inner child had no end to her feelings of abandonment triggered by my engrained desire to love and be loved. *It's only natural, right?*

In my willingness to feel the unbearable, I was met with the grace and support of my Family of Light who surrounded me. Amidst my existential downpour, I felt the presence of Mary Magdalene come through to offer her comfort and High Council. She appeared in spirit and was accompanied by two etheric dolphin guides. She sat before me as if to have a womanly heart-to-heart, moonlight chat.

I connected with her spirit through the ephemeral lyrics of Snatam Khar. 'Carry me across the ocean, carry me with your love. Give me your hand, hold me close. Give me peace, sweet peace.'

Mary soothed me with her words of wisdom and loving compassion born from her own human experiences.

'I was once here, where you are now, dear sister of the rose, sitting by the banks of this very river, looking toward the stars for answers to my deepest questions and heart's deepest longings. Imagine it — my beloved Yeshua nailed to the cross to model to humanity that love can never be extinguished. It was an initiation he had to complete, and he had much support from us all. Yet afterwards, all was chaos and danger. I had no other choice but to flee from the soldiers and move on with my life. And so my family and I set sail to this land to carry forth the teachings of my Beloved with the seed of his child ripening in my womb. At times, I felt painfully alone and forlorn as I longed for physical union with Yeshua. In truth, it catalysed a great opportunity for me to dive deeper into the depths and bond with the source of the Beloved within as I knew he could never leave me. Although Yeshua and I are Twin Flames — one soul incarnated in two bodies — I incarnated, as you have, to undergo the great initiation of embodying my divine sovereignty and learn that the Love I Am is whole unto itself. It cannot be divided, nor is it reliant on any outer source for its completion. This awareness is the true gift of the Christ child that grows inside of you. Like an everlasting spring, your

love is eternal, forever sourced by the Beloved that dwells within. So yes, dear sister, all that you are and ever will be is already here awaiting your tender embrace.'

Tears streamed down my face and merged with the river. I bowed my head and saw my reflection on the surface of the water being illuminated by the light of the moon. The purity of love and piercing light of Mary's words had opened my heart to a higher truth, while the presence of the twin dolphin guides reminded me of my true origin of joy, which is inherently Self-replenishing. I sat on the dock under the stars, allowing the transmission to fill me. Then, feeling raw and vulnerable, returned to bed, humbly surrendering to my fate.

As I slid onto my side of the sagging mattress, Aiden stirred from his sleep and slipped his hand into mine. I felt his compassionate presence gently being offered to me, meeting me where I had just met myself. Lying there with my hand entwined in his, I soon fell into a lucid dream. I dreamt that I was in sacred counsel with a group of highly evolved Ascended Master beings who were counseling me on how to keep my heart open, no matter what outer conditions and circumstances were presented to me. The trick was to feel the flames fully without attaching the heat to a person or a story. I awoke at dawn with the vivid image of a St Bernard dog imprinted like a postage stamp upon my third eye.

As the first morning light flooded our room, Aiden and I snuggled, and I shared my vision of the St Bernard. I also told him about my experience by the river with Mary Magdalene and the twin dolphins. He held me with warmth and listened with interest, before cracking a huge yawn. Filled with a dose of domestic bliss, I smiled warmly then left him to doze off, while I went to the market to fetch some fresh fruits and yoghurt for our morning breakfast. *Je suis afamé !*

CHAPTER THIRTY-SIX

LE SACRE' COEUR

O Birther! Father-Mother of the Cosmos
Focus your light within us — make it useful.
Create your reign of unity now —
through our fiery hearts and willing hands.
Help us love beyond our ideals
and sprout acts of compassion for all creatures.
Animate the Earth within us: we then
feel the Wisdom underneath supporting all.
Untangle the knots within
so that we can mend our hearts' simple ties to each other.
Don't let surface things delude us,
But free us from what holds us back from our true purpose.
Out of you, the astonishing fire,
Returning light and sound to the cosmos. Amen.

– Neil Douglas-Klotz, *Prayers of the Cosmos*

Gradually he lifted those discordant and incoherent fear-based energies into love's coherent expression of harmony. Skillfully projecting light, sound and color, he cleansed and purified the aura. Holding each individual in innocence, there was a release of fear. With the letting go of fear, there was room to breathe, the perception of time and space expanded into a greater awareness of the eternal presence of love. Through co-created harmonic resonance the Divine Healer, who dwells in every heart, worked miracles through Yeshua, Mary Magdalene, and the other initiated disciples.

– Claire Heartsong, *Anna, Grandmother of Jesus*

When I returned from the market, Aiden was still lounging in bed. He had no appetite and complained of an enormous headachey pain on his right temple.

My compassion immediately responded, ready to offer healing relief. I knelt by the bed, my bag of food forgotten. 'Can you track the source of this pain in your body?' I inquired.

He was silent for a long-drawn-out pause. 'It...feels related to navigating through the head instead of the heart. Overusing my third eye to scout out what could possibly harm me. I'm being called to surrender my pattern of hyper-vigilance and control. Um, my chest and belly are also really tight.'

'May I tune in with you?'

'Yes, please,' he said, letting out an uncomfortable groan.

I silently grounded, created conscious boundaries and tuned in to open a larger field of awareness. With innate empathy and understanding, I recognised this pattern within myself. I saw that these were places we both constricted our energy in order to protect our hearts and remain in control. The energetic circuits in his body had become blocked, mistrusting the primordial life-force to course through him without the need to do anything with it. He was locked into a defence mechanism, which guarded him against getting hurt or losing control of his personal space. The headache showed him how he took control with his mind in order to bypass the unpredictability of his body and heart. He was mirroring my own coping mechanisms back to me.

'Aiden, would you be open to receiving a belly massage? I will offer you a safe space to feel and release this protective armouring. All you have to do is focus on continuous breathing and make sounds or tones that come naturally to you.'

'Yes, I am open to receive your healing touch. Thank you,' he said with refreshing receptivity.

I knew that if I was to be in highest service and respect, I needed to be totally neutral and create a sacred space for him to relax into his own process through fully detaching from our personal dynamic. I took a few grounding breaths and said in a clear, resonant voice, 'I call upon the Divine Mother to work through me as an instrument of healing. I offer a pure intention to support Aiden in healing himself through releasing anything and everything that is blocking his energy to flow through his body. May all pain and suffering be transmuted and released, returned to source, and may he receive whatever he requires to come into balance with his body, mind and spirit. May it be so. Aho!

'Aiden, if you ever feel unsafe or uncomfortable, simply raise your index finger and I will pause to check in with you. As always, you are the captain of your ship.'

I felt Mary Magdalene and the twin dolphins come in to support and guide me to allow the Divine Feminine to flow through me while intending for him to reconnect the circuit of primal innocence between his heart and his sexual life-force energy.

She guided me to hold specific points on his feet to ground his connection to the Earth and guide his awareness into his roots. I worked up his legs and knees, affirming his sense of support and direction in life. When I reached his hips I could sense the energy building in his hara. I poured coconut oil onto his skin and massaged his belly with tender care and gentle deference. The best way to clear tension is by opening the wind gates around the navel. Resting my hand on his heart, I proceeded to loosen the armoured fascia around his lower abdomen by sinking my elbow into each of the eight wind gates that surrounded the rim of his navel while inviting deep and conscious breathing until I felt them each release with a gentle pop.

Aiden's breathing began to increase, and I could feel a warm glow wash over his entire body as he incrementally let go and allowed the trust and relaxation to open and expand his heart. His breath and energy continued to build until he had a full body release followed by a flood of primordial tears. He let go on such a monumental level. It was if he had released an invisible band that had kept his upper and lower chakras severed at the Solar Plexus, neither of them trusting in the other...until now, when they were invited to be unified in the heart of primordial innocence.

Through an avalanche of wrenching sobs, he confessed to me, 'All my life I've been desperately fighting with my mind to stay in control! I've bullied and denied my very own heart! I've mistrusted my instinctual body. I've mistrusted all others, and even my own sexuality. I have denied myself the wisdom of my deepest feelings! I've been so goddamn afraid of losing control!'

Aiden grabbed my hand as he continued to release lifetimes of deeply suppressed primal energy, which had been locked up in a tight knot so as to suppress any emotional outbursts. In between sobs, he groaned and roared like a lion as I held space as a sacred witness, continuing to ground the enormous energy into the Earth and guiding it back up into the heart where it could simply relax open and rest in peace *and* pleasure.

As Aiden processed this huge catharsis, I recollected a passage from a book called *Dear Lover,* by David Deida.

> Your surrender and offering of love's divine light is also the source of your life's art, your devotional gift to all beings, and the only way to live open as your heart's deepest pleasure. Would you rather live any other way? You already intuit your deepest divine love and gifts, right now. If you didn't, you wouldn't yearn as you do... You can open and express this love spontaneously from your deepest heart, through your whole body, so every movement of your life is a reflection of the sacred. Love is not something that happens or not. Love is a discipline, a constant practice and commitment to feel and love our shells, relaxing with humour and surrendering open through your love-softened shells that would otherwise suppress your energy and build walls around your heart.

We spent the rest of the day nourishing our bodies, doing yoga and lounging like two lazy cats by the river. Aiden was mostly quiet, but his energy felt softer, more receptive and willing to trust the journey before us. I was stronger, self-contained and more attentive to my own needs. I sensed that the more I refocused my energies toward self care while giving Aiden the space to process in his own way, the more a natural balance and harmony could flow between us. That night, we slept like babies in a tender open vulnerability that came from burning through the intense fires of our protective armouring and unconscious defences. I prayed that the morning would bring us to a new place of grace and ease, where we could relax in gratitude and savour the evaporating moments that we still had left to be together.

CHAPTER THIRTY-SEVEN

SAINT BERNARD

Imagine for a moment that the Grail chalice, a cup made of the purest gold and embedded with priceless gems, represents the heart realm. It is to find this precious Grail cup that Perceval embarks on the quest. He comes upon it in the Grail castle, which is the home of a strange wounded king. Our heart has been in the charge of a wound. The Myth is about how to heal this wound and how to heal the heart. Sometimes those vivid dreams contain an experience of a union with another person that is so deep there is no differentiation between the emotional/sexual/spiritual components of the experience, a kind of connection that goes way beyond what we normally are able to share. We feel a Oneness that transcends all other. We cannot truly experience this Oneness until our hearts are freed. Much rests then, upon the healing of the heart for the emergence of the Grail.

– Diana Durham, The Return of King Arthur

Embodying the Soul/Love essence is where the physical truly becomes a chalice and Grail, a vessel for Spirit and the Elixir of Life – the Womb of Creation and the Sacred Union double helix – activating the dark matter/ 'junk' DNA as conscious birthing from the creative cauldron of infinite light and wisdom. This dissolves all obstacles and blockages, transmuting the energetic fields and techno intrusions around us that hold toxins, low frequencies and negative energy. Allow your physical body to receive this heart-deepening flow and transformation of the physical so that it vibrates and emanates love and wisdom from the soul, clearing the body, Gaia and creative channels so they can hold the Light-force and Life-

force of Source without obstruction or manipulation, flowing through our unique expressions and personalities in a unified whole.

– Laura Magdalena

As the sun came up across the river, Aiden and I arose to meet the new day feeling refreshed and renewed. Both of us embodied a newly relaxed, grounded clarity. We took time to enjoy our morning ritual of yoga, muesli, fruit, yoghurt, and a swim in the river. Feeling refreshed and reborn, we packed up our things for a day trip to the region of Arles in search of where the river greets the sea. I knew it was an important pilgrimage for me to make as freedom's song played on and on, in the back of my mind, 'Where the river greets the sea, this is how I love thee.' Aiden's willingness to come along buoyed my optimism, and we set off for the day in high spirits.

Arles is a large town located north of Saintes-Maries-de-la-Mer. It is especially famous for its flourishing arts community and being a place that Vincent Van Gogh would frequently go to paint. I had only a few clues for our mission: the first one, enigmatically enough, was the St Bernard dog that had vividly appeared to me in my dream. The other clue was a simple knowingness guided by Mary Magdalene that I would uncover something that was now ready to be unearthed.

We bid our sweet bungalow goodbye and stopped to pay the small fee to the beautiful bleached-blond Madonna.

As she kissed both my cheeks and embraced me, she whispered, 'Il a change!'

'*Oui,*' I answered, grinning. Then I thought, *And so I have.*

We drove toward Arles, zipping along the highway in our rental car. The warm wind blew through my hair, inviting me to relax, let go and trust the journey. Yet I had no idea where to go or where to begin. I could only trust that my intuitive clues would trickle in like small drops of water, each drop carving out the way to where the river greets the sea.

It felt good to be out and about while taking in the beautiful Camargue landscape. I was excited to embark on yet another adventure with Sir Aiden Arthur, who had come to be a part of my growing Grail family. Something nameless had shifted between us. For one, we were less resistant and more available to expose the hidden barriers and all that kept us from coexisting in harmonic resonance.

Once we arrived in Arles, we decided to stop for a coffee and check out the map to locate where the river Rhône forks into two branches, forming the Camargue Delta. Compared to Saintes-Maries-de-la-Mer, Arles was a big city, full of bustling students who attended the infamous Ecole Des Arts. The streets were lined with outdoor cafés and enigmatic billboards advertising the latest art exhibits in town. I could feel my creative juices sparkling from the mélange of Bohemian culture, brimming from the outdoor cafés and bistros.

Aiden and I made a quick stop at one of the many local café's where we sat outside under the veranda and ordered a couple of lattes. As we savoured the deliciousness of our creamy beverage, we unfolded a map and asked for divine guidance as to what direction we should embark on. I felt a little nervous about heading up our expedition. What if we couldn't find the right place? What if I was leading us on a wild goose chase? I excused myself to use the bathroom, hoping I would get one of my brilliant insights or epiphanies while sitting on the porcelain throne. Instead, I got an entirely different kind of surprise.

As I walked to the back of the café, I was greeted by a beautiful St Bernard dog with a lolling red tongue and huge wagging tail! There he was, the robust St Bernard I had seen in my dream two nights ago. He waddled right up to me as if he was expecting me all along. As I bent down to pet him, he lifted his paw and put it on my shoulder. *What a wondrously warm welcome from an animal I'm only just meeting for the first time!*

The dog connected with me, like an old familiar friend. *Thank you, Great Spirit! This is just the confirmation I needed! Now I know we are on track,*' I said to myself as I smothered my four-legged Saint in kisses then headed to the bathroom, wagging my own happy human tail with elation.

When I returned to the table to introduce my new friend to Aiden, he felt as delighted by the synchronicity as I did. We recognised our St Bernard friend as the guardian gatekeeper to the mystery that was about to unfold, and thanked him with our enthusiastic cuddles and caresses.

So with a spark of hope in our hearts, we set off and drove through the narrow cobblestone streets lined with boutiques, museums and outdoor restaurants. After a good forty-five-minute drive through the tiny lanes, we still could not find the road that led to the end of the river. I was aware that Aiden's patience was growing thin. I could feel his simmering anxiety regarding all that we had been through over the previous days. To his credit, he persevered without snapping at me or retreating. After what seemed like hours of driving around and looking for the right street with no success, I succumbed to feeling as frustrated as Aiden. Just when I was ready to abort our mission, we came across a small road leading out of town. Aiden quickly made a sharp left, and finally, our persistence was rewarded! We both had a feeling that this was the road leading to the river's end.

We followed it cautiously until we came across a sign that read in French: 'Private Property: Do NOT Trespass.' We looked at each other, grinned and then simultaneously chose to ignore the sign.

'We'll be fine,' Aiden said as he drove onto the small dirt track. 'We'll just claim to be dumb, lost tourists,' he added with a mischievous 007 grin.

'I like your style,' I said, smiling back at him, so grateful for his spirit of adventure and willingness to follow the tiniest of clues. The country road was lined with orchards of aligned fruit trees that seemed to go on forever. At the end of the unpaved road was another 'No Trespassing' sign and singular old farmhouse. My body barometer indicated that we were headed in the right direction, so we parked the car and got out to explore a little further.

The place appeared to be completely deserted. There were several paths leading to the river. We decided to try the first one. After walking along the dusty path for a few minutes, the only signs of life we found were a worn-out child's doll, a beer bottle and an empty packet of chips. We finally got to a place where we could push through a tangle of trees that led us to the bank of the mossy green river. I spotted a small embankment downstream and instantly felt cosmic shivers light up my spine. Without a doubt, this tiny island held something profoundly familiar and dear to my heart. Beyond the island, the river widened and continued to make its way to the sea. My hair stood up on my skin, washed in goddess bumps. *This was the place! This is where the river greets the sea.*

We scrambled down a small ravine and then hopped onto the rocky shore of the small island. It was completely overgrown with wild bushes and small trees. We found a clearing in the middle of the overgrown plants and sat down to face one another. Aiden and I both sensed we had entered a portal that would allow us to tap in between the worlds and see beyond the veil of ordinary life.

As soon as we sat upon the earth, laden in rocks, twigs and leaves, and got as comfortable amidst the rugged terrain, ordinary reality began to change. We sat in silence, and cleared our chakras from the long drive and then dropped into a meditative trance. As soon as my energetic field was harmonised, balanced and attuned, my body shuddered. The presence and frequency of Mary Magdalene braided with my own. She gave me the feeling that she had once visited this remote embankment herself. While embodying her sublime presence, I spoke aloud what I was seeing and experiencing, pulsating from the womb of this land.

'In front of me sits a beautiful carved wooden box – a darkly stained wedding chest, intricately engraved with a simple motif on the outside. I can sense it contains the most sacred and treasured belongings. When I place my hand on the lid, I can experience the details precisely, just as if it has been unearthed and is sitting before us now.

'Grandmother Anna had prepared and given Mary this box on the day of her Sacred Union ceremony to Yeshua. Within it, she kept the most sacred relics of her life with Yeshua. Exiled from Mt Carmel, Mary and the others departed Egypt on a very small boat. They could only take a few items with them on their precarious voyage to France. This small chest and its sacred contents had travelled all the way across the vast sea in their little boat that landed not far from where we sit now.'

My heartbeat increased as I opened the lid of the chest. Pictures and feelings of remembrance flooded my being. 'On top of the pile of objects are two strings of Tibetan malas, made of finely polished yak bone. Yeshua had brought them back from the Far East upon returning from his studies with Babaji and the Tibetan Rinpoches. I can see Mary and Yeshua sitting before a fire. They're offering prayers into the beads for the liberation of all suffering and the happiness of all sentient beings.'

With reverence, I lifted the malas out of the wooden box and began to rub them between my hands. 'Despite their etheric nature, I can feel the millions of mantras and countless prayers of loving compassion that have been rubbed into these beads, making the yellowish bone smooth to the touch.' I placed them gently back inside the carved wooden chest.

'Next, I see two bleached white linen prayer shawls. They appear to be hand woven by Mother Mary as a wedding gift to Mary and Yeshua. I can see them both kneeling before an earthen clay altar. In a tender moment, I see Mary placing one of the shawls around Yeshua's broad shoulders and then Yeshua placing the other around Mary. "May you always be clothed by the sun and find shelter in our shared heart. We are one." I hear him whisper.

'Next, I unroll a parchment inscribed with Aramaic letters. I recognise it as a blessing prayer of Sacred Union. As they light a singular candle, they recite the Aramaic prayer inscribed on the parchment.' The scene fades and my awareness returns to the chest.

Once again, I envisioned this Sacred Union ceremony through the eyes and heart of Mary Magdalene. It was all so vivid that I could feel her subtle lightbody, allowing me to touch, see and feel through her eyes and her illuminated heart.

As clear as day, I could still taste the sweet meats and bittersweet wine lingering upon my lips. My nostrils filled with the smell of burning copal, frankincense and myrrh. During the Sacred Union ceremony, I experienced Mary placing the mala around her Beloved Yeshuas neck and anointing him with spikenard oil. I was so moved by their soulful gaze as they tenderly honoured their shared heart-flame. An all-consuming, transcendent love washed through my entire being, encompassing me in the vibrational feeling frequency of merging with my most cherished beloved. My heart pounded, as the past, present and future braided together as one and I am flooded with a full-body memory of Divine Sacred Union. I recalled the Heart Sutra mantra and whispered it under my pounding heart. '*Gate, gate, paragate, parasamgate, bodhi svaha.* Gone, gone, gone beyond, gone altogether beyond, oh what an awakening, it is!'

My awareness returned to the carved wooden chest. Under the carefully folded linen shawls, I unwrapped a delicate alabaster jar from a finely woven cloth. As I held the vessel, I can see Mary chanting mantras and reciting prayers while preparing herbs and fine oils for anointing her Beloved in a tantric ritual shared just before his crucifixion.

The last item in the chest sent chills up my spine. 'I am gently unwrapping yet another sacred object also wrapped in a fine piece of white woven cloth. I see a simple wooden cup with an engraved Celtic knot, painted in gold and silver. I sense it has come down from Mary's Celtic lineage of Britannia. It had been used frequently when the apostles gathered for communal supper, prayer and meditation. As time passed, this cup gathered more and more significance. With each use, it became increasingly charged until a golden Christ light emanated from it.

'I am now being shown that Mary and Yeshua, along with their disciples, drank together from this chalice on several sacred occasions. Once, on the Sabbath eve of their wedding and then again, at the Last Supper, just before her Beloved ascended from this world.'

I gently opened my eyes while continuing to embody the succulent presence of Mary Magdalene as bride of Yeshua.

Aiden had been so attuned to me that he opened his eyes at the very same moment. His heightened gaze greeted mine with a warm and all-embracing heart smile. His voice was soft and resonant. 'Let us hold this golden chalice together as a symbol of our shared heart.'

As we embraced the chalice, we felt a fire ignite in our hands. Our hearts exploded with a universal love and compassion for all beings everywhere. We went on to envision the massive golden chalice being etherically anchored into the river so that the energetic activation of Divine Sacred Union could radiate into the entire region and beyond. With great passion and heartfelt prayer, we lifted the chalice to the sky and offered it up for all of humanity as a symbolic offering of the Inner Marriage – the crucible of the awakened heart-womb, unified with the flame of Christ Consciousness.

We held the vision of the massive golden chalice being placed into the centre of the river. I felt my body shudder, knowing that I too was being consecrated as a living chalice. Aiden and I continued to hold hands as we looked out to the river that gently rippled towards the sea, making a sweet lapping sound. We knew that the golden chalice we had anchored together would serve as an energetic beacon to guide beings home to awaken and in turn wed the Beloved within.

Aiden was beaming. He looked like a mixture of a proud husband and a noble lion king. In a mysterious and unspoken way, revisiting these relics had allowed us to remember the importance of these divine archetypal rituals and the vow we had each made to the Divine Beloved long ago – and to always stay connected through the way of the open heart.

This was the balm and the bond between us – whether together or apart. I began to spontaneously chant the Heart Sutra mantra '*Gate gate paragate parasamgate gate bodhi svaha.*'

Its relevance at the time would only come clear to me years later when I re-experienced the memory of receiving the Heart Sutra initiation in a prior Tibetan lifetime. The mantra would serve all beings to experience the true nature of emptiness. In the Red Tantra of Sacred Union, it would assist the initiate to remain anchored in one's heart, free of all grasping and all that brings upon pain, suffering and the unbearable fear of loss. The Heart Sutra is an ultimate gift of loving compassion, born to honour the transcendent experience of Sacred Union with the Divine, the one relationship that can never be tainted nor lost.

In a silent reverence, we returned to our meditative state and placed the wedding chest back in the place we unearthed it. We remained in humble awe of what had just transpired and its significance for all beings. After several moments of integrative silence, we stood up and walked away from the tiny island where the river flowed into the sea. My heart overflowed in gratitude for getting to experience a Sacred Union ceremony born from the Inner Marriage, and what Mary Magdalene and Yeshua Ben Joseph had embodied and devoted their lives to. I was beginning to glimpse why the couple was typically depicted in art with their finger pointing in towards their own heart.

As we retraced our steps down the 'No Trespassing' path, I felt blessed to have discovered this hidden enclave and relive the rituals of long ago through the eyes of Mary Magdalene and her beloved Yeshua. I felt alive with the possibility to know a love that was large enough to include all beings within it. Yeshua had prophesied that the Cosmic Christ would return, not as man, nor religion, but as the Light of the Divine shining forth from the hearts of all beings. I sang softly to myself in a musingly way, *Amazing grace, how sweet the sound, that saved a soul like me! I once was lost, but now I'm found, was blind but now I see.*

Predictably, as soon as we got back into the car, the energy between us grew thick like molasses: sticky, dark and difficult for me to breathe in. Once again, Aiden had retreated into his shell like one of those crabs you find on the beach. Like an untended blister, his irritability festered under his skin, threatening to ooze out and make things messy.

I felt authentically moved to create a safe space for him to open up and share what he was feeling, yet there was no apparent invitation to do so – and so I too retreated further into my shell. Whatever his secret burden, I knew that my integrity lay with myself and my ongoing capacity to trust, let go and allow him the space to go through his process in his own way.

When I checked in with how *I* was feeling, I felt called to celebrate and bask in the high-frequency transmissions that we had just shared together. But since he was unavailable, I proceeded to do that on my own, feeling a bizarre mixture of sober humility and bubbling joy. I was getting trained in detachment while giving myself what I most longed to receive.

Luckily, the gnawing reality of our grumbling bellies brought us back to the basics. We sought a place to comfortably relax and enjoy a simple meal. At least that was the idea. However, our silence had once again turned into an uncomfortable awkwardness as we headed out of Arles towards Saintes-Maries to grab a bite to eat.

Aiden swerved off the road when he spotted a quaint little specialty shop with an adjoining outdoor terrace. We parked and grabbed our day bags. At once, I was elated to find an array of gourmet foods, fresh vibrant produce, and handmade soaps and essential oils displayed in hand woven baskets lined with lavender, as if each item was a rare delicacy prepared for the king and queen. I placed some items for our lunch inside a beautiful hand woven basket that rested in the crook of my elbow and then proceeded to check out.

'Let's celebrate!' I still sparkled with the joy from our communion by the river.

He grunted, 'I need food.'

As we sat at an outdoor patio table overlooking the parking lot, a dark heavy cloud followed us. We nibbled on fresh rustic bread, goat cheese, cucumber slices and oily sardines out of the can. Honestly, despite my attempts to remain neutral, I was growing weary of Aiden's unpredictable hot-and-cold spells. While taking a bite out of a crispy cucumber, I checked in with him energetically. I could feel a current of strong emotion pushing into the fortress of his hardened heart. Then I checked in with my heart and pondered whether I should call him out of his gloomy shell with a healthy dose of good ol' honest communication. I did my absolute best to remain open, vulnerable and present, especially when my heart could have just as easily shut down along with his. *Wham, bam, thank you, man!*

Well, his truth is not necessarily my truth, I thought as I scanned the universe for answers and a higher ground to stand upon. *Once again,* I reminded myself, *Be patient. Trust Aiden will open up and share if and when it feels right for him.* I knew that respect was the highest form my love could take while leaning in to tend to my own tender heart. *This is quite the roller-coaster ride,* I added. *I'm sure getting plenty of opportunities to stay home in the sunshine of my heart no matter what the sudden change of weather may be!*

I reflected on growing up as a highly sensitive empath, where my well-being was often contingent on my family's unpredictable moods. *Could I be myself, stay in the love, be happy whether another was choosing to meet me in that love or not? Or would I allow my energy to be syphoned by getting hooked into the powerful emotions of others, often overwhelming my experience and shaping how I would feel?*

I took a chunk out of the loaf of bread and reflected on my relationship with my parents. As a child, I suffered from such immense neglect that I created clever ways to coax them into loving me through ascertaining what they needed, while learning to override my own needs.

Codependent no more! I declared inwardly.

Once again, I was being invited to reel in my empathic nature and come to see that whatever Aiden was going through was not necessarily about me.

Perhaps this was yet another golden opportunity for me to not take his behaviour personally. Instead, what if I could take his apparent neglect as an opportunity to give myself what I most longed to receive? What if this was the only real integral way to be when someone is not present nor meeting me? What if I could remain open, grateful and be able to bless the moments we had together no matter what he was choosing? What if I could use everything in my life as an opportunity to love this being more rather than measuring my love out according to what he was giving? How freeing would that be? I still had so much to learn about staying present with myself while remaining open to love without basing that love on another's reciprocation.

I smiled warmly over at Aiden and fully appreciated that he was exactly where he needed to be...and so was I. Then I popped a succulent green olive into my mouth while savouring yet another blessed day in paradise. *Gone, gone, gone beyond!*

CHAPTER THIRTY-EIGHT

LET LOVE REIGN

When love beckons to you, follow him,
though his ways are hard and steep.
And when his wings enfold you yield to him,
though the sword hidden among his pinions may wound you.
And when he speaks to you, believe in him,
though his voice may shatter your dreams
as the north wind lays waste the garden.
For even as love crowns you, so shall he crucify you.
Even as he is for your growth so is he for your pruning.
Even as he ascends to your height and caresses your tenderest branches
that quiver in the sun, so shall he descend to your roots
and shake them in their clinging to the Earth.

– Khalil Gibran, *The Prophet*

THE GRAIL

They are like shy young school kids – time and space
Before the woman and the man who are intimate with God
The realised soul can play with this universe
The way a child can a ball.
A chalice – the Grail my body became, for it held the Christ
And HE drank from me.
Sanctified are our limbs
For every heart has touched God, though most with closed eyes.

A Holy relic is each creature, and beauty may worry about its comeliness waning.
We fear dying until we know the truth of ourselves.
The seams on my body are torn.
I have stepped from the region of me
That did not love all the time.

– St. Teresa of Avila, *Love Poems from God*

When we arrived back in Saintes-Maries, I was guided to check availability at the sea-front hotel, Le Dauphin Bleu. Le Dauphin Bleu was built in the 1930s. It had three floors which towered right over the glistening sea. Aiden asked for a room with a view, but we ended up declining because it was significantly more expensive.

'Never mind. The weekend hustle and bustle coming from the boardwalk below sounds like a carnival. We'll be better off with the peace and quiet,' I consoled us.

We ended up in a little room on the second floor at the back end of the hotel. The quaint room was nestled in close proximity to Mary Magdalene's Church.

'It's so tranquil here,' I said, noticing the faint sounds brimming from closing shops and the distant bells coming from bicycles riding by.

Exhausted from the fullness of the day, we showered off and decided to take a short siesta before going out to peruse the town. I noticed Aiden had become more amiable and relaxed. He seemed to have worked through the tension around his heart. Both of us knew that we had received massive energetic upgrades from Spirit on that little embankment. As for me, I was more tolerant of our differences, coming to accept that we processed our experience in our own unique ways. *To each their own, as Yeshua would say!*

'After our nap, how bout we go out and celebrate our last evening together?' Aiden suggested.

'Yes, let's,' I agreed. Though, I wasn't sure that celebrate was the word I would have chosen. It was hard to comprehend that in less than twenty-four hours, I would be flying away from someone I had waited lifetimes to meet. My heart quickened, along with the sand

I envisioned pouring through an hourglass. *So why not celebrate and enjoy our last moments together?* I consoled myself. The river of life will inevitably carry me to the sea to join with an even larger destiny.

After we enjoyed a leisurely shower, we laid our wet heads on the freshly laundered pillows. Aiden opened the window to let in the afternoon sea breeze and to air out the over-bearing lavender scent. I noticed the stained glass window from the adjacent church directly faced our hotel window.

I assumed my usual sleeping position next to Aiden – on my back with a safe amount of safe space between us. Each wrapped safely in the cocoons of our sarongs, we lay there suspended in awe, feeling the deliciousness of our refreshed bodies and elated hearts. While reflecting on the day's auspicious discoveries, I was brimming with the blessings of what the day had brought and could sense that Aiden was feeling the same.

Getting to energetically experience Mary's Sacred Union ceremony with Yeshua was one of the highlights of my Grail journey. There was so much to integrate, so I began my ritual of breathing deeply into my belly. The more I breathed, the more the serpent in my spine began to stir awake. It felt as if I still embodied the archetypal energy of Mary Magdalene as a bride. Now here I am in the wedding chamber with my beloved! I did my best to contain my elation as I felt into the sweet intensity of this highly charged moment. At that point, I had learned to harness my experience and stay free of needing to make it into anything or project it onto anyone. That was until Aiden and I reached for each other's hands in the exact same moment. We squeezed tightly with a mixture of passion, intensity and numb disbelief as we felt into the magnitude of all that we had experienced together.

Then all of a sudden, Aiden pulled me close to his naked chest. Pictures flooded my mind as I reviewed our epic Grail adventure – all of which had been packed into one timeless month! Quite naturally, our legs entwined under the sheets, while we synchronised our pounding hearts. Our breathing grew deeper as waves of electric sunshine surged through our bodies.

I simply had never been met by anyone that so closely mirrored my soul and stirred my heart as Aiden had. After releasing him daily to be on his journey, how was it that I had come to now be entwined with him under the sheets? I continued to marvel at the paradox of this mysteriously estranged and yet undeniably kindred companion to my soul. After all those nights lying by his side, I had learned how to harness my passion and fall asleep to the tune of my own sovereign heart. So even though our bodies were intertwined, I steered myself to this now familiar ritual of respectful self-containment.

Just as I was about to doze off, Aiden gently rolled his body on top of mine, pressing his lips into mine with a fierce presence that I had been longing to feel ever since he held me under the full moon at the Rainbow Gathering. His mouth firmly enveloped mine, claiming the truth of our soul connection. His kiss ignited our flesh in an avalanche of passion and primordial presence. Based on all that had transpired between us, I was naturally hesitant at first. This sudden sensual outpour went against all his prior resistance to share his affection, and I had worked hard to maintain healthy boundaries. In a flash, I asked myself the only question that made any sense at all: *what would love do now?*

At the time, this was what I heard. *Choose love. This river has a course of its own. Tonight, you will be the lovers and surrender all restraint. Tonight, you will break the rules of self-preservation and offer yourself to the fire of this unbridled ballet. Tonight, you will meet at the very edge of where the river meets the sea.*

My soul had longed for this Sacred Union. And so I gave in to the powerful current and made my choice to relinquish all arguments with this love, this beloved soul flame, my heart, my destiny – my end.

Aiden moved with torrential affection, as if the entire time he held back now gave way to a tidal wave of passion. All prior resistance evaporated in the steam of our undulating bodies. I gasped in elation as Aiden pierced through all the ways I had held back my love, staying safe in my frozen shell. As we rose together entwined in a timeless erotic bliss, we relented to a force of nature that insisted we be the love and the lovers that we were. I closed my eyes and saw the room fill with celestial light as a luminous white dove hovered over us with her wide-open wings.

Our frequency continued to rise in unison while Mary's resounding church bells serenaded us from outside our chamber window. Like twin dolphins tumbling in the sea, our spines arched together and then subsided in oceanic waves of electrified union. The cathedral bells rang clear, bright and true yet another seven times as the love poured through our awakened flesh, our bodies melting together as one.

I opened myself fully to Aiden's full body embrace, which became all the more sweeter in the knowing our inevitable parting was soon to follow. Our mutual consent to love and be loved magically dissolved our prior defenses, accumulated over love's countless battlefields. In those sublime, fleeting moments, our fires became one flame and I knew the sublime sacredness of sanctified sexual union.

The last traces of separation dissolved as we exploded into starlight and showered in the light of the Christos Sophia. The room filled with a euphoric glow as we lay suspended in silence, witnessing our Sacred Union love merge with the cosmic heart of the universe.

Utterly silenced by the immensity of it all, I lay motionless, cradled in a pool of liquid-love light. Time blended with eternity until quite suddenly, I shuddered from both joy and sorrow in the knowingness that this joining was only the beginning...of my end. Aiden rolled me off the bed, grabbed my hand and our sarongs, and said, 'Come on, Bella. Mother is calling us out for a sunset swim.'

We headed across the road to meet the setting sun and consecrate our Sacred Union in the sea. Like twin dolphins, we frolicked and bounced upon the surface of the waves, daring to feel all that we had held back for what felt to be lifetimes. Our newly explored passion energised us as we frolicked and played as children in the waves, until resigning to float on our backs and allow the natural current to take us where it will.

I looked up to the twilight sky and spotted the bright Venus star beginning to make her evening appearance. *Thank you, Bright Star, for guiding me to Saintes-Maries-de-la-Mer, and for the endless gifts you have showered upon me here.*

Giggling like two young lovers, we emerged from the sea and ran across the street. Dripping wet, we made a run for our room. The concierge smiled all knowingly at us. She had an acute sensibility of a French woman who knew that it was more than the setting sun that had produced our beaming smiles.

Back in our quaint little love nest, we showered off together. This mundane act felt more like a sacred baptism and as natural as two newlywed lovers could be. I could sense that we were both soaking up the wonderful feeling of sharing this domestic ritual. It felt so good to finally be relaxing into our animal bodies, open hearts and clarity of mind, *a perfect trinity*. After our lingering shower, we wrapped our dripping bodies in the miniature white hotel towels. Aiden opened a bottle of French wine that he had picked up at the outdoor market the day before. A celebration was definitely in order! After all, we were on an archetypal honeymoon of sorts. As we dressed for dinner, our moods were mutually cheerful, light and somewhat triumphant, as if we had at last surrendered to rest in a place beyond what our minds could fathom.

Aiden put on a fresh white tank top, baggy khaki trousers and tied a blue bandana around his forehead. As usual, I was mesmerised by his unique sense of style that accentuated his gallant beauty. I dressed in a flowing white skirt and a hot pink East Indian sari blouse, embroidered with golden thread that laced up the back. This dressing ritual felt sacred and significant, as it was my first opportunity to adorn myself since coming to Europe.

'Thank Goddess for tonight,' I announced. 'It's made lugging around a wardrobe of fancy dress finally worthwhile!'

'Bella Madonna,' Aiden added as he offered me his arm and we walked out of the Hotel Le Dauphin Bleu floating slightly off the ground.

As we approached the plaza, we were surprised to find the streets were unusually quiet. Hand and hand, we strolled down the main road and wandered over to Magdalene's Church to pay homage to her under the light of the full moon.

We leaned against the ancient cobblestone wall and watched small clusters of people leisurely walking off the evening meal.

A woman strolled past us and then stopped dead in her tracks. She turned towards us to pay us a compliment, 'You two make a breathtaking couple. Are you married?'

We looked at one another, uncertain as to how to reply. Aiden took the leap by responding, 'Yes, we are newlyweds.'

'I suppose we are, in some archetypal realm and dimension,' I murmured to myself.

'Oh, what a beautiful couple you make. All the best to you!' she went on, envying our afterglow.

We smiled in return and Aiden put his arm around my waist. 'It's true,' he whispered.

We continued across the plaza to look for a restaurant. Gypsy King music wafted from a neighbouring bar. Our bodies spontaneously began to groove to the sultry rhythms of the Spanish guitar. Completely uninhibited, we danced unabashedly together under the street lamp. This moment made a deep impression on my heart. It was so rare for me to be invited to express the fullness of my Feminine essence without a care in the world for how others would perceive me. We were being danced by an unnamable force – drunk on the gifts of a larger love – daring to meet life head on in all its beauty and complexity. We were engrossed in a mythic version of a Broadway musical, where the couple spontaneously busts out on the sidewalk to celebrate their bursting hearts and newfound love.

Aiden spun me around and I collapsed laughing in his arms. 'Tonight, let's be fearlessly alive in our fullest expression of love!' I pronounced.

'Yes, Bella! Je suis d'accord.'

We danced our way towards an outdoor café, still giggling from our brave-hearted, flirtatious Salsa on the plaza. As we entered the dimly lit restaurant, Aiden asked the bartender, 'Are you still serving?'

'Mais oui, oui!' He escorted us to a candlelit table outside. Aiden pulled out my chair with a chivalrous flourish. I sat down and offered him a queenly smile, my senses dazzled by the aroma of Mediterranean gourmet food and aged red wine. The melodic sounds of an acoustic guitar strummed in the background while I grew intoxicated by the sparkles shooting from Aiden's aquamarine eyes and heartwarming smile.

Out of the blue, I flashed on what Aiden had said to me as he shared his views on relationship back at La Maison Lumiere in Limoux. 'Romance is not in service to the divine.'

I felt into these words with genuine curiosity while observing the moths flying around a nearby streetlight lantern. *This whole world is one divine romance – an unabashed, unapologetic swoon, a heart-thumping flirtation, where all of nature is in a state of perpetual arousal, birthing endless beauty through novel co-creations. Ode to beauty – the universal language of the Divine!*

I carried on with my inner reverie. *Life is a living love poem, animated by the astonishing love, beauty intelligence of the Creator making love to all of creation. Are we not here to explore and discover how we may serve, gift, bless, create and share the big LOVE in all manners of infinitessimal expressions of beauty? Art, nature, music, chaos, flow, rupture, rapture all crescendoing into sublime moments of rising and falling into miraculous grace. Whether in shadow or light, the very nature of being alive is designed to turn us on beyond all measure! Romance is not to be limited to the budding of new love...nor a promise to fulfill a gaping black hole. Romance is the sensual nature of all beings and belongs to existence itself...to be shared generously rather than hoarded or privatised! When we dedicate romance to enlivening ourselves and all beings, we become Lovers of the World, creating endless realms of beauty for all to be replenished and renewed.*

I knew in that moment that I was born for this very purpose, and raised my wine glass to Aiden and proclaimed, 'I am a Lover of the World...born to romance the Divine and create endless beauty for all to enjoy!'

That night we feasted and basked in the presence of the other, as two French lovers might do, before attending their own inevitable funeral. After all, tomorrow we would be on separate airplanes, headed in opposite directions.

Never mind, I consoled myself. *I'll simply make tonight stretch into eternity.*

CHAPTER THIRTY-NINE

DISCO KING &
SOVEREIGN QUEEN

Put everything into the initial connection.
The posture thereafter must spring from that connection.
The initial connection has to be whole-hearted.
What happens thereafter must not be a distraction.
In other words, the heart keeps pumping out that connection.
The technique is a whisper.
What is completed between you has the feeling of an entirety – of a being.
The responsibility is to be open.
Be open to the connecting of your heart with the other person's heart.
If the other person wants information about you let them open their heart.
Connecting is not a personal matter.
In any real interchange it is the Third Heart that counts.
Light and embracing, but embracing as a giving from
the heart rather than capturing.
And the inspiration of the Third Heart is nutrition for your becoming.
The spirit must be allowed freedom to dart about
and tempt the heart at the right moment.
To be a believer is to be a positive being – a believer is someone who is becoming.
Becoming leaves no imprint.
Becoming swallows what is commonly known as destiny.
Spirit is the effervescence of real interest in something other than yourself.

– John Kells

Put aside your clever schemes!
O lover, be mindless! Become mad!
Dive into the heart of the flame!
Become fearless! Be like a moth!
Turn away from the self
And tear down the house!
Then, come and dwell in the house of love!
Be a lover! Live with lovers!
Clean your chest from all hostility.
Wash it seven times.
Then, fill it with the wine of love!
Be a chalice for love! Be a chalice!
You must be all love
To be worthy of the beloved.
When going to the gathering of drunks, be a drunk! Become drunk!
Your thought takes a course
Dragging you in its wake.
Move beyond thought!
Let your heart lead! Be the leader!
When the grace of love is revealed,
Be a mirror to reflect it.
When the beloved's hair is loosened,
Brush it like a comb! Be a comb!

– Jelaluddin Rumi

When the samba takes you out of nowhere
And the background's fading out of focus
Yes, the picture's changing every moment
And your destination, you don't know it, Avalon.

– Roxy Music, *Avalon*

Aiden and I were drunk on succulent food, Spanish guitar and sweet, sweet lovin´. After dinner, we walked to the sea front to get some fresh air and gaze at the moonlight shimmering on the water. The blue moon offered me her unsolicited advice. *'The night is still young. Why don't you go out and have some fun?'*

I reported this to Aiden and he wholeheartedly agreed. And so we hopped into our rental car chariot and drove down the dark and desolate highway. A couple of kilometres later, we came to the one and only disco in town. There were only a handful of cars when we pulled into the parking lot. We walked toward the bright-purple building, which was trimmed in flashing rainbow Christmas lights. In a glance, we acknowledged that this could be a very different scene than what we were accustomed to. Brave with the spirit of romance and adventure, we decided to go in and give it a whirl. A hefty doorman taking long drags off his Gitamme cigarette greeted us.

'Bonjour,' he said dully while motioning us into the darkly lit club.

I was stunned by the décor, which looked like a cross between a Las Vegas coffee shop, Wild West Saloon and Saturday Night Fever. The mysterious DJ was playing a seventies song by Kool and the Gang. I was unclear if the music was for real or if it was meant to be a trendy spoof. Even though cheesy seventies music was not quite what we had in mind, we decided to go with it. Aiden did a quick spin, grabbed my hand and twirled me into his arms. I was impressed by his classic disco moves, even though I had thought I left all that behind in junior high! In the end, it was the mirrored disco ball covering my flowing white skirt in rainbow fractal patterns that gave me that final nudge to loosen up and let go.

Honestly, they could have been playing Black Sabbath and I would have still been in Heaven. I was sharing this once-in-a-lifetime experience with a person I cherished, cold spells and all. All the while, I knew that tomorrow could be the last time I ever saw Aiden again.

Amidst the onslaught of cheesy seventies hits, Aiden grabbed me close to his chest and said, 'Come on, lass. Don't you think this sleepy place can use some activation?'

A lightning bolt surged up my spine and my energy level rose to the occasion. It felt like an invitation to take a ride on his super-deluxe Triumph motorcycle. 'Oh yeah,' I shouted over the disco beats. 'I'm in!'

Just as he spun me to the middle of the dance floor, the DJ suddenly changed the genre of music, and like magic, we were instantaneously transported to a trendy, London dance club that makes you feel famous just because you're there. All inhibitions melted as we gave ourselves full permission to be taken by the nectarous drum and bass and each other. At that point, I was not dancing...I was being danced! An invisible force took us over, moving us into a seamless, full-bodied prayer with the spiraling force of the universe.

At first, there were only two other couples on the dance floor and a few chain-smoking stragglers at the bar. Before I knew it, the two became four, and the four became sixteen! Soon we found ourselves swimming in a pool of sweaty bodies, all gyrating in full trance-like locomotion. The heavy drum and bass vibrated the floors and shook the mirrored walls and disco ball. I was totally entranced by the music and my beloved's glistening eyes and sweaty body.

Aiden, along with everything else, was the most phenomenal dancer! I had never danced the way I had danced with him that night. I was drunk on Eros and the rare and precious gift of being exquisitely met in every piercing gaze and wildly coinciding dance move. It was as if our cosmic love dance synchronised with the movement of the cosmos. All the great poets and mad lovers of this crazy world flashed before me. An entire pantheon of cosmic lovers danced within us: Shiva and Shakti, Isis and Osiris, Magdalene and Yeshua, Rumi and Shems...even Ginger and Fred. I felt the gods and goddesses of past, present and future dancing along with us as one glorious, unified, swirling, ecstatic flame on God's burning dance floor.

Then suddenly, as if waking from a dream, Aiden and I became aware that we had been fully transfixed on one another and little else for hours upon hours of ecstatic dancing. Quite unexpectedly, he excused himself and said, 'Bella, I'm going solo for a while. See ya later on, eh?'

'Oh, Ok.' I nodded my head and then *poof*, as if it had all been a dream, he vanished and was absorbed into the sweaty mix of the throbbing crowd.

Bewildered by his sudden disappearance, I sat down on a velvet barstool amongst the sea of gyrating bodies to take in my surroundings. In a fraction of a heartbeat, the spell of entrancement was suddenly broken. Shiva and Shakti vanished; and I found myself alone in a very smoky, steamy, alcohol-filled room surrounded by a slew of very intoxicated strangers. Our love bubble quite suddenly popped, and a tidal wave of exhaustion and overwhelm came crashing down on me. I felt intensely exposed without the presence of Aiden protecting me from this den of slippery snakes. Feeling utterly vulnerable, and left out in the cold, I wanted to leave the disco and escape this feeling of being so abruptly cut off from our ecstatic tantric entwinement.

I dashed for the exit door, passing him on the way out. 'I'll be waiting outside. I have to go. I can't breathe in all this cigarette smoke!'

'Okay,' he shouted over the throb of sound. He didn't follow me.

I exited the club on the razor's edge of sheer panic. I needed fresh air, I needed to come back to myself, and I needed to feel the earth under my feet. I headed to the car and took some long deep breaths. I became painfully aware that ever since we made love, I had opened so deeply to him that I was no longer *me* – I had become *we*. I had surrendered so fully into our sumptuous connection that I had allowed my centre to fuse with his. This was a natural result of our lovemaking; the womb of my Feminine power had been filled with his very essence and seed. Combined with the deep soul love I felt for this man, it was little wonder that I become ungrounded, especially when he abruptly pulled away from me. I stood under the blue moon in the flicker of the disco Christmas lights, hugging myself in a state of raw bewilderment.

Aiden came out of the club soon after and opened the car door for me. We got in and he put on a compilation CD that he had made. I gasped in surprise; the song was one I knew well. I listened to it a lot before coming to Europe, recognising that the lyrics foretold the love story that I was presently playing out. Now here I was with Aiden, as the sultry British singer Sia, from the band Zero 7, wailed in her sultry voice, 'I love you. I love you. I love you. Yes, I really do. I only make jokes to distract myself from the truth.' Tears welled up in my eyes. I was stunned by yet another perfectly orchestrated song synchronicity. We sat together in the car, still sweaty from our mind-blowing dance, and listened to the lyrics that told a very human story of longing and the heartbreak created by not being fully met in that love. It poignantly reminded me of how soon Aiden and I would be parted, our love a fleeting dream.

Aiden was the first to break the silence. 'How are you, Bella?'

I lifted my teary eyes to his. 'I'm fine, apart from when I stopped dancing with you. I became overwhelmed and exhausted by the smoke and the crowd of people, so I decided to come out for some fresh air.'

He nodded. 'I noticed you became quite flustered and ungrounded when I went off, like you needed me in order to stay centred in your own power.'

The way I interpreted what he said felt condescending and laced in judgment. I couldn't help but to feel shamed just for opening up and surrendering to him. *Ouch!* His cool words pierced like a piece of charred glass that went straight into my solar plexus. The romance, the beauty, the communion shattered in one brutal comment that broke all of the rules of me not taking things too 'personally'. My mind began to spin as I felt judged and made wrong by his comment. *How come all he could see was where I lost it, where I became weak in his absence?* I was triggered by the critical voice that zeroed in on what was 'wrong' with me rather than appreciating all of the ecstatic love that we had just shared.

I was hurt, I was exposed, but mostly, I felt shattered. Love and humiliation were not my favourite combinations. I felt cornered, confused and exposed beyond anything I had ever experienced before. *So what if I became undefended – let down my guard – and it made me more vulnerable and susceptible to being ungrounded.* I admitted to myself. Then I added, *Could I have created it to be any other way?*

Like two cats meeting in a dark alley, we hissed and batted our claws for a brief moment. I struggled to comprehend what had just happened. All I could feel was his judgment and in a moment of weakness, I had done something terribly wrong. The safety we had shared ruptured and along with it our intimate connection. *Splat.* Down I fell and landed smack on my very own spewed-out, blistering heart where Aiden and I resumed our now familiar and somewhat cool distance.

I was disappointed that our connection was sabotaged by what I interpreted as an unwarranted comment, void of compassion and finely disguised to insert a wedge in our intimacy. Recognising he had indeed zeroed in on a weakness, I wrestled inside with two plaguing questions: *why did Aiden continue to look for what could shatter the love that we shared? And why did this man I only just met matter so much to me?*

'Let's just call it a truce and go back to the hotel,' Aiden suggested as he started the car.

At which point we agreed to disagree about what happened in the disco. I felt more than relieved to drop it and get back to the beach.

I exhaled deeply with a sigh of relief. 'Good idea.'

The road was desolate as we headed back to the hotel in a silent melancholy. Inwardly, I vowed to always remember that once in a blue moon night, I had experienced ecstatic Oneness – as the dancer and the danced, the lover and the beloved. *It's really possible, I thought.* For a brief flash in eternity, we dissolved all sense of Self and other. The cheesy song lyrics from that movie, *Dirty Dancing*, popped into my head. '*Oh, I had the time of my life and I never felt this way before. Yes, it's true and I owe it all to you.... I had the time of my life...*'

Upon returning to the hotel, there was only one remedy apparent to the both of us – get naked and dive into the sea, the ultimate hospital for any brave and wounded heart. The ocean of absolution awaited our visit under the light of the full, honey-coloured moon.

We parked at the hotel and walked across the street to the beach. The blue moon shimmered on the water.

'Que bella luna,' Aiden whispered under his breath.

I squatted like an Indian princess on the shore and watched the shimmering silver light make stars upon the waters rippling surface. Aiden confidently undressed and headed straight for the moonlit path shimmering on the surface of the sea. My eyes glazed over with a kind of disbelief as I witnessed this exquisite god-man walk naked into the sea. With an aura of unwavering certainty, his glowing body disappeared until he vanished altogether into the deep blue abyss.

Despite our spat at the disco, my heart breathed a prayer of gratitude. 'Thank you, Goddess, for the blessing and opportunity to dance with this remarkable being with whom I have come to cherish, for better or for worse.'

Although I came to accept the truth in Aiden's comment, I was still recovering from the delivery of his observation. I would have preferred a gentler and kinder lesson, one that wasn't laced in judgment. I chose to wait for Aiden to come out of the sea before I went in, alone. By bravely swimming solo, I would call back my sovereign power along with my energy that had overly merged with his. Aiden staggered out of the crashing waves, the water on his naked skin glowing with moonlight. Now it was my turn to dive into the ocean and disappear. Aiden observed me with his hawk-like eyes. I felt excruciatingly exposed as I walked naked into the sea with only my courage to hold me.

While holding my breath underwater for as long as I could, I gave myself to the shining sea. She embraced me unconditionally as I felt Mother Mary's presence fully welcoming me into her folds – accepting and loving me just as I was. As I swam toward the moonlit pathway glistening upon the rippling surface, the Cosmic Mother sang to me. I felt cradled and calmed, soothed and caressed as I joined her, lifting up my voice to meet the shimmering moon. 'Deep blue sea, darlin' deep blue sea. Deep blue sea, darlin' deep blue sea. The time has come, the time is now, to cross the deep blue sea.'

Her grace poured into me along with the billions of stars that held sacred witness from above. The dance of the moonbeams shimmering on the surface of the water along with the gentle lapping of the waves transported me to that place of wild belonging – that place that exists beyond my bruised heart. I felt my inner strength return while I affirmed that my only true anchor was to be found in the love that I AM. My covenant with the Divine Beloved is a guaranteed lifeboat to carry me through the greatest of storms. And then I heard a distinct voice from my Family of Light whisper to me. *'Beloved sister, you are not alone! We are with you now. Your ability to love is a not a weakness nor a flaw.It is the bravest and boldest part of you. It is a gift to be able to let this world shatter your heart, but still stay open to a larger love. A broken heart that still loves is not really broken. Instead it is a beautiful tribute to the nature of Love. Be still and know this: that which you seek is also seeking you.'*

I looked back at Aiden standing on the shore, watching my every move. He looked smaller and less significant from this vantage point, a mere shadow on the distant horizon. I could not presume to know what he was thinking nor feeling. He was a master of disguising his feelings even after we had shared so intimately. In the midst of treading water in the middle of the sea, I sensed I was at a major crossroads. Every part of me wanted to keep swimming, to somehow magically bypass what the following morning held. Tomorrow, my beloved friend and I will fly in two opposite directions.

'Oh, Mother, I prayed, *thank you for giving me the strength to keep dancing no matter what the day brings.'*

With that, I swam back to the shore to bravely face my greatest gift and deepest challenge. As I emerged from the sea, I felt so vulnerable that my legs felt like Jell-O pudding. 'I choose to be real. I choose to burn open. I choose to be wild and honour the rawness of my wide, open heart. I choose to die to the small love so that a larger love may prevail!' I declared to the Venus star shining brightly as my sacred witness.

When I reached Aiden, he opened his large arms to enfold me, and we pressed our naked bodies and thumping hearts together... *again.* He then wrapped his sarong around my wet body, took my hand and we silently crossed the dark empty street to retire to our hotel room. We were in bed by 3.33am and woke up the following morning to the tune of Mary's church bells ringing seven times.

DEPARTURE LOUNGE

As the world came tumbling down
You prayed to God what have we done
Free me from these chains. I need to change my way.
Heal these broken wings.
I need to fly far away, far away, far away.

– Zero 7, 'Spinning'

If you are longing to caress the moon,
Don't turn away from it!
If you are not ill,
Why do you crawl under a blanket to hide?
You are in a quarry of sweets.
Why do you look so sour?
You live in the spring of life.
Why are you withered inside?
Don't fight against yourself!
Don't flee from what can be your glory!
Like a fearless moth
dive into the flame.
Why be linked to your obsessions?
Burn out in the flames,
Until your heart and soul are enlightened.
Get out of the old carcass
And form yourself a new body.

Why are you afraid of a fox
When you descend from lions?
Why be a lame ass
When you have the strength of stallions?
The beloved you seek will arrive
To open the door to your fortune,
For love is the key
That opens all your locks.

– Jelaluddin Rumi

As I awoke that morning, I inwardly wished I had just a few more days to enjoy holding hands with Aiden under the bed sheets. And then, quite unexpectedly, Aiden pulled me into his arms and held me close to his chest while Magdalene's church bells rang seven more times. I could feel our beating hearts pushing into each other's skin. Words fall short to describe what I was feeling on that particular morning entwined together in our little hotel chambre.

We had to force ourselves to get up out of bed, groggy from our disco honeymoon night. We needed to be on the road by eight o'clock to get to Perpignan by ten in order to return the car and be at the airport by eleven. We proceeded to pack our bags in a methodical way, as travellers do after packing and unpacking the same things hundreds of times. We were comforted by the familiar routine of getting dressed and loading up our things into the car. Before we took off, we had one last mouthwatering croissant and cappuccino in the downstairs café overlooking the turquoise sea.

I summoned my power to stay present and grounded despite my aching chest and the river of tears that welled up from behind my eyes. We finished our petit dejeuner in that oh so familiar silence that I had now grown strangely accustomed to. With one last napkin-wiping finale, we paid our bill, thanked the concierge and stood before the turquoise sea to offer our heart felt gratitude and goodbyes.

The morning sun glistened brighter than usual, perhaps because Father Sun knew just how much I loved to watch his diamond light dancing on her aquamarine skin. Early risers passed on bicycles with freshly baked baguettes tucked under their arms. I had fallen in love with this place and promised to return one day. *I will ride one of those white horses down the beach and feel the wild power and grace of the Goddess as my very own Self.* For now, all I could do was look out the car window, the ocean a blur through my damp eyes as Aiden sped along the highway, leaving all we had shared behind.

Goodbye Mary Magdalene. Goodbye Sarah, Spanish guitar and sunset swims. Goodbye church bells, Grandfather Sun, wild white horses, jelly doughnuts, disco nights and smelly lavender sheets. Goodbye glistening turquoise sea and hello Divine sovereignty.

We got in the car and with an aire of resolve, I straightened up in my seat and looked forward down the road. *Hello, highway. Hello, sunglasses, CD player, Simon and Garfunkel, and brand-new lovely day.'*

Aiden drove for three hours straight, saying very little as the Father Sun rose in his full glory. I took over the wheel when we got to Perpignan Airport where we dropped off our rental car. It seemed like we had picked up our faithful chariot a lifetime ago. We then grabbed our luggage in one hand and gripped each other's hand in the other. We walked deliberately to the airport's departure lounge to check in. My plane would take off in forty-five minutes. Out of the blue, Aiden confessed that he didn't have his ticket to Scotland yet. He went ahead to the airline ticket counter to explore his travel options amidst the early morning rush of commuters and travellers. His funds were extremely low and he had to deal with the costly penalty of not pre-arranging his ticket. I overheard him pleading with the man behind the counter to find him a flight that would financially work for him. All the while my body grew tenser waiting for him, wondering why he couldn't make his arrangements after I had departed. Our precious last ten minutes together quickly dwindled into five.

At last, he turned away from the ticket desk and came to sit next to me on the blue plastic chairs. It was time to say goodbye. We sat sideways and gazed deeply into one another's eyes, joined foreheads and placed our hands upon one another's hearts. We each took a turn to offer gratitude for meeting one another by the fire and staying in the fire as we allowed the potent medicine of our togetherness to play out. And then, we gazed into each others eyes and shared a tender kiss on the lips and one on each cheek as our final ritual together. Mustering all my strength and composure, I then stood up and walked to my departure gate.

Don't look back, beloved! Just breathe and walk...walk and breathe... no matter what keep moving forward.

Trust and faith felt hollow just then as I reenacted the familiar and heart-wrenching drill of departing from that special someone I loved with every fibre of my being. In truth, this was not a first-time scenario for me. For one reason or another, I had reenacted the 'departure lounge' saga with just about every man I had ever truly loved. The day of departure typically involved an airplane, a bus, a train or some other mode of global transportation. After one last final goodbye, we would go our separate ways and vanish from one another's lives. *Whoosh!* Like a mist, we would each dissapear into the vast, blue-green world, never to be seen or heard from ever again.

Yet this departure scenario felt distinctly different than the ones before. Even with all of the moody blues, I had never been met by someone who had opened, reflected and engaged my soul in the way that Aiden had. With others, there were obvious conclusions to our togetherness that made sense in the greater scheme of our lives. I had been able to walk away with a sense of gratitude and knowingness that our contract to be together was complete. I attempted to rationalise and convince myself. *Your life paths are clearly heading in two very different directions, especially with Aiden moving into fatherhood and all.*

There was no doubt in my mind that my feelings were genuine. In other words, I felt that my love was big enough to expand to include all of our unique circumstances and conditions. *If it's meant to be, we will find a way.* In that moment, there was only one way...and that was to let go and trust that we were both moving in the direction we needed to be. *If there is a higher plan, it's no longer in my hands. Thy will be done!*

While standing in line at the departure gate, waiting to board the plane, I sank into a kind of melancholy. *Why did the men I had come to love vanish from my life as suddenly and mysteriously as they had appeared?* The line stood still for what felt like forever. I felt as if I was holding my breath underwater for a ridiculously long time and that if it didn't move, I would simply burst at the seams. Suspended in limbo, I could still taste, smell and feel his touch so vividly. *He is so close – just sitting on the other side of the partitioned wall!* A part of me desperately wanted to run back and say, 'No! I don't want to leave you. It has taken me lifetimes to finally find you!' I toyed with the idea. *Wasn't that the truly courageous and happily-ever-after choice? The one you see played out in the movies time and time again?*

Then I stood in Aiden's shoes and surmised that if he really wanted to be with me, he would have made that perfectly clear. *Or was it the other way around?* Either way, I felt like I had just swallowed a very bitter truth pill. *Flex your big love muscles, Ambe´,* I coached myself sternly, mustering all my strength to remain calm, centred and ultimately detached. *Remember, gate, gate, paragate, parasamgate bodhi svaha! Form is emptiness; emptiness is form. Form is no other than emptiness...capiche?* With this little pep talk, I managed to curtail my anguish along with an instinctual urge to run back into Aiden's arms.

Yes, I know what you're thinking as you read this: what a hopeless romantic. Right? It's true...I am, but even so, I managed to stay centered in the moment while fixing my gaze upon a three-year-old toddler sucking a lollipop in line in front of me. Her tiny little fingers were wrapped around her daddy's thumb. For a split second, I considered asking her papa if he had an extra lollipop I could bum off him, as I felt I could really use one at the moment. I gasped in relief when the stewardess finally told us to get our passports and boarding passes out. Sting's song kicked in and gave me the last boost I needed to get on that plane. *'If you love somebody, if you love somebody, if you love someone, set them free. Free, free, set them free. Free, free, set them free.'*

Feeling a little faint and dizzy, I was beyond relieved to take my window seat and fasten my seatbelt. I stared blankly out the airplane window, patiently waiting for take-off. I then placed my hands upon my heart, took some deep steady breaths and began to sing to myself, *'Row, row, row your boat gently down the stream. Merrily, merrily, merrily, merrily... life is but a dream.'*

The stewardess went through the normal take-off procedures in a painstakingly slow fashion. As you could well imagine, it seemed to go on forever. *Joseph, Mary, Baby Jesus! Hurry up for Christ's sake!* I couldn't stand to sit there another minute longer. My self-preservation instincts went into hyperdrive. *Come on, already! Arriba! Vamonos! Let's get the out of here!* My heart sank into the pit of my belly as we rolled down the runway and took off. Who knows how long I was holding my breath before I let out a sigh, a whimper and a solitary tear.

This is insane! Why on Earth am I going back to England? At this point, I was completely uncertain. Murray, my first long-term boyfriend, would be picking me up at the airport in Essex. He had offered to take me on a tour of the sacred sites and then drop me off in Brighton. Once in Brighton, I had vague prospects of teaching a workshop but nothing was confirmed. For now, I was just floating. I hadn't thought much about spending time with Murray. It could be wonderful to reconnect after so long *or* it could be disastrous. More than ever, he and I lived in two different worlds. When making the arrangements to reunite months ago, I hadn't foreseen the emotional state I would be in. *My heart was cracked wide open and the pieces would never be put back in quite the same way!*

I looked out of the small window. Father Sun hovered behind a cloudy sky. To keep my mind off Aiden, I reached for my new book, *Anna, Grandmother of Jesus* by Claire Heartsong. I remembered Gaianna telling me that it was extremely 'code opening' as she gifted it to me. *All right, here I go,* I thought as I opened and the following words shot off the page, landing smack in the middle of my swollen heart: *'Are you ready to take Yeshua and yourself off the cross? Are you ready to shift your focus into resurrecting your consciousness into enlightened states of gratitude?'*

In a weak attempt at humour, I added, *'Are you ready to stop wallowing in this pool of pathetic self-pity?'*

'Yes,' I murmured and opened to the first page and began to read.

My dear friend, I bring you greetings of love and peace this day. I am Anna, also known as the mother of Mary and the grandmother of Jesus. The fact that you are reading this letter, as an introduction to my story, is something of a miracle. For I send this message to you across great spans of time and space. And yet, I am here, closer than you may think.

I offer you my version of a complex, compelling, and life-transforming story, between many that present Jesus, the human, and Jesus, the Christ. Along the circuitous path that leads us to meet with the Christ "face to face," much will be revealed about the ancient Essene initiations that I mastered.

These same initiations I facilitated for Mother Mary, Yeshua Ben Joseph, Mary Magdalene, and other adepts who embodied and exemplified the Christ or the "Way of the Teacher of Righteousness" (the way of right use of energy). I gave these wisdom and high alchemy teachings (internal energy practices) to many, and now I pass the secrets of physical and spiritual immortality, resurrection, and other mysteries to you. This I do because, you, my dear friend, have asked for freedom and empowerment. You are well prepared to use these gifts for the benefit of all as we move through a perilous passage during Earth's birth.

I invite you to join me in a most timely exploration of these pivotal questions, trusting that the answers are present, simply waiting to be unveiled. I offer my story as a threshing board for winnowing the wheat of eternal wisdom and releasing the useless, encumbering chaff. I hold up a mirror to you so that you may behold yourself in greater clarity, knowing that you are the answer to your mind's most perplexing questions and the fulfillment of your heart's deepest longing.

We have heard each other's request to meet. And so it is that I will come to your abode where we will embark on our journey without distance. Its location does not matter: as long as you meet me with your feelings of the present moment.

Although I have made my ascension, I have freely chosen to return to the Earth plane from time to time so that I can continue to participate in Earth's evolution. My profound love for every particle and expression of life moves me to remain close. I have returned at this time so that I might take this long-awaited journey with you. This I do, not as a sacrifice but because I deeply know that my complete Union in God is inseparable from yours and that of Mother Earth's. It is reward enough to know that my words have catalysed your memory of us walking this way before, dreaming our vision of a New Earth, and that our love has brought us together again. We can be comforted in knowing that all our adventures, both past and future, have prepared us for this consummating finale we promised to celebrate.

I gladly serve you as paradigm shifter, life-coach, midwife, and as a very accessible friend. I accompany you side by side on the path that leads to the knowing that you are the Beloved Christ you seek. I offer you my hand in full fellowship so that we can remember the enduring thread of light that is the path that weaves all life together into a seamless, ever-changing, impeccable tapestry that revealed Mother-Father Gods infinite love and grace. Regardless of its name, that eternal light reveals your destination to be closer than any limiting thought you may think. You, my eternal friend, are the path, the light, and the way. Let the door of your heart swing open, enter in... and know the awakened splendour that dwells within! And I'll be with you.

A rainfall of salty tears mixed with every emotion known to womankind streamed down my face. It didn't matter what the man sitting next to me would think of me. I clutched the book to my heart in total awe of the synchronistic gift of stumbling upon it. Once again, I flashed back to my journey at Gaia's Grove and recalled the Divine Mother flooding me with a Love so vast that I felt to be wrapped in a cocoon of ineffable Grace. I had pledged my life to being a conduit for this Love! I fully understood that this pledge had to begin with me discovering the source of this love! I had tasted it...and yet I sensed, I still had quite a long way to go before I would discover its hidden mystery.

Feeling hollowed out and raw to the core, I closed my eyes for the rest of the short flight. Through the cascade of tears, I called out silently, *Divine Mother, show me how to be an instrument of your love!*

Before long, the pilot announced, 'We will be landing in Essex Airport in just under ten minutes. The current weather conditions are overcast with a good chance of rain. Thank you for flying Bryan Air. Have a pleasant day.'

I opened my eyes and inwardly acknowledged the completion of one journey and the beginning of the next. My heart turned towards Aiden. *Goodbye, beloved friend. I will carry you in my heart as I walk towards an even greater love that is yet to be discovered.*

A SKYLARK'S ANCIENT SONG

*Wild heather floats by
On the wisps of the wind.
Journeying to other worlds.
Awaiting next Spring.
Hedgerows burst with the promise that the gorse heralds in.
To Summer from Spring.
The land reborn, new life sprung.
Here stand I at the helm of High Sun.*

Still I wait as a chorus, for a verse to be sung.
A memory stirs of a quest in the night.
Of a Stag-King fight.
High Priestess's hand for the Great Rite won.
Still the skylark sings this Ancient Song.
My song.
Where be thy King.
To where have you gone?
A fire burns.
In my Being yearns.
REUNION.
For a taste as sweet as the heather gone.
A touch as soft as the rose now grown.
With each breath in thine essence flows.
Gentling my heart.
Healing my Soul.
Thine eyes have met mine.
I have seen clear.
Your Warrior heart.
Protected by fear.
We.
Curious.
Cautioned.
Holding ground.
For a love not lost.
Yet not fully found.
Silence.
Sacred Silence.
Pregnant pause.
We as the ocean.
Meeting the shore.
Silence.
Precious silence.
Eternal bond.
Born on the dawn of the Great Rite won.
These distant echoes of lives been done.
The spider's weaved.

The web is spun.
An olde world song of true lovers found.
The beat.
Of One Heart.
On a Sacred Drum.
Yay.
We have seen.
A Starlit night.
Comet in flight.
Sea and sand, made fire on land.
This sacred dance.
Of woman and man.
Your sword now gone.
Your battle scars shown.
Your wounds run deep and your shield is still strong.
Surrender.
My love.
Surrender.
The way of Love or Fear?
The freedom of the morrow?
The cloak of yesteryear?
Surrender.
Thine heart.
Surrender.
Thy breast be open.
Bare.
An act of resurrection.
To Love.
Where once was fear.
High Priestess waits for her King's Return.
This Wise Woman say.
Thy Will Be Done.
And the Skylark sings an ancient song.
Of a King.
And a Grail.
And a Priestess won.

– Nicolya Christi

PART
II

CHAPTER FORTY-ONE

WHEN DOVES CRY

Breathe slowly. Relax... Relax... Relax...

Your soul has a permanent passport to eternity. Knowing you cannot go back to the limited Self you once were, you are able to welcome the chaos of great planetary change that is occurring all around and within you. With confidence and ease, you can allow the birth of your ascending Christ consciousness that has been lying hidden and sleeping in your heart's womb/tomb.

The caterpillar cannot become the butterfly without its crucifixion initiation that brings about its liberating transformation. As the butterfly's chrysalis is its birthing chamber, so is the chrysalis also the caterpillar's tomb.

– Claire Heartsong, *Anna, Grandmother of Jesus*

Deep down, we know what it is to inhabit the full spectrum of who we are and live in harmony with our true nature. Our conscience ensures that we are kept abreast. When we align with our core essence, we can trust our Self to deal with anything, because we know it's just an experience... an opportunity to raise our consciousness and anchor our Divine light. Like the static on the radio, our bodies give us sensations all the time of being in and out of attunement. Tension, stress, urgency, contraction are all somatic indications that we are latching onto a fear and have lost that safe space within us. Find every part of you that has gotten lost in something false, and become a harbor for those parts of you to anchor in your love. We must no longer settle for half-truths. Instead, we must be willing to open our eyes to what's real without getting caught up in the fantasy of how we 'wish' it could be. Through compassionate awareness, every aspect of our being that was once cast out can find a haven inside of us. We become the safe harbor for the perfect imperfection of all that we are – and this is how we remember ourselves home.

– Inaiya Ray

'Brrrrr,' I said as I exited the plane. The crisp English wind whipped through my hair, sending chills through my body. I was totally unprepared for the overcast weather that Northern England is renowned for. The whole world seemed to be sunny while living in the South of France. I had forgotten that an English summer is a brisk winter to a native Californian like myself. I tried desperately to think warm and good thoughts as I departed the plane and met the brisk day.

Murray was waiting for me in the small airport lobby in long denim shorts and a T-shirt with the word, 'Underworld', printed on it. Ironically, 'Underworld' happened to be the name of one of the bands he managed. *Is this some kind of prophetic message for the next phase of my journey?* I wondered. At that point, I didn't doubt it. I imagined Murray greeting me and swallowed hard in the knowing that there was no way to prepare for what was coming. *Welcome to the Underworld, luv.*

It wasn't long before I discovered how vastly our lives had drifted apart. To him, he couldn't see the point in 'floating' around the world, following the whimsical plans of some new age-y bullshit, often referred to by *moi* as Great Spirit. Murray, on the other hand, was an extremely successful production manager for many UK-based, world-class bands. He liked to see himself as a stable and pragmatic man along with being a connoisseur of fine wines, fine herb, fine music and oh yes, fine women.

Like all intimate relationships, past or present, we mirrored each other in both shadow and light. I had nearly forgotten how Murray and I played out our unique man woman relationship dynamic. Murray was strongly identified with being an atheist, which made him highly allergic to anything that faintly resembled God, religion or spirituality. In his scrutinising eyes, I was too honest, sensitive, transparent and way too open. My passion for the esoteric irritated him, rubbing salt in his calculated, cool and collected, 'I got it all together' flavor of super manhood. Furthermore, my outgoing personality was so terribly 'un-English'. Within a few minutes of our reunion, it became painfully clear that our polarities had reached their furthest extremes. There we were, two old lovers together again after fifteen years – one of us horribly heartbroken and the other deeply depressed. *Aye yaye yaye!*

Interestingly enough, or should I say, painfully enough, Murray displayed characteristics similar to so many of the other men I was mysteriously attracted too at that time – extreme moodiness, aloof and hyper-allergic to the disclosure of feelings and raw emotions. *How on Earth did I end up with yet another temperamental man for me to walk on eggshells with? Just what is it you are trying to show me about myself, Great Spirit?*

At first, I made a polite effort to engage Murray in evocative conversations and show a genuine interest in his life passions. But the truth was he wasn't passionate about anything other than his job, sucking on a spliff and listening to classical music. He made it perfectly clear that he wished to avoid any and all deep conversation, which he conveniently interpreted as 'woo woo'. Instead, he preferred to hide in a cloud of denial as his best attempt not to expose himself or feel too much. *God forbid!*

Quite honestly, I was in no better shape. I was suffering from a severe case of departure-lounge shock. My heartache showed up as a dullness that stole the sparkle from my eyes. I was pale too, as if I had just seen a ghost. It took everything I had to stay present with Murray, as I had lost my capacity for small talk. The truth was, I had no business venturing out on a road trip with my ex after everything I had just gone through with Aiden. But there I was, with yet another emotionally unavailable man, and all I could do was venture even further into my self-imposed rabbit hole. I guess Great Spirit wanted to give me yet another hard look at the kind of men I was attracting to love in my life. *God sure has a wicked sense of humour, or was that me?*

Over the next four days, Murray and I politely agreed to hang in the shallows as our best bet for not going over the deep end. After several futile attempts to engage him in meaningful conversation, I resigned myself to staring out the window. I'd make sporadic comments about the beauty of the English countryside as it whirled by in an endless blue-green blur. I knew that Mary Magdalene continued to travel by my side. She was my secret tour guide, making her presence known when we arrived someplace that held special significance. Salisbury, Avebury and Cornwall held so many familiar overtones as each place echoed the memories of Mary Magdalene's footsteps along with my beloved Grail family.

After four long days and three nights of soaking up the English countryside, I was still emotionally numb and just barely coping with the basics of being social, while Murray's judgmental countenance hovered around me, waiting for the perfect moment to pounce. The best we could do was privately review all the good reasons why we were still not together. Needless to say, our road trip concluded in a candlelit café where Murray kindly introduced me to Devonshire pie, crumpets and tea. *Sounds delightful?* Well, let's just say our exasperation with one another ended up exploding all over our crumpets and spoiling the strawberry cream. *Whoa! What am I missing here, Mother?*

By the time Murray dropped me off in front of Fiona's sixteen-floor apartment complex in Brighton, I was exhausted and beyond relieved to be free from my trippy road trip with my ex. Let's just say that at this point, the salt was well rubbed in. *Ouch!* What I needed was time to myself to feel and integrate all that I had just gone through in France. I was beyond grateful to have a star sister to turn to in Brighton. Fiona was the town's brightest Fairy Queen. She had a strong resemblance to Liv Tyler from the movie *The Lord of the Rings* and a personality that strongly resembled Mary Poppins. We had an ancient and profound sisterly love that spiralled all the way back to our lifetime together as priestesses in Avalon. I was super excited to have a chance to rekindle our friendship.

With luggage in hand, I knocked on the door of her flat. A man with long blond hair wearing a white shirt unbuttoned to his navel opened the door as if he was expecting me. 'Ello, you must be Fiona's friend. Please come in and make yourself at home, luv.'

'I'm Ambe´, a friend of Fiona's from America,' I said, as a cloud of ganja smoke walloped me in the face. The first thing I noticed, apart from the trail of smoke, was the music playing in the background at full tilt. I walked into the sitting room and found four other guys with a variety of interesting haircuts sucking down cans of beer and passing around a spliff. I plopped down on the worn-out purple velvet couch and found myself both distraught and oddly relieved to be there. Prince's song, 'When Doves Cry,' was playing loudly over the stereo. Like listening to a weather forecast, I listened intently to the lyrics that echoed back to me my present mood, 'How can you just leave me standing? Alone in a world that's so cold? Why do we scream at each other? This is what it sounds like when doves cry.'

'Where's Fiona?' I asked curiously.

Max, who reminded me of a mix between David Bowie and Kurt Cobain, replied, 'Fiona is still at the hospital where she does an overnight nursing shift. Would you care for a cuppa tea, luv?'

'Oh, yes, no sugar please. Thank you,' I replied.

Curiously, I found myself in yet another den of smoke and asked myself, *What was I unwilling to see?* With a feeling of total exhaustion, I retreated to Fiona's room and ran a hot bath while waiting for my friend to return.

After my bath, I put myself to bed on Fiona's bedroom floor. I clung to my book, *Anna, Grandmother of Jesus*, as if it was my lifeboat in a stormy sea. Just like my dream back at Gaia's Grove, I was desperately trying not to capsize and go down in a swirl of hopeless despair. I fell asleep with a prayer to Grandmother Anna. As I dozed off, I allowed my thoughts to drift back to Aiden. I wondered where he was and with whom. Most of all, I wondered what he was feeling.

Even though we are miles apart, I long to be by your side, holding your hand under the sheets, listening to the sound of Mary's church bells ringing outside our bedroom window. You see, my friend, my love for you is still very much alive. This is a remarkable and altogether terrifying feeling, especially since I may never get to see you again.

I fell asleep fighting back the tears, determined to check my email in the morning. Perhaps I'll hear from him. So much for non-attachment...that spiritual muscle had mysteriously disappeared. *Gone, gone, gone beyond and only goddess knows where.*

CHAPTER FORTY-TWO

SLAVE TO LOVE

There's still a little bit of your taste in my mouth
Still a little bit of you laced with my doubt
It's still a little harder to say what's going on
There's still a little bit of your ghost, your weakness
Still a little bit of your face I haven't kissed
You step a little closer each day
That I can't say what's going on.

— Damien Rice, 'Cannonball'

*Nothing ever goes away until it teaches
us what we need to know.*

— Pema Chodron, *When Things Fall Apart*

The following days were full of inner turmoil and challenge. I checked my email every morning and each night to see if Aiden had contacted me as he had promised before we departed. I had written him the details of the upcoming Earth Heart festival. While we were together in France, we had explored the possibility of him coming out to meet me there.

On the third day of my Brighton visit, I received the following email: 'Hello, Bella, I'm in Scotland now. I would like to see about coming out to the Earth Heart festival to be with you. Please send me the details or call me. Love you, Aiden.'

I was ecstatic and full of excitement for the potential of reuniting with him. I rang the contact number he left, but was rudely dismissed by a very uncooperative young woman. On the fourth day, in a damp phone booth on the high street of Brighton, I rang Aiden for what seemed like the hundredth time. Finally, I managed to get someone to pick up. A young woman with a Scottish accent answered and then abruptly passed the phone over to Aiden. I sighed with relief and then held back my tears while mustering a calm and composed voice.

'Hey, Aiden. I...'

He cut me off. 'Ambe´, I tried contacting you by computer, but each time I tried, it would crash on me. I feel like some dark and precarious energy is messing with me. I believe it has something to do with you.'

He seemed to be somewhere far, far away. Something massive had shifted since his last email and based on his dismissing demeanour.

Before I could say anything, Aiden added in a weak and frail voice, 'This monster-like interference is quite difficult to track. I suggest you do something about it.'

'Okay. I...' Then the line went dead. We were disconnected.

With heart racing, I put my phone card back in the phone, redialed – and still no answer. He was purposefully not picking up the phone! *How could such a beautiful love story take such a horrific and humiliating turn? Really...how can this possibly be?*

Prince's prophetic song played on in the back of my mind. *'How can you just leave me standing, alone in a world that's so cold? Why do we scream at each other? This is what it sounds like when doves cry.'* My body trembled as I did all that I could not to go into a full-blown panic attack. I just stood there, doing my best to digest that the love of my life had just informed me that an untraceable monster-like energy was wreaking havoc on his life and most definitely mine. To top that off, I was simply left to deal with it on my own. *Clank, buzz,* end of conversation.

I walked out of the call box feeling a mixture of startled, shocked and distraught, as if the sky had just fallen in. I was left with one burning question: what was this mysterious dark force and why was it determined to wreak havoc in my life? I was in over my head and one step away from joining the homeless people sitting outside the phone booth, begging for spare change to buy their next bottle of booze. Bottom line, the calling-booth event triggered some residual trauma lodged deep within my cellular memory and nervous system.

There I stood dumbfounded, in the middle of the Hove amidst homeless strangers, feeling like one myself. I knew myself well enough to know that I was suffering from a kind of post-traumatic shock and could really use some extra support. Luckily, I had a few friends in town I could contact from my previous visit to Brighton. I went down my small list and found James. He was a very gentle and kind man who had attended my workshop the summer before. I dialled his number on a total whim. James picked up on the third ring.

I took a deep breath and tried to cover up the messy reality that I was on the verge of coming undone. 'Hello, James. It's Ambe´. Remember me from the workshop last summer? Well, er...I'm here in Brighton and I'm in a bit of a tangle and wondered if I could come round and see you?' I finished in a rush and waited for his response. If he was busy, I didn't know what I'd do.

'Yeah, sure, it'll be great to see you. Why don't you come round for a cuppa,' he said kindly and with an air of English hospitality. To my amazement, he lived in a one-bedroom flat overlooking the Brighton Sea, only moments from the phone booth I was calling from.

'Oh my goodness, thank you. I'll be right over,' I said, mustering up my last morsel of emotional composure.

I walked over to James's flat while attempting to regain my composure. My story was so out of the ordinary; I wondered how I could possibly convey what I was going through. When I approached his door, he was outside waiting for me with a white coffee mug in his hand. As soon as we hugged, I felt more relaxed and lingered in his arms for a moment to soak in his warm hospitality. I followed him into his living room where we sat overlooking the sea. Feeling immediately comforted, he handed me a hot mug of tea with a picture of Walt Disney's Goofy painted on it, and asked, 'So what have you been up to on your holiday?'

'My holiday?' I muttered under my breath. *Here it goes*, I thought, taking a deep breath. I took a swig of tea and began to tell him an abbreviated version of my recent adventures and where they had left me. Feeling goofier than ever before!

James, being a curious, sensitive and empathic kind of man, just kept repeating one word over and over again, 'Whoa, whoa, whoa, whoa, whoa.'

Holding back my tears, I asked, 'James, I really need some greater insight as to what is happening to me. Can you recommend someone who could offer me some intuitive and energetic support?'

'Why yes. Actually, I do know someone. He may be just the man to assist you. As a matter of fact, I received a session from him a few days ago and it was quite profound. His name is Christopher. He's an older fellow in his late sixties and a channel of Sananda who is the ascended energy of Yeshua.'

At first, I thought, *Oh, God help me, not another one.* But then I paused for a moment, felt his energy and knew this could be the right person to offer me some well-needed perspective.

James felt certain that Christopher could provide me with the guidance and support that I needed. I rang him immediately from James's flat. A woman answered with a very strong English accent and said, 'I'm so sorry, Christopher is away, but I'm happy to relay a message to him.'

'Yes, thank you. Can you please leave a message with James as soon as Christopher is able to see me?'

I swallowed my last sip of tea, thanked James with all my heart, grabbed my bag and headed for the Brighton Sea, the only place I knew to go to call upon the Divine Mother and my Family of Light. I prayed that someone would pick up and answer my call.

SCARY MONSTERS SUPER FREAKS

The landscape of the quest in all version of the story is surreal and dreamlike. It is of dark forests, wild moors, barren deserts, and enchanted castles and is peopled by monsters and prodigies, fearsome and beautiful damsels. A place both frightening and fantastic, it symbolizes well the terrain of the subconscious. The subconscious terrain is the terrain of the quest and the journey of the quest is the process of purification and healing of this realm. It is in the subconscious level that the memories of wounding, pain and fear are imprinted, and it is this level that requires purification and healing through undertaking the quest.

– Joseph Campbell

Breathe life into this feeble heart
Lift this mortal veil of fear
Take these crumbled hopes, etched with tears
We'll rise above these Earthly cares
Cast your eyes on the ocean
Cast your soul to the sea
When the dark night seems endless
Please remember me.

– Lorenna McKennit, 'Dante's Prayer'

There I was again, casting my eyes upon the sea. Yet this chilly English ocean was a far cry from the glowing embrace of Saintes-Maries-de-la-Mer. Like the hidden forces of the Dark Mother that now haunted me, the ocean felt daunting – colder, rougher and slower to forgive. I walked along the seashore and observed how rough the multi-coloured stones were. They were nearly the size of my clenched fist. My big black boots made large crunching sounds as I trampled over them to get to the water's edge.

Feel it, I heard a voice urge me on. *Express your rage, your anger, your frustration! There is a good reason for feeling what you're feeling! Your rage points to all the injustices...all that you know to be out of alignment with a deeper and nobler truth. Your body and soul knows that we are given a choice to script our lives in such that we rise every time we choose to honour love rather than succumb to fear.*

Halfway there, I collapsed to my knees. The contents of my overstuffed bag tumbled out amongst the rocks. I didn't care. I was tired. I was so so *so* tired. I wanted to lie down on the cool stones and never get up to face another day. Instead, I looked out to the horizon. There, the last golden rays stroked the surface of the Brighton Sea. The bold, unyielding beauty of the setting sun met me with a fierce presence as if calling me to remember a deeper truth. Turquoise, pink and majestic blues pierced my tormented heart and caressed my grief with a fierce and relentless love from Grandfather Sun. I remembered the day Aiden and I had channelled the light codes from the Central Sun and he dropped to his knees to honour the Goddess in me. That magnificent day felt so far away, so irretrievable like a distant dream.

Ah, this is my life, I thought. *What an absurd blend of devastating disappointment and miraculous grace and beauty. Perhaps the rupture is also a part of the highest divine plan, cracking the shell for a more authentic Self to be born. Could I trust the rupture as much as the rapture?*

The one thing I knew in that moment was that despite everything, I was still alive and I would probably be alive for quite some time. My job was to be exactly where I was – as heartbreaking and as impossible as it felt. I was here to feel the full spectrum of my experience no matter how uncomfortable and sobering the process would be. *What a wild ride this life is! Sometimes it takes an absurd amount of heartbreak to open one up to the light of the Divine.* I sighed and then cringed inside at the extreme lengths the soul will go to illuminate what still lingers in the basement of the unconscious.

You really got me this time, Mother, I growled, while simultaneously reminding myself of what my father once told me. *'Ambe´, you are a survivor. It is in your blood.'* I recalled him lecturing me. *'You have inherited the noble strength of a lion, equipped to endure the most challenging of trials and tribulations. You were born with the stubborn tenacity of a bear, ready to bounce back under the most gruelling of circumstances. The nicks and dings you suffer along the way are what give you character and the strength to endure all of what life has to offer. Don't give up, you'll get through this, and remember, if it doesn't kill you, it will make you stronger!'*

Yet in that moment, I felt overwrought with emotions that threatened to take me down. I had no energy left to build my damn character. *I don't want to survive – I want to THRIVE! Why does this 'love stuff' always get my knickers all up in a twist? Why? Why? Why?'* I pounded the hard stones with my big black boots as I cried out in despair.

And then I heard a distinct inner voice succinctly respond to my plea. *'Because love can only meet you as far as you are meeting yourself in love. It's just like that!'*

The sun was going down quickly, so I decided to head back to town via a stopover at the grocery store to pick up a bottle of red wine and dinner for Fiona and I. If there was ever a day to drown my sorrows, it was this one. I would come to remember that day, as the day I was jilted by King Arthur Aiden.

Over the next few days, I was determined to reconnect with Aiden and book an appointment for a session with Christopher. Who I would reach first remained a perpetual mystery. My bull-headed persistence was combined with early morning yoga on the beach, long walks through the Brighton lanes, copious amounts of PG Tips tea, regular doses of listening to Prince's song, 'When Doves Cry,' along with plenty of late night giggles with Fiona, Max and my new Brighton friends. Somehow, they managed to keep me laughing through this dark night of this sulking dove's soul.

However, it wasn't until the night I marched myself into Fiona's bathtub that I managed to find any sense of real relief. I locked the door, lit some candles and incense and had a long overdue appointment with myself. As I reclined in the salty water, I filled myself with golden light and called upon my Divine Self to anchor a temple of light in and around me. I placed an inter-dimensional Cone of Light above me and an Earth cone below me so the energy could pass freely and return to Source. I then called forth Archangel Michael for some extra support and aligned with my sword of truth as I spoke the following decree:

'I, Ambe´, call upon my divine sovereign presence to anchor a temple of light in and around me. I acknowledge that I am creation on all levels and dimensions. I call forth the violet flame of transmutation and the diamond light of purification to clear my body, space, aura and hologram of any and all influences that are out of alignment, service and affinity with my highest divine will and the highest divine will of all others. With the heat of the Violet flame, I command any and all negative influences and discordant energies to be cleared, cleansed and released from my body, space, aura and hologram; including all ancestral wounding, genetic miasims, trauma, DNA distortions and karmic story lines accrued throughout all timelines, spaces and dimensions and cleared from the Akashic records.

After several deep belly breathes of release, I continued with my clearing decree. 'I now call forth, neutralise and rescind all discordant contracts, cords, circuits, transactions, vows, promises, oaths and thought forms that I have made with myself, others – or that anyone has made on my behalf, with or without my consent – that have violated my free will sovereignty or that of another's, on all levels of my being and throughout all timelines and dimensions. May all that remain be purified with the violet flame in benevolent service to all of creation. By the Light that I AM, may all beings flourish in sovereign freedom as the pure Light of supreme Love! So be it and so it is!' After the decree, I threaded diamond light through each chakra and sealed my bioenergetic field with a cocoon of golden pink light of unconditional love in the knowing with such a massive clearing there is would be much release and integration.

CHAPTER FORTY-FOUR

LAST CALL

Sometimes by way of betrayal, romance defeats the ego and thereby helps us to grow. When a lover betrays us, as unspeakably awful and agonising as that is, the resulting trauma cracks open the fragile but restrictive shell of the ego, providing an opportunity to embrace greater and more soulful possibilities. We can only be betrayed romantically, moreover, when we have been blind to something about our lover. That blindness not only set us up for betrayal but also blocks the larger story that we must embrace to inherit our destiny. Each stage of ego growth contains the seeds of its own betrayal. The soul tricks us into setting up the conditions for that betrayal, which forces a deeper Self-reflection that might lead to a soul encounter and the next stage of growth.

– Bill Plotkin, *Soul Craft*

When it is time for the transformational expansions of crucifixion and resurrection you will be challenged to look at your attachments to beliefs, relationships, and possesions. Everything that limits you will come up for review. You may feel betrayed when your limited identity and world are falling apart, or on the other hand, you may begin to realize that your Soul is liberating you. When 'the betrayer,' as the catalytic 'Judas' appears on your threshold and knocks, will you open the door and behold a welcomed friend or foe. Yeshua recognized and welcomed Judas Iscariot as 'the friend little understood.'

– Claire Heartsong, *Anna, Grandmother of Jesus*

I rang Aiden for what I resolved to be the very last time. More than anything, I needed a sense of closure from our prior conversation that had ended mid-sentence and literally left me hanging in limbo. I sensed the immense significance of the conversation, as if every word would be imprinted in the Book of Life. And so, I took my time and internally asked myself once again, *What would love do now?*

Finally, the woman he was staying with in Scotland answered the telephone and as soon as she heard my voice, abruptly handed the phone over to him. For all I knew, she was his next lover.

'Hello?' he said, not sure who it was.

In my relief, I spoke in a rush. 'Aiden! It's me, Ambe´. Hellooooo? I've been trying to reach you since we got disconnected four days ago. What happened?'

'I've been really sick,' he said in a weary voice.

'Again? I'm so sorry to hear that. What's going on,' I asked with concern.

'I don't know. I guess I never quite got over the spell of illness I had over in France. It's been quite intense to say the least.'

'Yes,' I said. 'I too have had my challenges!' I took a long pause to gather my composure and clear my throat. Like a deep sea diver, I dove into my center and reached for a way to communicate my truth without lacing it in victim or blame. In that brief pause, I consciously chose to stay centered in my heart rather than be swayed by the minds reactivity. A part of me knew that staying open in love, honour and respect was the most integral way for me to navigate this uncomfortable terrain. Afterall, we are different characters but we all share the same one eternal heart. *What matters most is how I choose to respond, because the gifts I give to every character in my story become the reality I experience in every moment. And as messy, raw, and vulnerable truth can be, this is what matters the most to me.* I coached myself.

'Aiden, I wanted to let you know that I managed to evacuate all of those pesky "energies" that have been interfering with my energetic field and potentially yours. So...I wanted to check in with you and see how you're feeling.'

'Uhmm,' he said, 'well, that's really great to hear.'

'Aiden, I deeply honour our connection. It has never been my intention to cause you distress in any way. I hope you know that. My sense is that there have been an array of banal and discordant energies deliberately trying to interfere with our connection and some that are trying to protect me. I have done my very best to release any and all negative influences that may be interfering with me, you or any other people in my life. I let them know that I am in charge and have the right to manage my affairs without their so-called unsolicited help. Having said that, I know we are each responsible for co-creating this interfering discordance. There is much hidden beneath the surface that is yet to be revealed. Neither of us is to blame for what has transpired between us.'

I went on to say, 'I have taken this experience as an opportunity to steward my energetic field with greater inner authority and way more discernment. And for that, I'm grateful to you and all of the lessons I am continuing to learn. Out of this experience, I'm committed more than ever to steward my physical, emotional and energetic sovereignty and show up for the deeper "why" we were brought together in the first place. This way, we can harvest the lessons and gifts and truly set one another free.'

I breathed into my heart until I found the courage to put myself out on the limb and ask my final question, 'Aiden, um…would you still like to meet at Earth Heart festival for ceremony and share some beautiful soul family time? We would have the opportunity to bring whatever "this is" all the way through for the One.' I tried to keep my voice from cracking mid-sentence.

I paused and waited out the long silence. I wanted to show up for the relationship – to embody the remedy, rather than react to the fracture. At that point, I didn't care if we would ever be together as lovers again. I wanted to part ways with open hearts, mutual respect and with our friendship intact. With all my heart, I wanted to know if any small morsel of our connection could be salvaged, not only for me but for the purpose of the greater whole. That was what mattered most to me at the time. Deep from within, I knew that I had to live with this moment for the rest of my life and recollected this stanza from a Rumi poem as my reminder: '*Gamble everything for love if you are a true human being. If not, leave this gathering. Half-heartedness doesn't reach into majesty.'*

During his ensuing silence, I had plenty of time to come to terms with the reality that my inability to reestablish contact with him was no accident and in truth, his answer. He had clearly chosen another path and *yes,* potentially another woman. I wondered how I could have been so blind and naïve to have ever hoped for anything else. *Why was I so willing to show up for someone who was clearly not choosing to show up for me?* I recognised a pattern at play that went back further than I could remember. In the sobriety of the moment, it was I, that nearly hung up on him.

I then heard Aiden take a deep breath. He had to push himself to communicate. 'I am choosing another way right now. I am choosing simplicity,' he said. 'I am tired, and the path before me is full of new challenges. In truth, I've moved on and I'm into new things. I really must gather my strength for all that is yet to come.'

At first, I felt a sharp sting shoot through my heart and bolt down into the pit of my belly as I took the shot of blatant rejection. I used all my strength to stay open though, and honour the few words that he shared. After a few deep breaths, I mustered my calm and strong voice. 'Thank you for sharing what's real for you, Aiden. I totally respect where you're at, and honour that it's exactly where you need to be.' A womanly part of me knew there was much more that was not being spoken and sensed he was speaking in half truths. In short, he was not being fully honest with me and I was left to simply accept whatever morsels of truth he was willing to give.

Nevertheless, I came to terms with the only power I had at the time. *If he wasn't willing to show up and be honest, I was!* It was my way of taking a stand for the kind of communication that I knew to be the bed-stone for true friendship. I needed to give myself what I most longed for from him. I needed to be brave, vulnerable, undefended and true.

For all I knew, this could be our very last conversation and I was going to make sure that there were no regrets on my end. I felt as if I was stepping onto a very hot bed of coals.

'I choose to be real and transparent with you,' I said. 'What's true for me is that I will continue to honour the love that I feel for you and our special connection. Anything else would be closing my heart and living a lie. I am choosing to be brave and stay true to my heart and my feelings whether they are reciprocated or not.'

After another long moment of silence, Aiden replied vaguely, 'Maybe I'll see you in the spring, Bella,' he said firmly. 'Perhaps at some point we can meet up in California and carry on with our Earth healing work there. Until then, I want you to know that it has been a profound and wonderful experience getting to be with you. I have never met anyone who has affected me as deeply as you have. You are a beautiful goddess, a powerful healer and inspiring Wayshower. I am grateful for your wisdom and the wonderful time we have shared together. Take good care of yourself, Bella, and keep those pesky gremlins at bay.'

In that instant, my heart shattered all over again. And yet, I remained open to receive his overture and inwardly bowed in honour of all that we had shared. For me, love and respect were one and the same. And although I was grateful that he offered some amicable words of closure, the cellular memories of rejection rippled through my veins, reminding me of where I needed to go next.

'Thank you for sharing what is true for you, Aiden. I wish you a beautiful journey into fatherhood. I want you to know that I will always treasure all that we've shared together.' My voice faded as I held back a sob. 'Blessings on your journey, dear one.'

After that, I could no longer speak and neither could he. There was a long silence between us as I pressed the phone to my ear and waited for his goodbye, which never came. This time, I was the one to hang up first. 'Goodbye, Aiden,' I said as the phone went dead.

CHAPTER FORTY-FIVE

GOLDEN NUGGETS

The next time you feel abandoned, feel it fully. Let it all the way in this time. Not the story of abandonment, but the raw sensations that have been longing for your holding. Embrace the shakiness, the brokenness, and the raw life that is moving through you. Don't turn away, not this time. For you need yourself now more than ever. There is a portal inside the abandoned one, buried in her heart, her body, and in the core of the emptiness. There is gold there, but it is hidden and requires new perception to unearth. In the willingness to bring breath and to flood the feelings with the warmth of your presence, you will discover that which has never been abandoned. Take this one as your lover. In the commitment to never turn from him or her again, everything will break open, revealing the erupting, tender aliveness at the core. Even abandonment, when met, allowed, contained, and held, will reveal its purity, and clarify its role as a sacred, though devastating ally on the path.

– Matt Licata

The Christ Path is about burning in a love that is large enough to embrace every experience and being within it. It is about being stripped down to raw naked presence – where all that remains is a tear, an unspoken irony as the Beloved smiles upon you...from behind the eyes of each and every beating heart.

– Inaiya Ray

The following day I had my consultation with Christopher, a.k.a. Sananda. I was eager to have the Ascended Master illuminate whatever medicine was embedded in the dark and mysterious turn of events in regards to my heart-wrenching affair with Aiden.

A gentleman with a white beard opened the door of his two-story flat. He looked like a thinner version of Gandalf the Wizard from the movie *The Lord of the Rings*. His provincial home sat adjacent to the Brighton Sea. It appeared to be the last remaining residence amongst the encroaching industrial park.

Christopher kindly welcomed me in with a warm, fatherly embrace. He apologised for not being available earlier and gestured for me to take a seat in his front parlour. The room was filled with soft light from the large bay windows, which looked out to the overcast Brighton Sea. I sat down in a worn-out teal-blue chair that looked like something he had inherited from his grandmother. Christopher sat just across from me on an overstuffed white loveseat. I did my best to mask my eagerness for answers while we took a few moments to get acquainted.

Christopher took a large swig of tea, then pressed the tape recorder with his long index finger covered in soft white hairs. 'Shall we begin then, my dear?'

'Oh yes, please!'

He settled into the couch, took a few deep breaths and spoke. His voice carried the resonance of pure fatherly love.

'Dear one, it seems you are restless as you struggle to find ways to fulfill your soul purpose here on earth. As you may know, you are a powerful Lightworker and master Healer. You have a strong capacity to weave discordant energies into Oneness. And yet presently, you are feeling the turbulence as you undergo this heightened initiatory experience in this elaborate dance through time.

'You see, in the past, you had the ability to project your consciousness into the future and assist to build bridges across time into a new order of Oneness. Utilising crystals and rock formations, you buried energy grids at sacred sites, with the intention to be reconnected and reactivated during this evolutionary time on Earth. In feeling the urgent call to protect and assist Gaia from the poisons of our developing culture, you could not help but to get somewhat poisoned along the way, making it difficult for you to trust humans. Even so, your love and compassion for all beings gave you the tenacity to carry on with your mission. Yet in your attempt to shift the balance from darkness to light, it became simply too much for one person to manage.

'And so throughout the course of lifetimes, you learned to summon the spirits and the elementals to assist in protecting Gaia from her descent into darkness. You built alliances, which unbeknownst to you required repayment over time. In doing so, you had a sense of increased power when in actuality, you gave your energy over as a massive trade-off. In essence, you are only now becoming aware of the energetic syphon that you have been paying off for gaining the assistance. These external influences all seem to have their own unique agenda in the various situations you find yourself in and this has caused turmoil in your energetic field.

'In short, wherever your will is unclaimed and ungrounded in your power and inner authority, it will create an opening for uninvited energies to interfere with your energetic field. This is an opportunity to build resilience as you learn to embody your sovereignty and dominion over your life. The key is to stay centered in your core values and not be allured into matching their frequency or scare tactics. Now you find yourself reorganising the light of your being to find peace and resolve within, and in so doing you are reorganising the light of Gaia herself.

'Much of the purpose of meeting Aiden had to do with triggering and catalysing a new phase and period of service for you. You come from the same soul family and have shared many past lives. You specifically chose this lifetime to catalyse one another in releasing aspects of yourselves that have remained entrapped within the unconscious parts of your being. Your soul required the connection with this kindred heart to be strong enough to crack open the armouring that has prevented your core essence to emerge and shine through. A large part of this process has to do with sweeping away the debris that are shrouding your true gifts, awaiting to be reclaimed along with your sovereign power. This reclamation has catalyzed an awareness of what is required for you to live in integrity and alignment with your divine essence.

'It is time to complete any and all karmic and ancient contracts with external ties that interfere with your true power as a sovereign being. It is time to free up your energy on all levels and dimensions, and step into this next phase of service and greater self-love. In time, you will feel relieved and grateful to be accompanied by only those you intentionally invite in and by benevolent forces of light that match your purity of intent.

'You are a being of universal love here to midwife a new Earth humanity. A part of your purpose is to prepare this world for the new Starseeds who are coming in, and assist them to anchor their essence and share their unique soul gifts. In fact, there is a soul that wants very much to come through you. It is a being that has incredible amounts of love for you and has been intimately connected to you for nearly all of your lifetimes.

'Meanwhile, what we are suggesting for you is to organise a holiday by the sea for some good retreat and recovery time. We are sensing that you are in somewhat of a shock and feel it would greatly benefit you to take some time off to relax and restore your weary heart and nervous system. Imagine you are taking your best friend out on a holiday. Where would you like to take her? Then go to a local travel agent and ask them for their best "special" on a holiday package by the sea. It's important that you take time to be in silence and solitude while integrating the last few months. At first, you may feel like a worn-out weary traveller, but in time, you will reflect back on this time and see the profound gifts and invaluable soul lessons it provided.

'Thank you, for being so dedicated to a higher love and devoting your life to being a lantern for this world. You are loved beyond all measure and we are with you always. Good day.'

I slowly opened my eyes and looked up at Christopher. He sat upright on the couch, smiling at me. 'Thank you for this warm and wise sacred counsel, Christopher. Your words have brought me comfort and have strengthened me to go on with my journey with greater clarity, peace and resolve.'

'You are most welcome, dear one,' he replied tenderly. Then he added with a sparkle, 'Enjoy your holiday! It sounds like just the golden ticket.'

By the time I left Christopher's home, the public bus service had discontinued for the day. I had no other choice but to hitchhike back to the Hove district where Fiona's flat was. As if nothing could injure me anymore than it had, I decided I would brave it and walk down the industrial road with my thumb out, hoping to catch a ride.

I hummed to myself sweetly in order to keep my mind from spiralling down into that oh so familiar dark hole. 'This little light of mine...I'm gonna let it shine. This little light of mine, I'm gonna let it shine. This little light of mine...I'm gonna let it shine, let it shine, let it shine, let it shine.'

About twenty minutes into my walk, a little orange Mini Cooper swerved over to the side of the road. A man in his early forties with bleached-blond hair pulled over to the side of the road. I noticed he was wearing a Hawaiian shirt and smelled strongly of ale. He put his head out the window and shouted over the humming motor. 'Where you headed, doll?' he said in a very London-meets-California kind of way.

'The Hove.'

'I'm driving past there,' he said and motioned me to get in. Even though he reeked of the pub, I felt quite comfortable accepting his offer.

'My name is Elliot. Where ya from, luv? Ya have a funne' accent.'

'I'm Ambe´. From a place called Marin County, California.'

'Sure, I know where that is. My business brings me there from time to time. I'm a beer and wine rep,' he said. His wide grin revealed his polished teeth and I wondered how he got them so white.

'Oh right,' I responded nonchalantly as if we had been friends for years.

'Yes, indeed. Marin County is quite a spectacular place,' Elliot said.

In that moment, I felt like he had doused me with a magical elixir to momentarily divert me from my present reality.

'Oh yes! Marin is stunning. Especially the nature,' I went on in a nostalgic ramble, reminiscing about the wonderful life I left behind in Marin, as if I was the one who had a little too much to drink at the pub.

Elliot listened enthusiastically until he dropped me off on the Brighton High Street in the Hove. 'Fancy a drink some time, luv?' He said while tempting me with those pearly whites once again.

'No, thank you. I'll be heading off for a beach holiday in a day or two with my girlfriend,' I answered assuredly, inwardly reflecting on Sananda's strong advice.

I walked the rest of the way to Fiona's flat in a daze, still integrating my session with Christopher. I was grateful to have spoken about my hometown with Elliot and temporarily distract myself from the intensity of all that I was attempting to digest. I marveled at how Great Spirit always provided us with the medicine we needed, exactly when we needed it, because my life was becoming more and more foreign, far out and downright freaky by the moment.

Then I heard that small still voice within me chime in and whisper, *Let it shine, let it shine, let it shine.*

CHAPTER FORTY-SIX

THE GIFT OF FIRE

The heroine must venture forth from the world of common sense consciousness into a region of supernatural wonder. There she encounters fabulous forces – demons and angels, dragons and helping spirits. After a fierce battle, she wins a decisive victory over the powers of darkness. Then she returns from her mysterious adventure with the gift of knowledge of fire, which she bestows on his fellow humanity.

– Joseph Campbell, Hero with a Thousand Faces

What I discovered in this initiatory fire were two shattering truths, which many people discover when they come into the crucible of the Black Madonna. The first thing is that all your plans, agendas, projects, and visions are systematically and with terrifying precision, unraveled by Her. They are annihilated because they belong to a world of division and separation. They belong to the pride of the false Self and to a way of acting that has to become immeasurably deepened by radiant awareness.

The second thing that you discover is that She is not only transcendent, She is also the most passionately profound natural process, and that the birth into Her and through Her is very much a physical birth.

So it is clear to me that this birth into the Black Madonna is a birth simultaneously into this "dark transcendent" mystery – the source and womb and spring of all manifestation – and a birth into the splendour of tantric fullness and the glory of Divine union. The two together, as they deepen, create what only can be described as the resurrection consciousness, an authentic Divine humanity.

What She goes on to destroy is all of the fantasies that block the Transcendent as well as destroy all of the fears, loathing, self-hatreds, and all of the terrors of the body that block the light pouring out of the body's own most sacred truth. This is essential information for all seekers at this moment, because unless we embrace this powerful alchemical process to birth our Divine humanity, with fully consecrated sacred powers and creativity of every kind, we may not make it. The good news, however, is that if we are able to cultivate the inner strength and courage to undergo such a momentous task, our transfiguration becomes inevitable and we will birth a wholly new consciousness and a world beyond our wildest imaginings.

– Andrew Harvey

First thing in the morning, even before I had my cup of PG tips, I walked myself straight to the travel agent on High Street only to find that the shop was still closed. I paced up and down the sidewalk for twenty-five minutes until a very large-bellied man wearing a white button-down shirt and navy blue tie opened the shop for me.

'Please, have a seat in the reception area, Miss.' He pointed with the only free finger he had.

He settled in to his workspace with a cup of tea and a pastry. The bright-red jelly oozed out of its flaky middle, threatening to spill over onto the large stack of brochures sprawled out in front of him. He gestured for me to take a seat across from his desk. 'Good morning. How can I help you, Miss?'

I looked him in the eye and said in a rush, 'What is your least expensive holiday package to a warm beach where I can be self-contained, have plenty of privacy and a minimum of distracting night life?'

Unfazed, he nodded, took a bite of his pastry, a slurp from his teacup and began to search his computer.

A part of me wrestled with the alluring fantasy of heading straight to Ibiza, dancing all night at the infamous Café Del Mar nightclub and spending lazy days on the beach getting lost in trashy novels. However, I sobered up from my momentary fantasy and placed my attention on the travel agent. I was a little nervous about him as he held his dripping jelly pastry in one hand and shuffled through a large pile of brochures in the other. Our present realities appeared to be worlds apart. *He probably specialises in the exact opposite of what I am looking for,* I thought to myself as I waited anxiously while he searched his computer.

'Aha…' He took a swig of his tea and another bite of his pastry and chewed excitedly while shuffling through yet another pile of large travel brochures on his desk. With a whisk of great confidence, he pulled out three of the brochures and placed them in front of me. The first thing I noticed was that two out of three of them featured a slightly different version of a spray-tanned, large-bosomed woman posing in a white bikini on the white sandy shore of a tranquil turquoise sea.

'How about this one?' He pointed to the plainest of the selection. 'It's the last of the summer specials and comes with a self-catering room. It's in the Peloponnese Mountains of Greece. They're offering a super special deal right now. You can go for seven days for only 160 pounds, round trip! You're not going to find much better than that, Miss.'

When I hesitated, he added, 'And for only another forty pounds more, your trip could be extended a whole additional week!' The travel agent then swiftly opened the brochure to the centre page and showed me a picture of the tranquil-looking beach. I studied the illustration of a map highlighting the village of Stoupa, in the small town of Mani, located in the greater district of Kalamata, Greece – an area I was entirely unfamiliar with.

To be honest, the pictures looked good, but not great. They certainly had more dry and dusky browns than the alluring white-sand beaches with calm turquoise water depicted on the other brochures. I had a hunch that this was a newly developed resort town and they were doing their best to give the place a kick-start by attracting budget travellers.

Feeling noticeably strained, I begged the friendly man to search a little deeper. 'Isn't there anything comparable in that price range on the Spanish or Italian Mediterranean coast?' I politely pleaded.

He tapped away on his computer and came up with a few alternatives that were significantly higher in price. While he searched, I paused for a moment, looking idly at the brochure.

Then I held my breath. *Holy shit!*

Suddenly an orchestra of bells went off inside my head. I reviewed the names of the Greek resort he was suggesting. *Kalamata?*

Doesn't that mean the Black Mother, Kali? Isn't she the face of the Divine Mother deity from India whose love has the power to stomp out our egoic delusions? In the town of Mani? I believe that means 'precious jewel' or 'great teacher' in Tibetan! And didn't he say 'Stoupa'? That's a Tibetan temple that represents the graduated stages of enlightenment! I gasped. Who on Earth is writing this story anyway? With names like that, how could I not get my money's worth – and very likely a lot more!

'Yes!' I pronounced quite suddenly. This desolate place was exactly where I was to take my best girlfriend Self on my prescribed beach holiday!

The agent noticed me staring at the brochure. He quickly said, 'You know, Ms. Ray, this is a rather special place. It is still fairly undiscovered by most tourists. I'm sure you'll find the tranquillity and beauty of the mountains and the surrounding bay quite suitable to your needs.'

I looked up with a smile. In that moment, my travel agent had shape-shifted into Santa Claus, plump rosy cheeks and red jelly lips and all. 'I'll take it! Umm, give me the seven-day package, though. That way, I can leave right away if I don't like it,' I said, as if issuing myself a flexible prison sentence.

Then I heard a stern motherly voice inside of me say, *'Oh no no no, Ambe´. You must be there for at least two weeks! You will leave only when you have dealt with this monstrosity that is wreaking havoc on your life.'*

'Okay, okay, fine. I'll take the two-week package please,' I said hastily. I threw my credit card brashly on his cluttered desk with a defeated smile, reminding myself of my mother. She would fling her credit card down on the counter whenever she had spent way too much money on something that she felt she couldn't possibly live without.

My jolly ol' travel agent winked and smiled at me with a kind of all-knowing gleam that beamed from his beady blue eyes. In our short time together, I had grown rather fond of him. He appeared to know more about me than I did, and I couldn't help liking him for that. Like a top chef, he masterfully whipped out the brochure again and recited the itinerary at high speed. I knew I had to go to the Black Mother, Kalamata, so it didn't matter that I could only decipher one out of four words he was rambling off. He then handed me my credit card with a pile of papers, shook my hand and wished me a 'very fine holiday, Miss' – all in about twenty-three seconds flat. I think he wanted to seal the deal before I changed my mind, or ran out of there and jumped off the nearest building.

'Oh, thank you so much, sir! I'll think of you on my trip,' I said, smiling warmly at him.

In some mysterious way, we had bonded in that very short time. I closed the shop door, amused by that brief encounter. My initial feeling of estrangement from him had completely transformed into something quite unexpectedly intimate. Tears welled up as I realised that he must have recognised my not-so-subtle symptoms of a broken heart and went out of his way to ensure I got to just the right place to mend it.

Every encounter is an opportunity to meet a friend, someone who makes our lives possible along the way, I thought, as I sent him a silent blessing of gratitude for the lifeboat he had provided me with. For better or worse, I was on my way to discover this precious hidden jewel called Mani.

My plane did not depart until the following morning, so I spent the rest of my day in town procuring a few items I needed for my trip. On that Saturday, Brighton was bustling with young shoppers, brimming cafés and crowded boutiques. At the time, I was in no shape to enjoy Brighton in my usual upbeat fashion. I just wanted to pass out on a secluded beach and never get up again! However, on my way back to Fiona's, I found myself wandering into a used bookshop. My feet seemed to have a life of their own as they walked me directly to a book on the shelf entitled, *The Coming of the Feminine Christ* by Niamh Clune. I took the book down, opened it to the middle, and read, 'The Grail is not an object to gain, but something we become. Such individuals will be Feminine Christs – not born of the womb but of the sanctified heart.' With that, I purchased the book and carried on with the last of my errands. There was nothing more for me to do than pack up my things and say goodbye to Fiona and my gracious hosts back at the flat.

Feeling anxious for what was to come, the night stretched into endless hours of tossing and turning. I probably slept less than an hour as the gremlins in my feverish mind kept me awake all night. Like a puppet attached to some psycho's string, I flopped around in my bed, until sunrise. Whatever energies that had been wreaking havoc on my life were restless and toiling with me. *Perhaps they knew their days were numbered.*

The following day, I would be heading straight into the belly of the whale – retreating to the tiny little town whose name resembled the Indian Goddess Kali, where I would soon invite the Black Mother to have her way with me!

Just before sunrise, at the crack of dawn, I quietly slipped away with my bags, along with my war-torn heart. A ghost-like mist hovered in the air on this typical, chilly Brighton morning. I was headed to my secluded paradise, ready to face this mysterious monster in what I declared would be our last and final battle. I felt like a warrior heading to the front lines, weary from head to toe, yet unwavering in my determination to confront the dreaded enemy and put an end to it once and for all! I took heart as I remembered how the priests and priestesses of the mystery schools would retreat to a cave to fast, or bury themselves underground for days on end until they faced their greatest fear and looked death squarely in the eye. I opened my book, Return of the Feminine Christ and turned to this passage;

The shadows of our denials hide inside our unconscious, festering away, creating a kind of invisible decay. They cry out to be acknowledged and set free through our recognition and loving embrace. As we dare to meet what lies below the surface, we in turn are given second life.

I was half crying and half laughing when I entered the chartered airplane and heard Simon and Garfunkel's classic song from the seventies playing over the small aircraft's sound system. 'Here's to you, Mrs. Robinson. Jesus loves you more than we can say. Hey, hey, hey.' The last time I had heard that song was in Aiden's car. It was playing when we took off together from the Rainbow Gathering and set out on our Pyrenees mountain adventure! I heard a voice in my head insist, *'Go on, feel it, baby. Feel it! Feel it all the way, Bella, right down to the marrow of your weary bones!'*

I found my seat and got settled amongst a large group of elderly vacationers. One after another, the songs dropped in through the loud speakers like missiles. I was being pummeled by a musical medley of precise heart bombs from a mysterious, all-knowing jukebox...or was that a *joke* box? I could hardly believe it as the

Bryan Airlines musical oracle fired off a tragic romantic soundtrack, designed to rub salt into my open wounds. *Fire one! Fire two, fire three!* At first, I didn't know whether to laugh, cry or do both.

The medley kicked off with Whitney Houston's heart-piercing wail: 'And I…I, I will always love you! Bittersweet memories I took them with me…so goodbye. We both know I'm not what you need. And I, I will always love you… I wish you joy, happiness and above all this, I wish you love!'

My throat swelled up as I sunk deeper into my seat. Before I could digest that one, I heard, 'Must have been love, but it's over now. Must have been good, but I lost it somehow.' All of a sudden, my somber mood began to lighten as my ears perked up to listen intently to the Great Mother DJ in the sky. A warm smile washed over my being and melted my icy demeanour. *You sure are in top form today, Great Mother of all DJs!*

The music continued with yet another heartwrencher from the movie, *Dirty Dancing*. 'And remember you're the one thing I can't get enough of, so I tell you something – this could be love. Because I had the time of my life. No, I never felt this way before. Oh no, it's true and I owe it all to youuuu!'

Tears rolled down my face through my crooked smile, and then the eighties band Berlin bellowed, 'Turning and returning to a secret place in time. Through the hourglass, I saw you, in time you slipped away.'

OK, OK, I surrender! Could you rub it in anymore? I shouted in my head, stunned by the outrageous, cutthroat humour of the satirical music oracle.

Finally, to top off all the others, the last song before take-off blared, 'I believe in miracles, since you came along, you sexy thing. Where did you come from, baby? Did you know you're everything I prayed for? How did you know I'd give my heart gladly?'

I wanted to take out my barf bag right then and there! *All right, all right, already. I get it. I now entitle, the next chapter of my life 'The Great Purge', a full body and soulular detox from the world's sappiest romantic love songs!*

CHAPTER FORTY-SEVEN

SAFE PASSAGE

With the intention for communion as your guide, the next time you are met by the burning, the restlessness, the claustrophobia, and the shaky, survival-level vulnerability, remember your aspiration. Weave together a sanctuary where the visitors can rest from a long journey. Provide safe passage such that their richness and meaning may be revealed. Inside the heart, you will see that the lost ones do not need to be transformed. They do not need to be shifted. They do not even need to be healed. Only held. Go slowly. One second at a time, then rest. They are not in a hurry. They have been looking for you since beginningless time, and will never give up.

– Matt Licata

It takes immense strength to let go of absolutely everything and walk fully in one's self-realised truth. It is a profound initiation that brings up all fears of being alone, failing, not being safe, held and supported. It feels like jumping off a cliff blindfolded, trusting that the wings will open up and each cell of the being remembers how to glide within the quantum space – no one to hold on to, nothing to grasp at, only the great unknown. There is a moment when one's inner being cannot withstand a moment longer in timelines saturated with deceit, it becomes unbearable. And even though most other selves do not recognise the deceit and view the timelines as truth, the inner being chooses to take that solo leap. What is on the other side is beyond what one could dream of.

– Avatāra Ānanda

Grind yourself, strip yourself down
to blind loving silence:
stay there, until you see
you are gazing at the Light
with its own ageless eyes.

– Jelaluddin Rumi

Two hours later, our miniature plane landed with the kind of bumps, thumps and rattles one would expect from a small aircraft. As we disembarked, we were welcomed to Greece by a balding man with a protruding belly who was perspiring profusely. He greeted the flock of tourists with a crooked smile while herding us single file into a large tourist bus. The first thing I noticed as I looked around for my seat was that I was the only person on this budget holiday that still maintained my natural hair colour.

As we bumped along, I overheard an elderly couple reading, *Let's Go, Greece Travel Guide* aloud. 'Kalamata is a newly developing beach-town resort. According to Greek mythology and local lore, it is considered to be an actual gateway to the underworld.'

'*Ohhh, that's why my holiday package was going for so cheap,*' I snickered to myself, in awe of this divinely orchestrated destination. *I guess I'll get what I paid for – a two-week, self-catering trip – to, you guessed it, the deep, dark, not-to-be-traversed-by-the-faint-of-heart– UNDERWORLD! I wonder if there's a guidebook for the underworld*, I said, feeling a little lost. *Maybe I'll write it and call it, Let's Go Underworld!*

Forty-five minutes later, the bus driver screeched to a halt on a dusty dirt road and called out the name written on my hotel voucher. 'Elena!'

I grabbed my backpack, bid the busload of travellers goodbye and beelined to my studio apartment. The bus driver handed me my bags and then pointed up the desolate road. 'Make left at corner,' he shouted encouragingly as he got back on the bus, taking his place at the wheel. The bus roared away, leaving me alone in a cloud of dust.

The only shop in site was a small grocery store with a sign that said, 'Still under construction'. As I headed up the unpaved road, I spotted my humble abode. For a brief moment, I panicked and *wondered indignantly, Where on Earth was my beachfront studio? Didn't my travel agent angel promise me a white sandy beach? I'm going first thing in the morning to straighten this bloody mistake of a holiday out! Perhaps I can get a refund and get on the next plane out tomorrow. What was I thinking? This is no place to take my best girlfriend for a holiday!*

With a sigh, I lugged my suitcase up a short flight of stairs and opened the door of my sparsely decorated room. I noticed the large brass nameplate bolted to the front door that spelled out the name *Elena* in cursive letters. I didn't know it at the time, but *Elena* translates to '*ray of light*' in Greek. Much to my surprise, *Elena* had quite a unique charm. She sported a simple décor of two single beds, two nightstands with a vase of plastic flowers on top, a portable two-burner stove, a small colour TV, and standing lamp with pink furry pom-poms hanging from the shade.

Well, it's certainly not the Ritz, but I suppose it has everything I require for my journey to the Underworld, I consoled myself as I sat down upon the quilted bedspread with its decorative strawberries and blue ribbon bows. I sat there staring blankly at the motif with a mixture of shock and awe. *How on Earth did I end up here of all places?*

Here in *Elena's* kitschy charm, I was coming to terms with the precarious 'monster' Aiden had claimed to be messing with his *and* my life. It sat there hiding in the background, creating a level of sabotage and interference whenever I dared to ascend to the next dimensional level of consciousness.

I'm ready to face you, I thought. *Put up your dukes! But wait – I must prepare myself for battle and get some necessary provisions! Oh yes, and a good cuppa while I'm at it! I'm already going through PG Tips (pampered goddess) withdrawals.*

I opened my backpack, grabbed my bathing suit and a sarong just in case I stumbled upon a white sandy beach while stocking up on some provisions. I thought I was ready to get out and explore the area until my burst of energy dissipated, replaced by an all-consuming weariness. *Maybe I'll lie down for ten minutes, close my eyes and have a little siesta before I venture out.*

I reclined on top of my strawberry, blue-ribbon bedspread and offered up a prayer inspired by my beloved soul mentor Matt Khan. '*Thank you beloved Universe for awakening within me. Please spare no expense at unraveling what needs to be unraveled, transforming what needs to be transformed, and healing what needs to be healed. I surrender to the fate of my highest potential and divine authority, inviting the change that only brings forth greater harmony, wholeness, liberation, and well being. I hand over the aspects of ego that were never meant to go any further in my journey, allowing a greater embodiment and integration of heart-centered consciousness to abide within me now. Even when it feels like all hope is lost or as if I'm going to die, I step forward into the mystery that cannot be understood 'beforehand', only to receive more awareness of the light I AM, have always been, and shall always be. Thank you for this opportunity to transform ancestral lineages and help uplift the consciousness of humanity by ending the inner battle of ego. And thank you for no longer supporting the negotiation of self-defeating choices. Thank you dear Universe. I am the vessel of your highest divine will. Take me, I'm yours. And so I let go. I am surrendered, surrendered I am. And so it is.'*

Within the span of one full breath, I heard the now familiar, loving maternal voice whisper to me. This time she introduced herself. *'Welcome home, beloved one. I am Sophia, your Divine Mother and guide for your Underworld journey! Are you ready to retrieve the diamond light of your soul?'*

I lay absolutely still and listened with full intent.

'I invite you to take part in the sacred alchemy that will return you to the sanctuary of your awakened heart. It is time to embody and connect to the higher dimensions of consciousness where you will see all that needs to be seen, heard and compassionately held in your loving embrace. You will be guided to collapse ancient timelines and release parts of you that have weighed heavily upon your soul light.

'Let's begin by grounding into the 5th dimensional New Earth and clear your chakras and auric field as you come into vertical alignment with your pillar of light and crystalline soul star. Now we will weave the emerald rays of the Holy Father and sapphire rays of the Divine Mother presence around your body and throughout your heart. Feel your monadic core stabilise and align with Gaia and the highest expression of the Divine Christos Sophia so that you are fully held and supported throughout your journey of transfiguration. We now anchor a crystalline cathedral of light and four aurora pillars of light in and around you and your room, and invite you to attune yourself with the natural and organic blueprint of your soul coming into harmonic resonance with the Law of One.'

Whilst bathing in Sophia's scintillating presence, I joined her in setting up a pristine energetic space around my self and the studio. As I was doing so, I became aware of a pesky energy gnawing at every fibre of my being, pulling me into a vortex of dense, dark and frozen emotion. Unlike the benevolent presence of Sophia, this presence felt distinctly different – like a cunning and mysterious force that dragged me into her violent undertow.

'Who's there?' I demanded to know, struggling to sit up as I confronted the unidentifiable dark energy. '*Who tears at the flesh of my soul, holding me captive to an ancient unpaid debt? Who insists on sucking me into the dark river of my unresolved past while sabotaging my joy in the present?*' I confronted the daunting energy with a commanding presence. '*Who and what is syphoning my precious human life force? Who persists on making claims on my life as if they were the keeper of my soul?*'

'*I am the face of the fallen Dark Mother. My job is to diminish your light through making you believe you are living in a dangerous world and your life is at risk. Do not attempt to outsmart me, for I will be there to dismiss your creativity, demand your silence and feed off your shame and powerlessness. I will ensure you feel rejected and inadequate, as I revel in your ongoing sense of worthlessness. Feel my claws rip into your flaws and tear away at your self-confidence until you become paralysed by fear, disconnection and shame. I will ensure you feel under attack or threat until the war you wage against yourself becomes your ordinary reality. Just try to free yourself from my grip through your endless pursuit for perfection, and I will laugh at the futility of your persistent striving. Your striving for self-improvement only serves to reinforce your sense of chronic lack and low self-esteem until it manifests as a self-fulfilling prophecy. I am the dark lunar consciousness that lurks in the shadows of your unclaimed power. My agenda is to control you by snuffing out your light whenever your power and authority goes unclaimed.*'

Whoa! I shivered. In that moment, I realised I had spent lifetimes trying to please, appease or run from the monstrous grip of the Dark Mother who in truth was an aspect of Mother's fallen body now calling out to be re-membered and reclaimed. *Oh, the futility!* In acquiescing and appeasing her, I neglected to value myself while learning to disregard my own instinctual needs. I had become an expert at over-giving to compensate for an innate sense of never being enough. Like a hidden parasite, this underlying feeling of lack had driven me to find love 'in all the wrong places'.

I felt the light of Sophia and the Crystal Star beings holding space while surrounding the Dark Mother's consciousness. *Whoa, no wonder I'm so exhausted. I have been under the influence of the Dark Mother's reversal arc patterning for God knows how long!* With this influx of awareness, I had to slow way down to see the parts of my psyche that had been ravaged by scarcity and neglect.

Enslaved by her hypnotic presence, life had become the Dark Mother and me her needy child. Carried and passed on through my genetics were the shadows of having been ravaged and raped, left out in the cold and cut off from feeling my inherent lovability. Over lifetimes, this disconnect was reinforced by the projections, judgments and deceit of others, particularly those with narcissistic personalities. It was time to reclaim my power along with all the aspects of me that had been afraid to be seen, heard or left behind. With a fierce presence, I was being called to embrace all of the faces that loomed in the shadow lands and lovingly meet each one of them, whether it be sadness, rage or devastation and say, 'I see you. I'm here for you and you too belong.'

As I began to understand the Dark Mother's icy tendrils embedded in nearly every aspect of my life, I sensed the deeper reason behind why this soul-sucking pattern of scarcity made frequent appearances in my life. It was easy to point the finger and blame the Masculine for my insufficiencies because all too often, their actions were blatant and overt. But now, I was being pointed to the grip of the Dark Mother, who remained hidden in the shadows of victim consciousness. Her cunning was so subtle and overt, often masked in justified insecurity, hiding behind an over or under-inflated ego. *Aha! It is the monstrous dissatisfaction of the Dark Mother that has eaten away at my innate radiance, leaving black holes of deficiency that demand being filled by sources outside of my very own Self.*

I pondered how I had responded to her terrifying death grip by doing everything I could to correct my so-called flaws, leading me to pursue an unattainable perfection. *Well, well, well, I'm onto you now, Dark Mother, and it's far time I faced your evil eye once and for all!*

My womb rumbled and contracted as the pain of the collective Feminine came rushing in. It revealed itself as a dark seed implanted within my womb, carried into this physical lifetime through my genetics and reinforced by the dark lunar forces.

Sophia, who carried a benevolent frequency and loving tone, went on to illuminate, *'The seed of the Dark Mother is a reversal patterning held within the light body. It creates an imbalance that twists and distorts Mother's body into grotesque forms through the control of her womb and the use of these demon seeds. The parts of your Sophionic body that have been reversed, twisted and distorted is what we will be restoring, reclaiming and reincrypting on this descent to the Underworld. With stealth humility, we walk this path into the shadow lands to understand what has occurred, and bring full integration, synthesis and restoration to your light body – that aspect that communicates and expresses as the unified Christos Sophia.'*

I breathed deeply while absorbing Sophia's wisdom light. I went on to imagine my Merkaba light body. The Feminine triangular pyramid shape points down and connects to the pelvis; the Masculine triangular shape points up and connects into the shoulder girdle. The distortions I was presently clearing was not only about me; its capricious tendrils were entwined within the very roots of the matriarchy and the shoots of the patriarchy, creating a distinct imbalance in the light body.

The Dark Masculine has been preying upon the Dark Feminine ever since the womb of the Feminine was first violated in the ancient temples and sacred sites. Women subsequently acquiesced their power and authority over to the Priests and hence were condoned to worship them as the ones closest to God.

I flashed on a past life reading I once had. The Akashic reader opened the reading by proclaiming, 'Kill all false gods before ye!' She demanded with a tone that sounded like something out of a horror movie. She proceeded to recount a lifetime when I was sold to an ancient Indian tantric temple as a young child from an impoverished village. I was groomed to be a living deity where beings from all over the world came to worship me as a goddess. Only the highest Priests were given the favour of keeping sexual company with me. I was told that to give my body and soul over to the Priests and the Brahmans was the greatest honour and would *please* God immensely. I was essentially bred to be a glorified sexual slave. The clairvoyant went on to remind me, 'Over lifetimes, your devotion to God has *always* been so all consuming. In your naiveté, you would do anything to please Him, including sacrificing your body to the extent of being ravished and left barren by false Gods. The temple Priests made it their purpose to destroy the power of the Feminine's sovereign covenant with the Divine. Perhaps this was the beginning of the patriarchy, where over time, an individual's right to plug directly into their source was substituted by man's authoritarian hand.

The deceit of this memory was nearly unbearable to fathom as I was confronted by the mass betrayal and self-sacrifice I had endured in the name of appeasing a false god. My body shuddered and grew icy with the very thought of it and all the innocent beings who are being sexually trafficked to this day. 'No more!' I declared aloud to my surrounding Family of Light.

I felt into the countless times I had given my power away by getting lost in a fog of fantasy, deceit and confusion all in exchange for an elusive form of false love and belonging. I wondered how many lifetimes I had succumbed to this impersonation of love and God that left me in the cold, resigned to being a victim of an obtuse and unnamable crime.

'These horrific crimes on humanity will end now!' I declared once again on behalf of myself and all those innocent beings that have ever been sacrificed in the name of God.

I, Ambe', now stand in my divine presence and reclaim every aspect of my disenfranchised self, entrapped within the Dark Mother and Death Father's fallen timelines, maneuvers and conditions on love. I now reclaim my full sovereignty as original innocence and lovingly embrace all aspects of who I AM in body, mind and soul. So be it and so it is!

I lay on the bed and breathed deeply into the marrow of my bones. With each exhale, I blazed the violet flame to burn away all falsities of Self until I felt another tugging at my womb.

Now who's there? I insisted.

'It is we, your ancestors, pleading with you to free us from our prison.'

What ancestors? I've never even met most of you. I know nothing about you. Mom and dad talked very little about you. You were always kept a secret from me. By the way, what prison?

'*It's where you go when you become trapped in the hell realms of persecution and victim consciousness. Please, help us! Please!* They went on to beg me with a barrage of desperation. *Release us from all that entraps our souls.*'

I remained motionless. 'You've got to be kidding! This is what my holiday at the sea is going to be about? Blue ribbons, false gods, blood scars and hungry ghosts?' I said aloud in an exasperated tone. *This cheapo ticket to paradise comes with quite a hefty price on it,* I thought, while I envisioned myself as the Hindu Goddess Kali – complete with bleeding wounds, bulging eyes, long tongue, and skull necklace wrapped around my neck, ready to stomp out any and all illusions.

So who are you? I asked once again as if to go back over my work just in case I accidentally made a mistake in my interpretation.

The answer came loud and clear, reverberating in my head. '*We are the ghosts of your ancestors, predecessors of your deepest genetic wounds. Our memory lives within your blood, passed along through your mother's mitochondria DNA. You feed us through your thoughts of desperation, fear, doubt and unworthiness. We are the millions of silenced voices, from the guillotine to the gas chamber. We are the orphaned children of your past – and all you have ever cast out, abandoned and rejected inside of yourself. We represent all that you judge and are afraid of becoming. We are your worst nightmare stuffed inside the basement of your unconscious, wreaking havoc on your life while screaming to be let out. Will you honour us and in so doing, set us free?*'

Whoa, you mean to say you are the ancestral descendants of the Dark Mother? I said to myself, as if I just stepped into my own multi-dimensional time machine. *I can do this. All they are wanting is for me to shine the light on the darkness so that they will be seen, honoured and heard.* I conjured the bravery and conviction of a superhero who had the strength and courage to face her greatest demons instead of running away from them. *What happened to taking my best girlfriend on a relaxing holiday to recuperate? Isn't that what Christopher was suggesting I do back in Brighton? Is this some kind of a crazy setup? Can I go to the Underworld and soak up the sun all at the same time? What the hell have I gotten myself into?*

'*Welcome to the Underworld, beloved,*' Sophia responded with a splash of endearing warmth and cheekiness.

I sat there stunned, feeling a mixture of dread, fascination and massive relief. Whether I was conscious of it or not, I carefully reviewed how I played my part in Dark Mother and Death Father's whole shenanigan, whether it be under the influence of the patriarchy, ancestral karma…or succumbing to my habitual fears and insecurities. A breeze blew in from the window, along with it the spirit of a magnificent ruby and gold dragon.

Through this Sophia dragon's eyes, my vision elevated to a place where I could see that these split offs had served a greater function to wake me up to the deeper truth of who I really am and grow my Sophia dragon wings. She then guided me to speak the following decree as she energetically assisted me to release all distortions held within my light body.

I, Ambe', stand in my divine presence and call upon my Divine Family of Light to assist me in releasing all reversal seeds within my womb, umbilical cord and all dimensional layers of my being that have been used and distorted within me, my ancestors and within this or any other timeline or realm. I hereby clear and release all distortions, miasmas and contracts with the Dark Mother, Dark Father, along with the false light and false dark matrix on all levels of consciousness that have created trauma in my light body and on all levels and dimensions of my being. I clear all victim/victimiser, tyranny, persecution, enslavement, sexual misery and dark lunar programing from my body, space, aura, hologram, DNA, RNA, genetic imprints, between and throughout all time, spaces and dimensions. I now make all necessary repairs, re-encryptions and recalibrate myself with the highest vibration and expression of the Divine Christos Sophia and the law of One. So be it and so it is!

Rays of golden sunlight streamed through *Elena's* window, joining with an aurora of prismatic rainbow light that flooded my being and the room. *May all beings be returned to the pure light of original innocence. Victory of the light! So be it and so it is.*

CHAPTER FORTY-EIGHT

WAKING DOWN

Darkness cannot drive out darkness; only light can do that. Hate cannot drive out hate; only love can do that. The ultimate measure of a man is not where he stands in moments of comfort and convenience, but where he stands at times of challenge and controversy. Faith is taking the first step even when you don't see the whole staircase. Our lives begin to end the day we become silent about things that matter. Injustice anywhere is a threat to justice everywhere.

I look to a day when people will not be judged by the color of their skin, but by the content of their character. I have decided to stick with love. Hate is too great a burden to bear.

Life's most persistent and urgent question is, 'What are you doing for others?' The time is always right to do what is right. We must learn to live together as brothers or perish together as fools.

– Martin Luther King Jr.

We humans carry many emotions that have built up over many incarnations and they are being released through our emotional body and nervous system at this time. This is a very important part of the process and it is critical that we clear the shadows as we embody the Supernal Light. It is true that we have enemies to contend with in this process and that the Dark Forces are strong and present as always. It is important to know that they cannot detour a determined soul from entering the Bridal Chamber. They can distract and cause chaos, but the one who is determined will be greeted by the Masters who will help to lead the way. We can fight best by going to our true center of power. As we rise in consciousness, we fight from a new vantage point instead of on the terms of the Dark. "The Great Work" is the Divine right of all human beings and it is only through its completion that real progress can be made.

– Shannon Port, *Art of the Feminine*

I spent that entire day in Mani, wondering how on Earth I ended up capsized at the Underworld Inn, nestled on a hillside overlooking the Ionian Sea. The insidious voice of the Dark Mother relentlessly reminded me of how badly I screwed up. *'How terribly unlucky you are to find yourself all alone in this kitschy little room. Only you are crazy enough to buy the 'E' ticket to the Underworld. You spineless woman! Why didn't you go for the exotic Santorini? Swanky Ibiza? Tranquil Tuscany?'*

I argued, as my inner cynic tossed me about like a giant beach ball confined to a very small room. I let out a deep sigh and momentarily distracted myself by putting the kettle on.

With a feline-like precision, I moved intently through the spiral of ascension while consciously descending into the multiple layers of darkness. I grew my courage to feel and to face everything in the knowing that I was reclaiming the lost jewels of my soul. My sacred marching orders became simple and straightforward: *surrender all weapons of mass distraction, slow down, embrace and feel everything you have been unwilling to feel, tenderly, gently and lovingly. Capiche?*

Meanwhile, the Prince song played on like a broken record in the back of my mind – a clear indicator as to my direction for healing my ancestral karma. *'Maybe I'm just like my father, too bold. Maybe I'm just like my mother, she's never satisfied. Why do we scream at each other? This is what it sounds like when doves cry.'*

As I settled in, I began to feel as if I was living my own rendition of Charles Dickens' *A Christmas Carol*. I recalled Uncle Scrooge being visited by the ghosts of Christmas past and imagined he must have felt rather anxious, stressed and incredibly vulnerable to be confronted in the middle of the night wearing nothing more than his bed clothes. He, like me, had no idea what he would have to contend with in order to set himself and the ghosts of his ancestral past free. Luckily, he had the good sense to confront whatever arose, to listen, to feel, to stay open, to forgive and to be grateful that he was being given the gift of a second life through choosing love over fear.

Likened to Uncle Scrooge, my ancestors, along with my familial past, encroached upon me, summoning me to spiral down into the forbidden trenches of my soul. It was like being pulled down into the undertow of a stormy sea. All I could do was to continually surrender to the Black Mother, the redeeming twin sister of the Dark Mother, who was beckoning me to claim her fierce, merciful and monumental GRACE.

'Come now, you worthless, unlovable piece of shit. You know better than to try to resist or run away,' the gremlins murmured with ghoulish voices that sounded like something out of a low-budget, horror flick.

And then my own higher voice would chime in. *'Come on, bebe, you've got this. You were born for this. All that you require is right here, right now, alive inside of you. The time has come to set yourself – your ancestors and your entire bloodline – free! Free, free. Set them free!'*

Quite suddenly, the kettle boiled over and made a splattering sound all over the surface of my two-burner stove. What a perfect metaphor for how I was feeling inside. Everything that I had suppressed and quietly tucked away was now bubbling up to the surface, sputtering and spilling over onto my perfectly made bed. The wind kicked up outside my window, mirroring the whirlwind of emotion swirling in my belly. I never knew it was possible to feel so fed up, pissed off, victimised, rejected, lonely, frustrated, enraged, confused, longing for a tropical cocktail, a swim in the ocean and a session of ecstatic lovemaking – all at once! Cornered by my inner demons, I knew there was no way out but through.

Perhaps a cuppa might take the edge off a little and knock some well-needed sense into me.

There was just no way of escaping all that was surfacing until I had the momentary relief of getting up from the bed to go to the loo.

I felt my ancestors hover around me. They cried out to me as I sat riveted on the porcelain throne. *'Help us. Please free us from this prison of helpless despair! You must find out why God has betrayed and abandoned us.'*

In truth, I knew very little about my grandparents. In fact, I had never met any of them. Growing up, my aunt and a few cousins were the only living relatives that I had any relationship with. From time to time, I would ask my Aunt Elaine questions. In return, I would get one-liner clues that helped to paint a small picture of my ancestral history. What was clear was that three out of four of my grandparents had died before the age of fifty from what was referred to at the time as 'incurable diseases'.

My grandparents were European refugees, forced to flee their home and country. How painful it must have been to leave their family, friends and communities behind to suffer the crimes and atrocities of war. Attempting to feel an inkling of what they went through, I imagined their horrific predicament to the best of my capacity. I pondered what my thirty-six-year-old dying grandmother did to cope with the pain of her 'flesh-eating disease'. I was told by my aunt that the excruciating infection felt as if she was being eaten alive from the inside out. And what about her husband, my grandfather? I felt into the grief of his loss and the guilt and shame for having to give up his youngest seven-year-old daughter – my adorable mama – to an orphanage. He simply felt incapable to care and provide for more than one child, my aunt, on his meager salary as a grocery clerk.

Then there was my father's mother who appeared in my mind's eye. How did she cope with her fatal brain tumor, knowing very well that she was leaving her two young children behind to be raised by their negligent father. As it was, they barely saw him as he was consumed with making a living and putting food on the table during this time of the Great Depression.

I went even further back to my great-grandparents and imagined standing in their shoes. Their precious lives prematurely stolen by the atrocities of war. More than likely, those who were left behind in the old country were shot on the spot or brought into concentration camps and eventually murdered in the gas chambers. How utterly desperate and powerless they must have felt to change the course of their lives in the face of so much unspeakable brutality. In the end, their only hope of redemption was to live through the lives of their remaining children.

I was washed with an avalanche of despair for the suffering and trauma my ancestors had endured. For many, looking back was simply far too devastating and so a daily dose of denial, perseverance and masked optimism became the normal way of coping. As the descendants of the Great Depression, I could understand as adults how an over-indulgence of sex, alcohol, cigarettes, uppers, downers, food, materialism provided them with a sense of filling an unnamable void. Addiction was the way people coped with what was once too difficult to feel. Copious consumerism was considered a sign of success as people worked tirelessly to keep up the appearance of freedom and happiness while they ambitiously charged ahead no matter what the cost.

Waves of compassion washed through me as I glimpsed an understanding of what my parents inherited and what it took for them to make something wonderful out of their lives and provide for their children, especially when their predecessors never had the opportunity to do the same. For my grandparents and parents, their very survival was dependent on never looking back, only ahead. And yet there I was, at the edge of my world coming face-to-face with all that made my ancestors and I so anxious and unsettled. Their presence was now undeniable as they cried out to be heard, honoured and put to rest.

I pondered the unfathomable resilience of my ancestors along with all they had endured to survive and carry on after such extreme trauma. I realised that so much of the mysterious 'suffering' I had experienced throughout my life were the echoes of my genetic memories calling out to be healed, their origins going back as far as I could fathom. That was until the pivotol moment when I realised I was born to break the chain, to cleanse my bloodline and set myself and my ancestors free. *Aha, this is the true meaning of happily ever after.*

With a heavy sigh, I got up and returned to sit on my childlike bed. I stared into the tiny black seeds of one of the bright strawberries printed on my bedspread. *Hmm, what if each seed represented a repressed emotion? Grief, sorrow, helplessness, guilt, shame, rage, anger, frustration? So,* I mused, *did I inherit my denser emotions from my birth, my ancestors, from the collective, or from all three? Am I a byproduct of the beings that came before me and therefore destined to live out my genetic ancestral karma? Or are these suppressed emotions simply crying out to be heard, loved and accepted as the lost children of my soul?*

All that festered was now beginning to gurgle up from the basement of my unconscious. I was being invited to turn away from the allure of the false light and become a genetic path cutter where I would choose to consciously descend into the dark fecund of the black light and restore the fallen aspects of my soul on behalf of all my relations.

Choosing to fully accept this invitation was clearly a risk – a risk I could not afford to forego. Yet as I dared to feel all that was once too unbearable to feel, I was met, every squirm of the way, by an undeniable presence of pure grace. A little voice of hope and determination sprouted from within my heart. It felt to come from my inner child who had been patiently waiting for the adult in me to take the reins of my life back. I imagined myself as a beautiful bluebird living in a cage that decided she wanted nothing more than to fly. The bird went to the edge of the cage day after day and pecked at the bars until her beak grew weary and so resigned herself to living in the cage. She had believed that the key to freeing herself was in the hands of her master. Then one day, when the urge to fly became overwhelmingly powerful, she decided to try something new and nudged the little door open with her tiny beak. She was astounded to discover that the door was open all along and that she could set herself free as soon as she fully claimed her power and inner authority to do so.

'Each and every one of us is born with a master key that unlocks our divine nature and unique genius. Our purpose is to find that master key that sets ourself free,' I announced to my ancestors. *'So how does one gain access to this key?'*

'If you want to soar, give up all that weighs you down,' Sophia whispered.

In that moment, I let go of any last traces of resistance and chose to make the most of my underworld journey, deep dark muck and all. *After all, isn't a brilliant shining lotus born from the deep dark mud?*

Like a scientist looking under a microscope, I carefully examined my misguided beliefs one by one, along with my darkest perceptions about myself and about life. Until at last, I cut straight to the central question that had surfaced at La Maison Lumiere while staring up at the Venus star: *Where was God in all of this? How and why would God have abandoned my ancestors and I?* I concentrated on this question with a laser-like focus, as if investigating an unresolved riddle as ancient as life itself. *More importantly, what must I believe to feel this way?*

Then it all came whooshing in, along with a massive gust of wind that literally blew Elena's door wide open, sending a ray of new light into my small room. I pointed each one of my questions back to me. *Hmmm, when did I first abandon and betray myself? How and why did I disconnect from my own precious being? When did I first walk out on me, and what did I make up about myself in order to do so?*

I sprawled out on top of my bed, looking struck by a bolt of lightning. My bedspread was now my Shiva tiger skin. Blown away by my revelations, my jaw hung open in a kind of metaphysical shock. I sunk deeper into meditation and bore witness to a slew of irritating half-truths that I had been living for as long as I could remember. I was stunned by how my life had seemed veiled by a kind of foggy amnesia, which felt to be the healing response to that initial traumatic intrusion. I asked myself, *Just how long have I been gone?*

Then I heard a wise voice of unwavering love begin to speak from within me. *'I am Sophia. I speak to you from the divine God spark that lives inside the innermost chamber of your heart. As a Starseed, you carry the memories and connection to me through your Sophionic Solar Christ bloodline. Your deep inquiry brings up a long history of complex timelines and events in which my image has been enslaved, usurped, syphoned and even cloned. These events have lead to the distortion of your being and it is through clearing these histories that you will be reconnected to the purity of your crystalline rose heart.*

'There is an event that feels to have particular relevance in response to your question around feeling disconnected from 'the real you'. You see, during the journey of incarnating into physicality, a great deal of humans experienced birth as an extremely traumatic event. During that experience, original innocence, trust in Self and your direct line to the Divine Source got temporarily fractured like a crack in a mirror. In turn, this became the first imprint from which you began to learn about yourself and life. This fracture did not allow you to perceive yourself as clearly as you truly are. As one with the light of the Divine.

'During that initial split when you perceived that you were separate from Source, you naturally called out for some help. The e-g-o was conceived to help you to survive the trauma of being human while temporarily displacing you from your core essence and origin. Typically, this perception gets crystallised by the tender age of three. Little beings get spooked and Captain E-G-O comes to the rescue and displaces the authentic connection to the monadic core Self. By the age of five or six, many cannot tell the difference between their true essence and the ever so convincing new commander in chief. Over time, Captain E-G-O came up with a myriad of masks and sub-personalities that have cleverly assisted you to cope and survive the challenges that come with being human.

'Dear one, you are not alone is this. Humanity's core wounds and coping mechanisms were predominantly born from this initial jolt of separation from Source.

'Initially, the e-g-o was created as a means of temporary protection and mutual support. Hundreds, if not thousands of sophisticated sub-selves came to "the rescue" to compensate for the false impression that you were kicked out of Heaven and left all alone in a fragmented world to fend for yourself. Believing that you were ill equipped to survive the challenges of being human, the survivor e-g-o has provided you with many of the qualities and attributes you believed to be required for your survival. Eventually, these e-g-os became quite sophisticated. They discovered more and more clever ways to provide you with everything that you perceived you lacked, only to perpetuate even more feelings of deficiency and helpless separation.

'Over countless lifetimes, some of your e-g-o friends grew dark and went rogue, and conspired to create complex ways to feed off humanity's fear and negative emotions! Like parasites, they tend to feed off one's unclaimed and disowned power, urging you to meet your needs from sourcing outside of yourself. This in turn has created the weight and density of the denied Self, which has found a palatial home hidden in the far corners of your unconscious mind!

'Throughout this last Earth cycle, humans have predominantly been caught in a perpetual state of lack and scarcity due to the severed connection to original Self, Source and Divinity. Existing in a state of chronic fear has greatly compromised the nervous system, keeping humanity cycling through various states of fight, flight, frozen, fawn *or flop. When one is caught in a loop of frozen limbo due to a shock or trauma, it tends to reinforce one's self-image as flawed, wrong, unworthy, unlovable, unwanted, rejected and abandoned. Furthermore, one learns to adapt to feeling "helpless", seeking a sense of worthiness from sources from outside of one's self to compensate for all that is felt to be missing from within. This survival-based way of being has led humans into a kind of codependency, a misuse of power from that initial jolt of feeling exiled from their original innocence and natural state of overflowing wonder and joy.*

'As long as there is a sense of seperation, the negative e-g-o continues to be at the helm creating ones reality. Human relationships are compromised, fueled by covert agendas that manipulate others into being their source of love and power. Humans learned a myriad of clever ways to give in order to get in order to satisfy an insatiable void and pervasive sense of being incomplete. Eventually, humanity needed to find a place to store the shame, denial and guilt accumulated from being disconnected from the Source that lives inside of you and so the unconscious was created.

'Consider this, over countless lifetimes, the weight of the unconscious became too heavy to bear and eventually wore out the physical vehicle. Death and decay was created as a solution to off load the guilt for not being true to one's divine nature. Death became the way to drop the pain body and free oneself from the burdensome weight of the unconscious. At the next opportunity, one could choose a new vehicle, hop back on the karmic wheel and start the whole process all over again. This is what the Buddha describes as the wheel of Samsara.

'That is until now, when at last humanity is entering into an entirely new evolutionary cycle and epoch. One where those who feel called, shine the light of love upon the unconscious and all that was once denied is forgiven and redeemed. Bravo! You are waking up, facing your shadows and in so doing, healing the fracture of the mind and remembering the true image of the Divine that you are.

'You are being called to trust that embedded within your sacred wound are the greatest gifts of your soul. As you become a welcoming presence for all aspects of your being to be honoured, felt, forgiven and integrated, you heal the core split by not abandoning any part of you. Through becoming awake, aware and conscious, you are learning to take responsibility and

turn on the power to co-create your better than imagined reality. With taking responsibility, your power is restored, allowing you to perceive every experience as an opportunity to co-create something beautiful that enriches and serves the whole of creation.

Along with the planetary body, you are in a stage of evolving beyond the cycle of divisive separation and coming home to the source within that is whole and inter-dependant with all of creation. By living in the tiniest truth that is authentically you, the dark and the light takes care of itself, returning to coherent symbiosis with the natural world.

'In truth, this alchemical journey began long ago. You stand on the shoulders of your ancestors, the ones who have paved the way before you, along with each and every being who has dared to question the nature of reality and their place within it. The time will soon come when you will know that you have always been protected and held within the benevolent arms of your divine and loving parents who love you beyond all conditions.'

I fell back onto the bed, raw and cracked open, while my limbs unwound from their tightly held cocoon. I smiled inwardly at the massive cosmic joke of it all. In truth, I was more than familiar with the concepts of these revelations, but what was happening was a primordial unwinding from my body, like unplugging from an archaic false circuit board. This time I was feeling my way through energetically, digesting the unprocessed emotions and arriving at an entirely new place in consciousness that included the vast feeling intelligence of my somatic body.

Like a deer in the headlights, I saw that I, along with countless others, were awakening to a deeper truth beyond the personality constructs of the negative e-g-o's that cloud our clear perception and capacity to live as sovereign beings. As we come to captain our lives through living authentically and transparently, we compassionately embrace the challenges that affect us on the spiritual, emotional and physical layers of our light body. And just as we must face these challenges alone, we also recognise that we are never really alone. We are fully supported and held in the loving arms of the Divine every courageous step of the way. And while each goes about the 'great work' in their own unique fashion, we also come to recognise that every character, along the journey is playing a vital role in conspiring to serve our individual and collective awakening as we remember and return to the glorious source within.

I opened Elena's windows and stuck my head out to absorb the last rays of the bright afternoon sun. Streams of golden light washed over my face as I gazed at a beautiful ancient olive tree. It stood alone with its roots spreading wide and its branches reaching out in all directions. I felt Divine Sophia's energy circulating through the chalice of my being, re-imprinting my cells with her purity, wisdom and light.

With a grin on my face, I began to hum a tune from 'Hello Dolly', one of my all-time favourite Broadway musicals. 'Hello, Ambe´'. Well, hello, Ambe´. It's so nice to feel you back where you belong!'

Is all the pain and suffering really all that necessary, Mother? I mused, wondering if there could have been an alternative to this absurdly complex trail of blood, sweat and tears.

'It is the sacred alchemy that creates one's priceless soul pearl... the pearl beyond all price. As you respond to unwanted negativity by shining the light of awareness along with your willingness to feel, the situation transforms and your soul light and power brighten as a result. Through the lense of inner alchemy, one can relate to suffering as an irritant, the soul grit that produces empathy, compassion and inspires change. However, each being has been endowed with free will. The soul is allowed to create with absolute freedom, with the understanding that it will be fully responsible for its creations and not attribute negative experiences to the will of the divine. It is the fractured and unconscious parts of Self that create the sacred scars attributed to so much human suffering and pain. This sacred wound also serves as an incentive and catalyst for alchemizing and producing the antidotal remedy that in turn transforms you and the whole. You see, the soul will use all of one's experiences to evolve consciousness, while Spirit is ever present to pave the way by illuminating soul-lutions that align you with the will of the Divine. This Divine resonance creates coherence and gives you access to infinite resourcefulness and loving support – with full respect for your free will, which enables you to grow according to your own pace and unique purpose. It is up to you to align and partner with the ever present genius of your Divine will and become the remedy and resolution to all that has ever ailed you and in turn transform yourself and the whole.

I was given a picture of what life could be like as I unraveled myself from the insidious programming of victim, perpetrator consciousness. Instead, I imagined all of my irritations being a necessary catalyst to creating the pearlescent radiance of my soul. *Whoa! Have I co-created all of these experiences over lifetimes so that I could become the pearl beyond all price and know myself as the Divine knows me?*

Sophia chimed in with her wisdom light, *'Just as the caterpillar is unaware that it is becoming a butterfly, as it undergoes the dissolution of all it once knew itself to be, you too are in the midst of a great metamorphosis. Your temporary amnesia was part of a higher plan to navigate your way home through awakening all of you as the Love, Lover and Beloved that you are. Within your Source womb lives the primordial light seeds of pure passion and highest potential. By reclaiming your original innocence, you return to the wellspring within, the living Source of creation where you fulfill your soul purpose to give life just as the Creator has given life to you.*

'The wisdom light of the Christos Sophia is what is guiding this awakening within you and upon the planet right now. Sacred Union love is what is moving you so that all that has remained buried will rise to the surface to be loved back into wholeness.

'Your Solar Feminine is likened to a Divine doula, here to assist in the birthing of the Golden Age of Gaia – while your Solar Masculine embodies the crystalline core frequencies that ensure a pristine and ecstatic birth. Embarking upon this Heiros Gamos journey is your legacy of love that will illuminate the way for generations to come.

'For now, we ask you to have faith and trust as you surrender even more than you knew possible to the alchemical flames of transfiguration. Our greatest wish is for you to see yourself as we do, a unique and precious pearl amongst an ocean of luminous pearls – always free – and forever shining in grace.

'I Am Sophia, the light that shines forth from the One in the many and the many in the One. I am another You.'

CHAPTER FORTY-NINE

FREE FALLING

I am the bastard of the sun and moon.
I can no longer hide my heritage of raindrops and cougar scat.
I am made of your grandmother's tears.
You conquered rival tribesmen of your own color, then
chained them together, marched them naked to the coast,
and sold them to colonials from Savannah.
I was that sister you sold, I was the slave trader,
I was the chain.
Admit it, you have wings, vast and golden,
like mine, like mine.
You have sweat, black and salty,
like mine, like mine.
You have secrets silently singing in your blood,
like mine, like mine.
Don't pretend that Earth is not one family.
Don't pretend we never hung from the same branch.
Don't pretend we don't ripen on each other's breath.
Don't pretend we didn't come here to forgive.

– Fred LaMotte

When an unwanted guest arrives in the vastness of your heart – whether
sadness, rage, shame, or grief – listen carefully for an ancient invitation:
will you care for this one and infuse it with your presence? Will you hold
it close as you would a little one longing for just one moment of your

love? The next time you are greeted with an uninvited visitor, see the habitual movement to deny it or act it out, to avoid it or get hooked into its compelling narrative of urgency and escape. Stay close, right in the middle – offer an intimate playground of tender awareness for the energy to dance inside the vastness that you are. Before you turn away – concluding it is an enemy from the outside, a barrier to the path, and evidence that you have failed – offer just one moment of safe passage.

As you cultivate the willingness to provide sanctuary to the burning within, you do so not just for yourself, but also for all beings everywhere, as well as for the precious Earth herself. For when you lay a new groove of self-care and compassion in your own miracle nervous system, it is simultaneously reflected in the mud and the soil and the oceans and the stars. And as you return over and over and over again, to kindness and to space, you may be astonished as you notice your struggle with life falling away on its own.

– Matt Licata

We must come to recognize that every crisis that we face both individually and collectively also serves to initiate us into making true contact with our darkness and the grief that accompanies the loss of our illusions. In exile we must do what Lilith did, surrender layer upon layer of armour and adornment until we are bare. We must then undergo a symbolic death of the old life in order to be reborn with greater resilience and our holy assignment to carry forward. Over the course of some time, the initiated adult has learned to withstand uncertainty, has paid a debt to the Gods through her loss and grief and has decided to make beauty with her life as the future ancestor that she is.

– Toko-pa Turner, *Belonging: Remembering Ourselves Home*

Each new day in Mani, I looked to nature and the surrounding silvery-blue mountains for the strength to surrender all that I once knew myself to be. I was in free fall, stripped to the bones with nothing but blind faith and radical trust to navigate my way through the labyrinth of my soul.

The next two weeks were like one long dream – from waking to wandering to sleeping to waking. Apart from the few people sprinkled on the beach, the hillside hotel and a few local cafés, I mostly went through my days in silence and solitude. I glided and sometimes stumbled through the hours in a timeless trance, where the waking dream and sleeping dream blended together as one. I wasn't interested in self-improvement or quick fixs. That would imply that there was something wrong that needed to be fixed. I knew that wasn't true and that any sense of feeling broken was simply the rupture that would allow more light to shine through. As I went about my days, I unraveled and dropped into a slower, deeper healing rhythm where I welcomed whatever arose to the surface to be felt, embraced and integrated back into a larger love big enough to include all of me within it.

Throughout this time, I made sure I took plenty of sacred pauses, moments to rest from the task of untangling the messy roots and rise to the surface to take in the glorious views. *Hmmm, I have so much to be grateful for.* I have experienced so many epic renaissances throughout my life, along with experiencing living my greatest dreams. I called these periods my 'mountain peak phases'. Life chapters bursting with outrageous creativity, inspired friendships, healthy intimacy, empowered service, abundance, beauty and the freedom to live in exotic places! One could say that life *was* and *still is* golden. Even in the valleys, one can be full of joy and gratitude for the wonder and grace of it all.

Over the years, I had come to accept that being a bridge from the darkness to the light meant living a life of extremities. *I sure have had my fair share of peaks and valleys, and both have served in making me the woman I am today. The more balanced and integrated I become in both shadow and light, the freer I am to jump timelines and frequencies in the knowing that all dimensions exist simultaneously – and I am free to learn and play in all of them. The more I trust the light that I am, the easier it is to descend into the depths and retrieve the gifts of my soul.*

One evening, after spending a beautiful day at the beach, I came home to feel waves of nausea and extreme tension coursing through my veins. As I dared to feel what lurked below the surface, I felt squeamish, anxious and uncomfortable. I cleared my chakras with some toning then called upon Sophia and Archangel Michael for extra support and clarity. At once, I became vividly aware of an intricate wiring system wrapped around my left ovary, running through my liver and up the right side of my gallbladder meridian. I could clearly see that my entire right side had been hijacked by a foreign energy along with a slew of unexpressed anger from feeling small and disengaged from my power.

It required a laser-like focus to trace the pulling sensation and follow the intricate pathway of this energetic wiring. Its tendrils loosened with every breath, as I followed the sensations to the inception point. This process required a willingness to feel into the discomfort of primal rage without censorship, judgment or analysis. I made a strong effort to remain grounded in my core innocence and inner authority in the knowing that these energies were aspects of my denied Feminine self crying out to be loved. I became aware that I had created this intricate webbing out of my distorted relationship with the Masculine patriarchy and with my father who was both a loving provider and a precarious predator.

I asked to be shown any and all soul contracts that I had made to allow his energy to entwine with mine. I was reminded of Sananda's reading back in Brighton. Somewhere along my soul's journey to assist the Earth, I lost faith in my capacity to accomplish my mission on my own and so agreed to allow this foreign energy to 'help me', in exchange for siphoning off my life-force energy. I saw how I had caved into the pressure to sacrifice my life force in exchange for fulfilling my life purpose. By strongly acknowledging that this contract no longer served a function, I cancelled and cleared it, while reclaiming another layer of my truth, power and sovereignty through speaking the following decree; 'I, Ambé, stand as an awakened Wayshower of the Beauty Way and with the fierce love of a lioness and the gentleness of a deer, now direct my life force to absolving all wounds of being banished, bulldosed and erased by the false and fallen light. I clear all memories of soul monadic trauma that have taken place throughout my lightbody. I now re-encrypt and override all inorganic architecture from the false light matrix and step fully into the Crystal Star timeline and the diamond light of my soul.

'May I, and all beings, come to steward and respect all of life. May we embody the humility and strength to stand wing tip to wing tip as one beloved family, such that all that remains is astonishing beauty. A beauty that dissolves all barriers to living open and flourishing together as the love, lover and beloved that we have come to be. So be it and so it is.'

Admittedly, there were plenty of moments when this unraveling process seemed overwhelming, tedious and outright endless. The following evening, while I was sitting on my little bed praying for guidance, I gravitated to the remote control that sat on top of the dusty TV. *Aha! Finally, a well-needed diversion!*

I switched the power button on and found the tail end of a documentary on the American Indians. The Native Indian narrator was describing how the white people arrived on the land, raped, pillaged and slaughtered their people and then proceeded to insert time, money, religion, industry and alcohol into their culture. Essentially conspiring to sever their connection to the wild Earth, where as we all know, the *real* power lies.

'Many of our native people are trying desperately to hold onto their connection to their native ways and Earth-based spirituality,' the narrator said, looking straight into the camera with his piercing hawk-like eyes.

Wow, I thought. *Here is a native culture that revered their connection to Creator, the living Earth, Central Sun and Great Spirit. Until one day, foreigners landed upon their shores, invaded, dominated and then attempted to convert them into being God-fearing humans.*

The narrator went on to tell his story. 'Those who did not comply suffered greatly. Many were brutally massacred. For centuries, the foreigners attempted to condition the natives into believing that they needed to reform their savage and uncivilised ways. They were coerced into following a God that would judge and punish them if they failed to submit to his almighty power. There were countless massacres of peaceful tribes who, until then, were living in respect and harmony with each other, the land and Creator.'

I questioned who the savages really were as I recollected the Cathar massacre and how similar their story was to the Native Indians along with countless other peoples of the world who have suffered the horrors of mass genocide and the plight of colonisation.

The chief went on to speak of a growing epidemic of addiction and high rates of suicide that were spreading like wild fire throughout the Indian reservations. 'Ever since our connection to Mother Nature was severed, our sacred lands stolen, our living waters polluted, we as a peaceful nation have felt disenfranchised, trying desperately to keep our Earth-based traditions alive. Our Sacred Hoop has been fractured, our connection to Earth shattered, leaving us feeling displaced and without a home. Those of us who remember are doing our very best to keep our culture and native ways alive.' The chief's presence was so authentic and raw that his words pierced my heart and I began to weep.

I was astounded by how the television was likened to a crystal ball, reflecting what was fractured within me while shining the light on the wound of the collective unconscious. I was being shown how my own and humanity's exile from our wild roots was likened to a virus that would spread throughout the world. The only remedy would be to reconcile and reconnect with the sacred soul of the wild divine and make it one with our own.

I went on to dialogue with the chief. *We are all guests of this beloved planet Earth and share in the longing to feel safe, respected and live in harmony with each other and the natural world. When we lose our connection to Mother Earth, Father Sky and Great Spirit, we sever our Self from the very source that nourishes and sustains us from within. To take and consume without giving back, or offering gratitude for what has been given, creates suppressed guilt and shame that shows up as disease, addiction and imbalances within our body, mind and spirit. The Earth is reflecting to us how volatile and unsustainable life can be when we disconnect from revering the very source that gives Life to all. It is this guilt ridden disconnection from our true nature and the natural world that is at the root of what ails us. If we are going to continue as a species, we must live in a sustainable and symbiotic way while generously sharing and circulating all that we have in the knowing that all that we have is a gift to be cherished beyond all measure.*

The Indian chief left the viewing audience with two questions to contemplate: 'Will we as a species come to acknowledge our inter-connectivity and restore the Sacred Hoop in our lifetime? Will we learn that harming the Earth and one another is the very same as harming ourselves? I pray to the Creator that we wake up in time, that we hear the call of the Great Spirit to be the custodians of Mother Earth and all her native children. *Aho, Mitakuye Oyasin.* All my relations.' The Native Indian documentary ended abruptly with the deeply engraved face of the wise elder playing a haunting melody on his Native Indian flute.

My heart beat in a fever of passion and heightened awareness. I changed the channel to thirty-three to see what else the Tell-a-Vision Oracle wished to illuminate for me. I sat on the edge of my bed, totally riveted by a movie entitled, *The Mission.* At first, I could barely recognise Robert De Niro as he crawled up the overgrown jungle ravine. Blood, dirt and sweat disguised his typical, Mafia movie star look. He was lugging a bundle of armour wrapped in a large fishing net up the side of a steep mountain ravine. This heavy armour placed inside the net symbolised the weight of the penance he was paying for the brutal murder of his brother. Once a capitalistic slave driver, he had killed his brother out of spite, jealousy and rage for winning over the heart of his one true love. When she appeared on screen, I was captivated by her striking beauty and paid special attention to a golden equilateral cross that hung elegantly from her slender neck. Her eloquence and grace was radiant with the light of a living Grail Goddess.

Sadly, De Niro's ill fate led him to a bitter life in exile, tormented by the loss of his true love, compounded by the horror of killing his own brother. Finally, a wise and compassionate missionary priest discovered him in the local village in a state of miserable disarray. The priest showed him mercy and invited De Niro to accompany him on a mission to a remote church he was building in the heart of the Amazonian jungle. Seeing this invitation as his absolute last chance of absolution, De Niro accepted the invitation in the knowing that taking his own life was his only other option. He agreed to accompany the priest and make the arduous journey on the condition that he carried the large bundle of armour upon his back to pay his penance for his sins.

I envisioned myself as Ambe´ De Niro while feeling into my own karmic penance carried over lifetimes. It was compounded with the heavy weight of my ancestors, whose plight lingered in my DNA and cellular memory.

In the next scene of the movie, they showed De Niro arriving at the top of an Amazonian jungle ravine. He dropped to his knees in utter exhaustion from the weight of his sins and cried out for mercy. His path to salvation was to surrender what was left of his personal will to the will of the Divine. A group of tribal people hovered around him, observing him with compassionate curiosity. One of the elderly tribesmen adorned in face markings and a feathered headdress, cut the rope attached to his back. I let out a huge gasp of relief as I watched De Niro's heavy bundle roll down the mountain ravine, taking along the weight of his sins. Raw and humbled to the bone, he clung to the earth, tears rolling down his muddy face and thanked God for giving him another chance to live.

My jaw dropped in awe while witnessing De Niro's epic moment of redemption. *If DeNiro can do it, so can I!* I smiled warmly as I envisioned my karmic weight being lifted by the grace of the Divine along with a healthy dose of perseverance.

Suddenly, the TV went into white fuzz and I lay down on the bed, my eyes brimming with tears. I looked to the full moon outside my window for the strength to forgive myself for all the times that I had energetically or emotionally killed myself or another off, out of a sense of fear, the motive behind all jealousy, envy and insecurity. Wave upon wave of sorrowful regret washed through my weary bones. With a heart full of humility, I spoke the following decree inspired by Matt Khan:

'May all victims, predators, all forms of persecution, racism, bigotry, including every moment of bloodshed and war and battle and desire for domination, persecution and greed, and all patterns of unconsciousness, be cleared out of my energy field, returned to the source of its origin, transmuted completely and healed to completion now. Whether I come from a lineage that victimised or was victimised, may my life be the remedy for every trespass that has ever happened to me, or another.

May I pardon and set free any and all aspects of the past so as not to hold anything against my fellow human and not to perpetuate cycles of violence and harm. And from this moment forward, may I allow my words, actions, responses and behavior to be the remedy to every atrocity, and be consciously expressed as the solution to every evolutionary problem. May I be the gift of tolerance, sensitivity, equality that allows all aspects of our divinity to bring forth its diverse and unique qualities as jewels in the infinite crown of God, and may it be done for all beings and may it be done now. With massive gratitude for my angels, guides and Crystal Star Family of Light, I now consecrate and seal this clearing and decree with the highest Divine Light and in harmonic resonance with the Law of One. So be it and so it is.'

That night, I left the windows wide open so the fresh evening breeze could sweep all that remained heavy on my heart and soul into the clear evening sky. I aligned with my pillar of light and imagined a golden doorway that opened up in front of my auric field. A flame of ultraviolet light blazed through my entire auric field while I repeated the Kahuna mantra, Ho'oponopono, from the deepest place of my being. 'I'm sorry. Please forgive me. Thank you. I love you. I'm sorry. Please forgive me. Thank you. I love you. I'm sorry. Please forgive me. Thank you. I love you. Blessings on your journey.'

My body jolted as I felt a vapor of energy unwind, lift and then dissipate from my energy field. Just like that, all was returned to its rightful source, *gone, gone, gone beyond!* Feeling lighter than ever before, I took a deep breath into my belly and envisioned divine golden light filling in all of the places where the discordant energies had been released from my energy field. I could feel the midnight sun beginning to rise inside of me, making space for my golden wings to unfurl from between my shoulder blades.

With a wave of gratitude and self-acceptance, I lit some sage, smudged the room and then placed myself in a cocoon of golden pink light.

It is done, it is done, it is done for the One. Blessed be the gift!

CHAPTER FIFTY

BLACK LIGHT

The Black Goddess is the veiled Sophia who, in many forms, is the primal manifestation of the Divine Feminine. Sophia has seeded her sparkle of fire in us all. When we are spiritually kindled, then her pathway of fire spreads throughout the charcoal of our physical beings. When we deal with Sophia, we will find ourselves alternately dazzled and blindfolded – the effect is the same, whether we stand in darkness or light. We must trust in her voice within us to guide us forward. It is a long process of stripping off the veils one by one. It is a journey of descent, a valorous fall in order to remember.

The way of Sophia is the way of personal experience. It takes us into areas, which we may call magical reality, those creative realms to which ordinary mortals are called by right of their vocational and creative skills. However, the poetic, the magical, the creative inscapes of vision are often denied us by our culture. Anyone who has been into the world of vision, defined by many as 'unreal,' knows that its power can enhance our lives. It is Sophia who acts as a way shower and companion on this inner quest, especially helpful for women. Because Sophia's creativity has been denied, we see her in a cloak of the Black Goddess, moving silently and mysteriously about her work.

Within the darkness of night or the cloud of unknowing, we discover the heart of our spirituality. This is the seed experience of spiritual growth, to be held fast in the dark Earth, to suffer the coldness of winter that germination may take place. It is the return to the spiritual womb, in which we find the dazzling darkness. Re-entering this womb is both a rebirth of the spirit and a death of the ego. The school of dark night spirituality is found in most traditions that venerate the Black Goddess, not because she is sinister or evil, but because she is the powerhouse from whence our spirituality is fueled. It is a way of unknowing, of darkness and uncertainty. Yet the experience, which is obtained by this path, is one of illumination when the sun shines at midnight. Our fear of being exploded, diffused or made chaotic may be our reaction to the idea of the Black Goddess who, like dark matter, controls the structure and eventual fate of the Universe. The Black Goddess is the mistress of the web of creation, which is spun in her Divine matrix.

The Black Goddess helps us in the process of kenosis, or emptying: in this phase, we are stripped bare, reduced to basics, forced to lie fallow that knowledge may be seeded in the bare, cleansed fields of Wisdom. Sophia helps us in the process of Pleurisies, or filling: in this phase, we experience the growth and replenishment of our resources, when we are reinvigorated and our knowledge strengthened.

The loss of the Divine Feminine from consciousness is a wound, which we all carry. Without her dimension of love and justice, we exile ourselves from the Earth, from physicality and from each other. Fear of the Feminine is often fear of the chaotic and ecstatic nature of sexuality itself, in which men and women temporarily 'lose control' of their rational, ordered being. Sacred sexuality depends on our acceptance of life. If we don't accept life as wholesome, then we become agents of our own decasualization. As women resume their power – guardianship of the secret fire– a more dynamic and just society will result in which the Black Goddess will be joined with Sophia freely and effectively.

– Caitlin Matthews, *Sophia, Goddess of Wisdom*

The descent of the soul is how the Divine spark comes into matter. This is where you merge your Divine consciousness with your humanity. You have been groomed for this moment throughout lifetimes of life lessons and initiations. It is no accident that you stand at this threshold. This is a time that is pre-destined by you and the Christos Sophia, who will lift the veil for you to remember union in a moment of Grace. In this instance, you will see the truth of all and experience Oneness and know that there never was a struggle. In this moment of Grace, you will become the Soul unveiled, regenerated and able to walk among the infinitesimal gifts of life. Right now, everything within you is being brought up to the surface to be alchemised with the sacred Divine fire for this very purpose.

– Shannon Port, *Art of the Feminine*

E ach morning, I wrote in my journal. It was my closest companion during these days of contemplative solitude. I didn't always date my entries because I often lost track of time, but September twentieth felt especially significant for me. On this random day, this was what my entry read:

> Phew. Today I awoke with a silent mind, a blank slate, zero point! I believe I've been stripped down to plain ol' nothingness where everyone and everyting is a wonder to behold. What a relief. I am so grateful. The ancestors have been put to rest and have left me in the grace of fallow emptiness. I dedicate this renewed freedom to each and every relative who has paved the way before me. I am here because of you! May the light of pure love shine upon you all light surround you and pure love guide your way home. All my relations.

I put down my pen and placed my hand over the dusty window where the children were playing under the olive tree in the neighbouring yard. The sun poured in through the gauzy white curtains. I could hear my matronly neighbour firing off words in Greek as she said goodbye to her small son, who rode off on his girlish red bicycle. *It's also time for me to get a move on,* I thought, as I observed that an ancient burden had been unravelled from the DNA motherboard of my being, leaving me with a sense of wide-openness, the kind where anything and everything was possible.

With lightning speed, I dressed and headed up the hill to the Grand Hotel that towered above my modest studio where each morning, I enjoyed doing yoga and meditation practice. As I rolled out my YOGA mat on the wooden terrace, I took in the magnificent ocean view. I didn't mind the mysterious Greek man loitering at the outdoor bar who was gaining immense pleasure from observing my backside come up and down as I offered salutations to the sun. He lingered patiently, with the hope of catching my eye so he could offer me a flirtatious grin.

As I gently cycled through my sun salutations, my muscles unwound with slow rhythmic motion. Tears of humble gratitude streamed down my face as I looked to the bay and up to the Taygetos Mountains. Jagged indigo blue and brown cliffs, sprinkled with olive trees, sloped down to the aquamarine Ionian Sea shimmering on the horizon. I was seeing Kalamata in a whole new light. She had transformed from the deep dark underworld into Heaven on Earth.

Feeling complete with my practice, I reclined on my back in Savasana, closed my eyes and heard Sophia's voice whisper encouragingly, '*Hurry up, dear one. Go and visit the neighbouring village. Go NOW!*'

I knew that the bus left three times a day. The next one was due to depart in less than seven minutes. So I rolled up my yoga mat, grabbed my things and scurried down the steep hill to the bus stop. Just as I arrived, the bus was pulling away from the curb!

'Wait, wait!' I called out. *Whooo! I just made it!*

As I settled into the rickety old seat, the sound of the bus screeched around the corner, hugging the coastal road. I stared out the soiled window, soaking in the magnificent view. How amazing. Just days ago, I saw this place as a desolate wasteland! Now, after diving into the depths and clearing the cobwebs of my soul, I can now see the shimmering beauty glistening all around me.

Twenty minutes later, I was dropped off in front of a charming outdoor café. I sat down at a small table outside and soaked up the early morning sun. The sound of rustling olive tree leaves danced with the warm morning breeze. The waitress sauntered over to me to take my order. Smiling at her, I ordered a cappuccino and then looked around the café terrace. The only person in sight was a handsome Greek man who had approached me on the beach the day before. I smiled to him curiously, as this was the third time I had run into him over the last few days. He certainly stood out amongst the community of retired folks that inhabited most of the town. I discretely gazed at this coco-skinned, Greecian man/*bebe´* with curious fascination.

I wonder why he keeps turning up wherever I am. Or is it that I keep turning up wherever he is? Hmmm. Perhaps we are meant to connect in some way? I reflected on the powerful magnetism between man and woman, and how this irresistible force had led me to this very place, *alone in paradise*. Love, sex and God are the most creative and destructive forces in the universe. I wonder if I will ever get to fully experience true love in this lifetime?

Savouring the last sip of milky foam, I nodded warmly to Mr. Macho Man God then left some money on the table. I proceeded down the cobblestone road towards the ruins of Kardamyli, keeping my womanly eye on the real prize! Feeling a sense of magic and serendipity, I headed down the old stone road, past some dishevelled shops, wondering what I would discover on this bright new day. The shop windows displayed souvenirs, most of which were covered in a filmy dust. It appeared the items on display hadn't been touched or rearranged in years. In my bemused state, they beckoned for admiration, as if they called out, *'Take me home, shine me up and I will reveal the treasure I am.'*

I slowed my pace and peered into one of the shop windows. I was stunned when my eye glimpsed the exact equilateral cross medallion that I had admired on the beautiful actress from the movie, *The Mission*. Tingling with the serendipity of my discovery, I popped into the store and bought the medallion for a mere seven euros. Once purchased, I admired how it rested perfectly in my hand and rubbed it briskly between my palms to restore its regal shine. This unique cross was unlike a traditional Christian cross where the stem is longer. It was significantly distinct in its shape and geometry. Later, I learned that this unique geometry is called a primary cross; it is a symbol for divine truth, the blueprint of creation, the codes of nature and yes, Sophia's Holy Grail!

The dusty road now became a golden pathway leading me to a sign that read, 'Aeon Sophia Church', with an arrow pointing to the left. *Sophia!* An overwhelming sense of long-awaited reunion washed over me. I approached the small white stucco church, nestled at the foot of the silvery-blue mountains. The weathered periwinkle doors provided a splash of colourful contrast next to the bright white stucco walls. I entered with reverence, uncertain of the protocol for a Gypsy priestess from across the seas.

The inside of the church was modest with bare minimum decor. Two small paintings hung crookedly from the white stucco beams. The painting on the left was a traditional portrait of Jesus Christ. The painting on the right was a portrait of Mother Mary. Centred on the back wall was a larger painting of Sophia with outstretched arms, encircling the world. Twelve symbols of the zodiac surrounded the world.

Sophia was portrayed as a woman who offered the fullness of her presence to embrace the world in her wise and benevolent arms. Quite spontaneously, I reached out my arms toward her and whispered under my breath, 'Lovely to make your acquaintance, Aeon Sophia.'

In her radiant life-like presence, she winked, offering me a Mona Lisa smile in the soft morning light.

Aeon Sophia is not only the Patron Mother of the Greek Orthodox Religion. She is the heart of universal Love, known by her many names such as the World Soul, Bride of Logos, Mother Gaia and the Feminine Christ. One can sense her presence permeating all of creation as She shines the light of all embracing Love into all that appears to be separate from the circle of life.

I feel so blessed to be getting to know you as my closest confidant and soul guide. A timeless love flooded my being, warming my heart-womb with a golden honey-like nectar . *Oh my, you have lived inside me all along.*

This simple little church housed an ancient key to the living mystery that I felt so profoundly connected to. Her clear and loving voice whispered gently to me. '*Dear child, how wondrous it is to find you here. Return here tomorrow to receive guidance for the next part of your journey. Until then, know that all that you seek is seeking you!*

As I approached the blue doors to leave, I noticed a metal cart with a singular golden chalice resting upon a white doily. I looked at the glistening chalice and appreciated that it was not only a symbolic vessel which carries the blood of Christ, but a symbol for Divine Mother's body, the heart-womb of creation from which all life is born.

After closing the thick wooden doors behind me, I walked out into the bright sunshiny day. A loud rumble in my belly reminded me that I hadn't eaten anything since the night before. I decided to grab some lunch at a restaurant in the nearby village.

On the way back, I was surprised to feel a dark, heavy cloud overlay my energy field. I immediately sensed that something very tragic had happened, yet I could not identify its source. I scanned the energy fields of my parents and close friends for any clues. Nothing seemed apparent and so I chose to let it go for the moment and resolved to return to Kardamyli the following day.

CHAPTER FIFTY-ONE

CALLING MY BLUFF

Sophia is incandescent — her light illuminates our insight. All that she asks is that we answer the invitation to play the game of hide and seek. She is what is beneath the surface of consciousness that we do not necessarily see unless we look inward. United with the Logos, her celestial Self, Sophia, the Mother of all spiritual creation, leads her children back into fellowship with the Divine. Sophia represents the possibility of Divine Love — the possibility all creatures have of emptying themselves of egotism so that love might enter in. This power is the wholeness and integrity, the beauty of creation itself. This Feminine element, which is love, is the very life of humanity and the ground of all wisdom.

— Alice O. Howell, The Dove and the Stone

We are here at this time to journey into a transitional void. To experience the becoming of a new Self within a New Earth. We are being called to go deeply inside and consider who we are becoming. The Earth is calling us to get still, to listen deeply and create a clear connection for our Divine voice to guide us — alchemically clearing whatever stands in the way of our reception of the Divine.

We are like the caterpillar that has voraciously consumed everything in sight. As this excess builds, within her evolution stirs the imaginal cells within you. The imaginal cells become the genetic directors of your metamorphosis.

This calling of her instinctual encodement to embody her Divine blueprint moves her to make a cocoon out of a finely woven web to cradle her as she journeys into the unknown void. In this cocoon her head literally splits in half, and she begins to twitch. All that she has become up until this moment liquefies and melts into the nutritive soup. This nutritive soup becomes the genesis medium for the butterfly to be...her emergent Self.

Still, quiet, listening, opening in innocence...she gestates in the dark void of the chrysalis, until the chrysalis becomes translucent with the light of her true nature. The shape and form of the butterfly become visible underneath the chrysalis veil. A sensuous ripple begins from within, an undulating impulse to expand into more than she has known herself to be.

This miraculous being begins to tear the translucent walls of its birthing shroud, cracking open the chrysalis with an implosion of Divine light. In a breathless moment of being vulnerably suspended, literally by a thread, the butterfly hangs wet and new in an unknown world. Pulsations from her heart center begin to pump energy into her wings. Her impeccably adorned wings begin to fill out, opening, expanding, reaching out and drying in the sun. Luminous shimmers of light radiate from her new found wings as they open to take flight into the magnificence of being who she truly is – a miraculous winged butterfly, embodying the most expanded expression of her Divine essence and beauty.

– Kari Mathieson

In the early evening, after visiting the Aeon Sophia Church in Kardamyli, I sat to meditate on the edge of a high mountain bluff overlooking the Ionian Sea. The electric orange and purple sunset was framed by a silvery, blue-green mountain range. The air was filled with an intoxicating warm breeze. The sky glowed with incandescent light that illuminated everything in a golden sheen.

From the edge of the bluff, I looked to the far horizon and called myself into a lucid awareness and accountability for all the choices I had made to create my life exactly as it was. In that transcendent moment, I saw clearly that there was no such thing as a wrong choice or decision. Every bloody up and down and all around was working on my behalf to bring me to this moment of lucid clarity.

I flashed upon the countless times I required some outer validation to determine that I was desirable or worthy of being loved, only to reinforce a chronic mistrust in my own inherent value. I felt compassion for all the disappointments I experienced along the way, when someone failed to love me in the way that I wanted. *I now take full responsibility for creating my own worthiness through valuing myself more than I value the opinions or projections of others. Disappointment is never worth the happiness I might miss out on!*

I shook my head as if to sober up from some long hallucinogenic trip that I was only just emerging from. In a flash, I recognised the mind f—k being broadcasted into social consciousness that seemed to only reinforce, glamourise and even reward humanity's chronic obsession with outsourcing our fulfillment and happiness. It was cleverly designed to encourage individuals to project and blame others for one's lack, to externalise one's power and thus move away from taking responsibility for our part in creating our best life and reality!

Finito! I said, as if I waking up from being under the influence of a collective spell.

I accepted the paradox that within these ancient wounds, carried over throughout lifetimes, lives the starseeds of triumphant being. From this vantage point, sitting high above the cliffs, I could see that each period of darkness and light had birthed me into a more conscious, expanded and aware version of myself – someone who could joyously participate in life with an ever-expanding capacity to love and be loved.

'I am one with the source of creation, worthy of the deepest fulfillment and highest love,' I declared to the setting sun, knowing that this was only the beginning of creating a passionate life, one of unlimited abundance and unbridled beauty. Goddess bumps covered my skin. My body tingled with delight as an all-consuming, cosmic humour rippled through my bones, giving rise to a massive smile. At last, I was able to recognise that all of those countless, unreturned calls that I had put out to Aiden lead me to this golden opportunity to answer my very own call home to myself! I wondered if I would come to feel this inner peace and homecoming if what happened never happened.

From then on, I resolved to be a loyal, true and loving friend *and* my very own best lover! I affirmed, *I commit to answering each and every call for greater Self-love and compassion, especially when the chips are down and things don't appear to be going my way!*

I stood at the edge of the bluff, extended my arms and imagined diving into a free fall over the cliff. Instead of falling to the bottom and splattering onto the ground into a million pieces, I sprouted wings and soared into the vast unknown with a wide-open heart, brimming with joy for the gift of new life.

While savouring the last of the setting sun, I looked to the dark mountains as steadfast guardians of unwavering truth. The sea was my mirror into all that stirred within me and what was yet to be revealed. I watched the sun disappear into the ocean, leaving behind a sheath of orange and aubergine-coloured clouds. It was time to head back to Elena before it got too dark. After a few steps, I stopped suddenly, turned around and offered a closing prayer, *Thank you, Sophia, for helping me gain the eyes to see what was there all along!*

The night was upon me. Instead of feeling intimidated by the darkness, I felt lovingly held within it – an infinite spark of light within its supernal dark mystery. As I lie in my little bed, I heard the loving voice of Sophia gently whisper to me, *'It's really that simple, be still and know God.'*

I closed my eyes and imagined wrapping my arms around my inner child as she nestled herself close into my beating chest. I spoke to her like a wise and loving parent in the same gentle tone that Sophia spoke to me in. *There is profound beauty in all that you feel. Trust your heart to lead the way, and you will find it will never leave you astray.*

Like a large-bosomed Greek grandmamma, the starry night sky nestled me in a little closer. In turn, I snuggled the little one within me up to my naked chest as I carried on with my inner counsel. *You are the golden child of Sophia and the love of my life! No matter what happens throughout our lives, I will always be there for you, to hold, comfort and cheer you on. I honour your sensitive heart and how it feels all the pain and all the wonder of the universe within it. I know at times the world can feel scary, like a lonely, cruel and unkind place. Let us be brave together and meet every unkindness as an opportunity to radiate the love where once there was none. I've got you now little one, and I promise I will never ever leave you out in the cold again!*

That night, I fell asleep to the tune of 'Over the Rainbow' from the movie, *The Wizard of Oz*, my all-time favourite lullaby.

Somewhere over the rainbow way up high
There's a land that I heard of once in a lullaby
Somewhere over the rainbow skies are blue
And the dreams that you dare to dream really do come true.
Someday I'll wish upon a star
And wake up where the clouds are far behind me.

PART
III

"There is some rare and inexpressibly exquisite beauty
I long to bring into this world...
it lives behind my heart...far, far behind and beyond
out where the stars flicker, and further still
beyond the stars and whirling galaxies,
the myriads of worlds and suns and moons
beyond the beyond...
Deeper and deeper into the dark mystery of space
to the other side of darkness and time and form
to regions beyond the mind's perceptions
a distance incomprehensible, and yet
I would dream countless universes into being
in My attempt to express
my Heart...
My Heart that is more tender than a mothers,
the Heart of all hearts,
the Breath of all breath
and the Beauty that shines through all Beauty.
I cannot be named or defined,
yet I define and re-define you,
create and re-create you,
in My image,
each time your innocent heart is opened in love.
It is a longing for Myself who longs through you,
and the unutterably sweet mystery of our union
causes you to weep.

Your every tear is Mine
I created the stars thus...
and through your overflowing heart waters
I pour into your world.
Surrender to My current...
be overwhelmed, softened and melted down
by the waves of feelings
flowing through your vulnerable heart.
It is I...entering your world as a tidal wave,
destroying all structures of time and mind
that cannot contain my unimaginable Love.
Relax...
Surrender...
and be taken
as gently as a leaf falling, or a tear
falling,
falling,
falling...
So am I
Falling into you...

– Grace, *The White Rose*

CHAPTER FIFTY-TWO

THE ROSE CROWN

The tincture, or Elixir, produced at the end of the alchemical process has the ability to turn the gross human body into an incorruptible body of light. The purification and realignment of the chakras is solely to alter our subtle body, sometimes called the astral body, so that it takes on a crystalline or diamond form, filled with sparks that run through our physical body. But before the body of light can be attained, the adept has to work to reconcile and integrate the elements, which are missing from the individual and cosmic spirit. This work is then nothing less than the re-sacralisation of matter, the integration of the Feminine and Masculine, the craft of the Sophianic restoration.

– Caitlin Matthews, *Sophia, Goddess of Wisdom*

Verily all you seek is within you. Therefore, know yourself. Your body is indeed the Temple of God. Simply open the door of your heart, and enter in. Your Father-Mother awaits you. Even now the Father-Mother runs out upon the stony path you have trod and welcomes that part of yourself you have judged prodigal and returns you to your birthright. Once you turn around and begin to press homeward back into the light, you know this light is the Beloved you have futilely sought in the night.

– Claire Heartsong, *Anna, Grandmother of Jesus*

Sophia, lift us up the Tree of Life like drunken sap. Honey dredger, consume us within your ecstatic lightning snakes of love, traversing the rainbow staff of light twined round the tree of the caduceus of our spine, to explode as mystical sight Divine...Aeon Sophia...limitless light.... Aeon Sophia Aeon.

– Ariel Spilsbury

The next morning, I sipped slowly on my morning cup of tea as if to draw some long sought-out answers from it. I was overcome by the same peculiar feeling from the day before. Something's not quite right back at home. *I can just feel it!* I chose to stay open and continue to observe the feeling while carrying on with my mission to return to Kardamyli as requested by Sophia.

Perched upon the mountaintop that hovered above the white chapel sat another Aeon Sophia Church. The waitress at the café informed me that it was occasionally open for public visitation. I hoped that my timing would synch up with the local village woman whose job it was to light the candles and refresh the flowers.

I'll visit the mountaintop church first, then I'll return to the white stucco one in the afternoon, as promised.

My heart was thumping with excitement and anticipation. I looked forward to spending the day communing with my sacred companion, Sophia. Swallowing my last bite of Greek yogurt, I skipped down the hill to the bus stop. My womb felt swollen, pulsating with electric energy as if I was pregnant with all of creation.

A few moments later, the bus screeched to a halt and the bus driver gestured for me to come aboard while simultaneously screeching away from the curve. I slid into one of the tattered vinyl seats and bumped along the winding road.

What magic would this day bring? I wondered as the bus pulled into town and came to a high-pitched screeching halt. The heavy metal doors opened up with a clanking mechanical sound as the driver hollered in his familiar Greek accent, 'Kardamyli!'

First things first, I thought, feeling to make my first stop at the café to fuel up before my next expedition. The same waitress I had the day before sauntered over to my table to take my order. She had a glazed-over look on her face and a melted body, as if she had been up all night making love – most likely with the Grecian god-man I saw yesterday! *Good for her*, I thought, as I ordered my usual cappuccino. I sent her a silent blessing. *May love be kinder and a little less complicated for you than it has been for me!*

Moments later, she brought my warm frothy drink, which I savoured in a deep contemplative silence while attuning to the energy of the day and the presence of Sophia, my most beloved travel companion.

After coffee, I walked past the row of bedraggled shops. Each storefront window displayed an array of ruby-red objects. Just as Mary Magdalene was the featured celebrity of Saintes-Maries-de-la-Mer, Sophia was clearly the shining star of Kardamyli! I wandered into one of the shops to take a closer look at the postcards displayed in the metal spinning racks. My eyes got brighter and brighter as the mysterious Red Queen revealed herself through a pictorial story displayed on each postcard.

A middle-aged shopkeeper, wearing a bright red apron, approached me and stood staring blankly at me. He finally cleared his throat and with a robust confidence pronounced, 'Don't I know you? You have definitely been here before. I'm quite sure of it!' Before I could reply, he added 'Where are you from, Madame? Who are you?'

'Hello. Well, no, I haven't been here before.' *At least not in this lifetime,* I thought to myself. 'I'm from California,' I replied, a little more fascinated with the display of colourful postcards than with him.

'My God, you look so familiar to me! Are you quite sure we haven't met before? Maybe in a dream!' He persisted with his questions, as if my second reply might be different.

I recognised the archetypal significance of being seen and witnessed in this waking dream where the veils between timelines and parallel realities are so thin. I ran through one of many possible scenarios in my mind, keeping the divine humour to myself. *Oh yes, I too remember you! Let me introduce myself. I am the Divine Mother, Sophia. I have returned to one of my villages after thousands of years of wandering the world, remaining hidden from the ordinary eye.* I smiled deeply inside and carried on with my imaginary conversation. *Perhaps you don't recognise me with my veil on. After all, this wandering Gypsy has been travelling for lifetimes in disguise, awaiting the time when humanity would gain the eyes to see me. When they do, they will see all beings in their true form.*

I turned to the shopkeeper and smiled warmly into his wide-open eyes and said aloud, 'Perhaps we have met before.' And left it at that. After purchasing two white candles as an offering for the church, I proceeded to the foot of the mountain where a winding stone pathway wound up the mountainside. I gave myself fully to the long uphill ascent, grateful for my Capricornian strength to carry me up the steep and winding path. *Hurry up, beloved one, a very special gift awaits you!* The voice of Sophia urged me on.

The late morning sun grew hotter and more intense until I broke out in a full body sweat. I envisioned the scene from the movie *The Mission*, where De Niro feverishly climbed up the jungle cliff, lugging his penance in a huge black fishing net laden with arduous armour.

With each step, I grew lighter as the weight of countless lifetimes melted in the heat of the midday sun. Like a snake shedding its too tight skin, my cocoon was breaking open to reveal the butterfly I was becoming.

Out of nowhere, a beautiful black butterfly made an appearance. I gasped in delight as her tiny wings flittered about me as if to offer a sacred temple dance. At some point, she fluttered her ebony wings, making flirtatious circles around me, enticing me up the jagged path. I fell head-over-heels in love with her blackness! *How exquisite! Here is the Black Madonna dancing before me as a shimmering onyx butterfly.*

She became my bedazzling escort and whispered, '*It is within the womb of blackness that the diamond light of your soul will be born!*'

I began to sing to myself one of my favourite eighties songs. 'Goddess on the mountaintop, burning like a silver flame. The summit of beauty and love, and Venus was her name. She's got it. Yeah, baby, she's got it. I'm your Venus, I'm your fire, at your desire. Black as the dark night she was, got what no one else had. Wa! She's got it. Yeah, baby, she's got it! I'm your Venus, I'm your fire, at your desire.'

Panting like an overheated panther, I finally made it to the top of the steep mountaintop. I was given a choice to proceed to the left or go to the right. As I walked to the left, I felt a stirring in my belly, the kind you get when you are lost. I decided to walk a little further around the bend anyway, so as to take in the view of the valley. My underworld holiday was now sparkling before me like a rare and precious jewel, my prize for having the courage to descend into the heart of darkness.

While taking in the view, I raised my arms to the sky, opened my heart as wide as I could and inhaled the beauty of my surroundings. *Thank you, Creator, for showing me that there is beauty in the most unexpected of places, and that there are bright places even in the darkest of times...and that if there isn't...I can be that bright place with infinite capacities. Thank you for the gift of this fire! With this flame of love, a tremendous compassion is rising within me. A compassion that blazes so fiercely that it has changed chaos into calm, horror into beauty and agony into grace.* With that, I kneeled down, placed my forehead to the earth and felt deeply into all that was transforming within me such that I could give back even a morsel of the immense beauty that I had been given and contribute to the transformation of the collective. I whispered one of my favourite quotes by Pierre de Teilhard Chardin: '*Someday after mastering the winds, the waves, the tides of gravity, we shall harness for God the energies of love, and then, for the second time in history of the world, man will have discovered fire.*'

I then retraced my steps and approached the quaint church perched between two ancient olive trees. Upon arrival, I discovered that the double doors were secured with a thick metal chain held together by an old antique lock. I stood on my tippy toes to peek through the small window built into the ancient cobblestone wall. The appearance of fresh flowers and lit altar candles was an indication that the caretaker from the local village had already attended to her duties for the day.

Oh, well! Undeterred by the locked doors, I found a large rock to stand upon to glimpse a better view through the small barred window. I nuzzled my nose between the vertical bars and gazed upon a large ancient book that rested on top of the podium. *There it was again!* That same equilateral cross, inlaid in gold upon a worn-out leather book cover. Golden Greek letters were embossed below the cross along with the words, 'Aeon Sophia.' For a split second, the letters appeared to twinkle, as if someone had sprinkled fairy dust upon them. I marvelled as I placed my hand around the medallion cross hanging from my neck on an old piece of leather string.

My eyes darted across the room to a beautiful painting hanging on the white stucco wall. It depicted a boat carrying Joseph and the three Mary's – just like the one I had recently seen in Mary Magdalene's church in Saintes-Maries-de-la-Mer. The four beings in the painting emanated an aura of tranquillity, as if they knew that this new land was only a brief stopover on their eternal journey, and home was a place that each carried within their heart.

After several timeless moments, I stepped down from the rock and approached an olive tree to meditate. As I closed my eyes, I opened myself to the subtle energies of this sacred site and the surrounding land. While taking several rhythmic breaths, a wave of deep peace washed over me. The warm breeze rustled through the surrounding olive trees and glided over my bare skin. I attuned to my energy body and envisioned the organic architecture of my light body in the form of a Merkaba. The Merkaba is a supporting field of energy that keeps us coherently connected to Source energy. When the Merkaba spins correctly, it creates a trinitised field that moves us into higher levels of consciousness and opens our connection into zero point. In zero point, our light body vehicle can travel beyond the time space continuum and move through the various grid structures that exist within our universe.

As I sunk deeper into my meditation, I began to travel between worlds and received a vision of the clouds lifting for a brief moment. I was being shown a parallel dimension that existed outside of ordinary 3D reality. In the far distance, an etheric pyramid-shaped mountain revealed itself in its full majestic glory. I was then guided through an inter-dimensional portal where my awareness travelled inside the pyramid likened to the one I sat before at the base of Mt Bugarach. Upon entering, my surroundings felt familiar, as if I had been there on several previous occasions to hold sacred counsel with my Crystal Star family. Organic light architecture wove with nature's finest display of iridescent pastel colours and sacred geometric patterns. Vibrating within this etheric paradise were the frequency codes of Universal Christ Consciousness oscillating as a Sacred Union trinity wave.

A luminous tapestry of interwoven expressions of consciousness opened up to me. Each sovereign filament maintained a coherent centre that would fold into itself like a fractal and then reemerge into a newly expanded expression of light. These geometric light formations endlessly regenerated as they interwove with other distinct patterns, creating an infinitesimal tapestry of life-giving beauty.

My heart burst as I realised that the gift awaiting me today was the eternal part of my soul that had returned to remember my place within the whole of creation. By the grace of the Divine Christos Sophia, the appointed moment of my anointing was upon me, seeded in me to ripen as a single epiphany. I received this gift as a full-bodied frequency that shimmered as iridescent rainbow light dancing in the nucleus of my cells. It quickened my being and then dissolved my physical form so that all that remained was electric diamond light. This sparkling aurora danced within every particle of my being, just as the radiant sunlight sparkles upon the water.

I sat motionless under the olive tree when the presence of the Divine Mother Sophia appeared before me. She greeted me with a gentle, all-encompassing love, likened to the frequency I felt when she blessed me with her presence at Gaia's Grove. She wore a ruby-red cape and golden crown, laden with jewels that glistened in the high noon sunshine. Her strong earthen hands held a vertical staff with a Heiros Gamos rainbow sphere that glowed around it. I marveled at the intricate carvings of golden inlayed glyphs, representing the diamond light codes. She held a young infant wrapped in a ruby and gold silk cloth who sat nestled onto her left hip. Her mahogany eyes gazed deeply into mine and pierced the innermost chamber of my heart. Tears welled up as she enveloped me in a cloak of shimmering starlight. She then placed a rose crown upon my head and presented me with her golden staff. I sat riveted as she spoke these words, carrying an indelible vibration of pure grace:

'Dear one, you have travelled long and far to arrive at this sacred nexus point of Sacred Union alchemy that is birthing the diamond light of your soul. Divine love is what moves you, wisdom light is what shines upon you, so that everything that remains hidden now rises to the surface to be sanctified and made whole once again.

'I wish to consecrate that which has always been... the essence and truth of who you are. This golden staff is a symbol of your sovereign pillar of light that aligns you with the pristine will of the Divine. This rose crown is a symbol of your innate wholeness. It's thorn and bloom, born

from integrating the darkness and light, forever awakening the majesty of your soul.'

I breathed deeply into my heart-womb and was reminded of the feeling of being pregnant with a golden child. Sophia's wisdom-light continued to stream forth gifting me with the pure light of gnosis.

'You stand on the threshold of the Divine Marriage, where spirit and matter, Self and Beloved join together as One. The time is upon you to become one with the unified heart of the Christos Sophia. The crystalline consciousness that gestates within you is poised to give birth as the fruit of this Sacred Union alchemy in its purest form — blossoming forth as a golden child of the sun who embodies the eternal memory of the One. As you walk on beloved, cherish the golden egg that is growing from within your sanctified heart-womb. She is the Christ child, the song of your soul coming into harmonic resonance with the song of the universe.

'There has never been a breath from which we have been apart. We have been together since the beginning and will be together forever more. In times of darkness, I will be shining upon you and within you, just as the sun shines at midnight. I am the heart light that glistens from your eyes, the twinkle in the Venus Star forever reflecting the wonder of all that you are. I am you, the light of my soul, the pulse in the heart of the eternal sun. I am all and all is One.

I bowed deeply to the presence of Sophia and the gift of receiving her anointing grace. I was then startled out of my meditation by a middle-aged woman wearing a turquoise windbreaker. She had long golden locks that cascaded over her shoulders. She paused in front of me and politely asked, 'May I take a photo, Madame?'

'Yes, of course,' I agreed with an open curiosity. I was grateful to have this precious moment archived, even if it was in some random person's photo library. After she photographed me, I stood up and encircled the Church one last time, feeling beyond blessed to have communed with Sophia inside the etheric cathedral of light.

The woman who had just photographed me smiled warmly and then struck up a conversation. We stood side by side and admired the view of the lush green valley. I was moved to share the story of how the merchant in town insisted that he knew me and how familiar I had appeared to him.

She chuckled and said, 'Yes, yes, we recognise one another by simply taking the time to honour the unique essence and vibration that emanates from each person's soul.'

'Wow, what is your name?'

'Krista. I'm from Bavaria.'

'Oh, yes! Thank you for that amazing reflection, Krista,' I said. At this point of the journey, I wasn't surprised that I found her soul to be familiar, as if we had met once before, perhaps in another lifetime. I took a moment to close my eyes and scan the Akashic records for matching pictures. *Ahhh, I see.* I was able to see in a singular movie-like frame that she had snuck me small pieces of bread through the fence of a prison encampment. We met on opposite sides of the fence, each playing our destined role, while silently knowing there really are no sides – we had consciously chose to come together while being divinded and kept apart.

'I once had a little six-year-old Tibetan Lama friend remind me that there really are no strangers here on planet Earth. He would say, "We are all related in one way or another."

I smiled warmly at Krista, delighted to have bumped into an old friend who could have very well been someone who had saved my life. What I knew for sure was she was a kindred lover of the world, a beloved friend passing through to share a momentous blink in eternity.

We stood together at the edge of the ravine, breathed in the fresh mountain air while soaking up the picturesque view. Krista and I shared a silent moment reveling in how miracles happen in the most unexpected ways We exchanged a long hug, our hearts pressed together in gratitude in the knowing that when two or more are gathered, so is the Spirit of Grace. We then joined hands while gazing deeply into one another's eyes as if catching up after lifetimes.

Krista had appeared in my life in that perfect moment to witness and consecrate a miraculous milestone on my journey simply by sharing presence. After parting ways, I silently thanked her for risking her life for me in a prior lifetime. I then kneeled down and placed my hands upon the Earth, and offered a prayer of gratitude for all the so-called strangers who have blessed my life along the way. *My life is made possible through an infinitude of gestures seen and unseen. Thank you, beloveds, for recognising our shared calling!*

I sensed it was time to go and began my descent down the steep mountainous path. I felt in awe of how I magically found my way to the land of Aeon Sophia, thanks to Sananda and my travel agent, who I will always remember as loving jelly donuts. I felt like an entirely different person going down the mountain than I did going up. For one, I felt a whole lot lighter. I no longer carried the heavy weight of my past I felt more sovereign and free to admire and appreciate how every shrub, flower, bird and insect on the path was a part of me, and I them, and that the Beloved was not a singular being; the Beloved lived and breathed in everyone and as everything.

With this profound feeling of wild belonging, I squatted down behind a bush to relieve myself and saw the most remarkable vision on the adjacent hillside. The hill was totally barren except for three perfectly shaped olive trees growing side by side. A vibrant sapling tree grew between them. I observed that these two noble trees flourished side by side, with plenty of open space between them. They shared the same earth, air, sun and water, and yet remained distinctly individuated from one another, maintaining their unique characteristics. The younger tree that grew slightly in front of them occupied their shared ground.

From above, the trees appeared to be growing autonomously. From below, they shared the same root system, along with the rich earthly nutrients that nourished their growth. These majestic trees were showing me the potential of a thriving, harmonious relationship, where sovereignty and unity join to create a wondrous sacred third. Together, they made a perfect trinity.

I envisioned the sacred geometry of the vesica pisces which symbolises the sacred third that's created from opposite forces overlapping just enough to make a small conjoining oval shared between them. The shared circle represents the entrance into the womb, the pleroma, the fullness of divine life that arises from the absolute into form, creating the union of spirit and matter. It is the centre that is both empty and overflowing with highest divine potential. In essence, it is the child of innocence, forever being reborn within the heart of each and every being. To find the Grail is to exist within the centre of this trinitised field, a pleroma of empty fullness, born from the purified heart realm.

I was receiving this transmission through the lens of Gaia Sophia. Her garden, a cosmic playground for all of nature to make perpetual love, while birthing endless novel creations propelled by the sheer pleasure and joy of it all. As I gazed upon the family of olive trees, I felt into the qualities of mutual respect, openness and gratitude, the bedrock and foundation for safe and authentic intimacy. Life was showing me the dance of co-creation through sacred trinities, born from the union of complementary opposites engaging through mutual consent and the miraculous wonder and awe of it all.

Nature was shimmering in this trinitised field of awakened love beauty consciousness. I was so moved that I spoke this decree on behalf of the Wild Divine. 'I, Ambe´, stand in my Divine presence and offer my life to the creation of perpetual Beauty. With love, honour and respect, I harmonize and balance the Feminine and Masculine within me, while nourishing all that is born from this Sacred Union. May my life be an offering, a welcoming bridge, unifying Heaven and Earth through the stewardship of original innocence. May I be a sanctuary for all beings – a safe haven to join together for the sake of co-creating something wondrously beautiful that blesses the whole. So be it and so it is.'

Suddenly, a warm wind blew through the mountain so fiercely that it practically knocked me over. I knew beyond a shadow of a doubt that Great Spirit had heard my prayer. In awe, I stared up into the infinite, clear blue sky. It was a beautiful mystery, undefined and unknown – just like my life.

The high sun beckoned me on with my day and so I skipped down the path, astounded by the supernatural gifts that were being illuminated in Sophia's garden. I was fascinated to now see myself through her eyes, the eyes of the Beloved, the eyes of infinity. Everything was scintillating with her sprinkle of Love, magically interconnected through Her majesty. Sophia was smiling back to me through every leaf, insect and chirping bird and I knew from that day on, I would never walk alone again. *Beloved, when you see reality as it really is, you will see yourself in everyone and everything, and your endless longing will magically transform one of wild belonging.*

When I reached the bottom of the mountain path, I returned, as promised to the little church with the blue doors to offer my prayers of gratitude. Upon entering, I was literally brought to my knees. The meandering river of my soul had at last found its way home to an ocean of endless possibilities.

Flooded with a mixture of humility and grace, I sat down on the dusty clay floor and communed with the miraculous force that brought me to this remote and desolate land. It was only three months ago that I lay face down in the dirt at Gaia's Grove while Sophia poured her Love into me and called me home. With humble awe, I glanced up at the golden chalice and asked that same question that had burned in my heart for as long as I could remember: *How may I best serve this life?*

The answer came to me in a single epiphany that spread like a warm honeysuckle smile throughout my body. *Embody the Love that blesses all beings.*

By the time I got up and walked back through those periwinkle doors, a majestic hawk with large golden wings encircled me and released a piercing screech that sent a cosmic shiver up my spine.

Ah, my animal spirit guide has come to carry my prayers into the world. Thank you hawk medicine, for being a gracious messenger of the awakened heart! Thank you for carrying the highest vision of Oneness upon your wings through your sacred heart call.

I can see clearly now the rain is gone
I can see all obstacles in my way
I think I can make it now the pain is gone
All of the bad feelings have disappeared
Here is that rainbow I've been praying for
It's gonna be a bright, bright
bright sunshiny day.

– Johnny Nash, 'I Can See Clearly Now'

CHAPTER FIFTY-THREE

OCEAN OF REBIRTH

Having journeyed across the wasteland of inner being, those of us called to the portal of initiation realise the full weight of our transgressions against the soul. We dissolve our sins in tears of self-forgiveness. This is the first baptism – in water. Tears baptise the emotions and enable us to awaken to the world of feeling and meaning. Energies from the solar plexus are raised into the heart. The heart becomes the centre wherein the life of the individual is focused. During this process the astral body is vastly expanded and becomes an emotionally pure receptacle of soul experience. The heart is thus prepared for the second baptism.

The initiate now recognises the sacred vibration of her or his own secret name. She has come at last to the sacred place – to the centre of the heart where the four quarters of being stand still. This stillness cannot be achieved by an act of will or visualisation. It is born only of inner baptism, and from real transformation.

The spirit descends only in response to the call of the awakening soul. The soul will continue to over light its vehicle of expression. A chord of sudden knowing reverberates throughout the Initiate. It tunes up her whole being, bringing all dissonance into alignment. Energy trapped is set free. Each of the chakras is opened and illuminated. From octave to octave they sound their notes in perfect harmony. The fire of spirit baptises the crown chakra – known also as the thousand petalled lotus. The pineal gland is vitalised. Energy of the Divine Will pours through the crown chakra into the brow centre and stimulates the pituitary gland. The pituitary is the kingly gland that rules our threefold mental, emotional and physical being. When stimulated by the down-pouring fire of Spirit, it discharges elixirs into the blood stream. This is the elixir of life – the healing promised to those who find the Grail. These elixirs purify the blood. The blood will carry them to stimulate all other glands in the endocrine system. The secretion of those elixirs signals the endocrine system to set in motion a process that will open the chakras and raise the kundalini.

– Niamh Clune, *The Coming of the Feminine Christ*

If you would enter the kingdom of Heaven on Earth, allow the differences that provide contrast to inspire you. Make the two, one, by joining the inner with the outer and the outer with the inner. Allow your feelings of love to flow, giving and receiving as one. So likewise, make the upper like the lower and lower like the upper, merging the Heavenly Father and Earthly Mother, male and female, light and darkness into a single One. In this way you shall enter the bridal chamber where the Bridegroom claims you as himself. Then you shall surely enter the kingdom.

– Claire Heartsong, *Anna, Grandmother of Jesus*

The sea becomes filled with pearls.
The dry land receives the water of life.
The stone becomes a ruby,
And the body becomes all soul.

– Jelaluddin Rumi

The heat of the day spoke louder than anything else, and so I followed the dry rocky bed of the river to the sea for an afternoon swim. Freedom's melody flooded my mind, reminding me of the theme song of my Grail journey: 'Where the river greets the sea, this is how I love thee.' This time I heard it in a whole new way. No longer was this song all about my longing for the outer beloved nor about my love for Aiden. This song was always about the inner beloved serenading me home to the love that I am! This was a massive shift in consciousness, and I was beyond grateful to now begin to live into it!

The sea before me shone like a carpet of shimmering jewels. The shore was laden with a colourful blanket of stones, from robin's egg blue, creamy whites and light heron greys – all of them smooth and soft as a baby's bottom. Undressing slowly, I relished the opportunity to give myself fully to the ocean's embrace and entered the water with slow and deliberate presence. This time, I laid belly down on the warm silky rocks, letting go with a trust for life that was refreshingly intoxicating. The gentle break of the waves gave me the opportunity to fully surrender to the lapping water gently breaking over my body onto the shore.

I am all yours Mother Mer. At times you have shown yourself as a tidal wave, a tsunami of fear and doubt, an endless storm in my heart, a cleansing waterfall, a warm bath to soothe my soul, a river of feeling that twists and turns and knocks me against the rocks, breaking me open in all the right places. Today, you greet me as I am, naked and raw. I offer my life, body and soul to your life-giving waters and surrender into your wild grace. In your arms I am reborn. Mni Wokoni. Water is life!

With each receding wave, hundreds of smooth stones tumbled over my flesh. They offered me a sumptuous hot stone massage as the afternoon sun danced upon the curves of my body with intoxicating heat. The more I opened to this communion with nature, the more my essence flowed into the Earth, connecting me with all of her sacred elements. I began to sing aloud, 'Earth my body, water my blood, air my breath and fire my spirit... Heya, heya, heya, heya, heya, heya ho!'

As I lay belly down, sprawled out like a newborn babe, Sananda appeared before me. He stood ankle deep in the lapping waves, wearing a long white tunic with golden embroidery stitched around the trim. A golden rose light emanated from his radiant heart smile, creating a soft warm glow that surrounded him. His mahogany eyes and golden brown skin shimmered in the sunlight. While bathing in his presence, he beamed me a telepathic message: '*I honour, love and accept you exactly as you are, beloved.*'

With strong hands opened by his side, he stood before me as my sacred witness as I offered up the last vestiges of my alchemical cocoon to the sea. I was engulfed in a toroidal fountain of diamond sunlight as wave upon wave came crashing over my body. I was being reborn into the infinite rainbow plenum of the Cosmic Heart – no longer separate but wholly embraced by the sublime presence of pristine Love, Beauty, Intelligence. Nothing of 'me' remained, apart from the pure luminous light of empty presence. *Home!*

I remained lucidly present to the sensations of the water washing over my bare skin and caressing my sun-kissed body. Sananda offered me a warm smile then placed his palms together in a mudra of gratitude, then bowed his head with a mixture of reverence and celebration. I looked up to the blazing sun that was reflected inside Sananda's smiling eyes with a sense of profound awe and gratitude. *Thank you for witnessing this Self-baptism, beloved one.*

'*We are one becoming three, a perfect trinity,*' he replied. I sensed by his radiant smile that he felt my unspeakable gratitude for the blessing of his presence in my life. More than anything, he embodied the true essence of sacred relationship – friendship – something I had come to cherish above all else on this journey. I heard his quiet voice whisper to me, '*Heaven is not a destination, it is a relationship between your true nature as eternal light and the universe as infinite love.*'

I recalled his Grandmother Anna's words: '*Ascension is not a destination at the end of a path that eludes you in a distant future. The only time Union in God may be realized is NOW! You are already in this present breath, in the midst of your personal and planetary ascension into Christ consciousness! What remains is for you to simply choose union and allow your Creator to express through you, just as you are.*'

The rays of the setting sun dried my body and blanketed me in a cocoon of hot pink and golden sunlight. I was prompted to dress quickly in order to catch the last bus home to Kalamata. As I walked back to the main road, I soon discovered that I was too late. I had missed the last bus back to my little seaside village. Having no other apparent option, I resorted to putting my thumb out to catch a ride back to my room, which had now become my alchemical temple of light. After a few moments, a black sedan swerved over to the curb as if it was pulling in from the glamorous Italian Riviera. I looked in the window only to find it was the same man who had been gawking at me while doing my morning yoga at the nearby hotel! I immediately recognized him, complete with hairy chest, thick gold chain, strong aftershave and balding head.

'Come in. I'll drop you off at the hotel,' he said with a strong Greek machismo accent.

I smiled back and thanked him, feeling a little hesitant as to what I was actually getting myself into. *What the heck,* I thought. I slid into the smooth tan leather seat next to him. The radio was blaring at top volume as he changed the station to something that sounded a little more romantic for two! I could hardly believe what I heard. The vocalist passionately wailed these lyrics, 'Oh yes, because I believe in vision and I believe in love. I believe my time on Earth is destiny and I believe we are strong enough for all of it!'

I was absolutely flabbergasted. The synchronicity of this song coming on at this particular moment in time, just after meeting Sophia, Sananda, and my newborn Self was more than my awestruck mind could fathom!

Words were unnecessary as this pudgy Greek god man bobbled his head to the melody while I gazed to the sun and bid farewell to the tangerine ball of light setting over the sea. Our brief sunset ride was enough to celebrate him as an unexpected angel, here to be a part of my magical Grail ride. It was past twilight when he dropped me off in front of the still-under-construction convenience store at the bottom of my street. I took a brief moment to appreciate this man's generous heart, cloaked in strong aftershave.

'Thanks for the ride, my friend!'

He offered me a large grin while keeping a steady eye on my behind, through his rear-view mirror as he slowly pulled away from the curb. 'Hey, want to have a drink with me later on tonight?' he shouted out his window while looking back at me with that same mischievous grin.

'No, thank you,' I said, waving back and offering a warm smile.

That evening, while rinsing off the salt and sand in the shower, my moon blood released from my womb. I looked at the bright red trail running down my leg, mixing with the water as it trickled down the drain. *Ah, my blood is flowing in sweet, sweet surrender! On this day of rebirth my bloodline is purified and all are set free.* I recollected what I had learned in the Divine Feminine mystery schools.

My blood is the Sangraal that carries the solar codes of Christ Consciousness. Encapsulated within it is the mitochondrial DNA passed on by my mother, her mother and all the way back to the first mother. Each human carries the living Akashic records within their blood, a living library of all that ever was and ever will be. That is why it is so important to know and remember that blood reacts and responds to thought. The chemistry of negative thinking wears out the blood and makes it dirty. Negative thoughts and toxic emotions carried over from lifetimes of traumatic events encapsulate and make blood scars that block the light of our soul. This same blood gets passed on generation to generation. We incarnate to set the ghosts of our past free by loving all that was once exiled by previous generations.

On the other hand, our feelings of love, gratitude, curiosity and innocence purify our blood, making it run clean and bright like the living waters gushing from a mountain spring! When I inhabit my divine innocence, my blood becomes translucent, allowing the light of my inner sun to shine through.

I reached down and dabbed my finger into my moon blood and then anointed my heart, throat and third eye. I felt her presence as she whispered softly to me, '*The Grail is your womb, the source of all creation. Your moon blood is the Sangraal, the blood royal that carries the Light codes of the Divine Christos Sophia! You are a living chalice, a holy vessel of the Feminine Christ.*'

I watched with fascination as my ruby-red moon river trailed down my leg, making its way to be washed down the drain – taking along with it lifetimes of learning about the deeper truth of who I am *and* who I am not. My blood appeared to be cleansed and purified, now a river of truth and love uniting me with the essence of all.

Blessed be the gift! Now where can I go celebrate with a piece of raw chocolate pie?

CHAPTER FIFTY-FOUR

ENSOULMENT

We yearn to live sacred lives. To align ourselves with meaning. To consecrate our actions. To sing to the stars our ascent. To live sacred lives requires that we live at the edge of what we do not know. I believe we discover our bearings as we learn to bear the reality of our depths, and more importantly, that those depths we bear reflect the depths of the universe itself. The experience of integrity is the embodiment of those depths. The invitation to journey down is a journey without direction in order to find direction. The place we turn is within, and it is within that we find the tender connection between the one and the many. It is in that tender connection that we find our bearings to function as an integral part of the whole, to fly as members of the human flock.

– Anne Hillman, *Dancing Animal Woman*

All seeming problems are just symptoms of the larger You trying to emerge. They're the baby kicking inside the womb, the morning sickness, the labor pains – all of which aren't problems but signs of something trying to be born, and the necessary changes that make you an instrument through which it can come through. From this larger perspective then, the 'practice' is to appreciate and prepare the way through staying open.

From now on, whenever you're confronted with a seeming-problem, ask what new/greater dimension of you is trying to emerge and how you can more fully allow it. Affirm to yourself, 'I have no problems. All problems are symptoms of my larger Self trying to emerge. I keep my attention on the good unfolding within me and say, "Yes! Bring it on!"

– Derek Rydall, *The Law of Emergence*

That night, I had two vivid and potent dreams. In the first one, I was attending a party with the most radiant golden stallion as my date. I stroked and caressed him adoringly as he was just so beautiful! Then we rode off together into the enchanted night. I asked him, *'Am I too heavy?'*

He replied, *'Oh no, not at all. You are just right and I am delighted to carry you.'* Then the stallion gently reminded me, *'There will be times when you will be carried and will be invited to be fully receptive. Other times you will feel happy to stand on your own two feet and carry your own weight! This is your call to build the strength and soul stamina to walk on your own and the humility and graciousness to recognise the times to let go and be carried. Such is the dance of balancing your inner Masculine and Feminine power.'*

The second dream featured my aunt and uncle. They gifted me with a brand-new, customised motor home with an elegant floor-to-ceiling, intricately carved sandalwood interior! I was fascinated by how this palatial travelling home was presented to me by my relatives on my mother's side. I received it as a sign that my bloodline had been cleansed and my ancestors set free! Thank you for this opportunity to transform my ancestral lineage and help uplift the consciousness of humanity. Now we may grow and evolve beyond the pain of desperation that had once entrapped our souls. *Amazing grace, how sweet you are. What once was lost, now is found! What a gift it is.*

I marvelled at my new inner upgrade. I knew then that 'home' was not a place, but my very own blood. The same blood that coursed through my veins as unstoppable passion pumps through my heart as the love of the Universe and carries a living record of all of creation.

Pure, pure like the water

Let it run forever more

To be clean, clean as the waves come crashing to the shore

It leaves me smooth, smooth as a pebble

Polished in the depth of love

Carried by the winds of grace

On the wings of a dove

So pure, pure like the water
Let it run forever more
To be clean, clean as the waves come crashing to the shore
It leaves me smooth, smooth as a pebble
Polished in the depth of love
And carried by the winds of grace
On the wings of a dove
So shine, shine as a diamond
Project the light of One
From the Source we are sent through the center
As the moon reflects the sun
Arise and awake from your slumber
Kindle ancient flame
Is witnessed through the waves of what's to change
Though the essence remains the same
All lies and games
All fades away
All lies within
And all finds a way.

– ShimShai, 'Pure'

I dedicated the rest of my day to organising travel logistics for the next leg of my journey. And yet this charming little gateway to the underworld wasn't going to let me go without one last tug-of-war between my heart and my head. I got my knickers in a twist trying to decide whether to take the ferryboat or the airplane to Italy, my next destination. My mind teetered back and forth: *Is it better to take the ferry or fly? Ferry or fly? Ferry or fly?* I compared and contrasted – *time or money? Money or time?* The plane was double the money and half the time. The ferry was half the money and double the time. *What did I value more, my time or my money?* The irony of this dilemma was that I actually toiled over this potential choice for a ridiculous amount of hours. Then I froze in indecisiveness, wondering what would happen if I made the wrong decision! I put an imaginary measuring stick up to every possible scenario, only to come out of my analysis feeling drained and exhausted.

Sensing the absurdity of my quandary, I decided to call upon Sophia for some good ol' wise woman counsel and support. Just as I was settling in for bed, she came to me and offered her gracious consultation.

'Dear heart, your compulsion to manage every last detail reflects how you continue to see yourself as separate, habitually putting your head before your heart. We invite you to let go and step into the flow. It's time to trust your Feminine energy, and the benevolent nature of the universe that is always lovingly co-creating on your behalf. We suggest that you step onto the Earth, preferably barefoot, relax your awareness into the sensations of your body and breathe deeply into your heart-womb. Invite your Divine Self to take the reins of your open receptivity so that you can sense the wonder of adventure rather than the paralysis of fear. In this way, there cannot be a "wrong choice".

'The Divine does not co-create life through the lens of "problems" or "limitations". The Divine is here to innovate novel potentials for you to grow and expand into more of the wonder of who you are. Every time you risk going beyond your comfort zone and try something new, you literally create magical new pathways that go on to bless countless others along the way.

'We invite you to relax, open and feel that your perception is what holds the master key to creating your better than imagined reality. When you consciously place your perception on the perfection of creation, you can trust that no matter what happens there is a gift and opportunity to be harvested from every situation! To come into alignment with your better than imagined life, relax into the feeling of your somatic body. Once you feel grounded and centred, begin to raise your frequency by dwelling on the feeling of gratitude, what lights you up and turns you on! Give yourself permission to try on different possibilities without overlaying an agenda imposed by the mind. Now pretend you are perusing in the Goddess's infinite costume closet. Notice what attracts you, which expands your energetic field, opens your heart and brings you a sensation of excitement and joy. Your womb is your barometer, your heart is your compass and your imagination your GPS (greatest potential seen). Make them one and you will grow wings to fly into any situation and create all matters of miracles no matter what the conditions or circumstances may be.

'It is especially during those challenging times when you feel the most stressed and overwhelmed that you are called to remain open instead of constricting your energy. In this way you become the co-creator of magic and miracles. Simply ground into Mother Earth, breathe deeply into your belly, come into stillness and tenderly open and observe what you are feeling. Create a loving space for those feelings to be welcomed and land so that you may compassionately tend to all that you feel as worthy of your love. Now imagine the qualities you wish to feel and affirm: "All that I desire is already here now, waiting to be claimed by my willing and loving heart. All is unfolding in divine and perfect order to reveal my highest divine destiny. I say 'yes' to life, 'yes' to love, 'yes' to joy. Before you know it, you'll be on your way! Bon voyage, beloved one!"*

In that moment I felt my wings of light unfurl and saw myself crossing the great blue sea with my dolphin companions surrounding me.

22 September 2003, Fall Equinox

I sense that I am passing through an ascension gate...as I stand in that humble place of forgiving the unforgivable through accessing the deepest love, compassion and understanding for myself and all beings. It is in that moment of feeling the most forsaken that I have come to embody a LOVE that is large enough to include everyone and everything within its tender wake. Every small gesture of kindness, every warm smile, every gratitude, every humble bend, and mighty stand for the love that we are brings me closer to the beloved. YES! I have loved, and I have lost and now I rise to stand in the larger Love that I AM. I am ready for life to lead me into the wonder of new beginnings and to illuminate a Love that is beyond my wildest imaginings.

In this morning's meditation, I was surrounded by a pride of white lions. They transmitted to me the golden elixir of Divine nobility...forged in the fire of fierce unconditional LOVE, the kind of fire that blazes in the highest respect for ALL life and gives rise to a purity that cannot be compromised by the false light and the false dark matrix whose design is to undermine rather than enliven and uplift.

Instead, the lions invited me to embody my divine sovereignty and radiate an inner royalty that blesses rather than berates. They showed me that celebrating the triumph of others as my own opens the doorway to paradise – a world of unbridled benevolence and wild belonging.

On another note, here in the jewel of Mani, the clouds in my mind are finally parting. The demons in my head have stopped fighting for their last days of tyranny. I have made my choice, to follow my heart and take the ferryboat to Italy!

I have come to see this secluded town with fresh new eyes. The jewel in the lotus of Mani is sparkling in a whole new way. Today, I will take the bus to the neighbouring fishing village of Aghios Nikolaos. A local told me that just above the confluence of fishing boats rests a small village nestled in the crevices of the mountains. The local also happened to mention there is a very ancient cathedral dedicated to Aeon Sophia that towers over the sea. I am super excited to discover the magic of this new day! I gotta run now before I miss the morning bus.

The local bus was over a half an hour late. This contributed to a percolating restlessness I felt about leaving this quaint 'underworld' town that I had grown so very fond of. When the bus finally arrived with that now familiar screeching halt, I hopped on and disappeared into my grey vinyl seat.

Hmm, I wonder what life will be like in Damanhur, Italy, my next destination, I pondered as I floated off into a daydream while the bus thundered up the bumpy road. Around thirty minutes later the old rickety bus reached the top of the twisting mountainous road and came to a screeching halt that sent me flying forward in my seat.

The middle-aged driver, wearing a perspiration-soaked tank top, waved to me to get off his bus as this was his final stop for the day. As I stepped down, I smiled at him graciously and sent him some good vibes. He gave me a toothless grin and roared off in a thunder. After the cloud of dust settled, I was glad to be on steady ground again. With an elated heart, I soaked in the view of the glistening sea shimmering on the horizon: she, my constant companion, and I, a tiny drop in her ocean of love.

The only sign of life on the mountaintop was a small wooden gate covered in overgrown vines that appeared to lead into the hilltop village. *Where is everyone?* I wondered, noticing how unusually quiet it was with very few signs of people or animals around. I wandered down the cobblestone path, observing the few villagers who were absorbed in their daily chores. Eventually, the miniature path opened into the village square. What I saw next came as quite the surprise. *Holy Mamacita!* A massive stone cathedral towered over this humble little village and happened to be twice the size as the Aeon Sophia Church on the mountaintop of Kardamyli. *Whoaaa!*

I had no idea what I might find as I peeked my head through the giant thick wooden doors. The church appeared empty apart from a priest dressed in a long red robe. He appeared to be giving instructions to a young altar boy. The priest approached the cathedral doors as if to leave, when our eyes collided for a timeless moment. I thought that he might be startled by my unexpected presence. Instead, a shower of loving-kindness poured from his massive smile, making me feel delightfully welcomed and at home. The priest motioned for me to come into his impressive place of worship and so I followed with wide-open curiosity.

Sunlight streamed through the stained glass windows, filling the large wooden cathedral with a plethora of warm rainbow light beams. The presence of the great Mother Sophia permeated the air with her universal love, warmly welcoming me into one of her infinite universes. I looked up and there she was in the form of an enormous painting that occupied the entire back church wall. I noticed all of the zodiac symbols encircling the Earth that she held between her long arms. More exquisite than ever, she embraced the entire world with her larger than life, loving embrace.

'You know Sophia?' The priest looked at me curiously.

'Oh, yes!' I mentally reviewed what I had recently written about her in my journal: '*Sophia, the Divine Feminine, is the Mother of all Creation, who leads her children back into Sacred Union with the Divine. She is both world Soul and Bride of the Logos. In her Heavenly state, she is the guardian angel of the world – covering all creatures with her wings in order to elevate them gradually into true being. She is Mother Gaia. She speaks to us as the animating force in all of nature and in her Earthly state is found in every breath and pulse of life. She holds all the wisdom of the light and the dark and assists us to navigate through the murky waters of separation so that we may each return to the throne of our own awakened heart. Sophia represents the highest potential of Divine Love. She is the black void of the womb and the light that shines upon all of her children. Her language is beauty. She is the Beauty Way!*'

After a moment of silence, I kindly responded to the priest, 'She is the Mother of All.' I questioned how much of my English he actually understood, due to our difference in language. It didn't matter. His proud smile spoke a thousand worlds and I could tell that he was impressed to meet a foreigner who shared a mutual adoration for his Patron Mother Sophia.

The priest grinned from head to toe as we stood side by side in a silent awe, admiring the larger than life painting that covered one entire wall of the cathedral. I beamed immense gratitude for Sophia's unwavering grace to embrace the world in her arms, while we, her children, stumble along at the cost of so much war, bloodshed and environmental destruction.

Surely, humanity's endless compulsion to destroy our natural resources and kill off precious life was weighing heavily upon Her. I mean really – how much longer could she possibly hold us together when humanity's unconscious choices continue to rape, pillage and pollute her Earthly body? It's no wonder she takes things into her own hands when she needs to let off a little steam and remind us who's really boss.

I felt into my own exhaustion, accumulated over years of carrying the weight of the world upon my shoulders. *Someone's got to step up, so it might as well be me,* I would say to justify my weariness. And now, standing in the presence of Sophia, I felt the paradigm of self-sacrifice and over-caretaking was coming to completion for all those, like me, who felt it was down to them to save the world. I appreciated how evolution comes with its own form of urgency. And yet, I was being shown another way of evolving through relaxing the nervous system as the foundation and roots of integral stewardship. I imagined all beings as planetary guardians, taking equal responsibility for caring for one another and genuinely caring for the beloved planet we share. I imagined a humanity sharing their unique contributions from a place of being fully resourced and relaxed.

I heard Sophia's voice whisper to me, as if giving me a preview of what was coming down her evolutionary pipeline *'You are here to steward the life you were given in a way that gives life and enlivens the whole. Through radical self-care, living in harmony with nature and embodying the change you wish to see in the world, you are being called to graduate from your habitual sacrificial ways The natural movement to serve life on this planet will be sourced from the overflow of one's radiantly alive chalice. Embodying and expressing your creative passion and joy is how you turn on the tap. Everything flows from there!'*

Although the priest appeared to be a stranger from the opposite end of the world, the painting magically joined us as timeless friends. Few words were exchanged as we energetically bathed in our mutual admiration for our radiant Queen Mother. After sharing a silent prayer for peace on Earth, I touched my heart and bowed to him in gratitude. I then quietly walked out the cathedral, passing through the large wooden doors to reunite with the vibrant midday sun. Out in the courtyard, I saw an adjacent small chapel and entered with curiosity. It was considerably sparse in contrast to the previous large cathedral. I took a seat on one of the wooden benches, closed my eyes as if to recover from a lifetime of seeking outside of myself and softly sang a song written by a friend of mine, Kevin James Carrol. 'Some days I walk on flowers, some days I walk on stones, but today I walk on love – taking the long way home.'

And then the voice of Sophia chimed in, *'Sometimes what one seeks does not turn up until the end of a very long road. It's not that it suddenly appears – it's just that one needs to gain the eyes to see what has been there all along. It is time to go, dear one.'*

I smiled inside. *Now that's Divine timing!*

I walked slowly down the meandering path and out of the quaint village, savouring my brief moments of communion with the priest. The precious feeling of sharing our silent adoration for Sophia and the Sacred Feminine would forever be imprinted upon my heart. I marveled at the divine providence of meeting each and every random person along my journey. Whether a bus driver, a priest or a perfect stranger, I had come to know that these arbitrary rendezvous were pre-destined contracts, appointed by the Divine, each one of them playing a vital role on the journey home to the beloved.

By the time I got to the road, there was no bus in sight. So I chose to walk down the steep mountain and try my luck at hitching a ride. A few metres down the winding road, I was scooped up by a couple of vibrant expat women from England in their VW bug. They dropped me off at the fishing village, where I could catch the next bus back to Kardamyli. I was being called to return to the beach where I had been baptised with Sananda standing in as my sacred witness. Tiny butterflies flittered in my belly, indicating that there might be yet another surprise for me on the horizon.

Goddess only knows what on Earth Sophia has in store for me now!

CHAPTER FIFTY-FIVE

THE WATERFALL ROOM

Whatever your terror and whatever the sacrifice,
grow the royal rose-heart and step into the eternal garden.
For this dissolution you were created.
For this flowering beyond death you were born.
Refuse this destiny, and you refuse yourself.
You thought that when your house was burnt down
There would be nothing left but ash.
But look, moonlight is dancing on white roses!

– Jelaluddin Rumi

My soul ain't got no room for apocalypse doom and gloom,
let the truth be known.
I have remembered the power of the flowing water
to smooth the stone.
So come to the waterfall child, wash away flesh and bone.
Come to the waterfall child; water smooths all the stone.

– Joules Graves, 'Waterfall Child'

Join with the Goddess and God
Who are making love in every particle of creation...
And with every breath Bless the life that surrounds you.
The light of consciousness illumines the world.
The world reflects this splendor.

Energy and matter, essence and manifestation
Reveal each other to each other.
Individual soul and cosmic energy
Pulsing heart and infinite awareness –
Are secret lovers, always merging in Oneness.
When the secret slips out, there is laughter
And a flash of brilliance in the air.

– Sheikh An-sari, *The Radiance Sutras*

When the bus dropped me back off in Kardamyli, I followed my intuition into one of the dusty old shops. This one looked much like the others, as if it hadn't had a good cleaning for at least half a century. It sold fishing equipment, woven bags, Pepsi Cola and a variety of antique relics revered by the Greek Orthodox religion. I noticed a basket full of rings by the cash register. Mixed up among various, rusty brass rings of different designs, one leapt out at me. It was a golden double spiral, the only one of its kind. I wondered how long it had sat there, invisible to the ordinary eye.

'This must be my Heiros Gamos ring!' I pronounced aloud to the shopkeeper. I had no idea whether she understood English or not, but it didn't matter. In that moment, this voluptuous woman, who stood slightly bent over from a lifetime of kneading bread and pressing olives, was my grandmother. She blessed me with her ebony eyes and large toothless grin as I slid the double spiral ring onto my ring finger.

What a perfect symbol for this day, I thought. I reflected, *The double spiral is symbolic for the spiral of creation, death and rebirth, entering the mysterious underworld of the Earth womb, penetrating to its core and passing out again by the same route. It represents the relationship of the finite to the infinite, all things coming into balance – and as synchronicity has it, it's a symbol for the equinox!*

I walked to the beach admiring the golden double spiral that hugged my finger beautifully, as if the ring was made just for this day. This time when I arrived at the beach, I was not alone. A Swiss man in his late sixties with a long grey beard was camping out with his small caravan. We greeted one another warmly.

'Ello. Would you like to share my pomegranate with me?' he inquired in broken English.

'Sure,' I responded, feeling totally comfortable in his kind presence.

'Look, I found this praying mantis,' he said, and then placed it on my hand as if it was yet another wedding gift prepared just for me. I accepted his offering quite naturally. Amazingly, the Praying Mantis remained poised on my hand for the entire half hour of our conversation. I noticed how animated he was, like a friend out of a fairytale, fearlessly hanging out and being fully present with me. I was extremely curious as to what medicine this noble creature carried since it lingered with such lucid and aware presence. Later on I discovered that the word "mantis" comes from the Greek language, and its meaning is "prophet" or "seer." It is also related to the word "menos" which means, "spirit" and "passion." Therefore, the praying mantis is often seen as a symbol of someone with clairvoyant abilities as well as someone who is a master at meditation. Spirit will often use the praying mantis to send a message to whomever it chooses as a reminder to slow down and enjoy each moment of each day and the connections you make with other people. The praying mantis teaches us to be patient and to wait. As the old adage says, "good things come to all those who wait."

I thanked Eric for the conversation and delicious fruit, and then walked to the sea with my vibrant praying mantis friend hitching a ride on my hand. We had grown rather fond of one another. How magnificent to be blessed by this beautiful long-legged creature that seems to be so at home hanging with me.

The praying mantis rested on the top of my palm as we walked further down the beach. After finding the perfect spot, I placed my new friend gently on a rock, laid out my sarong and undressed. Once again, I laid belly down upon the round blue and white stones and soaked up the heat that radiated from their smooth surface. The warm stones magically melted away all of the tension I had been holding in my belly from arranging my travel plans the prior day. My skin drank in the afternoon sun shower. My womb melted, softened and opened like a flower, soaking in the mana of the Earth that cradled me. My heart synchronised with the heartbeat of Gaia.

I listened to the surrounding sounds of birds calling to one another and a young child laughing in delight in the near distance.

I was mesmerised by the gentle waves lapping over the stones, bringing out each of their unique colours and patterns until they would dry with the sun, fade and then be revivified by the next wave. These stones had endured thousands of years of being tossed and tumbled by the tide, and as a result, they have lost their rough edges and have become almost translucent and silky smooth all the way round. I honoured each of them as conscious beings, triumphant for their sovereign togetherness. Each had miraculously washed up to the shore to be reunited with the rest of their tribe. I lazily turned over to allow the sun to warm my front and felt into my sun-kissed belly. Just like the stones, it was soft and smooth, which I attributed to breathing deeply through the rougher tides of my life.

As I inhaled long deep breaths, my belly inflated like a large balloon and then I would let it all go, dissolve into emptiness and merge with all of existence. In my next deep breath, I concentrated on the still singular point at the centre of my heart. I repeated this cleansing until my breath synchronised with the ebb and flow of the incoming tide. My eyes gently closed and within seconds I fell into a state of lucid awareness. An invisible door opened in the centre of my heart where I entered into a Crystal cathedral and sat upon a beautiful lotus throne.

A shimmering milky white pink and golden presence appeared in front of me. It was Sananda. He was wearing a white linen robe that hung elegantly off his broad shoulders. A long mala of sandalwood beads hung from his robust neck. He was vividly present – as if the very sun was shining through his skin. I relished the gentle warmth emanating from his radiant open heart. He knelt down next to my body and began the energetic transmission of anointing each of my chakras. His broad hand glided over my crown and then moved down to my third eye, throat, heart, solar plexus, navel and root chakra. He focused on each energy centre with a penetrating light that unfurled the petals of each chakra until each one blossomed like a rose in full bloom. Wave upon wave of pulsating pristine energy rippled through my body, infusing it with an all-pervading love likened to what I felt back at the ceremony in Gaia's Grove. Sananda then telepathically transmitted the following words:

'Beloved One, I invite you to join me in the silence of your innermost heart. Here, you will find your forever home while being connected to the

whole of creation. As the old layers of the chrysalis fall away, you may feel raw, vulnerable and exposed. You are embodying the birth of a new expression...the birth of love, wisdom and power into the dominion of your humanness. As your heart softens, the radiance of your true essence shines through. Your choice to stay open even when you feel fear is what forges the gold from which the Grail cup is made. By embodying the soul/love that is the light shining through your essence, the body becomes a living chalice, the Grail, and you become the vessel that blesses and gives life to the world. Always remember, your power lies in choosing the way of the open heart. Just as I was initiated into greater realms of love and compassion, so will you be. Time and time again, you will be asked to stand strong in the fire of chaos and remain true to a Love that transcends all illusion. Your capacity to remain grounded in a larger Love when the shaking storms come creates a rainbow bridge for yourself and others to travel out of density and into the light. I am the heart of the diamond Sun and I Am with you always.'

Sananda placed his right hand over his heart while the other palm stretched open along his left side. He sent me an energetic blessing that made me shudder from head to toe in goddess bumps. After a timeless moment of silent communion, he flashed me an inner smile that felt like a bear hug from the sun. We closed our little ritual by bowing our heads and sharing communion in the sanctum of our shared heart. He then vanished from my awareness. *Poof, gone, gone, gone, beyond.*

It took me some moments to integrate what had just transpired. I sensed that my bio-energetic field had been totally recalibrated and upgraded. I walked in awe to the water's edge and gazed at the shimmering sunlight dancing upon the glassy surface. As I squatted down and put both hands into the wet sand, I could feel all of the dimensions spiraling within me, unifying the inner and the outer, the microcosm and the macrocosm in a symbiotic dance of all Oneness. I heard a celestial sound blessing from the cetaceans of the sea conjoin with the radiant presence of the Christos Sophia wedded in perfect unison. This celestial symphony audible to the inner ear was the sound of Sacred Union.

Still squatting at the shore with my palms pressed into my heart, I remained mesmerised by the shimmering diamonds made by the sunlight dancing on the water, forever reminding me of the Solar Logos making love to his bride, Sophia. I placed a hand on my womb and one on my heart and I knew that the inner and the outer were now wedded as One. *Heiros gamos... Om ah hum.*

CHAPTER FIFTY-SIX

A PERFECT STRANGER

We can learn how to heal the heart; our own heart and the heart of every creature. Healing the heart is about cherishing in every sense: cherishing the soul which has been neglected for so many centuries; cherishing the body which has been despised and rejected; cherishing the lives which have been entrusted to us; cherishing the Earth which is the great field of all our endeavor.

I have a final and inescapable responsibility to treat all beings and things with Divine love, Divine respect and Divine tenderness. The more I do so, the more I will grow in my own human divinity and the more I will experience, with ever greater intimacy and wonder, the Divine presence in every rose, every bird, every shifting play of wind in the grasses, every fern and pokeweed. To know the truth of your Divine consciousness is to see it reflected back at you from all living things. To deepen that experience constantly, through adoration, wonder, insight and direct service and action is why we are here.

– Andrew Harvey

Women are the most beautiful embodiment of empowered awakening. We breathe life into the world with the heave of our body, sing the sacred into song with our soul, and heal the deepest of wounds with our boundless heart. Love is calling us all to remember the eternal ecstasy of Being. Love calls for women to claim their deepest truth and to rise to fulfill the authentic self. We women are awakening. We women are rising. I am a woman rising.

– Ani Kaspar

Gratitude unlocks the fullness of life. It turns what we have into enough, and more. It can turn a meal into a feast, a house into a home, a stranger into a friend. Gratitude makes sense of our past, brings peace for today and creates a vision for tomorrow.

– Melody Beattie

Before making my way back to the village of Kalamata, I devoured a greek salad and plate of french fries at the local café. Eating french fries was my silly way of celebrating my wedding day. I enjoyed dipping each one into the ketchup, just like I remembered doing as a little kid. 'Yum. What would a celebration be without french fries? I mean, Greek fries!'

Upon returning to Mani, I was guided to stop at the Internet café to check my emails. I was surprised to receive a group email forwarded to me from one of my yoga students from back in Marin County.

> We deeply regret to inform you that our beloved friend Barry has crashed his plane while attempting to land it at Burning Man. His eight-year-old son was with him. Neither Barry nor his son survived the crash. Please join us in attending a Memorial Service for them on September 26th, 2003. They were greatly loved and will be missed. May they rest in peace.

My heart took a nosedive into my stomach. Now I knew why I had felt such a strong sinking feeling of loss the other day when I visited the Sophia Church! Barry had been a special friend of mine. He attended my yoga classes in Marin. After class, he would take the time to check in with me and ask me how my life was going. I remembered paying him a special visit while he was relaxing outside his cabana during our Wild Divine yoga retreat that I facilitated in Costa Rica. He felt so raw and vulnerable as he confided in me, 'I could not imagine that so much would come up for me to feel and to heal. I thought I was just going on a simple yoga vacation. I feel all that I have buried within me is now rising to the surface. It is almost too much to bear. How is it possible for one heart to feel this much?'

At the time, I could not recall my response to Barry. I imagined answering his question from the glimpses of wisdom I was now gleaning from my own dark night of the soul.

Dearest Barry, I so understand how overwhelming it can be to confront what lies beneath the surface. As beings of love, we are learning to love our Self in both shadow and light! We are also learning to trust that everything that rises from the depths of our soul carries a hidden gift, waiting to be embraced by our tender heart. By being in gratitude for the simplest things, throwing our self into nature, breathing deeply, asking for support when needed and championing our self along the way, we become the remedy and the cure to every atrocity and trespass of our soul.

As we both know, yoga is all about the yoking of opposites. Our practice supports us to cultivate the inner strength and soul stamina to embrace everything that comes our way or was once cast out as too unbearable to feel and digest. Our raw vulnerability and willingness to traverse the most hidden aspects of our being is our pathway to grace. When life brings us to our knees, we can have faith in a divine higher power to lift us up. As we dare to stay open while touching the bottom of the well of our pain, we will be met by a tender love and an unending wellspring of creative passion. Just as a caterpillar is consumed by its own flesh, we are each called to trust the larger version of our Self being born. Thank you for blessing my life, Barry. I love you and I miss you already.

Suddenly, I was interrupted. 'Excuse me. Excuse me! Are you done with the computer?' The young traveller finally got my attention, startling me back from my daydream with Barry.

'Yes, of course,' I said, still lost in paying homage to my dear friend. I logged off the computer and then walked out onto the beach and let my feet sink into the soft white cushion of sand. I took out my journal and wrote feverishly by the light of the setting sun.

22 September 2003

The veils are so very thin right now. I can feel the narrow window between life and death. For now, I am here, in the flesh! I am aware that in order to live in the full translucent light of my authentic being, I must die to each and every moment – while I'm still alive! I must surrender all that I am and all that I know myself to be – over and over again – to be reborn into this sacred now. This full-bodied surrender is what makes life so very precious. I fully accept that there is nothing or no one out there that will offer me safety or security. Everything is in a state of flux, ebbing and flowing and turning over into something brand new. The inevitability of constant change creates an ongoing opportunity for me to stay grounded in my open heart and rooted in my golden core. That much I can trust and the rest is about faith. Every moment that I get to fully be alive and experience the miracle of life is a gift to be cherished beyond all measure.

My stomach began to growl, reminding me that it was time for my last supper here in the precious jewel of Mani. I tucked away my journal and headed up the winding boardwalk to find a restaurant. Out of a handful of possible options, I chose to dine at the café where I had previously exchanged a heart smile with the waiter.

The pandemic of isolation and loneliness upon this overpopulated planet seemed to be the most perplexing and preposterous phenomena of all. In my current state of awareness, there was no longer an 'other'. *All are the beloved – no matter what kind of asleep or sour mood they might temporarily be in.*

I once heard that the root meaning of human is 'dispenser of gifts'. And the meaning of God is to be 'generous'! I imagined an awakened world of divine humans in which the true currency of wealth was defined as the generous dispensation of one's gifts that circulate as blessings for the benefit of all beings. *Wow, what a wonderful world it would be!*

As I walked to the café, taking each step as a prayer, I pondered why anyone would opt out of the opportunity to exchange a heart smile with another precious being. I cherished each and every magical glance, spontaneously shared with a so-called stranger. Every encounter was a golden opportunity to exchange a spontaneous gift! In a flash, one could offer a burst of gratitude, beam a warm smile, offer a silent blessing or simply celebrate the miracle of being alive in the most mundane of moments! More importantly, I was acutely aware of the intrinsic value of each and every being and that our very survival as a species was contingent on moving beyond the separate me into the interconnected we. As we do, we will rediscover the contagion that everybody wants to catch – the joy of being alive.

As I looked for a place to sit down at the restaurant, the sound system was playing the oh so familiar 'Mrs Robinson' song. I marvelled at how that same song would resurface again and again at different points of the journey. I used to listen to Simon and Garfunkel growing up as a child in the 1970s. Now after so many years, it was as if this particular song was a time capsule, destined to magically reopen for exactly this moment in time.

Wow, I thought, as I looked up at the canopy of stars. The return to the heart of the wild Divine Sophia was encoded to ripen within me lifetimes ago, and Simon and Garfunkel have been there to serenade me all along the way.

We'd like to know a little bit about you for our files
We'd like to help you learn to help yourself
Look around you, all you see are sympathetic eyes
Stroll around the grounds until you feel at home
And here's to you, Mrs. Robinson
Jesus loves you more than you will know
Whoa, whoa, whoa
God bless you, please, Mrs. Robinson
Heaven holds a place for those who pray
Hey hey hey, hey hey hey

– Simon and Garfunkel, 'Mrs Robinson'

The barefoot and ever-so-charming waiter sauntered over to my table as if he had all the time in the world. *Ah, the beloved has come to take my order,* I grinned to myself, amused by the poetic irony of the Divine.

'Hello, Madame. What would you like for your dinner?'

Looking into his smiling eyes, I decided to splurge a little and celebrate. After all, it was not only my Inner Marriage wedding night; it was also my last supper in Mani. 'I'll have the grilled salmon and garden salad. Oh yes, and a glass of your house red wine, please.'

'Good choice. I will be back shortly with your wine.' His gaze lingered with mine for a timeless moment. I relished the feeling of closeness as our beings opened to see the kindred soul light in the other. While he put in my order, I considered the greetings I knew that translated to, 'I see the Divine in you' such as, namaste, aloha, salute, sat nam, salam, shalom, om swastiastu, kiora, and so forth. I imagined a new heart-centred humanity greeting one another this way and genuinely feeling the profundity of what it means to see and be seen through the eyes of Divinity.

The waiter returned with my glass of wine. As he placed it on the table with a flourish, he flashed me a smile that melted away the remnants of sorrow from hearing about my brother Barry's transition.

Wow, is he flirting with me? I pondered bashfully, noticing my raw and tender heart becoming all warm and tingly.

Oh my goddess, he most certainly is! I concluded, and so I flirted back. This flirting was novel; it had little to do with the personal self. Instead, we were connecting with the divine spark that we had recognised in one another. In a singular glance, we drew back our heart feathers and allowed the other to see directly into the other's unique soul essence. Pure love flowed, and within an instant of dedicated presence, all was fully felt and known. *I love this being. He loves me. We are the beloved. We share a timeless supernatural connection. It's as simple and sexy as that!*

Within the span of an hour of being in each other's presence, we lived an entire love story that sparkled with an entirely new kind of romance, totally free of all agenda, or need to get something out of being together. There is an unstoppable creativity in this kind of cosmic universal connection, a unique power is released when one feels the other as oneself within the miraculous Oneness of it all. *Wow, it is such a turn-on to see and be seen, feel and be felt, love and be loved just because we can!*

This barefoot King brought me a beautifully arranged plate of food as if to present it to his Queen. I bowed my head, silently thanking him for making my last supper in Mani an extra special one. Then I noticed the music changed to a new song. My ears perked up toward the stereo speakers as I listened intently to yet another seventies classic by Cat Stevens:

> People get ready, there's a train comin'
> You don't need no baggage, you just get on board
> All you need is faith to hear the diesels hummin'
> You don't need no ticket you just thank the Lord!

After dinner, I walked down to the ocean. I cried, I laughed, I prayed, I sobbed, I twirled, I moaned, I danced and stomped my feet until I fell to my knees, placing my face into my hands and wondered if the world would wake up in time? *Would I – would we make that train?*

Across the ocean and the brilliant night sky, I looked to the stars and sent a prayer out to Barry.

Oh Barry, I know you are on that love train bound for freedom! I feel so blessed to have known you and practiced jungle asanas with you! I will always cherish your adventurous spirit, loyal friendship and your warm glowing heart. When I look to the stars, I will look for your bright-eyed smile shining back at me, encouraging me to be brave and feel everything as a gift to grow ever onward. Bon voyage and blessings on your journey. I will always love you.

PS: Please give John Lennon and Robin Williams a Heavenly bear hug for me!

BRING ON THE NEW

Be the king who has made his own kingdom.
Be the moon that has made her own summit.
How much longer
Will you coo coo like a pigeon?
Empty your head of all mortal lusts,
And become life without breath.
You will not call out for God anymore
For you have become immersed in God.

– Jelaluddin Rumi

I burnish bright the mirror of my heart
until at last, reflected for my rapture,
the Self's eternal beauty appears.
If you think of the rose,
You will become the rose.
If you think of the nightingale
You will become the nightingale
You are a drop:
Divine Being is the ocean.
While you still live,
Hold steadily before you
The vision of the whole
And you will be whole.

– Zeb-un-Nisa

My journal had carried me through this Grail journey as my loyal companion. On my last day in Greece, I wrote for a long while, curled up like a cat on a blanket on the sea shore while soaking up the morning sun.

23 September 2003

Last night, in my excitement, I could barely sleep a wink and rose early with the sun. Today, I will board the super deluxe ferry and head to my next destination, Turin, Italy!

I am still uncertain as to how this happened, but somewhere between getting up in the night and going to the bathroom, I sliced my finger. Ouch! It was a tiny cut and yet it bled and throbbed throughout the night. I noticed the colour was bright red, like a cherry lollipop held up to the sunlight. Last night, while examining my finger, I took time to appreciate the bright colour of my blood and acknowledged how the last two weeks have been such a precious opportunity to clear the gunk that has clouded my natural state of joy. I had come to understand that whatever we actually survive through our challenging experiences, we transmute for the whole. What a profound honour it is to stand upon the shoulders of my heroic ancestors and do my part to clear the cobwebs of illusion carried over lifetimes and generations!

I am aware that something profound has shifted in relation to what I once called the ghosts of my ancestral past. The spell has been broken, the karmic knots untied, my beloved ancestors set free. I remember a master guide once telling me, that it only takes one being to see from a new perception for the whole pattern to change. The Creator has bestowed each one of us with the innate power to liberate an entire species. Wow! I'm so grateful for what each individual has courageously chosen to experience and therefore transmute for the One. As each sheds the husk that has protected our most bejeweled essence, the seed of our highest potential blossoms forth as a gift that blesses and enlivens the whole.

Before departing Elena who became my crucible for rebirth, I smudged the space and called my energy back to me. I imagined my family constellation now dramatically shifted in its new configuration, and in turn, all of the stars of the universe growing all the more brighter for it.

Goodbye, Elena. Goodbye, tea kettle and blue-ribboned strawberry quilt. You were the perfect companions for my underworld journey. I then grabbed my gear, closed the door behind me and scampered down the hill to catch the local bus to Kalamata City. From there I would connect to the super-deluxe overnight ferry. I had grown fond of the scraggly ol' bus driver along with his grimy shirts, stubbly face, grumpy disposition and savoured my last ride.

After settling into my seat, I noticed an infant who sat contently on her mother's lap. Like Madonna and child, they were glowing with a supernal beauty. I literally saw a halo of light surrounding the both of them. The voice of Sophia spoke gently to me:

'There is a new generation of awakened children who have come to seed the New Earth with their fully activated Divine attributes. They are born with the full body remembrance of being part of the whole of creation, where all life is interconnected, held in sanctity and nourished by the Source of original Love, Life and Joy. They are free of the density and karmic imprints embedded within the carbon-based DNA. Instead, they inhabit their fully activated crystalline DNA and live in a multi-dimensional relationship with Source, Self, Divinity. These new beloveds will bring gifts to our world that are truly beyond our imagining. They will be Children of the Sacred Now, carrying every frequency with harmonic perfection in a fully balanced spectrum of light that comes from the Source of all things. As gifted empaths, healers, teachers, and spiritual leaders, their presence will forever change the lives of those around them. They will be magical creatures, Guardians of the New Earth, Wayshowers of the

awakened heart who will demonstrate what has always been and what can be in our world again-if we will only open our hearts and remember that we are one and love is all there is.'

I quietly observed a mother and child sitting in the adjacent seat. She was nursing her daughter while smiling into her sparkling emerald eyes. Their gazes were locked in bliss-filled communion as I discretely admired their seamless communion. *Wow, I can hardly imagine the exquisite gifts to come from this new generation with all of their life force plugged straight into the infinite source of the divine!*

My meditation with mother and child was soon interrupted as the perspiring bus driver shouted out in a thick Greek accent, 'Kalamata City!'

'That's me!'

I changed buses and boarded the super-deluxe air-conditioned bus from Kalamata City to Patras, where I was to catch the super-deluxe ferry to Ancona, Italy. Just after settling into my seat, I had to shield myself from the 'super-deluxe' air conditioning that blasted onto my bare, sun-kissed skin. I went from being hot and sweaty to absolutely freezing my bum off in a matter of seconds! Above each seat was a small-screened TV that featured Arnold Schwarzenegger blowing up multiple objects and people. *No way! Isn't that the new governor of California?* I closed my eyes to make it all disappear and put myself into a hypnotic trance nap.

'Ambe´ tuning out Ah-nold. Ambe´ tuning out Ah-nold,' I repeated softly to myself as I dove deep into my imaginary goddess spring, just like the one I visited in the Pyrenees. I envisioned myself submerged under the warm thermal water as if to drown out the sound of machine guns going off in repetitive fire from the TV.

After twenty minutes of determined naptime in the refrigerated bus, I felt a warm, sensual mouth meeting mine, which instantly awoke me from my nap. The kiss felt totally life-like, warm, deliciously fulfilling and most of all, the kiss of a prince. I inwardly asked, *To whom do these lips belong?*

Then I heard Aiden's boyish Australian-accent reply, *'Tis I reaching out to you. The truth is I miss you and I want to see you again, Bella. Meet me in Barcelona.'* I immediately sobered up from my deep trance to better ascertain the presence of my surprise guest. His soft, warm lips felt vividly sensual and ever so real.

Is this my fantasy, my imagination, a deep unconscious desire conjuring up his voice? Am I projecting his undeniable life-like presence?

I needed some clarity, so I called upon Sophia for guidance and support. I heard her clear and compassionate voice speak to me over the television.

'Dear child, it is good to be discerning when you get such an unexpected visit. Put your question inside a golden chalice and ask your Divinity to reveal the truth to you now. You will know this truth by the feelings you get in your body. If you feel nauseous and sick, well, there you have it. If you feel your heart warm or washed in exhilaration or joy, well, that also speaks truth.'

Okay, I thought, as I dropped back into a meditative state and scanned my body for clues. I concluded that I felt Aiden's warm presence to be true. He was definitely making affectionate, energetic contact with me. And yet, I was unclear as to his authentic motivation. I sensed that I was being tested in some way and needed to meet him with laser-like discernment. It would be so easy to give in to my fairytale inclinations, but now was the time to be very, very honest with myself...to renounce the fantasy for the sobering reality.

Just like a Venus fly trap, was I being allured into his sumptuous web of deceit?

I became aware of the part of me that still longed for a 'happily ever after' with Aiden. For a brief moment, I allowed myself to imagine him grabbing me closely to his chest, just as he did on the first night we met in the forest at the Pyrenees Rainbow Gathering. This time he would kiss me passionately and say, 'Ambe´, I wish you to take this very, very personally. He would kiss me deeply on the mouth, then twirl me by my fingertips and dip me into a graceful backbend while holding me tightly around the waist. Then he would look me passionately in the eyes while piercing my heart wide open and say, 'What a fool I've been for leaving you all alone in a world so cold!'

A deep sigh escaped my lips, and I felt the ghost of a smile. Then I felt totally sick to my stomach. My wise parental voice chimed in with a touch of loving irony. *Are you out of your mind? Wake up and feel the freezing cold air conditioner! Earth to Ambe´. Come in, Major Ambe´. This is Ground Control to Major Ambe´. Can you hear me, Major Ambe´?*

David Bowie's 'Space Oddity' song played on in my mind as if to add some well-needed levity to the situation. *'And I'm floating in a most peculiar way. And the stars look very different today. For here am I, sitting in a tin can. Far above the world. Planet Earth is blue and there's nothing I can do.'*

I admitted to myself, *Aiden may have come for a visit on the inner planes to share an affectionate kiss, but he was definitely not coming to find me on his gallant white horse and sweep me off my feet.*

This yearning was not about love as much as the false promise of love. I was being shown how my naïve innocence lacked vital discernment, which had led me to override my essential core values. I was being nudged to inhabit a more mature version of myself – to fall more in love with reality than with any wishful fantasy.

What felt genuine was a desire to reconnect with Aiden for the sake of making healthy closure, a closure that honoured our friendship from a place of radical self-responsibility, respect and gratitude for what we shared together as a gift that profoundly shifted the course of our lives. I noticed the part of me that still longed to end this leg of my journey on a sweet rather than a sour note. Little did I know at the time that I would have to bear this lack of conscious closure for years to come.

Suddenly, in an attempt to avoid running a red light, the bus came to a screeching halt, jolting me forward in my seat – and back to my present reality. I looked out of the window and observed that we were travelling through a large city. I reminded myself that I was on my way to Italy to visit The Shroud of Turin.

I'll be with you soon, Beloved Yeshua, I consoled myself humorously. *I'm OK with the fact that you are a shroud and not a living, breathing human being!*

With the jolting of the bus, a sober knowingness washed through my bones. *I must return to Saintes-Maries-de-la-Mer! There is something of great importance I must retrieve before returning to America.* I took several deep breaths to gather a second wind and affirmed to myself, *My epic love story is far from over yet! In truth, I have only just begun.* Once again, I snuggled deep into myself and dozed off to the sound of Rambo firing rapid ammunition from the TV screen hovering above my head.

Descending into my inner cave of treasures, I immediately returned to a vivid trance state where I experienced a diamond star illuminate my heart and third eye. A multi-dimensional doorway opened in my mind's eye. I stepped through and attuned my frequency to the Divine Christos Sophia. I felt Aiden's presence enter my awareness once again. I wondered if this was yet another test in choosing Self over the allure of joining with the fantasy of another. This time, I responded by bowing respectfully, then firmly requesting him to leave my energetic field just as he once exemplified to me when he was dismissing my entourage of invisible helpers.

I heard the voice of my soul speak clearly, *this is your moment to reclaim your power. Your experience is dependent on how deeply you are caring for and loving yourself. When you love yourself instead of relying on others to give you back your power in such a difficult and heartbreaking way, you become the soul mate that you were once seeking in the other. When you become the source of your own fulfillment and love, you can manifest a balanced counterpart to provide you with what you have already given yourself.*

This is the time to complete your story of needing to complete 'oneself' through joining with the 'other'! Within you lives an entirely unique, pristinely precious gift of Divine Source. In other words YOU, my dear, are the super-deluxe, first-class, all-inclusive ticket to the love that you seek!

At first, I hesitated. I knew I was being tested. I felt into that stubborn part of me that was still reluctant to fully release Aiden – the charismatic lover, the promise and the dream. I felt into the last vestiges of resistance to fully claim the Beloved I AM, the one I had come to embrace on the shores of Kardamyli.

The bus screeched into the station. This was my last stop before crossing over to Italy. *Okay, Sophia, I get it, I let go, I let go! I let it all go! Whooooosh!*

I recalled the Tibetan sand mandala being destroyed and then offered up to the San Francisco Bay and recited this prayer under my breath, *Just like the sand put out to sea, I lovingly let go and set Aiden free! Just like the sand put out to sea, I lovingly let go and set myself free! Just like the sand put out to sea, I lovingly let go and set my LOVE free! Goodbye, beloved friend. May you and all beings be happy and free. Om tare tuttare ture svaha*

I gathered my backpack and departed the super-deluxe bus, relieved to get out of the blasting-cold air conditioner and *The Terminator* movie. The afternoon sun instantly thawed my tight muscles and frigid bones. I noticed I felt more relaxed within myself and at peace with the choice to shift my relationship with Aiden. I was at a crossroads; there was nothing more that I could do but to leap into the boundless and make it my home.

CHAPTER FIFTY-EIGHT

DREAM WEAVER

So the sea journey goes on, and who knows where!
Just to be held by the ocean is the best luck we could have.
It's a total waking up!
Why should we grieve that we've been sleeping?
It doesn't matter that we have been unconscious.
We're groggy but let the guilt go.
Feel the motions of tenderness
Around you, the buoyancy.

– Jelaluddin Rumi

May the Grace of God be with you always, in your heart
May you know the truth inside you from the start
May you find the strength to know that you are a
Part of something beautiful...

– Celtic Blessing

A very, *very* handsome man in a tuxedo, complete with an impeccably ironed, crisp white shirt and black bow tie, welcomed me aboard the super-deluxe ferry! *Wow, that man is super deluxe gorgeous. Did I just swoon?* I found myself grinning from head to toe.

I walked through the maze of lined-up cars and up the shiny metal stairway to the second floor. I proceeded onto the rear deck to watch the ferry pull away from Patras. Tears poured down my cheeks as I watched the Greek island that I had grown to cherish fade away like a mirage in a dream. I recalled how I had wrestled with the angelic travel agent in Brighton, strongly doubting his intuition to send me off to the sleepy town of Mani as the perfect restorative holiday for me. *Who would have ever known that it would be the place where I would meet the Queen of Heaven, Sophia, and kiss the feet of the Beloved!*

The Greek shoreline was barely visible – my paradise had now vanished into the horizon. I offered a prayer of gratitude for all of the precious jewels I had retrieved from Kalamata. I sent my travel agent a telepathic memo: *'Sometimes the most exquisite gems are the ones that are hidden from plain sight. I want you to know that I received more than I could have ever bargained for and I am so grateful to you. Best underworld holiday ever!'*

I was excited to explore the ship and find the best place to have a celebratory drink. After a quick peruse, I found the smoke-free lounge, ordered a glass of Italian red wine and glanced around to see if there was anyone interesting to converse with. Since it appeared that I was the only one in the entire lounge area, I took up company with the flat screen TV hanging from the wall. The movie *Vanilla Sky* was playing, dubbed in Greek with English subtitles. Tom Cruise wore a wool ski mask that covered his mouth while the prison psychologist, played by Kurt Russell, interrogated him. I could not believe my ears as he flashed back on his love obsession with a woman named Sophia, played by Penelope Cruz.

Really? My ears perked up. *Sophia? What about Sophia?* I listened intently, straining my ears to hear over the swanky lounge music that drowned out the sound of the movie. I was able to surmise that Tom Cruise was trying to discern between a waking dream and a lucid dream. The dialogue between the psychologist and him concluded by saying, 'Love is so powerful it can totally obscure what is "real" and what is a "dream." In this scenario of cinematic love, Tom Cruise's character had lost all sense of self and reality.

This is sounding absurdly familiar, I thought, as I listened even more intently to the dialogue. The movie got even more serendipitous as Tom Cruise's character called David, while in a lucid dream state, called upon Dream Tech Support.

An AI angel appeared and said, 'You have a choice. You can continue to stay imprisoned in your lucid dream or wake up within it and deal with what is real. However, in order for you to wake up David, you must be willing to face your greatest fear. In this case, you must face your fear of heights and jump off the top of this building.'

David responded, 'I want to live a real life, I don't want to dream any longer.' And then, just before David leaps off the edge of a hundred story skyscraper, he says, 'Every passing minute is another chance to turn it all around.'

I sat there astounded as I witnessed David's choice to wake up inside his dream and face his greatest fear all in the name of Love.

I used the TV Oracle as an opportunity to ask myself, *Ambe´, what is your greatest fear that keeps you wishing something happens or doesn't happen?'* I answered, *Going through this life alone, with no one to share it with.*

Again, the voice of Sophia spoke. *'Everything on the inner has a corresponding vibrational match on the outer. That is how it all works. When you meet yourself intimately in unconditional love, the frequency is created for another to meet you there. The outer is always a direct reflection of the inner. Know and feel yourself as the beloved and you will see and feel the beloved reflected back to you in all. By the way, next time you happen to find yourself feeling lonely, remember, in your solitude is where you find your All-Oneness! From this higher vantage point, we are truly All-One. Now get some rest, beloved one. Tomorrow is yet another full day!'*

I swallowed the last of my red wine and walked on deck to take in the sea view. The night sky was clear and the Venus star was glistening in plain sight. Being ferried across the ocean was the perfect metaphor for leaving one world and entering into another.

Tibetans talk about the bardo realms being the in-between place you go after you die to integrate all that you learned from the prior life. It is also the place to prepare to be reborn into your next incarnation. I looked to the Venus star and felt myself between the worlds where all timelines, realities and dimensions dissolve into one vast open and unformatted space. I was being ferried from one shore to another, sailing between the tick and the tock. *Set sail, set sail, set sail, set sail. One thing becomes another in the arms of the Mother.*

I reflected with awe on the extraordinarily synchronised, thought-done-reality that I was experiencing. There seemed to be no gap between my thoughts and how they manifested in front of me. Every internal process that I moved through was being reflected back to me as a facet of the diamond of my true Self. Whether through dreams, movies, songs, symbols, signs, animals or chance meetings, I was living in a hall of mirrors. The movie of my life was slowed down just enough so that I could see every reflection as an invitation to create something novel through my clear perception and deliberate response. Every unknown doorway was an opportunity to trust deeper and open more. With each threshold I courageously dared to cross, I discovered a more expanded version of myself as an awakened dreamer, co-creating my greater-than-imagined reality. In essence, I was being shown the plasmic nature of the connected universe and how all of my movements, whether conscious or unconscious, rippled through, impacting the fabric of the whole.

The rocking of the sea, glass of red wine and cosmic downloads made me more than ready to retire to my sleeping quarters and enter dreamtime. I was filled with joyous anticipation for the next chapter and enjoyed the pause of being ferried through the night to Italy – the country renowned for mouthwatering food, stunning fashion and breathtakingly beautiful living Madonnas.

That night, I dreamt that I was pregnant. I had one contraction and waited for more to follow, but they never came. I lay suspended between waking and sleeping, wondering what it would take to give birth to the golden child that lay perfectly still within my heart womb. I understood that my life would continue to be a series of inevitable births whose timing was utterly in the hands of the Divine.

CHAPTER FIFTY-NINE

RAINBOW STARBIRD

The Grail is not an object to gain, but something we become. Such individuals will be Feminine Christs – not born of the womb but of the sanctified heart.

– Niamh Clune, The Coming of the Feminine Christ

When a Priestess is truly seated on her own throne, she realises that she carries the throne within her. Our bodies are the temple of our souls. To be seated on the throne is to be well placed inside our own sacred chambers, deeply grounded in the root of Mother Earth, well seated in the center of our belly, as we connect to the stars and the sky and let the Goddess's inspiration, her words and actions flow through us.

– Gaia Codex: Node 34215.955

DIVINE EMBODIMENT

How do I view myself...
The words that I speak...
The being that I embody...
My deepest feelings...
My inner self-talk...
My attitude towards life...
My accountability...
and my presence...
Are the vehicles of my manifested reality.

Realising that it is a choice to empower
and love myself unconditionally,
with the courage to accept the glory of exactly where I am.
Knowing that the unfoldment of my journey is perfectly whole.
May I continually shed all that is no longer serving me
for the most efficient movement of our unified destined path
with the stewardship of Mama Earth in highest mind
I move away from the traditional ingrained victimhood mentality,
and one who is angry at all the atrocities of life and make a decision
to instead step into this journey as an activated
Co-Creatrix of my life. I remember who I AM.
I am the Daughter of the Earth and Sister of the Stars.
I choose to be empowered by everything, as everything is already in its
Divinely aligned perfection.
So when I look in the mirror,
I can smile back at myself with admiration,
washing myself clean of old stories that no longer serve me...
rooted in my womb, standing in my presence
As an empty vessel alive and free
Breathing in infinite possibility.
I trust this life.
In all ways, with each gentle step I take.
Easily bringing dreams into fruition
because I am connected to the power of Divine Feminine and Masculine
aspects of myself understanding that the dissolve of both these polarities
allows me to once again
marinate in the all One essence of Light
I honour the fuel that comes from intuition and inspiration and when I
begin to embody this my life turns into a joyous orgasmic ride – to honor
this temple body and listen to its needs because I recognize that I am of
better service to others when I am in luscious overflow.
As only from a full cup can I truly give.
It is safe now to embody all I am – as the Earth needs conduits
for her divine reflection, knowing that us, just being ourselves –
"IS" the revolution,
so that we can remember the Eden for which we came.
We are un-tethered. It's time to spread our wings and take flight in our light.

*Living in our Divine duty to restoring the balance and sacredness of life
through the stewardship of our lands remaining present in the fullness of
this moment in breath.
Welcome Heaven on Earth
I can see you now
All divine beings... It is time...
We are in this together as one song.
Can we truly love ourselves...
So we can truly love others?
Embody what you already know
From your Divinely awakened Heart
Your courage.
Your fire.
Your light.
Shine.*

– Snow Forrest

An extremely loud siren trumpeted through my sleeping quarters and stirred me from my sleep. As I awoke, I noticed that the back of my heart felt more open, instead of feeling pressed in a waffle iron. I quickly dressed, gathered my things and headed for the Starbird deck to do some yoga and unwind my stiff body. I noticed something felt remarkably different about me. I felt lighter, less constrained, more myself, as if I had emancipated myself from an old-paradigm operating system! These distortions of the dark mother was the part of me that had been circuited to an artificial fear-based intelligence that had kept me looping in false narratives. This journey had lead me to emancipate myself from being entrapped in artificial timelines, controlled realities and undertake the necessary healing to embody my true divine sovereignty, the solar light of feminine Christ consciousness.

As I began to stretch, my head felt more connected to my heart and my heart felt more connected to my womb. Each centre communicated with the other, like long lost friends reunited after years of being mysteriously kept apart. The sense of coherence I felt within this trinity gave me full access to the motherboard of my being. My senses felt more heightened and my feeling intelligence more subtle and refined. Even the neuroplasticity of my brain seemed to fire on more cylinders.

Ah, what a gift! I knew that my newly awakened heart was at last at the helm and promoted to captain of my ship. *Whoa, I can really feel the difference!* In my newfound somatic expression, I experienced a new way of navigating reality. As long as I remained centred in my open heart, I was able to move with grace and fluidity.With this declaration of divine sovereignty, I felt a current of boundless love – large enough to include everything in its wide-open wake.

I recollected another one of my favourite Rumi poems and whispered it under my breathe while looking out to the shimmering sea. "On a day when the wind is perfect the sail just needs to open and the world is full of beauty. Today is such a day!"

While savouring each and every oceanic breath, I glided through each asana with full-bodied presence, enjoying each posture for the sheer joy and pleasure of it. I took my time luxuriating in each pose until my body naturally desired to change its shape. When I felt complete with my practice, I looked out to the vast blue sea that stretched out before me and concluded my practice by chanting three deep om's.

Before long, I noticed a man standing on the deck quietly observing me. He had a brown bushy beard and wore a long black tunic that fluttered in the wind. I decided to approach the priest who, like me, seemed to be reveling in the great mystery of being alive. 'Excuse me, sir.' I asked, 'Do you know how much longer before we dock in Ancona?'

He smiled at me and kindly replied, 'One hour and a half.'

My heartbeat quickened as if to speed up the ferry. I noticed an enormous amount of energy building at the base of my spine. The tip of my sacrum began to tremble and stir like an active volcano, *Shakti kundalini is alive and kickin' today!*

It was really strong, going off in the same kind of way it would when Aiden and I would be suddenly enticed to enter another dimension. I felt to be going into some kind of energetic labour and wondered how I was going to navigate the intensifying Shakti waves washing through my body. I excused myself and began to walk while grounding this upswell up to my eyelashes. Feeling as if I might explode, I began to pray. *May the rising tide in my sacrum subside into a gentle ripple and not overwhelm me.*

I smiled back to my priest friend and headed below deck to take refuge in the swimming pool. *Perhaps if I plunged myself into the cold water, that would suffice to calm the fire in my sacrum down.*

When I arrived at the pool area, I held myself back from jumping in with all my clothes on. As I stood there, I noticed an extremely loud otherworldly sound coming out of the pool. It spewed and sputtered like a large whale in labour about to give birth! I was totally perplexed – and suddenly not as inspired to jump into the convulsing abyss. The pool was making the perfect sound effects for the tidal wave rising in my spine! My body released electrical surges that came in sporadic undulating waves, perfectly synchronised with the whale-like sounds coming from the pool! Then the wind intensified, matching the intensity in my body. In truth, I didn't know what on Earth to do for my bizarre condition! I attempted to lie on the lounge chair and breathe it through with quick, repetitive sipping breaths, and then let them out with long-drawn-out exhales. The wind continued to agitate, the pool moaned and groaned, and the kundalini energy surged through my body, creating very unladylike contractions. I felt like a human volcano suddenly ready to erupt. I must have looked ridiculous to the teenagers smoking cigarettes on the deck chairs on the other side of the pool.

In a last attempt to distract myself, I pulled out my journal as if to divert some of the energy back into my head! As soon as I did, two pieces of lined notebook paper that had been inserted between the pages blew out of my journal. They were the two pages entitled, The Night I Met Aiden. As if in slow motion, I watched them fly away in the strong breeze and then like two leaves land face down upon the surface of the bright blue water. Upon contact, the purple ink ran like blood from the paper and faded into the water. Then the pages floated like two corpses on the surface of the swirling pool. I grabbed the pool-cleaning stick in an attempt to rescue them before the last of the purple words dissolved off the pages into oblivion. I questioned whether I was rescuing something wonderful or something terribly tragic and cruel. Nonetheless, as I held the wet paper with lines of blurry purple words dripping into nothingness, I hoped that I would still be able to make something out of them for memory's sake. Little did I know at that time that making something out of those words would lead me into thirteen years of alchemising them!

I carefully placed the soggy paper over the edge of the lounge chair to dry. As I did, I noticed a large praying mantis sitting on the floor staring up at me like a caricature from a Walt Disney movie. 'Welcome back, Mr. Praying Mantis. Now what have you got to say about all of this intense upheaval?'

This was what I heard the praying mantis say, *'Dear friend, won't you consider this? You have just played your role in a story that was created to serve as a catalyst for your soul's growth and evolution. For now, I wish to tell you the story of my beloved compadres, the Scorpion and the Frog. It goes something like this.*

'A scorpion lived in a dark and dingy cave near a mountain. He grew tired of his surroundings and wanted a change. One day, he came out of his cave and noticed that the valley across the river was very green. He crawled up to the riverbank and wondered how to cross it. Suddenly, he noticed a frog leaping around.

'Hello, Mr. Frog, would you carry me to the other side of the river?' asked the scorpion.

"I would, but you see, I don't trust scorpions," replied the frog.

"Well, all scorpions are not bad. If I sting you on the way, I will die, for I do not know how to swim," explained the scorpion.

'Now the frog saw enough reason in the scorpion's statement and agreed to carry him across the river. So the scorpion hopped onto the frog's back, and they set out on the journey. The frog paddled his limbs through the water as fast as he could. Halfway through the journey, he suddenly felt a sharp sting on his soft hide. "Why did you sting me? Now both of us shall drown," cried he.

"What else can I do? This is my nature," replied the unrepentant scorpion. Then the scorpion asked the frog, "Why did you carry me across the river knowing I could sting you?"

'And the frog replied, "This is my nature." And then the frog and the scorpion immediately drowned in the gushing water.

'*Dear friend, you are swiftly approaching a time when all will appear to be in a state of crisis and distress like the drowning frog and scorpion. Do not be fooled by appearances, for this is the death that precedes a rebirth. This kind of experience reminds us that all apparent "crisis" is truly a catalyst for a new creation! Your victory is assured! Always remember to return to self-love and compassion while staying grounded, light on your feet, fluid and adaptable like me. Before you know it, you will find that the scorpions in your life become your greatest friends and allies! And you will be able to leap and bound into any reality at any given moment and embrace it from all perspectives.*

'*Be honest about your true nature and don't be fooled by the scorpions in life. Old systems and paradigms are crumbling. Know that the winds of change are upon you. Check me out. With my alert and discerning presence, I can move in any direction towards a more harmonious experience with a hop, skip and a jump. Your ability to stay open, fluid and return to love again and again is what will carry you through the chaos. Your innocence is your golden ticket, guiding you to see that life is exactly what you perceive it to be. Remember to travel light and that there is never a good reason to postpone your joy. Ciao for now!*'

I thanked my praying mantis friend for sharing his wise medicine, always sprinkled with a tad of levity and humour. *Perhaps balancing openness with discernment was my greatest learning in this life.*

While I felt calmer inside, the loud moans coming from the pool became too encroaching, so I quickly departed from the lower deck. Carrying my blotched purple papers, I paced around the upper deck of the ferry like a restless tiger in a cage. After several laps around the large vessel, I settled for a perch overlooking the choppy sea. I was grateful that my spinal convulsions were slowly subsiding. As I watched the shore of Italy slowly become closer, I fantasised about getting an espresso and croissant upon touching ground.

Before long the super-deluxe ferry pulled into port and a wave of sadness washed over me. I realised there would be no one there to welcome me back from the Underworld and greet me on the shore. I reminded myself, *I am here, and that is enough! After all, my newly renovated body temple had magically transformed into a rainbow starbird and that was the greatest welcome home of all.*

The man in the black robe approached me and said, 'Excuse me. I saw you doing some spiritual exercises in the morning and found them very interesting. It's as if you are talking to God with your body. Are you religious?'

I had to pause to consider my answer and then replied in the best way I knew how at the time. 'My religion is kindness. And you?'

'I am a Greek Orthodox priest.' He then turned to me, looked deeply into my eyes and said, 'I am very, very glad to meet you. Will you please pray for me?'

'Oh yes,' I said. 'And will you please pray for me?'

Instead of closing our eyes, we opened them wider, offering permission to drink in the essence and features of the other. The warmth of our mutual smiles became our holy communion. Our silence spoke volumes as our differences melted before us and for a timeless moment, we became one.

'Thank you, my friend.' I could feel our mutual awe of basking in the grace of it all. It was yet another precious moment with yet another 'perfect stranger'. Suddenly I felt welcomed to Italy as I stood by my new companion's side, marveling at the wonder that was the wand of our mutual Queen of Hearts, Sophia.

As the ship anchored and docked at the port of Ancona, out of the blue, I heard Eva's sultry voice lovingly serenade me.

'This I know, anything is possible. This I know, anything is possible. Anything is possible. Welcome to Italy, beloved Ambe´. Come home soon, sweet sister. We miss and love you.

CHAPTER SIXTY

ETERNAL FRIENDS

The goal of all this work in the Temples was to attain enlightenment, as the archetypal High God Horus demonstrated, when he attained his highest spiritual body called the Sahu. The halo depicted around a saint's head or the hooded cobra at an Egyptian deity's forehead symbolizes the attainment of the Sahu, and the precursory light anointing called the Uraeus. Activating the Sahu and Uraeus also signifies that the initiate has been anointed within the brain centers by a very high vibration that permanently changes neurophysiology and consciousness, thereby allowing the experience of conscious immortality. Those of us who have attained this mastery are called a Christ, Buddha or ascended master, whose destiny it is to function openly or secretly as a planetary server.

– Claire Heartsong, *Anna, Grandmother of Jesus*

24 September, Turin, Italy

At sundown, I finally arrived in Turin, a place I know very little about. Upon arriving, I went across the street from the train station to decipher my next move and grab a quick bite at the Thai restaurant. I wasn't anticipating that my first meal in Italy would be pad thai, but at this point of my journey, I have come to expect the unexpected. I'll need to find a room for the night and then set out in the morning for the Shroud of Turin exhibit, the Egyptian museum and then off to Damanhur in the afternoon. I'm exhausted from my long travels. I can't wait to get a shower, a good night's rest and a fresh start in the morning.

The following day, after my morning espresso, I splurged on a taxi to the Shroud of Turin exhibit, only to find a sign outside the glass door that read: 'The Shroud of Turin is presently on tour in Switzerland.'

'Really?' I said with a mixture of a giggle and a sigh. *Jesus is so famous he still goes on tour even when he's a shroud!* Again, the divine irony! I shrugged off my temporary disappointment and instead, appreciated my rich encounters with him on the beach in Kardamyli in his ascended form as Sananda.

Instead, I headed to the infamous Egyptian museum, which was known to have the largest collection of genuine Egyptian artifacts in the whole world! After purchasing my ticket, I skipped down three flights of marble stairs, somewhat reminiscent of entering an old Egyptian burial tomb. Apart from my fifth-grade field trip to visit the King Tut exhibit, and a few very vivid past life memories of being a high priestess in the temple of Isis, I honestly knew very little about the esoteric mysteries of Egypt.

'Wow, wow, wow!' I said aloud as I entered the museum gallery. Apart from the snoozing security guard, I found myself to be the only mortal amongst a large array of life-like mummies, cow-faced humans, sarcophagi and several standing golden tombs. Some of the gods and goddesses stood side by side holding long golden staffs and wearing elaborate golden crowns. Egyptian glyphs lined their tombs, depicting an esoteric holographic language that could only be deciphered by the initiates of the mystery schools. These immortalised Kings and Queens sat upon their thrones, their auric fields alive with spirit, giving me the feeling that they were still alive. I imagined at night, when the museum was closed, they would hold ceremonial High Council, just as they would have thousands of years ago!

With all of my senses stretched open across time, I walked through each room and absorbed everything with a surreal sense of familiarity – as if I was a part of an open-ended story still vividly alive in present time. I saw crown jewels, papyrus, moons, stars, sun disks, golden vessels, ankhs, hawks, cobras, lions, cats, ravens and hundreds of scarabs surrounding each elaborate exhibit. My body was covered in goddess bumps. Somehow I remembered these symbols as being portals into another time, space and dimension.

I stood mesmerised by a mummy of a young queen who was said to have transitioned to the next world in her late teens. She looked so petite and fragile. The next enclosed case was another mummy, apparently a fourteen-year-old king. Both the queen and the king were surrounded with a parade of golden scarabs. I was so curious. *What did this mysterious, iridescent insect actually symbolise? Why were they encircling each and every mummified king and queen?*

I looked around to see if I could ask someone. The only person in the exhibit was the elderly security guard dozing off on bridge chair in the corner.

I walked over to another exhibit of a young King and Queen standing side-by-side emanating an air of royalty. To me, they exuded an energetic imprint of the alchemical marriage. Each had passed through the initiatory gateway of death to resurrect and emerge as immortals. They stood together, representing the *Heiros Gamos* – eternal God and Goddess reigning as One.

The more I allowed myself to open to these life-like beings, the more soul codes and memories began to awaken within me. I gazed for a long while at the large-eared, cow-faced, regal goddess known as Hathor, who held a staff that exceeded the full length of her toned physique. Next to her was a similar statue, except with the head of a lion, known as the Goddess Sekhmet. A profound love and affinity washed over me as I recollected the special closeness and companionship that I once shared with both of these beloved friends.

Oh my, I so remember you! I recalled the Hathors close association with the Isis mystery schools. Originally, Hathor was a personification of the Milky Way, which was considered to be the milk that flowed from the udder of a Heavenly cow, hence her sweet bovine face. For me, I most associated the Hathors as being alchemists who healed with sound and frequency. Their shapely ears attuned to the subtlest vibrations, their loving benevolent presence able to transform density into light. I attuned myself with their over-lighting presence. They offered me the gift of overriding all reversal energies instilled from the false light matrix. They went on to upgrade and repair the organic architecture of my monadic core and re-encrypt the crystal tones of my 5th dimensional, merkaba light body.

Before long, I noticed Sekhmet had a sun disk and a cobra snake protruding from her crown. Goddess Sekhmet has strong connections for Starseeds with Sirian connections and especially blue-ray Starseeds like myself. My heart welled with love for her as I received her telepathic transmission. *'I am Sehkmet and speak to you as a healing force of love, courage and fearlessness. I am calling to you to embody your warrior spirit and break the cycles of the past. I bring you the power of the fierce lioness to stalk your shadows, those fears that keep you trapped in your small self. It is time for you to embody your Divine Feminine power and rise as the fearless lioness that you are.'*

I stared intently at both the cow-faced and lion-faced Goddesses. I knew I was amongst ancient friends and spirit guides. I even fantasised about hiding in one of the mummy cases so that when they came to life after closing hours, I could reminisce with Sehkmet about old times in the Isis Temple. *Or maybe I'll go for a sound healing session with one of the Hathors to give my energy body a well-needed reboot.*

Instead, I gently reminded myself that I had to catch the last train to Damanhur in an hour. I bid my ancient friends a heartfelt farewell in the recognition that they too were treasured amongst my Family of Light. I exchanged a smile with the security guard who was now awake and chose to politely ignore my bizarre interactions with the life-like statues.

Goodbye, eternal friends. I'll be seeing you in the afterlife.

I then sprinted up the three flights of white marble stairs in record time to catch the next train headed to Damanhur.

CHAPTER SIXTY-ONE

LADY ALCHEMIA

Isis was regarded as the vessel of creation, which provides the forms and matter of creation. As a Divine womb she becomes Lady Alchemia, the Queen of the Great work. She is the Black Goddess incarnate, in whom the radiant Sophia waits to be rediscovered. Alchemy is the proper craft of Sophia, for she transforms one thing into another, allowing the true gold of creation to shine through the prima material. Sophia is, will be, and has always been the elixir of life, the philosopher's gold, the oneness and essence of the physical world Self, the Quinta Essentia. To make the sun shine at midnight was the initiation of the Mystery schools. To make light shine in darkness, or to draw light from darkness is the initiation of alchemy.

– Caitlin Matthews, Sophia: Goddess of Wisdom

At times, the only home you can find is one crafted of light particles of pure homelessness. No matter how much you thought you knew about love, about yourself, about why you have come here, and about how it was all going to turn out, these reference points are ground to dust in the radiant here and now. Dissolved into the crucible of rewiring tenderness.

Though this home is not a solid one laden with promises, dreams, and future oriented around 'me' and my 'needs,' it is an environment of love from which you will move to connect with beings everywhere. Out of this home you will wander and seed your heart and your essence out into a precious, weary world.

The only ground left is that of a vulnerable, yet raging alive groundlessness. Anything could happen and nothing will ever be the same – that much is clear. You are utterly exposed, blown open, yet excruciatingly present to what is happening. It is so clear now that things will never turn out the way you thought they would. You are being asked to allow the old dream of 'me' to die, over and over and over again, with no idea, yet, of what will be reborn out of the ashes of integration.

It feels as if you are falling apart, yes, but even that idea dissolves into empty space as you realize you were never 'together' to begin with. No matter how it may appear, love is always holding you. But this holding will never be understood by the mind or apprehended through the known. It will never conform to your hopes and fears, as it is an emissary of pure, transmuting creativity. It is the portal into a new world.

– Matt Licata

The Turin train station was elegant and grand, like something from a romantic Italian film set at the turn of the century. Age and grace emanated from the grandeur walls, arched ceilings, and cool white and grey marble floors. I sat on a wrought-iron bench on the platform and daydreamed about my experience in the Egyptian museum. As I waited to board my train, a chill rippled through my body as I suddenly felt extremely homesick. Homesick for where, for what, or for whom – I did not know. Throughout my life, this same nuance of homesickness had haunted me, though I could never trace it to any particular origin. I later discovered that homesickness is a common symptom for a starseed. I closed my eyes and asked, *What are the ghosts of melancholy and despair doing here again? I thought I had found what I was looking for.* I pleaded with the Goddess Sophia.

The answer came swiftly, with a fiercely loving and oh so familiar jolt. *'As soon as you 'find' truth, it will slip into something else. Despair, joy; joy, despair – they are one and the same! Feel and receive it all as a gift served up by the wise hand of Lady Alchemia. There is nothing that you can hold on to. We invite you to embrace the tides and cycles of life with the fullness of your presence and gratitude. For as you come to know a thing, it will surely change into another.'*

Really? Could I surrender even more? I didn't know whether to laugh, cry or jump in front of the approaching train. Apparently, I wasn't quite complete with the death and rebirth theme of my alchemical journey and as Sophia lovingly reminded me, *'In the ever expanding now, the Creator is always creating on your behalf. Like any contraction prior to birth, we invite you to breathe, relax, open and enjoy the ride!'*

The train whistled with an eerie screech as it eased into the station. The noise jarred my hypersensitive nervous system and alarmed my inner child. Admittedly, she was feeling a little more lost than found at that particular stage of her journey. I felt like Dorothy from *The Wizard of Oz*. After miles of wondering down the yellow brick road, she felt like she would never find the wizard and get home to Kansas. I considered, clicking my heels together three times just to see what magical thing might happen. Instead, I gave way to something way more authentic, my weary melancholy self. I was on the brink of collapsing from within.

'Oh toto, there is no place like home!' I wailed inside to the Great Mother Sophia. *Hang on,* I reminded myself for what felt like the millionth time. *There is no home 'out there'. Like a tortoise, I carry my home with me wherever I go. Have you forgotten so soon, my love?*

Amidst the surge of people whooshing by me on the platform, I clicked my dusty sandal heals three times before surrendering even deeper into the raw core of my being. I then boarded the train, found a quiet seat in the corner and patiently waited for my destiny to take me onward. I felt like curling up, going to sleep and waking up somewhere completely different than where I presently was.

I went on to console my forlorn inner child. *We're going to Ivrea, little one. Then we'll catch a taxi to Damanhur and explore this amazing modern-day mystery school. You'll see, my luv. It'll be fascinating and fun! We get to explore yet another country where our Blessed Mother, Mary Magdalene and the Black Madonna are so celebrated and revered.*

Finally, I managed to relax and resigned myself to feeling perfectly forlorn. The hypnotic chugging of the train made my eyes grow heavy. Still feeling the transmission from all the artifacts in the Egyptian museum, I found myself reflecting on all that I had encountered there. *I can't wait to discover the deep esoteric meaning of the scarab! What in the world is the significance of this mysterious beetle that lined the Egyptian tombs?*

Just then, I looked down at the filthy train floor, and lying right at my feet was something around the size of my middle toe. *What could that be?* Whatever it was, it glowed like a tiny jewel amongst the grime and chewing-gum wrappers. I leaned in closer and nearly fell off my seat. It was a scarab, shimmering in iridescent black, lime green and cerulean blue. I blinked my eyes repeatedly to make sure I was seeing correctly and not dreaming. This rare and revered legendary Egyptian icon sat at my feet, unscathed, glistening in its iridescent wonder. As if I had found a precious diamond, I discreetly took my train ticket, carefully scooped the insect up and folded it into a nicely secured paper pocket. This scarab had come to me as an ally, a reminder of a time long ago, and to escort me from one life to another. I grinned to myself. *Like I was just sayin', I cannot wait to discover the deep esoteric meaning of the scarab!*

My whole being shifted its demeanour and suddenly I felt recharged with renewed faith. At once, I became alive and leaned back on my seat, closed my eyes, took a long deep breath and asked the scarab about its special kind of esoteric medicine.

'I am your escort into your afterlife, at your loyal service, my Lady! I am the one that carries you beyond the threshold of fear and death into the glory of your highest destiny. As your trusty guardian of the afterlife, I exist beyond the veils of ordinary perception. I am all that is left when your heart shell shatters and you discover that you are not destroyed — you are set free. And when you come back to life, you will find that you are able to love without conditions because you no longer require protection from the anticipation of loss. Actually, you will have transcended the illusion of loss altogether. Now that is bravery. Bravisimo!'

I peeked into the paper where the dead scarab lay and whispered, 'Thank you, paisano scarab, for being here, of all places, and so graciously escorting me into my afterlife.'

I waited patiently at the Ivrea train station to be picked up by one of the Damanhur staff members. He would transport me to the remote, Damanhur, City of Light. It began to drizzle as I stood waiting under the mini-shelter where the train dropped me off. At last, a white minivan pulled into the station. A casually dressed man in his late forties approached me as if he already knew me. He greeted me in a heavily accented English, kissed both of my cheeks and then silently escorted me to the van. We drove several kilometres up the twisting mountain roads without saying a word. I occupied myself by looking out of the window and taking in the luscious green scenery. Compared to the city, the countryside appeared timeless and unchanging. I watched generations of old homes and ancient old growth trees pass me by in an enchanting green and gold blur. The rolling hills were lined with vibrant orchards. Clusters of small houses were tucked neatly into the hillsides as if they grew right out of the landscape. Despite the beauty, I was a little queasy from the barrage of winding turns and felt beyond relieved to pull into the large parking lot.

Franco pulled out my bag and pointed to the local café. 'You waita dera untila da offisah open againa,' he said, pulling the English words out like nasty weeds from his perfect Italian world.

'OK, *grazie*, Franco. Ciao.' As I grabbed my backpack and hurled it onto my sturdy back, my eye caught the blue unicorn painted on the awning of the café. *Cool, they're into unicorns. That's a really good sign*, I thought. The magical totem turned my queasiness into an excited anticipation of the magic that was yet to come. After so many long days of solitude in Kalamata, I was looking forward to connecting with some kindred souls. *This is clearly a place where mysticism is an embodied lifestyle*, I affirmed to myself excitedly.

I'm absolutely famished! I went into the quaint little café and ordered a cappuccino and soon found that there was nothing available to eat at that time of the day. Nearly an hour later, I was greeted by a very attractive woman. She wore pressed black slacks, designer high heels and a crisp white blouse that showed just the right amount of cleavage. She smiled and gestured for me to follow her.

'Ciao! I'm Francesca and I'll show you to your room. Please remain outside the main grounds until tomorrow morning, when you will be given a tour inside the Mountain Temple. You may take breakfast in the Unicorn Café between 8–10am. Ciao for now.'

I followed the loud clicking of her heels to my dorm room and thanked her. I noticed how unpolished I felt next to her elegant efficiency. Since the options for nightlife were non-existent, I showered in the public bathroom and went to bed early. After settling into my neatly made bed, I distracted myself from the grumbles of hunger in my belly by reading a chapter from *Anna, Grandmother of Jesus*. My breath deepened into my belly while I cleared my chakras, auric field and spinal pathways from the long journey.

Within moments, I fell into a deep meditative state where I entered a dimensional doorway that opened through my pineal gland. With continued deep breathing, my consciousness now rested in my light body where I became lucidly aware of a group of ethereal beings filling the room with golden white light.

I was being energetically greeted by a few of the spiritual guardians of the Damanhur mystery school. The first etheric being I noticed was a Hathor. I could tell by her cow-shaped ears and large amber eyes with long eyelashes. She towered over me and extended her open palms in a gesture of warm welcome. A High Priestess wearing a long flowing white dress and a cobalt blue cape stood at my left side, holding a jeweled box within her delicate hands. Like guardian angels, they silently held sacred space for me. I inwardly bowed to them in gratitude for their warm and gracious welcome.

Suddenly, my pelvic floor quivered and energy released like a rushing torrent that had been undammed. Then my liver began to rumble as if a small earthquake had erupted inside it. I heard a voice clearly say, *'Perdona tuo padre,'* which translates to, 'forgive your father'. My heart swelled up and tightened in my throat as my breath quickened in my belly. *Is that even possible? Will I ever be able to totally forgive him and be free of this frozen despair?*

As his youngest daughter, I admired my father and was often confused by his unsubtle ways of displaying his objectifying affection towards me. And yet I learned to tolerate it in exchange for a morsel of kindness and fatherly approval. All at once, I flashed on the moment I first closed my heart off to my father and why I felt so painfully unsafe with him. My consciousness regressed to being around seven years old. At that time, my father travelled a lot on business. Because he was gone so often, I pined for his approval and attention, and loved to impress him with my latest gymnastic moves. I became queasy as I recollected a family gathering at my aunt's home. As usual, Dad drank more red wine then everyone combined at the table. After dinner, he assumed his typical social role, cracking belligerent dirty jokes and taking political digs at Richard Nixon. After dinner, he beckoned me to come sit on his lap and began to bounce me around on his knee as if I was still an infant. He wiggled me playfully about acting oblivious to what was growing beneath me. Loudly and in high humour, he carried on with his verbal rampage.

Because I admired him and pined for his loving attention, I endured this strange kind of closeness until the moment I felt a cold terror pass through my bones. Suddenly, it dawned on me: he was actually getting sexually turned on and amusing himself at my expense. *For the love of God, I was his daughter!*

As soon as I registered what was actually happening, I jumped off his lap and ran to the nearby couch. An icy cold darkness rippled through my bones. In that moment, my love and admiration for my father shattered like a large crystal glass. In slow motion, I watched our perfect father-daughter love tumble to the floor and shatter into a million shard-like pieces, along with my own sense of safety and child-like innocence. I sat frozen on the couch, horrified that no one had dared to intervene. There was nothing I could say or do, as I was expected to silently endure his unconscious behaviour or pay the forbidden price. The whole family continued to carry on with their banter, oblivious to what had just happened and the shock of the rupture that coursed through my little body. My world with my father had just come crashing down. That night was one of many shameful transgressions and secrets that came down to me to bear all alone.

Worst of all, as an extremely open and sensitive child, I felt my father had little to no awareness around how his unconscious toxic behaviour had affected me. I rarely felt safe enough to relax in the comfort of my home let alone in my feminine skin. His typical response when I attempted to communicate my discomfort to him was to yell back at me. 'Come on, kiddo. What the hell is wrong with you? Have a goddamn sense of humour, will ya?'

Whether he was conscious of it or not, he was a master at gaslighting others along with my earnest request for greater respect for my body. I had been made to feel that I was the one that had the problem. All I knew was that most of my upbringing, I lived in a kind of pseudo-terror, wondering when he would have too much to drink and cross those forbidden boundaries once again – *which for me was simply not funny!*

It was the night at my aunt's house, my innocence and trust in the Masculine was ruptured. I was at the age that I could finally cognise that this was not the first incident that I had been used as an accomplice for my father's arousal in the name of 'fun and games'. I had concluded that it was no longer safe to be completely open or loving with my father...and perhaps with any man for that matter. Something very sad and devastating settled over my heart and though it got buried for some time, I realised that it had never completely gone away. In those days, a father's inappropriate drunken behaviour was considered 'normal' and children were expected to silently turn the other cheek and pretend that all was 'feelin' groovy'. After all, to speak up would be far too disruptive to the family's reputation – whose predominant purpose was to keep up appearances no matter what the cost.

The spirit guides that surrounded me prompted me to come to terms with the instilled memories of trauma and my fundamental mistrust in the Masculine. A slew of memories flooded in, not only from my father, but from countless scenarios of being raped, abused and tortured throughout lifetimes by the unconscious Masculine. This terror was altogether confusing because I simultaneously yearned to be close, to share my affection and to love the wondrous men in my life. *I absolutely love and adore my brothers and long for their brilliance and companionship in my life.*

With laser-like focus, I retraced this core mistrust into the roots of a patriarchal world that was embedded into nearly all of social consciousness. I was able to see this deeply engrained patterning had influenced my relationship with God. *After all, God was a man, right? Conclusion: if men could not be trusted, then God could not be trusted either!*

This misguided belief left me to fend for myself, alone in an unsafe world. In my best attempt to protect myself, I had inadvertently banished my own inner Masculine from my heart, just in case he could not be trusted as well. Over time, this split had left me feeling susceptible, weak, unprotected and abandoned – by my own best protector, my inner Masculine Self. *Woe is me!*

Thank Goddess there has always been a distinction from that patriarchal God I was programmed to believe in and the God of my deepest heart. It was far time I cleaned up my relationship with my father and the Masculine face of God. I was being called to make a clear distinction between the unconscious Masculine and how it has distorted and tainted my relationship with the Divine Masculine that dwelled within me.

The God of my heart is not a genderfied singular being. Instead, I experience this God as a benevolent, all-prevailing presence whose essence is luminous grace. This God is pristine consciousness… omnipresent, omnipotent and omni-sentient. This God is the universal, love beauty intelligence that I was born to commune with and in so doing become one with all. This God was a relationship that was ever evolving based on my ongoing relationship with awakening to the deeper truth of who and what I Am.

The insights continued to rush in as I dove deeper into the layers that were now surfacing for me to witness, release and forgive. I reflected on how I could be a wonderful friend and lover, joyously showing up to give all of myself and then some. But when it came to receiving, there was a hidden withhold, a part of me that tended to contract with mistrust, feeling afraid and contracted. I felt susceptible to being harmed because I had had residual childhood trauma and inadvertently distanced myself from the presence and protection of my inner Masculine Self.

After all, if I couldn't trust myself, how could I trust another?

By rejecting and closing off my heart to father/God, I had closed my heart off to my inner Masculine! Eureka! No wonder I attracted and sought validation from men who could not meet me nor be reciprocal with their love!

The mystery of 'unrequited love' was beginning to make a little more sense now, along with the awareness that my forgiveness needed to begin with fully forgiving me.

Still reclining on my bed, I felt the familiar and all-loving presence of the Divine Mother Sophia. Her arms embraced me, and the entire world, with her eternal Love. I drank in her luminous words of wisdom.

'When sexuality is linked to fear, violence, addiction, controlling others and robbing the innocence from the young, it becomes a distortion of the goddess's body, my body. It is time for humanity to come from the understanding that when we exploit or harm another on purpose or for our own personal gain, we are actually harming ourselves.

'Humanity is waking up out of a great distortion that has locked down this planet in a prison of shame, guilt, victimhood and powerlessness, operated through the narcissistic abuse of innocent men, women and children. And whenever one is abused, there is a natural decay and corrosion of the other. We cannot control others. Even if we lock them up, we cannot change others. However, we can heal our own understanding. We must restore our connection to our real Shakti force, known as the risen Christos Sophia, the Sacred Union of the Solar Feminine, Solar Masculine and Solar Child.

'The change comes from radical forgiveness, self-responsibility and the awakening of the cosmic heart that is inseparable from the whole. That is the way to embody the living wisdom and the risen Christos Sophia. Once we embody the power and fullness of the Solar Feminine, the lower energies do not have a chance. We are meant to explore sexuality in the same sacredness as all of life. In fact, our Self-worth, Self-love, Self-care, Self-expression and creativity is all connected to our reclaimed healthy sexuality. This is what the Golden Age is all about. As you rise, so does the New Earth in a symbiotic Love affair between nature, cosmos and soul.'

Once again, I felt consoled by Sophia's inspired presence and surrendered even further into the gratitude for all beings playing their perfect role during this epoch of rebalancing the Feminine and Masculine. I acknowledged that my soul had given me a gift by choosing my particular father. He was the catalyst to evolve beyond the narrative of victim/victimiser and flower my heart of compassion. The experience of being violated by the unconscious masculine had catalysed me to commit my life to honouring and respecting myself and all beings, beyond gender. I knew from experience that my words, choices and behaviour had the power to negatively or positively impact others. My relationship with my father motivated me to be empathic, to listen, to feel, and to sense whether my actions were harming or enlivening the cherished people in my life. It became top priority for me to honour the tender sensitivity of each and every human heart and the innate preciousness of their being. I became passionate about creating sacred containers for individuals to safely share who they are as sovereign beings in a resonant field of healthy togetherness and mutual appreciation.

I brought my palms together over my heart and conjured my father in my mind's eye. *Thank you father, for all that you have taught me to be... and not to be. You gave me life, loved and provided for me in the best way you knew how and for this, I am truly grateful. I know now that I am not a victim. I choose to forgive you and I choose to forgive myself for all that has ever transpired between us. I own my part in creating our relationship to be the way it is. I am now finally able to have compassion and be grateful for all that you have given me.*

I closed my prayer with several rounds of ho'oponopono, my favourite mantra to absolve the subconscious cause of my creation: 'I'm sorry, please forgive me, thank you, I love you, I set you free as I set myself free, blessings on your journey. So be it and so it is.'

The Light beings of Damanhur smiled at me, and I felt a shower of love-light braze my tear-soaked face. *Phew! I feel so grateful to be unravelling the tangles of my Feminine and Masculine heart.* I opened my innermost heart to create space for the Divine Masculine to be welcomed home with wide-open arms and was then taken by surprise by the unexpected visitor. He appeared to look like...God! You know, the one with the long white beard, sitting on his throne, high up in the cloudy sky. Except in this vision, he came down from his throne to stand barefoot amongst the other guardian spirits in the room. His presence reminded me of Gandalf, the wizard from Lord of the Rings. He looked like an elderly shepherd. He felt so gentle, compassionate, humble – the embodiment of benevolent Masculine energy. I sensed all that he wanted was for his flock to feel safely at home with him, one another and the Divine spark within.

He beamed with a fatherly pride as he held open the Book of Life and pointed to the pages of the names written within it. *'Each living being recorded in this book is a precious gift to LIFE! The greatest gift of all is to be a benevolent Father to you and to all of my beloved children.*

His transmission came through as loving kindness, as pure as the morning sun. He invited me to get to know him as he really is, as if he was to say, *'The projections humanity has cast upon me are actually not who I am. The origin of these projections comes from a mind that has been fractured and therefore perceives reality through the perception of separation and fear. My love and light is a benevolent and pure expression of pristine consciousness, abiding in respect for the origin and sanctity of all life. Like the friends who surround you now, I am an aspect of your Divine Self, a most loyal and loving companion on the journey of remembering yourself home.'*

His tender countenance melted my every resistance.

After this auspicious encounter, a giant weight had been lifted, and another layer of my protective shell dissolved. *Poof, gone, gone, gone beyond.* A feeling of total relaxation washed through me and warmed my heart to its core. Just like that, through forgiveness, I felt empowered to love full out...from that wondrous place of childlike innocence, wonder and awe. My little one felt safe to be the LOVE that I AM and experience the LOVE that WE are – in all of our infinite faces and expressions.

The Damanhur entourage was not quite done with me yet. Yet another energetic presence appeared in front of me. This time it was the founder of the City of Light and the presiding Guardian of the Damanhur mystery school. His presence was clear and strong. He appeared to me with a falcon on his shoulder.

'Welcome to Damanhur, Sister of the Rose,'

His energy mingled with mine like the blending of two distinct complementary colours. The molecules and atoms of my body opened to arrange themselves around his lucid and coherent presence. I sensed that I was in the company of a master being and an ancient friend. This was clearly not the first time we had tangoed in the Temple of Oneness together! With ease, I surrendered to his familiar soul light. I became highly aware that he was about to offer me a profound and life-altering gift.

Kabloom! My third eye sprang open and lit up like a full moon at midnight. I saw a pyramid capstone protrude from my sixth chakra. The eye of Horus opened within the centre of the capstone. The eye proceeded to turn 180 degrees and looked straight back into the centre of my head! I felt no force, but a gentle wisdom that affirmed that the third eye was meant to gaze primarily within so as not to lose sight as to who was projecting the dream of awakened consciousness.

Whoa! An aqua marine light poured into the centre of my head and then vibrated open my third eye. I was delighted to be encircled by an etheric pod of dolphins. They beamed a sonic symphony of tonal sounds that opened every sub-atomic God-particle of my being. Simultaneously, a gold and white prismatic chamber of light flooded the central pillar of my spine. Bolts of electrified mana surged from different points of my body while geysers of light spewed from my chakras. Each energy centre bloomed open and became one with the cosmos. A controlling grip released from the back of my neck and my body was showered in a fountain of pink and gold, universal Love Light. I gratefully surrendered to this bio-energetic overhaul and DNA recalibration as a gift beyond all measure.

All the while, I observed the heightened presence of the whole gaggle of Divine friends: Sophia, Sekhmet, the Hathors, Isis, Osiris, Pan, Yeshua, Magdalene, Shiva, Shakti, Quan Yin, White Buffalo Calf Woman, Tara, Grandmother Anna, the dolphins and good ol' fashioned God, *of course!* The whole galactic gang was there to encircle me with their beaming hearts, loving me as my forever companions of destiny. Their unwavering presence welcomed me home to the temple of my heart and affirmed a new level of awakened embodiment. I vibrated in bliss, like a newborn child, totally suspended in a unified field of Oneness.

Well done! Bella Madonna has forgiven her padre and can finally relaxa and go homa. As I drifted off into a lucid sleep, I felt to be a shimmering star floating amongst billions of other stars, each one of us having a loving awareness of the glorious existence of the other - sovereign and yet all together. We were a glorious constellation of interconnected nodal points of light, the star dusted kisses of God.

CHAPTER SIXTY-TWO

ALCHEMUMBO JUMBO

Alchemy is a process developed to purify the ego/personality so that one might develop gnosis or direct knowledge of the truth. You are bound to Earth because of the gravity of your soul. Once your thoughts are purified, ascent and descent are as natural as breathing since the Above is subtle and the Below is gross. The subtlest part of matter is soul: the subtlest part of soul is spirit and the subtlest part of spirit is God. To travel in these realms, you only need to change the density of your thoughts. First you must free yourself from the lead of denial and fear, for they destroy all subtle things and make lead of gold! Look into the deepest of your wounds, for there lies the gold of your being. Though it pains you, you must mine this lead from where it has accumulated. Release this treasure to the light of consciousness and follow it as it flies upward and merges with the greater Sun, to the place where fear cannot follow.

– Hermes Trismegistus

You sever my head
and mind grows radiant;
push me underwater, heart learns to speak.
Your eyes bloomed in mine,
I saw your snow light soaking every garden:
Your ears bloomed in mine,
I heard your river running over every stone.

– Jelaluddin Rumi

The tour of the temple grounds was scheduled for 11am. I had just enough time to grab some breakfast and check my email. I humbly observed that tender part of me that still pined for an email from Aiden that would quench my thirst for greater closure, as if that was the final ingredient to my ultimate liberation – *not!*

As I approached the designated meeting place for the tour, I noticed a small group of visitors converged around the entrance gate to the Mountain Temple. I surmised that the beautiful young Italian woman with wavy mahogany hair was our guide. She wore Italian couture clothing and avoided all eye contact with the group as she introduced herself. 'Bonjourno! I am you guide, Daniella.' Apparently, we were one of hundreds of tourists who casually passed through the temples to satisfy their curiosity each week.

Sharing a half smile, Daniella pointed to the towering sculptures in the gardens, which looked very surreal in their life-like presence. She clicked along the path.

'Over there is the Goddess Sekhmet. She is the presiding deity of the lands of Damanhur. To the left is the High Priestess, she is the Goddess of the Sacred Feminine. And over there is Pan – he rules the nature and the Underworld. And over there is the labyrinth.' A few people approached the labyrinth for a closer look, but she stopped them abruptly, '*Por favora!* Step away please. We only allow the residents of Damanhur to walk on it. *Por favora*, step away!'

Daniella moved us quickly along. 'Beyond the garden are the workshops where the art is handcrafted for the underground temples by the members of our community.'

Wow! How amazing! I imagined a community of modern-day Michelangelo's creating one masterpiece after another. I was beyond impressed and secretly longed for a more in-depth window into this astonishing, modern-day mystery school. I soon discovered that if one desired a deeper dive into the inner mysteries of Damanhur, one would need to sign up for a weeklong course. I gazed at each of the statues, privately thanking them for making an appearance in last nights, profound healing transmission. Once again, I recalled the movie, *Night at the Museum*, where all the figurines in the Natural History Museum came to life at night and interacted with one another. Actually, it was not a far-fetched idea to me anymore. I had basically just experienced a multi-dimensional version of that phenomenon!

As our group concluded the tour of the surrounding grounds, we were invited to join the residents for a special monthly talk given by Falco, the founder of the community.

'Tonight, Maestro, will be speaking on the subject of alchemy. You are all most welcome to join our community. Doors open promptly at 19:00 pm!'

Alchemy! I can't think of a more aligned topic! I knew right off the bat that I was meant to attend. I was excited to thank the founder for his generous energetic welcome and receive his enlightened transmission on the 'Great Work' of transforming lead into gold.

The group was breaking up and chattering about the tour when Daniella raised her voice. 'Attention, one last thing,' she announced. 'If you wish to tour the Mountain Temple, we will meet at the same place tomorrow at 11am. *Grazie. Ciao!*'

The community of Damanhur paraded into the auditorium, filling it nearly to full capacity. I felt honoured to be among the members of this highly esteemed, esoteric community. Observing the room, I noticed how somber and serious everyone was as they settled into their seats. Perhaps the poker-face vibe was attributed to the disappointment people felt about Falco's absence. Upon entering the auditorium, there was a chalkboard sign that read, '*Fortunatamente, Falco non può assistere a così Professor Suvasio lo sostituira. Grazie.*' It translated to '*Unfortunately, Maestro is unable to attend. Professor Suvasio will be standing in for him. Thank you.*'

Feeling curious to be amongst the inner circle of the Damanhur community, I took my seat towards the back of the room. As soon as everyone settled in, a hefty elderly man in his late seventies hobbled carefully onto the stage with a cane. He wore a tweed blazer and suit trousers belted high above his hips. Before he greeted the audience, he turned to the large chalkboard and scribbled the following seven words: *Calcination, Dissolution, Separation, Conjunction, Fermentation, Distillation and Coagulation.*

After coughing several times to clear his throat, Professor Suvasio began his presentation by apologising profusely for not being Maestro. Instead, he dove right into his scientific equations, crunching numbers and scratching words out just like he was teaching a high school algebra class. Meanwhile, the beautiful Goddess Francesca sat at the back of the room, translating his lecture to me through headphones. Every few moments, the professor would pause, clear his throat, then turn toward the audience to reassure us. He would say, 'This talk on alchemy is meant to confuse you because the science of alchemy is complex and for most people, it takes a lifetime to understand.'

I wasn't clear on whether it was politeness or loyalty that had the audience nodding their heads in agreement following each succession of incomprehensible scribbles. I squirmed in my seat, trying not to show how agitated I was becoming. I hungered for something that I could actually sink my heart into rather than stretching my mind around indiscernible equations that were intended to keep me confused.

The community appeared to be accepting the material without question on the premise that Maestro had invited the Professor Suvasio to speak, and that was enough. Forty minutes later, my patience wore thin and I grumbled to myself, 'This is all feels so murky to me, like mental gymnastics or mind masturbation!' I silently questioned the well-mannered audience who appeared to have no problem with this one-way, convoluted mind maze.

At last, Professor Suvasio concluded his talk with one last scribble on the chalkboard, followed by an extensive coughing session before inviting the audience to ask questions.

A young man stood up and boldly said, 'Excuse me, but I don't understand.'

Once again, the professor responded, 'The path of alchemy is meant to keep you confused.'

Then a middle-aged woman with jet-black hair and a thick furrowed unibrow stood up and asked in a serious tone that displayed her keen intellect, 'What is the meaning of "*Nigredo*"?'

The professor pointed to one of the many equations scribbled on the green chalkboard and said huffily, 'Can't you see, signora? It comes before calcination!' He tapped his cane on the chalkboard to emphasise his point.

My heart began to thump hard. *What on Earth is all of this? I protested to myself. Why are these people settling for mental gymnastics and avoiding the very heart of the question? Is everyone really going to sit there and be silent, pretending to understand, settling for scribbles on a chalkboard? Are they really satisfied with accruing more fanciful facts in the hope that somehow they would magically add up to enlightenment?*

Feeling fired up, I debated whether I should raise my hand and ask a question or sit back in disbelief. Instead, I continued on with my inner rampage. *Where has the mental body ever really gotten us anyway but into countless bloody battles of true and false, right and wrong, and good and evil? When we disconnect from our heart, it causes so much needless pain and suffering. The 'know it all' intellect is the part of us that will bulldoze another to get our own way. It justifies the kill, going to war, exploiting the innocent and destroying entire ecosystems all in the name of domination, control and privatised agenda. How much more bloodshed and destruction of life will the human species tolerate in the name of outsmarting the 'other'?*

Whoa, easy now, Ambe´! Chillax, I counseled myself, as I pulled back on the reins of my own Righteous Rhonda sub-personality. I wanted to jump out of my seat like a wild bucking mare refusing to be tamed or restrained by this status quo rodeo.

If one's thinking is not married with the heart, with no care or concern for our impact on life and on others, we literally become human weapons of mass destruction, dangerous to each other and to life. We must come down from our analytical pedestals, whose sole purpose is to defend one's position and singular perspective. Humans are the only species that destroy their own kind. What is being called for is more empathy and compassion in such a way that we respect, honour and celebrate diversity, seeking ways to compliment rather than polarize from one another.

I looked around the room at the somber faces. *Who here would like to experience what alchemy is?* With passion and vigour, I rehearsed this invitation inside of me, envisioning myself standing before the entire community and requesting them to join me in dropping into their hearts, breathing into their tightly held bellies and feeling into what was presently alive for them, instead of trying to figure it all out by staring at the scribbles on the chalkboard.

Then I heard the professor clear his throat and say, 'We have time for one last question.'

My heart began to race vigourously, and before I knew it, I leapt out of my seat and made eye contact with the translator at the back of the room. She gestured for me to proceed with my comment. All eyes were upon me.

'My experience is that to know spiritual alchemy, we must be willing to descend into our bodies and the feeling nature of our hearts. And then, from a place of open curiosity and fierce compassion, descend even further into all that remains concealed within the dark matter, or *nigredo* of our lives. Alchemy is the great work that calls the initiate to bravely descend into the darkness within – to harvest the hidden jewels and discover our true essence as the gold shining through our open hearts.

'When we courageously dare to create a safe and somatic space for the dark matter of our lives to rise to the surface and be lovingly felt and embraced, this is where the alchemical process naturally begins to transmute all that was once held in darkness and welcome it into the light. In essence, all that we have avoided, denied and judged within ourselves, deeming it as too painful to feel, is embraced and invited into our somatic awareness...to be felt, forgiven, released and ultimately loved back into wholeness.'

The room was so still one could have heard a pin drop. There was only a distant cough coming from somewhere in the back row. The flustered Professor Suvasio quickly chimed in and said, 'Oh no, no, no. Here at Damanhur, we don't believe you must suffer or feel pain to enlighten. We are out of time. *Grazie* for coming. *Ciao.*'

The crowd immediately resorted to the usual social protocol then scuffled out of the room in a serious sobriety. I sat in my seat, utterly stunned that my inquiry was reduced to the simple one-liner, 'Oh no, no. We don't do pain or suffering here in Damanhur.'

How very interesting, I thought, staying open to the professor's perspective while I took my inquiry even deeper.

I sensed the Maestro of this ever so mysterious mystery school would have his own enlightened wisdom on the topic and it was not in service to draw harsh conclusions from what had just transpired. I was more curious than ever to meet him in person and exchange our unique perspectives.

That evening while lying in bed, I reviewed the lecture and cleared the part of me that went into my own emotional reactivity and defensiveness. I saw that my stance for guiding with an open heart was partially mixed with an indignant sub-personality whom I named, Miss Rhonda Bucking Righteous! I owned my emotional charge about the whole matter. It had invited me to see the part of me that felt passionate, as well as the part of me that still participated in the slippery slope of righteous indignation, aka as being a 'know it all', and ironically getting swept up in the whole seductive 'right versus wrong' shenanigans.

Yes, I thought, holding myself accountable for living with greater integrity, *all beings have the right to be exactly as they are. I may have glimpsed wisdom from my own experience, yet wisdom held with an emotional charge is often reduced to the same kind of closed-mindedness that triggered me in the first place! Instead, I affirmed, I choose to stay open, curious and honour the unique perspectives of others while stewarding the highest expression of my passion, truth and unique perception of reality. So be it. So it is. Bless us all!*

CHAPTER SIXTY-THREE

THE ELEVENTH HOUR

This movement, connection and penetration of your feeling awareness, moving down into your humanness, this is the movement that delivers your light, your acceptance, your love and nurturing into this previously denied part of your being. This is an integral part of the evolutionary journey of feeling. This is the path of emotional maturity and awakening. This is the process of descending in your humanness. This is your choice to cultivate a conscious feeling relationship with your own humanness. This is the ending of your denial, dissociation, fragmentation and separation. Your devotion to the fire of the heart is my joyous awakening into grander expression. This is the beginning of integration, wholeness and unity.

Your inherent and Divine design is to live your life in the deep satisfaction and authentic dignity of your Origin...and this is your fearless heart. It is your Divine design to be continually and abundantly nourished by the deep satisfaction of Being, which is your Origin...your Original nature...located conveniently in the centre of your own Heart. The Beloved calls. The Beloved sings. The deep satisfaction of Being...is only a breath away. Relaxing into your Origin is a choice, a relaxing, a surrendering, a letting go of outward grasping. It is an eternal remembering.

– Neil Steven Cohen, *Voice of the Heart*

Self-love is all you need to birth a New Earth... To walk through the threshold, all you need is to align yourself with the Love that you already are and embody it as Self.

– Kari Mathieson

O sudden resurrection!
O countless blessings!
O blazing fire
in the jungle of thoughts!
Today, you arrive with laughter
To break open the jail!

– Jelaluddin Rumi

That night, I did a little research to find out what made Damanhur so very special. I found this description, which explained much about its hidden mystery. But as we all know, there is so much more that lies beneath the surface.

The Damanhur Temples of Humankind are an underground work of art, created entirely by hand and dedicated to the Divine nature of humanity. They are a great three-dimensional book that recounts the history of Humankind through all of the art forms, delineating a path of re-awakening to the Divine — both inside and outside of us. In the Temples of Humankind, every aspect of the art has a meaning; the colours, the measurements and every detail follows a precise code of form and proportion. Consequently, every Great Hall has its specific resonance and its own sound.

The Temples of Humankind symbolically represent the inner rooms inside every human being. Walking through its halls and corridors corresponds to a profound journey inside oneself. The Temples wind for over 8,500 cubic meters on five different levels, connected to one another by hundreds of meters of corridor. They arise in the place where the Eurasian continental plate meets the African plate, pushing up a mineral 300 million years old: mylonite, a rock that carries the physical energy of the Earth. The Temples of Humankind have been built right inside a vein of this particular mineral, whose presence perfectly follows the flowing 'Synchronic lines' of the planet. The Synchronic lines are like great rivers of energy that cross the Earth and connect it to the Universe, carrying ideas, thoughts and dreams. They are similar to Ley lines or Dragon lines. The Temples arise within a 'shining knot', the point where four Synchronic lines meet. The Temples serve as a great laboratory where art, science, technology and spirituality are united for the evolution of humanity.

The following morning, I went on a tour through the Mountain Temples of Damanhur. These temples were truly an impressive undertaking of exquisite beauty that completely lived up to their title, The Eighth Wonder of the World. Each of the rooms depicted the esoteric history and evolution of humanity throughout the ages. Each uniquely themed room was created and handcrafted by the Damanhur community of artisans. The whole endeavor was beyond impressive.

I sensed that there was so much more to this impressive tribute than met the eye. However, I felt mysteriously agitated and restless within the confines of these temple walls. I entered deeper into the sensation of longing for a new paradigm, where mystery schools transformed into Open-Source sanctuaries for awakening through mutuality, free from complex pre-requisites and spiritual hierarchies.

I'm ready to explore in realms of shared astoundment ad open curiosity. Where we listen with all of our senses and highly attuned feeling intelligence as embodied conduits of Divine gnosis. Mostly, I'm ready to be in a welcoming haven of mutual discovery, where each and every being is recognised, honoured and celebrated as a living master, God/Goddess, an invaluable and vital thread in the tapestry of Oneness.

I went on with my visionary meditation. The statues became my imaginary friends. They responded to my inner rant by grinning, some of them even winked back at me. They seemed happy to be relieved from their tedious job of being put up on a pedestal, untouched and out of reach. Instead, they preferred to be admired and celebrated for their unique contributions and qualities.

Yeshua once said, 'The kingdom of Heaven lives within you.' Or, 'You shall do this and more.' As each claims dominion over one's life, we become the living masters and masterpieces of our time.

I sat down on the cool marble floor and felt massive gratitude for the spiritual insights and energetic downloads the Damanhur community had ignited within me. The most valuable being a profound knowingness that the greatest 'wonder' of this world lives within each and every being.

That night I lay in bed, eyes wide open, peering at the ceiling while feeling the immense uncertainty on the horizon. I took some long deep breaths into my belly and put my hands over my heart. '*What* now, *beloved Sophia? Where shall we go? How may I serve?* The answer was not yet clear to me.

There was nothing to do but to hold myself tight with all the passion and fervour of a devoted mother. The loving voice of Sophia chimed in to comfort, soothe and console my restless heart. '*Whose will are you serving, beloved? Because when you are serving the will of the Divine, you are always on the path of resolution. It is in the silence of your heart that you will feel what is in highest alignment and resonance for you. Allow your joy to guide your way and seek comfort in the natural world. Soon you will be amongst family and friends, and will feel happy to be back in the Bay Area. When the time is right to return, you will know. For now, breath deeply, be grateful as you take rest within the sanctity of your newly awakened Heart.*'

With that, I closed my weary eyes and slept like a baby until sunrise.

CHAPTER SIXTY-FOUR

TREE OF LIFE

Stay close to those who know about the heart.
Choose the shade of a tree
That is in constant bloom.
Don't meander aimlessly
Among the herb sellers and potion venders.
Go directly to the shop
That sells nothing but sweets!
Don't sit waiting by every boiling pot
To have your plate filled!
Not every boiling pot
Is cooking what you want.
Not every sugar cane is filled with sugar.
Not every down has an up.
Not every eye has vision.
Not every sea contains pearls.

– Jelaluddin Rumi

The apple that grew by the miracle of God refers to the pituitary gland stimulated by the down pouring threefold fire of Spirit. It rules the third eye. When fully awakened, this is the eye of the heart by which the initiate will see into spirit realms. The initiate thus enters in. She will die upon the inner tree in order to be reborn into the life of spirit. The inner tree is the alta major, whose roots burrow deep into the root chakra, with branches reaching up to the crown. This is the tree of knowledge in which the initiate stands alone in order to accomplish salvation for the bloodline.

– Niamh Clune, *The Coming of the Feminine Christ*

The Tree of Sophia (Wisdom) is identical to the Tree of Life, for it is known that "She is a tree of life to those who lay hold of her." The apple from this tree contains Sophia's five seeds of wisdom, and she instructs one to eat these seeds, thus taking her wisdom within and assimilating it in one's deepest being. This is an organic process by which wisdom is the fruit, which grows from a "new perception." As we are instructed to "Acquire Sophia, acquire perception," it is apparent that Sophia (Wisdom) is identified with perception. This "new perception" that Sophia brings is precisely the wholeness of her apple, which integrates the dichotomies of existence. It is the perception of the interconnectedness of all life and the wisdom that comes from that awareness; it is the perception of creation as a blessing and the joy that comes from that recognition. Eating the seeds of the apple of wisdom leads to an "eco-Sophianic perspective of nature" as we recognize Sophia's presence in all things. Truly it is the apple of joyful wisdom that she blesses us with!

– Cynthia Avens, *The Call of Sophia*

On this new day, I wanted nothing more than to commune with nature in all her radiant glory. *Oh, how I long to immerse myself in the morning mist rather than the mystery!* I stepped out into the fresh air and took in the majesty of the surrounding trees gently swaying in the breeze. Like a teenager ditching school for the day, I walked across the Damanhur grounds, discretely slipped out the main gate and walked briskly up the country road. A sense of refreshing freedom washed over me. *Whooohoo! Freedom!* I was back in Gaia's garden, elated to be reveling in her full-blown beauty.

The whistling birds and rustling green leaves welcomed me back into the wilderness of my soul. My inner child relaxed, feeling safe and delighted to drink in the mana of the ancient emerald trees, which swayed amidst the silvery-blue mountains. My legs grew roots that reached down into Gaia's fertile belly. I took long strides up the steep hill, relishing the sinewy vigour of my stretching muscles. As I called my energy back, I gave myself permission to release any and all self-imposed constraints that I had inadvertently placed upon myself. My wild and free spirit resumed her natural countenance and my unbridled inner feline began to purr once again.

One of the many gifts I had received from the City of Light was a deeper reclamation of my core sovereignty in relationship to tribal and group consciousness. I was aware of the countless lifetimes I had spent as an initiate, giving my power over to appease a false god or an outer authority. I wept for all the times I sought acceptance and validation from fitting into a group mind or an external 'higher power' in the hope for a breadcrumb of acceptance, approval and belonging.

The symphony of bird songs lightened my heart. I realised how weary I had become from all of the pressure and conditions I had placed upon myself to be a 'someone' that lived up to someone else's expectations and interpretations of what God is and what God is not.

Never mind. My thirst for communion was now being quenched by the wild majesty of the natural world. *This is where I AM whole, alive with the power of unbridled wild resplendence. This is where I can simply be one with the essence of all of creation. HOME!*

I walked on and before long was magnetically drawn to a cobblestone church nestled on the side of the hill in the neighboring village. Upon arriving, I perched on the front steps to offer a prayer of gratitude to all my relations, invisible friends and allies who have blessed my life along the way. Instead of entering the chapel, I stood to face Grandfather Sun and allowed my skin to be kissed by his golden rays. The penetrating heat felt as if I was being showered in luminous grace. His solar nectar spread through my high heart to unfurl my iridescent rainbow wings and reveal that hidden paradise in the stargate of my heart.

I whispered a prayer. 'May our lives be a living prayer ground, a place of sacred communion to enliven and celebrate the precious gifts of life.' With that, I walked through the old cobblestone streets of this remote rural village. It was charming, but on this day, I longed to be in the wild arms of Gaia Sophia. And so I continued until the stones ran out and delivered me to the edge of an expansive green meadow where an old-growth apple tree invited me to come and sit by her. Quite naturally, I accepted and curled up under her canopy of shade to have a wee rest.

'Thank you, ancient one, for sharing your shaded canopy with me. I'm ever so sleepy,' I murmured. 'Would you mind if I lie down underneath you and take a little nap?'

'Why yes, of course! It is my greatest joy to provide you sanctuary.' I heard the tree spirit reply. I snuggled into the cradle of earth's nourishing embrace, closed my eyes and then drifted off just as a child would, safely in the soft lap of her mother. After some timeless moments, I opened my eyes and asked, *Who am I now?* I posed the question to the clouds drifting by in the dusky blue sky. My eyes gently closed again and I was given a lucid vision while resting between two worlds.

My beloved and I were skydancing together as one. We landed in the temple of the Christos Sophia's where our Family of Light, along with all Starseeds, species, races and cultures, were gathered around an ancient future Tree of Life as tall and luscious as one could imagine. There was an overall sense of deep peace and serenity sitting amongst her curvacious roots amongst eternal friends. I became lucidly aware that each being was uniquely encoded with an energetic signature of pristine Light that coincided immaculately with the all-pervading Love of the cosmos. The luminous light from each radiant heart flowed together like a toroidal fountain that cascaded down in an aurora of rainbow spectral light. As we resonated together, we became one shared heart, collectively beating as one. The coherent resonance of our synchronised hearts opened the dome of the temple. Together we gazed up to the canopy of shimmering stars and saw two suns shining all at once. I knew that the energy that flowed from within this temple was the same love-light that beat within each and every heart. Just before the vision faded, I heard Sophia's soothing voice remind me, *'You can relax now, trust life and take delight in the cycles of nature. Embrace the unknown with wonder and awe. Creation is infinitely expanding into more and more resplendent Love and Beauty.'*

Scintillating in empty fullness, I gazed into the clear blue sky and pondered the one truth that included all of existence within it: *What if there can only be...more and more beauty?*

Suddenly I was startled from my daydream by a stern and robust grandmother who tapped me on the shoulder with a fallen branch from the apple tree. She wore a red-and-white-checkered scarf wrapped around her thinning grey hair. As she towered over me, her robust bosom overflowed from her soiled apron and spilled over onto my face. She then proceeded to wave her plump arms around in a flurry and fire off a slew of indistinguishable Italian words.

With dazed eyes, I looked into her ebony eyes and said, '*Si, si, madre. Grazie.*' And then added a few animated hand gestures that somehow conveyed to her the circumstances that led me to lie down and have a rest under her ancient apple tree.

Well, this wise ol' grandmother caught on rather quickly and gave me her ever so precious seal of approval along with a warm, toothless grin. Grandmother then waved her flappy arms in a gracious gesture that welcomed me to stay for as long as I desired. Then with a toothless chuckle, she waddled away like a plump ol' goose to resume her afternoon chores.

Feeling utterly blissed by Grandmother's blessing, I luxuriated under the apple tree until the pink grapefruit sun disappeared behind the mountainside. Just before I got up to head back to Damanhur, I heard the answer to my question: *Who am I now, Madre Terra?*

'*You, my love, are the apple of my eye!*'

CHAPTER SIXTY-FIVE

GYPSY QUEEN

The ability to shift frequencies between the higher vibration of spirit and the lower vibration of matter is possible because of the existence of a transformer found not only within every human being, but also at the centre of the galaxy. This unique piece of equipment is the heart. When we are disconnected from the pulse of our heart, we forget that we are immortal magicians and we readily relinquish our wand and our power. It is time to remember who you are: this can only occur through listening to the heart.

The heart could be called a stargate, transporting us naturally within this multidimensional existence. Creating heartfelt space wherever we go. The heart resonates with the energy emerging from the heart of the Great Mother, whom embraces us all equally: within the energy we call Love.

– Christine R. Page, *Return of the Great Mother*

Inside the mandala of aliveness, you may always be called to bear witness to the falling away of old dreams of who you are and how you thought it was going to be here. It can be both terrifying and exhilarating to watch as all of the familiar reference points, beliefs, and ideas about love dissolve into a pregnant field of hopelessness and deflation.

This deflation is one of the secret envoys of the beloved, one of the clarifying arrows in her quiver, sent from beyond to seed your essence with particles of wholeness and luminosity. Through your ripening body, other envoys arrive – old unmet guests of sensitivity, vulnerability, sadness, and bliss, washing out your nervous system so that you may attune to beings everywhere. She has even called in her allies of the phenomenal world – including the colours, aromas, and majestic visions – so that you may finally rest in the radiance that you are.

– Matt Licata

While sipping my morning tea, I took a pulse on my travel plans. In only four more days, I was scheduled to fly back to San Francisco. My money was definitely dwindling and my online Airtech ticket had very sparse return flights to the U.S. If I didn't take this next upcoming flight, I would have to wait for another two weeks, and I simply didn't have the funds to extend my trip any longer.

What are you aware of right now? I asked myself, closing my eyes and coming into empty presence. As I sat in stillness, it became obvious that I was not quite complete with my pilgrimage. *Okay, Great Mamacita, where shall we go now?* My mind's eye lit up with a herd of white Camargue horses accompanied with a melody from a Gypsy king's song – *Saintes-Maries-de-la-Mer it is!*

Of course, I was being called back to the mystical lands of Mary Magdalene! I sensed that I still had some dangling soul threads to retrieve, especially the ones I left on the burning dance floor. I looked at my map and calculated that Saintes-Maries was approximately twelve hours away by car. I was seriously wondering how I was going to pull the whole escapade off and still make it back to catch my flight to the US. My plane left out of Frankfort, Germany in just four more days!

I spent my last night in Damanhur coming up with my master 007 plan to pull off this insane *Mission is Possible* plot. *I will rent a car in Turin, return to Saintes-Maries, then drive back to Turin to catch my first flight out – all in a matter of three days. Now that's bending time. Crazy! Crazy! Crazy!*

The next morning, I aligned with my super-heroine mindset and took the first shuttle out of Damanhur to the local Turin Airport. I then rented a car that nearly maxed out my 'emergency only' credit card. At that point, I didn't care about the price; there were still some soul fragments lingering between the sheets and under the moonlit sky of Saintes-Maries-des-les-Mer. *I simply cannot deny the strong call to return the land of wild white horses and reclaim my full sovereign heart.*

I bolted out of the Turin Airport, infused with a blooming passion and stoked for my next adventure. My red Italian sports car was the perfect vehicle to catapult me to Southern France and back in record time. Even at my steady pace of 130 kilometres per hour, I managed to devour the stunning scenery of the Mediterranean Coast. The opulent beauty of the Italian Riviera was breathtakingly beautiful. It felt like a mysterious force was irresistibly calling me forth and it was way larger than my appetite for sightseeing. With laser-like focus, I shape-shifted into an Italian racecar driver, stopping only for bridge tolls, refuels and an occasional cappuccino. Luckily, the gas stations doubled as espresso bars in Italy. With each kilometre, I became fueled with my passion to live as my own greatest partner for life, wholly authentic, divinely wedded, nothing more, nothing less.

I sped along the sparkling coastal motorway while signs for Cannes, Nice and Marseilles flashed by in a blur. The magnificence of the French Riviera coastline swooned me at every curvaceous bend of the highway. I entertained myself by imagining that I was in my own Divine Feminine version of the Goldfinger 007 film. *Golden heart woman, you're the kiss of life!*

I zoomed along, screaming like a wild banshee or an exotic bird freeing herself from an invisible cage that she had become too tightly ensnarled in, for far too long. *I call back my power, my heart, my body, my freedom, my soul! I call back my innocence, my joy, my passion, and my courage to love full out like never before!*

Nine hours later, I pulled into Saintes-Maries-De-La-Mer and swerved into a parking spot right in front of where Aiden and I had taken our midnight swim. I will never forget the euphoria of dancing the night away with him at that purple disco. I recalled watching him walk like a naked god into the moonlit ocean and saying to myself, *yikes, there is something about this exquisite man-god-bebe´ that has the power to annihilate me.* How prophetic. In a way, I was certainly right about him! Yet now I knew that it really wasn't about his power to annihilate me because I gave him that power, whether he wanted it or not. He may have been the scorpion, but

I was the frog, and I played my perfect part in walking myself into the alchemical flames. *Thank you, Mr. Scorpion. I get it. What burns are the illusions I built around love. We came together to fulfill a sacred contract and for this, I am grateful for all that I have learned. If it wasn't for you, well...* My thoughts trailed off.

Nevertheless, the fires burned inside, a passion so fierce it could light up Las Vegas! I slammed the car door behind me, ran across the silky white sand to the edge of the shore and fell to my knees. *This sea has loved me a thousand times before. Time and again, I have offered myself to her mysterious moonlit tides.*

I dropped my sundress to the sand and walked into the arms of Mother Mer. She wrapped me in her liquid folds, as a mother would, to comfort her cherished daughter. *Oh, Mother, you are the only place I know that is big enough to receive my salty tears and make them one with yours.*

Letting the tension of the drive go, I exhaled deeply into her warm embrace and gave way to the avalanche of tears that soon turned into a rolling revelation. *Aha! I love this glistening lemon-burst sun! I love this succulent salty sea! I love this luscious wonderment of a moment, and yes, yes, yes, Sophia, I love myself and I love him. I love you and I love all beings as the beloved. Love needs no object nor does it need to be owned or possessed. Love cannot be parceled out, nor can it be measured. I allow LOVE to BE, without feeling compelled to ascribe it to a person, place or thing. I am the Love and Love is endless! Wow, this is what it means to truly be 'in' Love!*

Salty tears came rolling down my face, along with the recognition that there was a place for my grief to coexist with the depth of my love. After all, this was the place of the Gypsy kings, where the dark and the light dance the eternal tango with the Divine. This ancient future home was big-hearted enough to include everything in her big bosomed, beer-bellied, bottomless embrace of all-prevailing grace.

After what seemed like hours of frolicking in the deep blue sea, I swam to the shore and rested my belly down on the warm silky sand, still buzzing with my revelation. *Love just is, and I am brave enough to bare it All! In fact, this shimmering play of opposites held in the light of ever-expanding Love was exactly how God/Goddess creates new worlds of endless possibility. The nothing becomes a something through the impulse of love...and voila, new life is conceived, and what a gift it is!* With this full body awareness I sat up and spoke aloud this Higher Light Decree, inspired by Steve Nobel:

'I call upon my Divine Presence, Family of Light and the highest light of the beloved other to be present through mutual consent for this decree of intent. I call upon the angels of loving compassion and ultraviolet fire to cleanse, clear, purify, resolve and bring complete healing to Self and beloved other.

'I now call back my power and life force from all timelines, lifetimes, dimensions and parallel realities. I call back all soul fragments and soul fractures to be cleansed and purified in the cleansing waters of the Holy Grail and returned to my I Am presence for clearing and reintegration. May all energetic cords and circuitry be respectfully released and returned to the beloved for clearing, healing and reintegration. May all soul growth and highest learning be lovingly integrated, free from any and all hurt or trauma.

'With abiding respect for the divine sovereignty of Self and other, may healthy intimacy, abundance, connection, flow, freedom, harmony, happiness, miracle consciousness be recalibrated into the highest light of love; and all be restored into the light of original innocence. May this and all sacred connections be protected and held within the immaculate light of the Christos Sophia. I now declare the pristine chalice of my being, to be fully recalibrated to the highest Light of Divine Love now and forever more.

'I AM the light, the light I AM. I am the light, the light I AM. I Am the light, the light I AM. From this moment on, I declare myself, beloved other and this world to be an awakened expression of pristine light and immaculate Love. So be it and so it is.'

Upon concluding this decree, I received the most magnificent vision that would forever be imprinted upon my heart. All of the horses of the Camargue were set free to run wild once again. They galloped together along the shores of Saintes-Maries-de-la-Mer, their manes whipping with water, their prancing hooves dancing alive and their untamable spirits blazing the light of triumphant being.

Ahhh, this is what it feels like to flourish together in sovereignty, Oneness and sublime beauty. Blessed be the gift!

ALL ROADS

Anyone who loves must learn to lose themselves
and then find themselves again.

– Paulo Coelho

ALL ROADS

This is the sound of one heart starting to hear
This is the sound of faith stepping out of fear
The journey of one soul's passage through time
And this is one lone dreamer learning to fly
And this is the sound of love
Reaching out from the storm
Calling through the thunder
Through the anguished war
And I can feel the winds
Feel them beginning to turn
And this is one small light, starting to burn
And your love is shining
In everything I do
And I hear you calling for me
For all roads lead to you
Every moment of my days, every movement
Every miracle, every time I speak your name
I know that you are here inside

And this is the sound of a prayer
On its way to the sun
Calling all the children to gather as one
And I can see us there, see it clear as the blue
And this is one small part, here is my gift to you
So count the hilltops, count the towns
As we're crossing over
See no, hear no, speak no sound
On this golden flight.

– Tina Malia, 'All Roads'

L ate that afternoon, I took a long delicious nap and dreamt about my early banishment from the word 'no', which opened up a whole new cache of stored memories. I grabbed my journal, turned on the bedside lamp and began to write. So much of my past was unraveling into clarity.

I put down my pen and reflected on the intense feeling of being born a highly sensitive empath. Empaths typically find it hard to say 'no', because of their instinctual tendency to want to please others and harmonise their environment. They also have a tendency to take on the problems of others as their own. It is often difficult for them to set boundaries for themselves and say 'no', even when too much is being asked of them. There were plenty of times I played the survival game by 'conforming to please others' with great finesse, and yet I had never stopped saying 'yes' to my sovereign self and highest calling to live my most authentic and soul inspired life. Despite countless heartbreaks of being profoundly misunderstood for my overly sensitive nature, I was equally stubborn and tenacious. Qualities that ensured my wild untamable spirit remained fiercely alive. From early on, survival would simply not be enough, when I knew my authentic soul purpose was to flourish and thrive along with all beings.

I closed my eyes, acutely aware that I was in front of the same hotel where Aiden and I had made love nearly a month ago. That was an experience I had not wanted to say 'no' to, but now, alone in the darkness, I saw the cost of saying 'yes' and wondered if my life would have unfolded any differently if I had abstained from our night of passionate love making.

I needed to be honest about my choice. I allowed a being to enter my womb that ultimately did not respect nor care for my deepest heart. This level of discernment and stewardship for the sanctity of my womb-heart would be a lesson I would take with me into the rest of my lifetime.

I flopped onto my back and looked directly into the slanting sunlight. I saw that at the time of meeting Aiden, I felt no other choice than to choose love in the best way I knew how and ride the initiatory wave all the way home. I flooded my being with tender compassion, as I came out of that fire more than a little singed. And yet, I knew quite well that I was not a victim of circumstance. I was destined to be burn in this initiatory fire that allowed me to rise like a phoenix from the ashes and become the Lover of the World that I was born to be.

I reflected on the resilience of the Gypsy folks who gravitated from all over the world to play music, dance and celebrate the revered Black Madonna year after year. Their deeply engraved scars worn like shiny jewels won from triumphing over life's precarious battleground of the heart. Their lined faces, rippled bellies, tattooed skin and gold-capped teeth proudly paraded their soul scars. The light shining from their eyes told the story of their fearless and tenacious courage to choose love over fear of being burned. For many, a heart broken wide open was the greatest trophy of all. Like proud peacocks, the Gypsy people loved to flaunt their incandescent beauty. They beamed a noble pride for having what it takes to transmute the poison in their lives into the medicine that fuels their creative passion. These global nomadic people share in an unspoken secret that points to the greatest treasure of all – they know that within the darkest wound lives the potential for the greatest light to shine through. They earn their vibrant colours by dancing in the fire, risking it all for the passion that brings them to the threshold of God's wild embrace. For them, life is not about being perfect – it's about being boldly alive with the fire of risking everything for a red-hot kiss on the lips from the beloved. *Living and loving with full passion is how we grow our wings of compassion!* I reflected on one of my favourite poems by Dawna Markova entitled, 'I Will Not Die an Unlived Life':

I will not live in fear of falling or catching fire.
I choose to inhabit my days, to allow my living to open me,
to loosen my heart until it becomes a wing,
a torch, a promise.

I wrapped my arms around my little one and held her tight, until I finally dozed off to the tune of Bob Marley's 'Redemption Song' like a lullaby cradling me to sleep. The remaining warmth of the setting sun was my blanket, the sand my cradle, my raw open heart a bed of roses and intense vulnerability a crucible for all that was yet to rise from the ashes.

Old pirates, yes, they rob I;
Sold I to the merchant ships,
Minutes after they took I
From the bottomless pit.
But my hand was made strong
By the 'and of the Almighty.
We forward in this generation triumphantly.

CHAPTER SIXTY-SEVEN

THE SWEETEST NECTAR

I am a living chalice of embodied wisdom, compassion and truth.
Bound only by the highest Love and Light
Touchable only by the hands of God.
I am Sophia, the essence of Christ
I carry the white lily of the living trinity
The symbol of Heaven on Earth
Sacred Mother/ Divine Father/Child of God
I serve only you. I am YOU
This Love perpetually rebirthing through childlike wonder
I stand beside my sisters of the Rose Magdalene
Safe and protected in my unwavering trust and faith
Together witnessing the return of Christos Sophia
Corona's awakening, bearing the flame of Light
Birthing this Divine New Humanity.
I remember the essence of All that I AM.
Divine embodiment is now. So be it and so it is.

– Snow Forest

Before dawn I was wide awake, so I quickly dressed to go out and greet the rising sun. As I wandered the narrow streets, I noticed an eerie quiet. Only a few of the bakeries were stirring, getting ready for the morning's *petit dejourne*. The sky looked like freshly squeezed tangerine juice as the sun rose on the horizon of the sea. I walked to the church of Magdalene to offer my gratitude prayers, only to find that the thick wooden doors were locked with a heavy chain. A singular bench sat in the village square adjacent to the cathedral. If I couldn't be inside Mary's cathedral, I could sit within the crystalline cathedral of my heart and commune with her there. This was a day I felt to be extra close to my Family of Light. I sat quietly and meditated while soaking in the early morning light and then took out my journal to write:

> This journey has cost me absolutely everything! I am coming to accept that I will cross the ocean with very little in my pocket and very few noticeable changes on the outside. And yet, on the inside, I am not the same person that left Gaia's Grove. My Divine pilot light has been lit from within, and although the flame may fluctuate from light to dim and dim to light, I know it is forever alight with the Beloved who is anchored within my innermost heart. For this, I feel abundant beyond measure, eternally grateful and overflowing with the light of love Divine!

A warm breeze encircled me. It carried the fierce love and compassion for all the men and women who had dared to make the journey into the depths of their chalice well. I sensed the three goddesses surrounding me, and as I merged with this holy trinity of sacred sisters, I felt fortified with a love large enough to embrace the whole of the world. Mother Mary placed a ruby-red velvet cape covered in tiny golden white stars around my shoulders.

She reminded me, *'Those who brave their own darkness will rise as a vaster and more expanded Self. Always remember, as you dare to traverse these forbidden realms and love all that was once deemed unlovable, you will be protected and held by this royal gown.'* Mary Magdalene touched my womb and my heart with a long stem rose to annoint and consecrate the source of my divine Feminine power and unbridled creative fire. Sarah, the Black Madonna, gazed deeply into my eyes to transmit to me that living from passion fueled by my wild, fierce, uncompromising spirit is the only way to truly live.

The four of us held hands in an etheric circle of light. I felt them honour and celebrate me as a sovereign queen anchored in the heart of the Wild Divine Beloved. The marrow of my bones shimmered with incandescent rainbow light. A deliciously sweet amrita nectar flowed through my veins. This was the feeling of being one with the essence of all that I had come to reclaim, serve and remember. A symphony of tiny bird chirps filled the air around me as if they had come to witness and celebrate this sacred occasion.

I sensed it was time to say goodbye to the church of Mary Magdalene. I beamed my biggest love and thanked her for her undeniable presence that permeated this region in a sweet yet fiercely uncompromising perfume. I knew her Sacred Union flame would forever blaze in my eternal heart of hearts.

As I strolled through the narrow streets, I delighted in the first stirrings of early morning risers and bustling merchants setting up shop. The aroma of freshly baked pastries was intoxicating and opened up all of my senses to this brand-new sunshiny day. I stopped in at the first open café and ordered a hot tea and warm croissant to enjoy by the sea. Upon arriving at the boardwalk, I found a bench to enjoy my petit déjeuner while soaking in the beauty of the turquoise sea lapping on the shore.

As the seaside town stirred awake, I sat and admired the plethora of unique and eclectic people strolling by. They felt remarkably at home in their human skin. You didn't have to hide your imperfections nor fit into the fashionable status quo here. *Exiled, orphaned, outcast or poor, come, come, whoever you are – you are always welcomed in Saintes-Maries-de-la-Mer.* To me, that was a testimonial to Mary Magdalene's daughter, Sarah, patron saint of this region. Her untamable spirit represented the Universal Christ Consciousness being born in the heart of a new humanity – a humanity anchored in unconditional love, a love that savoured the endless flavours of diversity and celebrated the novel and sumptuous creations made from God/Goddess's infinite spice cabinet. *No wonder I felt so accepted, relaxed and totally at home here!*

As I stared at the glistening sunlight dancing upon the water, I was shown the light of the Masculine making love to the body of the Feminine, producing mesmerizing, glistening prismatic stars that represented all of Sophia's children. Feeling intoxicated by this liquid light ballet, I looked up to the clear blue sky with a mouthful of gooey, chocolatey croissant to see a flock of white doves flying by, displaying an array of winged beauty. I marvelled at the Christos Sophia's ingenious orchestration. Their living poetry had brought me and countless other to their knees in a singular breath of awakened splendour and awe. *Simply 'dovine'!*

CHAPTER SIXTY-EIGHT

LAST RITES

Passion is like the force that splits the atom. It splits the atom of the privatised self to release the nuclear energy of dynamic love in action. Anyone who's been through an experience of either divine or human passion, or both, knows that passion annihilates the small self and births you into the universal cosmic fire energies of a much vaster Self. It is peaceful, but it is also wild, wildly loving, and wildly hungry to see justice done. You cannot awaken to the Mother's love for everything that she has created without also awakening to the Mother's heartbreak at the agony and injustice and cruelty and madness of what we are doing to everything She's created. You cannot awaken to the Mother's truth without waking up to the Mother's urgency to see love, justice, compassion, and harmony put into action so that the fullness of her gifts to us can be known and so that the fullness of our potential to evolve into divine human beings can be realized.

– Andrew Harvey, *An Evolutionary Vison of Relationships*

The task you are given is to love the hell out of yourself, to turn the truth of your innermost heart into the beacon light you steer by. To rise up from the chaos of a dying world, peel the old skin off and at long last discover what you're made of.

– Mark Borax

fter packing up my things, I sat for a moment, recollecting how Aiden and I spent our last magical night entwined around one another's sun-kissed bodies here at the Hotel Le Dauphin Bleu. To honour that memory, I said a prayer of gratitude and wished him eternal happiness. My heart knew the time had come to let go so that I could find peace and experience spiritual, energetic and emotional closure. I sensed a beautiful new reality was opening up for me, but for me to enter it I would need to release my attachment to the past. I felt into what is meant for me to move on with an open, trusting and grateful heart.

I went down to the hotel restaurant and picked out the same table where we once sat, sipping our morning coffee. While waiting for my breakfast to arrive, I chose some oracle cards to get a pulse on what the day might bring. I pulled the card *Clinging to the Past, Postponement, Play and Discovery.* I took my reading as a clear sign to let go of the past, say farewell to Saintes-Maries and move on to discover new realms of enchantment and play. I affirmed inwardly, *Nothing from my past is worthy enough to postpone the joy of today!*

After paying my bill, I offered a farewell smile to the lady patron of the hotel. I recalled how she grinned at Aiden and I as we came giggling into the lobby like two intoxicated lovers, dripping wet from our sunset swim. Just like Sophia, she saw right through me into the razor's edge of love's great paradox. I silently thanked her for playing her perfect role in my Grail journey as I recollected something my brilliant friend Matt Khan once said that rang especially true for me as I stood at this divine crossroad, *'This journey is very personal because it is through the willingness to be a person, that the light you already are becomes real, real tangible, real palpable, real powerful and real transformative for your life and for the lives of all.'*

Before reuniting with my racy, Italian sports car, I took a few moments at the seashore to ground my energy deep into the crystalline core of the Earth. I connected to my breath, relaxed my body, cleansed and balanced my chakras, while aligning the central pillar of my spine with the Earthstar and diamond heart of the Central Sun. Smiling into every cell, atom, organ and bone in my body, I opened myself as a golden chalice to be filled by the light of my soul's sovereign essence. *Wow! I have the ability to embody this*

Sacred Union anywhere and at anytime! So this is what it feels like to clothed by the sun!

I departed Saintes-Maries-de-la-Mer in high spirits and headed to Arles, the town where the river greets the sea. I would always cherish the memory of how Aiden and I had uncovered Magdalene and Yeshua's treasure chest, filled with their sacred marriage relics. From that day on, I went on to anchor etheric golden chalices throughout the world in magical lakes, oceans and rivers that greeted the sea.

This time around, I had practical matters to attend to in Arles. First, I would check on my flights back to the States and then take care of some long-overdue banking business. The day grew increasingly challenging with a continuous downpour of rain, a dead car battery, closed banks, and an overwhelming feeling of anxiety that slowly encroached upon my day. *Keep the faith. Now is the time to stay strong and stay centred in your heart.* With a heavy sigh, I resigned myself to being stuck in Arles until the following day, when I would receive the emergency funds I required to get me back to the US.

With a little less than sixty euros in my pocket, I wandered the streets looking for an affordable hotel room. Fatigued to the bone and withered by the rain, I finally found a room for sixty euros, which I managed to talk down to fifty. That left me with a whopping ten to get me through the night. With my remaining ten euros, I bought a glass of red wine and a small appetiser for my supper at the hotel pub. I felt like Cinderella at the end of the ball. I was intensely aware of the sobering reality that the magic of my journey was slowly wearing off and in just three days, I would be on my return flight to North America.

No matter. Just like a saloon girl from the Wild West, I polished off my last sip of wine. *I may have discovered the source of the living Grail but it's a whole other thing to keep the chalice of my being in overflow!* Wearily, I walked up the three flights of stairs up to my tiny room perched just above the hotel bar. It took some time and patience to wriggle the rusty key in the old lock and wrestle open the door. When the key finally gave way, I was met by a nauseating wave of stale French cigarettes. At least it had a private bathroom. Relieved to have found a dry place to sleep for the night, I proceeded to shower off from my disheartening day. After a long hot shower, my pity party substantially lightened. I was grateful that I could relax and rejuvenate before the big push to return Gypsy Queen back to Turin. Like a crab crawling into her shell, I retreated under the synthetic blankets and found some comfort upon the worn-out mattress.

Mother of God! I pray I won't discover any other kinds of crabs apart from me inside my bed!

Click. I turned on the TV and peeked out from under the covers to get a taste of the present global reality on the local news station. The Tell-a-Vision-Oracle reported the latest stories and showed me pictures of the rising tensions in the Middle East.

'It looks like the US is headed into another war. Stay tuned for more updates,' the anchorwoman reported. I felt like I was inside a planetary pressure cooker that was inevitably going to release an explosion of steam. Government fear tactics were encroaching upon the entire world, pumping out mass doses of distraction to keep humanity overwhelmed in fear and feeling like powerless victims. The news was always such a sobering reminder to tune in to my sovereign truth and put energy into the reality I wished to create rather than feed the fear-based narratives. I envisioned myself, and all beings embodying their creative passion, making choices that honour the Earth's ecosystem, building cooperative and sustainable communities while using each and every day to be in service and create value for others for generations to come.

I visualised stepping into the shoes of the so called enemy to glimpse reality through their eyes. I would gaze into the so-called other's eyes from a space of openness, curiosity and compassion and say, 'I see you and I honour you. I feel the part of me that is in you – we are unique and we are also the same. Let's see what we can come up with that would be beneficial to all parties involved, including the Earth.'

The slick news reporter, dressed in a bright red suit and wearing glossy red lipstick, slowly faded into oblivion as I fell into a deep slumber and found myself in yet another lucid dream.

I was walking along an empty road, and I met Aiden, who embraced me in deep recognition. Joyous delight enveloped us in a wave of sacred reunion, yet I simultaneously saw myself burning alive in a funeral pyre. He screamed, 'I am here,' and his love poured out into me.

I let out a curdling death scream, 'MOTHER!' Mother never came. *Where is She?* All that remained of me were bits of my bones amongst the ashes.

I woke up startled and drenched in sweat. The TV still blared, so I turned it off and drifted back to sleep. The vivid dream continued. My biological mother and father appeared and brought me a vase of three pink roses. They placed them on the bedside table as a peace offering and then vanished. Then suddenly the roses caught fire from the candle next to them. Then the bed caught fire too! In a mad frenzy, I reached for some bottled water and put out the flames. All that remained from the flames was the vase of three pink roses. In the end, only that which is pure withstands the heat of the alchemical flames. I was left with a strange feeling of nobody being out there but me, floating in a vast, cosmic ocean as dark and mysterious as the midnight sea.

That morning, as I lay in my alchemical cocoon between one life and another, I felt the timelines of my soul dissolving with these powerful spiritual last rites so I could be cleansed and liberated into the fullness of my next phase. I had been inwardly preparing for this powerful rebirth and now I was in the final anointing before I leaving one life and leaping into another. It was time to let go in order to embody something of extreme value for myself and for the collective consciousness that I was a part of.

I lingered between worlds and reflected on my startling dream. I looked for the lesson and gift in the intense symbolism. free you from the grip of what has been.

I heard the voice of Sophia chime in, *'There is a moment, maybe a breath, beloved, when one realises there is no turning back and the path before you is imminent. This space between what you once were and what you are now becoming is the most fertile place of all. It is the ending of a stubborn pattern as you embrace your future and let go of the emotional and psychological burdens you have been carrying for yourself and likely countless others, ancestors and more for far too long. Let yourself off the hook of guilt, blame and shame. You have been preparing over lifetimes for the threshold you find yourself on. It is the stage of making your chrysalis translucent through the final release while incubating in the imaginal cells of that which is destined to be born. It is the transfiguration from death into rebirth, the metamorphosis from Homo sapien into Homo luminous.*

Give yourself permission to acknowledge that all people, including you, have done their very best. The universe is offering you a powerful spiritual gift. Your heart knows how to receive it. It's time to let go. It's time to be happy and free. As you do, you will find greater freedom and a new lease on life, as if you are being born again in this lifetime as the monarch butterfly that you are.

'There are countless narratives and timelines being played out and all have their relevance just because they exist. The narrative we wish for you to embody is the one that has all the essential ingredients to birth you into your next greater than imagined life. May you find the courage and strength to stay open to meet the contractions of this collective birthing while infusing each moment with humility and grace.

'Each and every being is likened to a cell in my body, the body of the One. In this phase of radical let go may you activate the cosmic stardust that fertilizes the seed for what's to come —the golden world that is now rising as the Universal Christ.'

I thanked Sophia for her wisdom light and then felt moved to do a Google search on the stages of alchemy to shed even more light on my dream, and resonated with the following passage:

> Distillation is the agitation and sublimation of psychic forces that is necessary to ensure that no impurities from the ego or deeply submerged id are incorporated into the next and final stage. Free from sentimentality and emotions, cut off even from one's personal identity, Distillation is the purification of the unborn Self – all that we truly are and can be.
>
> Distillation is the process where we become far more interested in the greater good then merely in our own. It is the transformational stage where we spiritually and emotionally mature enough to merge with the collective conscious and unconscious

without becoming devastated by what we find there. The reason we can keep our balance after having arrived at the Distillation stage is that the Ego no longer controls us and we can therefore appreciate the mysteries of the collective – and personal – shadow material without the ego's intrusion. A distilled person surrenders to the higher forces while celebrating and honoring the existence of the lower ones.

– Joseph D. Dismore,
The 7 Steps in Alchemical Transformation

CHAPTER SIXTY-NINE

CALL OF THE DOVE

As we bring these dissonant energies back into balance the energies of separation will naturally dissolve and humans will once again remember how to connect with their hearts and intuition. It is time to offer gratitude to everyone in our lives who has reflected our Divinity back to us in both the darkness and the light. For both are necessary for the expansion and evolution of our souls. And may I remind you that the roles of holding the light amidst the darkness have been the most challenging and most deserving of our appreciation. Through eons of life experiences, all these aspects have been expanding our conscious ability to experience and embody the divinity of Love.

This unique lifetime on earth offers an opportunity to expand our consciousness beyond the antiquated ingrained misconceptions, to gather all our expanded aspects into wholeness, and realize the Sovereignty of our Divinity from whence we were originally born. For we all originate from the same infinite Source, birthed as Divine Seeds of Creation to create art and music beyond anything the omniverse has ever experienced before.

– Sharon Lyn Shepard

LOVE

Love
Love all beings
Love everything
Be only love

Surrender all fear
Be love
Speak only light
Surrender all that is darkness within you
Be love
Speak only truth
Hide no longer
Live truth
Know who you truly are
Trust who you truly are
Live who you truly are
Be who you truly are
Love can never be lost
Love is never poor
Love is who you are
Love is Light
Love is pure
You are love

– Nicolya Christi

The following morning, I left the dingy hotel feeling a sense of closure around the karmic timelines and the parts of my soul that I was called back to retrieve. My fast and faithful red Italian sports car was parked in front, ready to deliver me to the airport to begin my journey back to the states. I had named her Gypsy Queen.

'Bonjourno, Gypsy Queen! I hope you slept better than I did,' I said to my red hot chariot while I gave her a pat and loaded my things into her boot.

By now, I was well acquainted with driving in France. I cruised at a comfortable and confident pace on the motorway. The familiar tunes of Michael Franti kept me company as if he was singing directly to me. 'Pain is what got me here. Love, sweet love, is gonna set me free!'

Midway between Toulouse and Turin, I spotted a freeway sign out of the corner of my eye that read, Saint-Maximin-la-Sainte-Baume. I sped by it while singing along to the blaring music and maintaining a steady speed. *No matter what happens, just get me to the church – I mean airport – on time!*

I suddenly flashed on Gaianna asking me over morning tea, 'Have you been to Saint Baume yet, my dear?'

I replied, 'No, I haven't been there yet, but the name sounds strangely familiar.'

Before I had a chance to say, 'Let's get this show on the road,' Gypsy Queen took command of the wheel and swerved off the freeway at the Maximus Ste. Baume exit, as if she had a mind and a mission all of her own.

Once again, I heard Gaianna's sisterly voice saying, *'Oh, Ambe´, you should really try to visit Saint Baume! It is the sacred cave where Mary lived and ascended!'*

In truth, I had forgotten about her suggestion until this juncture of my journey. Yet as Gypsy Queen purred along the exit road, Saint Baume's significance as part of this Grail journey suddenly dawned on me.

'Alright then,' I said aloud to my feisty little sports car, 'Saint Baume it is!' The little car sped along in satisfaction. 'We're a lot alike, you know, Gypsy Queen – always up for a spontaneous adventure and living life on the edge!' Still, this was cutting it insanely close. I went over my itinerary mile by mile and hour by hour in my head. In less than twenty-four hours, I have a flight out of Turin to Frankfurt via a brief stopover in Stanstead, England.

This is more than a little bit crazy – this is completely mad, as mad as mad can be! I reminded myself, all the while feeling undeniably pulled to this final place of pilgrimage. *Mary's ascension cave, really, Ambe´? How could you possibly pass this one up?* So away I went, and all the voices of pragmatism flew out the window until all that remained was a consistent thump, thump thumping in my heart of hearts.

Gypsy Queen and I zipped up the winding road lined with a barrage of luscious greenery and old growth trees. Mountainous ravines overlooked the small Provence below. I faithfully followed the signs to Saint Baume while hugging the country road corners with precision-like finesse.

Approximately thirteen winding kilometres later, I arrived at a small inn that appeared to be a café. I swerved into the parking spot. A large building set back in the trees was barely visible. I decided to investigate further. Sure enough, it was the convent that Gaianna had told me about. She happened to mention to me that it could accommodate overnight pilgrims for a very affordable price. By this time, it was already late in the afternoon, so I decided to see if I could book a room and continue my journey early the following morning. My plane to England left Turin at twelve noon. I would have to leave before sunrise. I knew I would be cutting it extremely close, and yet I felt deep in my womb that I needed to stay the night.

I wandered into the convent and noticed a small chapel inside. A nun was seated on one of the wooden benches. '*Pardon moi, avez-vous une chambre pour la nuit?*'

'You must inquire with the head Mother, who is presently away, Madame. Return in one half hour, *sil vous plait.*' She said in a cool and detached manner, complimented by excellent English elocution. Apparently, every guest had to be carefully screened and required a stamp of Mother Superior's approval.

As I walked back to the café, I suddenly noticed that my bra strap was hanging off my right shoulder and the contours of my legs and bum showed through my sheer white skirt.

I wonder if she will let me stay looking like this? Or will she look at me and think I'm some kind of California floozy? I pondered while adjusting my clothing and giving it my best shot at looking a little more presentable for a convent.

The small café was bustling with the last afternoon visitors of the day. I ordered the cheapest thing I could find on the menu with my last handful of loose change. Shortly later, I polished off my *pomme frites* feeling delightfully satisfied with my lunch. There was an energetic vibe about this place that was nourishing in ways that was hard to describe. I simply felt warmly and pleasantly at home. Upon returning to the convent, I found a very large matronly lady sitting piously behind her desk.

'*Bonjour,*' I said and then continued in my limited French, '*avez-vous une chambre pour la nuit?*'

She scoured me over from head to toe with a silent scrutinising glare. I held my ground and silently prayed that my bra strap would remain in place. At first, she hesitated. Without a word, she scoured me over from top to bottom again, and then gave me that kind of look that conveyed that I didn't quite fit the picture of a woman who had given her life to Jesus Christ.

I sincerely pleaded with her, '*Je suis ici parce que j'aime* Marie Magdalene. I only need a bed for one night.'

Finally, she said, '*Bon.* Okay, *alors.*' She fixed me with a steely gaze. 'Ze curfew hour is 9pm. Lights out by 10pm. A nun will be out shortly from ze chapel to show you to your dorm. You may sit in the chapel and wait if you like.'

I placed my palms together at my heart and bowed, not knowing what else might be appropriate. '*Merci. Merci beaucoup, Mere!*'

'*Au revoir, Mademoiselle.*' She dismissed me with a curt nod.

I was secretly thrilled to be staying in a convent. In truth, my only reference to such a place was from childhood. I had been enthralled by the hit television show starring Sally Fields called, *The Flying Nun.* I was beyond delighted to experience what it was like to be a woman of the robes for the night. Twenty minutes later, the nun approached and motioned for me to follow her. We silently walked up three flights of white marble stairs. She pointed to the austere public washrooms and then to my room, which came with two single beds, two night tables, two lamps, two Bibles and one window overlooking a beautiful courtyard at the centre of the convent.

'*Merci beaucoup,*' I said politely, thanking the nun for my modest sleeping quarters.

As soon as I heard her shuffle away in her long robes down the icy cold marble floor, I bolted down the three sets of stairs and ran back to my car to change my shoes and start my ascent to Mary's cave. Gaianna told me that this was the place where Mary spent the last part of her life in meditation and communion with her Beloved.

I sat in the driver's seat of Gypsy Queen and quickly changed into my good walking shoes. I had absolutely no idea what I would find at the top of the steep path to the grotto. Tiny butterflies fluttered in my belly accompanied by a tingly warmth that spread through my limbs and into my hands.

As I was tying up my laces, a wild white dove appeared from out of nowhere. She flew right over the car and landed on a tree branch directly in front of me. I had to adjust my eyes and blink a few times to ensure that I was really seeing this luminous white bird beaming intently at me with her deep ebony eyes. Honestly, at first, I thought I was hallucinating! There she was, the legendary white dove, the sacred symbol of the resurrected Divine Feminine Christ. *Oh my goodness, the Divine Shekinah has come to bless my journey to Mary's cave!*

I gave full presence to this singular, white-winged one who magically appeared out of the clear blue sky. Mesmerised, I sat motionless, calming my excited mind so I could open and receive her silent transmission.

'*Welcome home, shining one! What a blessing it is to find you at the foot of this most cherished dwelling place. This is the cave that our Lady spent countless days and moonlit nights in ecstatic union with her Divine Beloved. We honour each and every courageous step that has brought you full circle to be here with us now. We celebrate you as you have reassembled the fragments of your soul, scattered throughout countless lifetimes, dimensions and distant lands. With each star-dusted step, you have spread your wisdom light and have grown the wings to return all the more radiant and wise. Your pilgrimage has served you well, dear one, in cultivating the awareness, sensitivity, empathy, attunement and compassion for you to at last remember who you are beyond the veil of separation. You have come to embody yourself as a sovereign creator and dwell within the sanctity of your robes of light. This is the way of the Feminine Christ, where you alchemise your human experiences and turn them into the golden light of your true essence and beauty.*

'*The wisdom codes soul facets and cellular memories that you carry are woven within your Sophionic body and will shine forth as an illuminated Wayshower of the Cosmic heart. Gestating within you are the crystalline seeds destined to blossom at a time humanity and the planet will undergo a collective rebirthing, giving rise to the golden age of Gaia.*

'*Today is a homecoming for the part of you that has wandered over countless lifetimes. It is with great joy that we welcome you to one of many sacred Earth Temples where you may access the rapture of dwelling in Sacred Union. Seek no longer, and enter into the cave of your heart-womb where you will discover a long-awaited gift. Now you best be on your way before you miss the light of the sun. As always, we are with and within you.'*

My gaze rested upon the shimmering white wings of the dove as her message faded into the dusky blue sky. At that moment, I flashed upon a distant memory, a timeless vision that felt as if it had happened just yesterday.

My soul family was gathered around an ancient fire. We saw that for a while and perhaps lifetimes, we would need to be apart from one another. Scattered throughout the four earthly corners, each would be reborn within different cultures, ethnicities and stationed at different parts of the planet. We would do this to ensure that our Universal heart was seeded and kept alive within all people of all lands. We were the Keepers of the Flame, and our light would sustain the Earth throughout a long period of darkness and forgetting. Each would be called at their appointed time to return to the central fire and reunite as the One in the Many and the Many in the One. We would then combine our singular points of light, creating a unified light grid. As our interwoven codes of light anchored in the heart of the One and around the Earth, we would usher in the Golden Age of Peace – where unity and diversity flourish within the hearts of all beings in harmony and celebration for countless generations to come.

The white star dove lingered for a moment longer as we communed and shared in a most precious multi-dimensional smile. I witnessed the fragments of my soul spiral back into one singular point of awareness. In that moment, all separation consciousness felt to be a fleeting experience, as if I had been one with all, all along. When I opened my eyes, I witnessed the dove take flight as swiftly as she had flown in. From that day on, I would bring myself back to that feeling of all-prevailing Oneness whenever and as often as needed. *After all, evolution is endless and I would go on to dance with the dark and the light, remembering and forgetting with as much humility and grace as one being could possibly muster.*

As I set out upon the long mountainous path, I drank in the surrounding beauty of the emerald ferns and leafy foliage nestled amongst the remains of an ancient old-growth forest. Golden rays of the sunlight filtered into the spaces in between, making the foliage shimmer in an enchanting fairy-like glow. I relished each step up the twisting pathway, taking my time to integrate the auspicious visitation from the Shekinah dove. With each inhale, I breathed in the wonder of creation and with each exhale dissolved into a state of Oneness as I began to sing aloud, *'Ishk'allah ma budle' la* – God is the love, lover and beloved.'

In this new expanded awareness, I realised that my life was as miraculous as my capacity to surrender to the tiniest little truth inside of me. The closer I came to the mouth of the cave, the more butterflies fluttered inside of my belly. *Whoa, I'm beginning to feel Mary's energy braiding with mine. I felt as if I was walking in her bare feet and returning to a most cherished home after a very, very long time away. Thank you for guiding me back here,* I added with a massive smile, hardly believing that I was delivered to Mary's mountain cave in a cherry red sports car named Gypsy Queen!

As I approached the entrance to the grotto, I was met by an impressive pieta – a life-sized bronze sculpture of Mother Mary with her son draped on her lap after he was taken down from his crucifixion cross. Mary Magdalene was portrayed kneeling in front of them with her hands clasped at her heart in fervent prayer. Upon seeing this dramatic scene, I instantly felt a powerful connection to this sacred place. I knelt down by the bronze statue.

I feel so grateful to remember you, beloved Yeshua and Magdalena, as true friends, lovers of the world, teachers, yogic masters, mystics, healers, poets, tantricas, guardians of the awakened heart whose flame of love continues to inspire, guide and bless me and countless beings. Through the darkest of times, you dared to be the Wayshowers. Thank you for lighting the way for the big love to shine through! Now I know that there is only one of us here.

The long shadows of the sun startled me out of my reverie and reminded me that I only had a short window of time to enjoy my discoveries in Magdalene's cave. I approached the entrance with childlike innocence, full of wonder with what I might discover.

A warm glow beckoned me from the furthest part of the cave. I walked toward it as if I was walking through the mists of Avalon and was beyond astounded by what I discovered next. There it was, a larger-than-life white marble statue of Mary Magdalene. Her sculpted hair cascaded over her shoulders, guiding my gaze to her hand held open in a gesture of simultaneous offering and receiving. Someone had placed a crimson-red rose between her fingertips, which added to her sensual life-like presence. I stood there, absolutely mesmerised by her timeless beauty. The energetic presence surrounding the statue was radiant with agape, the light of Universal Love, Beauty Intelligence.

Quite suddenly, I flashed upon the ceremony back at Gaia's Grove. While lying face down in the moist dirt, I had been flooded with a cacophony of images of Magdalene's life as a Priestess of the Rose throughout her many lifetimes and lineages. Each incarnation was intertwined with her Family of Light until the time would come when the light of Christ would awaken as the Beloved in the hearts of the many and the One.

'Good goddess,' I gasped, *'This is the same cave, statue and rose I was telepathically shown towards the end of the ceremony back at Gaia's Grove!'* Over the course of my travels, the image had faded away from my awareness. *That is until now!* Now the vision along with the spirit of Divine Mother's all-embracing Love came rushing back to me as if it was only just yesterday.

There she is! I could hardly believe my eyes! I was standing face-to-face with the life-like statue that had lured me into leaving the comforts of my hometown and venture out into this mad pilgrimage. Dumbfounded in awe of the magic of arriving here, I stood before the statue and fell into a timeless gaze. I energetically merged with the sublime frequencies that emanated from the statues energetic field. When I felt the depth of what was coming through, I chose to sit cross-legged on the cold grotto floor while absorbing the gentle breeze that wafted through the opening of the cave. As there were only a few other meandering visitors, I felt free to drop into meditation in the knowing I would be undisturbed. I proceeded to close my eyes and then slipped into her world, the one that simmered just beneath the surface of ordinary reality.

Opalescent, turquoise and golden energy cascaded from the statue and then braided with my light body. Her spirit was alive, gently illuminating my inner eye while blossoming my heart-womb wide open with an intensely bright, nectarous love-light. This magenta and tangerine light elixir drenched every particle of my being with a feeling of being welcomed home into her Temple of Love.

'Welcome, beloved sister of the Rose. What a blessed gift to feel you joining me here in the sanctity of this precious now. I am aware that your sojourne has torn open the very fabric of your being – turning you inside out and at times leaving you feeling stranded out in the cold. You know, this too was in the grand design, for seeded within all great heroic journeys are the necessary challenges to forge the soul qualities that have brought you to stand in this special place with me now and recognise that we have always been...One.

'Can you feel it? This is the Earth Temple from which I brought forth my embodied wisdom school and danced naked with the Beloved under the light of the full moon. Open with me now. Feel the ecstatic communion that has permeated this cave for countless sunrises and sunsets. Here, you will taste the amrita, the sweetest of nectars, that which arises from the ultimate surrender to the god/goddess within.

I sat mesmerised before her, enveloped by her fierce love that shimmered like wild starlight inside the marrow of my bones. I began to quietly sing a heart song I had learned from my friend Jah Levi: 'Let the way of the heart, let the way of the heart, let the way of the heart shine through. Love upon love upon love all hearts are beating as one. Light upon light upon light, shining as bright as the sun.'

Occasionally, my eyes would open and become aware of the other tourists peering into the grotto from the main entrance. Most of them walked a few steps inside, took a flash picture and then quickly disappeared. I sensed a strong presence lingering at the entrance of the cave observing me from afar. He appeared to be the local pastor of the grounds who most likely lived in the tiny cottage adjacent to the grotto. We made eye contact long enough to mutually acknowledge the potent energies that continued to emanate from the cave walls nearly 2 000 years after Mary's blessed ascension.

I closed my eyes and resumed my meditation. I was shown Mary Magdalene wearing a sheer white cloth draped over her naked body and a bright-red woven shawl. She walked barefoot through the forest, collecting edible plants, herbs and berries while communing with the many fairies, devas, animal companions and winged ones that inhabited the surrounding area. She loved to sound tones and to hum a sweet melody – at which time the birds would often join in. She spent days in timeless bliss, communing with nature, her Beloved and Family of Light. From time to time, a travelling pilgrim or neighbor would come along and she would feed them, offer energetic blessings, healing sessions and anoint them with plant medicines. In addition to her miraculous healing capacities, Mary was a midwife, herbalist, teacher and wrote several illuminated manuscripts about her unique relationship with God/Goddess, Sacred Union and the rising of the Divine Feminine Christ. She spent endless hours bringing forth wisdom pearls for humanity in a variety of realms and dimensions: from art, metaphysics, midwifery, natural medicine, womb wisdom, sexual healing to the art of tantric relationship and lovemaking.

I pondered how she must feel about her legacy living on to illuminate the hearts of humanity over the course of thousands of years. Now, more than ever, as the Divine Feminine rises in her power and Sacred Union is blossoming awake in the hearts of the many. *Was she aware of how she would go on to serve as a magical beacon of womb awakening that would assist in healing the trauma of sexual abuse in millions of men and woman? Was she aware of how she would inspire the Sacred Feminine to rise in her full sovereign, sensual and erotic power where the return to primal innocence, pleasure and passion gives ecstatic birth to the Golden Age of miracles? Was she aware of how her relational alchemy and sacred tantric relationship with Yeshua would serve as template for Divine Sacred Union? Or how the seeds of unconditional love that she and her beloved planted over 2000 years ago would be a lantern to light the way for countless others through a cycle of great darkness and eventually blossom into a glorious garden of awakened heart consciousness? She must be aware that her ministry is more alive than ever, because she lives on in each one of us and within the cosmic heart that unifies us all.*

I touched my forehead to the stone cave floor and bowed to Mary's multi-faceted presence touching my life in all of her wondrous ways. *Thank you beloved sister for being a sister and such a clear reflection of awakened Love.* Then I sang to her one of my favourite Tibetan chants of the marriage of wisdom and compassion. *Om mani padme hum, Om mani, Om mani padme hum...Om mani padme hum, Om mani, Om mani padme hum.* I sensed that she and Yeshua had chanted this mantra throughout many starry nights until they greeted the morning sun rising over the mountaintop.

After several timeless moments, my eyes gently opened. I stood up to stretch my body and noticed my bum was icey from sitting for so long on the cold cave floor. I stood up and wandered over to a glass case discretely placed in one of the crevices of the cave. The plaque read: 'These are the bones and relics of Mary Magdalene.' My body shuddered in awe.

Then I walked over to the part of the cave that was set up as a chapel with chairs placed in seven concentric rows. I sat down to offer a prayer and one last meditation before closing. There were a handful of others seated quietly, muttering prayers in their native languages. I continued to attune to the subtle energies emanating from the cave walls and imagined what life was like for Mary. I wondered how long she lived in solitude in this damp and cool grotto nestled into the face of the mountainside.

What did she eat? Where did she sleep? Did she entertain company? What would she feed them? Where would they visit? Where was her altar? Where did she hang her clothes, or did she fold them up neatly and place them upon a natural cave shelf? Where would she bathe? Did she feel scared or alone in this cave late at night? Did her heart long, as mine did, to be entwined with the warm welcoming body of the Beloved?

I recalled the long hours spent alone as a child, feeling spooked by my fear of the night and what might be lingering in the dark. Over the course of this journey, I had come to embrace my fears and to trust the gifts that lay hidden in the black fecund of my being. I sensed that Mary had her moments, as all humans do, and yet after so much 'soul-itude', her long and lonely nights at last transformed into All-ONE-NESS!

'Now that you have befriended the darkness, your light can never be extinguished.' She whispered as I prayed for all beings to come to know that we are always surrounded by love, grace and beauty, especially in our darkest of hours.

The pastor walked over to the chapel area and gently gestured for us to come out of prayer because the grotto was about to close for the day. Reluctantly, I complied with his gentle request and took a moment to say goodbye to this magical temple grotto that still emanated the light codes of Sacred Union and the Divine Feminine Christ.

I walked out to stand at the edge of the cliff that overlooked the steep ravine. The sun was beginning to descend behind the adjacent mountain. I noticed a mixture of feelings simmering in my innermost heart. A part of me wanted to stay and live as Mary had, in a wild intimate communion with herself, Beloved and animal companions amidst the wild grace of Mother Gaia.

The pastor stood serenely at the foot of the cave door. As I passed, he graciously reached his soft hand out to me for a handshake. *'Bonjour, Mademoiselle.'*

'Au revoir, Monsieur. Pere. Merci beaucoup! Merci.' I shook his hand and thanked him with a warm smile that beamed through my teary eyes. I felt I was parting ways with an old friend and that he too sensed a mysterious familiarity.

In a state of profound awe and gratitude, I looked back into Mary's earthen temple for the very last time and then began my descent down the winding mountainous path. From that day on, I knew that I would never be too far from my star sister Mary of Magdalene – and that I would feel the gift that we share as I sip from the chalice of my heart-womb.

By the time I reached the bottom of the mountain, the sun was barely visible. I felt famished from the long walk down the mountain and by my surprise encounter. Like a constant companion, Gypsy Queen was waiting to greet me at the foot of the path. I hopped in and drove into the nearby village to fetch a bite to eat before retiring to my room just in time for our strict curfew.

CHAPTER SEVENTY

THE SACRED EROTIC

Beloved, as you hear these words, you must know that many of Mary Magdalene's sacred practices and templates for healing are stored deep within your DNA. She instilled within you the Divine patterning of the Sacred Feminine. She taught you how to lay your hands on bodies and personal energy fields so that Light codes could flow through them, thus activating the inner spiritual potency of each and every individual that came to you. She demonstrated the importance of honouring and worshipping the female sexual life-force, and how this magnificent energy-source is connected to every matrix, every grid, every vortex, every spiral of Light that could ever exist in the entire Universe. She practiced the ancient sacred art of opening up the chakras and vibrating them with the pure note of the Infinite. You learned with her that you do not need to fear the awakening of your Kundalini life-force energy: that this is the most profound gift of the Creator and will open you up to entire new worlds if you allow it to rise and take you into explorations of the Divine. This wise Priestess encourages you to not be afraid of the sexual forces that flow through your body because you are coming into a time in your life during which you will use this sexual energy with much sacred intention, Divine wisdom, and understanding of its transformational powers. Mary Magdalene speaks to you now through your intuition, instinctive feelings and through waves of Sacred Feminine Love. There is a wondrous, beautiful, bejeweled and radiant path ahead for you. Allow Mary Magdalene, Priestess of Isis and the Inner Feminine Temples, to hold your hand as you walk gracefully towards all that is truly yours and always has been.

– Sophie Bashford

And at the end of all our exploring
Will be to arrive where we started
And know the place for the first time.
Through the unknown, unremembered gate
When the last of Earth left to discover
Is that which was the beginning;
At the source of the longest river
The voice of the hidden waterfall
And the children in the apple-tree
A condition of complete simplicity
(Costing not less than everything)
And all shall be well and
All manner of thing shall be well
When the tongues of flames are in-folded
Into the crowned knot of fire
And the fire and the rose are one.

– T.S. Elliot, 'East Coker' in Four Quartets

My alarm went off at 5.30am and I awoke with a massive inner smile. I looked out my small window and noticed the sun making its way up over the mountain. *Holy Mother of God! How hysterically funny, divinely ironic, and hilariously absurd!* I thought, as I recalled my dream with an enormous grin on my face. That night, as I lay upon the ever so sterile, pure and chaste convent dormitory bed, I had quite a surprising dream that entailed an interesting challenge to resolve. I dreamt that I was visited by a variety of deliciously radiant, well-endowed men whose sole purpose was to pleasure me with a menu of erotic sexual asanas that felt to be out of the Kama Sutra. My dream challenge was to find a way to negotiate engaging with each of my dreamtime consorts in a way that felt loving, honouring and balanced for all. In essence, I spent the night in bliss-filled, erotic tantric play.

Oh my goodness, I thought. *My dream body has the most outrageous sense of humour! So this is what the nuns are up to when they tuck in early after evening prayers and contemplation. After all, our Mary was quite the Dakini, well versed in the tantric arts of Egypt, India and Tibet.*

Perhaps this was a parallel reality conjured to counter-balance the strict protocols of a Catholic nun's chaste and pious life!

I stretched my limbs to integrate the evening's sultry, sizzling asanas into my subtle energy field. Perhaps this was Spirit's creative way of infusing me with Shakti to fuel my long drive ahead. I managed to take a brisk cold shower, dressed and then skipped down the cool marble stairs just in time to hit the magnificent French Riviera highway by sunrise.

Before departing, I took a moment to meditate under the tree where the beautiful Shekinah dove had come to pay me a visit. I was genuinely sad to part from the grotto so abruptly. It didn't take long for me to be swooned by this beautiful Fairy Queendom that exuded the essence of Mary in every dancing leaf and arabesquing butterfly. Before bolting out of the convent parking lot, I looked around for the white dove who had blessed me with her presence the day before. She was close by, I could feel her, so I placed my hands to my heart and offered her a massive prayer of gratitude for her companionship, awestruck to at last been led to the statue of Mary and make my vision a reality. My ending had returned me to my beginning, and I was beyond grateful for the surprise. *Goodbye, beloved, until we meet again.*

While buckling up, I speculated that I would just make my plane if I averaged 130 kilometres per hour and limited myself to one fuel and espresso stop. *No worries,* I thought. *Nothing that a cappuccino and a warm fluffy chocolate croissant can't sort out. Thank Goddess for the European power breakfast!*

'Zip-a-dee-doo-dah doo da, zip-a-dee-aye, my oh my...what a wonderful day. Plenty of sunshine heading my way, zip-a-dee-doo-dah doo da, zip-a-dee-aye!' *Here we go.*

CHAPTER SEVENTY-ONE

THE BIG GIVEAWAY

Once the soul awakens, the search begins and you can never go back. From then on, you are inflamed with a special longing that will never again let you linger in the lowlands of complacency or partial fulfillment. The eternal makes you urgent. You loath to let compromise or the threat of danger hold you back from striving toward the summit of fulfillment. When this spiritual path opens, you can bring an incredible generosity to the world and to the lives of others. Sometimes, it is easy to be generous outward, to give, yet remain ungenerous to yourself. You lose the balance of your soul if you do not learn to take care of yourself. You need to be generous to yourself to take care of yourself in order to receive the love that surrounds you. You can suffer from a desperate hunger to be loved. You can search for long years in lonely places, far outside yourself. Yet, the whole time, this love is but a few inches away from you. It is at the edge of your soul, but you have been blind to its presence. Through some hurt, a door has slammed shut within the heart and you are powerless to unlock it and receive the love. We must remain attentive in order to be able to receive. Boris Pasternak said, "When a great moment knocks on the door of your life, it is often no louder than the beating of your heart, and it is very easy to miss it."

– John O'Donahue,
Anam Cara: Spiritual Wisdom from the Celtic World

There is only this one life going on, this one loving, all giving, perfect intelligence. This one perfect pattern of infinite potential, and as it emerges, where there is resistance, or in some cases where there is a need to develop certain abilities in this three dimensional realm called human existence, it appears like crisis, it appears like problems, it appears like bad things. But when you really understand this Oneness, you get to understand and discover that, in fact, all of it is really a conspiracy of good; a conspiracy of wholeness. All of it is conspiring to awaken you to your full potential and set you free.

– Derek Rydall, *Emergence: The End of Self Improvement*

Zooming onto the esplanade, I headed straight for the Turin airport. This fiercely stunning, Mediterranean highway spans the coast of Southern France and Italy, and the scenery is beyond spectacular: mountainous towering hills stacked with old stone houses, dripping gold, and green valleys filled with terraced farms, all overlooking the intense sparkle of the turquoise sea.

People often liken the esplanade to a raceway for the Italian Grand Prix. I carried on with my playful pretending that I was in my own 007 movie, *Live and Let Die* or was that, *You Only Live Twice*? *Nevermind.* it was clear that I was not the only one driving like a 007 agent this morning. High as kites on double espressos, we were a swarm of mobile bumblebees, comprised of speeding sports cars, delivery trucks, luxury sedans, motorcycles and everything else you could imagine under the Mediterranean sun.

I had to be super sharp, unwaveringly focused – and drive like a maniac – in order to get Gypsy Queen and I back to the airport alive and on time for my twelve o'clock flight. The mission was beyond insane. Any fellow passenger would have pissed in their pants while screaming, 'Ahhhhgh! Slow down, you bloody madwoman Madonna!'

Miraculously, seven hours later, I arrived just in the nick of time at the airport to catch my flight to Stanstead, England. Little did I know then that compared to the rest of the trip, my wild race down the esplanade would be a joyride!

First of all, the issue of my excess baggage weight made its debut at the Turin Airport and followed me around like a pesky nuisance I couldn't seem to shake. For one, my guitar, which I had carried since the beginning of the journey and strummed a total of twenty-two times – put my luggage eight kilos over my allotted weight. Each additional three kilos cost fifty euros, so it would take about one hundred and fifty euros to get my travelling companion guitar a seat onboard. That translated to around two hundred and fifty dollars, and at this point, I had less than a hundred dollars to get me home. I needed what little cash I had left to eat and make my way to Los Angeles!

I shared my predicament with the manager of Bryan Air and quite graciously, she allowed me to check all of my baggage while negating the additional charge. *Whooo! Thank Goddess for her empathy and understanding!*

'*Grazie, grazie!*' I repeated my thanks. She returned my appreciation with a warm smile and a very Italian pinch on the cheek.

With massive waves of gratitude to have made it in time for my flight, I sank into my seat on the plane and contemplated the next segment of my journey. My flight back to the US was referred to as a charter airline ticket, which typically flew out of non-commercial airports located in the outskirts of major cities. These tickets are substantially lower in price than commercial flights because they divert some of the air traffic from the international airports. When I landed in Stanstead Airport in the London suburbs, I was scheduled to take a charter flight from there to Frankfurt and then fly out of Frankfurt to the US. Fingers crossed!

As I read the fine print on the back of the ticket, I didn't know whether to laugh or cry. First of all, I had to arrive in Frankfort specifically on a Sunday to get my voucher certified and approved by an official Airtech representative. Only then could I be placed on a flight back to the US. Secondly, Frankfort was currently the only place Airtech flew out of, and New York was the only place in the US that they flew into! *How did I ever miss that fine print? And how would I get from New York to Los Angeles on my meagre funds?* I guess I had been far too hasty and neglected to read the fine print when I purchased our tickets. So here I was on the way to England with a very dubious airline voucher in hand, and basically no ticket back to the Bay Area! *This bloody 'online deal' came with quite a hefty price!* Thus began a divinely orchestrated obstacle course, which in the end was worth every insane moment of it. As the plane bumped to a landing, I instructed myself, *Here we go. Remember to breathe and enjoy the ride!*

I collected my baggage in Stanstead Airport to then recheck it in for the 7pm flight to Frankfurt. Here in the grey and overcast English suburb, the graciousness of sunny Italy quickly ran dry. The blond woman with hot pink lips behind the check-in counter sternly reminded me of my eight kilos of additional weight. She then topped that off by scolding me for not knowing the Bryan Air policies for overweight baggage. I backed away sheepishly from the counter to review my options. That's when I spotted a friendly looking young Swiss couple standing in line behind me. *Hmmm, they don't have any extra carry-on bags.* A light bulb went on in my head, and before I knew it, I approached them with a warm smile.

'Excuse me. Uh, I imagine this may sound overly presumptuous, but would you mind helping me out of a predicament by checking in my extra carry-on bag for me? I'm over my allotted weight allowance and don't have the additional funds at the moment.'

'Sure, why not?' The young man from Switzerland grinned. 'No problem at all.'

Before I could say, 'How very kind of you – thank you ever so much for helping me to get home', airport security surrounded me like a gang of highly agitated English bulldogs.

A pudgy man, wearing a maroon security jacket held me briskly by my elbow. 'Excuse me, miss, are you aware that you have breached airport security regulations? I'm terribly sorry but we are obliged to arrest you.'

At this point, partially from exhaustion and sheer desperation to catch my flight, I broke down in a torrential downpour of tears. I begged them between sobs and sniffles, 'Please, please, please give me another chance, sir! I am terribly sorry for not knowing the Bryan Air regulations! Oh please, pleeeeeease don't arrest me!'

The English authorities became unmanned at such an emotional outburst. The pudgy man with the long baton let go of my elbow and brought out a handkerchief, which he ineffectually handed over to me. 'Now, now. No need to make such a fuss, miss's. I can see you are quite discombobulated. Just settle yourself down, miss.'

He motioned the others away and escorted me to a private cubicle to give me a good talking to. In the end, I managed to persuade him to release me from my impending arrest on the grounds of a combination of intense PMS and plain ol' foolishness. I blew my nose loudly and offered him a grateful puppy dog smile. He sent me out of the cubicle with a stern, though fatherly admonishment. 'Never ever try that unruly stunt again or else you won't be as lucky next time round. Do ya here me, luv, or...or...I'll...' His words trailed off, leaving me to imagine the rest.

I nodded vigorously and returned his sodden handkerchief. 'No, I won't, sir. Never again and thank you again, sir!' I was beyond grateful for his leniency in the matter.

As fate, karma or rather my brilliant creation had it, this pseudo-arrest took so much time that I consequently missed my flight to Frankfort. My only option was to purchase another ticket for a hundred and fifty euros, which was not surprisingly the exact cost of the additional luggage fee! *Ha! Like creates like.* What else could I do, but to whip out the 'emergency only' credit card once again. Let me just say, for reasons I rather not go into – this was the last thing I wanted to do, especially since I had already used the 'forbidden' card a few times before!

The flight attendent that sold me a new ticket to Frankfort must have been familiar with the prior 'boss lady' attendant who denied me passage and called security on me. She was very understanding of my situation, and oddly enough encouraged me to try putting my baggage through once again. 'You might as well try your luck again, luv. They had a shift change at the check-in counter and this next attendant is quite the pussycat,' she assured me.

With her encouragement to lessen as much weight as possible, I walked out into the most crowded part of the airport and imagined myself in a fairy godmother costume, complete with my etheric cape and magic wand. I proceeded to open my overweight backpack and gave away my belongings to random people passing by. If I hadn't been quite so exhausted and borderline hysterical, I would have had a lot more fun staging this impromptu giveaway in the middle of Stanstead Airport. As it was, with tears still trickling, I brought out my cherished belongings and offered them up one by one to a random selection of strangers.

'Step right up and get your free snorkel!' I gave away my mask and snorkel to a young Korean couple. They were thrilled. I gave away my paints, sketchbook and brushes to a family with two kids. Their delighted smiles were more than worth it. I gave away a Sony Walkman and headset to a lanky teenager with a bad case of acne. He accepted by giving me a peace sign and then nodded his oversized head with a teenage seal of approval. I offered my spiritual books to miscellaneous people walking by, keeping only my precious journal. They all seemed intrigued and happy to have a little something extra to read on the flight. The best moment was when I gave my jacket to a janitor who worked in the airport. She was the most excited of all. She grinned so big that she looked like she had just won the lottery. I sensed that this maybe the very first time that she had been gifted with anything at all. Bless her beautiful heart.

As my pack lightened up, so did my heavy heart. This homebound flight simply insisted that I leave all excess baggage behind! Clearly, I was undergoing yet another bizarre initiation into radical let go, trust and surrender. I sternly marched myself to the nearest recycling bin, where I proceeded to throw away my notebooks, extra batteries, an organic apple, water bottle, toothpaste, shampoo, conditioner and sunscreen, along with my half-eaten French fries and iced tea. Basically, if I wished to get on the next plane without paying another hundred and fifty dollars, everything and anything extra just had to go. *'Gone, gone, gone beyond.'* I heard the voice of the Divine Mother instructing me, this time in a stern Irish accent, *'You won't be taking any excess baggage home with you, will you, lass? That was all to be left behind in the underworld. Or have you forgotten already?'*

I replayed the song that I heard during my last supper in Greece. *'Ambe´, get ready. The plane is comin', don't need no baggage. You just get onboard.'*

Okay, okay! I get the message! Though still a little shaky from nearly being arrested. I approached the check-in counter and prayed that the new flight attendant would be more lenient with me than the last. 'Ello,' I said, mustering a casual cheery tone.

'Good evening, Ms. Ray.' She looked at me kindly and then weighed my baggage piece by piece. 'I'm sorry, but you are over by the weight of the guitar. Would you prefer to leave it behind or pay an additional fifty euros?'

Once again, I made a heartfelt request. 'Please, miss, would you allow me to carry my guitar onboard?' The nice lady gladly complied without a blink. She completed stamping my boarding pass with a friendly smile, happy to serve me as well as my guitar companion.

I breathed out a deep sigh of relief. My eyes watered with gratitude and I thanked her profusely for making an exception and choosing the way of compassion. I was back in the game of ease and grace, and on my way to Frankfort. *Free, free, free at last! Thank you, Goddess. I'm free at last!*

As I headed down the long lane to my departure gate, I observed the people streaming by and contemplated the importance of loving-kindness. *How sweet life can be when humans are genuinely inspired to make life a little sweeter for the ones around us. While I appreciate that rules have a functional purpose in life, I wonder what this world would be like if life was about how much value we can create for others. After all, wasn't the soul purpose of a human to be generous, bless each other up and conspire to make miracles out of the ordinary? What a wonderful world it would be.*

I had one more hour to go before my flight boarded for Frankfort. By this time, my mood had considerably shifted to being deliriously tired, intensely raw and beyond relieved to be getting on the last flight to Frankfort. I still had time to gather my wits, take a few deep breaths, have a cuppa and quietly mourn the loss of my one good winter jacket. I recollected the look on the lady janitor's face when I handed her my jacket. Her joyous response had gifted me with way more than she had received. *Oh, well,* I sighed. *I have my etheric Magdalene cape to keep me warm throughout the night.*

At last, the flight attendant announced the boarding of my flight. I was filled with gratitude for not being behind bars in a foreign airport jail. As I approached the gate for boarding, I spotted the impeccably groomed flight supervisor who originally rejected my baggage and squealed on me to the airport security. *Oh no!* She was now assigned to the departure gate and collecting boarding passes. Like a panther calculating her next deadly move, she glared at me from afar. With sudden dread, I could tell that she was ready to pounce on me from behind the podium. I smiled weakly, sensing I was to be her next prey.

'Good evening, Ms. Ray. I see you have managed to get on our next flight and still keep your guitar with you. I presume you have paid for the additional weight. Would you please remain here while I make a quick phone call?'

I nodded coyly while standing frozen, as the other passengers shuffled past me to board the plane.

The woman hung up the phone and smiled a fake, superficial smile. Her energy was a mixture of triumph and revenge. *Pounce!* 'I'm terribly sorry, Ms. Ray,' she said in a saccharine tone. 'We simply cannot allow you to board this flight. You have an additional four kilos of baggage that you still have not paid for. We cannot let you fly until you pay for it.'

My heart sank into my belly. I tried to explain while holding back the tears. 'The flight attendant at the ticketing counter permitted me to take my guitar on board.'

'Well, well, well. However, as the Bryan Air supervisor, I have the authority to refuse you permission to board this plane. You still owe Bryan Air an additional fifty euros. Or would you prefer I call the authorities for smuggling in excess baggage?'

Feeling battle worn and defeated, I handed over my credit card. I knew on some level that whatever was playing out was yet another opportunity to purge old programming and respond in a new way. The situation also highlighted the parts of me that could choose to feel victimised and betrayed. And yet this time, it was not by a man. I noted to myself that repairing the wounds between sisters was next in line for healing.

As the supervisor smugly processed my excess weight fee, I was being shown a leak, or a place within me that still required healing and strengthening. *Were all of these challenges coming up to mirror back to me just how integrated I was with all that I had just learned? Ha! This is where the rubber hits the road.*

I saw how I had inadvertently projected my power and worth outside of myself onto the airline attendant. *Why else would I be so triggered by her cool and uncaring behaviour?* I was being given yet another opportunity to release persecution karma. This time I would remain centred in my core without getting pulled into another's way of being, simply because it did not match my own.

Time stood still. I could choose a new response. And that's exactly what I did. I called back my power and adjusted my posture to create an entirely different scenario. With an aura of being a rock star diva who had just won a Grammy Award, I proceeded to pay for my guitar, compliment the attendant for doing her job and thanked the universe for providing me with yet another invaluable reflection of how I create my reality through my energy and vibration.

With my precious guitar in hand, I boarded the aircraft and settled into my costly seat. My journey was practically over, yet based on what I was experiencing, I clearly had some excess baggage to leave behind before crossing the sea into my brand-new reality. As I curled up into my dimly lit seat and licked my wounds, the voice of Sophia spoke softly to me.

'Dear one, life is a holographic projection of patterns reflected at every level of consciousness. The light shines through the picture you hold within your psyche. So, as you move along the crystal spiral of ascension through all of these energetic levels of where those patterns have been held, you repair them by purging discordant thought forms and collapsing old timelines. Your excess baggage is symbolic of your residual belief in lack and limitation which carries a heavy vibrational density.

You are here to raise the vibrational light not only for you but for the soul group from which you came in. Abundance consciousness makes your heart as light as a feather and propels your wings to soar through life rather than drag your feet. To embody the wellspring of the Grail is to balance and stabilise your core and connection with source energy. As you do, your chalice overflows with unlimited resources, possibilities and potentials...living and breathing inside of you and filling you with gratitude. So remember dear one, travel light and light you shall be!

CHAPTER SEVENTY-TWO

GOLDEN ARCHES

In the silent core of your heart, discover the unshakeable. Discover the pure consciousness of the Self, in whom we are One. One human family. One divine sun with eight billion human rays. Touch the imperishable blue sky beyond the passing clouds. You are That.

This is not a belief, but a direct experience, attained not by philosophy, or science, or politics, but by tapping the original seed, in the stillness of meditation. This is not "spiritual by-passing." It is touching the ground. The real. The eternal.

We don't have to rise to the occasion, but fall. Fall inward. Collapse. Touch Being. The most fruitful work we can do, is to Be.

I am afraid. I am uncertain. I am weak. But I Am. For just a moment, let me place no noun, no adjective after the verb. Here is what the stars are singing about. Here is what the silence of boundless night is breathing. I Am. Here is courage. Here is the heart.

– Fred Lamotte

And something ignited in my soul,
Fever or unremembered wings,
And I went on my way,
Deciphering,
That burning fire

– Paulo Neruda

Before enlightenment, chop wood, carry water
after enlightenment, chop wood, carry water.

– Zen Proverb

At around 9.30pm, my plane landed in Frankfort International Airport. With fierce determination, I walked directly to the Air Iceland ticket counter where I was told I would find a travel representative who would instruct me on how to get my ticket certified for tomorrow afternoon's flight to New York.

I presented my voucher to the young man behind the counter.

He looked confused. 'I'm sorry, Madame. I have never heard of a company called Airtech. Try again tomorrow, please.'

I mustered up all of the fierce clarity I could in that late hour and carefully explained again how the Airtech agent had instructed me to fly to Frankfort and go to the Air Iceland counter to redeem my ticket voucher today! 'My flight is tomorrow, sir. I have to be on that plane.'

The airline representative saw that I wasn't leaving until he did something. 'Let me make a call, Madame. I will see what I can do.'

While he was on the phone, I took some deep breaths and offered myself some on-the-spot coaching. *I trust that everything that is happening is truly greater than anything I can imagine!*

After what seemed like forever, the representative returned to the counter and reported. 'The office for certifying your ticket voucher is closed due to a German holiday. You'll have to wait until after the weekend. I'm sorry, but at this late hour, there is really nothing I can do for you. Perhaps the main office in Reykjavík could give you the approval you require in the morning. Good night, Madame.' He dismissed me with a polite nod.

I proceeded to whip out my warmed up, emergency-only credit card and called Air Iceland in Reykjavík. I dialled once – no answer. Twice – no answer. After the third time, there was still no answer. At 10pm, with very little money left to spare, I opted to sleep in the airport. At that point I was even too tired to pray.

I found myself standing on the marble floor at the base of an escalator, dumbfounded and utterly drained. A wave of fatigue washed over me like a blanket of heavy clouds. At that moment, everything in my life felt a million times heavier than it actually was. All I could think of was that I needed to sleep, so I began to investigate my options for the night. Fortunately, the daily bustle of the airport had subsided. Even though the downstairs restaurant-lounge area had cushioned benches ideal for comfort, they were crowded with immigrant night owls and late-night commuters who preferred to stay awake on Coca-Cola, cigarettes and all-night card games. I took the escalator upstairs to explore my options. I walked by a lounge area encased by a metal railing that reminded me of an animal corral. Inside the corral, people could smoke and drink; outside the corral, they had to keep walking. I wandered down a long carpeted corridor that led to some departure gates. It was empty and quiet. *Perhaps here I can find a sanctuary to rest until sunrise – then I can try phoning the Airtech office again.*

Finally, like an oasis in the desert I discovered a deserted departure area. As I investigated further, I found a bench that looked like it was designed to prohibit people from being comfortable. *Oh, well. Thank Goddess for yoga!* I secured my carry-on bag and guitar close to my body and contorted my limbs so I could sort of recline, draped over the armrests of a seriously cold metal bench. *Ah, sleep at last!* I closed my eyes and reflected on the incredibly crazy day I had just experienced. I could hardly believe I was at the foothill of Mary's cave on this very same day!

That morning, I had woken up after an erotic dream in the convent of Saint Baume, drove seven hours to Italy, nearly arrested in Stanstead Airport and detained by a frightfully cold flight attendant. Now here I was, curled up on this cold metal bench in the maze of Frankfort Airport. *How on Earth am I going to get myself home on a meagre $28?* I wondered, as I drifted off into an exhausted snooze. I reflected on my own grandparents coming to the USA on boats as refugees. What a feeling it is to feel so displaced and at the mercy of other people's kindness and cooperation. I wondered how these countless immigrants refugees must have felt crossing the seas into the great unknown. For them, there was no looking back. To look back would have meant to feel the shocking atrocities of war and a loss far too unbearable for any human heart to fathom.

They were the 'lucky ones'. They had managed to escape with little more than their precious human lives. In order to survive, they would have to put the past in the past and look only towards the horizon with hope in their hearts and faith in their wings.

Little did I know I would be called to look back into my ancestral past and feel all that was once buried under the forbidden carpet of my bloodline. *May they rest in peace.* I imagined introducing myself to my great-grandparents whom I recently learned were people of great kindness, courage and faith. I made sure to offer my gratitude and love and let them know that their memory lives on, along with their hopes and dreams.

In only a matter of moments, I was startled awake by a monstrously loud, encroaching noise. I opened my eyes to see a massive vacuum cleaner swiftly approaching down the long carpeted corridor. Like Godzilla, the great beast grew louder by the second. In my delirious state, I was unsure if it was aiming to suck me up into its ruthless, roaring jaws. I closed my eyes again, clinging to sleep, and tried to ignore the beastly machine. Hopefully, it will simply stroll on by. Instead, it stopped right in front of me and made several passes back and forth. My invisibility skills were failing miserably. In one swift movement, I rose from the metal bench, swung my guitar and my backpack over my body, and like a delirious zombie, fled the corridor. I proceeded to stumble downstairs to the café and was nearly blinded by the fluorescent lights and cigarette smoke coming from the late-night card players.

In a desperate attempt to find somewhere to rest my weary bones, I took another escalator to the top floor where there was a cluster of restaurants that were presently closed for the night. I could have sworn I heard angels sing when I spotted some large golden arches glowing in that unmistakable mustardy yellow. I walked toward the arches as if I was walking towards Heaven's gate. *Hallelujah!* I never thought I would ever be so elated to see those infamous golden arches! I put my hands together in Namaste as I greeted the Ronald McDonald statue as a god-like deity. I had to hold myself back from hugging the scary-looking plastic clown. Then I stretched my body out on one of the long benches and gave in to the weariness throbbing in every cell of my being. Inwardly, I grinned from head to toe at the humour of Mr. Ronald McDonald being my knight in shining armour.

'God Bless Micky D's,' I mumbled, feeling truly elated to find some sense of the familiar. I couldn't help but notice this was Spirit's way of preparing me for the USA, where for many of us, our roots went only as far back as these infamous golden arches. I drifted off to sleep on the bright yellow bench that felt like a five-star room in the Ronald McDonald Royal Embassy Suites.

Before long, I was startled awake by a light tapping on my shoulder. I sat up slowly, a little disorientated, my eyes blinking like an innocent child's. An elderly dark-skinned man smiled at me and extended his arm. He pointed to the massive glass windows where people could watch the planes land and take off while enjoying their food. The sky glowed with a plethora of rainbow sherbet colours that gloriously welcomed me into a new day. Groggily, I smiled at the man and sat up to greet the most magnificent sunrise that I had ever seen in my life!

Like a loving grandfather, he gently returned my smile. 'Good morning to you! Can I buy you a cup of coffee?' he said in a thick Russian accent.

How kind of you to invite me to share in your morning ritual, I thought. At that moment, he seemed more like an angel than a stranger to me. *Are you an angel?* I thought, still flabbergasted by the rainbow aurora splashes of colour. My disorientation quickly dissipated as this gentleman tenderly welcomed me into the new day with his offer to treat me to coffee.

'Sure,' I said. 'Anything to raise my spirits!' *Wow, wow, wow! How wondrous it is to wake up to the beauty of this amazing sunrise.* I sat in awe, mesmerised by God's masterpiece that painted the sky. I held my warm coffee between my hands like the chalice of the Holy Grail, while absorbing the beauty of the hues – golden yellow, tangerine orange, whispers of violet, fuchsia and a hint of clear aquamarine all promising me a miraculous new day.

The elderly Russian gentleman winked at me and then sank into a corner to read his newspaper. I smiled back, then pulled out my journal and began to write. As usual, my pen had a mind of its own. *It's good to be alive! Even though I may have slept like a homeless person, I feel more like a queen today.* I imagined sitting cross-legged on my inner throne within the centre of my heart and envisioned my inner council standing around me. Each reflected a part of me nor better or worse. I had come to appreciate all of me, no longer seeing myself as a fixer upper, that requires perpetual self-improvement. One of my sub-selves, a.k.a. e-g-o, bravely stepped forward as if to represent all of the others around the council and began to speak. I marvelled at her life-like cartoonish persona. She was well- mannered and kind when she spoke her mind.

'*Before you cross the seas into your new life, might you consider embracing us as friends instead of the 'enemy' you try to control, suppress or run away from? Without us stepping in, you would never have been able to survive the dangers and pitfalls of this uncertain and chaotic world. Don't forget – when the shit hit the fan, we were the ones that came running first! We have been your most loyal and trustworthy companions. Even though our methods may be old paradigm for you now, our desire has always been to serve and protect you. We were there for you since the beginning, from the very first moment you began to have thoughts of feeling separate and left out on a limb! I remember the good ol' days when you felt you couldn't possibly live without us. Remember how we came to the rescue when you first felt helpless, powerless and abandoned. Don't you forget it was team E-G-O that came rushing in to save the day again and again. We made you look strong, capable, worthy, lovable, and really, really hot when you needed it the most! The more that you felt incapable of coping on your own, and sought outside of yourself for completion, we stepped right up for you and compensated for this perceived lack.*

'*OK, we admit it. We enjoy the power and prestige, so much so, that we fabricated more and more sophisticated versions of ourselves to impress you....and of course, to serve your highness. Over time, you became so impressed with our abilities that we decided to take over your entire reality. As a service to you, of course! Admittedly, over time, we became just a little addicted to the adrenaline rush of running your reality show! We simply can't resist a good drama.*

'*Quite frankly, I'm relieved that you have finally snapped out of it and come to your senses. Between all of the graveyard shifts, emergency calls and under pay, we would rather be working for someone who shows a little more loyalty and appreciation! So here's the thing – we e-g-o's like to mature and evolve just like you do. We just don't know how to go about getting upgraded until YOU take the reigns of your authentic Self and promote us to a new job. We understand if you feel that there are a few of us that you need to let go of altogether before getting on that airplane. I know that some of my more super destructive e-g-o buddies won't be sticking around after this eye-opening trip. As for me, I'm glad to be hanging around to take digs at you from time to time so that you can use me as a reminder and an opportunity to give yourself even more love instead of less! Hey, thanks for hearing me out on behalf of your team e-g-os. This is Sensible Sally now signing off. Oh, by the way, don't eat the French fries! They are totally genetically modified! Believe me, I would know!*

Feeling amused by Sensible Sally's sassy little sermon, I thanked her for sharing and took note of her bid to re-evaluate my inner team. I sipped my coffee slowly while continuing to savour the psychedelic sunrise that painted the morning sky. It felt perfect to be right here, right now. My three-and-a-half-month journey turned out to be more like a journey of a thousand lifetimes.

I rewound the timeline to where it all began at the ceremony in Gaia's Grove. With a rush of love, I recalled how Sophia, Green Tara, Mother Mary, Magdalene, Sarah, Yeshua, White Buffalo Calf Woman, Isis, Quan Yin, the Fairy Queen, Pan, the Hathors, Grandmother Anna, Grandfather Sun, Sananda and The Black Madonna had each guided me in their own special way to return to the temple of my beloved heart.

With a mixture of melancholy and profound gratitude, I recollected the festivals and how they prepared me to build body and soul stamina for my journey to come. I needed my strength to face my destiny appointment with Aiden and remain anchored in my heart as I met one of the most potent soul mirrors of my life. I felt that our brief cosmic dance together had fulfilled a higher purpose that would continue to unfold over time. I knew that creating greater sovereignty, balance and harmony within the marriage of my inner Masculine and Feminine was the greatest gift of all. I silently bowed to Aiden, fully releasing the last of our sacred contract with a silent prayer of gratitude. *Thank you for playing your part ever so perfectly. May you be free; may you be happy. Blessings on your journey!*

And what a gift it was to have explored the Grail lands of Mary Magdalene, the Black Madonna and the Aeon Sophia and be given the sublime honour to walk in their footsteps. Their living legacies of Love will forever live on within me.

Who could have ever known that a budget holiday brochure would lead me to the underworld where I would meet the Black Mother, clear my bloodline and be baptised by my Divine Self with Sananda as my sacred witness. I touched the ring on my finger, which remained as a reminder of my Inner Marriage and babtism that had transpired amongst the robin-blue stones that lined the shore of the Ionian Sea.

The other parts of the journey sped through my mind like a revolving kaleidoscope: Eva and the festivals in England, meeting Aiden at the fire of the Rainbow Gathering, soaking in the glorious hot springs, dancing with the Fairy Queen, driving to Barcelona, getting soaked in the rain, visiting the Grail sites with Murray, the Brighton Sea, Kalamata beaches and praying in the Sophia Churches. There was the Egyptian Museum, Damanhur, napping under the apple tree and my 007 pilgrimage back to Saintes-Maries. Finally, my impromptu visit to Saintes Baume, where I discovered the Shekinah dove, Mary's cave and the fortuitous statue, topped off by the most erotic dream of my entire life! I smiled deeply as I remembered the crazy race back to Italy in Gypsy Queen, my near arrest in Stanstead Airport and the astonished look on the janitor's face when I gave her my brand-new winter jacket. Now here I was in Frankfurt, Germany, hopefully headed to Los Angeles on an Airline ticket that so far, no one seemed to recognise as valid. *Oh well, who needs validation when I know I'm the one writing my own ticket to paradise!*

I soaked in those first glorious rays of the morning sun as it dawned on me. At last, I've returned to ground zero; I had discovered the ultimate Happy Meal – the freedom to be *me* inside all that I Am. I scribbled a note in my journal just to be sure I would never forget. 1) Trust open 2) Love relentlessly 3) Create endless beauty.

CHAPTER SEVENTY-THREE

LOVE BOMB MADONNA

When we awaken the magical chalice within our heart that is prepared to receive Divine compassion, everything changes for us. All that we see and do has new meaning. The worries and challenges of the past become portals into a new power to create harmony on Earth. We realise that we have been living in an illusion the whole time. This is the gnosis of the Christic-Sophianic Consciousness of the Divine Sophia, our Divine Mother. It is Her gift to us as awakened sons and daughters of the Supernal Light. Our life in the polarity of the light and the dark is uplifted to our true destiny as a Divine human being.

– Shannon Port, *Art of the Feminine*

This is what humans are being raised to be conscious of and embody – this foundation of Creative Power that transforms and transmutes dense physical matter with ease into awakened higher forms and expressions of consciousness. The Sun we see in the sky is a reminder of what is within. We are also a portal to the Creator – Earth, Air, Fire and Water and all the animals, plants and creatures on Earth also remind us of what is within. Nature is the naked soul of the Earth, and reflects the macro of the micro. The Venus Light Heart Sun, with the Galactic Core Black Sun, is shining for all to be restored and made whole again, from within and without. This is the Alchemical Marriage of the Divine Heart and World Soul – pure Creative Power that is changing not just the Earth, each other and ourselves – but everything in the Cosmos!

> – Llewellyn Vaughn-Lee,
> *The Return of the Feminine Spirit and the World Soul*

It felt good to stretch out my stiff body in the departure lounge while I waited for the Iceland Air ticket counter to open at 9am. I was super relieved to see the flight attendant who came to open up the ticket counter. She appeared to be rather gentle and well mannered based on her kind, doe-like eyes. *May she have more compassion and empathy than the piranha at Bryan Air*, I prayed, placing both palms together at my heart.

At 9am sharp, I approached the Icelandic Air ticket counter with an air of inner calm and confidence. I then proceeded to report my unique story and present my predicament in a clear and grounded way to the extremely attentive flight attendant.

Despite her good listening skills, she was not as helpful as I had hoped. With a kind smile she said, 'Oh, I'm so sorry, Ms. Ray, I have not heard of this Airtech voucher and all of the city offices are closed today due to a holiday. You may purchase a new ticket for $1,300 if you like, or try to speak with my supervisor who will be arriving at 10am.'

More committed than ever to honouring my three options for the day to trust open, love relentlessly and create beauty out of everything, I thanked her and walked over to the pay phone to call the Airtech office in New York for what seemed to be the hundredth time. Once again, there was no answer. I then decided to call upon the Divine Mother hotline and request a super-deluxe miracle intervention. At 10am, I re-approached the Icelandic Air ticket counter and was greeted by a friendly face behind the counter. I was pleased to discover he was the supervisor. Once again, I relayed the finer points of my story for what seemed the umpteenth time. *Thank Goddess! At last, someone has actually heard of the Airtech voucher.*

'The only person who can give me clearance to apply your flight voucher is a gentleman Airtech representative. However, he cannot be reached in the office today because it is German holiday. I'm sorry, Madame.'

Despite a growing desperation, I stayed open and asked, 'Is there any other way to contact this Airtech representative?'

'No,' the supervisor replied.

Then he paused for an extremely long moment while I inwardly repeated my morning mantra, *Trust open, love relentlessly, life can only become more beautiful!* I actually saw the light bulb go off inside of his head as he picked up the phone and asked directory assistance for the phone number of a Mr. Rolf Schmidt.

Brilliant, I thought. *Now we are getting somewhere!* My whole body shivered with goose bumps. The supervisor had managed to get the Airtech representative's personal mobile number and connect with him on a golf course. Apparently, he was playing golf somewhere in a small town in Bavaria. The supervisor spoke fervently in German for over five minutes. He then hung up the phone and reported to me the miraculous news in his thick German accent.

'Well, it's your lucky day, Madame. Here's what I can do for you.' He cleared his throat and then proceeded grandly. 'I can sell you a ticket for an additional $188.00 to New York. And if you wait momentarily, I will see if we can get you on that flight for today.'

'Oh, thank you! *Danke schoen!*' And once more, I handed over my 'emergency only' credit card. My heart pounded as I stood at the counter and watched him click away on the computer keyboard for what seemed like an eternity.

'Hmmm. I'm sorry to inform you that most of our flights to New York are already sold out.'

Trust open. Love relentlessly. Create beauty, I affirmed with great enthusiasm while visualising myself lounging on the plane!

He clicked away at the keyboard. 'Aha, I think we can possibly sneak you onto the 4pm on standby. Of course, you'll have to check in with the flight attendant who has to make the final decision.'

I exhaled a deep sigh of relief for the miracle I received and asked, 'What do you think my chances are of actually getting on that plane to New York?'

He pointed over to the gate and said in a very dry manner, 'It's all up to the flight attendant who will check you in over there. Good luck,' he said, as he pointed to the counter diagonal from his.

'Thank you, thank you, thank you for making that phone call!' I refrained from grabbing his rosy-cheeked face and giving him a great big kiss on the mouth. Instead, I reached over the counter and shook his hand. While basking in my victory, I visualised some random Airtech employee on the golf course in a crisp white golf shirt and waist-high khaki trousers being interrupted by his cell phone just as he was about to hit an ace in the hole.

A huge wave of relief washed over me as I sat down in the lounge and reached for the book I had just purchased at the kiosk. The book was entitled, *Warriors of the Light*, written by Paulo Coelho, the well-known Brazilian author who also wrote *The Alchemist*. I opened to a random page and read the following excerpt:

> A warrior of light knows he has much to be grateful for. Angels help him in his struggle, Celestial forces place each thing in its place, thus allowing him to give it his best. Companions say, 'He's so lucky!'
>
> And the warrior does achieve some things far beyond his capabilities. This is why at sunset, he kneels and gives thanks for the protective cloak that surrounds him. His gratitude, however, is not limited to the spiritual world. He never forgets his friends, for their blood mingled with his own on the battlefield. A Warrior does not need to be reminded of the help given to him by others. He is the first to remember and he makes sure to share with them any rewards he receives.

'So true!' I affirmed whole-heartedly. Instead of waiting to find out if I was going to make it on the 4pm flight, I thanked all who conspired to assist me in making a miracle ahead of time. I then envisioned myself taking my seat with ease and grace, knowing that it was not only up to the flight attendant, but up to me and the universe to co-create something even *greater* than imagined. This time I was going to create my transaction with the flight attendant to be a wonderful opportunity for both of us. I connected with

Source, opened my heart and felt the stars of the Universe aligning and supporting me every blessed step of the way.

While I envisioned miraculous doors opening before me, I took a double take at a woman of colour sitting across from me in the departure lounge. She seemed oblivious to me while she hummed a happy little tune and paged through a tabloid magazine. I observed her discreetly, enthralled by her radiant beauty along with her rhinestone-studded blazer. Her bosom overflowed from her blouse like large clouds of soft coco cream puffs. Her mahogany hair was perfectly arranged in shiny sculpted waves. I was fascinated by her turquoise frosted eye shadow and how her plump glossy lips picked up the overhead lights. I couldn't help but be mesmorised by her magnetic aura and beaming self-confidence. I imagined her to be a famous celebrity diva out of a glitzy movie called, *Like a Rhinestone Butterfly*. All that I knew was that this luscious beauty Queen was living her own version of *Mission Is Possible!*

By the time 3.33pm came rolling along, I had nearly finished reading my book. The time had come when they would announce who would get on standby for the last flight out to New York. Just as if I was waiting to hear my winning number called from the lotto, the suspense was palpable. I was grateful for my night at Micky D's, but imagining another night there was simply too much to bear. As I eagerly waited in line to check in at the gate, the first thing I noticed was that the flight attendant had large emerald green eyes. I connected with her luminous soul essence and found her to be stunningly beautiful. Like a living goddess, I envisioned her as Green Tara, remover of all obstacles and bestower of Supreme compassion.

When it was my turn in line, I took a deep breath, opened my heart, looked in her eyes and proceeded to tell her my abbreviated story in such a way to perhaps inspire her to become a part of it. I had to summon my courage to then ask her, 'Would you like to be a part of making a miracle with me?'

She took a long pause; I sensed she wanted to help me. 'I'm sorry. Every seat is absolutely full. I'll have to consult with my manager to see what other possible options there were. I'll do what I can, Ms. Ray. Please take a seat until I call you up for further notice.'

'Wonderful. Thank you, Madame!' I retreated to my seat, sat back down and waited for the final verdict, all the while envisioning myself, flying way above the world so high like a diamond in the sky. I sensed the goddess was genuinely intrigued by my invitation and was busy taking the necessary steps to make our miracle actually happen. As everyone else boarded the aircraft, I beamed my love and sent out a prayer. *May all beings be delivered effortlessly to their highest destiny and destination.*

Then the flight attendant announced my name over the loudspeaker. 'Ambe´ Ray, please come to the ticket counter. Ambe´ Ray.' Apparently, I hadn't been breathing because I gasped for air when I heard my name called out. In that moment, I felt to be the winning contestant on the game show, *The Wheel of Fortune.*

'Well, Madame, we have miraculously managed to find you a seat! My supervisor and I found your story quite inspiring, and we felt moved to offer you a first class seat for the duration of your flight.'

'Wow! Really? That's even greater than I had imagined! I'll take it! Thank you so very much!' I said, catching my breath. *What an angel, a living goddess! Om tara, tu tara, ture svaha!*

'The pleasure is all mine.' She smiled, her emerald eyes dancing in joyous celebration along with mine. After three official stamps, I was issued my golden ticket and then escorted to the entrance of the plane to take my first class miracle seat.

I was surprised by how quickly I snapped back into feeling extra fabulous. The super soft leather seats, warm face towels, freshly pressed orange juice and feathered pillows created a much-appreciated sense of luxury and comfort after my long overnighter at Mickie D's. With a renewed spirit and grateful heart, I cozied back in my seat. *New York, New York, here I come!*

Within a few moments, my eyes closed and I drifted into a deeply relaxed doze. It felt like a whole hour passed by when I was revisited by the stewardess who first welcomed me aboard. 'Excuse me, Ms. Ray, would you care for an extra blanket?'

'Oh, thank you. Yes, please,' I responded, feeling beyond grateful for the upgrade into 'pampered priestess' status. I smiled inside as I registered that the man in the aisle seat sitting next to me was in a military uniform complete with multiple badges of honour pinned to his finely ironed lapel. I swallowed another big gulp of orange juice and decided to strike up a friendly conversation with him.

'Hello,' I said.

'Er, hello.' He cleared his throat.

Funny enough, the first thing I noticed was his nose. It was bright red compared to the rest of his face, which was a pale yellow tone. I remembered my studies in Chinese face diagnosis. An extra red nose related to a severe heart condition usually connected to over-consumption of alcohol. For a brief moment I considered telling him that he may need to get his heart checked, but then I appropriately held back.

'Are you in the military?' I asked.

'Well, yes ma'am. You could say that,' he replied with an American accent that seemed to come from somewhere in the deep South.

'Wow.' I pondered the unique opportunity to connect directly with somebody in the US Military. 'Thank you for your service, sir. You know, you and I have similar careers. We are both working to serve and protect the land and the people of this world.'

'Now, is that right?' he said.

'Yes, except if you don't mind me saying, I could never comprehend how the government can utilise the military to wipe out entire countries along with thousands of innocent civilians in the name of democracy, peace and freedom for all. In truth, it's utterly heartbreaking. It just doesn't make any sense to me. Humans are the only species that actually destroy their own home.' It felt as if I was getting something off my chest for the both of us.

His face turned bright red to match his nose as he picked up his bourbon on the rocks and took another generous swallow. He finished it off as if it had the power to magically erase some of his reality. I could feel his disciplined etiquette taking over as he cleared his throat and responded to my comment in a good Samaritan kind of way. 'Well, you know, we are still learning. The truth is, we have yet to find a better way.'

'I understand,' I responded somberly. I sincerely appreciated the General's reply. His composed response had a tone of apologetic humility that genuinely shared my concern. He was not defensive, in as much as awkward in the knowing that he was giving his life to a highly flawed system – one that impacted the environment, families, communities, future generations and entire eco-systems in unfathomable ways. We shared in the silent mourning of the countless innocent lives that have been devastated as a result of this highly 'flawed' system. In his own way, the General let me know that my concerns as a civilian were more than valid. In the end, I was grateful to have had the opportunity to voice them while appreciating his service and sacrifice.

As we continued to chat, I became a safe and anonymous person for him to confide in and release some of the pressure that weighed heavily on his troubled heart. He privately confessed to me his pain for contributing to a system that was predominantly financially motivated. The conversation felt to be healing for both of us, and I appreciated his intention to be in service to his country and fellow citizens. It must be challenging to give your life to a system that enforces so much mass destruction under the guise of promoting peace and democracy. *It's no wonder he has a heart condition*, I thought with genuine empathy and compassion. In my heart of hearts, I knew that there was no financial gain that could ever be worth the horrific atrocities of war, destruction and massive bloodshed.

The beautiful flight attendant who had gifted me with my first class seat politely interrupted our conversation. Another woman, whom I presumed was her supervisor, stood closely by her side. 'Excuse me, Ms. Ray, we are so very sorry to have to do this, but we had to reissue your seat to a woman who has purchased your seat for full price. We will need to move you back to 13B, an economy class seat. Once again, we are terribly sorry for the inconvenience.'

For a split second, I felt disappointed and then quickly shifted to my oh so familiar mantra, *Be disappointed or trust open. All righty then, trust open it is.*

I said a warm goodbye to the General and gathered my things. My thoughts ran something like this: *why trust open? Because when I close, I create just that, closure! While staying open creates novel possibilities where once there was none. When I choose to flex my trust open muscles, all matters of miracles are made out of the mud. I* swallowed my last sip of orange juice, reached my hand out to the General for a handshake and wished him all the very best. I then walked through the partition into the narrow economy aisle to my new seat, which sat just above the left wing of the aircraft.

I stopped in the aisle to stow my bag in the overhead compartment. And there she was, radiant as ever, sitting in 13A, the aisle seat next to 13B, the beautiful diva, shining brightly in her ruby red lipstick and glittering rhinestone- tailored jacket.

She burst out, sending my heart leaping out of my body, 'Haw! Hot damn. I knew it! Have a seat right here next to me, young lady. I've got to show you somethin'. Looky here,' she said, pointing to a page in her journal. 'I told God that I wanna sit next to a goddess on the plane on my way to Iceland.'

She held up her journal. 'You see that here?' She pointed with her long fuchsia nail. 'You're that someone special. Howdy do? My name is Miranda Wilde. What's your name, hunne'?' She put out a hand bearing a large diamond ring and hot pink fingernails gleaming with diamond rhinestones on each tip to match her lapel on her jacket.

I wriggled my way into my window seat and turned to face her, meeting her bulging eyes with a big grin on my face. 'Hello, my name is Ambe´. Lovely to meet you, Ms. Wilde.'

'I'm so grateful you have come to sit by me. I just knew it. I knew it! God always supplies when I ask in prayer!'

'Oh, I know what you mean,' I said, riveted to discover what was to come out of her mouth next. I literally gasped when I realised that I was sitting next to the Black Madonna herself. *Oh my goddess! There she was, alive, in person, face-to-face, bosom-to-bosom. Did all of those setbacks happen so that we could fulfill our destiny appointment to sit next to each other? Ohh, this is so good…so good. It absolutely must be true!* I thought with astonishing delight.

'You may not believe this,' I said, 'but I feel I was supposed to sit next to you on this journey back to the US, and that every obstacle I have just encountered – including almost getting arrested and then spending the night at McDonalds – was actually perfectly orchestrated so that you and I could meet up in this very moment!'

Her eyes sparkled and beamed back at me. Then she replied, 'Aw haw! I know what you mean suga'. I feel the same way! God works in mysterious ways, I tell ya. Hey hunne', where you from?'

'I'm from the Bay Area, California.'

'Really? That's where I'm from, San Francisco to be exact. I've lived there half my life,' she said, making the sign of the cross over her overflowing, velvety bosom.

'Me too! Actually, I've been living just over the Golden Gate Bridge in Marin County for some time now.'

'Oh, it sure is pretty there, just like you. I'm so darn happy you're sittin' right here next to me. I can hardly believe my eyes. Thank you God for anserin' my prayer!'

'So am I! So where are you headed?' I asked.

'I'm going to Iceland to sing at a corporate party for Toyota. I'm a singer, ya know. Yes, I am. God has blessed me with the most perfect job. Ah haww. I'm livin' in Germany now with my man. He's a wonderful husband, ya know. But sure is cold there and there aren't many people like you. It gets a bit lonely there sometimes. That's why I am so darn happe' to be sitting next to you, a real, live, genuine goddess!' she repeated, bubbling over as she smiled deeply into my eyes. We nearly hugged in that moment.

Someone like me, I thought curiously to myself while momentarily pondering who 'someone like me' was now. 'Wow,' I said. 'You're a singer?'

'Yeah. But I wasn't always a singer. I was turning tricks the better half of my life over on Larkin Street in the Tenderloin district. You know where that is? You won't believe it, but I was a prostitute for over seventeen years on that same ol' dungy street corner. I was hooked too, ya know. Hooked on cocaine, crack, meth, ice – you name it, I smoked it, sniffed it, drank it and I even shot it up my veins. It was baaad and it took everything under the kitchen sink to numb myself out from my crazy ass reality. Whoohoo, you should have seen me then. You would never have recognised me. I've changed so much I can hardly recognise me now.'

'Whoa! Really? Tell me, how did you change?' I asked.

'Well, one day, a friend of mine dragged my sweet ass over to that famous church on Larkin Street. You know the one, Grace

Cathedral.' I remember it like yesterday, cuz it was that day my life changed in a very big way. It was Sunday service, ya know. I was a wreck, hung over from the night before. I thought I'd just go along for a giggle, ya know, get off the street for a little while. Maybe I could repent one of my millions of sins or somethin' like that.'

She laughed flamboyantly and then quickly paused to rearrange her large hair and admire her extra-long nails. She tapped one of them on the armrest as she talked, 'Well, ya wouldn't believe what happened next. I started to sing along to that choir of theirs. I sang so loud and clear, I thought the roof was going to blow off. Somethin' came over me and it was a hell of a lot bigger than little ol'me. You know the feelin'? I was so taken aback. Even my friend sittin' next to me looked at me with her big eyes bulgin'. She could hardly believe it was me. I just couldn't stop singin', nothing could stop me. Ya know what I mean?'

'Uh-huh,' I said, nodding my head in disbelief of the utter coincidence of our story lines.

'Anyway, that next Sunday, I came back to that big ol´church and I sang some more, and the following Sunday too and the following Sunday after that. Then one day I decided I wanted to be a part of that choir. They were singin' with so much pride and glory. It scared the daylights out of me how much I wanted it, almost as much as I wanted my fix. So I stayed away for a very long while and instead went back to my old familiar ways.

One sunday mornin', months later, I just had that feelin' I had to go back and sing some more. You won't believe what happened to me next. Out of the clear blue came that fine lookin' preacher man. He told me straight up to my face, 'I'm really glad you've come back to church, Miranda. I've been noticin' your voice and missing it too. It's the voice of an angel. How would you like to be our special guest and come sing with our choir next Sunday?

'Well, as you can imagine, I nearly flipped my lid and passed out right there and then! 'Who, me? Me sing with you?' I said. 'Oh no, I don't think so.' I didn't think I'd be able to hold it togetha' without my regular fix and all. I regretfully declined his kind invitation and went out that night and got myself extra wasted. My pimp would never allow it anyway. What came next was quite a surprise. I had one of those dreams, ya know, the ones when Jesus comes to you all special like and says, "Ms Miranda Wilde, if you are spectin' to live another day longer, you betta' join that choir and join it tomorrow. Otherwise, you may just not see the light of anotha' day, the way you be headin' and all! Are ya listenin', Miranda Wilde? Not anotha' day."

'Well, I wasn't gonna argue with God ol' Mighty, so I marched myself to that big ol' church the following day and made arrangements to go to choir rehearsal. After that, I found help there, ya know? The kind that could support me to kick the heavy drugs and get off the street-turning tricks too. It worked for a while and then my pimp would find a way to get me back on the crack. Nasty stuff, ya know. I felt absolutely helpless. I thought I could never beat this shit out of my body. But then somethin' came over me and gave me the strength and the will to try again. They say we fall down a million times to see what we are really made of. Somehow, in some God-be-Jesus way, I managed to pick myself up for the millionth time and get off them nasty drugs. I continued to turn tricks for a while, but this time, without the dope. I kept up my singin' in the choir and gainin' more and more important solo roles. I had to be sober to keep up with my responsibilities to the others in the choir. And with that fine preacher's help, I finally got free of my pimp and those dev'lish drugs!'

Miranda paused, and then began to sing her story to me. 'I wanna know,' she broke out in song and bellowed, 'I wanna know where God was in all of this? I wanna know!' She abruptly stopped and giggled. 'Well, God must have been there all along, cuz I'm here now and I'm on top of the world! I'm a top paid professional singer who's livin' in Germany with my sweet darlin' of a husband. To top that off, I'm being paid to travel all over the world and do what I love to do most, sing my heart out! Hallelujah, praise God!'

Hanging on to each word, I nodded my head over and over again, utterly astonished by her heroics.

'How 'bout that? Now I'm on my way to sing my heart out for the Toyota Corporation. Haw! Can you believe it? I'm their lead entertainer! I give thanks every day, ya know. I tell you, God works in mysterious ways. My faith is my mountain. Now tell me, darlin', what do you do for a livin'?' Her eyes streamed liquid pools of shimmering love light, reviving every part of my being with her divinely inspired presence.

I was so blown away and so deeply moved by Miranda's story that I could hardly find the words to answer her loaded question. Her fierce love and sizzling passion epitomised all that Sophia had revealed to me about the heroine's journey in the underworld. With tears streaming down my face, I gave it my best shot to reply.

'Hmm, I'm somewhat of a gypsy priestess,' I said, envisioning my red sports car and Magdalene's cave all at once. 'I'm just returning back from a spiritual pilgrimage through the Dragon ley lines of England, France and Greece. In my own way, I too have experienced a life-altering initiation that has brought me to my knees. Oh, and when I'm living in the Bay Area, I teach yoga and facilitate transformational temple arts retreats.'

'Oh, so you are a goddess!' Miranda declared and slapped her hand on her voluptuous thigh. 'I knew it! God Almighty has put a living goddess here to sit next to me. Do ya have a business card, sweetie? I'd like to contact you when I'm in the Bay Area.'

I smiled deeply into her ebony eyes shining from that first mist of tears. Right then and there, I knew beyond a shadow of a doubt that my entire Grail journey had lead me to sit next to this rare and precious diamond. We continued to savour each and every precious moment together, like two old girlfriends reunited after being separated for lifetimes. We wanted to catch up with all of our adventures and near-death experiences.

As I handed her my card, we promised one another that we would get together the next time she came to visit the Bay Area. 'Miranda, I would love to introduce you to my friend Michael Franti. I really feel you two would hit it off big time. He is a passionate singer/songwriter guided by his big open heart just like you.' I whipped out my laptop from my backpack and opened up itunes. I played one of Michael's more famous songs called, 'Bomb the World'.

In her inspired frenzy, Miranda glued her ear to the tiny speaker and soaked in the lyrics while absorbing Michael's deep, honey-toned vocals. Her rich and resonant voice harmonised along with the chorus to get a better feel for the song. I secretly imagined the

General seated in first class chiming in to sing along with us. 'We can chase down all our enemies, bring them to their knees. We can bomb the world to pieces but we can't bomb it into peace. Whoa, we may even find a solution to hunger and disease, we can bomb the world to pieces, but we can't bomb it into peace.'

Oh, how I adored every ounce of this hot-blooded Madonna. She shone like a beautiful black diamond full of spirit fire, sublime substance and a healthy dose of sultry sassiness! *Miranda Madonna, you are not only a rhinestone diva, you are a majestic monarch of the most high!*

Miranda carried on about her new dream to perform in concert with Michael Franti and that this too, was now going to be recorded in her magic journal. And then like a songbird, she chimed in with another medley from a piece she had written and performed in a concert. Miranda continued to speak and sing her amazing heroine's journey of how she had resurrected herself from the dead to become the succulent, full-bloom rose that she was!

'It's a miracle, I tell you! I should never have made it out of my livin' hell, especially with those seductive drugs pullin' me back over and over again. I tried to defy God so many times, but he just wouldn't let me go down. No, ma'am, he kept at me till I finally gave in to his wish. It's sura is a miracle, I tell you. I did so much lethal shit, I should never have lived, I tell ya. But I neva gave up. Oh no, ma'am, I neva ever gave up. And now I'm sittin' here next to you tellin' you all 'bout it! My sweet Lord! It's a frickin' miracle that I'm alive to tell the tale.'

Each time Miranda would share a vignette of some massive challenge that she had overcome, she would soak in a reflective pause, readjust her hair, spin her gold diamond ring and then strum her long fingernails on the armrest that sat between us. I joined her, astonished by all the wild and wondrous ways the Divine works magic in our lives. I then imagined showering her in crimson red rose petals.

I bow to you, SHE who has delved into the depths of the underworld to tango with the Queen of Death and retrieve the crown jewels of your soul. Like a phoenix you have risen from the ashes to meet your highest destiny and offer your inspired songs of freedom and redemption to bless up the people of the world.

'Miranda Wilde, you are a one-of-a-kind, bonified G-O-D-D-E-S-S, a precious jewel and gift to us all!' *Yes, indeed, the Black Madonna is back in town and she's gonna light up this world with her sonic love bombs!*

With that, we embraced each other with a fierce love born from surviving the depths of an unspeakable darkness. We knew that if either of us had given up, we would never have gotten to experience this heart-melting, heavenly embrace. I felt her heart pressing into mine while whispering softly in my ear as if she could foresee the path that lay before me, 'If I can do it, so can you, my darlin'. The road may be dark and lonely at times, but there is always a light at the end of the tunnel. Before ya know it, you will find that you too have become the lantern, lightin' the way for others.'

We clung to one another as we soared through the clear blue sky from one chapter in our lives to another. My heart was so swollen that my chest felt as if it was about to burst. My eyes filled with salty tears as Miranda continued to serenade me with her sultry voice. We held hands tightly as the plane descended and touched ground in Iceland. We were both incredibly grateful for the relatively smooth landing!

'Why don't you join me, sista? Come be my guest and stay with me at my five-star hotel in Iceland! You can be my special date at my singing engagement for Toyota and after that, we can pamper ourselves in the glorious Blue Pools!'

'Whoa, thank you! That's quite an invitation, soul sista', I pronounced, as I pondered the ever-so-irresistible invitation for as long as I could before the plane pulled into the gate. I visualised all of the magic that could unfold if I embarked on a five-star Icelandic holiday with the one and only, Miraaaanda Wilde. Most of all, I felt incredibly touched and beyond honoured by her outrageous invitation.

Miranda Wilde Madonna and I hangin' out together at a classy, high-end hotel, dancing the night away, soaking it all up in the Blue Pools – how could I ever pass this once in a lifetime invitation up? I found myself at yet another huge crossroads, where I was being invited to choose between two potential life destiny paths. I closed my eyes, dropped into the silence of my heart-womb and imagined two roads coming together at the point of now. And then I asked Sophia for some on-the-spot guidance.

The tender voice of the Divine Mother whispered to me, '*Oh, I know it's an irresistible invitation, one that seems rather insane to pass up...and yet it is time to go home, dear child. You will have another opportunity to return to Iceland and experience the Blue Pools and discover more of this enchanting land. Much awaits you at home. Do not postpone embracing your new life any longer.*

With tender acceptance, I gently released the image of myself floating under a canopy of shimmering stars while moon-bathing in an expansive oasis of glacial hot springs co-mingling with the deep blue sea. For now, it was more than enough to have met the great Miranda Wilde and be so warmly invited to share in her miraculous world.

I pressed my brimming heart into her overflowing cocoa bosom, and we exchanged another timeless, Divine Mother bear hug as I whispered, 'I will have to take a rain check this time. Thank you, dear one. Your invitation means the absolute world to me.'

She looked deeply into my eyes and then leaned in close to me, filling my head with her poignant soul perfume. I listened intently, as if she was handing me a magic key that would change everything. 'A wise woman once tol' me, don't downgrade your dreams to match your reality. Upgrade your faith to match your destiny. You bes' be goin' home now, sweety. I know the Goddess will have us meet up again when the stars align!'

I sang a little tune as we exited the plane. 'Twinkle, twinkle, little star, now I know just who you are. Miranda Wilde who shines so bright, blessing this world with her diamond light. Twinkle, twinkle, little star, now I know just who you are.'

CHAPTER SEVENTY-FOUR

HOLY DESIRE

There is a longing that has been placed inside you...a cry for pure aliveness, to fully participate in this very rare and sacred love world that we have miraculously found ourselves in. Please do not postpone your participation – until you have "fully healed your past," become "awakened," landed in some state of safety, invulnerability and are experiencing only "positive" emotions and have gotten rid of the yucky, icky, negative ones, found the perfect soulmate, or the most groovy, spiritual career. There is only now and what is arising within you. Now is pure glory, an illuminated portal into pure, shimmering presence. If you do not infuse this world with your gifts, with your heart, and with your unique signature and fragrance, something will be lost forever. For it is up to you to provide wild, raging love with safe passage here. The stars, the ocean, the sun, and the moon – these ones are looking to you.

– Matt Licata

Your longing for me is my message to you.
All your attempts to reach me are in reality my attempts to reach you.

– Jelaluddin Rumi

Parting ways with Miranda Wilde was beyond moving for both of us. It felt like lifetimes for us to find each other and in the silence of our hearts, we knew our brief meeting had changed our lives forever. Meanwhile, my layover in Reykjavík made quite an impression on me! After Miranda went on her way, I sat alone in the small airport lounge and felt engulfed in a silence so surreal it took my breath away. I had never experienced anything like it in my life. Outside of the large glass windows, there was nothing in sight for miles apart from the endless expanse of sky. I felt like I had been dropped off on another planet, somewhere in between the tick and the tock. In such a lucid, pristine space, my extrasensory perception was amplified in an exponential way. Everything I thought, I could see ripple into the fabric of reality like a pebble dropped into a still pond. Every thought, feeling and intention is a brush stroke painted on the canvas of God's hand.

The things that change the world are the subtle and invisible movements in our inner terrain. A small shift in my emotional or energetic field can lead to a massive shift in the collective experience, I mused, feeling into the significance of each person's life impacting the whole.

As I walked to my departure gate, I felt considerably lighter and couldn't help but notice that I was free from my typical departure lounge sickness. Instead, I amused myself by being fascinated by a harem of female airline attendants, each meticulously made up in Chanel-like makeup and immaculate updos. *Where in all this wide-open space are all the upscale beauty salons? Never mind,* I consoled myself, feeling more than a little rough around the edges. I just got the inner makeover of a lifetime!

I stared out the large airport window into the vast open terrain, marvelling at my meeting with Miranda while letting go of needing to know what my life would look like upon my return to the US. After a two-hour layover in this fascinating bardo lounge, I boarded my next airplane headed to New Jersey, which we know is like another planet altogether.

Seven hours later, I set foot in the bustling Newark Airport. In customs, I was interrogated for quite a while before they allowed me to cross into the 'land of the not so free.' My Australian friend Kevin summed it up nicely when he first came to America for a visit. 'America seems like an orange. On the outside, it's got a tough skin that squirts acid but once you're in, it's surprisingly sweet and juicy.' I never could have imagined how delighted I would be to be welcomed into the US by a mélange of people who shouted at each other as their normal way of communicating. Many of them were on the fast track to Starbucks to get their double shot, half-caf, fat-free, extra foam, agave-sweetened lattes before retrieving their imitation designer luggage from the baggage claim.

Since my connecting flight was not until the following morning, I saw no other choice but to arrange a nearby hotel for the night. This time, I consciously chose not to constrict around the unexpected expense. Instead, I chose to stay open and trust in the abundant flow of the universe. *This is Spirit's way of building up some good ol' fashioned soul stamina. After all, it's one thing to see the light; it's a whole other thing to keep the lights on while navigating in the dark.*

By 10.30pm, I was checked into the Howard Johnson's hotel in the (not) so beautiful downtown Newark, New Jersey, where it appeared the neighborhood gang were having a strategic meeting over coffee and doughnuts in the hotel lobby. I had no idea where on Earth I was, and quite frankly, it didn't much matter. I was ecstatic to run a hot bath, use the tiny rough towels, switch on the small TV and fall asleep to the tune of 'I Love Lucy'.

By 7am the following morning, I was checked out and headed back to the airport to catch my last flight to Los Angeles via a stopover in Las Vegas. I felt grateful to have made it through the night without being kidnapped; mugged; or solicited for sex, drugs and/or money.

While waiting to board my final plane, I wrote the following entry in my journal:

> Dear Sophia, thank you for illuminating the way for me. Soon I will be back in Los Angeles, and although I feel an immense gratitude and soul transformation, my heart continues to feel a deep longing. Is my heart meant to feel as if it is broken in a million pieces while my spirit feels to be soaring?

I remained silent for a moment until I heard Sophia's loving voice respond.

'Oh yes, dear child, we are well aware of this churning in your heart, and we would say this is how we keep the channels open! We invite you to shift your focus away from the feeling of something's missing and open to the gift of longing itself. We suggest that you use this feeling gift to open your heart even wider to let more of the Divine's Love in. For in truth, all longing is ultimately a longing for closer intimacy with the Divine. Do not attempt to squelch or overcome this feeling or any other feeling for that matter. Allow your feelings to be a constant flame that burns brightly within your heart. This is the Beloved's way of communicating with you. After all, how can the big Love get in if your heart is not cracked wide open?

'Remember, the love that you long for doesn't belong to any one person, object or thing. It is the flame of the Cosmic Christ dancing inside of you. As this love continues to flow toward creating an ever more depth-filled relationship with your Divine Self, you will discover that you come into a greater intimacy with the glorious nature of your authentic being. The full spectrum of sorrow to joy is ALL to be embraced as the heart of the Beloved. Remember, everything is here to assist you to grow your wings of light. For now, be still and know: here and now is where you have access to all the Love of the Universe. I am Sophia and I am speaking to you from the crack in the centre of your heart. Be still and feel me reaching for you, just as you are reaching for me!'

CHAPTER SEVENTY-FIVE

THE BLACK PEARL

Wherever we want to go, we go. That's what a ship is, you know.
It's not just a keel and a hull and a deck and sails; that's what a ship needs.
But what a ship is...what the Black Pearl really is...is freedom.

– Jack Sparrow

I have more mothers than any girls off the street. They are the moon shining over me. I guess I have forgiven myself, although sometimes in the night my dreams will take me back to Salvice and I have to wake up and forgive myself again. But Mary is always there. I feel her in unexpected moments. She will suddenly rise, and when she does, she does not go up into the sky, but further inside of me.

– Sue Monk Kidd, *The Secret Life of Bees*

Walk until the darkness is a memory,
and you become the sun on the next traveler's horizon.

– Kobe Bryant

B y midmorning, I had landed in Las Vegas for a layover. What else could I have done other than gamble away the last of my small change in one of those glittery slot machines? After all, I had gambled everything else that I had on this journey. It simply made sense to finish off the job right then and there in viva Las Vegas – the

Disneyland of risking it all for the vague promise of being rewarded with something more. I heard an assertive voice in my head chime in as I manoeuvred the slot machine handle up and down. *When it comes to awakening, don't hold back. Give everything you have. Don't save anything for a fictitious rainy day in the future. Go all the way! Gamble everything. Go on. After all, what is the purpose of holding anything back?*

Hmmm. At first, this input sounded alluring, even fearless – having all the heroic archetypal qualities of Zena, the Fearless Warrior. And yet I wasn't feeling much like Zena at the time. I was feeling more like Aphrodite. This 'all or nothing' aspect of me had lacked a most essential ingredient of radical self-love and self-care. What if I were to participate from the fullness of my being rather than being willing to sacrifice it all in the name of God? My Taoist teacher once told me, 'Fill your cup first and give generously from the overflow.'

I stood in front of the shiny red slot machine. I had sixteen quarters left. If I put ten aside, I would have enough for a refreshing drink when I arrived in Los Angeles. *I choose to nourish and flourish, to give all and receive all for the benefit of all. Now that sounds like a very satisfying way to play the game of life.*

With that decree, a cascade of quarters spilt out of the slot machine as all my lucky cherries lined up in a row. *Yes! She who has shall have even more! Ambe' Aphrodite Ray, you just won yourself a nourishing lunch and a massage!*

The flutter of butterflies whirled in my belly as I gazed out the plane window before takeoff to Los Angeles. Ever since leaving Europe, my environment and reality had dramatically shifted. It was like turning the channel from one dream to another. *Only three evenings ago, I was meditating in Mary Magdalene's cave. Amazing!*

I overheard the voice of the stewardess consoling a Korean passenger about his dissatisfaction with his assigned seat. She said, 'I'm sorry, sir. It must be your karma to sit where you are. But I'll see what I can do to change your seat for you.'

The world is waking up, I thought with a bemused smile. *Humanity has come to a place in our planetary evolution where the conscious Masculine energy is becoming balanced with the equal power of the conscious Feminine. We are not only experiencing this world awakening to our Oneness, but also our equality. Humanity is at last growing up, taking responsibility and becoming aware of our interconnectivity and how our choices impact one another and the planet we share. We are tapping into the awareness that our perceptions, thoughts and feelings ripple out and impact all those around us. With this growing consciousnesss, we are stepping out of victimhood into self-empowerment. Instead of pointing the finger and blaming another, we now take a breath and become curious about the potential for greater cooperation and connectivity within every encounter. As conscious co-creators of our reality, we open to feel our interconnectivity and are naturally inclined to contribute to our fellow journeyers because we no longer see ourselves as separate. As Self and Divinity partner on the dance floor of life, we become aroused in a whole new way. A way where our highest synergistic potential changes the way we inhabit our lives, liberating the best of what we have to offer each other while enlivening the whole.*

When the plane touched down in the City of Angels, I felt a rush of excitement to be back in California. *I guess I'll always love the far-out, freaky, fully expressed, uniquely dressed, uptown, downtown, hip-hoppin', always-shoppin', fast-food-lovin', outrageously rude, hot-tub-soakin', always-outspoken, good-ol'-American, land-of-the-gluten free... kind of folks. Home!*

CHAPTER SEVENTY-SIX

INDWELLING PRESENCE

Forgive everything and everyone including yourself, for all the ways separation consciousness has played out. Offer gratitude for the rich variety of experiences offered within the fragmented matrix, you can now discern separation consciousness and its operating systems. Witness all that is present within the now moment without resisting what is. Surrender to the living plasmic light as it reconstructs the physical/mental/emotional/spirit bodies and reconnects all to the living source of creation, the Divine Mother.

– Avatara Ananda

We are coming out of a deep sleep. We are opening the door to a new era of possibility. In order to walk through that door, we have been told repeatedly by our elders to forgive ourselves and forgive the story that wounded so many of us. In allowing and receiving the consciousness of that moment, our compassion is awakened and enlightenment flowers.

– The 13 Grandmothers

Integrity can be used to describe the unbroken quality of life in all its dimensions. This interwoven nature of reality is reflected in a sense of Self, which embodies all of creation: a living tapestry of creatures and cosmos, inside and outside, logic, imagination and mystery. Such an identity redefines what it means to be human.

– Anne Hillman, *Dancing Animal Woman*

On the following night, just after my return to Los Angeles, my mother and father invited me to attend Temple with them in honour of the Jewish holiday, Kol Nidra, the day of atonement. It is a day especially devoted to forgiveness and reconciliation with God for living in separation from the One, Adonai. In this tradition, it is said that atonement allows us to pass from death into life. Even though I considered myself spiritual rather than religious, I felt the serendipitous timing of this ritual and the opportunity to be part of honouring my parents, ancestral lineage and my heritage. And so I said yes with very little reluctance...*for a change.*

A heart-melting melody from a singular cello filled the room as my parents and I entered the temple. Apart from the warm welcome from the ushers who escorted us to our seats, the room exuded a kind of eerie melancholy. I overheard the people sitting next to me discussing the news that Israel had been bombed the day before by the Palestinians – or perhaps it was the other way around. I'm not quite sure and it really didn't matter at this point. I knew that either way, it was yet another horrific atrocity and loss of precious human lives in the name of politics and religion.

I sat down between my father and mother on the hard wooden benches that faced the low platform stage. Two vases brimming with bouquets of greenery and white flowers marked both ends of the platform where the Rabbi was seated. My father placed his hand on my leg with a gesture of gratitude. I had finally come to temple and he was beaming with fatherly pride. Initially, I noticed my response was to flinch. My body became cold and froze underneath his hand from a distant memory. I became aware of the terror that coursed through my nervous system and felt my energy contract. Instead of closing down to protect myself as I had done over the years, I made a conscious choice to try something new. I dropped my defenses and opened more. I chose to meet my father's affection with the love that I am and to inwardly bless him with all the love and joy in the universe. In that flash of an eternal moment, we were both set free from all that had transpired between us, throughout all lifetimes, dimensions and realities. We were two birds, one black as night, the other white as snow, who knew that one would not exist without the other.

It's a new day, I thought. *The day of 'at-one-ment'. I choose to live and love with an open heart no matter what comes my way.* What was to come next was nothing short of a miracle. The Rabbi stepped onto the platform stage and told the story of Shekinah, often depicted as a white dove carrying a green wreath. He explained that the wreath we typically see accompanying the dove is a sign of forgiveness and of letting go of bitterness. It is this forgiveness offered in full sincerity that opens the gateway to our original innocence – the golden pathway to eternal life. I sat there, flanked by my parents, absolutely stunned by the uncanny synchronicity of being welcomed home by this story that so immaculately reflected my recent Grail journey and encounter with the Shekinah dove at the base of Mary's cave in Saintes Baume.

PRAYER *to the* SHEKINAH

O Shekinah,
yours is the feminine face of the Holy,
the luminous moon who lights up the night
as we travel from captivity to liberation,
the pillar of fire who guides our way home,
the cloud hovering over the mountain peaks,
living sign that the drought is over.
You are the Sabbath Bride, the Beloved,
returned from exile.
You restore balance in our relationships
and wholeness to our fragmented souls.
You infuse our lovemaking with honey.
You fill the cup of our hearts,
which tremble with longing,
with the wine of your answering love.
You are the song of our homecoming.
You are the Sabbath Queen, the Great Mother,
who sits at the heart of the table
tearing off hunks of the secret bread
that contains the exact flavor each of us loves best.

You feed us all,
the proud and the repentant,
the believer and the skeptic,
from your own hands.
Your unconditional forgiveness dissolves otherness.
May we remember you and lift you up.
May we recognize your face and celebrate your beauty
in everything and everyone,
everywhere, always.
AMEN.

– Mirabai Star, *Wild Mercy*

The rest of that day was spent relaxing with my parents. For the first time in a very long time, I felt free to love and accept my father just as he was. After all, he too is playing his perfect part within the One shared heart. My mother basked in the unity of it all.

Before falling asleep in my childhood bedroom, I whispered to the darkening night, 'In the end, all that really matters is how much I have loved, let go and allowed love in.'

CHAPTER SEVENTY-SEVEN

THE COSMIC HEART

Dolphins are 5th dimensional Beings who contain the immensity and power of the cosmos in their physical bodies – and what makes this possible is their heart. This is where we are headed from Homo sapiens to Homo luminous. Their bodies and hearts are containers, which are capable of holding a magnitude of energy on a scale beyond anything humans can imagine. Dolphins can move at the speed of light through the Heavens whilst at the same time swimming in the oceans here on Earth. The frequency of dolphins is so accelerated that they can time/space travel and exist in parallel realities simultaneously. The dolphins invite us to live the fullness of our celestial Self in a physical body. The way to contain the intensity of cosmic energy would be through the power and the strength of having the heart of a dolphin. The unconditional heart of the dolphin is shaped like a diamond with the cosmos contained within it. Imagine your entire body becoming a cosmic being, your entire organs, cells, limbs and whole physical form transformed into the cosmos.

– Nicolya Christi

I invoke the light of eternal service so the world around you can be blessed by your presence. So that I can hand you an invitation to make the most of the time you've been given. Please do not wait to be popular. Just become the most intentional and powerful being you have ever encountered, one I love you, one intention and one blessing at a time. And in doing so, all questions will disappear, all judgments will fade and you will become what you were born to be, which is the fully realised, one cosmic heart, beating in the bodies of all.

– Matt Kahn, *Awakening the Cosmic Heart*

> *Footprints lead to the shore of the sea!*
> *Beyond that point,*
> *No trace remains.*
>
> – Jeyaluddin Rumi

It was my last day in Los Angeles before heading back to the Bay Area. The sun blazed brightly in the crystal blue sky, which was unusual for an autumn day in October. The ocean called to me and so I set out for a solo day of wild replenishment at the beach.

Upon arriving, I walked to the water's edge and relished the feeling of the silky warm sand massaging my bare naked feet. I nestled my feet deeper into the soft, warm sand, wiggled my toes and cleansed my body in a golden wave of sensual bliss. The glistening sunlight dancing on the turquoise sea was a cherished site to behold, a reminder of Sacred Union alchemy and bathing in the rarified light of the Christos Sophia. I was grateful to be on Venice Beach, which I took the liberty to rename Venus Beach. Gratitude for the gift of life flooded my being as I looked to the horizon and drank in the light of the afternoon sun. The sun had become my most beloved companion, always filling me with honey-like elation and diamond lucidity.

Every hair on my body stood on end as I let out a squeal of delight. I had spotted two spinner dolphins twirling in the air in joyous unison! Two by two and sometimes three, the dolphin pod dazzled me with their synchronised ecstatic ballet. They dove below the surface – only to re-emerge in another confluence of circus-like arabesques. I offered them a standing applause, in mutual celebration of the miraculous gift of simply being alive.

Oh my goodness! The dolphin kin have come to welcome me home from my Grail journey!

The entire time I had grown up in Los Angeles, I had never ever encountered a pod of wild dolphins at the beach! I was filled with childlike elation as I beamed my big Love and gratitude to my loyal escorts and etheric travelling companions. This time 'the voice' came from deep within the cathedral of my eternal heart, beaming with childlike wonder and awe.

'Daring to serve the Light of the Divine with an open and innocent heart is the crest of the wave you will ride like a dolphin into the Golden Age of Gaia. As you embody and resonate with the crystalline core of your awakened heart, you will experience the song of the universe dwelling within you. This is a golden opportunity to take all that you have cultivated within your individual journey and ask 'how may I vibrationally, personally and spiritually offer my life for the benefit of this ever-evolving, expanding planet? How can the truth of who I am simultaneously assist the world into awakening the highest truth of who we are on a collective level and as one unified Family of Light?

Each incoming wave becomes an irresistible invitation to embody these questions as the propelling force of all that you will go on to create. Every experience and encounter becomes an opportunity to give life and be a part of co-creating endless life-giving beauty.

'Life is the wisdom school, your body the temple, your heart-womb the Source of the living Grail where you will discover the beloved companion of your Soul has been dancing with and within you all along. Truth be told, there is only 'happily ever now'. If you wish more blessings to come into your life, look around and ask, "How may I bless this life, this world, this being, this sacred now?"

'Now are you ready to gift this precious life with all that you are like never before?'

'Yes!' I shouted out to the dolphins spinning before me in a confluence of embodied bliss. 'Yes!' I declared to the setting sun that painted the sky in a wash of purple, orange and pink sorbet-like brush strokes. 'Yes!' I whispered to myself, whom I was coming to know as one of the infinitesimal wonders of this awakening world.

I stood up to anchor this diamond light frequency and raised my arms over my head to encompass the orange ball of electric fire that was now descending into the glistening sea. My arms became shimmering opalescent wings, my body a platinum and golden pillar of light that spiraled into the crystalline core of the New Earth and kissed the heart womb of the Sun.

As I beamed my big love into the setting sun on the horizon, I became keenly aware of a warm and kindred presence enter into my energetic field. A majestic white horse with a long glistening golden mane approached me with an air of noble grace and majestic power. 'Maha!' I gasped with delight.

As she came to stand in front of me, I was awestruck by her glowing innocence and regal stature. We locked gazes for a moment that stretched into eternity. Respectfully, she then bowed her long graceful neck to greet me…I her master and she mine. She knelt down and steadily placed one knee in the sand and with a gentle nod of her long muscular neck, gestured for me to come sit upon her bare silken back. I accepted graciously and mounted her as my Sophia dragon horse. With an unwavering trust in her fearless and untamable spirit, Maha proceeded to stand up ever so gracefully as I took hold of her silky white mane. She then began to walk, trot and then bolted with passionate aliveness down the ocean's shore. She galloped with full power straight toward the centre of the setting sun and then leapt into the air where her majestic golden white wings expanded in full flight. I completely surrendered as my wild love burst my heart wide open to embrace all of creation as the Love, Lover and Beloved. And then *poof!* Just like that, we vanished into the heart of the diamond sun. No more me, no more you, only this Love of all Loves soaring into the great beyond.

An eternity seemed to pass before Maha, my majestic white horse, bowed her head to acknowledge my return and gracefully knelt down so that I could dismount her. I felt exhilarated, and relished the feeling of standing on my own two bare feet – naked, present, raw and in a state of pure gnosis with the all that is. I looked to the horizon and felt that I stood on the crest of a new beginning – one where I was yet to experience this wild divine splendour in the precious moments I had left to play upon this magical Earthstar. This was the Beauty Way, the golden chalice I had come to embody, overflowing with all the divine ingredients to delight this child-like heart, while enlivening and blessing the whole of creation. *For this, I was born, for this, we are here now.*

WE ARE HERE

How could you ever be more than you are
Will you ever see how blessed you are
Similarities between your soul and a star

You are always free
to call out the name of the one that you are
Beloved I Am, Beloved I Am That I Am
This is your sacred name
Beloved I Am, Beloved I Am That I Am
Mother Mary, St Germain
Beloved I Am, Beloved I Am That I Am
Still climbing, will I reach the peak?
Beloved I Am, Beloved I AM THAT I AM
You are that which you seek
We are here to bring some Heaven down
Yes, we are here to spread the love around
We are here to activate the Grail
Yes, we are here to praise the whales
Praise the mother, praise the sun, praise the whales in the ocean
I think it's time that we open our eyes
take a look around and see through the lies
so many beautiful things will arise
If we keep our feet on the ground and lift up our heads as we reach
for the skies
Beloved I Am, Beloved I Am That I Am
This is your sacred name
Beloved I Am, Beloved I Am That I Am .

- +Elijah, Band of Light, 'We are Here'

EXISTENCE

Stepping out of righteousness
Recognizing Oneness
No separation of you and I, of that, of this
We are playing one game
Everyone wins the same
I allow all things to exist today
I allow all things to exist in their own way
I exist in my own way
And I am a powerful creatress

Living in the matrix
Source of all wisdom
In this bliss queendom
We will all manifest
We will all rise
Raising our consciousness
Opening our eyes
We can do anything as long as we try
Whoever said that the limit was the sky
I have a dream and I'm living it everyday
Learning not to let my fears get in the way
Oh, and I reach into myself and
Oh, I smile for what I'm feeling
Know that you are God and God is love
When you pray, do you pray to above?
When you pray, do you pray below?
When you pray, you can pray to yourself because you know...
You are so powerful
You are the One you've been waiting for
You are so powerful and
You are the One you've been waiting for
There's more to be aware of
Nothing to be scared of
We have a relationship with Spirit
Guided by the instinct
Intuition, don't think you are living this life alone, oh no
We were born into a world so vast
We got to slow down and not move too fast
We have been given the gift of life
Blessed are these days and
Sacred are these nights
Oh, and I reach into my soul
Oh, just to find all that I knew I know
We are part of a circle, a family
And how long will it take for us to see?
And how long will it take for us to be?
And what more could we possibly think we need? Just breathe!

We are so powerful
We are the Ones we've been waiting for
We are so powerful and
We are the Ones we've been waiting for
I am so powerful
I am the One I've been waiting for
I am so powerful
I am the One I've been waiting for

– Shylah Ray Sunshine, 'Existence'

The Beginning

AFTERWORD

It is the task of every woman that is awakening right now to establish a reverent relationship with herself, to cut through all the self-negating, false beliefs once and for all. To throw all the pity seeking, illusory wounding out the window, to cease giving herself away to fit in and to be accepted, and to instead devote herself to discovering the potent power that she holds. It is her time to take that journey within, to take time to listen to her body, to listen to her intuition and her heart and to live from that place...to bring forth what is inside out into the world. When a woman is connected to her true nature, for the most part she feels whole and complete, alive, peaceful, joyous, grateful, inspired, creative, actively dynamic, all embracing, expansive, beautiful, wise, truthful and sensual...these are all signs that she is in alignment with her Feminine and integrated with her Masculine. Such a woman has the power to transform the world.

– Caroline de Lisser

During this time of great chaos, as most of humanity feels despondency and despair, it is vital to instill courage and hope....as a courageous experience of the Greater Power and Eternal Life in which a certain trust and expectation of "something better" can be fully grounded. From a more expanded viewpoint, you may, on a very personal level, bring Yeshua's and Mary Magdalene's eternal example of forgiving, empowering love into your present choices and life's experiences. Through doing so, you can effect harmonious change in the world and midwife the Earth into...a peace that passes the intellects understanding, because it fully comforts what has felt comfortless through the power of the Divine Feminine heart.

– Claire Heartsong, *Anna, Grandmother of Jesus*

We need to fertilize the soil of our reality and raise the vibration of this planet so the world and all its inhabitants can be readied and prepared to receive what you are going to create. This is the love revolution, this is what will resolve the plight of this planet and this is what will restore your power so that you can have the greatest experiences of every encounter and bring forth the highest qualities of every character you meet. Dare to serve your own innocent heart as you serve others. Let this life of service be like a game of tag, just like in childhood. You've been tagged now pass it on.

– Matt Kahn, *Awakening the Cosmic Heart*

16 August 2015, Balangan Beach, Bali

Goddess only knows why it has taken me thirteen years and thirteen countries for *The Grail Rider* to be born into this world. All that I know is that it was a supernatural force of relentless L-O-V-E that moved me to midwife this story as an offering to the Beloved in all!

After the number twelve comes thirteen and the thirteenth letter of the alphabet is the letter is 'M' which is for Mother Mary and Mary Magdalene and the returning of the Divine Feminine. Thirteen is also the number of transcendence, the foundation of essence-self combined with the rhythm of the Trinity. Thirteen is symbolic of being moved by fate, open to transcending the identifications of Self and the workings of destiny offered by universal Christ Consciousness. Being impregnated with this 'story' for thirteen years often stretched me beyond my wildest capacity because like all stories, it continued to evolve and change along with my own continued evolution of bringing the unconscious Feminine into greater consciousness.

Sometimes, the best way to let go of a story is to exhaust yourself with it, and that is exactly what I did! By the end of what I thought to be the last edit, it felt as if I was in a fire so hot that it was actually cremating every part of my being, like a caterpillar being ferociously consumed by its own flesh. Yet as with all birthing mothers, trust and faith carried me along, with a required shift from resistance to relaxing into the sensations of the discomfort – and eventually lovingly accepting what is. In the end, I am so very grateful for the large and small blessings along the way that gifted me with the dedication to hang in there through the cyclic metamorphosis from caterpillar into butterfly, while being inspired to steward a mysterious friend that carried the gift of blessing others along the way.

Surprise, surprise! The song, 'Mrs. Robinson' just came onto the café stereo. *Now how did that ol' seventies song find it's way to me all the way in Balangan, Bali?* As you may recollect, the last time I heard that song was when I was boarding the airplane bound for the underworld in the Peloponnese Islands, nearly thirteen years ago! Once again, the music oracle reminds me of how grace and synchronicity can miraculously show up as a constant reminder that the Divine Beloved is the beauty engine fueling this ever-evolving Grail ride.

I feel moved to share with you what happened at this rustic beachfront café just before completing what I had *thought* to be the final edit on the last few chapters of this book. I went for a sunrise walk on the nearby beach that was in proximity to the hotel I picked out called Paradise Inn, which turned out to be more like a glorified youth hostel for young travellers. Nevertheless, I have learned to stay open and trust what lies beneath the surface of appearances. Anyhow, as I was walking along the beach, I knew I was on the home stretch and honestly felt as if I was on my last leg. I prayed to the Muse for a surge of inspiration that would give me the strength to finish.

I heard my soul voice whisper. *As soon as you tenderly accept and embrace the reality of what is unfolding in each and every moment, you will find your exhaustion will melt and your passion will be reignited.*

'Yes,' I said, and instead of wishing that I felt differently, I welcomed my feelings that were showing me where my inner Feminine had gone out of balance with my Masculine through neglecting to take deeper care of myself while focusing solely on finishing the book. Just as I made the choice to surrender to stewarding that delicate balance between effortless flow and deliberate action, I stumbled upon a white cloth bag tied up with string. Two ancient Balinese coins were attached to the ends of the string. The curious bundle had washed up from the sea and was sitting on the edge of the shore. I picked it up and gave it a shake to see if I could determine what could possibly be inside this mysterious cloth bag. At first I thought it might be someone's prized seashell collection. I sat down on the sand and untied the bundle with much effort and patience. Much to my surprise, I did not find seashells inside. Instead, I found a grey ceramic clay vessel that was broken into several pieces, although the top of the vessel was still perfectly whole and intact. Two other objects were also inside the bag: a beautiful dark mahogany seedpod a little larger than the size of my thumb and a rusty razor blade. Fascinated by my treasure, I stared into the bag and pondered the symbolism of the broken ceramic vessel, the sharp blade and seed pod.

When I returned to the youth hostel, everything looked and felt a little more paradise like. I asked the Balinese receptionist if she recognised the cloth bag full of broken clay and she said, 'Oh, yes. This is the offering they make for a cremation ceremony. The seed is from a very special tree that makes a very sacred red fruit full of juicy red seeds.'

'Yes, I know this fruit. Thank you.' *Of course! The pomegranate is associated with the Divine Mother Sophia! And that's why I was guided to this remote beach to find this sacred offering and retrieve the seed of Sophia. Today, I will return the broken pieces to the sea with a prayer of gratitude for all that has cracked my heart open to be filled with the light of the Divine. And I will take this seedpod into my new life as a symbol of perpetual rebirth. Blessed be the gift!*

That miracle finding was then followed up by another miracle finding only a few weeks later when I was walking along another beach in Bali. Much to my astoundment, I stumbled upon yet another clay vessel of the exact kind, lying face down in the sand. This time, the vessel was not broken; it was totally whole and complete apart from a small crack running down its side. For me, it symbolised resurrecting into greater wholeness while the crack represented the perfect imperfection that each one of us has come to embody as divine humans.

As always, I remained awestruck by the parallels, chance encounters, synchronicities and soul lessons that continued to mirror back to me whatever I was presently writing about. The setting, characters, time zones, countries and circumstances may have changed, yet the initiations and situations would re-manifest, inviting me to navigate through them with a whole new level in consciousness! Each successive year *and* edit, the story would work its magic and alchemise me into a more expanded, integrated and illuminated version of myself and the embodiment of the Inner Marriage. As I evolved, so did the story, until at last, I could set it free to soar into the world as its own sovereign being.

At last, *The Grail Rider* has now taken flight! May it land with the people and places that it can best serve and bless up!

Last words before I dive into the sea for a sunset swim. I would like to dedicate and offer my endless gratitude to *you* and to all beloved hearts who found their way to reading this whale of a Grail tale. May the longtime sun shine upon you, all love surround you and the pure light within guide your way home.

With boundless love,
Inaiya

BIBLIOGRAPHY

Adyashsanti. Accessed July 22, 2016. https://www.adyashanti.org

Ai Sari, Shakh. *The Radiance Sutras: 112 Gateways to the Yoga of Wonder & Delight*. Boulder, CO: Sounds True, 2014. N. pag. Print.

Amoraea. 'Sovereignty'. Accessed April 22, 2020. https://pheonixcode.org

Avens, Cynthia, and Richard Zelley. *Walking the Path of Christo Sophia: Exploring the Hidden Tradition in Christian Spirituality*. Bloomington, IN: Author House, 2005.

Bach, Richard. *Messiah's Handbook: Reminders for the Advanced Soul*. Charlottesville, VA: Hampton Roads Pub., 2004.

Bashford, Sophie. Accessed July 22, 2016. https://www.SophieBashford.com

Beattie, Melody. *Codependent No More: How to Stop Controlling Others and Start Caring for Yourself*. Center City, MN: Hazelden, 2011.

Bertrand, Azra and Seren. *The Magdalene Mysteries*. Rochester, VT: Inner Traditions / Bear & Co., 2019.

Borax, Mark. Accessed July 22, 2016.https://www.markborax.com

Campbell, Joseph. *The Hero with a Thousand Faces*. Princeton, NJ: Princeton University Press, 1972.

Cathar Creed. 'Cathar Creed'. Accessed July 22, 2016. http://lightascension.com/arts/catharcreed.htm.

Chardin, Pierre de Teilhard. 'The Gift of Fire'. https://www.brainyquote.com/quotes/pierre_teilhard_de_chardi_114239

Christi, Nicolya. *New Human – New Earth: Living in the 5th Dimension*. Lulu Com, 2012.

Christi, Nicolya. 'Love'. Accessed July 22, 2016. https://www.nicolyachristi.com

Christi, Nicolya. 'A Skylark's Ancient Song'. Accessed July 22, 2016. https://www.nicolyachristi.com

Chodron, Pema. 'When Things Fall Apart: Heart Advice for Difficult Times'. Accessed July 22, 2019. https://www.goodreads.com/quotes/593844-nothing-ever-goes-away-until-it-has-taught-us-what

Coelho, Paulo. *Warrior of the Light: A Manual.* New York: HarperCollins Publishers, 2003.

Clune, Niamh. *The Coming of the Feminine Christ.* Vancouver: Amrita Publication, 1998.

Codorniu, Vanessa. 'NY Alternative Spirituality Examiner'. http://vanessacodorniu.com

Cohen, Neil Steven. *The Voice of Heart: An Intimate Invitation.* Book Surge, 2006.

Deida, David, and Marianne Williamson. *Dear Lover: A Woman's Guide to Men, Sex, and Love's Deepest Bliss.* Boulder, CO: Sounds True, 2005.

Deida, David. Accessed July 22, 2016.https://www.deida.info

Dismore, Joseph D. '7 Steps in Alchemical Transformation'. Accessed July 22, 2016. http://ordosacerdotalvstempli.net/seven.html.

Douglas-Klotz, Neil, and Matthew Fox. *Prayers of the Cosmos: Meditations on the Aramaic Words of Jesus.* San Francisco: Harper & Row, 1990.

Dreamer, Oriah Mountain. *The Dance: Moving to the Rhythms of Your True Self.* San Francisco: Harper San Francisco, 2001.

Drew, Sarah. 'Gaia Codex: A Novel of Ancient Wisdom Text Revealed'. Accessed May 11, 2017.http://tinyurl.com/gaiacodex2020

Durham, Diana. *The Return of King Arthur: Completing the Quest for Wholeness, Inner Strength, and Self Knowledge.* New York: Jeremy P. Tarcher/Penguin, 2005.

Eagle, Brooke Medicine. *Buffalo Woman Comes Singing: The Spirit Song of a Rainbow Medicine Woman*. New York: Ballantine, 1991.

Eliot, TS. 'East Coker'. 'East Coker' in Four Quartets by Esme Valerie Eliot. Harcourt Inc. 1968.

Ellis, Normandi. *Awakening Osiris: A New Translation of the Egyptian Book of the Dead*. Grand Rapids, MI: Phanes Press, 1988.

Eve-olution. Accessed July 22, 2016. https://www.facebook.com/ EveOlutionEvokingSacredArt.

Forrest, Snow. Accessed June 22, 2020. http://www.labyrinthholistichealth. com

Ghazal of Zeb-un-Nisa. 'Technology of the Heart'. Accessed July 22, 2016. http://www.techofheart.co/. Accessed July 22, 2016.

Gibran, Kahlil. 'When Love Beckons'. *The Prophet*. Alfred A. Knopf. 1923.

Grace. *The White Rose*. The Starlight Foundation Press. Mount Shasta, California, 2015.

Goose, Mother 'This Little Piggy'. Accessed July 22, 2016. http:// https://www.poetryfoundation.org/poems/46943/this-little-piggy

Hafiz. 'Not with Wings'. *Love Poems from God*. Daniel Ladinsky. Penguin Books. 2002.

Harvey, Andrew. 'Institute for Sacred Activism'. Accessed July 22, 2016 https://www.andrewharvey.net

Harvey, Andrew, and Chris Saade. *An Evolutionary Vision of Relationships:* Toronto, Ontario: Enrealment, 2016. Print.

Harvey, Andrew. *The Direct Path: Creating a Journey to the Divine through the World's Mystical Traditions*. New York: Broadway Books, 2000.

Heartsong, Claire. *Anna, Grandmother of Jesus: A Message of Wisdom and Love*. Santa Clara, CA: S.E.E. Pub., 2002. Print.

Hillman, Anne. *The Dancing Animal Woman: A Celebration of Life*. Norfolk, CT: Bramble Books, 1994.

Hopi Prophecy. 'We Are the Ones'. Awakin.org. Awakin RSS. Accessed July 22, 2016. http://www.awakin.org/read/view.php?tid=702.

Howell, Alice O. *The Dove in the Stone: Finding the Sacred in the Commonplace*. Wheaton, IL, U.S.A.: Theosophical Pub. House, 1988.

Hunter, Derek Walcott-Poem. 'Love After Love Poem.' Poemhunter.com. Accessed July 22, 2016. http://www.poemhunter.com/poem/love-after-love.

Kahn, Matt. 'The Path of Courage'. Accessed July 18, 2017.https://youtu.be/SiFoCTuAipg.https://www.trueDivinenature.com.

Kahn, Matt. 'Whatever Arises, Love That: A Love Revolution That Begins with You'. 2016 https://www.trueDivinenature.com

Kells, John: Accessed July 22, 2016. https://www.johnkells.co.uk

Kasper, Ani. Accessed July 22, 2016. https://www.facebook.com/pages/Ani-Kaspar/285508834795666.

Kidd, Sue Monk. *The Secret Life of Bees*. New York: Viking, 2002.

Ladinsky, Daniel James. 'The Grail'. *Love Poems from God: Twelve Sacred Voices from the East and West*. New York: Penguin Compass, 2002.

Lakota Sioux Prayer. 'Mitakuye Oyasin'. http://harmonicconcordance.org/. Accessed July 22, 2016. http://harmonicconcordance.org/all-my-relations.

LaMotte, Alfred.K. https://yourradiance.blogspot.com/2019/11/ancestry.html. Accessed April 22, 2020.

Lao Tzu Quotes (Author of Tao Te Ching). Accessed July 22, 2016. https://www.goodreads.com/author/quotes/2622245.Lao_Tzu.

Licata, Matt. Accessed July 22, 2016. https://www.alovinghealingspace.blogspot.com.

Linden, Stanton J. *The Alchemy Reader: From Hermes Trismegistus to Isaac Newton*. New York: Cambridge University Press, 2003.

Magdalena, Laura: Accessed July 22, 2016. https://www.cosmicgaia2012.com.

Markova, Dawna. 'I Will Not Live an Unlived Life'. *I Will Not Live an Unlived Life Reclaiming Passion and Purpose*. Newburyport: Red Wheel Weiser, 2000. Malecek, Stefan https://www.stefanjmalecek.com.

Martin Luther King Jr. Quotes. Martin Luther King Jr. Quotes (Author of the Autobiography of Martin Luther King, Jr.). N.p., n.d. Web. 18 July 2016.

Matthews, Caitlin. *Sophia, Goddess of Wisdom, Bride of God.* Wheaton, IL: Quest Books, Theosophical Pub. House, 2001.

Mathieson, Kari. Accessed July 22. https://www.karimathieson.com

Neruda, Paulo. *Se Mejor Poesia.* Bookspan. 2005.

Nobel, Steve. 'The Higher Light Decree'. https://www.soulmatrix.com

Odier, Daniel. *Tantric Quest: An Encounter with Absolute Love.* Rochester, VT: Inner Traditions, 1997.

O'Donohue, John. *Anam Cara Spiritual Wisdom from the Celtic World.* Bantam Press: Australia, 1997.

Oliver, Mary. *Dream Work.* Boston: Atlantic Monthly Press, 1986.

Osho. Osho Quotes on Trust.OSHO. Accessed July 22. http://www.osho.com/highlights-of-oshos-world/osho-on-trust-quotes.

Page, Christine R. *The Return of the Great Mother.* Rochester, VT: Bear & Books, 2008.

Plotkin, Bill. *Soulcraft: Crossing into the Mysteries of Nature and Psyche.* Novato, CA: New World Library, 2003.

Port, Shannon. *Art of the Feminine.* Accessed July 22, 2016. http://www.artofthefeminine.com

Povey, Nicola. Accessed June 22,2020. nicolaandreapovey@gmail.com

Robbins, Tony. Accessed July 22,2016. https://www.brainyquote.com/quotes/tony_robbins_147773.

Rilke, Rainer Maria, and Robert Bly. 'Love Song'. *In Selected Poems of Rainer Maria Rilke.* New York: Harper & Row, 1981.

Rūmī, Jalāl Al-Dīn, Andrew Harvey, and Lekha Singh. 'Whatever Your Terror'. *Call to Love: In the Rose Garden with Rumi*. New York: Sterling, 2007.

Rūmī, Jalāl Al-Dīn. 'Come, Come, Whoever You Are'. Come, Come, Whoever You Are by Mewlana Jalaluddin, Rumi. Famous Poems, Famous Poets. Accessed July 22, 2016. https://allpoetry.com/Come,-Come,-Whoever-You-Are.

Rūmī, Jalāl Al-Dīn. 'The Guest House'. 'The Guest House by Mewlana Jalaluddin Rumi'.–Famous Poems, Famous Poets. Accessed July 22, 2016. https://allpoetry.com/poem/8534703-The-Guest-House-by-Mewlana-Jalaluddin-Rumi.

Rūmī, Jalāl Al-Dīn. 'Grind Yourself'. Quote by Mewlana Jalaluddin Rumi. Accessed July 22, 2016. http://www.Earthportals.com/Portal_Messenger/gyoung.html.

Rūmī, Jalāl Al-Dīn. 'So the Sea Journey Goes On'. Rumi Quotes – Timeline | Facebook. Accessed July 22, 2016.

https://www.facebook.com/RumiQuotes/photos/a.145481988858591.36288.145479798858810/

459062147500572/.

Rūmī, Jalāl Al-Dīn. 'Rumi Quotes' (Author of the Essential Rumi). Accessed July 22, 2016. https://www.goodreads.com/author/quotes/875661.Rumi.

Rydall, Derek. 'Law of Emergence: The End of Self Improvement'. Accessed July 22, 2016. http://derekrydall.com/.

Shepard, Sharon Lyn. Accessed June 22, 2020. https://www.sharonlynnshepard.com

Sarton, May. https://www.wiseoldsayings.com/door-quotes/. Accessed July 22,2016.

Sparrow, Jack. '25 Memorable Quotes by Captain Jack Sparrow That Made Us Fall in Love with Him'. ScoopWhoop. Accessed July 22, 2016. https://www.scoopwhoop.com/entertainment/jack-sparrow-quotes/.

Spilsbury, Ariel. 'The Alchemy of Ecstasy'. Accessed July 22, 2016. https://www.holographicgoddess.com

Spilsbury, Ariel. *The 13 Moon Oracle: Holographic Meditations on the Mystery.* San Raphael, CA: Mandala Pub., 2006.

Starr, Mirabai. 'Prayer to Shekinah'. *Wild Mercy: Living the Fierce and Tender Wisdom of the Women Mystics* by Sounds True, 2019.

Starbird, Margaret. 'Mary Magdalene, Bearer of the Holy Grail'. Accessed July 22, 2016. http://newagejournal.com/mary-magdalene-bearer-of-the-holy-grail.

Steward, Corrina. 'Our New Humanity: Becoming One with the Heart'. New Humanity Press. 2014. Accessed July 22, 2016. http://www.newhumanitypress.com/.

'Thirteen Indigenous Grandmothers'. Accessed July 22, 2016. http://www.grandmotherscouncil.org/.

Tillich, Paul. *The Shaking of the Foundations.* New York: C. Scribner's Sons, 1948.

Turner, Toko-pa. *Belonging: Remembering Ourselves Home.* Her Own Room Press, 2017.

Thomashauer, Regena. *Pussy: A Reclamation.* S.l.: Hay House, 2017. Print.

Vaughn, Llewellyn. *The Return of the Feminine Spirit and the World Soul. The Golden Sufi Center.* 2013.

Yoon, Nicola. *The Sun Is Also a Star.* United Kingdom, Random House Children's Books, 2016.

Zen Proverb. 'Chop Wood Carry Water'. Zen Revolution. April 28, 2012. Accessed July 22, 2016. https://zenrevolution.wordpress.com/2012/04/28/chop-wood-carry-water/.

BIBLIOGRAPHY OF LYRICS

Arlen, Harold, E. Y. Harburg, Judy Garland, and Victor Young. 'Over the Rainbow' (from the MGM Picture, *Wizard of Oz*). Decca, 1939. CD.

Bananarama. Venus. 'True Confessions'. Recorded July 1986. In Greatest Hits. London, 1986, CD

Bassey, Shirley. Lyrics by Leslie Bricusse and Anthony Newley. 'Goldfinger'. Capital. 1964, CD

Berlin. 'Take My Breath Away'. Sony BMG Music Entertainment (UK), 2005, CD.

Bowie, David. 'Space Oddity'. Philips London, 1969, CD.

Darpan, 'Blessing'. Love Light. Darpan 2011. CD.

Denver, John. 'Take Me Home, Country Roads'. LaserLight Digital, 1997. CD.

Enya. Lyrics by Enya and Chuck Sayre. 'Orinoco Flow'. *Enya*. Intersound, 1996, CD.

Ferry, Bryan. 'Avalon'. *Best of Roxy Music*. Virgin Records America, 2001, CD

Franti, Michael. 'Bomb the World – Everyone Deserves Music'. Boo Boo Wax/iMusic, 2003, MP3.

Freedom. 'Where the River Greets the Sea'. Lyrics by Freedom.1996. CD. Reprinted by permission.

Graves, Joules. 'Waterfall Child'. Rabble Rouser Records.1995.CD.

Hansard, Glen, and Markéta Irglová, writers. 'Falling Slowly'. Once Music from the Motion Picture. Sony BMG Music Entertainment, 2007, MP3.

Hot Chocolate. 'You Sexy Thing'. EMI Records, 1993, CD.

Houston, Whitney, and R. Kelly, writers. 'I Will Always Love You'. Arista Records, 2012, CD.

Jagger, Mick, and Keith Richards, writers. 'Satisfaction'. Editado Por Libra Libra, 1997, CD.

James, Kevin C. 'Long Way Home'. Lyrics by Kevin James Carroll. https://www.kevinjamescarroll.com

Khar, Snatam. 'Deep Blue Sea'. Snatam Khar. Spirit Voyage Records, 2005, MP3.

Malia, Tina. 'All Roads'. Lyrics by Tina Malia. Amida Records, 2006, MP3. Reprinted by permission.

Marley, Bob. 'Redemption Song'. *Bob Marley: Songs of Freedom from Judge Not to Redemption Song*. Island Records, 1992, CD.

McKennit, Loreena. 'Dante's Prayer: The Book of Secrets'. Quinlan Road, Warner Bros. 1997.CD

Mitchell, Joni. 'Woodstock'. Luxury Multimedia, 2005. CD.

Murdoch, Alexi. 'Something Beautiful'. Something Beautiful Lyrics | LyricsMode.com. Accessed July 22, 2016.

Nash, Johnny, writer. 'I Can See Clearly Now'. *The Best of Johnny Nash*. Johnny Nash. Epic, 1972, CD.

Prince, and Bob Belden, writers. 'When Doves Cry'. *The Music of Prince*. Metro Blue, 1994, CD.

Ray, +Elijah. 'We Are Here'. *+Elijah and the Band of Light*. Elijahraymusic, 2008, MP3. Reprinted by permission.

Shim Shai. 'Pure'. Promesa Records. 2006, MP3. Reprinted by permission.

Shim Shai. 'Yeshu-Maria'. *Shim Shai*. 2001, MP3. Reprinted by permission.

Simon, Paul. 'Mrs. Robinson'. *Simon and Garfunkel's Greatest Hits*. By Art Garfunkel. Simon and Garfunkel. Columbia, 1985, CD.

Sterling, Suzanne. 'The River-Bhakti'. Suzanne Sterling, 2000, CD.

Stevens, Cat, and Yusuf Islam, writers. 'Peace Train'. *Teaser and the Firecat*. A&M Records, 2000, CD.

Sunshine, Shylah Ray featuring Mother Medicine. 'Existence'. Shylah Ray Sunshine, 2012. MP3. Reprinted by permission.

Rice, Damien, writer. 'Cannonball'. *Damien Rice O*. Damien Rice. Vector Recordings, 2003, MP3.

Warnes, Jennifer, and Bill Medley, writers. 'I Had the Time of My Life'. RCA Records, 1987, CD.

Zero 7. 'Spinning'. *Simple Things*. Quango, 2007, MP3.

CITATIONS FOR ILLUSTRATIONS

Celtic Knot. digital image. Dreamtime.© Mykola Lytvynenko. Web. 22 August 2018.

Clay chalice photos. Digital image. http://wwwthelivingchalice.com © Inaiya Ray. 21 September 2016.

Evening sea coast. Digital image. Shutterstock. © Yuriy Kulik, n.d. Web. 15 August 2016.

Galloping white horse. Digital image. Thinkstock Photos. © Abramova_kmnf Kseniya, 16 February 2001. Web. 15 August 2015.

Golden chalice. Digital image. Shutterstock. © Paul Fleet, N.p, n.d. Web. 15 August 2015.

The Grail Rider cover art. Digital image. www.thelivingchalice.com © Inaiya Ray. 22 August 2018.

The Grail Rider cover art contributions: www.Lucinda-Rae.com and www.gaelynlarrick.com.

Vintage frame with dove. Digital image. Dreamstime. © Olena Antonova, n.d. Web. 15 August 2016.

Vector dove symbol. Digital image. Dreamstime. © Oleksandr Melnyk, n.d. Web. 15 August 2016.

ABOUT INAIYA RAY

Inaiya Ray is a Wayshower of the Beauty Way and steward of The Living Chalice, an embodied Wisdom School for New Earth Temple Arts. Her life-long journey of personal and planetary awakening has led her to travel the world while pioneering the inner alchemy of Conscious Evolution and the birthing of a Divine New Humanity. Inaiya draws upon three decades of facilitating experiential trainings such as: The Evolutionary Priest/Priestess, New Earth Wayshower and Akashic Awakening, a sonic and somatic unwinding of the body and soul that delivers one into greater consciousness, coherence and connectivity with one's authentic self and whole of creation.

As an emissary of Gaia Sophia, Inaiya transmits the living intelligence of the Wild Divine. Her sacred ceremonies and global retreats are instilled with the magic and majesty of the moment. Weaving the wonders of the natural world with a plethora of experiential discovery, she guides individuals into creative self-mastery and mutual awakening that anchor new paradigms of Oneness and life-giving beauty.

Inaiya thrives in serving an international community, offering Akashic Awakening intuitive readings, Bio-energetic Attunements, Awakened Life Coaching and transformational courses that illuminate and polish the gifts of the Soul. For further adventures of The Grail Rider and to stay connected, please visit Inaiya at: www.thelivingchalice.com

www.ingramcontent.com/pod-product-compliance
Lightning Source LLC
Chambersburg PA
CBHW051452030726
47592CB00006B/1897